Kosova 1: Dardania in Ancient and Medieval Times

Series Editors

Jason L. Frazer
Besa Pinchotti
Diane Tafilaj
Ramadan Musliu

Series translated by:

Avni Spahiu
Getoar M. Mjeku
Faton Bislimi

Originally issued 2012 in Albanian
by Jalifat Publishing in Houston and Faik Konica in Prishtina as
Kosova 1: Antika, Mesjeta

© 2012 Jalifat Publishing
English translation © 2013 Jalifat Publishing
All rights reserved

Published by Jalifat Publishing
Houston, Texas

JUSUF BUXHOVI

KOSOVA

Volume 1

Dardania in Ancient
and Medieval Times

JALIFAT PUBLISHING
Houston USA
2013

*To my wife, Luljeta,
and children: Arsim, Njomëza, and Arta*

CONTENTS

CONTENTS 7
FOREWORD 9

PART ONE: ANTIQUITY

INTRODUCTION 15
CHAPTER 1 31
   Pelasgians and the Puzzle of Antiquity 31
   Pelasgian Antiquity from an Historical Point of View 43
   Pelasgian Antiquity from a Mythological Point of View 55
   Pelasgian Antiquity from an Archeological Point of View 63
   Pelasgian Antiquity from a Linguistic Point of View 81
   Homer and the True Pelasgian Antiquity 106
CHAPTER 2 117
   Pelasgians and Dardanians 117
   Dardanian-Illyrian Ethnic Relations 130
   Dardanian-Illyrian-Greek Relations 147
   Illyrians, Epirotes, Macedonians, and Etruscans (Tyrrheneans) 157
CHAPTER 3 177
   Dardanian Kingdom 177
   Long Wars Against Rome 202
   Roman Conquests and Uprisings against Them 215
CHAPTER 4 227
   Illyrians and Dardanians during the Roman Empire 227

    Romanization and Illyrian-Dardanian Ethnic Identity 244
    CONCLUSION 257

PART TWO: MIDDLE AGES

CHAPTER 1 265
    Illyricum and the Emergence of Byzantium 265
    Christianity in Illyricum and Dardania 281
    Dardania and Byzantium 296
    Illyrians and Dardanians within the Framework
    of Early Byzantine Mentality 312

CHAPTER 2 323
    Slavic Invasions and Deepening of Divisions
    between East and West 323
    Illyricum and Bulgarians 343
    From Themes to the First Arberian Principalities 349
    Arbenians between Byzantium and the West 360
    Despotate of Epirus and Arberian Kingdom 379
    The Agony of Byzantium and Arberian Principalities 408
    Ethnic Relations between Arberians and Slav Invaders
    during the Middle Ages 438
    Social and Political Relations between Arberians
    and Slav Invaders 457

CONCLUSION 471
LITERATURE 477

FOREWORD

The declaration of independence of Albania in November 1912 and the acceptance of the London concept of the Albanian state, with half its territory outside the political borders, on one side emerged as a result of the conquest of Albanian territories by their neighbors during the First Balkan War and, on the other side, resulted from the agreements of the Great Powers, to bring an answer to the finality of the Eastern crisis as imposed by the circumstances of the Balkan wars. These circumstances drew on the political issue of Kosova, first as a matter of the unresolved Albanian question, in order that after World War II, having turned into a "special" issue, which, after the disintegration of former Yugoslavia, in accordance with the circumstances that led to this development, a statehood answer would be given. Even more so since Kosova itself, with its Constitutional Declaration of July 2, 1990, the Kaçanik Constitution of September 7 of that year, the Referendum on Independence in 1991, and eventually with the first mult-iparty elections in May of 1992 had declared Kosova an independent state. Thus, the presence of the remnants of Yugoslavia reduced solely to a repressive police and military apparatus, was back to the classic occupier of the state of Kosova, which would be fought with general institutional resistance (parallel state), without excluding the armed resistance, as happened in the last stage when this burden was taken over by the Kosova Liberation Army. The international intervention of NATO from March 24 to June 10, 1999 against the Yugoslav military and police forces, when Kosova was liberated from the military occupation of Belgrade and the circumstances that led to this development, such as those that appeared on Resolution 1244 of UN Security Council of June 10, 1999, when Kosova was placed under an international protectorate, made it possible for Kosova, in cooperation with the international community, to declare itself independent on February 17, 2008. This declaration was nothing more than an exercise of its legitimacy of the will of Kosovar citizens to their state as proclaimed in 1990 and began being implemented in 1992 through the organization of the "parallel" state despite the police and military violence exercised by the military occupation regime of Milosevic.

However, the emergence of a second Albanian state in the Balkans, although its political tabloid gave the appearance of a mosaic, where there may be other parts, no matter how it seemed from the outside and how it may be measured and rationed, did not diminish the Albanian issue of its ethnic, social, or cultural integrity. Rather, it brought it into a common, most natural, historical framework.

Therefore, the attempt to write the political history of the state of Kosova, as well as that of the Albanian state, does not mean segregating it from the whole, nor opening a separation process, but on the contrary, its commonalities will be brought out, which allows the ethnic Albanian edifice with all its features of internal linkage (spiritual, social and cultural), where the core of ancient Dardania, geographically, historically and politically, in all stages, played a very heavy, if not a decisive role. Although the term Kosova is of a very recent date (it appears in the 19th century in one of the four Albanian vilayets), unfortunately, the appeal of Great Serbian hegemonic policy and the international community that supported it, had become synonymous with the violent partition of Albanians at the moment it was wrongfully identified with "old Serbia."

Given this position, the history of Kosova from antiquity, Middle Ages, the time of the Ottoman Empire, the time of Serb-Yugoslav occupation, and the occurrence of the state, even as parallel, which was announced in the early nineties of the last century, and independence, all build up to the view of a common history of natural Albania, the beginnings of which relate to Pelasgians and their major role in prehistory and history, upon which arose what is known as antiquity and Western civilization.

Needless to say this view corrects the historical focus from the first millennium BC, which usually is seen connecting the Albanians with the Illyrians and Illyria, to carry it over to the sixth millennium, that of the Pelasgians – the oldest inhabitants of Europe and Mediterranean in general, which, recently, many scientists are rightly attributing the merits of classical Indo-Europeans upon which Hellenism was rebuilt, what is called the cradle of human civilization and all other developments.

So, this focus is also important for the Albanians and their history, which remains unwritten as yet, as it extends the view beyond the four millenniums, from where the Pelasgian factor, or even Pelasgia in terms of a cognomen representing members of the same family, as named by promi-

nent and revered authors of antiquity (Homer, Hesiod, Herodotus, Thucydides, Isocrates, Demosthenes, Scylla, Aristotle, Polybius, Cezat, Titus Livius, Tacitus and others), highlighted their role beyond the scope of the first frictions with those who would later appear as Greek (primarily Dorians), as with Troy, at that important knot that connects the Balkans with Asia Minor, where the Pelasgian Dardanians appeared as founders of Troy and carriers of a very important factor of antiquity, from where Greek and Roman delimitations appeared.

Of course this very challenging observation, with Dardania, Illyrians, Macedonians, Epirotes and others as exponents of the first and main Pelasgian factor appearing externally as "barbarians" as defined by the Greek newcomers, most likely sometime from the early Eighth century BC turned into Dardanians and Dardania, and thus the present-day Kosova as an integral part of Albanian ethnicity, into an epicenter of one of the key developments in the history of antiquity. With this, what had until now been viewed as an Illyrian-Albanian continuity, is not only confirmed, but with a coherence of four thousand years, has strengthened and, thus, an often controversial view, gained its permanent foundation.

After all, it would be the big events since the Trojan War and on (even if as imagined by Homer), that Dardania, as a hub linking the East and West, and Dardanians as a separate branch of the largest Illyrian family trunk and descendants of the Pelasgians in general, would be placed in a large historical scene, through which all the empires and civilizations would pass, and from the Greek, Roman, Byzantine, Ottoman and Austro-Hungarian times, would continue until our time.

Kosova in three books: the first involving Antiquity and Middle Ages, the second including the period of the Ottoman Empire, and the third book, capturing the time of Kosova's separation from its Albanian ethnicity, the period of Serbian-Yugoslav occupations up to the NATO international intervention and confirmation of independence proclaimed in 1990 in cooperation with the international factor, on February 17, 2008, reflects an historical framework that deals with the history of the Albanian people in general.

The author hopes that this study will contribute to the overall view in the historical framework of natural Albania, as a social, cultural and political reality, as part of the wholeness of Western civilization, where its roots are, regardless of the state mosaic on which it stands and regardless of its current or future appearance.

PART ONE
ANTIQUITY

INTRODUCTION

In the second half of the 19th century, the famous German Albanologist Johann Georg von Hahn, while working with tenacity in search of the origin of Albanians and the determination of their identity within the Indo-European family stated, "The more I study the Albanians the greater the need for further study."[1]

This was the time when the first scattered evidence of these peoples' links with antiquity began to come to light. However, scientific overlay and additional research was needed before this evidence could be accepted.

The assertions of the German scholar, which have evolved into an open invitation to develop further Albanological studies, made scientific sense. They were of social and political importance as the science of linguistics, in cohesion with other disciplines of historiography, ethnography, mythology, and anthropology that responded to what he discovered to be an important link to historical times and developments in relation to European and other ancient civilizations (Middle East, Far East and especially Egyptian civilization). Simultaneously, in response to significant social changes (including those that would emerge on the political scene from the time of the Eastern Crisis), the Balkans began to conceptualize the first national states emerging from the collapse of the century-old Ottoman Empire. The issuance of Albanian autochthony as an important part of ancient antiquity influenced diplomatic and political trends of the time. It eliminated the inaccurate thesis and other deliberate attempts aimed at disputing Albanian autochthony, ethnicity and antiquity, in order to exclude them from future state configurations on the European map.[2]

---

[1] Hahn, Georg von: *"Albanesische Studien,"* Jena, 1854, p. 286.
[2] This refers to the Serb historiography, which with the proclamation of *"Nacertanja"* of Garasanin and Greek *"Megalo idhea,"* of 1844, set the basis for the Great Serb and Great Greek hegemonic policies, following from the Eastern Crisis and continuing as such to

Apparently, what the well-known scholar said about the proximity and distance of Albanians was not a metaphor similar to the one of a deceiptive shadow deception becoming inconceivable any time you intend to catch it. Instead, von Hahn was speaking to the reflection of a particular situation where proximity of distance comes from research because of the recognition and "unexpected contingencies" it reveals. It also opens up many issues that frequently offset scientific logic and create confusion rather than clarity.

As for the "unexpected" about the Albanians and their antiquity, von Hahn was among the first to encounter news about Albanian as the language of the ancient Illyrians, spread by the famous German philosopher Leibnitz among many scientific circles,[3] declaring them descendants of the Illyrians. By showing respect for the courage of Leibnitz and his work with a vocabulary of about 100 words to highlight the first points of the Illyrian-Albanian proximity in the field of linguistics,[4] von Hahn went even further in support of the Illyrian thesis presented by Leibnitz. He associated these findings with those left behind by the knight von Harff,[5] findings being shared by Xylander about the Albanians,[6] Thunman,[7] and

---

the present day. Serbian "*Nacertanja*" and Greek "*Megalo idhea*" focused on the so-called new role of these two peoples in the Balkans which, by gaining the support of the European powers and Russia would turn into a regional factor, replacing the Ottoman rule in these spaces and turning it into a sphere of their own interest. Both the Serbs and Greeks based their projections of expansion as states on the back of the Albanian ethnicity. For the Serbs and Greeks, Albanians and their space should be partitioned under the justification that they, by accepting Islam, turned into a tool of the Ottoman Empire against the European Christianity. Therefore, as punishment, they were not entitled to statehood and scattered throughout Christian-Orthodox states of the Balkans. Those who did not consent to this moved to Turkey, by force if needed.

[3] The well-known German philosopher, *Gottfried Wilhelm Leibniz* (1646-1717), was the first to be dealing with the history and studies of the Albanian language and people. In his letter of December 10, 1707, quoted in 1897 in the review "Albania" of Bucharest, states that his studies of Albanian books, and the vocabulary vocabulary within them, convinced him that "Albanian is the language of the ancient Illyrians."

[4] Leibniz, Gottfried Wilhelm, cited according to "*Albania*," Brussels, 1897.

[5] See Riter, Arnold Von Harff: "*Die Pilgerfaht – in den Jahren 1496-1499,*" Köln, 1860.

[6] Xylander, Ritter von: "*Die Sphrahe der Albanensen oder Schkipetaren,*" Frankfurt am Main, 1835.

[7] Hans Erik Thunnman (1746-1778), a Swedish historian, professor at the Hall University in Germany, was among the first Albanologists that studied the origin of the Albanian

Franz Bopp's research, through methods of comparative linguistics.[8] In his lengthy and profound studies in the field of linguistics, mythology and historiography,[9] and his direct contacts with the Albanian world[10] (to which he paid the most attention), von Hahn was satisfied with the current thesis on Albanians as descendants of the Illyrians. In his opinion, this theory was important because it represented a starting point in linking certain antiquity points such as the great movement of people from India towards the West. This concerned Albanians about their origin and prehistoric times because it helped determine the historic period and unsettled issues that were seemingly turning into taboos.[11]

Of course, the linkage between the Albanian and the Pelasgian role in passing from prehistoric to historic times opened up the possibility of

---

language and people. Surprised by the presence of a non-Greek and non-Slavic people in the Balkan Peninsula he researched Greek, ancient, and Byzantine sources and studied the three-language dictionary by Theodor Kavalioti (Greek, Slavic, and Albanian), published in 1770. In his work "Research on the History of Eastern European Peoples" (1774) he concluded that Albanians were an indigenous offspring of the ancient Illyrian population who were neither Romanized nor assimilated by later immigrations.

[8] *Bopp, Franz: "Über das Albanesischen in seinen verwandtschaftlichen Bezihungen,"* 1854. In this work Bopp reached the correct conclusion that the Albanian language in its basic component parts has no background connection with any of the Sanskrit sisters of our continent. And, this conclusion, accepted universally a bit later, Bopp supported with a range of data, mainly by the grammatical structure of the Albanian language.

[9] *"Studime shqiptare,"* Tirana, 2009, pp. 420-443.

[10] *Johan Georg von Hahn* (1811-1869). The Austrian, a graduate of the University of Heidelberg, served the court in the newly formed Greek state, under the direction of the king of Bavaria, Otto I. There he fell in connection with the Arvanites of Greece and their Albanian language, which was so different from Greek. In 1847, he was appointed vice-council of Austria in Ioannina, where he was engaged in Albanian language studies, along with Constantine Kristoforidhi, a linguist, and made long trips across Albania. In 1854, he published his fundamental work in three volumes, *"Albanesische Studien"* (Albanian Studies), on the Albanian culture, language and history. He was convinced based on ancient sources that Illyrians, Epirotes, and Macedonians were not Greeks but were rather older than them and had descended from the ancient Pelasgians. He was the first to study the vocabulary of the old Illyrian, concluding that many place names of Albanian territories were a direct continuation of old Illyrian names and drew up rules for the explanation of the phonetic changes that had happened to the names of places over the centuries. This led to his conclusion that the Albanian language was direct bearer of Illyrian, and that Illyrian came from Pelasgian.

[11] See *"Studime shqiptare,"* Tirana, 2009, pp. 13-27, 278-339

different reviews on previous stances which generally withstood the complex of antiquity. Its main pillars were put in question including those about the prehistoric movements of people in different directions, their role in creating the first ethnicities starting hitherto human civilization, and other issues that were waiting to come out of the mist. Another German linguist, Karl O. Müller, anticipated possible disarrays in an already set hierarchy about antiquity where Hellenism turned into an impassable reference and a foundation for all the starting points of definitions of antiquity. He said, "The more intelligence used to penetrate the history of Greece, the more attention will be paid to the Pelasgian element, hitherto sacrificed.[12]"

Viewed from this perspective, von Hahn was the first to investigate the seemingly forgotten great role of Albanians, in order to shed light on the so-called Pelasgic "dilemma" and its importance. It held the key to other issues related to Indo-Europeanism in general, which was overlooked because "the question was about a prehistoric people that had vanished. Although its remote existence was not being denied, its traces were lost among others for the lack of tangible evidence.[13]"

Even at the time when von Hahn raised the issue of Pelasgians it could now be accepted in principle because the concern was about an old prehistoric people, which ancient authors clarified, could have lost its traces through merging with other people. In this instance, the first mentioned were the ancient Greeks. However, he was drawing attention to Albanians and their origin from antiquity, which was accepted by its authors as the most typical specimen of its remains in a form of a "human fossil." This not only kept its "un-melted traces" among the rest, stated as priori, which were still alive and tangible from material, spiritual, and historical standpoints. Adding to Leibniz, whose issue of Albanians as descendants of the Illyrians dating back over a century ago, von Hahn saw this important link for science as an important link connecting Albanians with the Pelasgians, a link that deserved everyone's attention over the unstable assumptions that attempted to close the scientific circle.

However, distrust over the views of Johann-Georg von Hahn provided the necessary scientific support to consider Leibniz's warning about the Albanians as being the daughter of the Illyrians with great seriousness, thanks to thorough research in the field of linguistics and to a great extent

---

[12] Müller, Karl O: *"Prolegomena,"* 1825.
[13] Johan Georg von Hahn: *"Studime shqiptare,"* Tirana, 2009, pp. 401-423.

the Illyrian theory by some of the most zealous German researchers dealing with the Albanians. This research continued the Pelasgian theory for the origin of the Albanians. During his 30 years of work, he assured that even if the Pelasgic issue remained under doubt as being elusive, it would still affect the Albanians and their past would turn into an open object of this evidence, even if hypothetical. Attachment to Pelasgians as the cradle of antiquity and also as the main carrier of the first large influx of peoples from India (who moved to Europe in the 6th millennium), Albanians are living proof of their existence for many renowned world scholars. Additional arguments for the displacement of the Hellenic factor from the fundaments of antiquity, according to them, were placed not on grounds of scientific proof but rather on political ones. The contention of Pelasgic autochthony and the revaluation of their role in passing from prehistoric to historic time diluted the late arrival of the Greeks to a level of settlers relocated in that part after their departure from Egypt as Heraclites or their occurrence during the so-called Doric movement from the northwest in the 18th and 19th centuries (considered classic Hellenism), would not be attributed to the Greeks. Instead, they would be attributed to the Pelasgians as the matrix of ancient civilization with Illyrian-Albanians as the dominating factor. This replacement became even more indispensable through more credible assumptions that the Hellenes were using the cradle of Pelasgian culture. It was also stated that the Phoenician alphabet also came from the Pelasgians, a view that would increasingly find scientific backing.

So this daring and initial explication from a scientific perspective continues to remain an open dilemma because of the difficulty of providing "tangible" evidence. However, it is in no way excluded or removed from the agenda because it maintains an anathema as to why Albanians, in the focus of science, are paradoxically juxtaposed by distance and distanced by juxtaposition. This paradox becomes even more special since the release of the hypothesis linking the Pelasgians with Albanians as their descendants. Certain scientific circles, rather than leaving this to be assessed through the research as an issue that does not concern Albanians alone, would react with concern. Meanwhile, whenever this issue was connected to social and political issues it would be experienced as something short of a disaster.

It's apparent that the second aspect (primarily the connection with certain social and political issues) would be the one that would make the theory of Pelasgian origin embraced by the Albanian revivalists with so much interest, kindness, and enthusiasm. One should not exclude the knowledge and competence of the extraordinary case of personalities including Sami Frashëri, who led the Ottoman Encyclopedia, and Vaso Pasha Shkodrani, Hoxha Tahsini, Kristoforidhi, and others, who had a high degree of education as much as they had intellectual creed. For the Revivalists, the theory on the Pelasgian origin of the Albanians, (despite the distrust of traditional science and despite consequences that could result from being attached to it rather than being Illyrian, although it was not yet thoroughly recognized) would turn into an all-compassing motto of their national program, from which they would never stray. Instead, they would attach to it their political future in order to turn it into a device to be used in search of the European civilization and the Western support as an historical right based on the spiritual one with roots in antiquity.

Therefore, it is known that Sami Frashëri,[14] and also Vaso Pasha Shkodrani, author Naim Frashëri,[15] and others, in efforts to get Albanians united around a national program, focused entirely on the Pelasgian origin of the Albanians. By this lineage they were connected to the foundations of antiquity. Furthermore, they turned the theory into a powerful weapon against Greek hegemonic and nationalistic tendencies, which were trying to use Hellenism (much supported by relevant cultural and political European circles to which the very creation of the Greek state is attributed in the 1930s) in order to Hellenize Albanians, denying them the right to decide upon their political future, in compliance with their (Greek) declared chauvinistic platform, *"Megalo-idhea,"* and other projects conjured up in collaboration with Serbs and Russians aimed at excluding Albanians from the political map of the Balkans.

The Pelasgian theory was also being supported by the Albanians of Italy (Arbereshi) focusing on opening new venues through Italian language studies on a wider scale.[16] However, evidently the Italian-Arbereshi

---

[14] See encyclopedic studies: Sami, Semsedin (Sami Frashëri): *"Kamus al-Al'am – Esma-yt hassa-yt Camidir,"* Stamboll, 1889-99; *"Kamüs-i Türki,"* Stamboll 1899-1901.

[15] See: Frashëri, Naim: *"Dëshirë e vërtetë e shqiptarëvet,"* Works 1, Prishtina, 1986, p. 137.

[16] See: Dhimitër Kamarda: *"Një ese e gramatikës krahasuese rreth gjuhës shqipe,"* 1846. The well-known Italian-Albanian scholar with this and other studies documented the antiquity of the Albanian language. Walking in Hahn's footsteps, he also made an important philological comparison of roots in Sanskrit, Persian, Latin, classical Greek

also focused on the Illyrian theory (convinced that it could help to be seen as a link with the Pelasgian) that remains a matter of a wider and more open sphere.

Over time, particularly since the emergence of an independent Albanian state which, although halved, would return to the Western European family, the Pelasgian theory began to gain significant support in the international scientific circle. However, Albanian scholars, by remaining faithful to the important German "Illyricists" and their school, remained mainly proponents of the frame of the Illyrian origin without showing any interest to go deeper. This determination, with some exclusion,[17] would continue following World War II and lead into present times.

Obviously this definition should be seen as a result of political reasons rather than scientific ones, where the fear "from distance" (as von Hahn presented more than a century before) can influence the proximity, social, cultural and political actuality in its various forms. In this context the definition of the Illyrians, as an ancient entity that cannot be denied any longer and of Illyria as a tribal or state formation associated with Greece and Rome, was suitable to the Albanian communist state and generally to Albanians remaining outside the boundaries of Albania (mainly in areas of the former Yugoslavia and Greece) as a country. Although halved, provided a continuation linked with antiquity without any impact on it, the Albanians as a people (with disputes between the Illyrian and Thracian affiliation in a narrowed space compared to the

---

and Albanian. From the critical analysis of dozens of scientific sources, he concluded that the language of the Albanian people was among the oldest of all the peoples of Europe.

[17] This "exception" refers to the work "Albanians and the Pelasgian Problem" of Philologer Spiro N. Konda, graduated in Philosophy at the University of Athens on the eve of World War II, to be published in Tirana, in 1964, but remaining almost forgotten, without the slightest reference by the science of Albanian linguistics in Tirana and also in Prishtina. This "forgotten" work represents one of the important scientific contributions to the study of the Pelasgian issue in the field of linguistics. The Albanian philologist, with clear scientific authority, animates much of the evidence on the Albanians connecting it with the Pelasgian. The background upon which Konda creates his paradigm between Hahn's studies on this issue, from the mid-19th century, and those who appeared at the beginning of last century and accepted by revivalists (Sami, Naim, Pashko Vasa, Kamarda, and others) with studies by Krahe, Müller, Budimir, and others, restored legitimacy to the Pelasgic issue, which has been increasingly accepted on all sides.

historical one) preserved the ancient autochthony beyond true justifications of antiquity. Limitation on the Illyrian origin outside the Pelasgian and Dardanian linkage to roots of Troy antiquity on the cultural, social and political plain maintained "the peace" with neighboring people, especially Greeks, whose history was recognized regardless of it being contested from many sides without considering that this was still being used for expansion purposes against Albanians.

Despite these speculations (which could have occurred in such circumstances when the ideological political judgments were also set by research and other issues that affected the intellectual and spiritual spheres of great importance, the consequences of which have been devastating) this determining and narrow view of the ancient history of the Albanians, with special emphasis on the Pelasgians, has been even more incomprehensible than those of the available ideological recipes today. Here one may be tied to the Illyrian theory of Albanian origin without moving at all from what has been said a century and a half before (even though a lot of corrections have been made to the advantage of the antiquity of Albanians based on Illyrians' linkage with the Pelasgians as well as with Indo-European antiquity where they appear with a much more complete presentation, and even by many scientists they were acknowledged deserving crucial role in it) the actual science of Tirana has not only been ignoring these changes but continues to ignore the achievements in the field of historiography, linguistics, anthropology and archeology. Pelasgians, as the first Aryan people who came to these parts during the first movements of peoples from the 6th millennium in an area dominating the entire old continent, extended into Asia Minor, the Caucasus and North Africa which is considered the cradle of Indo-European civilization.[18]

Furthermore, under this incomprehensible attitude, even a sabotage occurred against the followers of the theory about the Dardanians as proven descendants of Pelasgian root inhabiting Italy in the West, Iberia, and reaching as far as Libya while in the Aegean they are found in Anatolia, where they are viewed as Trojans and even its founders by many ancient and contemporary authors. The Trojan War itself, not only in the form that it appears in Homer but from other testimonies as well, is seen

---

[18] *"Historia e Popullit Shqiptar,"* Volume I, Tirana, 2002, p. 43.

as an internal war of Pelasgic tribes.[19] Current Albanian historians appear not to be interested in what they call "an historical presence and extension of Dardanians in Asia Minor and elsewhere," with which the importance of their ancient civilization is growing and along with it that of their descendants.[20]

In this case, more elusive than the disinterest to "bypass" the Dardanians in the East, i.e. Troy and further on in the Caucasus and India, is the justification for this action when said: "as their historical destinies (speaking of Dardanians and Paeonians) in the *new territories, where they settled*, are completely separate *from the real Illyrian-Balkan world*, these migrated groups will not be included in any further treatment of Illyrian history."[21]

Even though in further treatments more space will be provided to answer to such incongruities that follow the Albanian institutional science, it must be pointed out that precisely a turn towards the Albanian-Pelasgian formula (which of course runs through its trunk and large Illyrian and Dardanian branches and their numerous known and unknown ramifications enlighten it thoroughly on the scientific plain in accordance with the definition that we are dealing with branches of the same lineage) not only does not endanger the Illyrian theory (even with known deficiencies it has and regardless of its view on issues resolved) but strengthens it. Through it comes to light new truths about Albanian antiquity and simultaneously brings other information of great importance to light for the path of human civilization from its origin to our time, where Pelasgians, as a "divine people" (as Homer called them) appear in the role of its cradle [22] from which the Greeks and others would attain much of its values in order to carry them forward.

---

[19] Jacques, Edwin: "*Shqiptarët*," Tirana, 2002, p. 64. This view is justified by the historian Jacques by the fact that Pelasgians came to the Balkan Peninsula sometime in the early second millennium bringing along traces of early civilization that were developed on the shores of two great rivers of the East, the Euphrates and the Nile. On this long journey, Pelasgians spread throughout the Aegean basin, in the Balkan Peninsula, even in Italy, focusing mostly on the southern region, the Balkans, which later was called Greece. The author estimates that the entire region was known as Pelasgia, where Athens, Sparta, Mycenae, and Argos were Pelasgic centers.

[20] Ibid, p. 43.
[21] Ibid, p. 43.
[22] Homer: "Iliada," Tirana, Book II/ 430, 1979.

However, superficial reading of Homer's major work - without excluding the testimony of ancient authors from Herodotus and Strabo to those of Rome and from AD period onwards - reveals a different historical reality as that of the Dardanians and other tribes that participated in the Trojan war on the Trojans' side or the Achaean side as others assumed to be Greeks. So, this reading makes it plain enough that what the ancient epochs contain in regard to the Dardanians and their fighters, whom Homer calls Pelasgians, is not a matter of fantasy of muses which could also have been contrived two centuries later in the time of Pisistratus. Instead, it provides the framework for a historical reality that is tied to an autochthonous pre-Hellenic people that accurately represents what might be called the cradle of antiquity, which rightly or not, from the beginning of the 18th century, would be attributed to Greek Hellenism.

From a historical perspective, the Pelasgic traces which now can be followed more closely with Albanians in terms of important linguistic, archaeological, and mythological evidence, including remnants of other material and spiritual cultures, not only connect the "four dark centuries" of antiquity from the 12th to the 8th centuries B.C. and dealings with the so-called Mycenaean culture (when its unclear demise occurs with a sudden emergence of Greek culture from the Dorians also explain the classical antiquity from the 6th century B.C. to the 2nd century A.D. as a continuation of a Pelasgian civilization acquired by the Hellenes as Herodotus and other ancient historians admit[23]) but were also carried to the centuries following the Roman conquest, and especially the emergence of Byzantium. About the latter it is known that the predominance of Dardanians as an important political and social factor in the eastern part of the Empire is the first ever associated with the large Illyrian family tree as its separate branch during the 4th century developments, (with the famous reforms of Diocletian and Constantine the Great) as well as those

---

[23] See *"Iliria and Ilirët te autorët antikë,"* Prishtina, 1979 (*Hesiod*, p. 13 inserted from Carmina recensuat Aloisius Rzach, edito terita; *Herodotus*, p. 15 – inserted from Herodotus "Historioriarum" book IX; *Herodotus*, pp. 16-22; *Tucídides* p. 23 inserted from *"Thucydides Historiare,"* Thucydides, pp. 26-29; *Isocrates*, pp. 30-31; *Demosthen* "Oritiones," p. 33; *Scylax*, pp. 34-37, inserted from *"Geographi Greaci Minores,"* Aristotle, pp. 39-49, inserted from *"Politica,"* Book II,V, *"Die Animalum Historia,"* Book II,IX, *"Die Mirabilius Auscultonibus,"* Polybius, pp. 43-70, inserted from *"Historiae,,* Book I, II, III, IV, V, VII, VIII, IX, X, XVIII, XX, XXI, XXIII and XXXII; *Scymni*, pp. 72-74, inserted from *"Obris Descriptio"* – Europa.

of the 6th century (when Justinian I declared Justiniana Prima as the church center of Illyricum upgrading it to the vicar rank connecting it directly with Holy Rome), and up to the 8th century (when by a decree of Emperor Leo III it was placed under the jurisdiction of the Eastern Church, i.e. Constantinople), appearing as an identity of the Eastern Empire that would be rightly called "Illyrian Byzantium."[24]

Of course, being called "Illyrian Byzantine" does not present a metaphor, but a specific historical reality based on social, political and cultural factors. These factors, seen to them in accordance with the weight and virtual importance, had to be judged in accordance with the role of ancestors of the Albanian descendants of the Pelasgians (Illyrian-Dardanians) like an internal construction of a natural development rather than "times of invasion" as it was described in the traditional and ideological evaluations. It draws out the traces of their citizenship within the Byzantium edifice (which will be given special attention throughout this review) aimed at eliminating historical straying of the past deliberately fabricated by Serbian, Greek and other historians who have served Great-Greek and Great-Serbian ideas emerging from "Načertanja" and "Megaloidhea" ostensibly about historical non-appearance or absence of Albanians from early Byzantine times until the late Middle Ages following the establishment of Serbian, Greek and other principalities in the Byzantine space, where they were "met" on the periphery of events, usually as strayers or usurpers!

At this important historical outline, with many ambiguities and even more deliberate distortions, along with many open questions that await answers of scientific merit, the autochthony of the Albanians clearly emerges still relating to antiquity (At least in an ancient historical proportion related to the emergence of the first Indo-European people on our continent where Pelasgians were the pioneers of this lengthy process that began in the 6th millennium B.C. and ended sometime in the early millennium B.C. with the first in what is called the invasion of the Dorian or Aegean peoples.).

Despite the "shrinking" of the Illyrians, which has for so long delighted Albanian politics and science enough to turn it into a convention, it does not take away their antiquity or the importance they had as an historical entity. However, the interconnection with the Pelasgians brings

---

[24] Budimir, Milan: *"O etničkom odnosu Dardanaca prema Ilirima,"* Belgrade, 1951.

their offspring into a different light, a light of being a very important factor that links pre-history to history. It simultaneously determines the direction of antiquity, (besides the relativism of the role of Hellenism in antiquity) clarifies the Egyptian and Semitic components of Greek civilization as dominant, and opens the range of the role of Pelasgian civilization and its ancient Dardanian-Macedonian-Illyrian stratification acquired by Hellenism and the political factor that also preceded the Greek one, known as Classical Hellenism.

As the Greek called the Pelasgians and all of the common trunk stratification (Dardanians, Illyrians, Epirotes, Molossians, Macedonians and others) throughout the north and east as "Barbarians," (not in the present-day terms of indicating backwardness but as a different foreign civilization that is not identical with the Hellenic one and had been attained by them by being assimilated into it) then the Pelasgian theory in relation to the Greeks in a "more conciliatory" form turns them into partnership with that civilization by elevating them onto a social and political plain into its direct followers.

However, a good part of the science of linguistics and certain disciplines of historiography (especially that of the 19th and 20th centuries for various reasons, the least scientific in nature) had a cold or disregarding attitude toward the issue. It could not have been forever excluded from research as often desired, because true scientists saw a real key where they could open many secrets and find many answers to open questions, no matter what would result.

This complex scientific explanation for the Albanians and their past is significant not only for being recognized, but also in explaining the time and developmental terms including all aspects of social, cultural and political nature. It related to their relations with others in antiquity and themselves, especially in thick lines known as "Iliad," being a popular epoch, which later in the time of Pisistratus (5th century) was collected into a whole maintenance of what the Hellenes found in the local epoch.[25] Pelasgians laid the cultural foundations of antiquity as they established (with Pythagoras and Aristotle) the main pillars of science and philoso-

---

[25] For more on this see: Johan-Georg von Hahn: "*Studime shqiptare,*" Tirana, 2009, pp. 396, 407; Budimir, Milan: "*O Ilijadi i njenom pesniku,*" Belgrade, 1940, pp. 9, 11; Bernal, Martin. "*Athina e zezë,*" Tirana, 2009; Kola, Aristidh: "*Arvanitasit and prejardhja e grekëve,*" Tirana, 2002; Mathieu, Aref: "*Shqipëria, odiseja e pabesueshme e një populli parahelen,*" Tirana, 2007, p. 14.

phy.[26] This also applies to the City of Athens founded by Pelasgians, and to Rome, founded by Aeneas upon leaving the Trojan War. The same can be said for other social aspects in addition to the Hellenes and later the Romans, Pelasgic heritage noted with its ramified trunk in which Illyrians, Dardanians, Macedonians, Molossians and others that were distinguished with their political and social structures, stable and unstable from tribal to state and royal ones that often appeared as a community or federation, including Molossians League, Epirus League, and Epirus Federation. Apparently, together with the Greeks and Romans, from the 4th and 2nd centuries B.C. when they were ultimately defeated by the Romans,[27] they were joint participants in the political arena of antiquity, which according to many testimonies of the time, were denied to them even by their rivals who would later turn invasive.

Even after the loss of independence to Rome, for more than a century later, Illyrians and Dardanians and others of the Pelasgic family continued to be present in the historical arena with their constant revolts against Rome, which, from the administrative point, would allow autonomy and internal self-government where subsequently many Illyrians would rise rapidly to its highest political and military hierarchy.[28] Dardania, however, as a separate branch of Pelasgic root, continuously maintained its importance in the central part of the Balkans and enjoyed a special status similar to that of a state within a state that would be crucial for further maintenance of the Roman Empire in this part of the Balkans. Meanwhile, in 395 A.D. after the administrative division of the Empire into two parts, the remaining Dardanian lands in the Eastern part enabled the emergence of Byzantium with Constantinople as its powerful center, which was built from ground up on the foundations of Dardanian institutional structures, which would protect the edifice of the Empire in the East for ten centuries. At this time, the Byzantine Empire was ruled by Illyrian-Dardanian emperors: Constantine the Great from Nish, Anastasius from Durres

---

[26] Budimir, Milan: "*O Ilijadi i njenom pesniku*," Belgrade, 1940, p. 9; "*Grci i Pelasti,*" Belgrade, 1950, p. 10.

[27] After the capitulation of Gentius in 167, in Shkodra, the Roman Senate decided to divide the Illyrian lands into three parts, while, Dardania, in the meanwhile continued to resist the attacks of Rome and in three major battles, in the years 97, 85, and 84, inflicted huge losses to the Roman military.

[28] In the 3rd and 4th centuries the Roman Empire was ruled by Emperors of Illyrian origin: Decius, Claudius II, Aurelian, Probius, Diocletian and Constantine.

(491-518), Justin from Dardania (518-527) and Justinian I and Tauresium from Shkup of the Macedonian dynasties (527-565).[29]

However, the rise and fall of the Roman Empire in the Illyrian-Dardanian land between the 2nd century B.C. and the 5th century A.D. and the emergence of Byzantium out of structures of the Dardanian autonomous state recognized by Rome - which were the Dardanian Emperors that established the military and political foundations of the East - raises the issue of continuity of the power of Dardania similar to what was once Troy in this part of the world, hence the position that the Illyrians and Dardanians founded and built Byzantium between the 3rd and 9th centuries A.D. One should not only see their administrative, political and ecclesiastical identity, but also elements of their statehood in it, using as a prerequisite wavering from the past position of a conquering Byzantium of Illyrian-Dardanian ethnicity in favor of the stance of Byzantium being created by Illyrian-Dardanians as a continuation of ancient Troy, while other barbarian nations from the East (primarily Slavs and Avars) invaded and destroyed it from within even after Byzantium accepted and created opportunities for them to stay in it.

Although historiography often holds different attitudes about the connections of Dardanians and Dardania and Illyrians and Illyria, which are sometimes differentiated from one another, there are cases when Dardanians are unilaterally separated from Illyrians and attached to the Thracians and others in the East. However, growing into one of the most important factors in the central area of the Balkans, Aegean and Anatolia[30] (mentioned also as founders of Troy), this did not diminish their common Pelasgic roots or the Illyrians with them and others from this great family regardless of their closeness and mixtures with others around them, which were quite natural. However, the differences seem to occur at the point that the Illyrians, since the very first reports about them from ancient and later day authors, appear as scattered tribes from the Adriatic to the Ionian Sea, the Alps and the Danube, connected to each other sometimes as tribal communities and kingdoms that rose and fell quickly, or even in other not always steadfast political connections. Initially, Dardanians appeared as children of their first direct heirs related to the center of ancient Troy, where even after its fall from the Greeks continued to search for that decision-making center to move

---

[29] *"Historia e Popullit Shqiptar,"* Volume I, Tirana 2002, p. 739.
[30] See Grga Novak: *"La nazionalita dei Dardani,"* published in *"Arhiv za arbanasku starinu,"* Belgrade, 1950, pp. 4, 72, 89.

elsewhere as Aeneas had done. He moved to Italy in order to build Rome, while the Dardanians love for Troy was overwhelmed 20 centuries later when, another Dardan, Constantine the Great (the founder of Byzantium) who, contrary to Aeneas, claimed the West by building Constantinople at Dardanelles, as their forefathers did with Troy.

The great emperor had a vision of restoring the fame of the ancient empire as a continuation of Dardanian power that was destroyed 2,000 years earlier by its Hellenic rivals as others after him, especially the Justinian. Furthermore, it is not by chance that he, "as a Christian" like most Dardanians, being the first to have accepted Christianity in order to strengthen his authority, continued to maintain a pagan belief. This is also evidenced by a message buried in a sarcophagus adorned with Dardanian idols. Even though at that time the sarcophagus of the powerful Emperor of Byzantium with the Dardanian gods was seen as a metaphor of trust between the force and strength of faith, it does not exclude the importance of power in the homeland of the Emperor in all historical developments from antiquity to our time as a permanent arena in which many of the world events of major importance would occur. These events include the administrative division of the empire in the 4th century A.D., the creation of the province of Illyricum, restoration of Dardania to an ecclesial center from the 5th century to the 9th century, separation of church in the 11th century, Barbarian Slavic and Bulgarian invasions, and the Battle of Dardania between the Balkan Christians and the Ottomans in 1389, the collapse of Byzantium in the fifteenth century, and others that would follow in the wake of the collapse of the Ottoman Empire and beyond, which gave the epithet of a "knot of two worlds."

In this respect, most objective observations of Dardanians and Dardania since ancient times are important not only because they further clarify their Pelasgic origin, which has already been scientifically accepted, but also simultaneously clarify their ties to the Illyrians, in terms of kinship, that is accepted as a matter of common ethnicity deriving from the large Illyrian family. Even from the standpoint of a social and political rivalry it can be inferred to from the "Iliad," which often found opposing sides, it renders true the dilemma that the direct descendants of Pelasgians were of the same trunk from Central Europe, the Mediterranean, and the Aegean to Asia Minor. Socially and politically they lived in different circumstances, as they often succumbed to their interests without excluding the mutual conflicts and wars in the 2nd and 1st centuries B.C.

CHAPTER 1

Pelasgians and the Puzzle of Antiquity

The circumvention of the Pelasgic issue aimed at granting the Greeks the title-deed of Hellenism and antiquity. - The authors of antiquity, focusing on the Pelasgians and their values upon which Hellenism was based, brought down the unscientific theories of Phil-Hellenism. - The major role of the Pelasgians comes to highlight the explanation of prehistoric and historic times and their merits to the ancient civilization. - Greek deities of Pelasgic origin. - The meaning of the word Pelasgian and explanation of Goddess Demeter through cosmogonist theory.

The understanding and explanation of antiquity from the Copper Age leads to the Pelasgic question, although it can be said that it has finally been accepted since the time when Johann Georg von Hahn and well-known German researchers raised the central issue of the Indo-Europeans and its deeper understanding,[31] had been sabotaged, circumvented and often ignored in various ways (mainly on unscientific grounds). This happened in the 18th and 19th centuries when Hellenistic studies took great momentum and almost the entire edifice of European civilization was attributed to the ancient Greeks, despite clear warnings that the Pelasgians, under the influx of early peoples in prehistoric times coming from the northeast across land and sea and the early Neolithic (i.e. from the sixth millennium and beyond) lived across the European space (the Balkan, Apennine, and Iberian Peninsula, the Mediterranean, Aege-

---

[31] See: Hahn, Georg von: "*Albanensische Studien,*" Jena, 1854; Karl O. Müller: "*Prolegomena,*" 1825, stating among others the following: "*The more intelligence that is penetrated in the history of Greece, the more attention will be paid to the Pelasgian element, hitherto sacrificed.*"

an) and extended even further to Anatolia and the Caucasus,[32] leaving deep and irascible traces behind. These traces began about three millenniums before the Greeks emerged in the Balkans, whose arrival was related to the so-called Dorian immigration, sometime in the 12th century B.C.

Although ancient authors have accepted the Pelasgian factor (not only as a residue present in the Greek culture but also as people, who faced upon arrival of the Greeks, began in these parts in which they blended well with them, and as Herodotus admitted calling the Ionians "Pelasgians turned Hellenes by adopting Greek language")[33] this recognition has not been duly followed by respective research on the grounds that the name Pelasgians was a generic name defining a heterogeneous population, even "strayed" like storks using as "proof" of this an inappropriate pun in Greek ("*pelargos*"), announcing in this way Pelasgians and their language extinction.

By the second half of the last century to present times, when the famous euphoria of philhellenism passed what the Germans created as reasons of wishing to strengthen the race-centered Aryan theory, greatly overestimated the Greeks at the expense of others. Pelasgians seemed to "wake up" in order to return to the historic scene where they had been "forgotten" or ignored initially as important actors in return to the point between prehistoric and historical time dealing with people's movements of Indo-European family in the directions of the old continent from the center of which they subsequently ramified in different directions, so that this attention continued to focus precisely on the relations with Hellenes and their role in classical antiquity in the 8th to the 5th centuries B.C. and other larger issues as well.

In all these movements or journeys, the Pelasgian factor is particularly important, not just as an impenetrable authentic prehistoric stratification which marks the only known link between indigenous element in the European space (from the middle Neolithic time to the bronze and iron one), but simultaneously important for the historical era that has to do with the formation of ethnic and state-organized formations at the so-

---

[32] See on this: Kretschmer, Paul: *"Die Illyerier in iren Sprachbeziehungen zu ital. Und Griechen,"* Gottingen, 1896; R, Krahe *"Die alten Balkan-Illyrischen geograpchischen namen,"* Heidelberg, 1925; "Müller, K. O: *"Geschichten hellenischer Stämme und Städte,"* Breslau, 1820; A. Fik: *"Vorgrichische Orstnamen,"* M. Budimir: *"Ilirski problem i leksička grupa Teuta,"* Split, 1953, p. 13, Bernal, Martin: *"Athina e zezë,"* Tirana, 2009, p. 108.

[33] See: Herodotus: *"Historiae,"* (I, 57 – VIII, 44 and VII, 95).

called Anatolian-Mediterranean union. Troy and its emergence, (imagined by Homer) opened the curtain to the scene of archaic Hellenism from the 8th to the 5th centuries, which was reflected in Greece and then Rome and continued in that state until 300 A.D. when it yielded to Byzantium for the formation of which the descendants of Pelasgians, Illyrians and Dardanians played a major role in strengthening and protecting it to its last breath. Meanwhile others (Slavs and Greeks), in various forms, were trying to benefit from this development.

From this point of view, Pelasgians are the only people to whom the turn of history appears in a dual role; as a factor that its participation has directly influenced the emergence of the Hellenic and Roman civilization and also left offspring that would be able to compete with them. In the first case, by bringing cultural stratification (language, mythology and even something of a social order) to be called the "Classical Indo-Europeans,[34]" this is also evidenced by ancient authors Homer, Herodotus, Strabo, Aristotle and others as well as Roman authors. In the second case, by leaving behind a legacy of important ethnicity, tribal and state formations including those like the Dardanian-Illyrian-Macedonian ones (which were in constant battle from the south and southwest with the Greeks, Romans, and the north and north-east against the noted Avarian, Celtic, and particularly Slavic incursions that continued in the Byzantine time to the Middle Ages) would have to recognize actors in this historically important part of European and Western civilization in general.

The assumed dual role of the Pelasgians as being an important ethnic, tribal, and state factor (tribes, tribal kingdoms, and kingdoms), which was bound by the Greeks and called "Barbarians" or un-emancipated because of the way the Greeks referred to non-Greek neighbors, is also of importance for the developments dealing with the last three centuries of the old time (i.e. that of the outline of tough confrontations) on one hand between Hellenes and "Barbarians" from the North in their drive towards the near and far East for world domination (as happened at the time of Alexander of Macedonia), and on the other, those with Rome driven for domination in the Mediterranean Basin and beyond (through the spread of colonization).

In both these scenarios the relationship between the non-Greeks with the "Barbarians" of the north, whether in fierce wars between them or in

---

[34] See: Milan Budimir *"De Illyriies et Protoillyriis,"* in *"Vjesnik za Arheologiju i Historiju Dalmatinsku,"* Zagreb, 1951, p. 3.

occasional alliances with them, would again be determined by the descendants of Pelasgians from their common trunk with its numerous and varied branches as the Dardanian, Illyrian, Macedonian and other Epirotan ones. They shared ethnicity and language but differed on a social and political plain, which was quite natural stretching in such a wide space linked to other cultures (from the west of Europe, across the Mediterranean to Asia Minor and north of Africa.)

Even in this case, it would be the Greek sources (historians, poets, philosophers and statesmen) who testified on dealings with non-Greek inhabitants, the "Barbarians" from the north, which besides the Hellenized Pelasgians as Herodotus was making it known,[35] appeared Illyrians, Macedonians, Epirotes, Thracians and especially Dardanians. Similar ancient evidence often appeared as "confusing" because after losing the war of Troy, these peoples were found in different parts and in different roles, simultaneously (In Italy under the Aeneas track-lifting, founding Rome, in Epirus and the Greek border, leading the Dardanian state, and in Anatolia to the Caucasus always bringing some proof of their unknown antiquity that would always evoke curiosity to separate them from the Pelasgian trunk and the great influence they had and continued to maintain in the Central Balkans and other parts.). However, they were "foreign," a term that is very ethnically, culturally, socially and even politically defining.

Authentic historical records since antiquity, archeological ones from the past two centuries, and linguistic records, which in terms of ancient proto-Indo-European "fossils" decipher ancient language status before and after the onset of Linear A and Linear B,[36] (without excluding mythology and anthropology) now more than ever support a comprehensive social and political review between Hellenes and "Barbarians." According to ancient Greek sources, Epirotes and Macedonians at the time of

---

[35] See: Herodotus: "*Historiae,*" p. 46, cited according to "*Ilirët dhe Iliria te autorët antikë,*" Prishtina, 1979, p. 16.

[36] *Linear A,* deals with syllabic writing that replaces the one with symbolic drawings. It is a disk of Crete from 1650 BC, found in the city of Faistose. It has been assessed that the language should be proto-Ionian, that in the opinion of many linguists (Budimir, Krahe, etc.), since it is not related to the ancient Greek and other languages, it can only be related to the ancient Pelasgian. Mycenae were using Linear A to write down their accounts on clay tablets. Such were those dealing with Linear B.

Strabo[37] were non-Greeks, (i.e. "Barbarians," showing Epirotes, Macedonians and Illyrians appeared as relatives based on numerous indications of the time); Epirotes and Macedonians made up the core of Tyrrhenian-Pelasgian people, and some tribes, (especially Etruscans and Dardanians) played a role in the history of Italy and Thrace,[38] something that despite these variations of ancient authors, the Greek image of the Illyrians shows that in the broadest sense and as scattered as they were, they were Pelasgians.

This definition, which relies on Strabo's data,[39] which applies as an almost unique template for others, helps to understand and rebuild from the ethnic, political and social point of view, a good portion of what is taken for the Pelasgic root of the common trunks and numerous branches and sub-branches in a larger space. This root preserves the key to many historical explanations that have followed and continue to follow some issues regarding the appearance of some of the characteristic linguistic stratifications of the Illyrian in relation to the Bask in the Iberian Peninsula, Caucasian dialects, or the Celtic-Baltic ones in the North. This has caused inconsistency on a part of scientists, who based on these hypotheses often see the Illyrians in various places and in different roles, sometimes located in the central parts of the Balkans, coming from the Iller river which flows into the Danube by the Ulm River in Germany[40] from where they continue to flow out into Italy (Venetians, Messapians).[41]

---

[37] See: Strabo: Chapter I, V/8.

[38] See: Johan Georg von Hahn: *"Studime shqiptare,"* Tirana, 2009, p. 291.

[39] See: Strabo, *"Geografica,"* p. 150-164, in *"Ilirët dhe Iliria te autorët antikë,"* Prishtina, 1979.

[40] See: P. Kreschmer in *Glota XXX*, p. 147, who accepted Pocorn's thesis according to which the epicenter of the Illyrians was the parot of River Iller near Ulm of Germany feeding into the Danube. Moving away from the previous thesis about the epicenter of the old Illyrians coming from Visla, Kretschmer was based on an analysis of the Illyrian hydronym *Tilurius*, the etymology of which he links with the origin of the inhabitants of that part, supposedly called *Iliuris*. This theory and that of pan-Illyricism of Frank Schahermayer provoked a response from Milan Budimir (see *"De Illyres et Protoillyres,"* pp. 1-3, *"Vjesnik za Aerhologiju i Historiju Dalmatinsku"* - LIII 1950-1951).

[41] For more see: Krahe, Hans: *"Der Venetische. Seine Stellung im Kreise der verwandten Sprache,"* Heilderbert, 1950; Krahe, Hans: *"Der Sprache der Illyrer,"* I, Die Quellen, Wiesbaden, 1955; J. Schmid: *"Einleitung in die Geschichte der griechieschen Sprache."*
German scientists rely mainly on German archaeological sources, according to which Venetians and Etrurians, on their way to the Italic Peninsula were carriers of a culture

Sometimes they set their epicenter in the Balkans, north and northeast of Greece,[42] without missing the fact that one of their important branches, called Aegean-Anatolian, with great influence on the Cretan-Mycenaean period and its culture, reached as far as Caucasus and Mesopotamia.[43]

This separation from the standpoint of historical perspective, (even if seen through evidence of ancient authors) would also look formal if not fraught with fundamental aspects of the role of Hellenism in antiquity in relation to the presence of the proto-Indo-European factor in it, where Pelasgians not only appear insurmountable, but also extremely important in determining it both in its early stage of the emergence of Greeks in the Aegean area, and later when certain groups of tribes and peoples, of the same origin, would appear in this stratification as they who would often actively participate in the social and political developments of the time.

Treated by Greeks in a barbarian way even after they were occupied and degraded by them (as admitted by the most important ancient authors), and their long wars against the *"Sons of the divine Pelasgians"* from the Trojan war on that would culminate with those of Macedonians during the time of Alexander the Great, they subdued but not assimilated them as the Egyptian Dorians had done with their ancestors after they invaded Peloponnese and Attica four centuries earlier. This shows that Hellenism, in the way it appeared in the last two centuries on a scientific, social and political plain, was much more exclusive from the outside towards the composing factors (i.e. by many European Philhellenes rather than by the Greeks of the time themselves, the latter recognizing the

---

called *"Urnenfelderkultur"* (urn field culture) of the Luzitc type in Germany, dating from the beginnings of the third millennium to the period of the Halschtat culture, which is generally perceived with a dominance of the Illyrian tribes in the Mediterranean parts.

[42] See: Johan Georg von Hahn *"Studime shqiptare,"* Tirana, 2009, pp. 291-296.

[43] See: Bernal, Martin *"Athina e zezë,"* Tirana, 2009; Aref, Mathieu: *"Mikeint = Pellazgët,"* Tirana, 2008. Budimir, Milan: *"De Illyriis et Protoillyriis,"* Vjesnik za Arheologiju i Historiju Dalmatinsku LIII 1950-1951, pp. 1-4, By addressing the spread of stratification that he calls proto-Illyrian from Italy, in the Central Balkans to Anatolia and connecting it with the Pelasgians, who according to Homer were called Pelastes, Budimir relies on the toponym *Tauromenian*, which was introduced into the Greek by the Illyrian vernacular. He also raises the question of the presence of classical Indo-Europeans - the Illyrians in the Cretan-Myceanean era, evidenced not only in geographical names, which have been explored for more than a century, but according to known chronological cycle counting as *"primitive time-reckoning"* that they had, also emphasized by Pythagoras, admitting that it had been taken from the eastern Balkan "barbarians."

merits of the *divine Pelasgians* from the beginning and later of "their family," Illyrians and other "barbarians," including Macedonians) who even when acquired after being conquered by the Greeks and after adopting their language (something that does not make them Greeks), their rivalry was admitted.

Therefore, pursuant to this observation, it is interesting to see a bit more plainly ancient historical evidence on the Pelasgians, in addition to spiritual evidence (mythology, linguistics) all would be rebuilt using archeological material remains and research by anthropology and other scientific disciplines.

It is also important because after that one can examine the entirety of what is called "The Pelasgic Legacy," which extends in many directions, one can point to historical, social and political relationships that can shed light on the internal relations of the whole "Big Pelasgic Family" (Illyrian-Thracian) and may also get a clearer picture about those developments occurring with the appearance of the big branches of this family with Illyrians, Dardanians, Macedonians, Epirotes and other non-Greek tribes. An ongoing confrontation over several centuries with Hellenes and the Romans, in which kingdoms, states or state alliances passed (including divided tribes who often did not pursue common social and political aims) were often found on opposing sides during long wars of Macedonians against Dardanians and Illyrian tribes, or those of Dardanians against the Illyrian Kingdom in the time of Teuta, something that complicates the entire social and political landscape of the time.

This clarified what happened with the Pelasgian factor and its presence at the time of Hellenic incursions in the Peninsula and Crete when one of the first stations of Hellenism was considered in passing to its direction (north-west or northeast). Deserving and unequivocal ancient Greek and Roman sources appeared where the main records regarding the large family of the descendants of the Pelasgians with Illyrians, Macedonians, Epirotes, Dardanians, Venetians, and Etrurians, came from them despite shortcomings and inconsistencies in keeping the familiar historical line mentioned since their conflicts.

However, Greek and ancient Roman sources, despite their shortcomings regarding this issue, remain the only ones that provide visual evidence of their wars with their northern neighbors, "Barbarians," which they sometimes called "Illyrian people" whom they separated in different tribes and kingdoms alongside Epirotes, Macedonians, Dardanians, and others who were also seen as barbarians and foreign.

Besides historical records that came "coincidentally" while dealing with neighbors, one can learn in detail about the "interferences" of Taulantii in the civil war in the Peloponnese, Molossians interfering in the internal wars of the Greeks, Dardanians against Macedonians and Pyrrhus and his penetration in Italy. Geographical and other records of great reliability speak of their spatial extension and their clashing with their neighbors to the north and northeast (speaking of Celts, Balts, and Slavs which are of particular factual importance). One may rebuild their outward appearance without excluding the possibility that this also applies to understanding their inner appearance including social and political forms of the descendants of Pelasgians of the large tree branching of Illyrians, Dardanians, Epirotes or Macedonians in relation to the Greeks and Romans.

Before going to the testimony of Pelasgic antiquity in terms of historical data, a prelude to the Pelasgian cosmogonist theory is needed, which according to Herodotus (father of history) the Greeks took their gods from the Pelasgians, saying:

> From the Pelasgians then the Greeks received them (understandably the gods). As to where each god came from, if all of them existed, was not known "till the day before yesterday," as the saying goes. Indeed, Hesiod and Homer might have been older than me in age of four hundred, not more. But they were those who gave theogony to Greeks and gave the gods their names, embellishing them with honors and crafts, and showed their face.[44] Receiving gods from the Pelasgians, the Greeks decorated them with fine appellations, determining their faces, skills, place, and origin, as they needed them.

The cosmogonist theory of the Pelasgians is *"Earth the Mother of all, Demeter giver of wealth."*[45]

However, this assessment requires more extensive explanations, which can be illustrated only by the writings of ancient authors. Philologist Spiro N. Konda assesses that *"Dhe mëmë"* (Alb. for *"Earth the Mother"*) of Diodorus is but an apposition to the word *"Demeter."*[46] In fact, the

---

[44] Herodotus: Book, II, Chapt. 53, 5-10.
[45] Diodorius: *Suqeljiti*, Volume I, Book I, 12,4.
[46] Konda, Spiro N: *"Shqiptarët dhe problemi pellazgjik,"* Tirana, 1964, p. 220.

word "*Demeter*" (Δημνετηο) is a synthesis of two separate words, the word *De* (δη) and the word *meter* (μηεηο). "*De*" is a Pelasgian word, which means "*earth*," the present-day Albanian word *dhe*. Based on these, "*Demetër*" is equal to (*de meter*) = *dhe mëmë* (Alb. for *Earth Mother*). And, according to philologist Konda, this implies that while the Greeks did not know the meaning of the word "*de*" (δε), declaring synthesis of "*Demetër*" Pelasgian. This, under philologist Konda, makes sense because Herodotus claimed the Greeks took the name "*Demetër*" from the Pelasgians. This *de*, in the old Albanian was originally feminine, without article, while with an article at the end it read *de*-a = *dheu* (*earth*). *Dea* is correlative because by *meme (mother)* there should be *at (father)*, i.e. co-creator. Therefore, the same word formed the masculine "*de-u*" meaning "*dheu*" (*earth*) in the masculine with the meaning of "*dheu*" (*earth*) as *at* (*father*).

Philologist Konda points out that Greeks received "*dea*" and "*deu*" from the Pelasgians, changing "*dea*" to "*thea*," and "*deu*" to "*theos*" through the conversion of consonant *d* in the consonant *th* (according to *det-thetis*, etc). However, to the Greeks "*dea*" and "*deu*" means "*thea*" and "*theos*," losing the meaning of *dheu* (*earth*) being taken as deities (gods, goddesses).[47]

Latins too acquired deities "*dea*" and "*deu*" from the Pelasgians, adding to *de* (*de-u*) their ending -*us* saying: *De-us*. However, "*Dea*" and "*Deus*" had no more the meaning of "*dheu*" (*earth*), but rather the meaning of a *goddess* and *god*. So, from *Deus* derived *Zeus*, hence, by the side of "*mëmë*" came "*Zeus*, father of men and gods," linked to "*dheu*, *mother of all*."[48]

Based on these, the basic understanding of the Pelasgian cosmogonical theory is that of "*the earth as the mother of all*," namely the "*creator of all*."

So, these are the general principles of the cosmogonical theory of the Pelasgians, explaining some of the names of gods and goddesses. Through the use of Albanian there is better proof of this:

So, besides the name "*Demeter*" as "*dhe mëmë*" (*earth mother*) with which the earth appears as *mother of all*, the name *Zeus*, by virtue of assessment by philologist Konda, *Deus* (Δευς) comes from the Pelasgian in its late masculine form *(De-u)*, with the first and basic understanding of

---

[47] Ibid, p. 280.
[48] Ibid, p. 280.

Dheu (*the earth*) as father, as *giver of life*. Hence, the form *Zeus* is the Greek form, not Pelasgian. Consequently, the form *Zeus* for the Greeks did not bear the meaning in the sense of *Dheu* as a father, but rather *their supreme god*. This means that the understanding of *dheu* (*the earth*) is not Greek, but of the people that were using the word *de* in masculine form, namely, *De-u; these are* Pelasgian.

Based on this, the first meaning of the word was *"deu pater"* = *Dhe (earth) is my father*, according to *Demeter* = *Dheu (earth) is my mother*. But, "earth is my father" means differently: "*I am an offspring of earth father,*" or "*I am earth-born.*" This is the first period during which *Dheu* (*the earth*) contained two qualities of birth, feminine and masculine, namely during which the earth was considered both *as a mother* and *as a father*. During this period the words *mater* and *pater* came separately, not together with the word *de (de-u)*.[49]

Concluding the explanation and etymology of the word *Zeus*, as a Pelasgic word, one should also add that the name of god "*Dipatyros*" mentioned by Hsyk of Alexandria has been preserved until today in the Albanian language, meaning *Perëndi* (*God*). This Pelasgian word, "*Dipatyros*" is the basis from which the names of the supreme god of the Japhetic peoples (Anglo-Saxons, Germans, Scandinavians, Lithuanians, etc.) were derived. Thus, for example, the old Germans have: *Ziu, Go*, the Scandinavians: *Tyr, Tyvar, Fjorgun*; the Lithuanians: *Perkunas, Devas*, Goths: *gup*, etc.[50]

There are some additional words other than the gods of Olympus, which according to the philologist Konda, supported visibly by some early assessments by Albanologist von Hahn,[51] directly related to the Pelasgic cosmogony, shared by ancient authors the real meaning of which can only be explained through the Albanian, though their acquisition from the Greeks and Latins was subject to internal linguistic changes (suffixes, metathesis, affixes, analogy, etc.), which, by utilizing this "naturalization" desperate efforts are made to find their origin.

However, as seen with the words *Demetra* and *Zeus*, related to the creation and all that followed in building an opinion of it from a mythological, creative, and philosophical aspect, according to philologist Konda, most of the gods and goddesses of antiquity were connected to the Pelas-

---

[49] Ibid, p. 284.
[50] Ibid, p. 284.
[51] For more see Georg von Hahn: *"Studime Shqiptare,"* Tirana, 2002.

gian root. Among them he brings the following names: *Poseidon* (Ποσειδων), *Afërditë (Afroditë)* (Αφροδιτη), *Apollon* (Απολλον), *Dionis* (Διοννος), *Hera* (Hεα), *Rea* (Pεα), *Athena* (Ατηνα), *Atrytonë* (Ατρυτωνη), *Thetis* (Θετιης), *Tethys* (Τητυς), *Persetonë* (Περσοωοη), *Dionë* (Διωνη).[52]

Furthermore, the Pelasgic cosmogony opens the issue of the etymology of the word *Pelasgian* itself from the viewpoint of different authors from ancient times until today and of its explanation by the Albanian language.

If the word *Pelasgians,* for ancient *Pelasgia residents*, mentioned by almost all ancient writers including Herodotus, Thucydides, Strabo, Hecataeus of Miletus and most importantly, Homer, who in "Iliad" and "Odyssey" does not explain everything. Ancient authors called Pelasgians the oldest inhabitants of their country but without explaining who the Pelasgians were.

Even when this was made there is nothing more than a vague description. Only from the 18th century and 19th century would it become clear that the Greeks were not the alpha and omega of Hellenist antiquity, (as some Philhellenes and their numerous supporters claimed) as it is clear there were others before them including the Pelasgians. Closer assessments began to appear on who the pre-Hellenes were and what the word Pelasgian meant.

Indeed, this issue was linguistically first opened by the German scientist von Hahn without any claim of having the last say. Instead, when he dealt with possible links of the Albanian and Pelasgian explanation of some Greek words with Albanian roots (and he finds a lot of them), he always showed caution. Thus, the word *Pelasgians* is divided by the famous German scholar into *pelasgos*, where at the word *pel* he sees the Greek word *pellos* (πελλος), *pelios* (πελιος), *peleios* (πελειος) = black and the Latin *pellos* (black). In the second syllable he sees the Pelasgian word *argos* (αργος), which to him it represents *arë, agros, ager* (field), in which a variable *r* appeared. Therefore, the word "*pellazgos*" to him means "one who belongs to the black earth."[53]

The Albanian philologist Spiro N. Konda thinks that the word *Pellazg* has a Pelasgian etymology deriving from an old verb *pel*, which in Albanian is pronounced *pjell (gives birth)*, which as medial or passive is *pillem* (from *pjellem*), which as *pill-e-m*, namely *Pell-e-m*, in a more precise way,

---

[52] Spiro N. Konda: *"Shqiptarët dhe problemi pellazgjik,"* Tirana, 1964, p. 59.
[53] Hahn, Johan-Georg von: *"Studime shqiptare,"* Tirana, p. 331.

means "*I am born.*" So, "born" is the verbal theme: *pell (=pel)*; "*jam*" *(am)* is "*E*" and "*unë*" *(I)* is "M."[54]

Thus, in the old verb *pelin* (πελειν) in Albanian *pel* the basic word of explaining the etymology of the word "*Pelasgian*" is found, where through the third element -*g*, which is the dative of the word *ga (g)* γα (γη) = *dheu* (earth), and could have also been *da*, namely Pelasgian *de*, expresses also the Pelasgians cosmogony theory as discussed earlier. Whereas, -ος in the Greek form *Pelazgos* (= Πελασγος), is the ending "*os.*"

Based on these findings, the word "*Pelazgos*" bears pre-Hellenic elements *Pel-as-g*, and the Greek element "*os.*" The Greeks, acquiring the form: *Pelasgia* (= Πελασγα), and *Pelagia* (= Πελαγα) and adding old endings, gave the following forms: *Pelasgos, pelago, Pelasgia, Pelasgis,* etc.[55]

The meaning of the word *Pelazg = I dhelindur (earth-born)* and *Pelazgia = e dhelindur* (fem. *earth-born*), in terms of analogy and semantics, is associated with the word *pelagon* (Πελαγων) and *Pelagoni*, to recharge antiquity which arises from the earth and the genesis, implying antiquity. This word, mentioned by Homer and continuing to the 5th century B.C., brings to mind the Albanian word *Plak (Old man)*. Here too the basic word is *pell*, and if the suffix *on (ov)* is removed its body *Pelag* remains. After the first root of this word was eliminated due to the strong emphasis of *a*, *plag* was formed, where the finite *-g* is equivalent to the finite *–k* of the word *plak*.[56]

The word *Pelag (pel-a-g)* in its meaning is the same as *Pelasg = Pelazg*, for S. Konda is explainable by the fact that that is a different form of the word *Pel-as-g*, in which the Japethic verbal form is with the form *a*.[57]

The focus is on explaining the etymology of the word *Pellag* with *pjell*, seen in the word *Pelagoni-plak-a*, related to Pelasgic antiquity, which means that the Greeks by the word Pelasgian, did not only determine the older one that they found when they came (which has to do with their internal appearance) the divine, which they are not accidentally called by Homer and all the old Greek authors "divine people," "divine Pelasgians," and seen as such in the Greek mythology as well.

---

[54] See Konda, Spiro N: "*Shqiptarët dhe problemi pellazgjik,*" Tirana, p. 336.
[55] Ibid, p. 341.
[56] Ibid, p. 348.
[57] See: "*Shqiparët dhe problemi pellazgjik,*" p. 347, indicating that this form is still in use among the northern Albanians. For example: *kusha a?* (Who is it?)

The certainty of this position can be found in many old ancient authors, starting from Strabo when he says, "They say that in the language of Molossians and Thesprotans, old women are called *pelini* and old men *pelini*,[58] and Hesiki of Alexandria who says the following, as the Coasii and Epirotes call their old men and women *pelius*."[59]

Pelasgian Antiquity from an Historical Point of View

> *Pelasgians, the oldest Indo-European people, who led the influx of peoples from India to the West from the sixth millennium. – Their traces in entire Europe, Asia Minor, the Mediterranean and North Africa testify to the crucial role they had at the dawn of world civilization. - What did Herodotus say about how he saw Pelasgians and their language? - Why did Homer call Pelasgians "divine people?" - According to the testimony of many ancient authors, Pelasgians were a source of inspiration for the Greek culture, which was built on the values obtained from them. - The Crete and the Aegean islands were included within the Pelasgic kingdom. - Mycenae culture was a pure Pelasgic culture.*

What is called the Pelasgian "secret" has to do equally with prehistory and history, as well as with the beginnings of the influx of people from areas of India where three major world civilizations originated: *Aryan* (Indo-European), *Sumerian* (Eastern) and *Torhan* (Chinese), with Pelasgians being the first Indo-Europeans to head West after this division, followed by others. The fact that the Pelasgians were the first Aryans to get detached from the nucleus of the origin of people is important as are the new territories where they were located. Traces of various symbols of original civilization, preserved both by *Sumerians* and *Torhans* including symbols dealing with the sun, water, and various cults of universal nature, spread throughout the old continent, especially in the central part of the Balkans and the Aegean and Mediterranean, which were then interpreted as "influences" that came through different routes out of a common origin by starting somewhere in India, were brought along by the Pelasgians and preserved; cults and symbols as found today in various forms among their descendants (Albanians) will be dealt with later.

---

[58] Strabo, Chapt. 329.
[59] See: Kupitari, Panajot: *"Studime shqiptare,"* Athens, 1879, p. 53, Paragraph 117.

It would be natural that this Pelasgic "secret" and uncertainties appear because of their proper interpretation if issues are to be seen detached from the beginning. The case with similar archaeological remains to the Sumerian and Torhane culture (the cult of sun, anthropomorphic and zoomorphic symbols) is valid for the early prehistoric time, though with more premedial ages, such as those from the Paleolithic and late Neolithic, had to do with one of the most primitive societies, outside any recognized organization and outside the footprint identities that emerged later and were characteristic for the dawn of civilization.

Despite this understanding, it is unnatural when some of the dilemmas like movement of people from the Copper Age and particularly from the Iron Age and the beginning of early antiquity on which data also exist - whether from material and spiritual culture inherited expressed in sign language and primitive art or from ancient sources by ancient authors through writings they left behind - are sometimes intentionally made more confusing in order to conceal important traces of truth upon which erroneous stances are built to serve certain purposes.

This paradox has by all means followed the Pelasgians and, more or less, continued to follow them, although by the second half of the last century, science in principle seems to have reached an agreement on three issues dealing with them:

First - that the prehistoric Pelasgians were part of the Indo-European family of peoples and were Aryans. In the distant past these people lived on the border between Europe and India. They all spoke the same language. They all lived a primitive life, raising goats, gathering fruits, fishing and hunting wild animals for food and clothing. Apparently, from the beginning of the 6th century B.C., a big split occurred, scattering these tribal families centrifugally in all directions. [60] As they scattered and settled in permanent settlements (in the entire European continent, Asia Minor, and reaching as far as North Africa), Pelasgians took with them elements of civilization from the common life somewhere in India, including the following:

- family: *pater, mater, motër, brhatr, brazer, sinus, nus-e,*
- dwelling: *dyer-dvar,*
- cattle-raising: *gaus, dam, vat-sa, mus, çvan, marg,*
- knitting: *vas-esthes,*

---

[60] Jacques, Edwin: "*Shqiptarët,*" Tirana, p. 64.

- farming: *jug-zygod, ajra-as = ar-a, ratha-as,*
- measure of weight: *mat=metron, bhar=fortos,*
- counting according to the decimal system: *dya, tria, katur,* etc.[61]

One should also note the hexadecimal (base 16) Sumerian system.

Alongside these they also took along the religion, which is discussed in length on Pelasgic cosmogony and its impacts on Greeks and other European peoples.

Secondly - prehistoric Pelasgians during this movement of peoples from India were among the first to approach the West so that from the beginning of the Early Neolithic era, they reached the Central European space, where they settled and continued to meet indigenous peoples and assimilating them. It is estimated that "stabilization" in the new environment extended over a millennium, but later on the most ancient Indo-Europeans, Pelasgians, after other cyclic invasions from the north, relocated to other southern parts of the continent, following with "peripheral" movements eastwards (in Asia Minor), the Aegean and Mediterranean area, to touch upon the coast of Africa, regardless how their direction is explained, and regardless of the fact that this sometimes is explained in a quite controversial way, they eventually ceased with the Dorian or Aegean one between the 14th and 12th centuries B.C.[62]

However, in these cases, there are also differences, disparities, and even contradictions of a different nature. The appearance and "stabilization" of the first Indo-Europeans on the central European basin, and their subsequent movements, comprising the time from the 6th to the 3rd millennium, would be seen in different directions (northwest towards the South and from northeast towards the South) without excluding the other observation that sees these movements in an "intermediate" direction, observing that the great movement of peoples followed a direction through the Caucasus, Asia Minor, and from there, via the Black Sea, through the flow of Danube towards the center of Europe. There it ramified in the three peninsulas and the North and from there turning southwards. "Intermediate" observation is based on geographical factors (climate, river valleys, surrounding plateaus, fish, game, etc.), which geography, sometimes rightly and sometimes unfairly, claims to turn into an arbiter over the historical one.

---

[61] Konda, Spiro N: *"Shqiptarët dhe problemi pellazgjik,"* Tirana, 1964, p. 50.
[62] Ibid, p. 64.

Third - despite numerous difficulties in identifying the Pelasgic legacy, which has long been a source of disagreements and differences expressed in extreme views, being on one hand denied on the grounds that "their traces have been erased and on the other, even when it had been viewed it was not duly animated. However, there is an agreement on the existence of a Pelasgian legacy and that it necessarily leads to the Albanians, though further interdisciplinary research must justify this development. The current concentration on the Illyrian-Albanian connection, not only does not exclude the Pelasgian theory of the origin of the Albanians, it also helps it to gain the proper scientific explanation.

Apparently, subscriptions in principle to the three above-mentioned issues, although creating a more or less settled realistic framework of Pelasgic assumptions in favor of the opinion that Pelasgians were the first Indo-Europeans and to the benefit of the Albanians as their descendants (without excluding any other residue), may still lack full consensus and acceptance. On one hand, they undermine the stereotype for Hellenes as carriers of antiquity, which highlights the increasing role of the Pelasgians on the rise of the Greeks on their merits. On the other, promoting on the Indo-European plain, Pelasgians as "classical Indo-Europeans," and being an epithet due to specialized linguistic studies concurring on the Albanian, it continues to maintain the three circles of the gutturals, consideration of *Satem-Kentum* divisions as becoming increasingly credible by which the two very pretentious theories lose a lot of credibility in their drive for this historic "trophy" (A very important one for our civilization: namely the Celtic-German and Baltic-Slavic one).

But, what do the ancient sources say about the role of the Pelasgians (historians, philosophers, and even Homer himself) in order for their entitlement as important carriers of antiquity to be accepted? This would deprive the Greeks of some of the merits they have acquired from others and spark many social, cultural and political taboos conjured up during the last two centuries, filling the libraries throughout the world.

However, the Greek authors themselves prove that following their arrival to Hellada (they even link this with Egypt, which is entirely inconsistent with their Aryan and Indo-European affiliation), they found Pelasgians as an indigenous population despite potential assimilation and constant shrinking. They continued to remain there with their renown features from Athens (which they founded) with their independent kingdoms, their social domestic life, and their spiritual cults, altars and gods, while in the North were the "barbarians," foreigners, in permanent neighborhoods and engaged in frequent battles with them.

The same can be said about the *Leleges, Curetes, Epeii,* and *Caucones,* whose connections with the Pelasgians are not known quite exactly, but were not excluded from being of Pelasgic tribes, having been renamed by the Hellenes. This does not change the fact that they were indigenous peoples among which the Pelasgians dispersed in their major settlements in Argos, Arcadia, Attica, Boeotia, and Thessaly, being most powerful.

Regardless of the dilemma about the Pelasgian factor and its tribal ramifications and social and spiritual coherence that it might have had in the new circumstances, this does not change the truth that a certain and stable basis of civilization existed there, which was used to move further.

Furthermore, these revered authors admit that the Pelasgians possessed their own idols in Dodona and elsewhere, as well as temples that caused the Greeks to call them *"heavenly people,,"* including Homer.[63] According to the famous author of antiquity they also had Zeus, the King of Kings. He was adorned as *"Dodona and Pelasgian King, living far away,"*[64] implying that cults, gods, myths, were adopted from them, including their writing. Many scholars assume that the Phoenician alphabet, which the Greeks supposedly borrowed from the Phoenicians, might have originally been borrowed from the Pelasgians. The Phoenicians are considered by many meritorious sources to be a Pelasgian "stem," without excluding the possibility of Phoenicians borrowing the alphabet from the Pelasgians, which they changed a bit for their needs spreading it throughout their settlements,[65] an open issue to be discussed extensively when dealing with the Pelasgian antiquity from the language standpoint.

According to the ancient authors, the history of Pelasgians began with Hellada and remains within it as an integral part, even though centuries later, the Philhellenes, for known political reasons, tried to circumvent this supposing that it allegedly meant "indigenous elements," which did not leave any marks and was of no consequence.

What Johann Georg von Hahn said half a century before regarding Albanians requiring more study,[66] the more he studied them, had to do

---

[63] Homer *"Iliada,"* Book X, Verse 429, Tirana, 1979.
[64] Ibid, Book XVI, line 233.
[65] For more on this see: Johan Georg von Hahn: *"Studime shqiptare,"* Tirana, 2009, pp. 370-389.
[66] See *"Studimet shqiptare,"* Tirana, 2009, p. 408.

precisely with the Pelasgic antiquity as an essential issue of which the Hellenes themselves were aware, leaving extensive evidence of them, although they were not always properly regarded. Much of the evidence was allegedly "contradictory,"[67] and beyond the reach of true documentation which regains weight when associated with living proof, as with Albanians as their descendants. This then opens the way of clarifying the many other issues which were considered or had to be considered as pertaining to the dust of time. From this perspective ancient sources and others of that time were of great importance for revealing a "silent" truth, and also for establishing a natural link between antiquity and the future.

Let us start with the father of history, Herodotus.

What does he have to say about this "closeness of distance" dealing with the descendants of those that Greeks found in Hellada when they embarked there for the first time?

The fact that he accepts that Pelasgians, as Homer says, "were heavenly"[68] with their temple of Dodona, which according to Hesiod, was built "by the will of Zeus who wanted it to be a precious sanctuary for the people,"[69] clearly shows that the Pelasgians were an indigenous population organized in accordance with the circumstances of the time with a degree of awareness of tribal society and its way to becoming a slave-owning society. This not only remained, but also influenced the newcomers to accept a lot of their culture from where they would then enter jointly in

---

[67] Those considered as "contradictory," of the "material" nature refer mostly to what Herodotus says about the names of the gods who, according to him, the Pelasgians brought out of Egypt, but this has to do with "some uncertainties" about determining that Macedonians were Hellenes at times and as part of the "barbarian" world at other times, and this "tampering" actually related more to the fact that the Greeks call Pelasgians by their real name as citizens of Greece in Athens, Peloponnesus, and wherever present in that vicinity, called "barbarians" all those in their neighborhood, their name being associated with the affiliation of the country. For example, the Pelasgian tribes in Epirus were called Epirotes, others Molossians, and the same about the Macedonians, who were often called Hellenes once some of their tribes were included within the composition of the Greek state, although acknowledging that they had "preserved their barbaric language." Here then arises all that is seen as "confusion" or contradictions, which, with a bit of care can easily be explained, but this explanation leads to the Pelasgian factor and its crucial role in ancient times.

[68] Homer: "Iliada," Book X, Verse 229.

[69] Hesiod: From the poem *"Carmin,"* cited according to *"Ilirët dhe Iliria te autorët antikë,"* Prishtina, 1979, p. 14.

the important social and political developments of the time. From this observation, the fact that Herodotus identified Spartans as Pelasgians and not as Greek is meaningful, giving further weight to the Pelasgian role in determining the social structure of Hellenism.

"With *Ionians*, the Greek newcomers also mixed with *Arcadians*, *Cadmus*, *Pelasgians*, and *Dorians*, *Epidaurus*, as well as many other tribes."[70]

So says Herodotus for those found in Hellada. But the mention of Dorians, who were found in Hellada together with Pelasgians and others, opens the question of the Dorians themselves who are so often mentioned as founders of Greece, arriving from northwest sometime between the 12th and 10th centuries B.C. upon the last influx of peoples, the *Aegean*, considered the destroyers of Troy and its civilization.

Even when bypassing this issue, which would be dealt with more closely in further observations, there is another issue of which Herodotus leaves valuable evidence by saying that "Pelasgians spoke a barbarian language" that "the Pelasgian tribes still preserve today."[71]

The issue of the Pelasgic language, which Herodotus mentions without saying what language it was, is of extraordinary importance as they spoke their own language that appeared as a separate entity with their distinct traditions and customs, and drives away the mist over the Greeks having allegedly found nothing in Hellada.[72]

Herodotus himself says the following: "In early times the Pelasgi, as I know by information which I got at Dodona, offered sacrifices of all kinds, and prayed to the gods, but had no distinct names or appellations for them, since they had never heard of any. They called them gods (Theoi, disposers), because they disposed and arranged all things in such a beautiful order."[73]

So they were people who "disposed and arranged all things in a beautiful order," and above all they held the laws of the universe, laws that would be valid for a long time among the Hellenes while they turned to thinking about a comprehensive explanation.

Herodotus said that Pelasgians having no distinct names or appellations for the gods in order to continue that "after a long lapse of time the

---

[70] Herodotus: *"Historiae,"* Book I, p. 46.
[71] Ibid, p. 52.
[72] See Johan Georg von Hahn: *"Studime shqiptare,"* Tirana, 401-403.
[73] Herodotus: *"Historiae,"* Book II, p. 52.

names of the gods came from Egypt, and the Pelasgi learned them."[74] This acknowledgment came "not long after the arrival of the names about which they sent to consult the oracle at Dodona,"[75] which according to the Greek historian was the only ancient oracle in Greece at that time. After receiving the answer, they used the names since "the Pelasgi made use of the names of the gods and passed them down to the Greeks."[76]

So, all of this opens the question of a direct influence of Pelasgians in the spiritual, social and political life of the Greeks, regardless of the fact that the issue has been rarely touched, or has been deliberately kept silent for the already known reason that in the past two centuries antiquity was entirely connected to Hellenes and Hellenization and those from whom had been taken the most.

The Pelasgian impact on the spiritual life of the Greeks and everything after twenty centuries has surfaced as the cradle of civilization and rightly regarded as an exceptional heritage. It is best reflected in Hesiod's "Theogony,"[77] a poem about the creation of the gods, which supports what Herodotus himself would accept about the names of gods adopted by Hellenes from the Pelasgians three centuries later, although some changes of their names and images, continue to bear the same "messages."

Viewed from this perspective the whole Greek mythology and its extraordinary power to reflect a world in motion between the known and the unknown, (displaying itself wonderfully with heroes, semi-heroes, and other surreal creatures spawning from a very rich imagination, stems from the Pelasgians, who according to Homer were "divine") could have served as a model to be accepted in order to then from there start a Hellenic differentiation of philosophical, social, and political thinking that had been so dominant at the time of Aristotle. His leaning towards philosophy and mathematics demanded a detachment from the "clutches" of mythic imagination, demanded by Socrates, Pythagoras and others coming after them as well. That can be explained not only as an escape from imagination for scientific research purposes, but also to overcome

---

[74] Ibid, p. 52.

[75] Ibid, p. 53.

[76] Ibid, p. 53.

[77] *Hesiod* was one of the important Greek poets. He lived in the 8th-7th centuries BC. He wrote two poems in hexameter, one of them (Theogony) dealing with the creation of gods in a completely mythological content, pointing out that Greek gods were mainly appropriated from the Pelasgians.

the impact of the acquisition of an old culture, which had to be "overcome."

The superiority of the Pelasgians over the Hellenic newcomers is admitted by yet another Greek historian, (one of the most important ones after Herodotus), Thucydides,[78] known also as the father of political history. He was among the most direct by saying that "Before the Trojan war nothing appeared to have been done by Greece in common; called all by that one name of Hellas; nor before the time of Hellen, the son of Deucalion, was there any such name at all. Pelasgicum (which was the farthest extended) and the other regions, received their names from their own inhabitants."[79]

According to the noted historian, Athens and its greatness too was inherited from the Pelasgians who, he says, inhabited Athens before, and the construction of big stones below Athens's castle was Pelasgian.[80]

Herodotus, like the others who called Pelasgic tribes "barbarians," described in the same way Chaonians, Thesprotians, and Molossians, who once helped the struggles of Corinth. For the Enchelei, who came to the help of Lyncestis, he said, "we're warrior people," and thanks to their bravery, Macedonians fled the field of war as losers.[81]

The presence of Pelasgians in Hellada, and the great role it played in the emancipation of the settlers, are documented by records from almost all ancient authors, filling the big picture of a large mosaic in antiquity, which was neither deserted nor reportedly deserted nor a situation when everything started from scratch which is connected with the Greeks having a sustainable economic, social and even political life. It had its kings, connected to a dynasty of seven generations, a time leading directly

---

[78] *Tucídides (Thucydides)* was born in Athens around 460 B.C. and died after 400. In 424 he was commander of an Athens naval unit near the island of Thasos. As he was unable to prevent the fall of Amphioples, Athenians sentenced him with death in absentia. He lived in exile until 404, and for a few years in Athens. As an historian, Tucídides touched on the issue of the Pelasgians leaving behind direct evidence of the Illyrians from the civil war in Epidamnos where the Illyrian tribe of Taulanti became involved in the war. He also writes on the participation of several tribes of Southern Illyria on the Spartan side during the Peloponesian War.

[79] Tucídides: *"Historiae,"* Book I, 3, cited according to *"Ilirët dhe Iliria te autorët antikë,"* Prishtina, 1979, p. 24.

[80] Ibid, Book IV, 126.

[81] Ibid, Book IV, 126.

to Troy as a Pelasgic center. Among these important testimonies are also those of Diodorus, which he shows alongside the continental part, where the islands of the Aegean, Lesbos, Argos and Lycos were inhabited by Pelasgians.[82] In these historic enclosures, focused on the island of Argos, Diodorus spoke of the son of the Pelasgian King Xanthius from which one learns that Triopus was the legendary king of the Pelasgians. He described the king as coming from Argos, having conquered a part of Lycos and bringing Pelasgians there. He had also crossed the island of Lesbos and divided the land among his people and changed the name of the island to Pelasgia, named after its residents.[83] Evidently, after seven generations, a reversal occurred causing the death of many people because of high waters that desolated the island of Lesbos.[84]

The mention by Diodorus of the "seven generations of dynasties" of Pelasgians, as pointed out also by other ancient authors including the Apollodorus, Pausanias, Dionysius of Halicarnassus and others opens the question of the genealogy of the Pelasgian ethnos of a "seven generations" dynasty, 23 generations, according to Pausanias. According to him Pyrrhus of Achilles was the 15th,[85] which based on a simple count mounts up to about six or seven centuries prior to the Trojan War.

These records, although incomplete, deserve special attention and may lead to the assumption that six to seven centuries before the hypothetical war of Troy, the late second millennium from the 20th to the 12th century, a Pelasgian Empire may have existed in Central Europe, the Mediterranean basin space and in Asia Minor. This does not rule out the possibility of these "people of the sea" as called by some ancient authors, having frictions with Egyptian dynasties of the time of Ramses.[86] Further

---

[82] Diodorus: *"Biblioteka historike,"* Book V/81.
[83] Ibid, p. 136.
[84] Ibid, p. 136
[85] Pausinianis says: *"Indeed Pyrrhus was the son of Aiacides, the son of Arrybes, and Alexander was Olympia's son; Olympia was daughter of Neoptolom and Arryba, Arryba's father was Alcetis, whose father was Tharypa. From Tharypa to Pyrrhus of Achilles are fifteen generations ..."* (Description of Greece, Book I/11).
[86] For more on this see: Bernard, Martin: *"Athina e zezë,"* Tirana, 2009; Konda, Spiro M: *"Shqiptarët dhe problemi pellazgjik,"* Tirana, 1964; Aref, Mathieu: *"Mikenët=Pellazgët,"* Tirana, 2008; Marsh, Herbert: *"Horae Pelazgicae,"* Cambridge, 1915; Beonloew, Louis: *"Greqia përpara grekëve,"* Tirana, 2008; Pilika, Dhimitër: *"Pellazgët, origjina jonë e mohuar,"* Tirana, 2005.

research would soon give an answer to this question, as findings and reports coming from them are increasingly leading to the conclusion of the existence of a Pelasgian Empire, and its beginning at the dawn of human civilization. However, the question is how and to what extent would its proportions be revealed?

Even despite what Greeks found among the Pelasgians (royal dynasties and a particular social order) obtaining so much from them and leading further to connect to Hellenism, in order to display myth and imagination on the Pelasgians, continued to be a preoccupation of most of the writings of antiquity. Gods of Olympus are those who related to the human mind with the universe and its secrets while Hellenistic society turned philosophy into an important tool of their political culture with democracy emerging as a social model restored 20 centuries later. Even though Plato assessed it to be the worst form of government because the majority of the poor led over the affluent minority from which comes bad governance.[87]

To avoid bad governance through democracy, which is a tool of the mass poor, Plato mentioned the monarchy as the most perfect model known until then. Based on ancient writings from Homer to Aristotle, Hellenes found in Hellada upon their arrival as conquerors, kings and kingdoms, around the 7th or 8th century B.C. (not on the 12th as stated without any support). According to Homer, Pelasgians were governed by kings, spiritually and politically, spiritually by Zeus – "Dodonian and Pelasgian,"[88] and politically by kings who were numerous and diverse, which continued by the descendants of Pelasgians - Illyrians, Dardanians, Macedonians, and others, in all the stages of their social and political organization.

Before the birth of democracy, which Plato called "bad governance" it is noted that the Greeks retained the power of a "divine king," namely that of Zeus at Olympus, extending there through numerous deities that were appended while kings were removed from the state and political power.

Indeed, the exclusion of the kings from social and political power marked the biggest turning point that Hellenes made toward their secession from the "clutches" of the Pelasgians and their legacy, besides introducing the culture of burning their corpses, which meant losing the traces of certain materials in royal forms, which Pelasgians had culminated at

---

[87] Plato: *"Kriza e shoqërisë athinase,"* Tirana, 1997, p. 9.
[88] Homer: *"Iliada,"* Book XVI, Line 233.

the time of Pericles in Athens. This has been considered today as the perfect model of a just governance, opening up the issue between Hellenism and "Barbarianism" between Hellenic thinking and governing through philosophers and democracy and non-Hellenic thinking and governing through laws of the universe and kings held outside the Hellenic world with the Pelasgians with their increasingly new names (depending on their territorial extensions).

The Pelasgian royal model with a dynasty of 23 generations, which was followed by the Greeks before passing to the model of democracy that Athens, and to a lesser extent, Sparta embraced, was adopted by the Romans and the founding of Rome in 753, when the kingdom Etruscans appeared to be what Herodotus call Pelasgians.[89] From different ancient sources and legends one learns that Aeneas, as a Dardanian, after losing the war of Troy, moved to Italy where he established Rome.

Regardless of what Herodotus said about the origin of the Etruscans, Herodotus, Homer and Virgil, and about Aeneas and his crossing over to Italy (in the Peloponnese through the sea and not land - from the Central Balkans – according to some other sources), from its foundation and for two and a half centuries, Rome was governed by kings, starting with Romulus (753-715) continuing with seven legendary kings (715-709), and then with Numa Pompulus, Tullus Hostilius - Horatius, Ankus Martius, Tarkin the Ancient, Servius Tallus, and Tarkin the Great. This continued until 510, when, a year later, the kingship would fall, and be replaced by a republic instead.

This, therefore, shows that the Roman civilization, which emanated from the direct descendants of the Pelasgians, Dardanians and other tribes of the same family, regardless of the ways and directions that led to it, was a continuation of the Pelasgian civilization not only from the spiritual but also from the social and political point of view.

The discontinuation from the royal model, which the Hellenes found among the Pelasgians and the introduction of democracy, was neither easy nor simple, because Herodotus and other ancient authors claimed that Hellada, despite its cultural and social development and its philosophers, and political culture, had involved the masses the same as the Hellenic leaders faced from within "Pelasgic remains." Those who would still retain their deities and genuine conceptions of the universe, and from

---

[89] See Herodotus: *"Historiae"* (Histories), Book I, 46.

without, i.e. in the neighborhood (north and west) faced the Pelasgian-Illyrian kingdoms, especially Epirotes and Macedonians whom they fought for more than two centuries as recorded and witnessed by the Hellenes. This takes the Pelasgians and their family out of any mystification as that coming from Homer and other authors to be brought back to history with their spiritual, social, and political traits.

Even though this return to history would, by most, be marked by its opposites, namely from the Greeks and Romans, against whom they had been fighting, it is still historical evidence that will end with the victory of a more developed civilization over the indigenous one. Plato himself would later admit this while assessing democracy as the worst form of governance and soon restore its kings in subsequent centuries. However, when that happened, thanks to Christianity, their crowns had the blessing of "the only God, the Creator," by which antiquity with its "heavenly people," as the Pelasgians were assessed by the Hellenes themselves for more than 10 centuries, were banned and their traces fought against in order to erase all traces.

Pelasgian Antiquity from a Mythological Point of View

How did the Greeks adopt Pelasgic deities and into what did they change them? - Why did the Greeks pray to the Pelasgian Dodona and what did they demand from her? - What were the first Pelasgian myths and why do many of them, in some way even today, continue to function among Albanians while their extension reached other peoples as well from the Germans, Balt-Slavs to Basques, crouched on the western edge of Europe? – A direct connection with Albanian mythological figures of Zana and Ora and numerous other phenomena of antiquity.

As assessed, monotheism with the obliteration of polytheism, after stripping the free social and political thinking of its philosophical background, also excluded antiquity from the foundations of human civilization for a long time. However, it would be the silent language of the soul of a banned world, stored in thousands of books and other writings that would send conflicting messages from the violence of a "single book," that would free itself of captivity.

This release from the century-old prison of a different truth, which has to do with a rich and magical world of the most creative kind that mankind has known, implies by all means the Pelasgians and their truth, as they too are brought back to light along with their extraordinary treasure.

Here, the same as happened with the first historical evidence coming from ancient authors, myths and mythology would perpetuate the Pelasgians to the indelible memory of mankind, from where their traces are not only notable due to different residues, but are both tangible and vivid among the Albanians and their oral heritage and folklore. This would make many research scientists associate them with the treasure of antiquity, giving an impetus to the assessment that their ancient ancestors were part of that civilization.

Prior to clarifying the relationship residues with antiquity and their role in maintaining the spiritual identity of a people who were ancient and able to testify openly as a living proof of life, focus shifted to how the Pelasgians entered mythology and what it says about them so that other conclusions may be drawn through other issues of antiquity, and may be clarified as a general value of civilization on which one may reconstruct their past too.

When dealing with the issue, it should be pointed out that originally the Pelasgians, along with their myths, deities, and idols, entered mythology through Hellenes, who in turn, acquired a lot and on the basis of a stunning creativity rebuilt in art and philosophy that was transmitted to the Romans in order for it to become mankind's treasure.[90] Therefore, the myth of the Pelasgians is of an anthropomorphic nature and its history is related to the Pelasgos, the legendary ancestor of the Pelasgians, the first inhabitants of Greece, who were of divine origin.

As the Greeks came to Greece and found there the indigenous Pelasgians in a social state of an early tribal development, with kings and kingdoms, from whom they acquired a lot, it was only natural that in various parts legends were also being hatched for Pelasgos and the powerful deity, connecting the divine with human power. Furthermore, it should be perceived in Arcadia as son of Zeus, in Argos, son of Palecton - founder of the king of Argos, in Thessaly son of Poseidon in Epirus

---

[90] For more on this see the following authors: Bettencourt M. M: *"Les dieux grecs,"* Paris, 1944; Chuvin, Pierr: *"Mitologjia greke,"* Tirana, 2000; Graves, Robert: *"Les Mythes grecs,"* Paris, 1967; "Fjalori i Mitologjisë," Prishtina, 1986.

Pelasgus, mentioned by Plutarch in Pyrrhus, etc. This transfer of power from divine to human needed a legend upon which to explain the crossover that could be in the hands of the gods and in accordance with their will.

Therefore, prior to reflecting the will of the gods, Pelasgus and Pelasgians established their connection with Cadmus, legendary founder of Thebes in Boeotia. Anthropomorphism is attributed and reflected through him and his work, (i.e. embodiment of the gods with good features) given that in the case involving the transfer of the divine power to supposedly human society's emergence, related to historical time.

In this mission, implying the origin of terrestrial life, according to the Hellenic myth, Cadmus was the son of the king of Phoenicia, Agenor, brother of Phryx and Europa. His sister Europa would be abducted by Zeus and in her search Cadmus traveled to Boeotia from where after killing the dragon that kept his water, he planted its teeth in the ground,[91] which caused some giants to spring. At the end of the vicious fight only five warriors were left alive, those who built the city which Zeus awarded to Cadmus together with Goddess Harmonia whom he married and had five sons: Polydorus, Autonoe, Ino, Semele, and later Illyrius. The latter's task was to establish Illyria, where a part of the divine power would be transferred under the ownership of humans, which remained under the supervision of gods. According to the Greek legend, after their death, Cadmus and Harmonia turned into snakes, while Illyria became king of the Illyrian lands. According to this myth Cadmus was also important for bringing an alphabet from Phoenicia containing 16 letters, which was accepted and brought about the Hellenic civilization.[92]

The myth addressed two actualities from the historical reality: that of the emergence of Illyria and the Illyrians as an ancient people who emanated from historical time. Before the involvement of the Greeks, there was also the alphabet that was brought by Cadmus from Phoenicia having been accepted by the Hellenes, thereby marking the blossoming of the Hellenic culture and everything considered of supreme civilization value which reached up to the present.

---

[91] Planting dragon's teeth has also been preserved in Albanian mythology, especially in northern parts, understanding heroes' birth that fought for the good. Viewed from this standpoint, the dragons in Albanian mythology appear as protectors and saviors from evil powers, such as the monster, whose defends people (often beautiful maidens) can only be beaten by a dragon.

[92] See *"Fjalor i mitologjisë,"* Prishtina, 1988, pp. 127-128.

It is exactly the Phoenician alphabet and its acceptance by the Hellenes that kept the key to the truth of the existence of the Pelasgic language, which was accepted by Homer and ancient authors as being spoken by them as "barbarian" and continuing to remain something that nourished the assumptions about the Pelasgians being the true authors of the alphabet. This not only was theirs,[93] but was also taken from them by the Phoenicians, as they too were considered to belong to a Pelasgian stem.[94]

Along with the legend of Pelasgus, the creator of the Pelasgians of divine origin, Dardanus appeared, son of Zeus and Electra. Forced to leave his hometown, Arcadia, he went to Phrygia, where he settled and founded the city of Troy on the shores of Scamander. He was considered a progenitor of the Dardanian tribes living on Mount Ida.[95]

This legend also relates to certain historical realities, viewed with suspicion by researchers for a long time, (although predictions of their authenticity were also found in Homer's "Iliad" and some other evidence by ancient authors) clearly implying that Troy was a Dardanian city. This opened the question of the role of Dardanians in one of the most important developments of antiquity, such as Troy, so magnificently eternalized by Homer, turning it into an artistic world monument.

Homer experienced the Trojan War with an immense artistic force, while history has never been able to prove the truth of this war, which according to the ancient poet is embedded in the memory of humanity and as such would remain forever. Still, the historical and archaeological evidence confirm its presence to social and political formations, which Homer enlists as defenders of Troy as well as the attackers, who, thanks to the deception of the "Trojan horse," would become both its conquerors and destroyers.

According to the Greek legend, Dardanus, son of Zeus and Electra, traveled to Phrygia and built Troy. Dardan's departure to Phrygia is associated with a movement of peoples during the Bronze Age, when evidently Pelasgians, after having settled in Central Europe, drove the

---

[93] See: Johan Georg von Hahn: *"Studime shqiptare,"* Tirana, 2009, pp. 379-401 Aref, Mathieu: *"Shqipëria odiseja e pabesueshme e një populli parahelen,"* Tirana 207, pp. 482-520; Kola P, Aristidh: *"Arvanitasit dhe prejardhja e grekëve,"* Tirana 2002, pp. 184-186; Kocaqi, Elena *"Roli pellazgo-ilir in krijimin e gjuhëve evropiane,"* Tirana, pp....

[94] See: Budimir, Milan: *"Grci i Pelasti,"* Belgrade 1950, p. 18; Johan Georg von Hahn: *"Studime shqiptare,"* Tirana, 2009, pp. 385...

[95] *"Fjalori i mitologjisë,"* Prishtina, 1988, p. 62.

Celtic and Baltic peoples and penetrated towards the center of the continent, heading on one side, towards the Iberic Peninsula and the Mediterranean and, on the other, from the Aegean Pelagos, crossing over to Anatolia and further to the East, in Caucasus. There they dominated a vast area that touched upon three continents.

Of course, here appeared Troy, the Phrygians and Phrygia as an important center which stood as a precondition for the Greeks to cross over to the East, from where they would extend their influence in that part of the world where the Persians and other powerful peoples of Mesopotamia lived.

Therefore, Troy had to be taken in battle, but this battle which the great poet imagined as a cause of love (the beautiful Helen taken by the Trojans and the Greeks taking her back), actually reflects the social and political relations of the time, which as testified by ancient authors and confirmed by other sources, represented the continuation of war by the Greeks against the Pelasgian-Illyrians, namely against the Dardanians as their carriers, for new conquests.

Military formations around Troy, "tribes of the neighboring Pelasgians, those who lived in the fertile Larisa," led by "Peleus brought by Hipotheus" where Paiones archers brought by Priam of Amydon,"[96] actually reflected the military rivalry between Greeks and Pelasgians, surrounding it by the North and West and beyond to Anatolia at the gates of the eastern world. Therefore, the Trojan War and the entire Homeric atmosphere presents a double war of the Greeks against the indigenous Pelasgians, on one hand to dominate from within over the tribes included in the Greek state, and on the other to externally destroy their state formations as tribes or kings: Epirotes, Macedonians, and, above all Dardanians the most defying and sophisticated, representing their main obstacle.

The appearance of the gods and their relationship with people would be insufficient and even impossible without the oracles. A mediating spirit between the human and God came either as a permanent reminder to help Him to bring to perfection his earthly power, or to maintain connections with the divine.

Homer and all ancient authors wrote about one of the most notable oracles of antiquity, Dodona,[97] an insurmountable spiritual center that

---

[96] Homer: "*Iliada,*" Tirana, 1979, Books II and X.
[97] Carapanos, Constandin: "Dodone et ses ruines," Paris, 1952.

belonged to Pelasgians and built directly by the Zeus' command, as Hesiod said, "wanted it to be a precious sanctuary for the people."[98]

Pelasgic tribes: Molossians, Thesprotians, Chaonians, and Pyrrhic Epirotes have always believed that they came from and were protected by the Pelasgian God-Dodona, and could be followed throughout his pre-Hellenic imageries. However, the Pelasgian God inherited in Dodona the cult and symbols of the great pre-Hellenic goddess, *Mother-Earth*, known as Demetra, whose name is explained through the Albanian language.[99]

Dodona, the oldest oracle, was situated in the Molossian land. Ancient authors like Homer recorded that Dodona emerged as an old center of the Pelasgians where they maintained their ties with their gods and prayed. Herodotus said that all theology derives from the Pelasgian Dodona.[100] It is also mentioned in Homer's "Iliad" claiming that Odysseus came to Dodona to learn how he could return to Ithaca; Aeneas too inquired as to how he could return to Ithaca.[101]

Dodona's oracles prophesized by telling the fortune through flying doves, throwing of the dice and sound coming from an ancient legend of the Bronze era while discovering the will of the gods through the murmur of a leaf of a century-old oak. Religious services were entrusted to a family of priests called *Tonuroi*.

Greek myths and legends with oracles, according to their pattern of being built by the Greeks (Delphi) not excluding the possibility of rebuilding of historical truth, highlighted the emergence of political leaders from the myth. This is clearly proven in the case of Zeus, whom as a sovereign creator of gods and men was seen by the Greeks also as a "Dodonian and Pelasgian King,"[102] meaning that this definition had to do with the status of certain social and political organization of Pelasgian tribes, which was equal to that of kingdoms. Therefore, it is not at all surprising why Homer ranks various Pelasgian tribes in Troy under the leadership of their kings from Hipotheus, Teutamides to Thymbre and others. Even later, in all

---

[98] Hesiod: *"Carmin,"* a poem, fragment 134, cited according to *"Ilirët dhe Iliria te autorët antikë,"* Prishtina, 1979, p. 14.

[99] See: Johan Georg von Hahn: *"Studime shqiptare,"* Tirana, 2009, pp. 223-228; Konda, Spiro N: *"Shqiptarët dhe problemi pellazgjik,"* Tirana, 1964, p. 322.

[100] Herodotus: *"Historiae,"* Book One, cited according to *"Ilirët dhe Iliria te autorët antikë,"* Prishtina, 1979, pp. 16-18.

[101] *"Fjalori i mitologjisë,"* Prishtina, 1988, p. 72.

[102] Herodotus: *"Historiae,"* Book XVI, Verse 233.

their wars with the Hellenes and Romans, the Pelasgian-Illyrians appeared as kings, maintaining the hierarchy of the ancient monarchy and its transmission and storage of the Dardanian Pelasgians, Illyrians, Macedonians, and Epirotes. All that inherited as a heritage by Albanians continued to prevail, even as tribal and patriarchal mentality, and its transmission to Pelasgians, and its storage by Dardanians, Pelasgians, Illyrians, Macedonians, Epirotes is considered Pelasgic legacy.[103]

However, ancient myths, Greek or Roman, suspended their communications with the spiritual heritage of the Albanians, either in the field of folklore, general social thinking, (upon which lie many of their values) or even conceptions that have to do with a consciousness inherited from antiquity. This has affected and still affects their moral and even social code, which in many respects appears more influential and more stable than beliefs. Therefore, today many of these concepts, which can be explained by ethics and even religion, are stored in their earliest form, where the clash between good and evil is seen as acting in accordance with the phenomena of nature (whether destructive or constructive), as the cult of nature was also preserved when Albanians worshiped the sun, earth and water, wood and stone, which many continue to worship. *Sun, earth* and *water* remained the most worshipped idols whom were connected spiritually since the time Christianity was adopted and associated with names of saints like Shëngjergji (Saint George), Shëmitri (Saint Demetrius), and retained by Albanians in their pagan names of antiquity: *Day of Summer, Day of Winter,* and became part of the calendar of nature.

In different parts of Dukagjin and Northern Highlands some plants and trees are revered in a particular way, while in most parts of what once appeared as Dardania, the serpent and eagle are sacred. This special reverence is not something concerned with totemism, as the phenomenon of goat horns (symbol of fertility displayed on the helmet of Pyrrhus) may be related to Alexander the Great of Skenderbeg with rather theriomorphic phenomena of a primeval nature when Gods transformed themselves into animals and vice versa. This was the case with ancient Cadmus, who

---

[103] For more on the preservation of tribal heritage and ancient tribal mentality of the ancient Albanians see: Johan Georg von Hahn "*Studimet shqiptare,*" Tirana, 2009; Konda, Spiri M: "*Shqiptarët dhe problemi pellazgjik,*" Tirana, 1964; Pilika, Dhimiter: "*Pellazgët origjina join e mohuar,*" Tirana, 2005; Aref, Mathieu: "*Shqipëria odiseja e pabesueshme e një populli parahelen,*" Tirana, 2007; Stylo, Niko: "*Historia e shenjtë e Arvanitëve,*" Tirana, 2004.

turned into a snake about to defend his son's state of Illyria from the evils, from where the Albanian belief was derived about the snake of the house, standing on the threshold and considered sacred saving it from evil and the unpredicted.

On this view relates the mythological figure of *Ora* (*oread*), which the Albanians imagined often as a woman, and as a snake. It was believed to live in the mountains, forests, fields, springs, or close to people. She was charitable and enlightened the minds of the people teaching them the art of healing diseases. Ora helped and brought good fortune to good people and provided guardianship for people, their homes, and tribes. This is best reflected by the expression of the people *"Ora e njeriut"* ("Man's Ora"), also of home, tribe, *"Ora e mirë"* ("Good Ora"), *"Ora e mbarë"* ("Lucky Ora"), but also *"Ora e ligë,"* ("Wicked Ora") from where come characters, such as *"Njeri me Orë"* ("Man with Ora"), meaning someone with authority in terms of knowledge and the like, and *"Njeri pa orë"* ("Man without Ora") meaning the opposite.

Another mythological figure widely spread and one of the most important of the ancient faith, relating directly and undoubtedly to antiquity is Zana (*Zana* Fairy). This figure of Albanian folk beliefs was envisioned with a rare beauty (in south of Albania she was called *Zëra*). She was the muse of the Albanian mountains who lived in the gorges of the Northern Albanian Alps, where every mountain had its own fairy. She was a divine being full of courage and ferocity. The highest honor to a brave man would be to be called *trim si Zana* (valiant as a fairy) or possess a weapon that would kill as a Zana (*vret si Zana*). Zana sang in the night at water springs, danced and played, gathered flowers and bathed naked. However, Zana punished too, by hurting anyone who dared throw a look while she bathed. Therefore, according to popular belief, a passer-by, before passing through these lands, coughed to Zana in order to give Zana time to wash and walk away. From this comes the curse: *"Të shitoftë zana!"* ("May Zana curse you!") However, she liked the Albanian warriors and assisted them in war, as Homer's Palladium Antenna helped her well-doers, Diomedes and Odysseus.[104] Zana inspired the bard of the mountain; as did the Greek Muse inspire lyrical poets, in folk songs sung with a lute.

The strong cult of Zana among Albanians spread throughout their expansion across the Balkan Peninsula showing clearly that she was a

---

[104] *"Fjalori i Mitologjisë,"* Prishtina, 1988, p. 248.

genuine native deity, meaning Pelasgian, pre-Greek, acquired by them and carried over to other Balkan peoples, especially the southern Slavs.

Of the native nature inherited from the ancient ancestors of the Albanians are also *lugetërit*, (vampires), *kuçedrat* (dragons), and other images that personify forces of darkness and evil, which man had to face since premedial moments when he was not yet able to cope with nature's phenomena and their causes, although he left behind a material legacy on these subjects that survives even today.

These and similar legacies, not only nourished the inner spiritual world, but they also protected it from other phenomena that came externally and tended to distract him in all forms. This probably turned the ancient values into a measure of what appears as part of a special spiritual identity, which could not be excluded by religion or any other social pressure of a transitory nature.

Pelasgian Antiquity from an Archeological Point of View

> *Pelasgian prehistoric footprints and expansion into Mycenae, Crete, Troy and beyond Asia Minor. – Pelasgian linkage to Cretaceous constructions and perceptions arising in theories on the origin of first creatures from dinosaurs; where do they see their origin to be? - Troy discovered traces of Dardanians from Dardania to Asia Minor, identical in many ways, while confirming a late arrival of the Greeks in these parts. - Pelasgian-Illyrian cults and their importance in explaining the ancient spiritual world of all Indo-European peoples. - Excavations reveal interconnections of ancient civilizations in the Mediterranean basin and their constant interconnection.*

Besides the historical evidence, coming mostly from ancient authors, and those of spiritual nature (gods, myths, legends, and mythology), there are materials from archeology to help bring light on Pelasgic antiquity as an important part of antiquity. This evidence comes from the earliest times when man made the first attempts to survive and cope with unknown nature and all that surrounded him for thousands of years in his long journey to reach the state of homosapiens.

Therefore, from an archaeological standpoint, the earliest period of development of primitive society is known as *Paleolithic* (from Greek *palaios* - old, *lithos* - stone) and covers the period from 1.5 million B.C. to 10,000 B.C. This era is divided into *Lower, Middle* and *Upper Paleolithic*.

Earliest traces of human existence in the Albanian ethnic space, namely that relating to the descendants of early Pelasgians, appear in the Mousterian period pertaining to the Paleolithic 160,000 to 30,000 years ago. Archaeological and speleological discoveries found the Krapina Cave in Croatia and the Gajtani Cave near Shkodra belonging to that time. Well-made flint tools from that period were found in this area with typical Mousterian shapes serving the primitive man for various work processes directly related to the provision of daily food. They included cutters, scrapers, and abrasives found in the prehistoric Xara station in Saranda, the Kryegjata station close to Apollonia (Fier), and at the Gajtani station in the Shkodra district.[105] Such objects were also found in the former Dardania location near Prishtina, Gllamnik near Podujeva, the Drin Valley (Ramjan), the Ibër Valley (near Mitrovica), in Theranda and in some localities in the vicinity of Nish.[106]

Similar tools have also been found in northern and northeastern parts, in Kosova and up to Nish, but their persistence runs into two branches: through the valley of the River Morava reaching to the River Danube and through Morava to the Vardar in the Aegean. Numerous exhibits were also found in Bosnia and Herzegovina reaching as far up north as the Austrian Alps.[107]

The Museum of Kosova contains a great number of these tools.[108] They are also found in other museums, especially in Belgrade. The latter was during the time of the occupation of Kosova by the Yugoslav state, the sole provider and supervisor of archeological excavations in Kosova and Macedonia. As one may learn from Serbian and Yugoslav studies of

---

[105] *"Historia e Popullit Shqiptar,"* I, Tirana, 2002, pp. 23-24.
[106] Mirdita, Zef: *"Studime dardane,"* Prishtina,1979; Stipcevic, Aleksandar: *"Ilirët – historia, jeta, kultura,"* Prishtina, 1980; Shukriu, Edi: *"Ancient Kosova,"* Prishtina, 2004; Cerović, I: *"Nalazi u praistorijskih tumula u Donjoj Bitiji kod Uroševca,"* Belgrade, 1991; Galović, R: *"Predionica, neolitsko naselje kod Pristine,"* Prishtina, 1959; Garašanin, M: *"Rugovo fushe Djakovica – praistorijska nekropola sa hukama,"* Belgrade, 1966; Glišić, J: *"Iskopavanja na lokalitetu Gladnice kod Gracanice,"* Belgrade, 1959; Glišić, J-Jovanović, B: *"Fafos II – Kosovska Mitrovica, Naselje vinčanske grupe,"* Prishtina, 1961.
[107] Shukriu, Edi: *"Ancient Kosova,"* Prishtina, 2004, pp. 10-13.
[108] Ibid, p. 12.

this nature Belgrade possesses thousands of exhibits from this area which are of great importance for the explanation of antiquity.[109]

However, most of the archaeological evidence in the Albanian area came from *Neolithic* times (the Greek *Neos* - young and *lithos* - stone). They cover a period starting from the 6th millennium and ending by the end of the 4th millennium B.C. when natural circumstances were significantly altered providing better conditions for human life.

Among these conditions were climate changes, from the cold and wet Neolithic period, which began as far back as Mesolithic time, to a softer climate similar to the present-day climate. These suitable natural conditions in this area with other parts of the Central Balkans and the Mediterranean helped man evolve from being nature's slave. At this time various forms of human productivity came about on a primitive scale, opening

---

[109] For more on archeological heritage of Kosova in Serb-Yugoslav sources see: Benac, Aloiz: "*Starija Kamena doba,*" Sarajevo, 1969, "*O identifikaciji ilirskog etnosa*" in Godišnjak, CBI XII/10, 1974, "*Predilir, Protoilir, Prailir – neki novi aspekti,*" Balcanica VIII/1977; Bojanovski, Ivo: "*Dolabelin sistem cesta u rimskoj provinciji Dalmacije,*" Sarajevo, 1974; Todorović, J. - Cermanović, A: "*Bojnica, naselje vincanske culture,*" Belgrade 161; Čerškov, Emil: "*Arheoloska zbirka Muzeja Kosova i Metohije*" GMKM L/1970, "*Rimljani na Kosovu i Metohiju,*" Belgrade, 1969, "*Antička bista zene iz Klokota*" GMKM III/1969; Čorovič, Borivoje: "*Osnovne karakteristike materialne kulture Ilira na njihovom centralnom području,*" Sarajevo, 1965; Dušandič, Slavko: "*Novi Antonijev natpis i metalla municipii Dardanorum,*" Belgrade,1971; Galović, R: "*Uvod u praistjoriju Kosova,*" GMKM I/1956, "*Predionica, neolitsko naselje kod Pristine,*" Prishtina, 1959 "*Halstatski depo iz Janjeva,*" GMKM IV-V/1959-1960; Gavela, Branko:" *O ilirskom substratu na Balkanu,*" Godisnjak CBI III/1,1965; Garašanin, Milutin:" *Iz prvobitne istorije Kosova i Metohije*" Muzeji 3-4/1949, "*O poreklu i hronologiji balkanskog neolita,*" Starinar, VII-VIII, 1956-1957, "*Istocne granice Ilira prema arheoloskim spomenicima,*" Simpozijum I, 135-175, "*Ka kronološkom sistemu gvozdenog doba u Srbiji i Makedoniji,*" ZFF VIII-1/1964, "*Istorijska i arheoloska rasmatranja u ilirskoj drzavi,*" Glas CCLX/1974; Gličič, Jovan: "*Specifičnost kulture vinčanske grupe na Kosovu i Juznom Pomoravlju,*" GMKM IV-V (1959-60) p. 264-271; Glišič, Jovan – Jovanović, Borivoje: "*Preistorisko naselje na Gladnicama kod Gračanice*" GMKM II (1957) p. 223-233; Jovanović, B: "*Stratigrafija naselja Vinčanske grupe kod Kosovske Mitrovice,*" in GMKM VI/1961; Marić, Zdravko: "*Arheoloska istrazivanja ilirskog grada Daorsa na gradini kod Stoca,*" Sarajevo, 1975; Novak, Grga: "*Pogled na prilike radnih slojeva u rimskoj provinciji Dalmacije,*" HZ I/1948; Tasic, Nikola: "*Zitkovac i neki problemi relativnog hronološkog odnosa neolitskih naselja na Kosovu i dolini Ibra,*" Glasnik SAN, Belgrade, 1959.

the path to changes that took place in agriculture. Also processing techniques from bone to stone tools appeared and began to be used in work.[110]

By the late Neolithic era, for the first time utensils emerged made of copper, marking the beginning of metalwork. However, it should be pointed out that besides work tools, there were also those dealing with spiritual lives of the local primitive population, mainly represented by tiny anthropomorphic or zoomorphic figures of baked clay. Their most characteristic feature was a schematization of form, sometimes off measure, as an accentuated geometrization of an ornament in the decorative art of pottery. These figures of beings appeared in cylindrical forms, plates or steatopygic, both standing and sitting. A number of them resemble types of frontal Asian peninsulas and the Eastern Mediterranean, displaying the impact of links and direct Neolithic cultures.[111]

These plastic products, often of artistic value, embodied mysterious powers that primitive farmers and cattle-breeders believed upheld the fertility of land and well-being of cattle. Therefore, the figures of women, who dominated the anthropomorphic Neolithic plastics, is associated with the fertility cult of mother-earth, while those reproducing zoomorphic shapes were associated with the cult of domestic cattle, and agriculture, playing an important role in the economy of the Neolithic community. The cult of the *earth-mother* - which was noted above among the Pelasgians was linked to Goddess Demeter, carried over to the Greeks, Romans and others attaining different names - related to zoomorphic and anthropomorphic vases discovered in Neolithic settlements in Maliq, Dunavec in the vicinity of Prishtina, the valley of the Iber River reaching as far as Vinca (near Belgrade), and everywhere in the central part of Bosnia up to Austria.

It should be pointed out that the material culture of these findings, widely expanded, represented an almost unique human development for the prehistoric era, indicating that it related to inhabitants of a population which was rightly called paleo-Indo-European that lived approximately under the same climatic and social circumstances.

The Bronze Age, which starts from 2100 B.C. and comes five to six centuries after the Copper Age, began to emit the first signs of ethnic identities, which as prehistoric, led to historical time, which appeared from the early first millennium. At this time, within the movements of

---

[110] "*Historia e Popullit Shqiptar,*" I, Tirana, 2002, p. 26.
[111] Ibid, p. 29.

peoples, which affected the assemblance of what is called Indo-European identity, Pelasgians, appeared from prehistory to the historical time as a key factor of a very wide expansion from the entire Mediterranean to north of Africa without excluding a good region of Anatolia and continued to maintain their presence in the circumstances of these developments as well.

However, the cultural material and its remains from the late Paleolithic, Bronze, and Iron Ages determined a lot of these changes and dilemmas that followed the Pelasgians and their role in antiquity and was mostly identified as Hellenic.[112]

As the Greek authors themselves recognized the Pelasgian factor in Hellada as an entity, which they met since their arrival, a lot was carried over from the deities to the spiritual and living culture (animal breeding,[113] farming,[114] and processing of metals).[115] It is natural for all of this to be reflected in traces of material residues (damaged or undamaged) scattered all around throughout their living space, even though items (tools, various ornaments, and dishes) – carried from place to place or shown as merchandise goods - always determined their authenticity. It even, in many cases, brought confusion and misinterpretations, which were then used for wrong assessments, which have not been without consequences.

In the material culture and its role to highlight the traces of ancient Pelasgians in their own light, in addition to anthropomorphic and zoomorphic figures, as well as various ornaments of mostly the same nature, there was also certain evidence including facilities, walls, and remnants of

---

[112] For more see: Vulpe, R: "L'Age du Fer fans les reions thraces de pa peninsule balcanique," Paris, 1930

[113] On this see Aristotle: *"De Animalium Historia,"* pp. 40-41. Here it speaks about how in Illyria and Paionia there were pigs with unsplit hooves, big cows for which they said "each gave seven and a half pitchers of milk," other big animals, and also small animals, such as sheep which were called "Pyrrhic" named after King Pyrrhus. The famous philosopher speaks of the work of Illyrians and Epirotans to maintain and enhance livestock herds and use their products for food and clothing.

[114] In *"De Mirabilibus auscultationibus"* (On Told Wonders), Aristotle says that the Illyrians, called Taulanti, produced a wine from honey after squeezing honeycomb thrown into the water and boiling half-way, and leaving for some time to ferment.

[115] Aristotle also spoke about the land of the Paiones saying it was so rich with gold, as many people found large and heavy gold pieces. (See: *"Ilirët dhe Iliria te autorët antikë,"* Prishtina 1979, pp. 38-42)

constructions called cyclopic (built with big square stones without connecting compound) that correlated to the shift from prehistoric to historical times, belonging to the 2nd millennium B.C. However, certain researchers are not inclined to see the remains of these cyclopic constructions through ordinary people, known from early Paleolithic time, but through mythological giants as they fought Zeus, as they then lost that war, while on the ground remained evidence of the "strong and stubborn" man, scattered in different parts of Pelasgian lands to set human power on Earth.

Although the ancient enigma of these cyclopic constructions remain an issue with the only explanation provided by mythology, while excluding the premedial man in the Neolithic era or any other more advanced from a technical aspect, nevertheless, traces of these cyclopic constructions as walls or other dispersed residues continue to bind "mythic reality" with true ones, that is, with subsequent cultures and settlements and fortresses, which are compatible with a certain degree of social development.[116]

Therefore, models of strong fortifications, instead of stones of cyclopic size with large carved stones bound by plaster and later combined with metal served the constructions found continuously in most of the early spread of Pelasgians, when their dwelling culture marked a much more organized scale.

Despite this tendency, Schliemann's archaeological maps,[117] of Troy, others produced two centuries ago in Greece and Italy, and recently on the Adriatic coast (Albania) and central parts of the Balkans (Kosova and former Yugoslavia) made it plain that cyclopic constructions characterized an authentic social development of the ancient peoples, conditioned not only by a more recent degree of their organization in pre-tribal and

---

[116] For more on this see: "William, Boyd C: *"Genetiques et races humaniens,"* Paris, 1882; Paul, Ulrich: *"Les grande enigmes des civilisationes disparues,"* Geneve, 1971; Benloëw, Luis: *"Greqia para grekëve,"* Tirana, 2002; D'Angely H.R: *"L'Enigme des Pallasges,"* 1990; Rene, Dussaud: *"La civilisation prehelleniques,"* Paris, 1910; Coon, Carlesons: "The Mountains of Giants," Cambrigde-Massachusetts, 1950.

[117] *Schlieman* was a German merchant, who, after marrying a Greek woman, inspired by Homer's work, started inquiring about the Trojan traces, researching from 1870-1881. On this occasion he discovered the location of ancient Troy, whereby he extracted from the ruins and depths over one hundred thousand exhibits, ranging from the largest to smallest. He published two books on this: "Troy and its Fences," and "Troy."

tribal communities but also by the need to be defended from movements of different peoples, who, as historically proven, aimed at Central Europe and Mediterranean from where they moved in other directions.

Viewed from this perspective and judging by the traces of cyclopic constructions, which continued to serve as foundations for later fortifications that appeared in antiquity, it can be assumed that this kind of construction is linked to the earliest prehistoric inhabitants - Pelasgians, who were already regarded as the nucleus of Indo-Europeanism,[118] not spared from subsequent waves of invasions of other peoples, who would later continue their movement towards their lands affecting their dispersion in different directions. In some cases they attained proportions of large movements of parts of this population, such as those that followed after Troy lost its importance, moving towards the south of Italy having an impact on the foundation of Rome, or those towards the Aegean islets and the North African coast, reaching as far as Britain, as ancient authors report.

Ancient authors, as direct witnesses to the real situation found in what was called Pelasgia and considering their divine origin as something that could serve to justify their supernatural power, recognized that in many parts the fortification artistry continued on stones like the case with the Acropolis in Athens and several other edifices in Greece built on the foundations of these cyclopic buildings, visible in any aspect.[119]

In this case, the superstructure over cyclopic foundations, i.e. Pelasgic culture, to be found anywhere in the Mediterranean Basin (Crete, Mycenae, Asia Minor, the Aegean, Italy and Palestine), wherever there were Pelasgians, extended to several coastal colonies in the western part, such as Epidaurum and Apollonia, underlying the fact that the Greek colonies in these parts exhibited a continuum of urban Pelasgic presence. Meanwhile, the so-called Hellenic colonization in various parts represented no more than the spread of trade in varied social and political circumstances, where the local population accepted the new rules, accelerating the absorption of a part thereof, even though it may also be taken as a matter of a certain political-administrative accommodation set in the new

---

[118] See Johan Georg von Hahn *"Studime shqiptare,"* Tirana, 2009, p. 405.
[119] See Bernal, Martin: *"Athina e zezë,"* Tirana, 2009, pp. 117-145; Aristidh P. Kola *"Arvanitasit and prejardhja greke,"* Tirana, 2002, p. 118; Gordon, Vere: "L' aube de la civilisation europenne," Payot, 1949.

circumstances, which was afterwards regarded by different chroniclers and scholars as complete colonization.

However, the focus on cyclopic constructions and the treatment of this problem with scientific competence, as most deserving regarding the static nature of material evidence, i.e. those that cannot be manipulated (by means of transmission and other forms of movement among the most different kinds), besides showing out the oldest factor, as Pelasgians are considered to be within the Indo-European stratification and reduced greatly the effort by means of which the Greeks pretended, although they arrived at the Aegean basin by late second millennium and beginning of the first, to be given a decisive role in antiquity for the spread of urban culture and even treated as its founders.

Evidently, fortifications existed before their arrival, as evidenced by cyclopic remains, traces of which are found not only in Crete, Mycenae[120], Athens, and cities where Greek colonies appeared later on the Adriatic and Mediterranean and also in the Central Balkans, exactly where Pelasgians were concentrated, but also their heirs of the great Illyrian family with its numerous branches, where Dardanians appear among the most unique, not only from the point of view of ethnic compactness that is maintained in almost all phases of the movement and migrations of peoples, but also by their social and political role.

Interestingly, traces of cyclopic buildings, as fragments, or as upgrades to ancient fortifications of the middle period of antiquity appeared concentrated in the whole of the present-day ethnic Albanian space (Albania, Kosova, Macedonia, and eastern parts reaching as far as Asia Minor), not only in the form of strong fortifications, but also of entire cities, which played an important social, cultural, and political role from the 5th century B.C. up to the Byzantine emergence in our era. *Naissus* (today's Nish), *Ulpiana Prima* (Scubi), *Ulpiana Secunda* (Prishtina), *Astibo* (Shtip), *Theranda* (Prizren), despite barbaric destructions occurring by the late 12th century A.D. following the Nemanjas invasion, represented vivid evidence of this urbanization, which has survived thanks to the fortifying older model, based on cyclopic constructions.

The material culture of the later time, through it's working tools, various ornaments of amber and metal, coins and others, can be identified once it expressed or reflected the language of signs, myths, idols, and

---

[120] Dothan, M: *"The Myceneans in the East-Mediterranean,"* 1982.

imagination, a creative symbolism, where then there were different symbols, such as those of cult among the Illyrians, found also among the Greeks, and even Romans.

Therefore, one may say that in Illyrian ornaments, ceramics, stone tiles, coins and other objects, an underlying symbolism is expressed, which is characteristic, and often, unlike others of that nature. This is particularly true for the pure motives of ornamental and symbolic significance, even though they, both anthropomorphic and zoomorphic, reveal a somewhat special kind of manifestation of cult reflection in accordance with a certain belief.

One of the ornamental motifs, whose partially preserved symbolic significance often appeared as an ornament, was the *spiral*.[121] As a religious symbol, the spiral appeared in various civilizations since the Paleolithic Age. It was used to decorate ceramic dishes in pre-Pharaoh Egypt, on burial memorials, ceramics in the Craetean-Mycenean culture, and in a range of Neolithic cultures in the region of Central Europe.[122] While, in the region where later lived Illyrians, Dardanians, and other tribes of this family, the spiral appeared very early as well and was to be found both in the Stone and Bronze Ages in almost all their areas. As such, it appears in various forms - as a *flowing spiral, double helix, spiral in the form of concentric connected circles, etc.*, and is thought of bearing deep symbolic meaning, especially in mortuary objects, symbolizing the underworld, namely the complex way that the soul of the deceased is obliged to pass through in this dark world.[123]

The connection of the coil with the underground life and its mysteries becomes even clearer by the fact that it appeared with a serpent, a typical chthonic animal.[124]

But the double coil, which also frequently occurred in Illyrian lands as a very ancient symbol, the timber of life so rooted in the earth and above its body, was important to women, as it was thought to assure

---

[121] Stipcevic, Aleksandar: *"Simbolet e kultit te Ilirët,"* Prishtina, 1983, p. 10.

[122] On the emergence of *spiral* and *Medaur* in this area, according to Stipcevic, see in particular V. Milojcic: *"Zur Frage der Herkunft des Mäanders und der Spirale bei der Bandkeramik Mitteleuropas,"* Jahrbuch des Römisch-germanisch Zentralmuseums Mainz, 11, 1964, pp. 57-80.

[123] Stipcevic, Aleksandar: *"Simbolet e kultit te Ilirët,"* Prishtina, 1983, p. 10.

[124] E.Küster: *"Die Schlange,"* p. 13, cited according to Stipcevic, Aleksandar: *"Simbolet e kultit te ilirët,"* Prishtina, 1983, p. 11.

fertility and helped upon giving birth to children.[125] A serpent is also frequently found in the double coil. This explains why in so many cases the spiral or the coil, as the figure appears in the role of the materialization of the serpent cults lacking his real presence, was vital to everyday life when it served as guardian of the threshold of the house and tribe.

Having the serpent appear permanently (alive, as an animal protected and revered in particular, and as a figure of decoration on tombstones and shrines), speaks of the great importance of this animal for the Pelasgians and their descendants, Illyrians, traces of which were found in cave drawings and later from the Neolithic time, with the serpent appearing also in a variety of clay images of men and women, one of which is found near Prishtina.[126]

In the South the clay figure of the serpent appears in slabs too, within the framework of figurative compositions, such as the one found at Hollmi Castle, near the city of Kolonja,[127] the one in Lower Selca,[128] and one on clay at Berat's Krotina (ancient Dimallum),[129] as well as a plate from Lower Selca of Pogradec, by the Lake Ohrid.[130]

In the latter, the serpent has a role to protect the Illyrian warrior, while his rising, threatening position means that he too is actively engaged in war. An identical iconographic presentation is also available on a tablet found in the necropolis of Gostili in Montenegro, in the vicinity of Lake of Shkodra.[131]

The serpent, symbol of a particular belief among the Pelasgian-Illyrians, at a later stage, i.e. from the 5th century B.C. also found a place in Greek-Illyrian coins. The oldest and most interesting one is a serpent's signification on the Greek coin of Pharos colony (present-day Starigrad in

---

[125] M. Wenzel: *"O nekim simbolika na dalmatinskim stećcima,"* Prilozi povjesti umjet. U Dalmaciji, 14, 1962, pp. 79-94, cited according to Stipcevic, Aleksandar: *"Simbolet e kultit te ilirët,"* Prishtina, 1983, p. 11.

[126] About the Prishtina serpent and its importance see: R. Galović: *"Predionica,"* Prishtina, 1959, p. 25; D. Garasanin: *"Religija i kult neolitičkog čoveka na centralnom Balkanu"* in his study *"Neolit centralnog Balkana,"* Belgrade, 1968, p. 247, photo 12.

[127] S. Aliu: *"Konferenca e Dytë e Studimeve Albanologjike,"* Vol.II, Tirana, 1970, p. 432, T. IV

[128] See: Ceka, Neritan: *"Studime historike,"* 29/1957, no. 2, p. 160.

[129] See: B. Dautaj: *"Studia Albanica,"* 2/1965, no. 1, p. 69; B. Dautaj: *"Studime historike,"* 19/1965, no. 2, p. 98.

[130] *"Shqipëria arkeologjike,"* Tirana, 1971, photo 47.

[131] Dj. Basler, GZM, n.s. 24, 1969, pp. 9, 43, T.XXV, 126/3, cited according to Stipcevic, Aleksandar: *"Studimet e kultit te Ilirët,"* Prishtina, 1983, p. 50.

Pharos). On the reverse side of the coin the serpent is presented standing up and threatening a billy-goat who is attacking the serpent.[132]

This dramatic scene, in which a battle of life and death has just started between the billy-goat, symbolizing the Greek newcomers, and the snake, the symbol of primeval native residents, occurred only in the first emission of the coin produced in the colony (by 4th century BC), at a time when Greek settlers were forced to wage relentless struggles with the old natives to stay on in the new land.[133]

In subsequent emissions the snake disappears from the Pharos' coin with only billy-goat remaining - a clear sign of consolidation of settlers in the Illyrian region.[134]

The serpent figures also appeared in the coins of Illyrian and Illyrian-Greek cities in southern Albania. Therefore, a currency emission from Apollonia during the time of Caracalla (AD 196-217) represented the snake coiled around Esculapio's stick, while another one shows Goddess Salus (Hygeia) leading the serpent.[135]

Further south, in the city of Byllis, coins were forged at the end of the third century and the beginning of the 2nd century B.C. representing the snake on the reverse wrapped around a pole.[136]

The last city to present the snake on its own currency was Amantia, where the serpent is rolled in a coil and stays calm.[137]

One should also mention here the Labeates tribe coin depicted an Illyrian ship on its reverse side. The ship had serpents engraved on the bow stern (ship's backside), and the stern (ship's front side) indicating that Labeates ships and other Illyrian tribes vessels (or at least some of them) in the southern regions had their serpent-shaped sides.[138]

The southern Illyrians also struck a local deity connected to the serpent. This can be said in terms of a statue of a woman, holding a basket on

---

[132] For more see: J. Brunschmid: "*Die Inschriften und Münzen der griechischen Städte Dalmatiens,*" Vienna, 1898, pp. 40, 41; F. Imhoof-Blumer – O. Keller: "*Tier und Pflanzenbilder auf Münzen und Gemmen des klassischend Altertums,*" Leipzig, 1889, p. 18.

[133] Stipcevic, Aleksandar: "*Simbolet e kultit te ilirët,*" Prishtina, 1983, p. 52.

[134] Ibid, p. 52.

[135] H. Ceka: "*Probleme të numismatikës ilire,*" Tirana, 1976, p. 126.

[136] Ibid, pp. 83, 84.

[137] H. Ceka: "*Quistions de numismatique illyreinne,*" Tirana, 1972, p. 147.

[138] Stipcevic, Aleksandar: "*Simbolet e kultit te ilirët,*" Prishtina, 1983, p. 53.

her left hand around which a snake revolved.[139] The statue represented the native Goddess of fertility.

The snake appeared significantly strong also as a totem animal as indicated by the name of the Illyrians, namely of the leader of their tribe *Illyrios,* hiding in itself the notion of the serpent. Both his parents, Cadmus and Harmonia turned into serpents, while the *Illyrios* (*Illyria*) immediately after birth received divine power from a snake.[140]

The belief of the Illyrian tribe deriving from a snake lived long in the Illyrians minds, therefore a reflection of this belief is found as far back as the 13th century in the work "*Historia Solanitana,*" in which when speaking of Cadmus and his serpentine shape it is said because of this story his people were called snake-derived (*anaguigene*).[141]

Speaking of this, it is important to note that the Illyrian tribe of *Encheleae,* who lived in the far extreme Illyrian lands, also had its own totem snake. The name of this tribe concealed, the same as the Illyrian one, the notion of the serpent, namely of the eel. However, as in ancient zoology the eel belonged to the serpents, this tribe too certainly worshipped this animal as its own champion.[142]

Besides the snake, which played an important role in the Pelasgic-Illyrian symbol and is most common in almost all the prehistoric and historic stages, and the birds which were also present, there are other animals permanently associated with the ancient world. Among them the most distinguished are the horse, ox, ram, boar, billy-goat, goat, hare, dog, rooster, dolphin, fish, and the bee.

Regarding the spread of the *horse* and its cult it is assumed that its common appearance in the northern part had to do with an impact that nomadic horsemen could have made coming from the steppes of Eastern Europe, especially after their invasions known in the Bronze and Iron Ages. Later-date archaeological findings from the Neolithic era in the southern

---

[139] H. Ceka – S. Anamali: *"Disa skulptura të pa botuara të Muzeut arkeologjik-etnografik të Tiranës,"* Buletini i Universitetit Shtetëror të Tiranas, seria shkencat shoqërore, 1959, no. 3, p. 83, photo 11.

[140] Stipcevic, Aleksandar: *"Simbolet e kultit te Ilirët,"* Prishtina, 1983, p. 56.

[141] Thomas Archidiaconus: *"Historia Solonitana,"* Zagabriae, 1984, (Monumenta spectantia historiam Slavorum Meridionalium Vol. 26), p. 5.

[142] K. O. Müller was the first to explain the name of the Aenchelei from the Greek word indicating the *eel.* W. Borgeaud agreed with this in *"Les Illyriens en Grece et Italie,"* Geneve, 1934, pp. 52-53.

Balkans, as well as those in Anatolia, where the horse appears carved in stone, clay, and other figurative forms, often accompanied with chariots, show that since horse prehistoric times, the horse, but also the dog, rooster, and other animals were an inseparable part of the Pelasgian man. This is best evidenced by the finding of a real image of a rooster from Neolithic times at the Fafos location near Mitrovica, and numerous others in these areas.[143]

The cult of *billy-goat, goat,* and *mountain-goat,* among the Pelasgians is also among the oldest. They appear as symbols of fertility, but also of all forces that influence the biological regeneration of nature, and human faith with a divine inclination to dominate the world. Therefore, the cult of the goat with horns was displayed on the helmet of kings with the conviction of their divine origin (the Pyrrhic Epirotes, Alexander the Great of Macedonia) that fought with dedication feeling they had a duty to achieve a global empire. Subsequently, the model of this gear also reached Skenderbeg.

However, a constantly held belief that the footprints of the Pelasgians could be found in Troy (and this has to do with the early Bronze Age Troy), namely more than ten centuries beyond what Homer presented in his "Iliad," only emerged after its discovery by Schliemann in the late 19th century.

Excavations in the ancient city in the area of the present-day Hisarlik (although the exact place is doubtful because this would place it seven miles away inside the Karayonur area), brought to light over 100,000 items, which were carefully catalogued, where the most conspicuous items were the stone tools and weapons, as well as other weaponry, such as the combat axe in wedge shape, skillfully crafted with gray stone or pea color. Also, large quantities of stone hammers, axes, and daggers were found made of high quality slab. There were also millstones or hand-rotated lava stones, oval-shaped on one side and flat on the other, mortars and stone pounders, calibers, discs, and other items.[144]

Many of these stone tools found at Troy (namely those from the 12th through 6th centuries before the Greek conquest) were largely identical to those found in Albania, Kosova, and Macedonia, of that same age but found only recently, as research in this area was mostly made after World War I. They are also identical to the findings coming from Vinca[145] (near

---

[143] T. P. Vukanović: *"Neolithic Terra-Cock of Kosova,"* in "Vranjski Glasnik," 7/1971, p. 1.
[144] Schliman,H: "Troja," 1976, p. 56, cited according to Jacques, Edwin: *"Shqipëria,"* Tirana, p. 15.
[145] *Vinca* is a settlement in the vicinity of Belgrade by the Danube. In this locality, from 1920 onwards research began due to some findings belonging to the recent Neolithic

Belgrade) and those in Bosnia and Herzegovina, and Dalmatia, relating to the areas where northern Illyrian tribes lived. These tools supported the fact that they dealt with a certain kind of material culture produced by the same people stretching wide in the north from Central Europe to the Aegean, Asia Minor, and Italy, whose carriers were Dardanians, related to the origin of Troy, and according to mythology, was Dardan, Son of Zeus.

What has been most frequently seen in this culture as "influences" of either Greek or Aegean, the Trojans not only proved them wrong, but also provided a denominator of a common heritage to which classic Hellenism was connected after the 6th century B.C. by acquiring and then developing it within the social concepts characteristic for that stage of antiquity.

But it was not only stone utensils, found in Troy, that reflected this cultural interconnection on a plane that may be called common to this old civilization, which appeared linked to both sides: to the West and the East, naturally with identifiable features, supporting claims placing them as a product of the same ethnic stratification with a wide dispersion, with Dardanians being unavoidable in all perceptions. Therefore, the positions were greatly weakened, raising the features to the level of an impact "from outside" as coming from the Hellenic south, or carried over from afar. Numerous archaeological discoveries in the Central Balkan region and the portion of the Danube (harnesses, headgears, shields of copper, war axes, cleavers, knives, tips of arrows and pikes of copper), along with some brass borers, known as Lauzier, Vinca, and Bosnia findings, appeared identical to those found in the locality of Maliq in Albania, those in the vicinity of Prishtina and the Ibër valley near Mitrovica,[146] indicating a material culture out of reach of the Hellenic culture, which is more recent for at least three or four centuries.

Schliemann himself admitted it, hoping he would find the remains of what Homer presented in the "Iliad" in the form of a heroic epoch.

---

time in 3800-3200. Around 50 thousand different exhibits were found in a space of several hectares, the most important being the various anthropomorphic figures, utensils of various ceramics and jewelry. It is estimated that as part of this culture, several similar exhibits were also found in the Morava valley, that of Ibar, and in Kosova. (For more see: Stojić, Milorad: "*Etnokulturni odnos Kosova i Pomoravlja u praistoriji,*" Belgrade, 1990).

[146] For more on these finds see: Stipcevic, Aleksandar: "*Ilirët - historia, jeta, kultura,*" Prishtina, 1980; Stipcevic, Aleksandar: "*Simbolet e kultit te Ilirët,*" Prishtina, 1983; Mirdita, Zef: "*Studime dardane,*" Prishtina, 1979; Johan Georg von Hahn: "*Studime shqiptare,*" Tirana, 2007.

Convinced that the creative imagination, not always goes along with historical realities, he concluded that the presence of Greek traces at Troy could be seen only hundreds of years after Homer's period,[147] that is, from the 6th century onwards, supporting the assessment of the Homeric epoch being part of an historic glory that entered the memory of mankind as Hellenic. It was actually the discovery of Troy, however, and those who were found and returned it to where it had been taken from, the Pelasgians, with the assumption that the war could have been imagined just as a reflection of the harsh realities of internal confrontations of Pelasgic tribes to dominate Troy, as it actually was, while the true Hellenic realities in that part showed up four centuries later, after the Greek invasions.

Findings of Troy, along with the material culture from the Copper, Bronze, and Iron ages, without excluding the more recent Greek and other stratifications which came centuries later, following its destruction, thanks to many exhibits dedicated to various cults and rites, highlighted the interconnections and affinities of the spiritual life of the Pelasgians with that of the *Sumerian* peoples, with whom they once encountered, however, without excluding the possibility of subsequent meetings taking place in the Aegean-Mediterranean basin.[148]

Objects found: sweltered reels of stone, with a carved sun in the center, or rays of intermingling stars, and the zodiac signs in some of them, frequently mentioned in the "Rig Veda" or Hindu Psalms, *broken cross* (*swastika*) bore similarities with many others found in parts of the Central Balkans and Italy, throughout the extent of the Illyrian tribes. The broken cross of Troy is identical to those found in many parts of the Balkans from the Alps to the Adriatic, Novi Pazar and Shkodra.[149]

These symbols of cult from the Neolithic era found in the former space of ancient Dardania (Kosova) and Albania[150] also came enriched

---

[147] Schliman, H: *"Troja,"* 1976, p. 268, cited according to Jacques, Edwin: *"Shqiptarët,"* Tirana, p. 17.

[148] For more on these issues see: Bernal, Martin: *"Athina e zezë,"* Tirana, 2009, pp. 114-144.

[149] Stipcevic, Aleksandar: *"Simbolet e kultit te Ilirët,"* Prishtina, 1983, pp. 18-19.

[150] For more on the finds at Hisar of Suhareka see: J. Todorović, Arch. June, 4, 1963, p. 25; on the finds of Maliq near Korça see: H. Ceka "Konferenca e I e Studimeve albanologjike," Tirana, 1965, p. 447, Photo 19; F. Prendi: *"Studia Albanica,"* 3, 1966, no. 1, p. 255, Figure 13.

with those of the Bronze Age, when the *broken cross (swastika)*[151] was found as presented on the well-known chariots of clay of Duplaja.[152]

Towards the end of the Bronze Age, i.e. the time when one can speak with certainty about the Illyrians in these areas, the *broken cross* (*swastika*) was presented in the rocks at Lipci near Risan at Boka of Kotor, and Zlijeb near Visegrad, Drina River valley.[153]

With many similarities to those of Illyrian Dardanian areas in the central part of the Balkans and Italy, there were many iron objects found at Troy. Even many of the objects of cult and weaponry pertaining to the Hellenic culture (6th century), retained much of what could be considered as a Pelasgic cultural continuity in this part, despite the primacy of the Hellenic culture, as observed in new forms of expression, especially in sculpture and construction, as well as in statues and engravings relating artistry with belief, which was featured in the classic Roman and Hellenic art. Therefore, it is obvious that in the statues discovered in the latter city, the Greeks had adopted a Pelasgian goddess, giving her human form, much more attractive, but without giving up some of the original shape of the old art, representing characteristic idols of this age to be found in the wide Balkan space.

Pelasgic antiquity in an archaeological aspect is certainly incomplete without a glance at the so-called Mycenaean archaeological finds from the late Bronze Age (approx. 1400 B.C.), as these finds helped complete not only the frame of the spatial and spiritual extension of the most ancient Indo-European people and certainly touching on a very important point,

---

[151] The word *"svastika"* for the broken cross, in Sanskrit "svasti," means health, wellness, and joy. It has been characterized as a sun symbol in motion, on which a cross was carved afterwards. In time its boughs were broken and thus the *swastika* with broken shapes within the circle. This would be the earliest appearance of the *swastika* graphics. The main meaning of the swastika among the Illyrians was solar. However, the swastika has other meanings as well. The form of swastika on Illyrian shields, shown in coins of the Illyrian city of Shkodra, the image of the tricvertrum (three cross symbol) Iliacus ears, etc., had significance of the time. Such meanings might have had the swastika appearance on fibulae, bracelets, and other jewelry carried by the Illyrians (Stipcevic, Aleksandar: "*Kukasti kriz*" (crux gammata) *kod starih Ilira*," Gjurmime Albanologjike, 9/1970, p. 109-128.

[152] Stipcevic, Aleksandar: "*Simbolet e kultit te Ilirët*," Prishtina, 1983, p. 18-19.

[153] For more See: I. Pušić: "*Godišnjak Centra za balkanološko ispitavanje*," Book 2, 1966, p. 187-191; D. Bošković: "*Starine Crne Gore*," 3-4, 1965/66, p. 13-21; M. Garašanin: "*Germania*," 46, 1968, p. 217.

from which some of the dilemmas that accompanied the powerful emergence and establishment of Hellenism in this important area were solved, rather as part of creative fantasy, as Homer, than of historical realities.

It should be pointed out that again it was the German Henrik Schliemann who was tempted by Mycenae after Troy, with the conviction that he would find the main center of Agamemnon,[154] according to Homer, the head commander of the joint expedition against Troy. Of course there Schliemann managed to bring back through facts the historical truth of some legendary or mythical figures emerging from the poet's imagination. However, in contradiction to what the descendants of the ancient poet would consider the "time of Hellenic heroism," the poet did not mention Hellada anywhere or the Hellenes in the form of the subsequent construct. At Mycenae two models of weapons were found (mostly swords, knives, etc.): one of brass of a much earlier date, and one of iron, of at least three or four centuries later. These weapons not only had a different composition (copper-iron), but also a different shape (edge), which spoke well for the manner of use and other forms of wars, which differed significantly from one time to another.

Metal objects, those of copper, found at Mycenae and produced between the 16th and 17th centuries found in Epirus and in Dardania, which showed the same time and method of manufacturing, regardless of where they were made (in Mycenae or in a blacksmith workshop in Epirus and Dardania from many of them mentioned by ancient authors). The important thing is that they were identical. However, the work of iron weapons (swords, knives, etc.) was different. Patterns found in Mycenae were found in some parts of Greece, but not in Epirus and beyond in Dardania. As later-date products, at the time of arrival of Greeks in these parts, who may have acquired their production, were made of iron, which comes a little later than copper, which shows this very important shift. This invention escaped even the drafters of the Greek version of the "Iliad" of Homer by the Athenian "publisher" of Pisistratus, when weapons of iron instead of copper, were in the hands of Troy's destroyers.

---

[154] *Henrik Schliemann* made excavations for finding the remains of Mycenae during the years 1876-1877. He approached the city from numerous points and managed to bring to light the royal tombs and a rich treasure in them of diamonds, gold and other valuable jewelry. In several graves Schliemman discovered bodies filled with gold and precious stones. He gathered from them a number of gold death masks, gold breastplates, cups, and bronze baskets with golden handles.

Besides this material evidence and their differential treatment according to ages (from the late Neolithic of Copper and Iron), such as porcelain and metals, on which was based almost completely the proof of a pre-Hellenic culture that could not be other than Pelasgic, as ancient authors admitted settling along stone walls characteristic of Pelasgic settlements in other parts of the Balkans. It's construction matched the middle of the 2nd millennium, and besides the royal tombs, which were strongholds of stone, large and stately, in Mycenae hundreds of clay tablets of *Linear B* were found, which having been deciphered only in our time,[155] opened the question of the presence of another script other than the one recognized by the Phoenicians, an issue which, based on the possibility of having existed among the pre-Greek Pelasgians, has been raised by various authors from the mid-19th century to the present day.[156]

Therefore, one may say that the cultural material that is provided today by the archeological subject matter coming out of research in a vast Euro-Asian space, certainly in terms of prehistory and historical time, removes several dilemmas, and adds some others. However, in this whole thing, it has been accepted that much of it had to do with the weight and importance of the Pelasgian factor in the Indo-European family.

---

[155] Initially some of the clay tablets of Linear B in Greece were deciphered in part by M. Ventris and Chadwieck in 1952. But two years later, E. Fahrer was more successful as he deciphered the kunai-domed inscriptions on clay tablets at the Museum of East Berlin, concluding that they were written in a non-Greek language, which raised the question of this other "barbarian" language, which Herodotus and other ancient authors admit to being spoken by Pelasgians. The different display of Linear B from that of A, used by Mineas of Crete, at least linguistically opened the thesis of a presence of another script, or parallel to the Phoenician, which was later accepted by the Greeks.

[156] See: Johan Georg von Hahn: "*Studime shqiptare,*" Tirana, 2007, p. 378-393; Budimir, Milan: "*Grci i Pelasti,*" Srpska Akademija Nauka, knjiga CLXVII, Belgrade, 1950, p. 16; Jacques, Edwin: "*Shqiptarët,*" Tirana, p. 26; Aref, Mathieu: "*Mikeint=Pellazgët,*" Tirana, 2008, p. 20-27.

Pelasgian Antiquity from a Linguistic Point of View

> *The first announcements by German Johan-Georg von Hahn on the Pelasgic-Illyrian-Albanian language links. - Why were Pelasgians called "classical Indo-Europeans?" – Were the Pelasgians the authors of the alphabet that the Phoenicians brought to the Greeks and then modified it to the form appearing in Homer's work? – Diodorius' evidence of the Pelasgian script and its broad scope. - Three guttural circles of Albanian indicating Illyrian links with the Pelasgian eliminated the great dilemmas over the division in the Satem-Kentum classification. - Explanation of many toponomastic names in Greek and other ancient languages from the Caucasus to Basque, from the Baltic countries to Crete and over the Mediterranean basin, to North Africa only through Albanian, shows the linkage of this language with the Pelasgian and the wide extension of the Pelasgians in the ancient world.*

If science, after many guesses often of unscientific nature, had been able to remove from the order of the day the dilemma about the continuation of the Albanian language with the Illyrian, and if the stages of transition from Illyrian to Albanian had been known, however, the connection of the Pelasgians with their offspring (Illyrians, Dardanians, Epirotes, Macedonians, and other tribes dispersed in the wide Euro-Asian space) coming from the same family had yet to be explained, in order to get a clear historical appearance of one of the most important factors of antiquity, without which many of its developments could not be explained in accordance with the truth.

As the archaeological, anthropological, and all the evidence falling into what is called material evidence are important, bearing often also ambiguities and inherent confusions even because of the possibility of their removal by means of transfer as cult objects, war tools, or as goods, (in case of trade from one part of the world to another resulting often in multiple confusion), then linguistic evidence remains the most important and deserving in offering even a partial explanation or clarification of the old truths, opening the way for the other explanations that touch on issues that come up to our day.

Indeed, in terms of linguistics and its evidence, it was possible to draw in thick lines pre-historic movements of peoples and the layers originating from them, where, in a sense, out of a common root, came to light the family tree of Indo-European peoples with ancient Arian peoples different since antiquity and on, with that of the *Sumerian* and *Tyrrhenian* peoples, even though despite this, it would be linguistics that with few exceptions would challenge some of the rules established by it, which then, in some cases, would further the still continuing troubles.

Although the division of languages continues to basically appear with many question marks - especially when it comes to early connections between the Arian and Sumerian peoples, with Greeks and Pelasgians usually implicated in it, it's worth presenting a map of linguistic genealogies in order to see more closely the traces of most ancient human identities, but also their affinities and features that have influenced the differences, which are easier accepted than explained.

Regardless of disagreements over explanations, there is already agreement on the point of the first departure of people from Africa, from where a part of them moved to its eastern part, the water sources of the Nile, dispersing in Africa in the west (Chadics) toward the northwest (Berbers), the flow of the Nile to the Mediterranean (Egypt), while the rest, namely Semites moved further into the Sinai to the Near East and the East. The next group is that of the family of Indo-European languages of the Aryan peoples of nine trees one of which is the Albanian language, which like the Armenian and Greek languages, remained without ramifications. From the other trees, from Celtic came Irish and Bretonnian of Wales, from the Italic came Latin and its neo-Roman derivatives (French, Spanish, Portuguese), out of the German tree came Gothic language and its branches of Anglo-Saxonian, Frisian and German; by the Balto-Slavic trunk came two branches: that of the Slavic languages with branches of eastern and southern Slavs, while from the Baltic-Slavic tree came Lithuanian, and Letonian, and in the Indo-Iranian trunk, from the Iranian Sanskrit came Persian, and New Hindu.

This map, often presented in different variations, was preceded by an Anatolian stratification representing the core of the Etrurian-Hittite peoples,[157] that is of interest, largely because it "implicates" the Pelasgian

---

[157] For more see: Bernal, Martin: *"Athina e zezë,"* Tirana, 2009, p. 29, map 1 and map 2.

factor so far as, in terms of solving numerous dilemmas, making them appear as "classical Indo-Europeans."[158]

This appellation had to do with the oldest Indo-European inhabitants of the Mediterranean not belonging to either eastern or western Indo-Europeans, as they are often unilaterally seen, as they distinguish three circles of gutturals,[159] which favors the conclusion on the their extension since prehistoric times, i.e. the first movements of peoples from India to the West, which as cyclical and with long interruptions in different parts, went on through several known and unknown routes, from where some of their traits derived, being seen as eastern and western respectively, or as being in between, which turns them into insurmountable and highly significant factors of pre-antiquity and antiquity.

However, the explanation of linguistic connections between the Pelasgian and Illyrian, although difficult in the absence of scripture, which does not, however, exclude the possibility that this be done by means of some fossils that only Albanian has kept and can be explained only through it, requires some prior clarification of relations of the Pelasgians with the Greeks on one side, and the connection of the Pelasgians with Phrygians and Phoenicians, on the other hand. Its relations to other peoples living in the Aegean-Anatolian space should also be made, including their implication in Crete, from where the pre-Hellenic civilization emanated, to which no attention was paid equally because everything was connected with the Greeks, while, as seen, subsequent research made it quite plain that it was precisely the Pelasgian factor that stood on its background from where the Greeks, and not only them, continued, and where certainly other influences have been present, an issue that remains to be considered by further research in order to shed light on its truth.

Additionally, such a linguistic trial may also explain some reasonable assumptions about the legacy of the Pelasgians and Illyrians in relation to other scattered tribes where Dardanians appeared as a separate node with some unknowns, to which more were added, namely those dealing with the truth about Epirotes and Macedonians, who often stand "as a bridge" between the Pelasgians and Hellenes, although ancient authors almost always see them as "barbarians," or even separated into the Illyrian family even when they engage in conflicts and wars with them, be it between the

---

[158] Budimir, Milan: *"De Illyriis et Protoillyriis,"* "Vjesnik za Arheologiju i Historiju Dalmatinsku" LIII (1950- 1950), p. 4.
[159] Ibid, p. 4.

Molossians and Illyrians, between the Macedonians and Illyrians, or others.

Since linguistics is based on facts of a spiritual nature, those coming as a product of a certain social consciousness reflected and developed within certain phonetic, grammatic, and lexical rules, which were different from the material ones cannot be manipulated or interpreted through allegations and adjustments. However, their investigation and interpretation often runs into trouble if certain priority factors are excluded from research with an explanation as being non-existent, or "indigenous," as they by being living spiritual testimonies continue to interfere, as happened with the Albanian and its case.

However, this challenged the linguistics to turn its necessary attention to reasons for keeping the key to many explanations relating to antiquity, where with other languages (excluding Greek which is taken as the basis of antiquity), no explanation can be given.

Indeed, since the early 18th century, when science was virtually and almost entirely focused toward the Greeks and Greece to explain antiquity and the role of Greek and Roman civilization as most prudent, although this was seen at the expense of others, the German philosopher Leibniz[160] drew the attention to the Albanian language as daughter of the Illyrian, which should not go unattended not only because this was owed to the truth, but it was also in favor of the Indo-European family in order to better understand its tree genealogy through a living language coming from antiquity.

It was a proper warning and timely. Behind him were German and other linguists (first Thunnman followed by Johannes Georg von Hahn, Franz Bopp, Norbert Jokl, Gustav Pedersen, Gustav Meyer and others), who by the 19th century onwards, were dealing with the tenacity of the Albanian language and its ties with the Illyrian, equally discussing the theory of the origin of the Pelasgians as ancestors of the Illyrians,[161] and by

---

[160] Jacques, Edwin: *"Shqiptarët,"* Tirana, 2002, p. 35.
[161] See Johan Georg von Hahn, who since 1854, with the publication of his book *"Albanesische Studien"* in Jena, came up with a thesis on the Pelasgian origin of the Albanians, thus opening the issue of the ancestors of Albanians as among the most ancient inhabitants of Central Europe, the Mediterranean (including Crete), Aegean and Anatolia, whose civilization was dominant (without excluding the possibility of their own script), which would be adopted by the Greeks, as they arrived to the Aegean area. At this time

doing so opening the question of primacy of the autochthony of Hellenes in Europe and its role in what is known as antiquity, where they stood firm until then together with the Romans.

Similarly, historians and archaeologists likewise found historical evidence of this ancient pre-Hellenic people among ancient authors, including Homer. However, all that evidence remained outside any scientific approach, arguing that the Pelasgian traces had been erased, or that even when detected, they dissolved in different directions among others, although this "dissolution," with Albanians as a nation stretching approximately in the same space and speaking a language that was neither Greek nor Latin stood as a living testimony demonstrated from both a physical and spiritual point of view.

However, it would be exactly linguistics, which, as Leibniz had warned in the early 18th century announcing the likelihood of the Albanian language being a daughter of the Illyrian, after a century of hesitations and wanderings, the issue of explaining Indo-Europeanism in terms of some of the many dilemmas began to be connected with Pelasgians and their descendants Illyrian-Albanians, as an insurmountable issue, which was in the interest of linguistics, but also historiography in general, which should get full scientific confirmation.

This interest in linguistics (though different information from the survey of perceptions of detached or sporadic research warned that Albanian holds the key to explaining the numerous dilemmas that come from antiquity) focused primarily on research of the origin of this language in order to find its place as part of the Indo-European family, and then, once this was done, to explain its relations with the other languages, primarily with those sharing affinities and similarities with it, resulting in some of the noted very contradictory stances in its relation and pertaining to the Illyrian and Thracian, to which, as would seen shortly afterwards, it would be exactly the Pelasgian that would remove those dilemmas, as their explanation moved toward their common background from a distant past.

---

there is another position by the German linguist Karl O. Müller saying that further penetration in the history of Greece attracted attention to the Pelasgian element hitherto sacrificed. (See: Karl O. Müller "Prolegomena.")

As in this direction Franc Bopp's studies,[162] and those of Gustav Meier, dealing with the origin of the Albanian language,[163] including also that of Pedersen on the historical grammar of the Albanian language,[164] Jokl on phonetics and historical morphology of the Albanian,[165] and others joining them, granted the Albanian language a place in the Indo-

---

[162] *Franc Bopp* (1791-1867), the prominent German linguist, was a professor at the University of Berlin and founder of comparative historical Indo-European linguistics. At age 25 he published his first work "On the conjunctive system of Sanskrit compared with Greek, Latin, Persian and German." After getting acquainted with Albanian, he noticed a similarity between the Sanskrit in grammar, word roots, and the sounds of diphthongs. He looked at Albanian numerals and pronouns and made an analysis of its grammatic structure and vocabulary. He noted similarities between the Albanian vocabulary, on one hand, and that of the Armenian or Baltic languages, Letonian and Lithuanian, on the other hand, particularly in the following areas: forestry, agriculture, woodwork, livestock products, household, names of plants, time, animals, livestock, diseases, body parts, as well as social and legal terms. Bopp published his work in 1854, proving conclusively that Albanian was part of the Indo-European language family and did not derive from any sister language on the mainland, like the Greek. (For the full story see Jacques, Erwin: "Shqipëria").

[163] *Gustav Mayer* (1850-1900), Austrian Professor of Graz University and member of the Academy of Sciences in Vienna, specialized in the field of historical studies of Indo-European languages, Greek, Turkish and Albanian. His fundamental publication *"On the position of the Albanian language in the circle of Indo-European languages"* in 1883, followed by eight or more scientific papers, as the one on the forming of the plural of nouns, comparative studies of Albanian numerals and other Indo-European languages, as well as the history of Albania, grammar, historical phonetics, legends, poetry and popular proverbs, collected in the dialects of the provinces of Albania and Arbëresh settlements in Italy and Greece. He is known particularly for the publication of an *"Etymological Dictionary of the Albanian language,"* 1889. Thanks to his profound scientific studies this remarkable Albanologist concluded that the Albanian language derived from the Illyrian and formed a separate branch in the Indo-European family of languages.

[164] *Holger Pedersen* (1867-1953) made significant contributions in the field of phonetics, highlighting the shape of the Albanian today linking it with antiquity which would support the position that Albanian is derived from European and Illyrian predecessors.

[165] *Norbert Jokl* (1877-1942) The Austrian Albanologist of Jewish descent devoted his entire life studying the Albanian language. He was distinguished in various fields, such as etymology and word-formation relations of the Albanian language with other ancient non-Greek languages in the Balkans, and the historical phonetics and morphology of Albanian, which he defined as an Indo-European language.

European family within a particular branch (among them nine in all). Although, this was followed by further dilemma about either *satem* or *kentum* belonging, as there was evidence for either one, and this was seen as more of a difficulty than not. Therefore, searching for its links with the Illyrian and then with the Pelasgian in order to prove its antiquity, inevitably required the trial of a measurement with the old Greek as a "standard" to which the complexity of antiquity was tied from where would then emerge other issues of common interest, such as that of the possibility of any "concealed" alignment of branches of Albanian among other languages, especially the Greek and Latin, though there is no denying of the significant participation of the vocabulary of these languages in the Albanian language fund.

All of this could have been a late development conditioned by social and political circumstances, such as those from classical antiquity onwards, while this influence would have been preceded by substantial borrowings by the two languages, especially Greek from Pelasgian, and all ancient authors, either admitted borrowing from it, or accepted its independent continuation "as a barbarian language."

Suffice it here to repeat some of the testimonies by ancient authors (Homer, Herodotus, Thucydides, Aristotle, Pliny, and especially Diodorius) to see the best of this issue, which for centuries, was ignored by others because by doing otherwise it would become necessary to look into the issue of its impact on others, that is, those who came later.

Therefore, in accordance with these developments, divided by entire centuries, it is only natural that this challenge, from a language standpoint, should investigate and bring to light Pelasgic remains in the general background of Indo-European antiquity continuing with Old Greek to see if these languages have common roots as assumed for these people, and secondly, that the conclusion is used to explain the Illyrian-Albanian continuity as a natural but extremely long and complicated development. This is the only way to open the road for clarifications dealing with the pre-Greek factor, i.e. Pelasgian, within the Indo-European family, though it is known and in several areas accepted, it was treated in a way as to give it a proper place because of strong Philhellene prejudices of the 19th century, which when dealing with the Greeks and Greek language as the foundation stone of antiquity, roads were blocked to other issues that could put that in doubt.

Non-scientific attitudes that many composing factors overlooked, this time by shifting the attention towards the Pelasgian antiquity of the Albanians removed of some clichés such as the group division of *Satem-Kentum* (eastern and southern) languages,[166] in order to build on it, not without flaws, was the characterization of peoples and their country from prehistoric to historic times, a division which unilaterally cut off Pelasgians. They were seen as an ancient people but "without a clear trace" or merged into others, detached from their offspring, with a similar thing happening to the ancestors of the Albanians, the Illyrians, although they would be mentioned by ancient authors as scattered tribes within their space, or in the neighborhood as "barbarians,"[167] with whom they would engage in wars for almost two centuries before conquering. However they did not eradicate them, fighting them as a delimitation factor rather than a factor that in various forms was part of all the developments having an impact on them in many ways that cannot be neglected anymore.

This sacrificing, as Müller would admit, could not, however, be permanent nor repulsive to that extent because of the living presence of the Albanian language of an ancient people, which despite being bypassed (intentionally or indeed because specific knowledge about it was lacking

---

[166] This division is made on two categories: *"kentum"* (with the word "cent" beginning with the K = *kmotom*) and *"satem"* (where the word "cent" begins with the syllable sound S = *satam, satem*), a method whose object is *kentum/satem* difference in order to distinguish languages. This division, made according to the situation of dead languages (Sanskrit, Avestic, Tocharian, Ancient Greek, Latin, etc.), counting also Pelasgian as missing without leaving any marks behind, called by some the "pre-Hellenic language," with Albanian in the meantime appearing as its descendant successor, which as an accepted Indo-European language, albeit belatedly, connected the "dead" antiquity, that is, stagnant with a living movement.

[167] See: Evidence by ancient authors from Herodotus, Plutarch, Aristotle, Plinis and others presented in the book *"Ilirët dhe Iliria te autorët antikë,"* Prishtina, 1979. The most accurate among the others in terms of the Illyrians and their dispersion, including their cities, is the geographer Claudius Ptolemy, born in the town of Ptolemais of Egypt, who lived and worked in Alexandria in the second century AD. This prominent astronomer of the time was also involved in geography, from where in his work *"Geography,"* consisting mostly of tables on which positions of settlements of the ancient world by degrees of latitude and longitude are marked and defined, among them also many towns and villages of Illyria, Macedonia, and Epirus. Among them there are also names encountered for the first time, as is the name of the Illyrian tribe of Albanoi and the city of Albanopolis.

for a long time), with its presence, intervened in the entire issue from where then all the doors were opened to it.

Therefore, unlike the material (archaeological) evidence, which mostly tried to keep the Pelasgians disconnected from their heritage - the Illyrians, seeing them mostly under the armpits of others and their impact, keeping in the margins of developments, the Albanian language as a living testimony had created its own space in order to be seen without any great reluctance as part of the Indo-European family of languages. Albanian, as a single branch among the nine that had in its static and also synthetic forms, being among the most specific, justly turned into an object of comprehensive linguistic scrutiny.

This treatment within the Indo-European genealogy, although it has caused the shrinking of the Albanian language from others unilaterally with no other entitlements but its own branch, does not preclude its possible participation from particularly Greek and later Latin, whose appearance is closely related to the Venetian. Once they fell in contact with it after the submission of Pelasgian lands, facts that have already been accepted by history, and the nature of those contacts and internal connections that were inevitable came out by further linguistic research outside familiar prejudices that have seen and continue to see the Albanian in accordance to the impact on it by the ancient languages (Greek and Latin) as well as those in the neighborhood (Slavic), in relation to those it received from them. Quite a natural borrowing was reflected in common language relationships, as evidently the ancient Greeks acknowledged the spiritual and social superiority of the indigenous population, namely of the Pelasgians, having found and adopted from them deities, idols, and even oracles, something that could also be valid for their language as a direct means of communication.

It is only natural that the first course, namely the influences and acquisition from old languages (Greek and Latin) and of its neighbors (Slavic) on the Albanian may be an issue of methodology to highlight certain relationships as conditioned by particular circumstances. However, in no way do they show the true situation from the standpoint of antiquity and less so reflect its true genetics. An objective methodology would surely imply an opposite approach, namely an historical one, starting from the origin in order to then look at the branches and subbranches in accordance with natural developments. Running away from the genesis and grabbing by the branches certainly placed Albanian in a bad position as compared to the major languages of antiquity, Greek and Latin, since they both were state languages, also official and administrative, languages of culture and later languages of religion, following the emergence of Christianity in the Byzantine time, having been written and even utilized in doctrine.

This development reflecting a social state in motion does not reflect the foundations on which this edifice stands and the true role of the basic factors, but that of new creations, which would, naturally, also show an image entirely different from that of the origin.

In fact, here begins the thread of these issues being viewed one-sidedly which tried to keep the Albanian dependent on old languages (Greek and Latin), namely beyond thinking that it might represent something of the epicenter of the old, as had happened with the historical view putting the Pelasgians and their descendant Illyrians, Dardanians, and others in relation to the Greeks and Romans, as seen at their periphery as "barbarians" and not as an indigenous factor that Greeks faced in their lands as they appeared there and who, according to the sources of ancient authors, accepted them and learned from them (cults, religion, gods, culture, life experiences, and much more), with the Hellenes then continuing to build what appeared as Hellenism on the platform of which antiquity and its civilization, so important for the history of humankind, would be assessed.

This also applies to the Latin, as the foundation of Rome, and later the Roman empire as directly linked to the role of the Etruscans (Tyrrhenians), but also Pelasgian Dardanians, who, again according to ancient sources and sources with historical backing, after the hypothetical loss of the Trojan War, an event that outside the creative imagination had to do with the Hellenistic conquests in Asia Minor that took place two centuries after Homer's stories, headed towards Italy by sea through the Dardanelles and Aegean and by land through Epirus and Peloponnese, and from thence to the south of Italy, as displayed in Virgil's tragedies;[168] Aeneas followed in search of building a new Troy in the West as redress for the eastern Troy, etc. There is more historical evidence to back this by ancient authors, such as Dionysius of Heraklion, Plutarch, and even Strabo.[169]

---

[168] Virgil: "*Aeneid*" (Aeneidos), cited according to "*Ilirët dhe Iliria te autorët antikë*," Prishtina, 1979, p. 97.
[169] For more see: Jacques, Edwin: "Shqiptarët," Tirana, pp. 55-57.

The attempts to keep Albanian at the margins because of acquisition from other languages, justifying all of this through almost alarming figures of acquisition in the lexical field was followed by a counter response that related to ancient Pelasgian and prehistoric antiquity placed in the role of an epicenter that either scared someone or made them ignore it because of a cold historical attitude towards the Pelasgians, suspicious of the Illyrians, and indifference to their Albanian offspring.

However, it was exactly the antiquity of the Albanian language viewed from the perspective of the disposition within the Indo-European family, of its division on the basis of the criteria in the northern or *satem reflex* and southern *kentum reflex* languages, that broke this internal rule thought to be concluded precisely because it was built on the basis of dead languages, such as Sanskrit, old Greek, and Latin.

The Albanian language showed that in historical, phonetic and morphological terms, it was presented as separate, because it met the "criteria" of the two groupings, appearing at the same time as a *satem* – eastern language (in the same group with Celtic-Baltic languages) and as a *kentum* – southern language (in the same group with Greek and Slavic languages), this being enabled by its distinction of the three guttural circles, which as a single Indo-European language led to quite an unexpected conclusion, that it constituted a separate language group, reflecting a preservation of the language situation of the Indo-European that preceded the formation of *satem* and *kentum* Indo-Europeans.[170]

This was also supported by the personal fate of palatal order that separated Indo-Europeans from the *satem* Indo-Europeans. This is seen not only by the remnants coming from the vocabulary of classical Pelasgians to the classical languages, but also by the undeniable fact that phonetics of the Albanian language today represent a close relationship with the Illyrian-Thracian-Phrygian language group, leaving no doubt of the Illyrian group bond.[171] Albanian words, such as *dritë* (light) (from the Indo-European *drita*), alongside *natë* (night), show support for the personal fate of palatal gutturals regardless of the **kt** consonant grouping.[172]

---

[170] For more see: Budimir, Milan: "*Grci i Pelasti*," Serbian Academy of Sciences, Special Edition, Book II, Belgrade, 1950, p. 16.
[171] Budimir, Milan: "*Ilirski problem i leksička grupa Teuta*," Split, 1953, p. 11.
[172] Ibid, p. 11.

Even the road to this "reconciliation in principle," if it can be so called, was not without difficulty, as it passed through two opposing linguistic positions: Nordism[173] and Classicism,[174] where on one side line up some of German linguists, supporters of extreme Arianism, who later would become politicized, and "reconciling" Classicism that links Indo-European civilization with Anatolian civilization and beyond that to the East as mutual and natural because of common historical circumstances.

However, spears would break over the Pelasgian factor and Albanian language, as it interfered with what had been supplemented to the old already dead languages (Sanskrit, ancient Greek, Latin), but it intervened also in the living languages, connecting antiquity to evolution, something that made its role more credible.

Therefore, for the "Southern" classics the Pelasgian factor turned into a main argument as "protection" against the "Nordics" and their theory that it would be the German-Baltic peoples that in the third millennium

---

[173] The best-known representatives of *"nordism"* as the basis of Indo-Europeanism, where the Greeks are attributed the role of first Indo-European settlers in our continent are German linguists: C. Schuhard, S. Fuchs, W. Kraiker, J. Jüthne, F. Schachermeyer and H. Krahe, supported to some extent by Swedish linguists: MP Nilsson and A. Pedersson. These attitudes were joined, although with caution, by the linguist P. Kretschmer. It is interesting to note that even within the school, which gives the Greeks the claim of Indo-Europeanism, there are differences regarding the Pelasgians and their role in this regard. Thus, the linguist H. Krahe recognized the merits of the Illyrian tribes calling them "missionaries of Indo-Europeanism in Central Europe." (See: *"Der Anteil der Illyrier in der Indogermanisierung Europas,"* published in *"Welt als Geschichte,"* VI, 1940, p. 54-73), while the head of the school, Archeologist Schuhard called pre-Illyrians "non-Indo-European groups" (See: *"Die Urillyer und ihre Indogermanisierung,"* Abhandl. Ak., Berlin, 1937.)

[174] The most noted representatives of "Mediterreneanism" are: A. Dauzata, A. Mayer, Fr. Ribezzo, A. Vaillont, M. Budimir, and others, who consider Pelasgians to be fundamental to Ind-Europeanism exactly because with their wide expansion from Asia to Europe they affected subsequent stratifications, including the Hellenic. "Mediterreneanists" or supporters of classical Indo-Europeanism linked the civilization of Crete, Troy, and Mycenae with pre-Hellenic times, arguing the Pelasgians as crucial. In this regard the linguist, M. Budimir was among the most direct, by concluding that Pelasgians were classical Indo-Europeans, who should be considered fathers of ancient civilization. On this occasion, he defended the view that Hellenism is but a reversal by the old Greeks of the Pelasgian culture (language, myths, culture, and generally their life experience) that was transferred to another more developed background carrying it into other parts. (See: *"Grci i Pelasti,"* Belgrade, 1950, *"Ilirski problem i leksička grupa Teuta,"* Split, 1953.)

would be moving Southwards and would affect the historic and prehistoric civilization of antiquity, in which the "*satems*" would determine the Indo-Europeanness (including here also old pre-historic peoples and the Pelasgians), while the "Nordics" would also be using the Pelasgians, as well as the Albanian, to counter the arguments of the "Southerners" about the *kentum* elements of this language, viewing it as "peripheral effects" of more recent times.

However, both schools agreed that the Pelasgians and Pelasgian language related to that situation that preceded the formation of Indo-Europeans, an admission that somehow turned into a conciliatory formula, valid today.

What was that language condition that preceded the formation of *satem* and *kentum* Indo-Europeans, where the Albanian alone maintained the three guttural circles, while others maintained one or blended with the second, but never the third, and hardly ever together, as happened with the Albanian language?

This issue necessarily turns one back to the late Neolithic time and onwards, i.e. from mid-third millennium to that of the mid-second millennium, exactly where the recent history sees Pelasgians in their role of people who, in their move towards northeast, settled in the greatest part of Central Europe and in the whole Mediterranean basin, without excluding Anatolia that affected the course of what would be called the "dawn of civilization" that concerned the transition from prehistory to historical time.

At this time, always according to linguistics, it could be said that the prevailing Pelasgians stretched into the vast Euro-Asian space, while to their North (beyond the Alps) emerged German, Baltic and Slavic peoples, and to the South, i.e. Mediterranean basin, in the early first millennium, emerged initially Hellenes and later the Romans, though at those times these peoples were at a developmental level significantly below that of Pelasgians or pre-Hellenes, as they are often called, and this did not exclude their tendency to deny their interconnection with Pelasgic antiquity.[175]

Besides numerous toponyms (names derived from places) and hydronyms (names of bodies of water), which preserve the seal of Pelasgic prehistory, whose explanation is provided only by means of the Albanian

---

[175] Budimir, Milan: "Iliri i prailiri," Belgrade, 1952.

language, besides much other evidence of a material nature, the supremacy of the Pelasgians against their earlier or later-date neighbors, among others, was also shown through vocabulary, which refers to the time of occurrence of metals (from copper to iron, i.e. from early second to the first millennium), where words of Illyrian origin, such as *hekur* (iron), *argjend* (silver) and some others, were found as borrowings in the western languages of the Indo-European family in a wide range of close to that mentioned above with what one may well relate theories on their arrival from different directions in pre-historic space often contradictory to the benefit of the position that the Pelasgians were the first people from the first influx to have settled in the old continent in all its space in order to be extended later on to other parts of Asia Minor and North Africa.

Therefore, in accordance with the assessment that from the Copper Age and on certain linguistic identities of certain people, according to linguist J. Pokorni, the Celtic and German name for iron (*Eisen*), with its radical element ***iso-*** by maintaining its intervocalic ***s,*** similar to the old Macedonian, is proof of the Illyrian origin lying in the Hallstatt, the center of the renowned culture of iron, which through archeological argumentation has been recognized by the Celtic-Baltic peoples.[176]

Pursuant to this, M. Budimir saw the word *argjend – argentums* (the old Illyrian form *subauros*), which was introduced from Illyrian to other nations (*silber* – in German, old form *silubra*, in old Slavic *sirebro*, and Lithuanian *sidabras*).[177]

Of this same nature and age, in addition to the words *Rhithymna, Caditus*, which bring to mind the Illyrian and Etruscan onomastic material, from Hessie's dictionary the Cretans, are the residents of the town of *Gortina*, which the Greeks call Γορτνιοι with its Eteo-Cretan indigenous form Καρτεμνι, where one may clearly see elements of Pelasgian origin in the pre-Hellenic name alongside radical and suffix elements of Indo-

---

[176] Ibid, p. 17.

[177] M. Budimir is of the opinion that the Illyrian word *subauros* for pure metal - silver is caradical (based on the eastern Caucasus) with the Armenian *surb* (pure) and *subhra* - shining of the Hindu (from its old form *kubhros*). According to him, the Illyrian name for the *Damavia* mine in Epirus (Srebrenica) also belongs to this lexical group. Budimir assessed these names to have come through the substitution of Illyrian anchor, while the vocalism of the first letter comes from a double monophthong of the old Illyrian diphthong **au**. The alteration from ***b/m*** in those names was documented in the ancient Balkans. (See: "Grci i Pelasti," p. 18.)

European origin, both documented in the Pelasgian lands outside Crete.[178] This renders the Pelasgian element in the "two linguistic wings," northern and southern, as acceptable, which coincides with pan-Illyrian European attributes granted to them by some linguists, who considered the Pelasgian people as the oldest Indo-European people dominating overall Europe reaching as far as Asia Minor.

This theory was also supported through the so-called paleo-European evidence, where the radical element *ghordho* (*gardh*, fence, town) is documented in Etruria, Arcadia, Phrygia, Galanti and elsewhere.

In the Pelasgian and Slavic vernacular *ghordho*, in its narrow sense means "wooden housing," while in broader terms, among the Pelasgian-Illyrians and their habitats, it represented fenced settlements, towns, and not citadels, which in Greek are called $\chi o \rho \tau o \omega$, and in Hittites are called *gurtas*. This Pelasgian word penetrated deeply in the Anatolian parts and was found in both ancient Palestines, the first less known in the Caucasus and the other in the eastern Mediterranean part: toponym *Tifranocerta* "Tiger Town" in Armenia, with Hessian gloss $\kappa \varepsilon \rho \tau \alpha \ \pi o \lambda \iota \varsigma \ A \rho \mu \eta \nu \iota \omega \nu$.[179]

The appearance of this Pelasgian word in the old Phoenician vernacular is of particular importance, giving their colony Carthage *(New Town)*, as a basic element the Pelasgian word *kart - city*. Evidently, it is not by accident that the center of the Phoenician colony is called $B\nu\delta\sigma\alpha$, in which the Greeks have noted the Pelasgian word $\beta\nu\delta\sigma\alpha$ *("skin")*.[180]

In accordance with what might be called housing culture, as the old Pelasgian word *kart-city* indicates, stretching from north to Africa, at some later time we also see the appearance of the word *larisa* for "fortress" widely used in the ancient world to mark a fortified city. This word that lingers still in maps confirms the wide spreading of the Pelasgian population. Shepherd's Atlas of Classical World includes eleven cities or settlements called "*Larisa*."[181] One of them, located near Troy, is mentioned by Homer as "the home of fierce Pelasgians from the rich fertile fields of Larissa."[182] Balkan towns that bore such a name were: one on the river Paeneass, in Pelasgian Agros area, Central Thessaly, Larissa Kremtase, in the southern part of Ftiotis Acetia, and another, currently called Tekos by

---

[178] Ibid, p. 45.
[179] Ibid, p. 45
[180] Ibid, p. 45.
[181] Jaques, Edward: *"Shqiptarët,"* Tirana, p. 45.
[182] Homer: *"Iliada,"* Book II 840, Tirana, 1979.

River Larisos, outpouring to the Ionian Sea, down the northwestern cape of the Gulf of Corinth, in Eliat of Aecea.[183]

The concentration on the vocabulary of the metal period, on one hand, and that of settlements and building systems (fences, fortresses and what are called cities) on the other, which have a continuity, except for the language importance, demonstrating the presence of the influence of Pelasgian linguistic stratification in other languages belonging to the Indo-European family, also has its historic importance in a broader sense, as it is a social set definition, on which one can rely a chronology of events and circumstances that took place before the emergence of written evidence, such as those from the 6th century B.C. and onwards, when the first writings appeared in Greece, although this did not mean that everything began and ended there. Because the use of metals, especially copper and bronze (in the 2nd millennium B.C.), which led to iron (in the early 1st millennium B.C. up to its half), speaks of a more organized society in many aspects, which gives the Pelasgian factor and their descendants Illyrians, Dardanians, and others of the large common trunk with many branches a different appearance from what is given to them for a long time when they were usually seen as being "off" events, but always with the Greeks, even when there was no way of denying to them their pre-Greek presence in the Euro-Asian space.

Therefore, the dominance of the Pelasgian factor from the Bronze Age to that of the Iron Age in Central Europe and the Mediterranean area and the Aegean in general, where linguistics accepted most major frictions within its systems (phonetic, morphological and lexical) on which the social and population map could somehow be constructed, opened the issue of language as a communication tool, originally through various signs and familiar symbols, universal or particular, and later through letters, occurring with the appearance of Greek writing in the sixth century onwards, when ancient authors began to leave behind evidence of historical, geographical and other circumstances before and after their arrival in these parts without excluding works of art, then, as is "Iliad" of Homer and others in Greek up to "Aeneid" of Virgil among Romans, which spoke of Pelasgians and their descendants, Dardanians, founders of Rome, with which then was identified an important part of ancient civilization where the Etruscans would also be deserving of spreading out

---

[183] Jacques, Edwin: *"Shqiptarët,"* Tirana, 2007, p. 45.

the story over those parts, as evidenced by their language declared mysterious, with the explanation that "it was associated with the pre-Hellenic language Lemnos," a Pelasgian island west of Troy from where, presumably, after Troy was destroyed, moved to Italy.[184]

Relying on this and similar data, coming from ancient authors and on, the French scholar Louis Beonlew, supported the view that "many names of places, mountains, rivers, and legendary figures, which cannot be explained by an etymology of Greek words, can be explained well by a non-Greek language. To date only one language is able to shed light on these names: it is the Albanian language. Therefore the author of this paper is compelled to support the thesis that modern Albanians are the descendants of the population, which lived before the arrival of Greeks in areas along the Adriatic and up to Halis.[185]

That we are dealing here with a Pelasgian language, mother of the Illyrian, which was alive at the time of Herodotus and also reflected in toponyms, it may well be proven also with what the noted historian said about hearing the Pelasgian language around the cities (Creston, Plakie, Scylace), which were established by them, as well as other cities of that population,[186] names which have specific meanings in the present-day Albanian, similar to that of the ancient Greek acquired by the modern Greek as derivatives. Therefore, the first word *Kreston* can be compared with the Albanian *kreshtë*,[187] the word *Plake* (as Stefan Byzantine records it), representing the oldest quart in Athens, has an Albanian root *plaka* meaning old, identifying with the meaning of the quarter in Athens, while the word *Scylace* in Albanian is *shkul*, the opposite of the word *ngul*.[188]

The same can be said about toponymic appellations in the new Greece and elsewhere, coming from antiquity, with etymologies and explanations by means of the Albanian language. These are names such as: *gur, mal, pyll, s(h)ur*, to which other toponyms may be added with other Albanian words at their base. Furthermore, there are Pelasgian words (names) of Albanian roots, such as: Pelasg (Πελαογς), Pelasgia

---

[184] Corelli, Filipe: "*Qytetet etruske,*" 1957, p. 14, cited according to Jacques, Edwin: "Shqiptarët," Tirana, 2007, p. 45.

[185] Beonlew, Luis: "*La Grece avant les Greces,*" Paris, 1877, p. 45.

[186] Herodotus: "*Historitë,*" Book I, 57, cited according to "*Ilirët dhe Iliria te autorët antikë,*" Prishtina, 1979, p. 16.

[187] For more see Johan Georg von Hahn: "*Studime shqiptare,*" Tirana, 2007, p. 335.

[188] See also Konda, Spiro N: "*Shqiptarët dhe problemi pellazgjik,*" Tirana, 1964, p. 347.

(Πελαογι), Aspelia (Ασπελια), Pelagon (Πελαγων), Pelagonia (Πελαογνια), Plakie (Πλακιη), Plak (Πλακος), Pelg (Πελαγος), Deukalian (Δενκολιων), Polydeukes (Πολνδεωκης), Apellon, Apollon (Απελλωη), Pallas (Παλλας), Pelias (Πελιας), Astypale (Αστνπαλη), Ampelos (Αμπελος), etc.[189]

For the same kind of trail the Pelasgians scattered in different parts, especially in the Central Balkans, with ramifications going towards Italy and Greece, which some linguists call "pre-Illyrian stratification," which cannot be explained by any other language (Greek, Latin, Thracian),[190] indirectly accepted the Pelasgian-Illyrian factor also for a number of anthroponyms related to the time following the Roman penetration in the central part of the Balkans and further in territories inhabited by Illyrians and other tribes of the family with a wide extension.

Of the same nature, i.e. related to ancient Pelasgic-Illyrian, are a good number of names that appear most frequently: *Delus, Dida, Getas, Maema, Mescena, Mestys, Pitta,* and others. Some of them, found also in Roman records from the 2nd and 3rd century AD, such as *Anna, Anneus, Annius, Annus, Dalmanus, Dardanus, Dasus, Dassius, Dida, Diza, Dizon, Denentilla, Enius, Epocadus, Licco, Nanra, Rhedon, Sareus, Scerulaedus, Tritus, Turrellius, Turranis, Varidius, Vocania,* and others, maintain their Pelasgian-Illyrian affiliation[191] even after various important social and political changes among the Illyrians occurred during the Roman conquest.

Here, important support comes from historical toponymy giving a great contribution in understanding the ancient Pelasgic-Illyrian side of linguistics, starting with a methodologically right way of the internal circumstances of the Albanian, determining that the names of those towns, rivers, mountains, and others of the region from Ragusa to Çameria, from Shtip, Nish, Sharr, Shkup (Skopje) and up to the coast of the Adriatic and Ionian Sea, which are known since ancient times in the form they currently have in the Albanian language, prove a continuance and a link to this area. These names mostly represent a linguistic development

---

[189] Konda, Spiro N: "*Shqiptarët dhe problemi pelazgjik,*" Tirana, 1964, p. 59.
[190] For more see: Krahe, E: "*Die Sprache der Illyrer*" I, Wiesbaden, 1955; Kronaser, H: "*Zum Stand der Illyristik,*" LB.4/1962; Meyer, A: "*Die Sprache der alten Illyrier,*" I-II, Vienna 1957-1958; Papazoglu, F: "*Dardanska onomastika*" ZFF VIII-1,1964; Mirdita, Z: "*Antroponomia e Dardanisë in kohën romake,*" Prishtina, 1981.
[191] Mirdita, Z: "*Antroponomia e Dardanisë in kohën romake,*" Prishtina, 1981, p. 82

of the ancient forms to modern ones in accordance with the phonetic laws of Albanian, and in a way that their patterns of today cannot be explained otherwise but by its means, finding no explanation by any other language of the Balkan Peninsula: *Ragusium*: Rush, *Skodra*: Shkodra, *Astibus*: Shtip, *Naissus*: Nish, *Skardus*: Shar, *Scupi*: Shkup, *Drivastum*: Drishti, *Pirustae*: Qafa e Prushit, *Lissus*: Lesh, *Candavia*: Kanavlja, *Durrachum*: Durres, *Isamus*: Ishëm, *Scampinus*: Shkumbini, *Aulona*: Vlora, etc.[192]

Evidence that the Albanian language provides for the explanation of those names and toponyms from antiquity, some of which were already discussed, are by all means stable only if the origin of the Albanian through the Illyrian is connected to the Pelasgian in view of its relation to other languages of antiquity, especially the old Greek, which contains so many words related to the Pelasgian,[193] an issue that also affects the origin of its script, supposedly acquired from the Pelasgians.

Evidence dealing with the dilemma raised, of great importance by all means is that of Diodorus,[194] one of the most renowned historians of antiquity, who provided the first evidence about the Greek script, which reportedly came from the Phoenicians, which they brought to the Greeks from Phoenicia having had strong trade relations. Diodorus says that the letters were Pelasgian, offering explanations as to why they were called Phoenician: *"I called them Phoenician letters mainly because it is they who*

---

[192] Çabej, Eqrem: "Studime gjuhësore," IV, Prishtina, 1977, p. 201.

[193] More broadly about old Albanian words in Greek as well as their distribution in Greek toponyms see Spiro N. Konda *"Shqiptarët dhe problemi pellazgjik"* ("Albanians and the Pelasgian problem"), Tirana, 1964. The well-known Albanian philologist mentions forty-eight Pelasgian words (names) of Albanian roots and 241 places where Pelasgians lived and acted (mostly in Greece) as kingdoms established by them. Based on this, he connects the etymology of the name Epirus, Crete, Athens, and others, connecting also almost all the names of deities arising from Greek mythology.

[194] *Diodorus* was born in Agrion of Sicily and therefore was known as Sycilian Diodorus. He lived and worked in the time of Caesar and Augustus. Only a few things are known about his life and these were learned only through his historic work entitled *"Bibliotheea Historica"* (Historical Library). It is a history involving a synchronic and analytical lining of the whole ancient history from the beginning of antiquity until 59 or 54 BC. Of the 40 books only books 1-5 *(Histories of ancient Orient and prehistoric time)* and books 11-20 (480-302 years BC) have survived. Diodorus' works, including fragments, despite their truncation have many valuable data about Pelasgians and the history of Illyria and Epirus, not found in other sources.

brought them to the Hellenes from Phoenicia, as it was the Pelasgians who used these characters first after having adopted them to their language."[195]

Historian Diodorus, relating to the Hellenistic history of invention of the alphabet, which was attributed to Linos, which as stated, after having acquired them from Cadmus who had brought them from Phoenicia, adopted them first to the Hellenic language, assigning a name to each one of them and devising their form, said the following: *"Linos, as stated in the writings he left behind, described the deeds of Dionysus the First and other myths and wrote them in Pelasgic letters. In this same way, these Pelasgian letters were used by Orpheus and Pranapides, teacher of Homer."*[196]

Diodorus' evidence on the Pelasgian alphabet acquired from them by the Greeks did not come out of the blue nor is at all confusing given that other ancient authors, from Herodotus and on, admitted the existence of the Pelasgic language spoken by Achaeans, Ionians and others in Athens and Argos, and the same was claimed about their neighbors, Epirotes, Macedonians, and other Illyrian tribes, who were indicated to have spoken their own "barbaric" language, foreign to the Greeks. If to all of this is added the spiritual power attributed to the old inhabitants they admittedly found there (myths, temples, and above all oracles, as was that of Dodona which was allegedly built by the Pelasgian Zeus), and above all, if one keeps in mind that they were also called "divine people," relating their origin to the gods, with something that they considered to be a superiority, something that was natural to be accepted without any hesitation and with respect, then it is clear that such a people, upon whom, as will be seen, although not accepted directly, the entire Hellenic civilization and antiquity in general was erected, from Troy, Crete and Mycenae, necessarily had to have possessed the means of expression (signs or letters) by which they would reflect their level of development.

As numerous archaeological resources and other material evidence already admitted the existence of a pre-Hellenic civilization in a wide Euro-Asian space, Mediterranean (Italy) and the Aegean-Anatolian belt, and that that civilization was also associated with pre-Greek peoples, where Pelasgians were in nearly all aspects unavoidable and represented the main link between the prehistoric and historic time, equally representing the main knot between Central Europe and Asia Minor, then it was

---

[195] Diodorus: *Works* III, Chap. 66, p. 257, according to Johan Georg von Hahn: *"Studime shqiptare,"* Tirana, 2009, p. 396.
[196] Ibid, p. 397.

only reasonable to search for the key to this civilization among the Pelasgians, among others. They were the only ones that dominated antiquity on that large-scale geographical antiquity through material evidence, and also through living evidence dominating the present, with Albanians and the Albanian language, as a living language in a single branch in the Indo-European family, appearing as the most emblematic sample of this development.

Furthermore, what historian Diodorus said more than 2,000 years ago about the Pelasgian script, that the Greeks must have received it from them and not from the Phoenicians, are not a matter of fantasy any longer, but a reality which, according to all forewarnings, can be proven by means of comprehensive scientific research, albeit by doing so many of the taboos based on different positions without proper scientific coverage of the Hellenes as the champion of ancient civilization may fall.

Based on various data, most of the time deliberately ignored, efforts to link the issue of legitimacy of early script to the Pelasgians, before being declared Greek and of Phoenician origin, would be found since the first two centuries after the publication that came out from Leibniz on Albanian as the daughter of the Illyrian language. In support of the evidence coming from ancient authors about a pre-Greek factor in Greece, where Pelasgians are mentioned with much piety in ways highlighted so far and, based on support of assessments that Mycenae too, and above all the Crete civilization, as one of the most important in antiquity, were pre-Greek relating all to the Pelasgians, some historians would not hesitate to even link the Phoenicians and Palasts (later-date Palestinians) to the Pelasgians and even to Cadmus of antiquity, according to Greek mythology the founder of Thebes and father of Illyrius, who got with goddess Harmonia, denying to them entirely their being Phoenicians in favor of their Pelasgian origin, the same as Crete and the entire Aegean and Mediterranean basin.[197] This then would make it quite clear what Diodorus meant when he talked about Pelasgic script, which he recalled was used by Orpheus and Pronaprides, Homer's teacher.

Relying on the possibility that the Albanian language as the only living language from antiquity, as the daughter of the Pelasgian necessarily preserves the most ancient phonetic and other forms of the common language pulp, i.e. Indo-European root, Jochan Georg von Hahn, besides

---

[197] See G.O Müller in M. Aref: "*Shqipëria, historia dhe gjuha,*" Tirana, 2007.

accepting Diodorus' assessments of the Pelasgic script, which the Greeks appropriated from them, also came to the following conclusion:

> Pelasgians, being historically the first inhabitants of Hellada used a script brought to them from their homeland by Phoenician pilgrims. Later on the Hellenes came to these countries swallowing, in linguistic term, the Pelasgian element, and in the meantime receiving, along with many other traces, the script that the Phoenicians brought, which side by side with Hellenic formative processes walked a new development cycle, in which the script, relying on a given basis, rose slowly to the level that some thought was perfect, and after achieving excellence along with the other arts, was gradually lost again.[198]

Before coming to this conclusion, which came to the research and academic world in 1854 in the German language from Jena, which was an important center of language and historical research of antiquity, Johann Georg von Hahn, as a diplomat and zealous researcher spent many years in Albanian lands, from Attica, and Morea to Northern Alps to learn about traces of antiquity among Albanians, as he was interested in addressing them from every point of view, especially in its language. From what he saw and learned, as he concluded in his *"Albanesische studien,"* he investigated a lot of the ancient soul preserved among Albanians in the form of whimsical nature conservation, which was only possible due to an historical memory and spiritual power originating and building on such values.

Viewed from this, proving that power and antiquity as part of a "safekeeping of a civilization among the most special ones," while focusing on investigating the residues of the old myths of antiquity among the Albanians, which continued to be reflected in various forms among them, he made a phonetic comparison between the Phoenician alphabet, that the Greeks would declare as the basis of their alphabet, and the Albanian alphabet.[199]

---

[198] Johan Georg von Hahn: *"Studime Shqiptare,"* Tirana, 2009, p. 397.

[199] The Albanian alphabet analyzed by the German scholar Hahn compared to the Phoenician, as said, is taken from an Albanian named Bythakuqe, who had no knowledge of the Phoenician alphabet. However, it is about the Mallakastra man, Dhaskal Todri, known for his cultural and patriotic activity of his time that he nearly paid with his head. We know about this alphabet in 1910 from Eqrem bey Vlora, who translated from the German Hahn's study of the Albanian language and its antiquity:

It should be pointed out at the beginning that the author made it clear that his review was not an arbitrary invention and that its similarity to the Phoenician alphabet and others deriving from it, was not casual, rather, it relied on the fact that the Phoenician alphabet was its ancient prototype. The author considered it legitimate to talk about a shift of certain signs of the Phoenician alphabet to that of the Albanian and he highlighted these changes in forms that have gone through this transition, but also discovered those that belong to antiquity.[200]

Therefore, according to Hahn, the comparison of the Phoenician alphabet with 52 sounds and that of the Albanian language with 36 letters represented very important evidence of phonetic linkage to antiquity, though out of its natural continuity, implying that the Albanian language, even outside this alphabet, in other appropriated alphabets, Greek or Latin, was able to preserve the early sound forms. If the old Greek alphabet retained 20 letters and the new one 22 of the Phoenician script, while other recent languages (neo-Latin and Slavic), more or less, would also be retaining approximately half of the letters of the alphabet, their reflection in the 36 letters of the Albanian language, but also in others of the Phoenician alphabet which can be found in the Albanian language and phonetically reflected in its most archaic form, testifies to the phonetic richness of Albanian and its conservation even in circumstances of lack of authentic letters or writing in foreign scripts (Greek, Slavic, Italic, and others).

From this research Johann Georg von Hahn reached the conclusion that the Albanian alphabet, which he considers almost faithfully, reflects the phonetic structure of the oldest known script, and that in many of its forms it was associated with the prototype (Phoenician) rather than the Greek. He also considers that the Albanian alphabet, although designed by someone who lacked a certain linguistic culture, except that he must have felt it and gave into that sensation in order to more faithfully reflect it through borrowed letters from other alphabets he had at hand (Greek, Latin, and Hindu), coincided completely with the Phoenician alphabet and others close to him, that is, out of its 52 letters there wasn't a single

---

"Notes on the old Pelasgian script" published in Istanbul. For the sounds found in his tongue, he produced a number of arbitrary signs, which he then lithographed and included in Auri's comparative table. (See: *Studime shqiptare*," Tirana, 2009, p. 375 and 394.)

[200] Ibid, p. 378.

one without some connection to those systems and, therefore, there was no reason to doubt its association to the family.[201]

The "digression" with alphabets from one historical angle to another, with two millennia in between, would look like some adventure if it lacked a natural explanation of the process of passing of language from its antiquity root - the Pelasgian to Albanian, known to linguistics as a *mother-daughter* transition path and in this case it passed through the Illyrian.

Although it is an extremely difficult thing in the absence of a relatively recent text document to determine even in rough lines the formation of Albanian as a language qualitatively distinct from her "*mother,*" without knowing the latter on the whole, however, the vast majority of linguists agree that the origin of the Albanian language is related to a language stratification, among the oldest one, in the composition of the Indo-European, such as the Pelasgian-Illyrian, and that its transfer from *mother* to *daughter* was a shift identical to that defined as "historical time" that must have happened to the Greek and Latin, a time identified in the 6th through 3rd centuries B.C.[202]

The Danish Pedersen links the historical period of the Albanian language related to that of the Roman rule when, according to him, a shift from a closed Indo-European ***u*** to ***i*** occurred as well as the "beginnings of a ***y*** that did not come from the closed Indo-European ***u.***"[203]

The well-known Albanian linguist Çabej too saw the historical period of the Albanian language in its contacts with the Greek, Latin, Slavonic, and others. Although Çabej divides the historical period of the Albanian language before its scripture from the prehistoric period of the language, he has not addressed the issue as to what time one may speak of an Albanian language, qualitatively distinct from her "*mother,*" the Illyrian.[204]

Linguist Selman Riza expressed the opinion that "from bottom-up the history of our language should be periodized in parallel with the history of our people," adding that the history of the Albanian language "should be divided into three known periods":

- Antiquity,
- Middle Ages, and

---

[201] Ibid, p. 388.
[202] Demiraj, Shaban: "*Gramatikë historike e gjuhës shqipe,*" Prishtina, 1988. 47.
[203] Ibid, p. 52.
[204] Ibid, p. 53.

- Recent or modern times.[205]

Each of these three periods he then divided into two phases.

Therefore, for the first period he distinguishes early and late antiquity Albanian.

He separated the second period into Medieval Albanian (5th-12th centuries) and the late Middle Ages (12th -15th centuries).

Furthermore, he divided the third period (recent times Albanian) into pre-contemporary Albanian (by the middle of 18th century lasting up to the Awakening), and the modern Albanian (from the Awakening and on).[206]

A somewhat similar periodization of the history of the Albanian language was also done by A. V. Desnickaja, in which she distinguished three periods:

1. *Proto-Albanian* (= Ancient Albanian), which ran from the separation of the Albanian from the Indo-European language community until its early linguistic contacts with Rome.

2. *Old Albanian*, which occupied roughly the 1st millennium AD.

3. *Middle Albanian*, covering the first part of the 2nd millennium AD.[207]

From this internal development the "prehistory" of the Albanian language includes a pluricentennial period and is identical to that of the history of the Albanian people, which means that traces of its roots must be sought among those leading to the Pelasgic antiquity. What was seen as influences or acquisitions from other languages, especially from the Greek, Latin and later Slavic languages, being close for centuries or through occasional frictions, concentrating on Pelasgian antiquity brought them in a new light: as natural developments from the common Indo-European root, or obtained from those languages at a later time, after having been acquired earlier from the Pelasgian, as acknowledged by ancient authors (Homer, Herodotus, Diodorus, and others).

An advantage to this explanation of the dead languages (ancient Greek and Latin), however, represents the present-day Albanian language as a living fossil, having been left aside or ignored for a long time, being eventually considered as inevitable.

---

[205] Ibid, p. 53.
[206] Ibid, p. 53.
[207] Desnickaja, A.V: "*Rekonstrukcija elementov drevnealbanskogo jazyka i obscebalkanskie lingvisticeskie problemi,*" 1966, p. 8, and "*Akten*" Innsbruck, p. 213, cited according to Demiraj, Shaban "*Gramatikë historike e gjuhës shqipe,*" Prishtina, 1988, p. 53.

Homer and the True Pelasgian Antiquity

Why may Homer's "Iliad" be called a Pelasgian spiritual history and therefore part of the identity of their descendants? - Imaginary Trojan War – a most convincing historical reality. - Founder of Troy Dardanus, whom Greek mythology sees as the son of Zeus, charged with building human power on earth. – Troy's defeat and its reparation by Dardanians by founding Rome. - Was Homer Pelasgian, as were Pythagoras and other important philosophers of antiquity, among whom Aristotle, teacher of Alexander the Great was also mentioned? - Although modified with many changes in the fifth century BC by an "editorial board" led by the tyrant of Athens, Pisistratus, Homer's work remains the strongest evidence of the Pelasgian world as the foundation of antiquity.

Pelasgic traces of antiquity exhibited by history, archeology, mythology, anthropology, linguistics, and other scientific disciplines, although largely scattered and unduly processed, though sufficient to assess that one is dealing with an important prehistoric and historical factor that has affected the entire ancient civilization, however, is another evidence of the most special that the world knows, turning Pelasgians into part of a major and magnificent spiritual all-time and all-human monument.

This implies the world epic "Iliad" of Homer, where Pelasgians were mentioned not only by providing evidence of their role in that war, be it imaginary, which would remain permanently in the memory of humankind of which one often hears of being a war among the Pelasgic tribes, but the work also explains a lot about the Pelasgian society, as preceding the Hellenistic society and Hellenism in general from where the abovementioned warnings from history, archeology, mythology, and linguistics may help build the stance that Greeks and Hellenism in general did not inherit from the Pelasgians only their material culture but also the spiritual one which subsequently and rightly so gave a specific coloration as it linked the pre-Greek civilization dominated by Pelasgians with that of the Greek and Indo-European future. The grandeur of Homer's art relies on these two pillars, where the old must be stronger, even though it is known little or not at all, because for a long time "Iliad" was seen as a Greek work, born and raised on the Greek soil without any outside support.

Before the world Homeric epic, which announced the Pelasgians as the cradle of Hellenic civilization and divine nation, there was also another poet, Hesiod,[208] who not only perpetuated the Pelasgic antiquity, but also identified himself with the founding Pelasgus of the Pelasgian people, born in that country from the earth itself, that *"son of earth"* of Arcadia.[209]

Homer's work, coming shortly after that of Hesiod, precisely related what his predecessor or contemporary said about the old Pelasgic and new - Hellenic, a link that would certainly seem neither down to earth nor in the sky without the major dramas and concerns that were conditioned exactly as one was dealing here with different worlds (that of Pelasgian *matriarchate* and Greek *patriarchate*, which ended in favor of the latter), where on one hand there was a monarchy with kings that the Pelasgian-Illyrians had, and on the other hand there were the local leaders from elected ones to tyrants that the Hellenes opted for. In this leap, it is not accidental that gods and men came together, why friends and enemies united, and why the human and bravery appeared facing each other, as virtues that deserve special respect, over which then the Greek philosophers built their famous positions on ethics, morality, and freedom.

In this clash of the worlds and the shift from one to another time, which was neither short nor easy, "Iliad," better than any other document, shows Ili or Troy, as an old Balkan castle at an important crossroad of the world that bears the name of Dardanians and her opponents, mostly Greek, but also non-Greeks, wanting to invade her as soon as possible in order to rise above her and move further, which they were not able to achieve by force but through trickery, such as was the "Trojan Horse," which, through that manner of conducting warfare, brought an end to the heroic time to pave the way for human cunning being so widespread and perfected. Therefore, it is not by chance that Hector's strong tower at the entrance of the Dardanelles, besides Trojans was also being protected by Dardanians and their Balkan-Anatolian allies, Paiones from Vardar and

---

[208] *Hesiod*, Greek poet, lived in the eighth or seventh century BC. He was born in Beotia, in a rural family and dealt with agriculture. He wrote two poems in hexameter. One called *"Theogony"* (Creation of the gods), is completely mythological. It deals with the origins of the gods and the creation of the world. In his second work *"Erga kai hemerai"* (Work and days), mainly guidelines for agriculture are provided. This work carries several verses describing the Pelasgian world, especially in Dodona and Epirus.

[209] Hesiod: *"Carina"* (Poems), fragments 134, 160.

others of this family, who identified with them precisely for being part of that civilization.

It is not by chance, too, that in this great epoch of the world there is a match between Hellenic colonist cult mentality from the North, personified in Achilles, continued later by Odysseus, who was on the move and concerned about the appropriation of innovations and reflection of the divine antiquity of Hector. Indeed, Achilles' struggle against Hector, and the killing of the latter by the first, represented the victory of the new social concept – the Hellenic against the oldest - Pelasgian, which the Greeks faced once they arrived in Greece, although it is known that they would acquire its key values (cults, beliefs, mode of production), without excluding from it the spiritual creativity and oral literature and philosophy.

Although this clashing was inevitable and its conclusion had to be a victory of the "new world," of what was both pretentious and invasive, both constructing and devastating, and aimed at bringing major changes in the social plan and ideas, the great poet behaved with great caution: showing respect for the old, while seeing the new as unstoppable, an undoing as already put into action in a different kind of relation between gods and people, between myth and reality, which had to belong to the future in accordance with the changes brought by time.

In the honoring and understanding of the "old" one should also see the power of what was still continuing to manifest itself not only in what Homer called a "barbarian" language and tradition, but also his demand to the society to maintain the morality and dignity even when feeling victorious. So, here lies the relation between the "victor" as a "loser" and the "loser" as a "victor" not only as a social and political issue, but also as a philosophical one in general. When Achilles killed Hector and according to the rules of the winner he could even throw away the corpse, after a plea by his father, he returned the body of his dead son, which coincided with the rules of "the barbarians" that the defeated should be honored, where the true power of the victor was measured also by his dignified behavior towards the defeated. This perhaps could have nourished the reasonable suspicion that understanding and recognition to that extent of the "barbarians" shows that the poet might have been "bilingual," so that besides Greek he also spoke and wrote the language of the Pelasgians, a suspicion that would subsequently go so far as to assume that Homer was Pelasgian, as was also Pythagoras, the father of Greek science and philosophy,[210] a guess which is not without support knowing that everything was connected with an ancient tradition that the most famous poets of this time were of non-Greek origin, the most distinguished among them being Orpheus, Thamyris, Museis, Linis, and others, an assumption further reinforced when considered that the word *muse*, which is almost entirely identified with the Greeks, is not of Greek origin.

Opening the case that the great poet could have been "bilingual," which brings him among non-Greeks, but namely to Pelasgians, also highlights some other issues, among which the most significant are those regarding the age of "Iliad," a dilemma which had also to deal with the issue whether it was a work of one single poet, or a summary of the many songs called epos, which were collected in order to attain the form in which the world had come to recognize it.

Raising these issues is not all about the authorship of the work, which was rightfully subject to different considerations of artistic nature that continue to remain inexhaustible, but for more, as through it one may clarify two other dilemmas, extremely important for the Homeric complexity with which much of antiquity and its appearance is connected, in the form that it was reflected during the last two centuries.

The first had to do with how and to what degree Homer was present in the emergence of Greece in *stricto sensu*.

While the second, always depending on the clarity of the first question, raises the issue of the presence of the Pelasgian factor in the fundament of antiquity and Hellenism, in which until recently the role of the Greeks was seen as alone and undisputed, although ancient authors have accepted what they found among Pelasgians and what had been acquired from them. Because, among those they found, as best expressed by Homer, are Pelasgian deities and gods, from Zeus and beyond, where, he expressed in a monumental way in the "Iliad" as on the origin of Zeus, the greater god of Pantheon Olympus as being Pelasgic:

Zeus, king, lord of Dodona, Pelasgian,
you who live far off, ruling cold Dodona,
around whom live the Selli...[211]

---

[210] Budimir, Milan: *"O Ilijadi i njenom pesniku,"* Belgrade, 1940, p. 9.
[211] Homer: "Iliada," Tirana, 1979, Book XVI, pp. 233-235.

These dilemmas, which are historical, but also social and creative in nature, however, require a comprehensive and primarily factual response, meaning they should start with the "Iliad" as a starting point as creative evidence and Homer as its author, regardless of the fact that the written form of this major work, as it is known today, comes from a final hand given by the "editorial board," the tyrant of Athens, Pisistratus, and his decree of the year 560 giving the famous work the final Greek seal, admitting that it was not Greek, but that it should be given such a seal, which, as we know, all would end somewhere in the 3rd century, which should have regarded the interests of his time, which evidently they knew what they were.

Since the time between when Homer lived (from the end of the 7th century), and the appearance of this work was seen, and its first official written version (year 560 BC) is relatively long, while three other centuries pass from the time of Homer and the Trojan hypothetical war, it can be stated that the "Iliad" and "Odyssey" in Pisistratus' version, despite inventions and those that have been added to the work by the "editorial board," in many cases indicate an old author, who was not present at the birth of Hellenistic Greece. This issue subsequently opens the importance of the factor of the presence of a native Pelasgian civilization in prehistory, or the birth of what is known as Hellada and Hellenism, and this can be proven by the presence of different overlapping, controversies and even anachronisms appearing in this great work with two faces: pre-Greek and Greek, one partially true, and one patched up by intervention.

Although linguistic and stylistic analysis have long since established significant discrepancies between the "true" author (Homer, who must have been greatly based on folklore and written heritage), and the interference coming from the version of Pisistratus' "editorial board," although many scholars in the field of mythology, folklore and onomastics have found many idols, deities, and even gods, incompatible with Hellenistic ones, either in names or in meaning and the like, as is the case with Zeus *"Dodona and Pelasgian king"* and others beside him. However, in addition to the corpus of evidence of a spiritual nature, as already discussed and under constant scrutiny, there were some anachronisms that had to do with social relations, especially with production and material culture, which in general belong to pre-Hellene, or Pelasgian time. These anachronisms were known and mentioned by important ancient authors, serving Hellenism as a background to move on, but in the meantime bringing to the surface the true view of a by-passed genuine civilization, located in the general background of Indo-Europeanism.

Therefore, besides the anachronisms such as the one Homer mentions regarding the use of iron that existed in his era but which did not exist in the Trojan War, or bronze and copper that were already in use, however, the biggest one is that Homer at no point in "Iliad" or "Odyssey" mentioned the Hellenes as a people forming a "Greek nation." This name is mentioned only once in the "Iliad"[212] as tribunes of Phtia, Achilles kingdom. Thucydides is explicit on this matter in Book I, Chapter 3 when he says "though (Homer) lived long after the Trojan War, he had nowhere described the Helenians country as a Greek entity."[213]

Another important fact that Homer did not know one of the most important factors of the beginnings of Greek civilization, had to do with the trilogy *"Aeolian-Ionian-Dorian,"* according to which, in the eighth century and later, the Greeks settled in Asia Minor (Aeolid, Ionia and Dorida) and there started the Greek civilization (ethnicity and language with three dialects: Aeolian, Ionian and Dorian), from where writing appeared, a legacy of the Phoenicians or the people living in that country (Lydian, Phrygian, Lysian, and others), which then, always according to the Greek version, was transmitted to the mainland Greece and the islands.[214]

Besides, Homer never mentioned Ionia and the only time he quoted the name of the Ionians is in the "Iliad," Song XIII, 685: "*Beotians, Ionians with soutane, Locrians,*" etc.[215] On the other hand, this line was treated by many critics as one of the fixed-intersections of many to have been added to the final text in order to flatter Athenians.[216]

Among other evidence suspecting Homer of being a witness to the so-called *stricto sensu* Greece is the one not recognizing the name of the Peloponnese, which he called Achaean Argos, and the tragic legends related to Pelops, the eponymous hero of the Peloponnese and Sparta. "Pelasgian Argos" for him was Thessaly.[217]

---

[212] *"Iliada,"* Tirana, 1978, II, 684.
[213] Turqididi, Book I, Chapter 3.
[214] Ibid, p. 502.
[215] Ibid, p. 503.
[216] Ibid, p. 503.
[217] Ibid, p. 504.

However, it was not only Homer who failed to clearly identify the Spartans as Greek, something that connected them to the Pelasgic affiliation. Three-four centuries after him the same happened with the father of history Herodotus, who by linking them with the drama of Troy saw them as Pelasgians. Herodotus noted that the "barbarians" (that is, Pelasgians) throughout Greece, and "the Lacedaemonians in particular," despised merchants and honored warriors, still qualifying the Spartan as more barbarian than Greek.[218]

This fact, at first obvious, shed light on yet another historical and very important process, that dealing with the role of Sparta to the birth and rise of Hellada and Hellenism, based precisely on the clash between the native factor, i.e. Pelasgian, and the Dorian newcomer, that determined developments of antiquity, especially those associated with colonization towards the West, that is, towards Italy and the founding of Rome.

Another evidence of this nature is certainly the one dealing with the fact that for Homer, the Athenians and their leader, Menestheus, were derived from Erectus, snake god and son of Hephaestus and the Earth. He does not mention either Secrops Cranaon (or Cadmus), which most authors define as the first kings of Athens,[219] although for Herodotus, Athenians and Ionians were of Pelasgic origin.[220]

This "error" in appearance, however, had to do with Homer, or the time of the birth of the true epos (perhaps collected from various eposes of oral tradition), which not only does not coincide with that of Pisistratus' Greece but it was a product of a different world that the Greeks faced, appropriated and rewritten, giving it a new strength, without highlighting it.

This uncertainty becomes even more sensible by the lack of knowledge of the Olympic Games, which were not at all mentioned by Homer, which represented another evidence that the time of the poet does not coincide with that of the founding of the Olympic Games relating to the year 776 BC, a "trifle" that the conjurers of the final version of the "Iliad" may have omitted, as were many others, causing doubt if this world epos had been adopted and conjured up by "another time and another world" from that which it has been attributed to.

---

[218] Herodotus: "*Historiae*" (Histories), Book II, 167.
[219] Ibid, p. 504.
[220] Herodotus: "*Historiae,*" Book VIII, p. 44.

These discrepancies between the time of Homer and the time of Pisistratus' Athens of the year 560 indeed raise the issue of pre-Hellenic stratification in this work, known as Pelasgian. This then raises the dilemma about what the Greeks had found when they arrived in Greece, the appropriation of which is admitted even by ancient authors, with its content and above all its level being kept silent, leading to the assumption that indeed there could have been a highly developed degree of creativity that did not exclude writing and other forms of creativity that originated in this part of the world.

Besides the "Iliad" and numerous testimonies of literary or imaginative nature, which best highlighted the true social relations of one of the greatest historic breaking points, such as those that would appear in the Aegean basin and Anatolian space before and after the onset of the Greeks, caused by the last movement known as Aegean with Dorians, the second part of the work "Odyssey" also opened the question of penetration of the Greeks towards the West, using as a node what Homer saw as a sacred Pelasgian place with the oracle of Dodona, which Herodotus called Pelasgia. For, East and West of what is known as Hellada are not only geographical issues defining different sides, but they also determined the direction of the extension of ancient civilization, where the true one, strictly speaking, the one related to Pelasgian autochthony lay in the West (Epirus, Ambracia with Mycenae), while that of Hellenes arrived to the East, with the first settlements there, and focusing westward. This direction has defined three Hellenistic colonies: Achaean, Ionian and Dorian, with the first two related to Pelasgians, where their epicenter was.

That this orientation continued to remain the epicenter one learns from Homer and his work, where in its second half, before Odysseus went to fight the Trojan War he went to Dodona to consult the oracle over the fate of war, as he was also seen doing after returning to consult him on his way to Ithaca. By what this epos represented, the Pelasgian world was more than a spiritual oracle for the Hellenes, taking their best lessons in the western part on how to behave in their private and social life.

"But Odysseus, he said, had gone to Dodona, to hear the will of Zeus from the high-crested oak of the god, even how he might return to the rich land of Ithaca after so long an absence, whether openly or in secret."[221]

---

[221] Homer: *"Odisea,"* Tirana, 1979, Book XIV, p. 325.

The return of the Trojan warrior to Ithaca, who had to go through, as said, *"Thesprotian land,"* whose king was Pheidon *"hero and noble,"* his generous reception there by Thesprotian king and the assistance he received from him (a fast boat with many people) that would bring him back to his homeland, show the continued respect that the Greeks showed to Pelasgians, which, as found in Odyssey's case, also speaks of their continued dependence, which can be explained by their internal power that the Pelasgian world continued to maintain despite the changes occurring, a power which was spiritual and as such reflected almost indestructibly regardless of how much and how it was accepted.

Viewed from this angle, Homer's epoch also highlighted another development of great significance for antiquity, one dealing with the creation of Rome and the emergence of Greek colonies on the Ionian, Adriatic and Mediterranean, in general, providing another explanation from what is known, where colonization was seen mainly as a Greek civilization breakthrough and not part of the development of the indigenous population during the relations they established with Greek traders, and also with military and administrative structures under new circumstances, considered as being in the interest of the natives, namely indigenous Pelasgian-Illyrian population in both parts of the seas, where they were.

That one is dealing here with a formed ethnic and social pre-Hellene reality is best demonstrated by the so-called Aeneas journey from Troy to Italy, even as a figment of imagination of a poet such as Virgil,[222] who many centuries later saw it in another form from Homer's version. So, a different warrior from Troy, defeated of course, Aeneas refusing to lose the image of his ravaged homeland of Troy, made his trip through the Pelasgian lands. After a stay in Epirus he crossed the sea permanently settling in the Italian Peninsula, from where a Trojan stem that the ancient authors recognized as Dardanians, sons of Pelasgians, as accepted in different ways from other historical sources, established Rome, another "parallel" power to the Greek one, which would affect antiquity in a special way. Homer shows as to where the "defeated heroes of Troy" were heading, i.e. towards the West, and it seemed this would not only be a

---

[222] *Publius Vergilius Marone*, Roman poet, born near Mantua in 70 BC. He studied rhetoric and philosophy in Rome. He died in Brindisi as he was returning from a trip around Greece. Besides other works, he left *"Bucolica"* (Pastoral song) and the poem "Eneid," indicating the travel vicissitudes of the Trojan hero, Aeneas, who before reaching Lat to form his kingdom on the Latin land he stayed for a few days in Butrint.

"comforting issue" and an "oath" that Troy would return again in a "distant world," as indicated by Aeneas oath, to find its subsequent reflection stronger in the poem "*Aeneid*,"[223] and, although a figment of imagination (like the "Iliad"), based on historical facts revealing that the so-called social and political Hellenic and Roman constructions inevitably connected to the Pelasgian stratification, not only as an "accidental encounter," but as part of a foundation on which the grounds of antiquity would be set.

Literary aspects of creating another center of antiquity, that of Rome, standing as a balance against Greek civilization, coming originally from Homer and later Virgil and some other, are nothing but a matter of creative imagination describing internal aspects of an historical drama. This drama was identified also through the destinies of certain heroes appearing as carriers of major events, and also as part of a historic development on which the rivalry of these civilizations, whose epilogue was exactly at their origin, i.e. in Pelasgia. The West tried to restore itself to the idea of global universalism, trying to win over the East to the idea as well, thanks to the work of Illyrian-Dardanian emperors, Diocletian, Constantine the Great, and Justinian. And then after all this work, Byzantium would emerge.

---

[223] Virgil: "*Aneidos*" (Eneid), Book III.

CHAPTER 2

Pelasgians and their Descendants

Pelasgians and Dardanians

> *Dardanians, descendants of the Pelasgian,s stretching widely from Central Europe to Asia Minor, Italy and North Africa. – Dardanians viewed by Homer as founders of Troy, and by Virgil as founders of Rome. – Linking of the Dardanians with the Thracians and attempts to unilaterally detach them from the Illyrians and common Pelasgic root, to which, according to many studies, Thracians also belonged.- Explanation of the name Dardan through d a r dh ë (pear) and its expansion into a broader European space exhibited an ancient basic reflection of the Indo-European, highlighting also the role of Dardanians in a broad social and political context of antiquity.*

Extracting Pelasgians from antiquity through their multiple traces and placing them in a historical background, where they belong, inevitably opens the issue of continuity of their direct descendants, i.e. Illyrians, Dardanians, and Macedonians as a large family of many branches. This is not because it is inconsistent with a natural transition, or because an invention may be imposed so as to define something that has nothing to do with either the Greeks or the Romans (which they stood "somewhere in between") but because in this way an important and deserving factor in the Indo-European family clarifies its position within the genealogy of its roots and multi-branch trunk, where Albanian appears as a single branch. In addition, it removes ambiguities about the place and the role of the descendants of the Pelasgians in relation to themselves and others. This is particularly viable given that they stretched in one of the most important geographical areas, the Euro-Asian, and also knowing that from an ethnic, social and political standpoint, they were actors in all the developments from prehistoric to historical times that have been and occasionally are denied today, for reasons already stated.

However, their dual qualification by the Greeks (Pelasgians scattered in several tribes on one hand and viewed as "barbarians" by ancient authors on the other) seems to take away the veil of some "secrets" because in the first case an ethnic, social, and cultural reality appears, upon which the Hellenes placed and built what is called Hellenism. They placed it on the foundations of antiquity as a great civilization value that until recently was attributed to the Greeks and only Greeks, while the second presented their "competitors" from the neighborhood, numerous tribes called Illyrian and Dardanian, who were named differently, depending on their local expansion and their relations to them, mostly exclusive and hostile. Although dealing with the same entity, whose deep antiquity and wide geographical scope must have manifested certain features quite natural for the circumstances, this caused them to be viewed in different ways and in different roles. This "variation" retains a form of a historical cliché assessing them from an observation coming "from the outside," i.e. by the Greeks and Romans, while their evaluations, no matter how praiseworthy, appear as arbitrary measures rather than being seen from within and in accordance to the importance they truly had and the role they played in those developments, not only for themselves but for others as well.

Until certain cliches are changed or removed, it must be said that even the familiar Greek mirror viewing them as divided, as Pelasgians and "barbarians," was not formal because in what would appear as Hellada or the land of the Hellenes, which were recognized by Homer, they appeared as a social reality from the 5th century onwards. Different tribes were founded during those times, including Poiones, Aones, Thesprotians, Curetes, Leleges, Kaukones, Molossians, Dardanians, and others, who with their kings, idols and temples, as was the Pelasgian Dodona created by Zeus, "cohabited" with the Hellenistic society until one day, at least culturally and socially (more by ancient sources) they were assimilated. Meanwhile others outside of their space in the neighborhood and within their kingdoms, or later as part of the Greek colonies, were called "barbarians," that is, foreign, as they maintained their own language, social and political order, although at a later stage under the imperial crown of Rome or Byzantium turned to be powerful social, political, and cultural factors to the extent that during the threats from the North (attacks by Goths, Avars, and Slavs in particular) they became the main and last defenders of ancient civilization, following the demise of the Roman Empire and were able to prolong the life of the Eastern Empire of Constantinople for 10 more centuries.

However, increasing information coming from ancient authors, the division into Pelasgians and "barbarians" retains a hold of an historical passage between the "*divine*" Pelasgians and their direct "*ground*" descendants - Dardanians and others from this extended family. This leap probably relates to historical Troy and its glorious history that simultaneously represents the displacement of power from Asia Minor and the East in general (the Tigris and Euphrates valley and Mesopotamia where it emerged and flourished) to the basin of the Aegean and the Central Balkans in the European space, and antiquity experienced its historical rise and fall. However, it didn't experience its final extinction because after centuries of falling into "oblivion," it was restored again.

At the time of classical Hellenism the Roman wars against Illyrian kings, Dardanians and Dardania were seen in the North also as "barbarians," while their kingdom in the 3rd and 2nd centuries were significant in relation to the other Illyrian and Macedonian kingdoms that were included in severe and persistent wars, which can only be explained by the struggle for dominance erupting among members of the same family. However, the Greek mythology, an historical and poetic memory (Hesiod, Homer, Aeschylus, Sophocles, Virgil, and others), was the true shift of the Pelasgians initially among the Dardanians as a development starting from their gods and their power and ending with their representatives - the living heroes, responsible for the power on the ground that inevitably went through endless dramas and tragedies, as this was "the will" of the gods in order to permanently keep their subordinates in internal strife. So, Dardanians were as founders of Troy, its leaders during the glory and its destruction, emerging as "mandated" by the gods together with their feats in the battle for power.

In this dramatic leap, of course, they continued to remain the main actors of many developments, since after losing the Trojan War a portion of them (Galabres, Thunates, Daos, etc.) continued toward the south of Italy, where they settled and, as shown, influenced the establishment of Rome.

According to Greek mythology, *Dardanus*, was the son of *Zeus* and *Electra*, daughter of *Atlas*, brother of *Iasion* and *Harmonia*. Forced to leave his hometown Arcadia, he went to Phrygia where he settled and founded Scamander on the shores of Troy. He is considered the progenitor of the tribes who lived on the slopes of Mount Ida.[224]

Greek mythology also considers the first king of Troy *Ilos* of a divine origin, seen as the son of *Troy* and nymph *Kaliro*, father of *Laomedon* and grandfather of *Priam*. In Phrygia (Asia Minor), he founded the city of Atena Palada, called in his honor Ilion (later Troy).[225]

More from Greek legends, some clues describe Dardanus sometimes as Arcadian, that is, Pelasgian, sometimes as Cretan, and even Etruscan, whenever seen as leading the early beginnings of the most famous civilizations of the ancient world and world civilization, whose origin still being discussed today in relation to his true origin precisely because he is not Greek, which they would have destroyed, though all indications lead to the ancestors of the Albanians - Pelasgians, i.e. Dardanians, who in early antiquity should have had a crucial, if not a decisive role, in that historic leap among the most foggy for lack of data, but among the most important for the development that was set in motion.

However, Dardanians, as sons of the Pelasgians with a very wide range (from Asia Minor, Greece, the Balkans and Central Italy) were not found only in Greek and Roman mythology, but also among poets and playwrights of early Greek antiquity to be seen as such by Roman poets as well, which was only natural for the muses to be dealing with main actors, ranging between the divine and the earthly power. They were seen as such by the Romans and others as well.

Thus, in Homer's "Iliad" the heroes were mainly Pelasgians and Dardanians, although in the Trojan War they were seen lined up "on different sides," and this may have to do with the Pisistratus version of the 6th century in order to accommodate the emergence of historical Greece, as it circumvented their role as a foundation of Hellenism. However, to Homer, Priam, king of Troy, was considered a descendant of Dardanus.[226] According to him, Dardanus was the first king of Troy, and had given his

---

[224] *"Fjalor i mitologjisë,"* Prishtina, 1988, p. 62.
[225] Ibid, p. 121.
[226] *"Iliada,"* III, 38; VII, 89.

name to the city of Dardania. Therefore, Priam and his people were called Dardanians, sons and daughters of Dardanus.[227]

Homer mentions the Dardanians in the following lines:
"In the beginning *Dardanus* was the son of Jove."[228]
"*Dardanus* had a son, king *Erichthonius.*"[229]
"*Dardanus*, whom Jove loved above all the sons."[230]
"Hear me, Trojans, *Dardanians*, and allies."[231]
"Trojans, Lycians, and *Dardanians*, lovers of close fighting."[232]
"The *Dardanians* were led by brave Aeneas, whom Venus bore to *Anchises.*"[233]

Details of the great poet about Dardanians and Troy, on the foundations of which he sees them, as the kingdom that they would lead, are not only a product of imagination, or part of Greek mythology. Rather, they also have historical support, which as seen in previous perceptions reviewed, continue to add to the tableau of the key factor connecting the triangle among the Pelasgic, Hellenic and Roman worlds.

Hesiod, too, a contemporary or a little older than Homer, described the Dardanians as sons of Pelasgus who governed Arcadia first, as a place situated in the middle of the Pelasgian centers of Argos and Sparta, from where, according to him, most dramatic events that preceded the historical time and all that represents antiquity originated.[234]

More by this important author of antiquity, being an instigator of incredibly important events, assumed this ancient people moved towards the West in Asia Minor tying its fate closely with that of Troy, one of whose gates was named "The Dardanian Gate." While the narrow strip in the Balkan Peninsula was called Dardanelles and, continuing further in the West, in the central part of the Peninsula (today's Kosova, along with Macedonia and southern Serbia) they founded the powerful state of Dardania, it was one of the most steadfast and most important ones.[235]

---

[227] Ibid, XVIII, 230.
[228] Ibid, XX, 215.
[229] Ibid, XX, 219.
[230] Ibid, 304.
[231] Ibid, VII, 456.
[232] Ibid, VIII, 173.
[233] Ibid, II, 819.
[234] Hesiod: "Fragments," 160.
[235] Jacques, Edwin: "*Shqiptarët,*" Tirana, 2007, p. 59.

With the dramatic events resulting in numerous tragedies, with the attention of artists always challenged by Troy and those that occured in and around it, Euripides (482-406) BC also dealt with it.

On one hand, he portrays in his dramas Menelaus, King of Argos, his ancestors through Hercules or Heraclius in *Heraclides*, his wife, Helen, Agamemnon's brother, one daughter in two dramas: *"Iphigenia in Aulide"* and *"Iphigenia in Tauride,"* another daughter in *"Electra,"* and the son in *"Orestes."* On the other hand, Euripides reflected the tragic consequences of Priam's family, King of Troy, in the dramas treating his wife *Hecuba*, daughter of *Andromache*'s son, widow of Hector, his ally, *Rhesus* and his own people in *"Trojan Women."*[236]

The great poet Virgil deals also with the Dardanians and their destiny in his "Aeneid" turning them into characters of one of the most important tragedies of antiquity.

"Then he, Aeneas, whom *Dardanian* Ancises, life-giving Venus by the waves of Phrygian Simeon gave birth."
(Book I, 617-618)
"O light of *Dardanians* heart and strength,
He himself incited Gods against *Dardanian* weapons."
 (Book II, 617-618)
"O much-suffering *Dardanians*, land when first
Your ancestors were born, that same rich land
Is waiting now for your return. Look for the ancient mother.
Here Aeneas house will rule over the ridges,
And sons and daughters and those born of them."
(Book III, 94-98)
"We've come after you and your weapons, as *Dardania* burnt."
(Book III, 156)
"These are our special domes, here *Dardania* was born."
(Book III, 167)

Besides evidence from Greek mythology, where Dardanians, as heirs of the Pelasgians, appeared on their own will as founders and leaders of Troy, from where they, after losing the war, headed towards the West (Aeneas and his noblemen from Dodona and Butrint moved on to Italy)

---

[236] Jacques, Edwin: *"Shqiptarët,"* Tirana, 2007, p. 61.

in order to establish Rome there, along with artistic evidence, as seen in Homer, Hesiod, Euripides, Virgil, speaking about the same, Greek historians, first the father of history, Herodotus, and others after him, from the fifth century BC onwards, left direct evidence, though often controversial, which helped to see the Pelasgian factor as multiple tribes with their own kings and kingdoms (Lacedaemonians, Dannay, Argives, Achaeans, Thesprotians and others), dispersed within what was called Pelasgia or Pelasgicum appearing later as Hellada.

Here, however, is where myth separates from historical reality, as Troy and Dardanians go deep into history and are seen as a civilization between the 23rd and 28th centuries, when the Aegean civilization of Troy reached its height, while the imaginary war of Troy happened 10 centuries later, after the arrival of Greeks in Hellada, following the immigration of the Dorians with their Semitic-Egyptian origin,[237] and not through their assumed penetrations from the North, which is increasingly losing its previously held footing.

However, it seems that even in the first 12 centuries, from the 24th to the 12th, with many contests, it was already accepted as a "pre-Hellenic period," which was characterized by Aegean-Cretan and Mycenaean civilizations. The participation of the Pelasgian factor in this development was significant and crucial since they were at its center both as builders and defenders, seriously shaking past assumptions on the Greek authorship of an ancient and powerful civilization, which by now had been considered by almost everyone as pre-Hellenic, as proven loudly by ancient authors indicating that the Hellenes were greatly influenced by it. However, between the 12th and 13th century, known as an "interim period," and also known as a time of "Dark Ages," a time preceding the "Archaic Period" *sensus stricto* Greece and dealt with the time between the 5th and 8th centuries, in these four "dark centuries," through Dorian penetrations, first the destruction of the Pelasgian civilization occurred (in Crete and Mycenae) and thence the Hellenic civilization that emerged in archaic Greece, known from epic poems of Homer and Hesiod, the two works, which two centuries later paved the way to philosophy (Socrates, Plato, Aristotle, and others), mathematics (Pythagoras), astronomy, and others.

---

[237] See: Herodotus: *"Historiea,"* Book VI, 53, Book VIII, 73.

In the "dark centuries" (12th – 8th) Dardanians, and Trojans in Asia Minor kept their trail, but not the power that they once had when connecting Europe and Asia Minor. The reasons for this should be sought precisely in Dorian invasions and other similar movements circumvented and with disastrous dimensions for the Dardanians concentrated at this important juncture, but also for the Illyrians in general, as a trunk of Pelasgic roots. It has been assessed that by Dorian penetrations along the stream of the River Morava and Vardar valley to the Aegean, the Dardanian ethnicity was cut off into two parts, and their power as well, upon which its eastern part (Troy and the main part of Anatolia), fell into the hands of the Greeks, while those who did not cross over to southern Italy (Sicily – Galabri and some other tribes) shrunk in the Central Balkans so that only after four to five centuries of "silence," by the 3rd century BC they appeared as a rivaling kingdom. They engaged in frequent wars with the Macedonians and also with Greeks and other Illyrian kingdoms, which remained enclosed and often in alliances and agreements with them, especially when they engaged in a joint war against Rome that lasted for nearly two centuries and endied in a common defeat. Meanwhile, Dardania and most of Illyricum still continued to maintain the status of an autonomous province in the Roman Empire, from which it turned into an important factor of defense from attacks of Goths, Avars, and Slavs, which started from the 4th century A.D. and continued until the 10th century.

Dardanians and Dardania continued to play this role especially during the Byzantium time, when the whole edifice of the powerful Eastern Empire centered in Constantinople was established on the foundations of the Dardanian civilization as inherited from antiquity. Furthermore, it is not by chance that the founders of Byzantium were Dardanians (Constantine the Great and Justinian I).

It is precisely due to the great importance of this factor in early antiquity, especially as Troy with power as a "Balkan fortress in Asia Minor,"[238] served as a bridge between the most important civilizations of old times, the Dardanians and Dardania, with their wide presence from the Central Balkans to Asia Minor with some of their tribes found in southern Italy and as a central factor linking the Illyrians with the Thracians (the latter, according to many indications, are likely to bear Pelasgic roots). They

---

[238] Budimir, Milan: *"Grci i Plasci,"* Belgrade, 1950.

attracted attention in many ways, observed continuously sometimes as "Thracizied" and sometimes as "Illyrianized," and even as part of a larger Illyrian entity with special weight within it so as to be separate, or as a separate entity within the Central Balkan tribes extending to the space of Asia Minor (Anatolia and beyond). These observations, although often discrepant, increase the importance of the role of Dardanians and Dardania within the Pelasgic family, and antiquity in general, where they appeared as a dominating factor in the very center of antiquity.

Besides their role as a "bridge" connecting Europe and Asia Minor, appearing with a lot of issues about the origin of their power and prosperous future activity (from the West towards the East or vice versa), ancient authors paid significant attention to the connecting role of the Balkan Pelasgians with those in Italy and their alignment in the Aegean, especially Crete, from where the ancient civilization is assumed to have come.

Dionysius of Halicarnassus[239] wrote in the 1st century A.D. that Pelasgians originally came from Peloponnese, the neighboring province of Argos. They took their name from their king, Pelasgius, the son of Zeus. After six generations they settled in Thessaly, where they blossomed. They stayed there for five generations, until they were expelled by Deucalion, progenitor of Greeks.[240]

Always by Dionysus, a part of the Pelasgians were distributed in neighboring provinces, in Crete, the Aegean islands, especially in Lesbos, as well as along the Hellespont,[241] from where after they founded Troy, and defeated by the Greeks, crossed over to south of Italy. The historian considered Aeneas' origin as deriving from Dardanus, asserting that the founders of Rome, Remus and Romulus, Aeneas's sons, were Dardanians, that is, Pelasgians.[242]

---

[239] *Halicarnassus of Caria,* Greek scholar from Halicarnassus. He settled and lived in Rome in Augustus time. In the late BC years he wrote the work *"Romaiki arkeologia"* Lat. *"Antiquitatum Romanarum"* (History of Old Rome). The history of Dionysus starts from ancient times and amounts to the First Punic War (264 BC). The history of Dionysus brings valuable data for Pelasgians, Troy, Dardanians, and their settlement in Italy, including some data on the Pyrrhus campaign in Italy.

[240] Dionysus: *"Antiquitatum Romanarum,"* Book One, 17, cited according to *"Ilirët dhe Iliria te autorët antikë,"* Prishtina, 1979, p. 166.

[241] Ibid, p. 167.

[242] Ibid, p. 168.

Of course, these often differing observations have never denied the Dardanians the likelihood of being sons of the Pelasgians, and even their first offspring, never questioning also the power they had in the second half of the second millennium and up to the hypothetical war of Troy, which refers to the 12th century BC when they really represented a factor that influenced the civilizations of Crete, the Aegean and even extending to the south of Italy (Galabri, Thunates, Daunes), an extensive stretch, proven through numerous material remains and spiritual culture, which judging by archaeological and linguistic remains, largely retained the characteristics of what Dardanians had in Asia Minor, but also in the Central Balkans, in Dardania and further on in Italy and as far as North Africa.

The Dardanians as heirs of the Pelasgians has been well accepted by the most stubborn proponents of observation outside the connections to the Illyrian tribes as an independent entity in the Central Balkans, which appeared from the second millennium, where the source of various doubts of their "Illyrianism" or their later "Thracism" originate, together with incessant attempts to reduce their importance in the later centuries.[243]

Their linkage to the Pelasgians, whose traces run throughout the entire Balkan-Danubian area, the Aegean and southern Italy, and their antiquity is seen somewhere in the 6th millennium, making them the first people who arrived in these parts after their separation from the common trunk of the Indo-European family somewhere in the vicinity of India. This linkage cannot deny the dilemma regarding the time of the genuine social and political factorization of Dardanians and Dardania and its proportions when connected with Troy and their civilization, whose roots were encountered anywhere from the mid-2nd millennium and continuing to the middle of the 1st millennium.

As is known, the movements of peoples from the earliest prehistoric times from the 6th millennium, continued in different directions to be closed in a way with that of the 2nd millennium and the beginning of the

---

[243] For more see: Patsch, Carl: *"Dardani,"* PWRE IV/1901; Papazoglu, F: *"Srednjobalkanska plemena u predrimska doba,"* Godišnjak CBI, Works, Book XXX, 1961; Papazoglu, F: *"Dardanska onomastika,"* ZFF VIII-1,1964; Mirdita, Z: *"Studime dardane,"* Prishtina, 1979; Mirdita, Z: *"Dardanci i Dardanija u antici,"* Zagreb,1972; Moscy, A: *"Munizipale Gemeinde Obermoesien in hellenistisch-römischen Zeitalter,"* Actes I, Vol. II; Krahe, H: *"Von Illyrieschen zum Alteuropäischen,"* Berlin 1964.

1st, with the Dorians or as it is otherwise called the Aegean movement - was linked to the emergence of Greeks in what they called Hellada, while their civilization Hellenism, gave a special seal to antiquity. Dardania and Troy, identified as one and the same, continued to remain extremely significant factors of the latter development. It also shows clear signs of their coming from antiquity, which requires proper explanation that can hardly be found outside Homer's imaginative verse.

Moreover, a lot of the truth about the Pre-Hellenic factor and its importance depends on this explanation, which is also closely connected with the truth about the Crete, Maecean, and Phoenician civilizations. This was known to have an effect on Hellenism without properly explaining what their real direction was that was more important to know also that in the end it was the Hellenic scheme that won, rather due to the famous Philhellenism of the 19th century than scientific arguments, which were not only absent but occasionally attempts were also made to keep them absent.

Despite these schemes, relations of the Dardanians with Troy, outside of what Homer or Greek mythology present, should not only highlight the truth of their expansion into Asia Minor, but also the overall Dardanian-Illyrian complexity, which, although largely seen as a matter of a joint entity of the same (Pelasgian) root, and of the same trunk with various branches (regardless of the circumstances that conditioned them), they could not possibly be separated. And when this separation is aimed at by all means, and affects other matters of Indo-Europeanism (ethnic, social and political aspects), Dardanians and Dardania represent an inevitable reference to geography and connect almost all developments between prehistory and history, between the East and West, revealing truths and doubts as well, which continue to draw the attention of researchers, although often the outcome can be confusing.

Why it is so, unequivocally reasons can be found in an already monumental assessment, on an ethnic and linguistic aspect, Dardanians should be seen as an old Balkan mixture of indigenous residents and first Indo-European settlers - Pelasgians, who turned into an Indo-European fundament, whose character would not be altered by the engendered features or often contradictory new realities.[244]

---

[244] Budimir, Milan: "O etničkom odnosu Dardanaca prema Ilirima," Belgrade, 1950, p. 19.

However, in order to give the assessment an entitlement for complex consideration, as it may also throw clearer light on the Dardanian-Illyrian relations within the Pelasgian roots, a linguistic explanation of the name of *Dardania* is required, as *Dard* in the onomastic of the period of antiquity spread beyond the Dardanian and Dardanian-Trojan areas. According to Çabej,[245] it comes from a certain *Dardas,* name of a "proetar Epirotarum" of Δερδενσ, a frequent name of Macedonian-Eliotes, associated with Δερδια, the name of a city in the Elimiote region, and Δερδαια, in Thessaly, Δερδενις on the Lesbos Island, on the opposite bank of Italic land, in Appulia, as the name of the people of *Dardi* of Daunes, as the name of the province of *Dardensis,* and as a name of the city of Δαρδανον.[246]

As to the source and meaning of this name, although accepted in principle that the names of some regions and peoples of ancient times were very dark, here appears the linguist Johann-Georg Hahn,[247] who, speaking of those old geographic names, arising as appellatives in the present-day Albanian, links the name of the Dardanians with *dardhë* (pear), underscoring on the occasion that in Albanian, frequently place names are derived from names of trees, and he also mentions a name of a hamlet and mountain in Middle Albania called *Dardhë*.

On a later date work, Hahn writes: "Poroshtica gave us an unexpected confirmation of the explanation we have tried to give for the name *Dardania* in the book "Albanian Studies," as far as we could see, he realized that especially the eastern slope was covered with wild pears, that we had encountered before, mixed with other trees, but not in such a great bulk and frequency. The wild pear is spread throughout the Balkan Peninsula, making the name *Dardania* derived from the Albanian *dardhë* seems very reasonable, and the pre-medieval understanding of the topname seems to be "pear country."[248]

---

[245] For more see: Çabej, Eqrem: *"Studime gjuhësore,"* IV, Prishtina, 1977, (Name of Dardania and Albanian-Celtic Isoglosses), pp. 388-391.

[246] For more see: O. Hoffmann: *"Die Makedonen"* (1906), 157 vf; H. Krahe:*" Alltillyrische Personennamen"* (1929), p. 142; F. Ribezzo: *"Italia e Croazia"* (1942) 74; A. Mayer: *"Die Sprache der alten Illyrier"* I, II (1959) pp. 33,108 (cited according to Çabej, Eqrem: *"Studime gjuhësore,"* IV, Prishtina, 1977, p. 389.

[247] For more see: J.G von Hahn: *"Studime shqiptare,"* Tirana, pp. 236-266.

[248] J.G. von Hahn: *"Reise von Belgrad nach Solanik,"* 1924, p. 69.

According to Çabej, this explanation, according to which the name "Dardan," belonged to the country from its root that then marked it as *"pear country"* has found larger approval than all other interpretations of this name.[249]

An interpretation of the case by Edith Durham is depicted, who as an expert on Albania and the Balkans, called attention to the fact that names of places of plant origin are more frequent both in the South Slavic areas and the Albanian areas, as attested, she adds, by the names in Albania of *Arnje, Kështenja, Mollë, Arra, Qerreti, Kumbulla, Dardha,* and for the Southern Slavic *Krusevo, Krusevac, Krusevica* indicating that *Krusevac* is situated in the very territory of Old Dardania. [250]

Besides the Illyrian-Dardanian area, *Dardha* (Pear) is a common village name in Greece as well, especially in its collective and diminutive form *Dardhëza* (Νταρδιςα) in southwestern Morea, in Attica and Ellada, as well as *Dardhishtja* in the province of Trifilia province has put names to the Albanian element pressed in those parts. From Italy comes Dardhës, the name of a now extinct family in the village of Cienti of Molise.[251]

However, the interpretation of the word Dardan from the Albanian *Dardhë*, as it connects Dardanians and Dardania from an historical aspect with early antiquity, i.e. of a pre-Hellenic period, in linguistic terms, also its etymology is carried within an old Indo-European or even Pre-European stratification. The proponents of the latter (Ostir and G. Novak),[252] make an effort to associate *pear* with Pre-European means, through the stages of change (Stufen-wechsel) of "aloradic" languages with the word *mad-ari, ud-are,* the Basque "pear" and Greek αχρας with Lithuanian *kriause* and Slavic *krusa* "pear" with a pear-base form of Caucasian languages. Without entirely excluding the equalizer built by Bugges (in which he connects the Albanian origin of *dardhë* as a reflection of the Indo-European basic form - * g'hard-), Çabej opens the issue of a different linguistic proximity between the Albanian *dardhë* (pear) as a continuation of a basic form * d(h)arg'a which may be close to the Celtic word *irand. Draigen* (sloe, wild pear, transferred the issues to the field of Albanian-Celtic isoglosses. [253]

---

[249] Çabej, Eqrem: *"Studime gjuhësore,"* IV, Prishtina, 1977, p. 389.
[250] Ibid, p. 389.
[251] Ibid, p. 390.
[252] See: *Arhiv za arbanašku starinu* IV, 1969, p. 85.
[253] Çabej, Eqrem: *"Studime gjuhësore,"* IV, Prishtina, 1977, p. 391.

Dardanian-Illyrian Ethnic Relations

> *Different views of "northerners" and "classicists" about the role of the Dardanians within the Pelasgian and general Indo-European ethnos. – Were the significant social and political differences as well as other features between Dardanians and Illyrians a result of being strongly conditioned by invasions of other peoples towards the west, which followed from the third millennium to the first, affecting the Pelasgians dispersion in both directions: from Central Europe to its western part - including, on one hand, their settling in the Iberian and Italic (Ancient Italian) Peninsula, and on the other hand, the extension in the eastern part of Asia Minor to Africa - or is this discussion about their unifying role among the Danubian-Anatolian civilizations, which could not pass without certain consequences?*

If in principle the assessment is accepted that Dardanians, in ethnic and linguistic terms, represent a natural blend between the old inhabitants of the Balkans and the first settlers from Indo-European antiquity – Pelasgians, from where the great Illyrian trunk came with many branches and ramifications, with some additions, such as interlacing with the Thracian element in the far east of their territory,[254] it still does not solve the whole issue. It remains to be seen what the blending is, when it occurred, and what their role was within what is considered the big Illyrian family, as an important Indo-European factor that had an impact on subsequent processes.

Therefore, it can rightly be said that those views on the Dardanians and the great overall Illyrian family with their knowns and unknowns both connect and split the overwhelming number of scientists, "confusing" also fanatic Albanian followers of the Illyrians regarding the fact that traces of them are seen simultaneously in the Central Balkans, Italy, Asia Minor, Crete, Phoenicia and North Africa. Even without a wish, following them is a good opportunity to connect through ancient ancestors to the history of a civilization as old as 6,000 years that stands on the foundations of antiquity from where Hellenism was born and grew.

If agreements were reached in dealing with ancient Pelasgians since prehistoric times, already recognizing the fact that Pelasgians were the

---

[254] See Mirdita Zef: "*Studime dardane*," Prishtina, 1979, p. 49.

first among the movements of peoples within the Aryan Indo-European family of peoples from somewhere in India towards the West and in those areas they found indigenous peoples which they were able to assimilate (speaking of the Neolithic period of the sixth to the third millennium). However, differences and disagreements arose primarily about what direction the first settlers of Europe used. This explains the involvement of other peoples in this historical process during several millennia. Secondly, what were the main "stations" of these movements leading to their form of social, cultural, and later political organization, spreading to other parts, as known from antiquity onwards?

Throwing light on the first issue is important because it more or less highlights the role of other peoples, also Indo-European, that came later to the European territory and their disposal, that alongside the Pelasgians, through new influxes, either in temporary or permanent settlements (which could be long lasting or very long, for centuries), from an ethnic and social point of view affected the overall direction of Indo-European civilization to reach an historical scale recognized through various testimonies, especially those from the Copper period and on.

Throwing light on the second issue is important because through the material culture and language, with evidence from archeology, anthropology, to linguistics, even reaching the present time, it enables the creation of a more complete picture about possible friction, primarily between the newcomers and indigenous peoples (connected by mythology to Titans whose duty it was to spread the human race on earth and shared a certain kind of civilization whose remains continue to be mirrored by cyclopic walls and other inexplicable forms for the degree of development), and later on with those between Indo-Europeans and non-Indo-Europeans. These frictions were inevitable even for the very fact that the space populated initially by Pelasgians and later by their descendants, Dardanians, and other Illyrian tribes (Central Europe , the Balkans, Asia Minor, the Aegean, Crete, Phoenicia, and even North Africa), was also attended by other peoples: the Semitic peoples of Mesopotamia and Hamitics of Egypt, with which they shared natural ties, which also left their marks, both material and spiritual, but that, nevertheless, the true Indo-European character of Arianism was preserved in its recognizable form.

Even here the role of the Pelasgian descendants, Dardanians and the large family of Illyrians with many branches and ramifications, appears to be crucial, despite all the movements known as Doric invasions, the pan-

European and Aegean-Anatolian expansion of this ethnos with its numerous branches that Dardanians occupy defended antiquity by retaining its genuine Aryan character, which found its most potent reflection at the time of Hellenism after having acquired a lot from them through the Greeks and Romans.

Within these major historical outlines, the Pelasgian legacy with its large ethnic trunk with a Dardanian and Illyrian branching is directly or indirectly involved in almost all the core issues relating not only to Indo-Europeanism, but also to prehistoric time and other developments. This has caused an engendering of known branches coming out of this ethnicity, less known and unknown, to build, protect or destroy theories that relate to matters of the genesis of civilization, when the first division occurred among peoples turning into carriers of three world civilizations: that *Aryan* (Indo-European), *Semitic* (Mesopotamian) and *Turan* (Chinese-Japanese).

It has been estimated that this division of peoples occurred sometime before the 6th millennium, while that corresponds with the time relating to the early migrations of Aryan peoples towards the West (to be finalized by the end of the second millennium), drawing the directions of major migrations from their starting point somewhere in India, or possibly somewhere else. This is no formal affair, but it is of particular importance since the complex and difficult historical process, involving many factors, many nations and ethnicities, many of them without traces, or with traces passing onto others, a process that paved the way to the historic time and all that is known as antiquity, is finalized with Hellenism giving its special seal to the entire world civilization.

But what are the theories about the various routes of ancient Aryan peoples from India to the West (remaining rightly hypothetical), and why did they rise and/or largely collapse also due to the Dardanian and particularly Illyrian factor in general coming from the Pelasgian root?

Of course here, the migration theories maintained a common starting point, that is, the space in the vicinity of India and its direction towards the West, but not their decisive "turnaround" during this century-old journey, a twist with its last resting place, on one side, passing through the northern "tracks," and on the other through the eastern ones, without excluding the possibility of some other "middle" crossbeam being increasingly discussed in various ways.

Even potential and numerous stations in these directions were of particular significance, as the transition from one to another, represented sources of certain identities, which often turned into features confusing the tracks of the train.

This also raises the next question about why the descendants of the Pelasgians (that large trunk with major Dardanian and Illyrian branches and its multiple ramifications, where Dardanians are seen as being "special") appear in the role of "arbitrator" going as far as in some cases, due to the weight they had, being granted the right of "one track," and in some other cases that of the "other track," without excluding the possibility that in some cases the right is granted for both, something that makes the first issue even more complicated.

These are but paradoxes that are natural in certain circumstances as were those through which mankind passed at the dawn of civilization with many things in that show still remaining hypothetical, although some of the later-date taboos, built on stereotypes, such as dead languages (the Sanskrit, ancient Greek and other possibly intentionally fabricated "facts") without due respect for the living ones, change the established concepts of antiquity. Or is one dealing here with the fact that the very nature of issues arising from antiquity follows a real inability to properly access them, as basic testimonies, approach of interpretation, or for other unscientific reasons, turn hypothetical, producing in return unsettled problems?

Despite these justified dilemmas, which still preoccupy science, the importance of the Pelasgians and their descendants, however, has to do with the already insurmountable fact that they came first to the new land, succeeding in becoming indigenous inhabitants, managing to become natives, and that with their expansion in the overall space from West to East, from North to South, and Mediterranean basin, throughout Asia Minor and as far as Caucasus. The very fact that linguistics is grappling with common phenomena and forms of antiquity, scattered from one end of the world to another belonging to the same root, the language of the descendants of Pelasgians appears the only one that can provide answers, or that may serve as a basis for further interpretation.

Therefore, the theories faced here are not issues of geography, but of an historical development belonging to all. This long and strenuous journey of peoples must first be understood and seen as a social and spiritual transformation, allowing for subsequent changes, especially those from new Neolithic Era onwards to the emergence of tribal and ethnic groups and particular social communities further clarified from a social aspect as early as the Copper and Iron Ages.

The routes of these long migrations of peoples remain a concern for research, being only reasonable that they be defined in accordance with various theories.

The first theory, called "Nordic," sees the huge influx of Aryan peoples from antiquity as starting somewhere in India and moving from the Caucasus and Black Sea coasts. From there, people went through the steppes to the North, to Baltic, and from there turned to Central Europe from northwest.

Proponents of this theory define the 6th millennium as relating to the first wave of migrations, while, according to this theory, a millennium later another large influx occurred following on the same path and focused on the Baltic lands. This part of the Celtic-Baltic stratification, by the 4th millennium, moved further reaching the Alps and the Danube River in order to influence new migrations in the direction of the Mediterranean and Aegean-Anatolian Basin. These movements appeared to have been cyclical and closed with the Doric ones, around 13th century B.C., a movement that marked the most important and tangible changes for historians, as they were concurrent to the Greek penetration to Hellada from where Hellenism emanated with a superior degree of social and spiritual culture of antiquity.

Concentration of "Nordics" on Arianism, as a matter of race and Hellenization as its distinctive emblem of Indo-Europeanism occurred in the early 19th century by a large part of German scholars aided by Danish and Swedish scholars. Later, however, this would be sensibly corrected, significantly weakening the credibility of this theory, especially as social and cultural factors affecting the formation of ethnic groups in accordance with natural developments that followed those changes, were mostly seen through the lens of racial purity, an issue that at those early stages of social development was quite impossible.

The second theory admits that the migrations of peoples from the East towards the West began in the 6th millennium, continuing four millenniums, until the more recent ones relating to the 10th-13th centuries BC. This theory considers migrations as running from northeast, which means that the migrations of people passed through Asia Minor and the Aegean, on one hand by following on land in the Central Balkans on the other hand, by reaching Crete, in order then to continue to the islands and other parts of the Mediterranean.

This observation holds the importance of the Black Sea and the Danube flow as an important artery of the intrusions towards the Balkans and central part of the continent and vice versa. Its supporters believe that the quality of civilization and the ability to further influence it is conditioned by the climate and more favorable circumstances that this direction provided. Furthermore, without reason it was noted that a higher degree of civilization that was presented in the Black Sea area in Central Anatolia and towards the Balkans and beyond to the West (Troy, Cretan, Mycenaean civilizations are mentioned), was greatly owed to suitable climatic conditions for a faster development shifting from the north, accompanied by a most difficult struggle for simple survival (which in their opinion, it is understandable why the main directions of Indo-European invasions ended in the Mediterranean and Aegean) or at least why they experienced their highest peak.

It must be said that supporters of these theories have their arguments coming precisely from the material and linguistic culture created over the centuries, traces of which are beginning to emerge thanks to archaeological research starting in the 19th century in many important habitats and, viewed separately or detached, seem plausible.

For example, "Nordists" or supporters of the theory of the Aryan Indo-European civilization with its nucleus being first in the Center of Europe, between the Alps and the Danube valley, are based on the Danubian culture and its important trails such as those related to the beginnings of agriculture and cultivation of grain from the 6th millennium, which are then accompanied by cordilleran pottery and later with painted pottery. The Danubian space also maintained extensive evidence of Neolithic and later the Eneolithic Age up to the Iron Age. The latter finds its strongest reflection in what is called Hallstat culture, traces of which extend into the Mediterranean, extending well into the East, but this does not mean that this culture could not be influenced by other parts, knowing that at that time there was communication between East and West. These assumptions were a source for multiple denials and claims among the various theories that lose weight when they become exclusive, as often happens.

The other theory, which rejects the primacy of "Nordism," relies on arguments from material culture, also dating back from the early 6th millennium and continuing apace until the beginning of the 3rd millennium. Therefore, the stone sculptures from the early Neolithic Age found in the Balkans, cyclopic constructions in particular, extending into Asia Minor, and also Crete and, in addition to ceramics, in the Eneolithic and Iron Age, there are different tools and above all weapons, showing the seal of an impact of what has been called Aegean-Anatolian culture. This culture, whose presence stretches in various forms in the Balkans and extending further in depth and well into the North and also found throughout the Mediterranean basin, owed to an eastern impact and arteries coming from there.

Despite these varying observations, which have not been without consequences as they nourished recessive views instead of engaging in scientific credibility – there would be living and social circumstantial realities, which since early antiquity and up to the Bronze and Iron Ages, besides the common values exhibiting a mentality awareness being primitive either on its roots (some of the zoomorphic and anthropomorphic and most primitive symbols associated with nature) or other forms of idols - highlighted features within families in the broadest sense. These features included differences among tribes, reflected in material culture, and even social relations, through which ethnic group formations began, appearing as the bearers of identifying cultures, which exclude opposing and biased theories.

Therefore, from the 2nd to the 1st millennium, in the South appeared the Cretan civilization with first palaces (approx. 1800) and a little later with the appearance of script called *Linear A* (approx. 1600), at a time when in the northern and central part there was the well-known Danubian civilization in the field of urns (approx. 1290-900), while in the South at its height was the Mycenaean civilization (approx. 1450-1200), with *Linear B* appearing.[255] In the meantime, in the South of the Balkan Peninsula small governing kingdoms began to appear, ranging from fortified castles and palaces, such as those found in Homer's "Iliad" and other famous poets of antiquity, which were not only a product of creative imagination, but of certain historical realities.

But at these times several great natural disasters occurred (eruption of Santorini around 1656) and several large earthquakes that may have

---

[255] For more see: Severyns, A: *"Grece et Proche-orient avant Homerie,"* Bruxell, 1960; Schneider, Edouard: *"Les Pelasges et leurs descendants,"* Paris, 1894; Van Effenterre: *"Mycenes, vie et mort d'une civilisation,"* Paris, 1985.

caused the collapse of civilizations, of which that of Crete in around 1400 is most notable given that its true causes have been known,[256] providing certain issues with secrets resembling mythology.

In the center of these developments with major changes would be the Pelasgians and their direct heirs, the Dardanians-Illyrians and all of what was later seen as the Illyrian ethnos as the Illyrian branch with its ramifications, stretching more widely, especially in northwestern parts of the Balkan, Italic and Iberian Peninsula, even in the Adriatic Basin, accompanied by dynamic changes (multiple tribes and similar entities), while the Dardanian branch with its fewer subsidiaries was subject to severe pressure of the Dorians and other invasions coming from the East. Therefore, Illyrians and Dardanians with their branches, but always as a common ethnicity among the largest ones recognized in both pre-historical and historical times, were important and inevitable actors of these historical developments. Therefore, it is quite reasonable that they turned into carriers of different theories often by opposing views, because as the oldest Indo-European stratification they had melted the indigenous population, spanning over most of the old continent and part of Asia Minor. Being included in both sides helped them keep and reflect their common and inherent differences.

Therefore the so-called *field urn* culture (Urnenfeld-derkultur), especially its branch, which archaeologists call the Lausitzer culture,[257]

---

[256] Seismologists and volcanologists, based on different evidence that current techniques allow, through which almost accurately the age of volcanic debris is defined, confirm that in 1450 BC, on the island of Teras near Crete (70 miles in the north) a volcanic eruption occurred among the most powerful of all times, several times stronger than the giant one of Krakatoa in 1883. While the Krakatoa blast shattered windows hundreds of kilometers away, sending tidal waves as far as the Indian Ocean, with the dust thrown around the world affecting the climate throughout the Northern Hemisphere, the impact of the outbreak of Teras must have been colossal. (For more see: Bernal, Martin: "*Athina e zezë,*" Tirana, 2009, p. 72; Van Effenterre: "*Mycenes, vie et mort d'une civilisation,*" Paris, 1985.)

[257] The founder of this theory is the well-known German archaeologist *Gustav Kossinna*, assisted by archaeologist and philologist *Richard Pittion* and *Julius Pokorny*, who defend the position that the founders of the Bronze Age culture of the urn fields were the proto-Illyrians from whom, in the Iron Age, Illyrians sprang. *Kossinna* based his theory on the opinion of archaeologist *Rudolf Much*, who explained the names of some cities in Germany appearing in Ptolemy as associated with northern Illyrians based on their similarity to those of Illyrian areas in the Balkans. (See: "*Mannus,*" 4/1912, p. 173; and

among the most substantial from the Neolithic period onwards, was largely attributed to the Illyrians, who were initially seen as inhabitants around the river *Iller*[258] (Danube tributary near Ulm in Germany), continuing then from the center of the German center Lausitzer (Luzice), sometime around 1200 BC, and perhaps even earlier. According to "Nordists," they were deferred by their northern neighbors Celts and Balts, from where on account of some common linguistic and spiritual residue, seemed to have shared some "close blood relationship" from ancient times, a "legacy" that was preserved even after they became subject to their invasions towards Gallia, Spain and the Balkans, which were also seen as tectonic, since it is estimated that they shook Europe for more than a century. Their furious spread in those regions caused additional chain movements, while their penetration in the Balkans caused major displacements in the direction of Greece, known in science as *Doric or Aegean influxes.*[259]

No matter how many impartial scientists have almost concluded that the Illyrians of the Central European part, like those of the Danubian part, did not cause the so-called Dorian invasion, nor did they receive an active part in it - though some of them were significantly affected by it (Dardanians, who in their northern penetrations were divided into two parts). As a result, some eastern tribes (around Troy) crossed over to southern Italy, and Sicily while the same happened to some tribes in the West that moved to the north of Italy and even Spain[260] where the opponents of "Nordism" seized this opportunity to show the contrary. First in order to counter the Proto-Illyrian theory of Lausitz of Germany, in order to oppose Pan-Illyrism first by the stance on the Dardanians as a separate Balkan identity,[261] which put in doubt their ethnic ties with the Illyrians,

---

"Herkunft der Germanen," 2. Würzburg, 1920, p. 21). The theory was further developed in several studies by the German archeologist *Bolko von Richtschofen.* See: *"Die Bedeutung der Lausitzer kultur für Vorgeschihte der Donauländer und das Illyriertum ihrer Volkzugehörigheit,"* Mannus, 27/1953, pp. 69-81, cited according to Stipcevic Aleksandar: *"Ilirët,"* Prishtina, 1980, p. 19.

[258] See: Pokorny, Julius: *"Zur Urgeschichte der Kelten und Illyrier,"* Halle, 1938.

[259] *Kossinna, Gustav: "Mannus,"* 4/1912, p. 173.

[260] For more see: Budimir, Milan: *"O etničkom odnosu Dardanaca prema Ilirima,"* Belgrade, 1950, pp. 11-18.

[261] See: Novak, Grga: *"La nazionaliteta deri Dardani,"* Arhiv za Arbanasku starinu, 4, 72, 98, based on some evidence by ancient authors, especially those of Strabo, he separates

going as far as denying altogether their kinship with the Illyrians and the common ethnic trunk on grounds that they were a people different from historical Illyrians and being close to the inhabitants of Asia Minor of the Bronze Age and belonging to the Paleo-Mediterranean populations.[262] Therefore, opening the way to the Thracian theory of the Dardanians and its exclusivity, [263] although this rather extremist assessment appeared somewhat more conciliatory by what was being said that "the Dardanian ethnicum, because of historical circumstances between the 5th and 3rd millennium can be characterized equally as Illyrian and Thracian."[264]

Of course the opponents of "Nordism" in order to show that directions of the penetration of Indo-European civilization went from northeast and not from northwest, seeing a role of the East in the West, saw the Dardanians as a factor that would dominate the space connecting Asia Minor with the Central Balkans (Troy). After intensive contacts with the Illyrians, they were assimilated by them, while their ethnicity emphasized Thracian virtues, and that, later, with this "mixed" identity, they would be seen in southern Italy, Western Sicily from where they would have an impact on the creation of Rome and all that in what emerged as the Roman Empire.[265]

Leaving aside the ethnic relationship between the Trojans and Dardanians, it should be noted again that these oldest Indo-European colonists, did not arrive to the Balkans from the northwest, as the Greek tribes, but rather from northeast. This assessment is led by two Illyrian ethnicums, *Elimes* and *Segines*, found down the Danube, but also on the eastern coast and Cyprus, and *Elimes* in western Sicily and the Central Balkans.[266]

This has led to the chronology of Indo-European colonization of the Mediterranean being viewed differently, legitimizing assessments that

---

Dardanians from the Illyrians in ethnic terms. He draws the conclusion of Dardanians being the most ancient Balkan-Anatolian people.

[262] Ibid, pp. 88-89.

[263] See Papazoglu, Fanula: *"Srednjobalkanska plemena u predrimsko doba,"* Djela, knj.XXX. CBI, Book.1, 1969.

[264] See: Vulpe, R: "Gli *Illiri dell Italia imperiale Romane,"* in Ephem Dacorom III (1925), Roma, 162 ss, cited according to Mirdita, Zef:"Studime Dardane," Prishtina, 1980, p. 27.

[265] See: G. G. Matesku: *"I Trci nelle epigraphi di Roma,"* 1923; D. Deçew: *"Die Trakische Spracheste;"* Vl.I Georgierv: *"Introduzione alla storia dell lingue indieuropee,"* C. Ptsch: *"Dardani,"* in PWRE IV (1901).

[266] Budimir, Milan: *"O etničkom odnosu Dardanaca prema Ilirima,"* Belgrade, 1950, p. 12.

until recently were almost unpredictable permitting the Illyrians to appear in the eastern Mediterranean and even in the mid 3rd millennium, while the inscriptions in Cappadocia are derived from the first part of that millennium.[267] This is also consistent with the view that emerged about Illyrian dialects being the oldest representatives from the community of all Indo-European languages as they maintain the *three orders of gutturals*, and as this distinctive feature entirely separates them linguistically from Indo-European Hittites who appeared in Anatolia at the latest 2000 years BC. A conclusion imposes itself that Indo-European elements, stored in Lycia and Lydia, must be treated as members of the Illyrian group, confirming the opinion that the Indo-European palatal layers preserved in *Lycian* and *Lydian* differ from labiovelar gutturals.[268]

Besides these properties, which led from Illyrian and Albanian mother languages, there are also Anatolian idioms both in morphology and vocabulary, especially the links to Balto-Slavic group, which, from a geographical standpoint seems very improbable.[269]

Although research in this regard is still to come, it is safe to point out by now that at 1500 years BC three dialectic groups of Anatolian Indo-European languages should be counted:

a) The Illyrian, as the oldest,
b) The Hittite, and
c) The Aryan.

This state of knowledge about language pre-Greek and pre-Anatolian proto-history has fundamentally changed Kretchmer's assumptions,[270] which for quite some time were almost compassing from this point of view.

It is exactly among the migrated Dardanian tribes in Italy (Galabri, Thunanes, Daunes) that the clear tracks of Illyrian characteristic ethnos was seen as a wide Euro-Asian stratification with the participation of various factors within the same family.

Therefore, it has been assessed that among the Dardanian tribes were also the pure Illyrian *Elmira*, who along with the Balkan's Dardanians, in

---

[267] See: Kretschmer, Paul: "*Die Leleger und ostmediterrane Ubefölkerung,*" Gotta XXXII-1953.

[268] See: P. Merini "*Heimai u Kultur.D. Indogermanen,*" Festschrift H. Hirt 2, 257).

[269] Ibid, 2,257.

[270] For more see: Kretschmer, Paul: "*Einleitung in die Geschichte der griechschen Sprache,*" Göttingen, 1869.

all probability, moved to Anatolia and after the conquest of Troy by the Greeks and destruction that followed, a part of them moved to western Sicily. Furthermore, the famous Maltese archeologist who raised the issue of the Illyrian origin of the Dardanian descendant Aeneas, the godly, direct founder of eternal Rome, claiming that the easiest and more natural route to Sicily would suit better the Trojan Dardanians than for those of the Balkans, even though he found their traces in the Peloponnese and the island Zakinta, asserting their wide scope in the Balkans and Asia Minor.[271]

A. Fik found in Crete a pile of pre-Greek *Dorthonai* toponyms (hesitant about *a/o*), i.e. in the same land where traces of Pelasgian Illyrians were found, as well as words formed by specific suffix elements, such as *st* and *mn*. In this case, with the Dardanian nucleus in the Central Balkans, and certain oases on the outskirts of the Balkan Peninsula, it would be natural to conclude that the metanastic currents reached Sicily through the same route as the other Illyrian groups, namely from the Balkans through the Otranto Gate to southern Italy and Sicily.[272]

However, linguistic views settled the dilemma that Dardanian ethnicity can be characterized as Illyrian as much as Thracian, they broke away a portion of the weight and historical importance they had in an important phase of major changes crossing from the Bronze to the Iron Age to the emergence of classical Greeks and Hellenism, while by the same arguments the Thracian association with Dardanians was reduced to a minimum. However, this does not exclude the possibility that in a distant past Dardanians and Thracians, lived together and sometimes as mixed in the eastern part of the Balkans and Asia Minor where they had a special relationship, reflected in linguistic influences, remained beneath those seen as natural splicing Illyrian-Thracian-Daco-Roman language elements, traces of which are still found today as a common vocabulary in both Albanian and Romanian reflected as such mostly in the Dardanian and Macedonian place names,[273] and especially in some toponyms ending in suffixes *-dava* (*-deva, -dova*) "city," which attain, nevertheless, a Thracian influence.

---

[271] See: Budimir, Milan: "*O etničkom odnosu dardanaca prema Ilirima,*" 1950, p. 12.
[272] Fik, A: "*Vorgriechische Ortsnamen,*" 33, cited according to Budimir, Milan "*O etnickom odnosu dardanaca prema ilirima,*" p. 12.
[273] Evans, J. A: "*Antiquarian researches in Illyricum*" I-IV, pp. 47-48.

Apparently, these linguistic analogy efforts were also made in viewing the common tribal affiliation of the Dardanians (Homer and Herodotus mention three Dardanian tribes) as Thracian element, in which the Thunates tribe that is also mentioned by Strabo as an important Dardanian tribe was to be described as being Thracian.[274] In this case, the name *Thunatoi* is compared to the Thracian *thynoi*,[275] although this name has been confirmed in Southern Italy as an ethnicon name in the form of *Dauni* and *Calabri*,[276] in which undoubtedly there could not possibly be a Thracian element. Furthermore, even the very name *Dardan* may easily be linked to the name of the *Dardi* tribe in Southern Italy.[277]

Although few in the Dardanian ethnicum, of the same nature there are also some photonomies stored in the form of glosses, collected by Pedan Dioskudirius of Anabrases, the time of Nero, in his work *"On the Healing Plants."*[278] They are: *aloitis* (a mountain plant used for sedation, a type of anesthesia), and *absentium rusticum* (a kind of wormwood), which are explained through the Illyrian language fund.[279]

Actually the Illyrian language fund is an internal development of many centuries, which solves most of these dilemmas, often equating between Dardanians and the Thracians, or serving as a "trigger" in viewing their first ethno genesis different from that of the Illyrians without ever hesitating even to contest their common connection with the Pelasgians. This spread in the western and southwestern part of the Balkan Peninsula and in northern Italy and the East (from the Alps beyond the Danube and Sava rivers to the Adriatic), where they frequently seemed to move, the Dardanians appear concentrated in almost the same area (in the Central Balkans - the flow of rivers Morava and Vardar and in

---

[274] See Strabo: VII, 5, 7 when he says ."..*Galabres and Thunates are also Dardanians... bordering with Maedeans in the East, a Thracian tribe...*"

[275] See: Delschew, Dimiter: *"Die thrakischen Sprachreste,"* Österreichische Akademi der Wiessenschaft. Philosophisch-historische Klasse. Schriften der Balkan-Kommission. Linguistische Abtailung XIV, Vienna, 1957.

[276] Plin, NH.III 103.

[277] See: H. Krahe: *"Ballkanillyrische geographische Namen,"* 103, 112, where he treats the name Dardi as an Illyrian ethnicon.

[278] Ped. Diosc.III 3-4 at Pseudo Apylon, 16 (HS 51), cited according to Mirdita, Zef: *"Studime dardane,"* Prishtina, 1979, p. 35.

[279] Mayer, A: *"Die Sprache der alten Illyrier,"* Bd. I.Vienna, 1957, p. 137 (Dardan Name einer Bergphlanze).

the east to Asia Minor and Troy) from the middle Neolithic Age. Therefore, it has been consistently seen as Dardania, or land of the Dardanians, while Illyrian lands are called Illyricum, a characterization certainly related to certain social and political factors, through which Pelasgian passed for generations, where Dardanians distinguished themselves with Troy and the dominance over the central part of the Balkans, what is connected to Greece and the Aegean, while other Illyrian tribes in the west connected Central Europe to the Adriatic and Mediterranean, highlighting what would be called "Indo-European Pan-Illyricism" with one of the largest spatial extensions of historical time, as it connects Europe and its West, South and Southeast with Asia.[280] This relation, which is not only geographical but also of a genuine nature of Indo-European stamp, has also passed to the Albanians, who's current ethnic space, despite what happened during the twenty centuries, has nevertheless retained the definition made by the ancient geographer Strabo in the 1st century AD.

This Illyrian-Dardanian geographic definition cannot be taken as final and without exception because numerous sources coming from ancient authors, and others related to the Illyrian tribes and their rise, such as the ancient *Paiones* and Dardanians of the part of the Mediterranean and even Italy (Galabres and Thunates), with Dardanians being surrounded by Illyrian tribes expanding to extreme wings (in the east), along with features of social and political nature, which arise from the Iron Age and on, bring to light a common linguistic stratification, which underwent similar phonetic, and lexical developments, regardless of geographic expansion. The case of the Illyrian Paiones, on one hand, and the Dardanian Galabri on the other, is very characteristic and perhaps deserves more attention.

The Paion *Paioplai* ethnicum, as Herodotus recorded it as the name of the most northern tribe, must not be overlooked when it comes to determining the ethnicity of ancient *Paiones* within the expanding Illyrian

---

[280] For more on this see: Krahe, Hans: "*Von Illyrischen zum Alteuropäischen,*" in IF Berlin, 1964-65; "*Die Ballkanillyrischen geographischen Namen,*" Heidelberg, 1925; "*Lexikon altillyrischer Personennamen,*" Heildebreg, 1929; "*Die Schprache der Illyrer,*" I, Wiesbaden, 1955; Mayer, Anton: "*Die Sprache der alten Illyrier,*" Bd. I. Einleitung. Wörtebuch der illyrischen Schprahe. Österreichische Akademi der Wiessenschaften. Schriften der Balkankommission. Linguistische Abteilung XV, Vienna, 1957; Budimir, Milan: "*Grci i Pelasci,*" Serbian Academy of Sciences, Belgrade, 1950.

ethnos. The name *Paioplai* with its ending is marked as Illyrian, as it cannot be separated from well-known Illyrian names, while for *Teutiaplos* (Tycidides), *Megaplini, Ortopla*, their Illyrian affiliation is uncontested. The vocal change in this **a/o** Illyrian format is of the same nature as the cases mentioned: *Baiteia - Bottiaia, gandei kontouros kassis koptis*, in which a detected Illyrian influence was indirectly confirmed, coming from the Adriatic through Dardanians to the Paion tribe. Being that this view is followed by a complication of the phenomena which in itself are quite clear, evidently in the east beyond the Dardanians lived Illyrian *Paiuoplais*.[281]

For the well-known philologist Budimir, this *Paion* tribe, situated furthest from the sea, was the least accessible to be influenced by the Greek colonies and therefore has retained its most complete form of the name Paion. One should have in mind that in the "Iliad" the Vardar *Paiones*, together with the Anatolian Dardanians, fought in the Trojan War against Achaean settlers and that Aeneas, Virgil's character and founder of the Roman state is of Dardanian origin. The name of the Galabri, who, like the Messapians, Yapiges, Daunes, Peucetis, crossed the Balkans over to Apennine Peninsula, shows the same suffix as the Illyrian ethnicums *Magaplini Orthopla Teutiaplos, Paioplai: Galabroi* was established through the liquid dissimilation from *Galabloi*. The difference in the labial sound of this name, despite the voiceless *Paioplai*, can be explained through examples such as: *Astybos - Shtip, Belleros - Pelleros, karabos - skorpios, sempala - sambala*, which can be significantly associated with the analogous phenomena of numerous residual consonants of the Illyrian vocabulary.[282]

The same replacement of the vocal consonant with the voiceless one exists in the name of the Illyrian *Autariatae*, also called *Audaristenses* "highlanders" rather than Precotar, as based on the space they occupied and because of obvious lexical connections with Macedonian *darillos* and the Illyrian name of the priest of Hephaestus, Daret, one cannot completely relate this ethnicon to the Tara River. *Audaristenses*, in fact, is the genuine ethnicon *Audaristai*, which rather recalls the names: *Skordistai - Scordisci* and *Tauristai - Taurisci*. The name Skordiska, which was a Celtic-Illyrian mixture (Cf. also *Keltoligyes* and *Celtiberi*) cannot be disassociated from the mountain *Scardus*, which in many cases has been

---

[281] Budimir, Milan: "*O etničkom odnosu Dardanaca prema Ilirima,*" Belgrade, 1951, p. 11.
[282] Ibid, p. 11

taken as a boundary between the Illyrians and Dardanians. Variation of the suffix in the names *Skodristai - Scordisci* and *Tauristai - Tauirsci* may only be visible as among ethnic Illyrians more common is ***st*** than ***sk-***, which some treat as Mediterranean, although it appears in far north of the Indo-European. Therefore it is permissible to explain the variants *Tauirsci Scordisci* as a consequence of a dissimilation of lines ***t – t u t - k***. (cp. Slavic *kataraka* with Greek *aktarta* and the doublet *çuzhdi* and *tudzi* to German *teodiscus* and Teutan *Teuta* Illyrian "queen"). The same result of the dental group dissimilation is also found in the toponyms *Dlamoç - Glamoç* and *Tnina – Knin*.[283]

Evidently, Dardanians were surrounded on all sides by the Illyrian tribes, and it would be strange if so great a Mediterranean oasis were to be surrounded by Indo-European "occupants" and then be assimilated by them.[284] The northern boundary of the geographic cultural strip of *Alarodians* would probably be the Rhine – Danube line, on which even in the Balkans in the south of that line Mediterranean residues were later kept. However, this cannot even closely imply that Justinian himself could have been born in an indigenous or Mediterranean environment with pre-Indo-European inhabitants.[285]

Therefore, linguistically, being the common denominator of Indo-Europeanism from antiquity onwards, in the wide land of the Balkan Dardanians, spanning the space between the Sharr Mountain and upstream of the Drina and all the way to Nish and Timok, there is a significant number of toponyms and hydronyms, which without any phonemic and semantic constraint can be interpreted by means of the Indo-European language. However, this does not preclude the maintenance of residues of a geographic pre-Indo-European nomenclature,[286] to be

---

[283] Ibid, p. 12.

[284] For more see Papazoglu, Fanula: "*Poreklo i razvoj ilirske drzave*," Godisnjak CBI XII/10, 1967; Patsch, Carl: "*Dardani*" in: GZM BiH, X/2-3, 1898; Patsch, Carl: "*Tracki tagovi na Adriji*," in GZM BiH XVIII /1906; Schütt, Carl: "*Untersuchungen zur Geschihte der alten Illyrer*," Breslau 1910.

[285] Ibid, p. 11.

[286] See: Pedersen, Holger: "*Die Gutturale in Albanischen*," 1900; Ostir, Karel: "*Beiträge zur alarodische Sprachwiessenschaft*," Bd. I, Vienna-Leipzig, 1921, p. 67; Schütt, Carl: "*Untersuchungen zur Geschihte der alten Illyrier*," Breslau 1910; Patsch, Carl: "*Historische Wanderungen im Karst und an der Adria*," Vienna 1922; Mayer, Antun: "*Die Sprache der*

interpreted with difficulties because all the names belonging to that group are characterized by a high attendance, for which they were subject to different influences of phonological pathology.[287] Such are ancient and modern examples: *Larissa* - Lassa, *Constantinopol*-Polis, *San Francisko* - Frisco, *Sankt Peterburg* - Picer, *Jastrebarsko* – Jaska, etc.[288]

Therefore, based on what has been said, the Illyrian carries at least one yet known. This is the general Indo-European, the reconstruction of which is more supported today than it was two decades ago, because of the written documents available and understood from the mid-2nd millennium.[289]

Therefore leaving the Dardanian toponymy aside, it should however be noted that the birthplace of Emperor Justinian, *Tuarision*, with its radical and suffix element testifies to its accentuated and undoubtful Illyrian character (cp. *Tauromenion* in Sicily, then *Epidaurus*, *Tauros* in Anatolia, *Taurunum* at Sava flow, and ethnos *Taurines* and *Ta/eureskes*), while because the fraction *Brentesion Brindisium*, where under fully convincing interpretation by Skok becomes a word for the locative plural of the Indo-European.[290]

Another important circumstance is that Anatolian Dardanians, in addition to the toponym *Batieia*, which cannot be disassociated from the evidently Illyrian name *Baton*, have maintained in the name of Mount *Ida*, which appears in Thrace and Crete as well, an important field sign of the Indo-European.[291] As is known, geographical nomenclature stores considerably longer the visible signs of field expressions. So is the case with the pre-Greek *Ida* "mountain," "forest," "wood," treated as pre-European.[292]

With this pre-Greek field sign documented Thracian and Anatolian Dardanian lands the assertion on the Balkan-Illyrian of the Trojan Dardanians gets significantly enhanced. Their most famous personalities, such as *Dardanos*, *Assarakos*, *Akhisos*, *Aineias* (Aeneas) bear explicit

---

alten Illyrier," Vienna 1957; Katičić, Radoslav: "*Liburner, Pannonier und Illyrier*," Insbruck 1968; Katičić, Radoslav: "*Peonci i njihov jezik*," 1977.

[287] Budimir, Milan; "*Ilirski problem i leksička grupa Teuta*," Split, 1953, p. 3.

[288] Ibid, p. 4.

[289] Budimir, Milan: "*O etničkom odnosu Dardanaca prema Ilirima*," Belgrade, 1951, p. 8.

[290] Ibid, p. 9.

[291] Ibid, p. 14.

[292] Ibid, p. 14.

Illyrian names. Aeneas father's name *Ankhisas* with its endings reminds one of specific names such as *Akrisos, Tarvisium, Naissos, Ilios*, etc.[293]

This Illyrian onomastic character, which, as seen from the examples raised, preserves the form of either common linguistic parts of the Central Balkans, or Italy and Anatolia, i.e. East, cannot take away the social contradictions of the Balkan Dardanians in regard to their antiquity, by claiming, on one hand, that they slept in trash, while on the other claiming they were owners of thousands of slaves, while their Anatolian offspring, as progenies of Zeus, transferred the seat of their eternal kingdom of Troy to Rome. Julius Caesar considered that as a legitimate inheritor of the divine *Aineas* (Aeneas) he should move the seat from Rome back to Troy, but he was prevented from carrying out the plan by his assassins. Later Constantine the Great built the *"New Rome"* on the Illyrian Byzantine land.[294]

Dardanian-Illyrian-Greek Relations

> *Did the ancient Greeks consider the Dardanians to be different from the Illyrians, the first coming from deities and being immortal, and the latter coming from the people and being mortal? – Were there internal social and political links between the Illyrian and Dardanian kingdoms and the Greeks, and how were they reflected? – Besides deities and religion, the ancient Greeks learned work and creative habits from the Illyrians and Dardanians, which they advanced and enriched through other forms.*

If in the famous Troy the Dardanians, based on legend, during the time of King Ilos,[295] are seen as its founders by the order of Zeus,[296] by

---

[293] See: Kretschmer, Paul: "*Einleitung in die Grschihte der griechischen Sprache,*" Götingen, 1896.
[294] Budimir, Milan: "*O etničkom odnosur Dardanaca prema Ilirima,*" Belgrade, 1951, p. 13.
[295] *Ilos,* King of Dardanians, son of Troy and nymph *Caliro*, father of *Laomademont* and grandfather of *Priam*.
[296] <u>Dardanus,</u> according to legend, is son of Zeus and Electra. Compelled to leave his land, Arcadia, he went to Phrygia, where he settled and founded Troy on the banks of

which their fame forever remained covered with the mystery of that hypothetical war, however, in another legend, that of Cadmus of Antiquity, related to the founding of Thebes in Boeotia, similar to the gods of Olympus, another kingdom appeared, that of Illyria, which according to the legend was supposed to be in the service of setting earthly power cared for by responsible human beings. And this kingdom was pre-Greek and happened to be in the land from where "deities" would monitor over the entire development.

In both these cases, the tasks were given to a divine people, who according to Homer and other ancient authors were Pelasgians,[297] who therefore assumed a mediator's role between the divine and the earthly power with the people, from which of course derived the belief in ancient philosophy that the state is sacred, and statesmen (kings) should be idealistic, which means also divine governing in the service of setting an empire of the best, a concept of which we know from Plato onwards.

The task of *creating* the people's power with which they would be charged, according to mythology, the divine Pelasgians, is also of a special hierarchy, as in the first case, that of Troy, the founder stemmed directly from the legacy of the gods, as was Dardanus the son of Zeus, who had the goddess Electra and had to be immortal like the gods.

And, in the second case, Illyrius, who would become king of Illyria, came from king-man and was a mortal, while his memory consistent with his work remained eternal. His father, Cadmus of antiquity, was the son of Agenor, king of Crete, who in search of his sister Europe abducted by Zeus, went to Greece and there after having faced the dragon who blocked the sources of River Acenor, he created people out of dragon's ribs (twelve of them), populating the Pelasgian lands with them, and as an award from the Gods, he would marry goddess Harmonia, the daughter of Ares god of war, with whom he had five boys, one of whom Illyrius, having been born in the land of Enchelei, took over leadership of that people which were then named Illyrians. After they died, Cadmus and goddess Harmonia turned into snakes to protect human heritage, namely their holy guardians.

The legend of the snake included Illyrius as well, being wrapped in it by his father immediately after birth, conveying the magic of his ability so

---

Scamander. He is considered the forefather of Dardanian tribes living at the foot of Ida Mountain. (For more see: *"Fjalori i mitologjisë,"* Prishtina, 1988, p. 62)

[297] See: Homer: *"Iliada,"* Tirana, 1979, Book X, 429; Herodotus: *"Historiae,"* Book I, p. 58.

that he and his people would survive the evils and difficulties they would face in the difficult struggle.

In addition to the Pelasgian legend as heavenly people, which recognized their immortality, to which the Greeks tried to refer appropriately constantly, there is also another legend that speaks of the contrary, for the terrestrial origin of the Pelasgians, which not only goes against the will of the gods or with immortality, as is the case with Dardanus and Troy, or Illyrius the son of Cadmus and goddess Harmonia, but is inconsistent with it. It is related to what Appian of Alexandria brought in his *"Historia Romana,"*[298] who after explaining that the Hellenes call Illyrians those who live over Macedonia and Thrace (from Caones and Theprotes) up to the river Ister, speaks also as to why this land took the name Illyria.

According to legend, *Illyrius*, along with *Celtus* and *Galas*, was the son of Polyphemus and Galatea, who left Sicily and became rulers over the tribes, who were by their names called *Celts*, *Illyrians*, and *Gauls*. Further, the same legend says that the sons of Illyrius were: *Encheleus*, *Autarieus*, *Dardanus*, *Maedus*, *Taulas*, and *Perrhaebi*, and his daughters: *Partho*, *Daortho*, *Dassaro*, and others, of whom came Taulantii, Perrhaebi, Enchelei, Autariates, Dardani, Partheni, Daors, and Dassaretae.[299]

This dual viewing of the Pelasgians by the Greeks, mostly as heavenly people, but also as opponents of the gods, as was Polyphemus and Cyclops identifying first gigantic beings as predecessors of the humans, adds to their divine dimension that of earthly nature, although this contradicts gods as creators.

Since in antiquity myth is mostly created based on certain driving forces, on which natural phenomena are then explained, including those of relevant social and living importance, the myth of Dardanus as the founder of Troy and Illyrius as founder of the Illyrian lands, with a serpent's skin as sign of protection from numerous evils was so much to the liking of the ancient Greeks that they identified themselves with it. Here the explanation as to why they acquired the Pelasgian faith, deities, idols, and all seen of divine grace may be found, while this acquisition was accompanied also by stripping the Pelasgians of this heritage, although it

---

[298] *Appian*, Greek historian, was born in Alexandria of Egypt by the end of the first century AD and lived up to the 70s of the second century AD. Appian wrote the History of Rome in 24 books. It contains valuable information on the Illyrians, their geographical extension, and their history as seen by the Greeks and Romans.

[299] Appian, *"Historia romana,"* 4 Illyrice, 1, p. 250.

continued to be recognized by ancient authors, especially by Homer and Hesiod.

In line with this it was necessary to reverse the legend, that of their origin from cyclop Polyphemus, who fought against the gods, leading the famous uprising of the giants that would end after a fierce battle in which Zeus used all the power of the gods of heaven to defeat the rebelling earthly beings. So, the people of the Illyrians, and what would be seen as Illyria, had to stay as "barbarians" - foreigners, not only in a spiritual, but also in a social and political sense, as would be seen in their future behavior.

This dual lens of the Pelasgians and their ancestors by the Greeks: immortal and mortal, divine and earthly, seemed to have forged their stance on considering immortal those who came out of gods, that is, Dardanians, and those coming from people, such as Illyrius (from father-man Cadmus) and his many offspring as mortals, in a way as to preserve for Dardanus a special place in the eternal memory (Troy and its immortal war), while giving to Illyrius and Illyria, scattered in the neighborhood, a place among the foreigners, i.e. barbarians, with whom spiritual and social connections were excluded.

This dual assertion did not reduce the weight of what the descendants of the Pelasgians, Illyrians had as a tribal community with royalty in constant motion, with whom the Greeks would have constant friction and even wars, since they had a wide spatial expansion, among the largest of the time, and according to Herodotus, possessed the major rivers and estuaries with important mountains of the continent, from where they scrutinized over the knots of main rivers and mountains,[300] and controlled the crossing of the seas (the Ionian and Adriatic) as well as the space in the interior of the Balkans to the northern parts of Europe, as Strabo testified,[301] as did other authors, dealing with ancient history and geography, a stretch among the largest of antiquity, which later would drive many important scientists of the 19th century, to call this Indo-European pan-Illyrism,[302] an enforced thesis.

---

[300] See Herodotus: *"Historiae,"* Book IV, 48.
[301] See Strabo: *"Gjeografia,"* pp. 150-164.
[302] For more see: Mayer, Anton: *"Die Sprache der alten Ilyrier,"* Vienna, 1959; Krahe, Hans: *"Der Anteil der illyrire an der indogremanisierung Europas," "Welt als Geschichte,"* 6/1940, p. 70; Robert Heien – Geldern: *"Das Tocharenproblem und die pontische Wanderung," "Saeculm,"* 2/1951, pp. 233-248.

Historically, both the Pelasgic antiquity connected with the divine people, and their geographical scope in three continents simultaneously (Europe, Asia Minor and north of Africa) highlight the position of Illyricum as a common ethnogeograhic concept,[303] that included numerous Illyrian tribes (over fifty of them), called by Strabo "Illyrian peoples,"[304] extending from the northwest to the central part of the Balkan Peninsula and further in other directions to Asia Minor and beyond. He simultaneously and rightly opened the dilemma of such a configuration among the greatest of any time off any internal social and political structuring, more so considering the fact that they had their own economy, traded with others, especially the Romans, who sold to them a particular kind of wine they kept in barrels and traded it with various products, including slaves.[305] Even what might be called ethno geography becomes unstable, as attributed to the descendants of the Pelasgians, Dardanians, Illyrians, and other numerous tribes connected to each other, scattered and mixed with others, in long term periods, such as centuries, without a social and political component.

In fact this issue opens the dilemmas that turn the attention away from "only" and leading factors of antiquity: Greeks and Romans, to the "others," mainly Pelasgians and their descendants from the large Illyrian family and its Dardanian branch, seen only callously as "followers" even though they were active historical players in all the stages of social and political developments. This applies not only to the Pelasgians and their wide heritage, but also to other European factors: the Thracians, whose kinship with the Pelasgians cannot be denied, regardless of what kinds of links they were – an issue that deserves special and comprehensive treatment – and the same with the Celts, Balts without excluding those that, however peripheral, have a stake in history.

Viewed from this perspective one can say that Illyricum as an ethno geographic concept deliberately circumvented and later violently and en block ruled out the social and political factor rivaling that of Greeks and Romans, the kingdom of Molossians, and the Illyrian, Macedonian, Dardanian, Taulantii, Dalmatian and many other kingdoms from this family, who were present at that historical development even before the

---

[303] See: Mirdita, Zef: *"Studime dardane,"* Prishtina, 1979; Stipcevic, Aleksandar: *"Ilirët – historia, jeta, kultura,"* Prishtina, 1980.
[304] See Strabo: "Gjeografia," Book V, 1.
[305] Ibid, Book V, 1.

Greeks and Romans, continuing to remain so even during the classical Hellenism to be lost after long wars of occupation of the Romans against them, but continuing nevertheless, as entities in the new circumstances, with some exceptions, to develop certain social and political identities, such as those during the Roman Empire and especially during the Byzantine period, when they acquired state subjectivity within the imperial subjectivity.

Before the complete fall of their social and political structures (kingdoms and states), which does not mean an end of their ethnos – as it was present in distinct forms, trying to oppose both the invasion and later assimilation even in adapting as a form of survival in certain circumstances, as they did under Rome and Byzantium – however there was a time of over three centuries (from the sixth to the third century) when the Pelasgians and their descendants, primarily Dardanians, Molossians, Macedonians, Illyrians, Taulantii, and others, even though seen as scattered, appear as socially and politically organized. First they appeared as tribes led by kings, and later as powerful kingdoms, like those of Pyrrhus, Monune, Teuta, Gentius, and others up to the Dardanian Baton, without excluding the Macedonian kingdom. The latter rose over the rest from the 4th-2nd centuries and as known at the time of Alexander the Great achieved world fame, which as such remained connected with the Pelasgic root and rightly seen as part of the Illyrian family.

The fact that neither Alexander the Great nor the rest of his family, ever denied their Macedonian origin, but always stated it with pride, makes them different from their origin, which did not take away their being labeled as barbarians even when appropriated by the Greeks.

Here, again ancient sources come to the rescue, from the well-known Greek and later Roman authors, who even when it seemed they were being looked at frigidly, they appeared as an ethnic and social identity, although as noted it was ignored repeatedly, at least since the time of the tyrant of Athens, Pisistratus. Homer here is the most open and insurmountable not only for the information provided about the Pelasgian kings of Hellada, who continued to govern their tribes in their own way, but also for the viewing of their active role in the Trojan War, defending it, but also on the Hellenic side, in which among the participating kings (Hippothous, Peleus), he said about the first:

> Hippothous led the tribes of Pelasgian spearsmen,
> who dwelt in fertile Larissa-

Hippothous, and Pylaeus of the race of Mars,
two sons of the Pelasgian LeTherefore, son of Teutamus…[306]

Pelasgian kings and their forces, in addition to the Trojan War, appeared and even interfered in subsequent developments dealing with the return of Odysseus to Ithaca, by roads leading him through Pelasgian lands, namely by the Thesprotian king, Pheidon, "noble hero,"[307] where he was well received and accompanied to Dodona, as he "had gone to Dodona, to hear the will of Zeus/ from the high-crested oak of the god/ even how he might return to the rich land of Ithaca/ after so long an absence, whether openly or in secret."[308]

The well-known ancient Greek and later Roman authors, such as Herodotus, Thucydides, Isocrates, Demosthenes, Scylax, Aristotle, Pliny, Strabo, Ptolemy, Diodorius, and others quite accurately described the presence of Pelasgic tribes led by their kings within Hellada, where besides their involvement in domestic social development, without excluding the long rivalries and wars, such as those between Sparta and Athens or the Peloponnese, they were seen to preserve their independent social fabric, although it is not mentioned but rather implied. Herodotus, in addition, reflected the spiritual life of the Pelasgians, being associated with Dodona, the most important temple, admittedly founded by Zeus, where the Greeks would also turn to him with reverence. Herodotus, was among the first to recognize the Pelasgic language, which he says he did not know what it was, but that it was a barbaric language, meaning it was not Greek,[309] by which he acknowledged the power of its influence over the settlers, which would continue for a long time to come, even when the Hellenes did their best to assimilate them even without shying away from the use of repressive measures.

Besides these data, Herodotus finds also some of ethnic nature, dealing with the extension of the Pelasgians beyond Hellada, giving a significant geographical definition, as in addition to the Pelasgians also Thrace and Thracians are mentioned, as living next to them.[310]

---

[306] Homer: *"Ilias" (Iliada)*, Tirana, 1979, Book II/840.
[307] Homer: *"Odyssea" (Odisea)*, Tirana, 1979, Book XIV/315.
[308] Ibid, Book XIX/270.
[309] Herodotus: *"Historitë,"* Book I/57, 58, cited according to *"Ilirët dhe Iliria te autorët antikë,"* Prishtina, 1979, p. 16.
[310] Ibid, p. 17.

In his "History," Thucydides accepted the Pelasgian organized factor from a social point of view in tribes-kingdoms, even in a selective way, where among the first to be mentioned are Enchelei and Taulantii involved in the famous Peloponnesian War in 429 and in the civil war of Epidamnos in the year 436. The Enchelei were on the side of the Lyncestis against Perdiccas II of Macedonia, where, thanks to the bravery of the Enchelei, Macedonians abandoned their ally, Brasidas and ran away from the battlefield in chaos.[311]

Based on what Thucydides tells us, Taulantii, Enchelei, and others that he calls "barbarians" were involved in important events of Hellada, such as the Peloponnesian War, and the long wars between Athens and Sparta, and were not only "brave warriors," they also represented an organized military force "with thousands of fighters," who also continued to monitor the seas through their mobile fleet, a feature that will also distinguish other Illyrian coastal kingdoms (of Teuta and Agron), which opens the possibility of being in an internal Pelasgian-Hellenic, which might have existed for a good time, but which was never formally admitted by the Greeks as this would undermine the concept of Hellenism as their own property. It would be unnatural to speak of independent Pelasgian tribes and kingdoms within Hellada out of a social and political agreement, which are often seen as being decisive for the fate of the war. Resolving this issue would certainly reveal the antiquity in quite a different light being close to the realities of the time.

However, the indication that in certain circumstances there could have been an internal social and political connection between the Pelasgian-Illyrians and Hellenes is also supported by the famous Isocrates of Athens in his lectures (Orationes) when talking about the organizational and fighting strength of the Illyrians in their long wars with Macedonians, emphasizing the fact that Philip failed to subdue Perrhaebi and Paiones preventing him from becoming the lord of the largest part of Illyrian lands, except for those on the Adriatic coast.[312]

A significant factorization of the Illyrian kings in several events dealing with the fate of Greece, was described by Demosthenes as well as they resisted Philip's campaign to demolish Athens's democracy, while they

---

[311] Thucydides: "Historitë," Book I, II and IV, cited according to *"Ilirët dhe Iliria te autorët antikë,"* Prishtina, 1979, pp. 28-30.

[312] Isocrates: *"Ligjerata"* (Orationes), 5 Philip/19-21, cited according to *"Ilirët dhe Iliria te autorët antikë,"* Prishtina, p. 31.

bragged about it. Here, according to the famous orator, they appeared as defenders of freedom, since they did not surrender to Philip. Here is what the great orator of Athens said about them, presenting simultaneously an assessment about their attitude towards the social and spiritual values among the most important of antiquity: "As regards Paiones, Illyrians, and all their neighbors it is generally believed that for them it is more satisfying to be independent and free than subjugated. They are people not accustomed to obey..."[313]

This is another argument of a certain social and political consciousness of the Illyrians coinciding with that of Hellenes not only from the perspective of some kind of neighborhood, but of internal links, given that a number of philosophers and thinkers of the period, among them Aristotle, tutor of Alexander the Great, came from the Pelasgic world, supposedly like Pythagoras and a few others.

The free condition of the Pelasgian tribes (kingdoms) in the interior part of Greece and its neighborhood, especially to the West, namely the Epirus and the Adriatic coast, had been also nicely described by Scylax.[314] This is also confirmed by numerous other authors of antiquity, recognizing it as a natural extension going into three directions: to the West (on both sides of the Adriatic) up to the Alps, towards the center (the valleys of Vardar and Morava rivers to the Danube) usually seen as places where Dardanians and their tribes settled, and to the East in Thessaly, Pont (Bulgaria) and further to Anatolia.

It is no accident that centuries later, the broad spatial extent of the Pelasgians and their descendants from northern Europe, through Central Balkans, across the Mediterranean and to Asia Minor, would be seen as an Illyrian ethno geography, regardless of the fact that everything turned into a social, cultural and even political misunderstanding, being minimized

---

[313] Demosthenes: *"Ligjerata"* (Orationes) - *"Filipiket,"* I/12, cited according to *"Ilirët dhe Iliria te autorët antikë,"* Prishtina, 1979, p. 33.

[314] Scylax is a Greek traveler, geographer, and historian from Carianda of Caria who lived approx. 4th-5th century BC. By the end of the sixth century by order of Darius I of Persia, he undertook a research trip in India and on the shores of the Indian Ocean. The work entitled *"Periplus tes thellases tes eikumenes Europes kai Azias kai Libyes"* (Sailing the rivers of Europe, Asia and Africa) is connected with the name of this geographer. In fact, this work is not his but of a later author accustomed to being called Pseudo Scylax to distinguish him from the Cariandes Scylax. The work is a description of the geographic regions with much interest on the Illyrian coastal provinces.

even when participating in the great events of the time and playing an important role in them, while being excluded as they continued to stay independent or were involved in outside conflicts with others (Greeks, Romans, Celts).

However, Scylax' records about the geographic extent of the Illyrian tribes in a broad sense, even to an unrelated domestic social and political ethnos, though it has been proven by their internal alliances as well as by their tribal links with Illyrian federation, such as the Alliance (coini) of Molossians 360-444, Epirotan Alliance (cymatia) of 297-272, and the Second Epirotan Alliance of 234, which was dealt with later,[315] have a special meaning as they complement a piece of the important mosaic of this ethnicity, such as that of the West with the Ionian and Adriatic coast, implying the importance of the Pelasgians and their descendant tribal-kingdoms influencing all developments, which, as noted, was crucial to antiquity.

From this aspect, Scylax' notes weigh heavy as they show the interrelationship of these factors into an internal wholeness, although attempts were made to ignore or even silence them trying to leave them offline and out of the historical flow. Therefore, he speaks of *Istrians*, who oversaw the entire area around the river Ister, which flows into Point (Black Sea), then Liburnians, with its coastal city of Idasa, which supposedly belonged to the Athienitis, subject to women's power, that is, maternity, which was a distinguished trait of the Pelasgians, compared to the Greeks who were subject to paternity. He says that two days were needed for navigation over the lands of Liburnia.[316]

It is interesting to note that to these geographic descriptions of nature Scylax relates those that have to do with social and cultural character of older inhabitants, who, despite being "detached," have an overall impact on the Hellenistic society. Therefore, describing the other Illyrian tribes along the coast to the island of Corcyra (Corfu) and Alcinous, he speaks of "the barbarian peoples" Hierastamnes, Bulines, and Hyllos, whose origins he connects with Hyllos, son of Heraclius. This interconnection then proceeds to the land of *Manyetes*, whom he calls an Illyrian tribe on the lands located adjacent to the *Autariatae*, another Illyrian tribe, whose scope goes to that of the *Enchelei*, adjacent to Rizon, three days' walk from there toward the south to Epidamnus, through a road which then increas-

---

[315] For more see: *"Historia e Popullit Shqiptar,"* Tirana, 2002, pp. 89-104.
[316] Scylax: *"Periplus,"* Istroi, Libyrnoi, 20-21.

ingly leads toward the South, including internal parts of the Athinienitis, over Orichya and Caonia, leading to Dodona, where the Ceraunes Mountains appear as Epirus.[317] From there, throughout the Orichya lands descriptions of the Ionian Strait towards the Yapugia Cape to reach *Caonia,* this important Illyrian tribe, related to Thesprotians who possessed the Elaia port, where River Acheron flows. After Casopia came the well-known tribe of Epirotan *Molossians,* with a small portion of their land reaching the sea. Descriptions end with Ambracia stating that Hellada starts there,[318] meaning where Illyria ends.

Illyrians, Epirotes, Macedonians, and Etruscans (Tyrrheneans)

> *For the ancient Greeks, Illyrians were descendants of the Pelasgians, while Epirotes, Macedonians, and the rest were part of the large Illyrian family. - Ancient authors called the "barbarians" by provincial names (Epirotes, Macedonians, Leleges, etc.) while ethnically and spiritually they saw them as common because they spoke the same language and worshipped the same deities. - Strabo saw the Macedonians as non-Greeks, namely barbarian, while in the broader sense he equated the Illyrians with Pelasgians. - Etruscans of Italy and their interconnection with Dardanians, who after losing the Trojan War some of their tribes (Galabres and Thunates) migrated to Italy, where Rome was established.*

The beginning of Hellada, according to Scylax, implying also the end of what is called Illyria by the Hellenes, opens the question of the attitude of the Greeks towards the Pelasgians and their legacy not only on a geographic plain, but also on a social and political one, a stance that implicates them in almost all of their important developments, regardless of the degree to which it is accepted. However, this does not prevent the historical appearance of the Pelasgians and their descendants from becoming its actors from early antiquity onwards.

This historical view of the Pelasgians has two internal analyses. An early one suggests that when the Greeks came to Hellada following the

---

[317] Ibid, 27.
[318] Ibid, 30-33.

Doric immigration (anywhere from 12th century B.C.), they found there the "divine Pelasgians" and Hellenism from the earliest to the classic. The Greeks, after having learned from the Pelasgians all that they had (faith, idols, deities, without excluding the possibility of the script that that they had from the Phoenicians, who were a branch of the Pelasgians),[319] turned to their own well-known social, political and cultural development, among the most important ones of antiquity, while the remains of the Pelasgians, with the exception of Dardanians and Macedonians, were called Illyrians (Illyrian peoples).[320] Their space, Illyria, however, had been distinctly tampered with, since the Illyrians were mentioned only when in an external relation to the Greeks and in no way in any reflected within them internally, from where some kind of truth about them could be drawn. Even this would suffice for the truth about a pre-Hellene people having emerged whom they met there and who served them in the construction of their historical frame.

Despite this approach, which can be labeled as documentary from a direct source, remaining inevitable and among the most important ones, from a different and deeper angle, the mythical image of the Pelasgians and their origin is self-asserting showing them as "heavenly people," by which their spiritual and cultural supremacy was recognized when encountered by the Hellenes upon their immediate arrival to the Pelasgic lands from where they received many of their values, helping them to move further. This observation contains Troy and Dardania, but also the civilizations of Crete and Mycenae, as a basic focus of antiquity, which although denied of Pelasgic authorship, by accepting the so-called "pre-Hellenic" or "paleo-European" stratification, was placed in relation to pre-Greeks, being admittedly Pelasgians, and likewise also acknowledging that Troy was Dardanian. The Dardanian foundation, according to legend is connected to Dardanus, son of Zeus and Goddess Electra, from where the mythological imagination turned them immortal. However, even without this version of the myth, Dardanians and other Dardanian tribes are seen at the center of historical truth, as active agents in developments arising from the rise of Troy to its final fall and their fate associated with it.

But if Dardanus, the founder of Troy, in Greek memory remained permanent and honored not only by the works of Homer, being divine

---

[319] For more see: Diodorus: *Vepra III*, Chp. 66, p. 257; Johan Georg von Hahn: *"Studime Shqiptare,"* Tirana, 2009, p. 396.
[320] See Strabo: *"Gjeografia,"* Book V/1

and as such immortal and untouchable, this does not apply to the descendants of Illyrius (Ilios), first king of the Illyrian lands, called Illyrians and their land Illyria. Since he came from *king-man,* ancient Cadmus, who although brought knowledge and script from Phoenicia, from here Greek civilization supposedly originated with what would appear in the world as Hellenism, his legacy (Illyrians and Illyria) could not be conceived as Hellenes nor their eternal honor kept as the Dardanians of Troy had as "divine Pelasgians."

Here and with this issue, the *father-king* (Cadmus of Phoenicia), missionary who brought knowledge, culture and script to the Greeks, and the *son-king* (Ilios of Illyria), barbarian and foreign in the "neighborhood," things seem to fall in place by actually opening the possibility for history to release facts from the midst of mythology to give them their true place and appearance. In other words, in those times *father-king kings* and *kings-kingdoms* could be of the same blood linkage and the same place, meaning also that Cadmus (*father-king*) and Illyrius (*son-king*) may have been in Phoenicia or in Illyria and in no way on one side and the other, more so when those countries were divided by a major sea and two opposite worlds.

So, here history, different from mythology, is based on evidence, and as even evidence coming from the ancient Greeks confirming Illyrians and Illyria at a particular time and place (Hellada and the wide European space) even before the Greeks came, it is closer to truth that Cadmus, even as a Phoenician, seen in a fashion as to deny the Pelasgian sons, Illyrians, of earthly kingdom, presupposes their common link, extending far beyond the sea, the same as it extended to Crete and possibly reaching as far as North Africa. With the natural division between mythology and history coming from antiquity, also the beginnings of the historical coverage of Pelasgians by the Greeks and their historical appearance come to us, mostly through their dioptry, not only because these are the first and only testimonies from ancient Greek authors, but even their appearance in history depends entirely on their relations with them, no matter how they appeared.

Therefore, if mythology and many popular images and forms are left aside, then the Greek stand on the descendants of Pelasgians comes somewhat clearer, seeing them in their near or distant neighborhood as Illyrians (although scattered in tribes and tribal kingdoms). In this generalization Epirotes (Molossians), Dardanians and Macedonians are often exempt. The latter, after being run off by them and after accepting the supremacy of the Greek language as an official language, were seen as Hellenes although they were considered by numerous ancient authors as barbarians, taking them unavoidably back to their Pelasgian root from which they cannot be excluded. And if their political behavior during the classical Hellenization (6th-1st centuries) brought them closer to the Hellenes than to their own kinship with whom they (particularly with Dardanians) engaged in permanent and fierce wars, these wars can be explained as wars of domination within the family, which were inherent in those days, the same as the bloody wars for the throne between brothers. It is historically known that many peoples of the same ethnicity would dissent; on the same basis, various states of the same ethnic group or people sprung up, as happened with the Celtic, Baltic, and Slavic families.

Even without this observation, which should be considered when reviewing internal reports of large families of peoples from antiquity onwards and realities that have emerged from them (different peoples and later nations and numerous states), direct evidence coming from antiquity make it quite clear that the ancient Macedonians, whose Pelasgian root cannot possibly be denied, had very little overlap with social and cultural schemes of Hellenism. While remaining rather within the definition of the divine empire of global scale, the views of the Pelasgians were dealt with as a divine people, with a royal order of events since the first tribal organization and onwards, which Illyrians, Dardanians and other tribes upheld as their state government during all the time until it was destroyed by Roman conquerors. Of this nature was also the project of Alexander the Great, regarding the world empire as a divine view that he had created out of conviction that he was of divine origin coming from his mother, Olympia, an Epirotan, who had entered Zeus' bed in the form of a serpent.

The conviction that they fought for a world empire for which Alexander the Great stood, would also be shared by another Pelasgus, the Molossian Pyrrhus, who not only according to Greek mythology had direct links with Dardanians. It has even been assessed that Epirus in a way would be only a part of compensation for the loss of Troy, which Aeneas, as a Dardanian, after passing through those lands, headed towards southern Italy to establish Troy in the West, as indeed happened with Rome.

Regardless of their implication with the Trojan myth, Dardanians, Macedonians and Epirotes would have special treatment from the known definition of Illyria, involving numerous tribes in the neighborhood of the Greeks and those of others that stretched onwards to other parts of the Central, Northern and Eastern Balkans without excluding those appearing in southern Italy, although Dardanians and sometimes Epirotes were seen as associated with other Illyrian tribes, while the Macedonians were seen as Hellenized "barbarians." Furthermore, since the appearance of Alexander the Great in 338 to the Roman occupation, Macedonians were seen as the leading providers of Hellenism, which has meant that in subsequent centuries the Philhellenes removed all possible doubts that separate Macedonians from the Greeks, as they would exclude any thinking that they could be related to Dardanians and Epirotes because of their common Pelasgian origin. However, this was excluded even when having to do with the evidence of ancient famous authors who continued to treat the Macedonians as barbarians and foreign, though seen within the Greek social concept of Greek and Hellenism in general (of course once they set their military domination over them).

At any rate, the linguistic assimilation of the Macedonian aristocracy and mandatory involvement of Greeks in the campaign of Alexander the Great to create a global empire eastward, where he, defeating powerful empires one by one reached as far as India, did not make them Greeks, as it was supposed, nor deprive them of their Pelasgic origin, as it was desired.

However, it has been assessed that Hellenism as a sudden development of time cleared the way for new insights towards the East and the state concept for which it was fought was of Pelasgian origin. This caused the Macedonians to be seen as Pelasgians, while their conviction of an earthly empire of divine origin, that of a superior kind of *king-man* originated from the gods, in fact, remained in the Illyrian war mentality for greater space and freedom. A political consciousness was reflected in the Molossian Pyrrhus not long after the failure of the project of Alexander the Great in the East, with the only difference being that for this purpose he chose the West, the way Aeneas had made some centuries before, the closest, the most possible, and above all, the most natural one.

However, other evidence primarily historical and linguistic, coming from ancient authors, or later by scholars of comparative linguistics, indicate that the Epirotes were of Pelasgic root, as were the Macedonians, despite what happened before and after the time of Alexander the Great and regardless of the numerous wars that Macedonians waged with the Illyrians, and particularly with Dardanians. They were able to subdue them partially, as during the time of Philip II, but were never able to make them accept Hellenism as their emblem, which appeared as a copy of what the Greeks had taken and appropriated from them, shrinking them to a narrow space and for narrow interests. Even wars and constant disagreements of Dardanians against the Macedonians, in which, at some point Dardanians did not hesitate to enter into an alliance with the Romans against them, as previously stated, should be understood as part of an internal rivalry and an inherent competition in order to restore the glory and power of Troy. This restoration of Troy for Dardanians was most likely possible and natural to be done with the help of the Romans, who shared Trojan blood and had fled from there after being treacherously defeated (through devising the Trojan Horse), rather than with the Hellenes, who for them were different and even destroyers of Troy.

Despite hypothetical observations aiming to restore something of the appearance of a beautiful and rather blurred historic landscape, even here, as in other cases, the key word would fall on the old ancient authors, as their evidence, although in many cases fragmented and contradictory, is more deserving because through it many of the facts are related to historical developments from where the following positions are also derived:

- That the Epirotes and Macedonians even in Strabo's time[321] were non-Greeks or barbarians;
- That Epirotes, Macedonians, and Illyrians were related;
- That there are numerous signs that Epirotes and Macedonians made up the core of Tyrrhenian-Pelasgians, from where suppos-

---

[321] Strabo, a great Greek geographer and historian, was born in Pontus approx. 63 BC and died in around 20 AD. Strabo spent a part of his life in Rome, and the rest making trips to different countries of the Roman Empire, Greece, Asia, Italy, and Egypt. Based on his personal observations from this trip, and in particular by relying on the works of different ancient authors, Strabo wrote his "Geography" in 17 books. Strabo's "Geography" has a paramount importance and is a valuable source for Illyrian geography and history. The issue of mixing of the Celts, which the prominent geographer mentions, probably has to do with the remains of Celts, who after penetrating from the north and down to the Aegean, mostly afflicting Dardanian lands and Dardanians, after suffering defeat from the Greek and Macedonian forces, were drawn again to the valley of Vardar, Morava up to the Danube, with some of them remaining in the East, in the section between the Thracians and Dardanians.

edly the most extreme remote tribes of this people played a role in the history of Italy and Thrace;
- That the Illyrians were in a wide sense equal to Pelasgians, as were the Dardanians as well, appearing as a separate branch of the trunk.[322]

Regarding the first question, which still remains open and with many disagreements as to from where various stances stemmed, Strabo explains that the southern peoples were "both the Illyrian and the Thracian tribes, and all tribes of the Celtic or other peoples that were mingled with these, as far as Greece, were to the south of the Ister."[323]

This description in some way responds to the picture of the time of shared Balkan space in its central and eastern part between the Illyrians and Thracians, with the only difference being that the Thracians could be adjacent to the Illyrians in the northeast, but not the Hellenes. This correlation (Thracians adjacent to Hellenes) was made impossible because of the configuration of Dardanians in the East completely covering the strip between them, which as seen, was also refuted by following the description of the eastern part, saying that "the remainder of Europe consisted of the country which was between the Ister and the encircling sea, beginning at the recess of the Adriatic and extending as far as the Sacred Mouth of the Ister.

In this country are Greece and the tribes of the Macedonians and the Epirotes, and all those tribes above them whose countries reach to the Ister and to the seas on either side, both the Adriatic and the Pontic. To the Adriatic were the Illyrian tribes, and to the other sea as far as the Propontis and the Hellespont, the Thracian tribes and whatever Scythian or Celtic tribes were intermingled with them."[324]

Despite these mistakes, which are natural in the light of accurate information and their arrangement, it appears that Strabo divided the whole peninsula south of the Danube into three parts:
 a) Hellada in the South,
 b) Illyria in the West, and
 c) Thrace in the East.

---

[322] Johan Georg von Hahn: *"Studime shqiptare,"* Tirana, 2009, p. 291.
[323] Strabo: *"Gjeografia,"* Book VII, Chapter I.
[324] Ibid, Chapter V.

But he did not think Hellada was entirely inhabited by Greeks, because in its northern provinces non-Greek, i.e. barbarian, tribes lived, namely Epirotes in the West and Macedonians in the East.[325]

This definition of the well-known geographer is of importance since, as seen, he separates Epirotes entirely from the Greeks, saying "if we enter the Ambracian Gulf we'll find Acarnanians to the right, who are Greeks, *Cassiopeians* to the left, who are Epirotes... Our description in the north and west of the peninsula ends with Epirotan and Illyrian tribes, in the east with the peoples of Macedonia, stretching up to Byzantium, where after Epirotes and Illyrians, were Greek tribes of Acarnanians, Aetolians, Dryopes, Caucones, etc."[326]

For Strabo, the *Amphilochians* are Epirotes; and so are the peoples who are situated above them and border on the Illyrian mountains, inhabiting a rugged country... the *Molossian*, the *Athamanes*, the *Aethices*, the *Tymphaei*, the *Orestae*, and also the *Paroraei* and the *Atintanes*, who lived as far as the wilds in the highlands of Illyria, who, besides separating them from the Greeks, naturally connected them with Macedonia and Macedonians with whom they built a joint power. The population of the provinces of Lyncus, Pelagonia, Orestias, and Elimeia, were called Upper Macedonia, though later on some also called them Free Macedonia. In these parts people spoke two languages: their native Illyrian and Greek.[327]

According to this evidence, the following peoples living in Epirus and Macedonia shared the same kinship or were Epirotes: *Chaonians, Thesprotians, Cassiopeians, Amphilochians, Molossi, Athamanes, Aethices, Tymphaei, Orestae, Paroraei, Atintanes* (Illyrian *Bylliones, Taulanti, Parthini,* and *Bryges*), then *Perisiadiei, Encheleans* and *Sesarians*.

Along with the above ones, came six main tribes of Macedonia to the east of Pindus: *Lyncestae, Dryopes, Pelagones, Eordi, Elimiotes* and *Eratyres*, being in kinship.[328]

In regard to the Epirotes, Thucydides too shares the same opinion as Strabo. When speaking of an unfortunate expedition of Lacedaemonians, Ambracians and Chaones against the army of Acarnanians he says:

"With the commander of Lacedaemonians, Cremus, the accompanying Hellenic troops consisted of the Ambraciots, Leucadians, and Anacto-

---

[325] Johan Georg von Hahn: "*Studime shqiptare,*" Tirana, 2009, p. 292.
[326] Ibid, p. 292.
[327] Ibid, p. 294.
[328] Ibid, p. 294.

rians, and the thousand Peloponnesians that came with him; from the barbarians, a thousand Chaonians… with the Chaonians to war also came some Thesprotians… Molossians and Atintanians led by Sabylin, the guardian of King Tharyps."[329]

In this part, Thucydides calls barbarians the main peoples of Epirus proper and the thousand Macedonians sent by King Perdiccas he does not count among the Greeks.[330]

As seen from the data coming from Strabo, Thucydides and other ancient, early and late authors, it appears that Epirotes and Macedonians, two of the most powerful nations that lay to the north and west of Greeks, that is, the whole Epirus and parts that go east to the Pelagonia Vardar and up to Pindus appeared not to be Greek or of Greek root, but they also do not appear related to the Illyrian tribes there, as was the case with the Dardanians, who, concentrated in the Central Balkans (from the Sharr Mountains, Drin and Morava Valleys and north to Asia Minor), appeared also distinct from the Illyrians, leaving the impression that there were three different non-Greek entities.

Indeed, as indicated also by the important ancient authors, and as can be seen from further historical developments, these peoples (Illyrians, Dardanians, Epirotes and Macedonians), who nevertheless Strabo calls "Illyrian peoples,"[331] comprised of numerous tribes often so mixed that they sometimes appeared on either side,[332] shared the same ethnographic link (language and customs), leading to the judgment that Epirotes and Macedonians were related and formed a separate branch of the great Illyrian people, which applies also to Dardanians, adjacent to them and lying in the central part of the peninsula, which above all had common Pelasgic roots.

The common Pelasgian root of these important tribes that bind but also divide the Pelasgic world with the Hellenic one is also confirmed by

---

[329] Tukidid: "*Historitë*," Book IV/126, cited according to "*Ilirët dhe Iliria te autorët antikë,*" Prishtina, 1979, p. 29.

[330] Ibid, p. 30.

[331] Strabo: "*Gjeografia,*" Book V/1.

[332] Strabo calls the Antinates Epirotes, while Scylax and Appion write of them as being Illyrians (See: Scylax, p. 10; *Appion bell Llyrer* 7). According to both Strabo and Appian, Dardanians are Illyrians, but Dio Cassius writes that they belong to Maesi, (see: *Dio Cassius* VII, p. 495), and the same goes for Poeint and Bryga called alternately Illyrians and Thracians.

Strabo, who sees in this node a special role of Epirotes and Epirus as a significant space.[333]

Therefore, the famous geographer, knowing the ethnic realities and also the past, after stating that the Pelasgians, as an old tribe were spread throughout Hellada, and after making it known that this expansion included Crete as well, the center of old civilization, confirmed that Thessaly, located between the Peneus Gorge and Thermopyles and extending to the Pindus mountains, was called *Pelasgic Argos*,[334] saying that Pelasgians overruled. The poet (Homer) called Pelasgic the Zeus of Dodona "Sublime Pelasgian Zeus of Dodona," while many old authors called the Epirotan tribes Pelasgian, as they reached as far as there (Epirus).[335]

Furthermore, the famous geographer (to prove geography as not only being a factor) turned to historical sources from antiquity, quoting Homer, Hesiod, Aeschylus but also Erphorius and others who recognized the antiquity of the Pelasgians, but also their legacy expressed through a wide extension of tribes and cities, among which Athens is also mentioned as their center. Even its founder was considered to be the Pelasgian King Mole, who they claim came from Regis-Villa (South Italy), where he had his center, but had crossed the sea with his tribe to settle forever in Hellada.[336]

The seed of the Pelasgians and their descendants in a geographical connection to southern Italy and in a continuous movement from one side to another, sometimes seems "confusing," however, it has to do with the truth that the Pelasgians, not that they moved there or thereafter, as Strabo says, but because they stretched over the entire Mediterranean and Aegean space even before the Greeks came to be embedded in Greece. This fact they did not know. When they learned about it later, it is natural that they created their own various stories about the movement. Furthermore, in accordance with this, it is likely that the familiar crossing of a part of the Dardanians to Italy, after losing the Trojan War, as interpreted by Homer, Virgil and other authors, as Aeneas' wish to redress the loss of Troy somewhere in the West. This must have been but a natural shift of that that part of Dardanians in the western part, namely southern Italy,

---

[333] Strabo: *"Gjeografia,"* Book V, Chapter 2, p. 221.
[334] Strabo: *"Gjeografia,"* Book V/7-8.
[335] Ibid, Book V/7.
[336] Ibid, Book V/8.

where their grandparents Pelasgians were extended, the same as they were extended in other parts of the Mediterranean and further in Asia Minor and up to North Africa. The "puzzle" of the Etruscans and the issue of Venetians "descending" from the north, are nothing but a part of the known prehistoric Pelasgic Paleo-European configuration, on which the later-date Pan-European theory of lyricism was based reaching as far as to address them as "Classical Indo-Europeans."[337]

Despite this assessment, which preoccupied many scholars who already understood that the "wandering" of the descendants of the Pelasgians from one shore to anther of the Sea (from the Ion to the western Adriatic), as ancient authors saw it, was no more than a natural movement from one place to another, where they lay. Even Stephen of Byzantium speaks of the *Pelasgic Epirus*, from where their "crossing over" to Italy began and vice versa, among whom the most famous was that of Pyrrhus Molosses in order to extend his kingdom to that part which he considered belonging to him, dividing it into two parts: Upper and Lower Pelasgum.[338] For Byzantium both these parts have preserved their authentic ethnic character, with the only difference being that the Upper grips also a part of Macedonians and some Illyrian tribes, which also relate to the old Pelasgic core, but that the circumstances made them socially and politically different. This applies especially to the Macedonians, who led away the idea of Hellenism, but without returning to Hellenes.

Even the region where the temple of Dodona built by the Pelasgians used to be was called Pelasgia.[339] This was also shown by Herodotus in writing that this place, called Hellada at his time, belonged to Thesprotia of the well-known Thesprotians, whose kingdom was counted among the

---

[337] For more on Illyrians as classical Indo-Europeans see: Budimir Milan: "*Iliri i prailiri,*" 1952.

[338] Stefan Byzantine: "*Urbibus et Populis*" (On cities and peoples), cited according to "*Ilirët dhe Iliria te autorët antikë,*" Prishtina, 1979, p. 417. Distinguished lexicographer originating from Costantinople (lived in the 4th century AD), is the author of a large geographical vocabulary titled "*Ethinka.*" Stefan Byzantine's lexicon is important for the history of Illyria as he informs us not only of the many cities and tribes of Illyria and Epirus known from other older publications, but also of cities not met in any of the preserved works of the past. Also of interest are certain names of Illyrian tribes, not mentioned before, located in what he calls Pelasgic Epirotan.

[339] Homer: "*Iliada,*" Book XVI, 254; Strabo: "*Gjeografia,*" Book VII, 5, p. 327; Skymnos, v. 450.

first and oldest of Pelasgia.[340] This is also evidenced by traditions that Plutarch relayed when talking of Pyrrhus, stating that "after the great downfall he ruled over the Thesprotians, among the oldest of those who came to this country together with Pelasgus."[341]

The kinship between the Epirotans of the East and those of the West is also testified by what Apollodorus says that Thesprot and Macedon were sons of Lycaones from Arcadia, who was son of Pelasgus,[342] and according to Stephen Byzantium, Atintan was the son of Macedon.[343] These different testimonies of antiquity, allow the conclusion to be drawn that Macedonians were Pelasgian. Among those testimonies, that of Aeschylus is very meaningful when he says that entire Macedonia is within the borders of the Argives. He brings forth the testimony of their king saying:

"I am Pelasgus, Palecton's son, this country's king, of me, of the king, the people was named, who toils this country's lands and all the regions along Axios (Vardar) and Strymon from the west. My Kingdom includes the land of Perebeii, Provinces of Pindus, Peoni, Highland of Dodona and the border ends at the sea. Even beyond my kingdom stretches, but this country is called Appia."[344]

Justin too calls the various tribes of old Macedonia or Emathia Pelasgian,[345] and, according to Ellianos, the father of Pelasgian tribes Lycaon was the king of Emathia.[346] According to Aristotle even the Boetians, who came from Athena (the main place of the Pelasgians) and Crete (Homer writes that Pelasgians were there too) while passing through Delphi and Japudia sang *"we've come from Athena."*[347]

So, wandering through the notes of ancient authors is not aimed at highlighting what the well-known lexicon of Stephen Byzantium fifteen

---

[340] Herodotus: "Historia," Book II/56, cited according to Johan Georg von Hahn: "*Studime shqiptare,*" Tirana, 2009, p. 16.

[341] Herodotus: *"Pyrrhus,"* p. 1.

[342] Apollodorus, III, pp. 8, 1.

[343] Eskili (Aeskylos), Verse 249.

[344] Ibid.

[345] Justin, VII 1 (*Macedonia ante, nomine Emathionis regis, Emathia cognominate est. Populus Pelasgi, regia Boetia dicebatur*).

[346] Aeilon, "De natur.anim." X, 48, cited according to Johan Georg von Hahn. "*Studime shqiptare,*" Tirana, 2009, p. 299.

[347] See Strabo: *"Gjeografia,"* Book IV/1.

centuries before presented as an authentic factuality of time, which ranges in depth, five-six other centuries, but rather to reflect the historical realities upon which the ethnicity associated with the Pelasgian root was erected, as can be seen from the biased observations. It appears more complex as its branches lie in a space ethno-geographically connected to Central Europe throughout the Balkans and in Asia Minor, opening up into other parts of the Mediterranean, particularly into Italy, where the most important is what concerns the Etruscans (Tyrrhenians), whose enigma has preoccupied many scientists. The more it seemed unresolved, that ancient people did not show any similarity or brotherhood with the Greeks, Italics, Goths, Balto-Slavs and others, has in fact returned the issue back to the Pelasgians. Exactly Homer claimed in his *Iliad* that the Trojans (mostly Dardanians) crossed the sea landing in Italy to reimburse the lost Troy with something (with Rome), or as this story was sung by Virgil in his *Aeneid*, were literary facts. As noted, this not only revealed the truth of the pan-European alignment of the Pelasgians from prehistory, but also the truth of their expansion into Asia Minor and beyond to the north of Africa.

However, beyond the imagination of Homer, Virgil and other ancient authors, while looking for a permanent place, departed from Troy through land or sea routes and landed in Italy remaining there forever, and reportedly took part in the building of Rome. The virtual journey of the Etruscans in Italy appears with many unknowns including the country from which they moved, directions they took (from north or south), and the pathways through which they passed, to the question of timing, giving this development a special dimension.

Location and time were also followed and continue to be followed with the dilemma of whether or not they were Pelasgians, which would rank them among the Indo-European peoples, as many ancient sources indicate, or were they a separate non-Indo-European people of the east, of which certain circumstances had made them part of the ancient world, where they vanished, leaving behind numerous clues which in many aspects still remain uncovered, but whose key is apparently only in the hands of the Albanians.

As usual in these matters, there are ancient sources that provide information which, though scattered, on the one hand make it clear that the Etruscans, or Tyrrhenians, as they were called by the Latins, had Lydia as their starting point (noting an embankment on the north of River Po, from where they crossed over to the Apennines, and entered into Etruria,)[348] and on the other hand there are those who report of a different journey from the East (the space of Anatolia), from across the sea to land on the Tyrrhenian coast and then spreading to the parts of middle Italy and further in the north.[349]

However, some sources of that time, such as those from Dionysius of Halicarnassus, dealing with the Etruscan autochthony in Italy, whose being, however, was related to Pelasgians, though he confuses it while trying to present them as different people, namely for ancient "natives," who were, nevertheless, called Tyrrhenians by the indigenous tribes, while the "true" Pelasgians had come from Peloponnese, as other ancient authors saw them moving, because they had not yet come to an understanding of the truth of their extension to other parts of the Mediterranean, dominating that space as did "their" Hellada as well.

Therefore, Dionysius says that the Pelasgians who lived in the Peloponnese, Thessaly and other parts, after five generations, were expelled from the Deucalion of Prometheus and Clymene of Oceanus and scattered into the neighboring countries, Crete, the Aegean islands, especially Lesbos, and along the coast from Hellespont from where later, many of them, crossed the Ionian Sea and settled in Italy, in the province of Umbria. They collaborated with indigenous populations to expel the Umbrians, for a time occupying several towns, among them Pisa. In that part they possessed huge expanses of the fertile land of Champagne, where they built several cities, among them one named Larissa excelled, but who was forced by the Tyrrhenians to leave those lands, to exile, whereby some of them returned to from where they came, to Hellada, while the others were assimilated by which Dionysius saw the end of the Pelasgians in Italy.[350]

Even this "difference" between the Pelasgians and Tyrrhenian, which Dionysius admits that the locals called Pelasgians "in memory of the country they left behind and in memory of the old tribe,"[351] although at first this seems ambiguous, in fact, it touches the question of ownership of the seas by some early Pelasgic tribes, who are called masters of the sea

---

[348] For more See: Tacit, Kron (IV, 55), Herodotus (I, 94) and Strabo (V, 220).
[349] For more See: "*Enciklopedia e Madhe Greke*," Vol, 11, p. 687, cited according to Spiro N. Konda "*Shqiptarët dhe problemi pellazgjik*," Tirana, 1964, p. 231.
[350] Dionysus of Halicarnassus "*Historia e vjetër e Romës*," Book I/30
[351] Ibid, I/25.

because they were seen moving their light and fast boats across the Mediterranean, from where the Phoenicians too were rightly seen as one of their branches. Therefore, the possibility of an early branch of Pelasgians located on the coast of Italy and from there called Tyrrhenians by the indigenous population is not excluded, as it does not exclude also the fact that they were all Pelasgian peoples, as would be other "later-date" settlers. These later settlers were Trojans led by Aeneas, whom Virgil and many other authors of antiquity call Dardanians, who succeeded in settling in those parts, where their relatives had already settled, and jointly they were involved in the building of Rome and other developments related to the establishment of the Roman Empire.[352]

Dionysius, like his contemporary Virgil, writes that the loss of the Trojan War was what determined the Trojans' fate who settled in ly,[353] something that makes this literary fact as historically more accessible by reflecting that the fall of Troy is related to the Dorian immigration, resulting in a displacement of numerous peoples in different directions, with, evidently, some of them ending up in Italy, including the Etruscans who during the time of this large movement came from Eastern Mediterranean. They relocated in the sea region of Tuscany, pushing the Umbrians a little from within, while it is not known as to when they organized a confederation of 12 cities forming before the 7th century a powerful hearth of civilization. Then, for two centuries they also took possession of southern Italy, from Campani to River Silaro, therefore becoming lords of Latium. They developed farms, vegetation, arts and civic life all around. After giving Rome a dynasty (Tarquins), in 509, according to tradition, they were expelled by a Latin revolt. So, after much vicissitude, Etruria fell under the Roman rule, and its language quickly disappeared. However, they contributed a lot in establishing this rule, leaving behind a precious legacy in almost all of Italy.[354]

It will be precisely the multiple tracks they left behind all over Italy that raised the "Etruscan riddle" as an issue that affected not only Pelasgians and their Albanian descendants, who despite all the unknowns remain mostly related. Affecting antiquity as well, they still remained in many aspects on the foundations of Roman civilization, in all probability, not by crossing from one shore of the sea to the other, as seen by ancient authors,

---

[352] Virgil: "*Aeneido*" (Eneida), Book III/295.
[353] Ibid, I/62.
[354] Konda, Spiro N: "*Shqiptarët dhe problemi pellazgjik*," Tirana, 1964, p. 235.

and as described in the world epos that Homer, Virgil and others left behind, but because they were the sole and true possessors of those lands since prehistoric times, a fact upon which "different" histories were projected. But in order to resolve this constant puzzle forever, finally, the Etruscan issue, like many others that appear as "confusing" when separated from the Pelasgian wholeness, is being addressed by looking into it within the Pelasgian problem, as its integral part. Here too the starting point is looked for among ancient authors, those linking Etruscans with the Pelasgians. Such authors are: Hellanicus from Lesbos, Sophocles, Thucydides, and Plutarch. So, the Lesbos Hellanicus says that "The Tyrrhenians, who were previously called Pelasgians, after settling in Italy, took the name they have today."[355]

Sophocles says the following in his drama "Inachus:"

O Inachus, parent, son of Ocean,
Offspring Father, powerful king
Of Argus lands and cliffs of Hera
And of Pelasgian Tyrrhenians.[356]

Thucydides mentions regarding this, "cities inhabited by tribes of mixed barbarians who speak two languages, a few Chalcidice, but mostly Pelasgians, from the Tyrrhenians who once lived in Lemnos and Athens."[357]

Plutarch too, in his work *"On the virtues of women"* speaks of the virtues of Tyrrhenian women, claiming Tyrrhenians and Pelasgians are one and the same. However, the Etrurian etymology of the word should be added to this, which according to the philologer Spiro N. Konda, although it concerns the Province of Etruria, originally settled by the Romans and were called *Etrurios-Tuscos*, had to do with the fact that *Tyrrhenians* of Etruria spoke the *Tosk* language,[358] that is, coming from Toskëria, from where also the name of the Italian region Tuscany came. This is justified by the fact that they'd be called as coming from the province of Etruria, and, therefore, in accordance with linguistic laws, they would be called *Thyrrhenos, Etruriso*.[359] Based on this fact and others, Konda defends the

---

[355] Dionysus: Book One, A,XXVIII, 3.
[356] Ibid, Volume One, A. XXV.
[357] Ibid, Book IV, 109.
[358] Konda, Spiro N: *"Shqiptarët dhe problemi pellazgjik,"* Tirana, 1964, p. 241.
[359] Ibid, p. 241.

thesis that the Etruscan language represents the core of the Tosk dialect of the Albanian language, challenging the views of a good part of last century linguists who, although failing to break down many of Etruscan inscriptions in Italy, ignoring the Albanian, rushed into proclaiming Etruscans as a non-Indo-European people, which separated them completely from Pelasgians, who already Aryan people, were considered to be classics of Indo-Europeanism.

Linguistics and linguistic arguments, especially the latest ones relating to aspects of Indo-Europeanism, have, however, started to restore the Etruscans to the bosom of the Indo-European family, where they were rarely seen before, restoring also their Pelasgic origin, being associated with their pan-European expansion since prehistory, where they dominated every corner of the old continent and the Mediterranean, although this issue, for many, continues to stay open, albeit without any signs of their proximity to other peoples (Greeks, Romans, Balto-Slavs, and others). But the return of the Etruscans in a linguistic point of view to the Indo-European family, puts them *in media res* of both "extremes" of their affinities with the "northerners," i.e. the languages of Balto-Slavic peoples, as well as with the "easterners," languages of the Mediterranean-Anatolian peoples, all of this finding support of a pan-European expansion of the Pelasgians, which in accordance with the known historical circumstances and developments has also acquired its own characteristics, which often arise quite naturally from the nucleus frames.

The noted philologist Budimir seems to have managed to reconcile these extremes with his stance that one is dealing here with old pre-Indo-European strata, which was encountered in the space of Central Europe and the Mediterranean to Asia Minor at the Neolithic time, subsequently affecting newcomers.[360] While considering both B. Niehbur's hypothesis, whereby Etruscan, neighbors to Rettes, arrived in Italy came from the northern part of the Danube and the thesis of the Italian Etrurologist, B. Nagora claiming that the Etruscans came from the eastern area of the Carpathians and Pontius,[361] Budimir settles the "compromise" through a pre-Indo-European and, of course, pre-Hellene stratification and, to which necessarily relate Pelasgians and indigenous European peoples with whom they first fell in contact and were assimilated, but always recognizing that they included linguistic elements in their dialect, which then

---

[360] Budimir, Milan: *"Pelasto-slavica,"* Belgrade, 1951, p. 3.
[361] B. Nagora: *"Gli Etruchschi e la loro civita,"* Rome, 1943.

appeared in the form of fossils in different regions, with different developments, but always maintaining the common root of antiquity.

Therefore, Budimir brings numerous linguistic forms connecting the old Etruscans with Balto-Slavic languages, but also with the Mediterranean-Anatolian ones, appearing as paleo-Pelasgian exfoliation, without the treatment of which, at least linguistically, a lot proves distracting and unnatural. Among them are those of a *nomina sacra* nature: *Tin(ia)din; Veltha-Voltumnus-Vertum nus - (V)Lada; Maris-Mavoris; Turms- tulmacu- Adrays- Kandaulas; Gortyn-Cortoni-Grad; Sambas-salpinix-santerna-skadyx; Brilettos-proelium-prylis; Bryllikhis-Brilon-brilec; D(a)maia-Camillus-Kadmos-zemelo-familia-mija; Sapo(i)oi-Imbros-Kimbros-prosapia-seba,* names that can only be explained by the Pelasgian and in accordance with the phonetic and morphological development of the Albanian language, which since antiquity as a whole appears as one of the largest ethno linguistic entities of all times, able to provide answers to "puzzles," such as the Etruscan one and similar.[362]

Obviously such an enigma, coming from the entire ethno linguistic Pelasgic space, shows unequivocally the Basque language and the Basques as well, as a people cornered in the "suburbs" of the West, whose language is very close to the Albanian language today with a similar vocabulary of over two hundred words. However, besides a vocabulary with linguistic affinities between the Albanian and Basque languages, there is the verb in the latter language built from a root by including suffixes and particles including the active, conjunctive, passive of action (plural), as in today's Albanian language. The article is located at the end, as in Albanian, Romanian, Armenian, paleo-Caucasian, and even Berber.[363] In addition, there are visible traces of a vegesimal (base 20) system, which is the rule in paleo-Caucasian and Elamite languages.[364]

As with the case of the Etruscans, the Basques too were advertised as an "offline people" without a clear historical link as they are not mentioned by ancient authors. Not being mentioned by ancient authors represents no difficulty in recognizing their antiquity, as they are Iberians (coming from a subdivision of this ancient people, who were pushed by invasions coming from the East, driven North and finding refuge at the Pyrenees in an obscure era), and as such they are directly entitled to

---

[362] Budimir, Milan: *"Pelasto-slavica,"* Belgrade, 1951.
[363] Afer, Mathieu: "Shqiptarët," Tirana, 2007, p. 565.
[364] Lahovari, Nikolas: *"Popujt evropianë,"* 1946.

receive the treatment of antiquity. Rather, the "troubles" emerged and continue as both Iberians and Ligurians constitute the western branch of the first European populations, related to Pelasgians, being forerunners of the first Neolithic civilizations.

Like the ancient peoples of the Pelasgian trunk: Pelasgians of Arcadia, Leleges of Laconia, Pelasgians of Crete and Cyprus, *Ligures* of southwest Europe, Basques too were drawn in depth, and that due to these surviving withdrawals, some ancient populations miraculously resurfaced in the twilight of antiquity, even prehistory, in both the cultural and language plains, as happened with the modern-day Albanians, some of the Caucasian peoples, Basques, Kurds in the Middle East or the Berbers in North Africa and others.[365]

But even with the case of the Basque language and Basques as a people, as well as in the case of the Etruscan language and the Etruscans, there are the explanations of philologist Budimir, which he liaised with the ethno linguistic integrity of the Paleolithic time from where common elements of the Pelasgian substratum originated that dominated all the European space from east to west, from north to south, from where it remains an issue once forgotten or ignored by unstable hypotheses.

Indeed, the case of the *Etruscans*, *Basques*, the *Albans* of Caucasus, and the *Berbers* of North Africa, shows very well the whole fate of the edges, which not only fell subject to multiple and often unavoidable influences, by which through assimilation or other violent forms they broke away from the trunk, but even when stored in terms of long closures, their origin is denied. Even when it is quite obvious that it is contrary to unscientific theories, such as that of the Hellenes and Hellenism as a single and leading pillar of antiquity, the aim is to exclude the Pelasgian factor and their descendants, as the foundation of human civilization.

---

[365] Aref, Mathieu: *"Shqipëria,"* Tirana, 2007, p. 526.

CHAPTER 3

Dardanian Kingdom

> *The Dardanian connection with Troy explains their direct connection with the Pelasgians. - What are the reasons for four centuries of "recoiling" of Dardanians from the fall of Troy to the recurrence of their kingdom, in the 4th century BC, in the central part of Illyricum? - Why was the Dardanian Kingdom in constant wars with the Macedonians and why did their king, Bato, son of Longar, for a moment enter into an alliance with Rome against them? - The successful war of Dardanians against the Bastams, who were brought there by Philip V to colonize their lands. - The first wars of Dardanians with Queen Teuta and an endless affinity of King Monun with King Gent of Illyria and their temporary alliance against Macedonia. – Renouncing the alliance with the Romans after the loss of the Illyrian Kingdom and the beginning of a long confrontation with the Romans.*

It may be said that the Pelasgian root came out of a growing tree with many branches, which were among those of the great Illyrian family involving Epirotes and Macedonians, who produced their own branches, according to a known topography.[366] The same can be said about the

---

[366] According to *"Historia e Popullit Shqiptar,"* Tirana, 2002, p. 44, the topography of most important Illyrian tribes is as follows: among the tribes mentioned earlier are *Thesprotians*, who occupied the coastal plains from the Gulf of Ambracia to the river of Thiamis (Calama). In the north of them came *Caointi*, whose settlements reached to the Drinos Strait. Molossians lived in the Jannina plateau. Along the Vjosa Valley lived *Paraunes*. In the east of Bylines stretched the *Atintanes*. *Taulanti* lay in the coastal zone from Vjosa to Mat. In their north, along the Adriatic, stretched the tribe of Aerdiani. In the Central Balkans two tribes were dominant: *Paiones* in the Middle Valley of Vardar and *Dardanians*, who lived on the plains of Kosova, stretching in the area between the

Dardanians as a separate branch of the Pelasgian trunk, whose antiquity is related to Troy, while the presence of this ethnos continued to be stable in the central part of the Balkans (from the Sharr Mountains in the West, to Pelagonia in the South, Morava and Danube in the North, and Asia Minor in the East).

An important entity of Pelasgic heritage, which should be viewed as an important hub connecting the two arms of Illyria (the South with the West), was also indicated by Strabo saying that "Dardania borders with *Macedonian* and *Paionean* tribes in the South, along with the *Autorials*, *Dessaretes, Autariatae. Galabres* and *Thunates* were also Dardanians, who bordered the *Maedes*, a Thracian tribe in the East."[367]

In addition, certain traces of Dardanians were carried to southern Italy (Sicily) and tribes of Galabres, Thunates and Daunes who moved there after the destruction of Troy, a time which is most likely related to 12th century B.C. beyond the literary version of Homer, Virgil and others. This "transfer" can be seen as part of the natural movements among the Pelasgians from one place to another (i.e. from East to West, and vice versa). The Trojans might have been the last movement, as it was caused by the Dorian influx in the 11th-10th centuries as a consequence of its occupation and destruction by the Greeks and themselves.

However, since the hypothetical Trojan War and the appearance of the Dardanian Kingdom in the 4th century, when they reappeared on the historic scene in the central part of the Balkans where they played an important role, the founders of Troy seemed to remain unnoticed. The major works of Homer and Virgil kept Dardanians and other Pelasgian tribes alive in the memory of mankind, but not consistently in the historical events.

This considerably long "abstention" of Dardanians, which had an impact on a part of Albanian historiography to unjustly see them as detached and at the level of a simple tribe,[368] can be explained by the developments brought along by the last migration of Doric, or Aegean, of

---

Danube and Morava going further up in the East. Among the earliest tribes of the Northwest Balkans and among the most powerful were *Liburnians*, who lived on the coast and on the islands up to the River Krka, with Dalmatians to the south of them, while in the interior areas of Bosnia, *Autariatae*.

[367] Strabo: *"Gjeografia,"* Book VII/7
[368] See: *"Historia e Popullit Shqiptar,"* Volume I, Tirana, 2002, Stipcevic, Aleksandar: *"Ilirët,"* Prishtina, 1979.

the late 11th century. However, the long Greek war for the conquest of Troy began, which happened after a century with its demise; the violent Doric invasions not only disrupted the ethnic map of the Balkan-Aegean-Anatolian region, but also the social and political reality of this space which was already at the turn of history.

In these circumstances, the eastern Dardanians, the Leleges and other tribes living in Troy and on both sides of Bosphorus were forced to withdraw from a part of Asia Minor known by some tribes (Galabrians, Thunates and Daunes) that moved permanently to southern Italy (Sicily), where they soon established Rome.[369]

The rest of the Central Balkans also experienced significant disorders because during the Doric incursions from the northeast to the Aegean, they crossed over the Morava River valley and across the Vardar, setting a wedge through Dardanian ethnicity. This had significant consequences, especially in its eastern parts, which were subject to Thracian influence, while southern Dardanians were subject to continuous Greek pressure causing continued assimilation or withdrawal from the north and north-west towards the center.

Withdrawal from Asia Minor in the direction of the early center, (i.e. in the Central Balkans, and the movement of several Dardanian tribes to Italy) made a number of authors generally connect this withdrawal with the direction of penetrations of Aryan peoples into Central Europe from the East. (i.e. from Asia Minor to the West[370]). Others opposed this, arguing that it would be precisely the Doric invasions, namely the latest wave of very long invasions of peoples that made Dardanians cross over to Asia Minor after the destruction of Troy, to where they were originally from.[371]

Proponents of these theories, as noted earlier, while trying to move the autochthony of Dardanians without hesitating to extract them entirely from Pelasgians or from native Illyrians and their internal relationships, forgot the Dardanians and the overall Pelasgic legacy of the great Illyrian family. These were viewed in the West on the continent in Iberia in

---

[369] For more see: Homer, Herodotus, Plutarch, Dionysus of Halicarnassus, Virgil, and others.

[370] See: Tomaschek, Wielhelm: "*Die alten Thraker,*" I/13, Vienna, 1893; Kiepert, Heinrich: "*Lehrbuch der alten Geographi,*" Berlin, 1878, p. 109.

[371] Kretschmer, Paul: "*Einleitung in der Geschichte der Griechischen Sprache,*" Götingen, 1896, p. 182-183; Schlieman, H: "*Troja,*" Leipzig, 1884, XV.

affinity with Basques, witnessed in Italy (Venetia in the North, Messapi in the central part, Galabres, Thunates and Daunes in the South), and displayed in the Central and South Balkans even when noticed in the East (in Anatolia and elsewhere), based on the overall Euro-Asian foundation of Pelasgian stratification, appearing in these large areas since long before the invasions of the peoples from India in the 6th century B.C. Significant influxes, as through them the first Indo-European stratification of the Aryan family were set, which then continued with additional stratifications, especially that of the invasions of the 3rd century B.C., and 2nd century ending with the last, the Doric, from the beginnings of the 1st century B.C., had major consequences for the descendants of the Pelasgians.

Despite observing these with great differences, which, has literally become part of screening through Dardanians and Pelasgians, as Aryans generally reconcile their toughest contradictions within the Indo-European family, such as those of the Kentum and Satem division, the Dardanian being as an important branch of Pelasgic root with a geographical entirety, similar to that of the great family of Illyrian tribes and kingdoms, with an extension among the largest of the time, remained stable from an ethnic, social and political standpoint with a separate ethnic and state identity.

Viewing the Dardanians as a separate branch of the same lineage does not mean that they were different from an ethnic and linguistic point of view of the large Illyrian family. In this respect, many of the dilemmas that were due to ignorance of the realities have been lifted, including the intentional ones. However, the Dardanian independence remains an open question in a geographical, social and political view, which cannot be ignored, for the fact that Dardanians were found at an extremely important historical crossroad between West and East where different civilizations of the time clashed. Being a factor in such a bond implied a defense capability, but at the same time, give and take, which turned the Dardanians into a bridge, reflecting the effects of different sides, making them unique and often within the family of eastern peoples, breaking them away from any connections with the Pelasgian root and common Illyrian family.

Of this nature are also the observations that rely on the approach that sees the Dardanians in permanent wars and conflicts with some of the Illyrian tribes close by and the Macedonians, against whom they engaged in alliances with the Romans. The external factors and their effects were forgotten when the same ethnicities were involved in internal wars and conflicts that divided them and often led to separate states. However, it did not go against their common ethnicity or origin. Of this nature could also be the wars between Sparta and Athens, as those same tribes had the dominating role.

Despite the direction of specific developments within the Pelasgian legacy which were known since the early Bronze and Iron Ages when different groups of this ethnicity within a wide geographical extension (extending in the entire European space, in the Aegean and Asia Minor), underwent influences of different material and spiritual cultures, Dardanians and other parts of this ethnic group scattered in the South, West and East, were subject to developments that led to significant social changes. Links with the developed South during the 4th and 5th centuries BC, and especially trade with others, helped this important change, which then led to the creation of urban centers. This was reflected also in the culture of life which was set at a higher level in terms of production, and construction method of houses, roads and other infrastructure that led to the strengthening of tribal aristocracy, creating the basis for the next slave-owning layer, which enabled a process of further social differentiation, as a natural development.

However, in order to see the nature of those developments and the changes they brought, it is necessary to shed a little light on social relations and structures that emerged from them, as they determined the future social and political direction of those considered Dardanian, but also Illyrian communities.

It should be pointed out at the very beginning that the social, political, and economic structures and spiritual development of the Pelasgian legacy within the great Illyrian family, the Epirotans and even Macedonians, would take in its known political course, with all the features of the northern, middle and southern parts, from the 6th-4th centuries. In accordance with the sample of a comprehensive model, where a tribal aristocracy comes out as a carrier of economic and political power, autonomous cities also appeared, seeming as independent units with organization resembling that of the Greeks, Illyrians, and Dardanians. In the absence of authentic written evidence by the Illyrians and Dardanians themselves (even though one should not exclude the possibility of finding one day the key to their internal communication, which was inevitable) history depends on ancient authors and their testimonies, which remain sole and insurmountable. They even remain the only source, which regardless of the known viewpoint considering the "barbarian" neighbors only in accordance with their relations with the Greeks or the Romans, though with considerable difficulties, enabled the reconstruction of their appearance from the inside.

Both this interior view, initially with the tribes and tribal aristocracy and then with autonomous cities and also the external view of the large Pelasgic legacy, is often confusing. It shares a joint attribution of "*ethnoi Illyrioi*" even when Dardanians, Epirotes, and some other characteristic tribe is mentioned, as this notion had a broad political significance which meant the wider community feeding support for the position that the term "includes a set of cities and large or small tribal units, which share a somewhat similar complex structure."[372] This entirety was seen in the eyes of ancient authors as divided into two political-territorial parts.

The first includes the territory of South Illyria, with Epirus and Macedonia often isolated and interconnected without any clarity, and with Dardania as constantly separated, a space in the immediate vicinity of the Hellenistic cultural and political world and significantly associated with it.

The rest includes the part of the northwest Balkans to the coast, from Neretva in the North and part of the Central Balkans, reaching eastward to Thrace.[373]

In light of this division it is roughly possible to see and understand many phenomena that are characteristic of Dardanians and Dardania and their very important role in this entirety, which according to ancient authors, is seen mostly in the region of South Illyria, a definition that in ethnic and cultural terms, may be more or less accepted, but not from a social and political aspect as well. In that case, Dardanians and Dardania would shrink to the level of multiple tribes and would often barely be noticed within what is called the Illyrian family, tribal community or alliances of tribes-kingdoms, something that does not correspond with the realities through which Dardanians and Dardania passed from early antiquity to classical Hellenism, and also later during the Roman occupation as an entity with some specific characteristics, although stable.

Despite this division, among the Illyrian tribes and Dardanians the following rather identical forms of political power were faced:

---

[372] See Papazoglu, Fanula: "*Politicka organizacija Ilira,*" 1967, p. 19.
[373] Mirdita, Zef: "*Studime dardane,*" Prishtina, 1979, p. 58.

a) *bazilikai - baselius* (Lat. Regia) of the *monarchs* and

b) *autonomesthai* (Lat.propriae leges) - *self-rule.*[374]

Although it is difficult to determine areas where this power was more accentuated, it may be said that the forms of *baesilius* power, namely of the monarchs, appeared by the early 4th century B.C.; they by no means exclude other existing forms that somehow "cohabited" at different levels from tribal government in the autonomous cities. They also aligned with tribes and kingdoms, which rightly opened the genuine dilemma about their political power within these heterogeneous structures that the Greeks faced from the 7th century BC onwards. In fact, they launched long wars to dominate the Mediterranean, which began with the establishment of the first colonies in the Illyrian lands on the shores of the Ionian Sea and later on the Adriatic reaching far up into the North.[375]

Even here, ancient authors shed light to help understand a little more of the "parallels" of state governance structures of the Illyrian and the Dardanian family in a wider view where the tribal link implies some kind of military *koinon* democracy,[376] which found backing on the primate of

---

[374] For more on the political structures of Illyrians and Dardanians See: Droysen, J.G: "*Geschichte des Hellenisumus*" III/2, Gotha, 1878; Droysen, J.G: "*Das Dardanische Fürstentum*" in "*Kleine Schrfiten zur alten Geschichte,*" Bd, I, Leipzig, 1893, pp. 87-89; Patsch, Cael: "*Dardani,*" in PWRE IV-1901; Niese, B. G: "*Geschichte der griechischen und makedonischen Staaten seit der Schlacht bie Chäronea,*" Vol. II, Gotha," 1899; Zippel, G: "*Die römische Herrschaft om Illyrien bis Augustus,*" Leipzig, 1877; Schütt: "*Untersuchungen zur Geschishte;*" Hammond, G. L: "*The kingdoms in Illyria,*" London, 1961; Papazoglu, Fanula: "*Politicka organizacija Ilira u vreme njihove samostalnosti*" and "*Poreklo i razvoj ilirske drzave,*" Godisnjak CBI V-3, 1967; Stipcevic, A: "*Ilirët – historia – jeta - kultura,*" Rilindja, Prishtina, 1980; Mirdita, Zef: "*Studime dardane,*" Prishtina, 1979: "*Historia e Popullit Shqiptar,*" Part I, Tirana, 2002.

[375] For more see Strabo "*Gjeografia,*" Book VI/269, as the known geographer points out the first Greek-Illyrian conflict in the year 734 BC, taking place between the leader of Corinth, Hersicrates, and the *Liburnian* kingdom, saying that he managed to drive them away from Corfu (Corcyra). The same author writes that such wars between Greek and Illyrian tribes continued for a long time until sometime by the mid-fifth century when the Liburnian power fell opening the way to new Greek colonies on the Adriatic coast, among first which was Epidamnos, founded by Corcyrans in 627 BC. Later, the Romans called it Dyrrhachium, the present-day Durrës.

[376] See: Polybius: "*Historia,*" Book II/4, cited according to "*Ilirët dhe Iliria dhe te autorët antikë,*" Prishtina, 1979, p. 45.

noble families, *"prostates."*[377] According to the popular principle *"premium inter pares"* (first among equals), the tribal connections represented some other forms of government among the *Molossians* and *Atintanes* *"the keeper of the king"* is mentioned, and even the king among the *Paraneii*,[378] whose appearance as a state institution came later with kings (Bardhylius, Teuta and Gentius in the Illyrian state; with Pyrrhus in Epirus, and with Bato, Longar, and Perseus in Dardanians), which will be discussed later.

Relying more on ancient sources, Gentius, at this point, is somewhat unique because he appeared as an absolute ruler. The position he built at the expense of his country, thanks to his tribal organizations, was the underlying political structures in the Illyrian and Dardanian communities as well. Therefore, it is not by chance that after losing the war with the Romans and being conquered by them, it would be then that the domestic political structures of the Illyrians and Dardanians be reinstated, even when Rome extended its military power over Illyria and Dardania.[379] That occurred because allowing local political and economic structures to develop independently was in the domestic and imperial interest, as it was a way to preserve "internal peace" and strengthen the power of Rome, whose main strength depended on the income coming from the Illyrian provinces and Dardania. These resources included the largest mines of zinc, copper and gold. One of these important centers of minerals was Damastion. Strabo says that it was rich in silver, where great work was taking place in many mines.[380]

Of course, the mines and assets in these parts were reflected in the economic and political power of the dynasties from among *principes gentium*, which like *Basileus*, cut their own coins, among which stands out Ballaiosin.[381]

The appearance of internal governance structures at all levels of the extended Illyrian family and the Dardanians from the tribal structures,

---

[377] S. Anamali: *"Iliria,"* 2, 1971, p. 90.

[378] Thucydides, II/80, cited according to Mirdita, Zef: *"Studime dardane,"* Prishtina, 1979, p. 58.

[379] Mirdita, Zef: *"Studime dardane,"* Prishtina, 1979, p. 54.

[380] Strabo: *"Gjeografia,"* Book 7, as quoted in *"Ilirët dhe Iliria te autorët antikë,"* Prishtina, 1979, p. 153.

[381] Ceka, Hasan: *"Probleme të numizmatikës ilire me një katalog të monetare të pabotuara apo të rralla të Ilirisë së Jugut,"* Tirana, 1956.

autonomous cities and royal levels in the South and North, remains incomplete without its social appearance, which determined its content.

Here, the main reference are the remains of social, economic and political Greeks sources, which necessarily complicated the "barbarians" within the compounds of the country and those in the neighborhood, admitted as numerous and strong.

Therefore, the appearance of the interior of the Illyrian tribes and Dardanians, from the Iron period and on, by many respects, was identical to that of the Greek society. Ancient authors, such as Pseudo-Scylax and others say that important tribes who lived near them or with them (Chaonians, Thesprotians and Molossians) lived in villages (*palifates*),[382] something that could also be said for a good part of the Hellenic population, which had also the first cities. According to Herodotus, Thucydides, and other ancient authors, the Pelasgian-Illyrians were not only seen in villages, but also in cities. Herodotus wrote that they were founders of Plakias and Scylaxea in Hellespont,[383] while Thucydides described them as residents of Agos and several other important cities in the Peloponnesus.[384] Furthermore, it is known that from the Iron period onwards, fortified settlements with thick walls expanded, called towns (*qyteza*), castles or *gradina*.

Southern Illyria and Dardania are characterized by townships or fortresses surrounded by walls of stones. They were raised on protected hills and vistas with dominant positions and wide horizons of observation. Walls were built with large raw and rough stones, overrun by sides and a central nucleus filled with smaller stones. Their thickness varied from 3.10 to 3.50 meters.[385] Ptolemy, an author of the 2nd century A.D. mentions four ancient important towns of Dardania: *Naissos, Arribation, Ulpiana* and *Scupi*.[386]

Unlike the territories of South Illyria, Dardanian settlements were protected by walls, known as "*gradina*.[387]" The majority was found in this

---

[382] Scylax: *"Periplus"* (Cruise). Haones -28; Thesprotoi – 30.
[383] Herodotus: *"Historiae,"* Book I/57.
[384] Thucydides: *"Historiae,"* Book II/68.
[385] *"Historia e Popullit Shqiptar,"* Volume I, Tirana, 2002, p. 45.
[386] Ibid, p. 151.
[387] The etymology of the name *"gradina"* comes from an old word of Pelasgian stratification **ghordho** (*gardh, fence, fort*). For more See Budimir, Milan: *"Grci i Pelasti,"* Belgrade, 1950, p. 53.

part, but goes even further beyond their normal expansion. *"Gradinas"* were located on the dominating hills. Their bulwark was formed by earth or stone mass, reaching 7-15 meters wide. A protection system was apparently completed by a fence of poles, standing on the bulwark, and a surrounding moat.[388]

Of course, at this time, the descendants of the Pelasgians (Illyrians, Dardanians, Epirotes and others) saw farming and cattle-breeding as a significant activity, while the population of cities was dealing with craftsmanship (pottery, work tools and metal jewelry) and commerce. Written sources and archaeological evidence mark agriculture and livestock as the primary activity of the descendants of the Pelasgians. Extending through the plateau and the fertile valleys of the rivers, they managed to produce many kinds of grain, though not lacking evidence for their expansion through mountain gorges and even mountainous parts. Hesiod, the Greek writer of the 8th-7th century B.C. describes the very fertile field of Helopia, while according to the Greek historian Hecateus (end of the 6th-5th centuries B.C.), in Illyria there were provinces that produced up to two crops a year.[389]

Besides agriculture, in coastal areas and low-lying regions with temperate climate, grapes and olives grew. "This country has been warm and fruitful," writes the Greek historian and geographer Strabo. "It is full of olive groves and vineyards."[390] Illyrians were distinguished in this period as good beekeepers, from which they took honey and wax. Aristotle shows how Taulantia also used honey to make a kind of drink similar to the sweet and strong wine.[391]

In addition, animal breeding was very important for the Illyrians, Dardanians and other members of the extended Illyrian family. Ancient authors offer numerous descriptions of livestock breeding, especially sheep and cattle. Aristotle shows how some Illyrian tribes were involved in frequent conflicts over the saltworks of Autariatae and Ardianes.

"Salt, - says Aristotle, - they need for their cattle, which they offer twice a year, or else most of them die."[392]

---

[388] *"Historia e Popullit Shqiptar,"* Volume I, Tirana, 2002, 46.
[389] Ibid, p. 46.
[390] Strabo: *"Geography,"* Book V/1.
[391] Aristotle: *"De Mirabilibus Auscultationbibus"* (On Told Wonders) pp. 832 a, 22.
[392] Ibid, p. 833 b, p. 45.

Agriculture, livestock, beekeeping, fishing, crafts, and exchanges of goods during the Iron Age were due to changes in the structure of Illyrian and Dardanian society. The basis of these changes became private property, which began to appear among more economically developed tribes.[393] Hesiod, speaking of large flocks in Helopia says they were property of special people.[394] The order of land sharing every eight years among Dalmatians and some other tribes[395] was another proof showing that the periodical ownership was an intermediate link in the process of private property.

Obviously facing these circumstances starts the appearance of the tribal aristocracy, depicted as the most developed form of tribal government toward creating tribal communities, enabling the emergence of tribal-stated and a little later, tribal-kingdoms, based on slave-owning states. Ancient authors demonstrate the excessive presence of slaves among Dardanians; they even kept prisoners of war. Agatharchides announced that as the Dardanian Army withdrew from Macedonia in the war in 216 B.C., they took with them around 20,000 prisoners of war,[396] which opens the question of their true economic, political and state power that was relatively strong, according to ancient sources.

The most important of these testimonies are those speaking of the first tribal-state formations from the 7th century B.C., such as that of the Encheleii.[397] This was followed by the creation of the wide region of Illyria, which according to ancient authors, called "Illyrian" differing from those of the "Dardanians," "Taulantii" and others, stretching extensively from Narona (Neretva) River in the North and River Aous (Vjosa) in the South stretching toward the east as far as Lake Lynhidia bordering Macedonia and in the North with the Dardanian Kingdom.[398]

---

[393] *"Historia e Popullit Shqiptar,"* Volume I, Tirana, 2002, p. 49.

[394] Ibid, p. 49.

[395] Strabo: *"Geography,"* Book V/5.

[396] *"Historia e Popullit shqiptar,"* Volume I, Tirana, 2002, p. 151.

[397] For more on the emergence of the tribe of Aenchelei with a state structure see: Georg Zippe: *"Die Römische Herrschaft in Illyrien bis auf Augustur,"* Leipzig, 1877, pp. 12-20; Shütt, Kurt: *"Untersuchungen zur Geschihten der alten Illyrer,"* Breslau, 1910, pp. 24-26; Rade Vulpe: *"Les haches de bronze de type albano-dalmate et le regime de Cadmos chez les Encheleens,"* Istros, 1-1934, pp. 44-59; Stipcevic, Aleksandar: *"Ilirët,"* Prishtina, 1980, p. 46.

[398] *"Historia e Popullit Shqiptar,"* Volume I, Tirana, 2002, p. 61.

Supposedly, the Illyrian kingdom originated here, which continued to King Gentius, who ruled from 180-168 B.C. and ended the dynasty and independent life of the Illyrian state.[399]

In southern provinces another important state was also formed, known as the State of Epirus, famous especially for the political events of the late 4th century B.C. and the quarter of the 3rd century B.C. At the time of its scope, it included the lands of the River Aous (Vjosa) to the Bay of Nicopolis (Arta).[400]

Compared with Mangesi's evidence about the first Illyrians, Dardanian and Epirotan state formations, ancient authors were missing authentic inside evidence, since independent city-state formations existed including Dyrrachium, Apollonia, Ambracia and others, whose political history took place sometimes in close relations and sometimes at odds with that of the Illyrian state and Epirus.[401]

In such circumstances the emergence of the Dardanian Kingdom outside its continuity was also witnessed from the time of Troy on, continuity which cannot possibly be separated, despite the lack of direct evidence, because it is Homer, Hesiod, Virgil, and various myths that do not allow this.

However, in order to see its historical role and importance of this kingdom, one should shed light on the reality called the Illyrian Kingdom, so that from there one can see the other social and political relations created in the space of the descendants of Pelasgians, drawing on their

---

[399] For more on this see Fanula Papazoglu: "*Poreklo i razvoj ilirike drzave,*" Godišnjak Centra za balkanoloska ispitavanja, 5/167, p. 123-144. This author defends the view that the Illyrian kingdom begins by late fifth century BC with King *Sirrhas* and that it continued to live without interruption up to the second century BC, meaning until it lost its political independence and to the time when the Romans took captive the last Illyrian King, *Gentius* (*Genthios*). According to the author, in this period the Illyrian state was ruled by fifteen rulers: *Sirrhas* (late 5th and the beginning of the fourth century BC); *Bardhylis*, founder of the first dynasty, died in the year 359 or 358 BC, first mentioned as King of Taulanti, and as an Illyrian King from 317 BC until 302 BC. Then comes *Bardhylis II, Monuoun* and *Myltis*, the latter reported as early as from 270 BC. After that dynasty came the one beginning with *Pleurat* (ca. 260 BC), succeeded by Agron, Pynis the Minor, who rules under the supervision of his stepmother, Teuta. After Scerdilaides came Pleurat and in the end his son Gentius (ruled between 180-168 BC).
[400] "*Historia e Popullit Shqiptar,*" p. 61.
[401] Ibid, p. 61.

internal relations, but also on those they had with the Greeks and Romans.

Indeed, these relations, starting from 4th century to the middle of the 2nd century B.C. are mostly characterized by "family conflicts" for larger properties that erupted between the Illyrians and Macedonians on one side and Dardanians and Macedonians on the other, without excluding those between the Illyrians and Dardanians. These relations support the basic thought that the vast Pelasgic legacy was from the "divine people" as seen by Homer and many ancient authors, with the exception of Alexander the Great, who had the concept of achieving a global kingdom.

Even though he failed, it led to his early death, while others shared a mentality of gaining strength to the detriment of others, defending themselves from the Greeks and Romans at the expense of gaining their alliances. Therefore, based on ancient sources, the first reports of Illyrian, Dardanian and Epirotan king came to light due to conflicts with the Macedonians who were considered "neighbors,"[402] they triggered what is called the "Lynchestes issue," namely to acquire a province that stood between the Illyrian King Sirrhas and Macedonian King Arhelau, led by King Arrabeus, which was important for both sides for further expansion. Notably, the Illyrian Sirrhas, thanks to his marriage with Arrabeus' daughter, signed an alliance in 423 B.C. with Lynchestes that would help them oppose the Macedonian King Arhelaus. Seemingly, a good occasion for this came in 399 B.C. when King Arhelaus died and Amyntas II took his place. Although the Illyrian King Sirrhas married him to his daughter Eurydice, it did not prevent him from entering Macedonia and occupying a good portion of its land at the moment when Macedonia was experiencing a crisis after internal turmoil that went on for several decades. He expelled his son-in-law from the throne and brought instead Argeus, of the Lyncheste dynasty,[403] something that forced the deposed king Amyntas II to seek shelter in Thessaly where he was restored to his throne two years later.

Ancient sources make it known that it is here that King Sirrha's tracks got lost, and with this ended also what, according scarce reports by ancient authors, is known as the first Illyrian king, yielding to the appearance of the first Illyrian dynasty, that of Bardylis, beginning in 393 B.C. and ending in 335 B.C. with his death. This period was considered the

---

[402] *"Historia e Popullit Shqiptar,"* Volume I, Tirana, 2002, p. 67.
[403] Ibid, p. 67.

most successful of this dynasty, as he managed to shatter twice the attempts of the Macedonians, in 369 B.C. and 360 B.C. to set them free of the situation created by him in 393 A.D. when he forced Amyntas II to pay perennial tribute to the Illyrian Kingdom. In the last battle, ending in profound defeat of the Macedonians, King Perdiccas III was also killed with 4,000 warriors.[404] A year later, this situation changed in favor of the Macedonians, when Philip attacked the Illyrians with a large army consisting of 10,000 footmen and 600 horsemen. Diodorius says it was a battle with much loss on both sides, with victory leaning on either side, ending up in victory for the Macedonians.[405] Peace was reached on this occasion at the expense of the Illyrians, as they were forced to leave the areas they held, while Philip returned to Lynchestia, from where he would be forced to withdraw by another king, Pleurias, who caused great losses to the Macedonian army, while Philip himself was wounded in the battle.[406]

Macedonians took back what they lost and even went further in subjecting the Illyrians and others, when Alexander came to power, replacing Philip, who died in 355 B.C. He managed to defeat them all one by one: Cleitus, Bardylis' son, and Glaukias, King of Taulantii.

Speaking of the latter, Glaukias, it must be said that his name is connected to the time of the second Illyrian kingdom, known as Glaukus' dynasty (335 B.C. -231 B.C.), with a significant change, as he was named the King of Taulantii, namely of a larger tribe after having liberated the lands to the East of the Macedonians, and managing to unite them to his kingdom which gave him the title of "The King of the Illyrians."[407]

According to the same sources and for these purposes, namely in order to unite the divided Illyrian tribes, Glaukus made efforts to reduce the Macedonian influence in Epirus, approaching Aiacides, King of the Molossians, through a marriage with Beroia, the royal Molossian family. Obviously, the Macedonians undertook prompt measures to prevent the approach of the Illyrian kingdom with Molossians, the son of Cassander; Antipatris, in 317 B.C. ousted Glaukus' ally, Aiacides from the Molossian

---

[404] Ibid, p. 68.
[405] Diodorius: *"Bibliotheca Historica,"* Book XVI/2, cited according to *"Ilirët dhe Iliria te autorët antikë,"* Prishtina, 1979, p. 138.
[406] Ibid, p. 138.
[407] *"Historia e Popullit Shqiptar,"* Volume I, p. 72.

throne. Glaukus took the son of the deposed king, the two-year-old Pyrrhus, under his protection.[408]

The taking of Pyrrhus under protection was of importance because it encouraged other wars between Glaukus and the Macedonian Cassander, in which Illyrians were victorious in circumstances when the Macedonian Kingdom, following the death of Alexander, was involved in internal struggles for power, leading to its downfall.

These successes were also associated with the instatement of the 12-year-old Pyrrhus on the Molossian throne. Therefore, opening another chapter of restoration to the scene of the Molossians Kingdom, also related to important events, led by Pyrrhus, dealt with the establishment and later decline of Epirus.[409] These events were extremely influential in the inner Illyrian-Macedonian-Dardanian triangle, and externally in relation to the Greeks and Romans. Pyrrhus, after Alexander the Great, for nearly a quarter of a century (from 296 B.C. - 272 B.C) shifted the attention to foreign wars in order to advance towards the West, being the first to cross over to Italy and extend his kingdom there. Everything followed Pyrrhus' campaign in Italy, including his defeat, as a consequence of which was the penetration of Rome in the western parts, i.e. Epirotan and Illyrian lands. However, its results were the elimination of the Epirotan factor from the stage and turning it into an "odds and ends" situation to be used by other factors (Greeks and Macedonians). They brought back the Illyrian Kingdom to the game, however, and Dardanians by Pleurat (260 B.C.), to his son Agron (250 B.C.), Teuta (230 B.C.), Demetrius of Pharos (219 B.C.), Pinus (205 B.C.), Pleurat (205 B.C.), to Gentius (168 B.C.), when his defeat in the war against the Romans, marked the end of the Illyrian kingdom.

In this internal squirm, besides the emergence of Illyrian tribes-kingdoms, as the case of Sirrha from late 5th century to the Illyrian kingdom led by Pleurat and Gentius, besides the occurrence of Molossians along with Pyrrhus, it was very important for developments on both sides

---

[408] Ibid, p. 72.
[409] The terms *Epirus* and *Epirotes* came later and has to do with what Greek settlers on the Ionian coast and other Pelasgian areas called the vicinity (continental) residents of - Molossia, (Epirus - mainland). Later on, Greek historians, inclined to name the Pelasgian population they found there according to their geographical rather than ethnic name used the name "Kingdom of Epirus," or "Pyrrhus of Epirus," as they called similarly the others, again according to geography.

of the Adriatic practically starting the Roman involvement in this historical circle ending up in their victory. There was the appearance of the Dardanians and the kingdom of Dardania, which different from the Illyrian, Epirotan, and Macedonian kings, was related to Troy. The legacy was denied by the Albanian historiography, because as discussed before, that threatened the "Illyrian origin,"[410] while others, ranging from the Greeks, Macedonians, Romanians, Bulgarians, and even Slavs tried to acquire, or at least somehow relate to it, as happened even with the Serbs, who stand furthest away from any such kind of connection.[411]

However, despite these issues which would preoccupy everyone belonging to the basin of antiquity, including those attributed to it, as is the case with the Slavs and other barbarian peoples emerging in these parts after 7th century B.C., the first news on Dardanians and Dardania as a separate kingdom pertained to the mid-4th century B.C., and dealt with the efforts of the Kingdom of Macedonia, at that time the largest military power in the region, to strengthen its northern border, after having lost the war in the East and was shrinking, two centuries later entirely collapsed by the Roman Empire. Under such circumstances, the Dardanian Kingdom represented an important political and military factor in the central region, which posed for Macedonians a constant challenge in coping with them and in setting their domination in that part, the same as it posed a threat to Rome later, pretending likewise to submit the center of antiquity and in moving further on towards the East.

Ancient historians indicate that the power in the Dardanian Kingdom was hereditary. The king commanded and possessed the military power of the Dardanians.[412] As indicated by the same sources the Dardanian army was a regular, well-organized army, at the base of which stood

---

[410] For more on this see *"Historia e Popullit Shqiptar,"* Volume II, Tirana, 2002, p. 41; Stipcevic, Aleksandar: "Ilirët," Prishtina, 1980.

[411] See: Relja Novaković: *"Gde se nalazi Srbija,"* Belgrade; *"Kaukazski Albanci, lazni Iliri,"* The Serb Academy of Sciences and Arts, Belgrade, 2007. The Serbian historian opens the thesis according to which Serbs can see Slavicised Dardanians in the 7th-8th centuries AD, while some Serb academicians, although not openly admitting, try to manipulate with the Albanians of the Caucasus, which according to them, must have come in the 11th century in the Balkans after being invited by Necyphoris to participate in the first crusade to help the Christians, in order to remain in the lands where they are now!

[412] *"Historia e Popullit Shqiptar,"* Volume I, Tirana, 2002, p. 150.

the phalange of 8,000 soldiers able to move with fighting skills.[413] The Roman historian, Justin[414] brought accounts about the wars that the Macedonian King Philip II waged to defeat Dardanians and other Illyrian neighbors. "Once he placed things in order and set power in Macedonia, Philip conquered through diablerie and shrewdness Dardanian and other neighboring lands."[415]

Justin's accounts too, like those of most of ancient authors, when it comes to the Pelasgians and their heirs Illyrians, Dardanians, are of a detached nature, incomplete and exclusive, even lacking other explanations of social and political nature. However, despite what Justin and others from antiquity have to say, one may build a picture of a broader and deeper historical context, in which Dardanians, although bypassed, are included among the most important developments, such as the birth, rise, and fall of Macedonia as a great world power, which as testified, rose from within but it also fell upon the Illyrian and Dardanian factor with whom they are connected through their common Pelasgic roots. However, their subsequent political behavior, fighting for a great global empire, such as the one of Alexander the Great, kept the rest in the twirl of local delimitations, mostly at war with each other. This broad and deep historical concept, besides the Dardanians and Illyrians also included the Hellenes, and, above all, Romans, as the next world power, who also built on the foundations of the Illyrian-Dardanian trunk, namely Pelasgian legacy, where their roots also were turned into a great empire thanks to their factorization from within, while the Illyrians and Dardanians were seen as

---

[413] Ibid, p. 150.

[414] In the year 9 BC, during the reign of Augustus, a history of 44 books titled *"Historiare Philippica"* (Philip's History) appeared in Rome. Its author was *Pompe Trogis*, a contemporary of Titus Livius, originally from Narbonne of Gallia. This work brings the history of Macedonia, starting from the time before Philip II to the fall of the Macedonian state, being in contradiction with the known Latin position. This probably led to the disappearance of Pompe Trogus work; only general outlines are recognized, its epitomes were written in the second century AD by M. *Junian Justin*. For Justin little is known. As an epitomator, summarizing Trogus' extensive work with rich contents he left behind valuable records of geographic ethnographic character. Despite large gaps, Justin provided an opportunity for getting acquainted with the work of Trogus' composition and its historical concept. Justin's work is of particular importance for the history of Illyria and Dardania, especially on the relations and wars of the Illyrians and Dardanians against the Macedonians.

[415] Justin: *"Epitoma Historiarum Philippicum Pompei Trogi,"* Book VIII/6.

included in all structures of imperial rule, as leaders and managers, including the emperor's throne.

Before this development occurred, as Illyrians and Dardanians were found on the throne of the Roman Empire, with quite a few (Diocletian, Constantine the Great, Justin, Justinian, and others), Illyrians and Dardanians were involved in numerous and various wars initially against the Hellenes, and Macedonians who were called Hellenized, and even against Romans, without excluding their internal wars with each other, lasting for more than two centuries. Descendants of the Pelasgians, Illyrians, Dardanians, and others of this large family were not able to establish an internal link, appearing individually and often against each other. In consequence, they fell under the Roman occupation, from where originated the attitude regarding the Illyrians, Dardanians and others of this large family, among the largest of all times, as an ethno-geographic factor, outside a domestic social and political relationship and outside imperial claims, as Macedonians had since the time of Philip I and Alexander the Great. Their direct ties with the Molossians were taken under their protection until things were ripe for the restoration of the throne. Even then, when they entered leagues and alliances, such as was the one with the Molossians and a little later Epirotes, they were not able to unify all the scattered Pelasgic legacy contrasted with their interests and ambitions between the southern and western factors, as contrasted with those of a the central factor, Dardanians, unable to turn into a dominating power similar to that of Troy.

However, in this important historical outline, from the 5th to 2nd centuries it would be the southern Illyrian wing (Molossians to be called Epirotans) and the central one with Dardanians, who tried to turn into important players doing so by initially waging war against Hellenized Macedonians and then against Rome, engaging in long wars and ending in military rather than social and political defeat, as Dardanians, along with ethnicity during the Roman occupation, retained many of their autonomous self-government structures. These economic and spiritual customs continued which led to the rise of Byzantium, considered by many authors a continuation of Illyria, and remained until the 10th century when social and political formations of the Slavs appeared.

In these preliminary developments, to be empowered as much by means of internal wars, the kingdom of Dardania had its greatest confrontation with Macedonia and its efforts to return to regional power. In the early 3rd century B.C., according to sources of ancient authors, Dardania appeared as a social and political organization of weight, which would simultaneously face two serious challenges: that of Macedonia, which was declining, but always ready to maintain dominance over the Greeks and Dardanians, and the Celtic invasions coming from the northeast with the intention of invading Greece. More by ancient sources, the Celts, of whom Justin says "increased so much that they had no longer any room in the land of their birth, and they sent 300,000 people to search for new places to settle,"[416] after having gone to Italy and having burned Rome, crossed over to the Illyrian lands as well, submitting inhabitants of Pannoni. Here, divided into two groups, one attacked Greece and the other Macedonia.[417] The Roman historian reports that Dardania, feeling the Celtic danger, provided assistance to the king of Macedonia, Ptolemy. Dardanian delegates offered 20,000 warriors as assistance, to which he behaved heedlessly telling them "it was a job for Macedonia and the Macedonians and that Macedonians who had subdued the entire East had no need to have Dardanians protect their borders."[418]

This contempt for the Dardanian assistance of 20,000 warriors, cost Ptolemy Keraunos a heavy defeat,[419] a defeat that was compensated somewhat by the Greek victory at Thermopylae against the Celts, who defeated and in their run through the Dardanian lands also received a lecture from Dardanians, and this highlighted the Dardanian social and political factor, as an important power. This was illustrated by their expanding boundaries to the North and South, who could in no way find

---

[416] Justin: *"Historiarum Philippicarum"* (Collection of Philip's history of Pompey Trogus), Book XXIV/4.

[417] On the great impact that the arrival of Celts had on Illyrian and Dardanian lands for more see: Huber, Henri: *"Les Celtes depuis l'epoque de la Tene et la civilisation celtique,"* Paris, 1950, pp. 46-54; *"Kelti u nasoj zemlji,"* Glas Srpske Kraljevske Akademije, Belgrade, 1926, pp. 73-89; Zipel, George: *"Die römische Herrschaft in Illyrien bis auf Augustus,"* Leipzig, 1877, pp. 12-20; Schütt, Kurt: *"Untersuchungen zur Geschihte der alten Illyrer,"* Breslau, 1910, p. 24-26; Garašanin V. Milutin: *"Iz istorije Kelta u Srbiji,"* Istorijski glasnik, 1953, no. 3-4, pp. 3-15; Gavela, Branko: *"Iliri i Kelti u Podunavlju i na Balkanu,"* Godisnjak grada Beograda 7/1960, pp. 5-28.

[418] Justini: *"Historiarum Philippicarum,"* Book XXIV/4.

[419] "Ptolemy Keraunos was defeated by Celtic Captain Belgiosis, falling in the battle, costing unseen destruction exerted by Celtic winners. According to Justin's testimony, Macedonians "raised their hands to heaven from atop the ruins of their cities crying out Philip's and Alexander's names as gods of their homeland defense." (See: *"Historiarum Philippicarum,"* Book XXXII.)

common language with the Macedonians, something that may be explained by what has been said before about rivalry within the same family, similar to that also among the Athenians and Spartans, expressed also in numerous bloody wars between them. In these circumstances, we have the outbreak of other wars between Dardanians and Macedonians, as a result of continuing claims of Macedonians to further continue the occupation of Illyrian lands in North and West or to place under vassalage some of the small Illyrian kingdoms in the vicinity. Dardanians were particularly unacceptomg of the Macedonian claims for conquering the Paeonian land, their most important neighbors. To prevent this, Paiones relied on Dardanians with whom they needed an alliance against the Macedonians, which kept the road open for Dardanians towards Macedonia. This is best seen by the actions of the Dardanian King, Longar, who once rescued Paeonia in 231 B.C. fought against Demetrius II of Macedonia, therefore rejecting the Macedonian state efforts to expand the northern borders.[420]

The Dardanian wars against Macedonia, where its ruler, Demetrius II, was killed, continued with the Dardanians claiming to restore a part of their former power. It is known that at this time, namely after Dardanians marked significant military successes against the Macedonians and some surrounding Illyrian tribes, they openly displayed their claims to penetrate further towards the southeast, towards the former Troy, but in doing so they were met by Macedonians,[421] who also had the same claims that Alexander the Great had, which, despite the great successes he harvested with his penetrations towards the East, it was his early death that deprived him of it.

Even though it was already clear that by now, with the appearance of the Romans on the shores of the Ionian and the Adriatic, circumstances had changed, meaning that a confrontation with the West was expected, Dardanians still saw their factorization in defeating the Macedonians and Greeks after that in order to move on towards Asia Minor. Dardanians counted on realizing these claims also through the help of the surrounding Illyrians.[422] But it became clear that the Dardanians could not count on the Illyrians, as they had thought. In the reign of Antigon Dozon, thanks to a deal that Macedonians signed with the Illyrian state, Dardanians were driven out of parts of Macedonia and Paeonia. In the Paeonian

---

[420] *"Historia e Popullit Shqiptar,"* Volume I, Tirana, 2002, p. 146.
[421] Droysen, J. G: *"Das Dardanische Fürstentum,"* Leipzig, 1893, pp. 27-35.
[422] Ibid, p. 30.

city, Bylazora, in the valley of River Axius, Macedonians set a strong military garrison, in order to close the road to the Dardanians from crossing into Macedonia.[423]

The Dardanian-Macedonian wars continued with the same rigor in the days of King Philip V, however, it appeared that all of this was triggered for Paeonia and its being held occupied by the Macedonians, which was unacceptable for Dardanians, as this put into direct test the ambitions of both parties for further rule over the Illyrian tribes, but also over the Greeks, from where domination over the Central and Southern part of the region could be ensured, which could prevent any threat to them from Rome, and simultaneously create the prerequisites to go further eastward, i.e. Asia Minor.

With these claims, in 219 B.C., when Philip V was in the Peloponnesus, Dardanians entered Paeonia and liberated the parts that the Macedonian Army kept occupied. Titus Livius reported that "there, namely in Peloponnesus, Philip V met messengers brought more disturbing news; he learned that Dardanians spread in Macedonia had become lords of Oristida, having come down to the fields of Arges and among the barbarians, rumors circulated that Philip was killed."[424] Philip V, aware of what the Dardanian presence in that part meant, attacked Bylazora again succeeding in removing the Dardanians. Furthermore, on this occasion he captured the city of Cynthia in the southwestern part of Dardania, and north of Pelagonia. This situation, however, did not go on for long. Dardanians, using the conflict of Philip V with Southern Illyria, after having allied with its ruler Aerop, in 208 B.C, attacked Macedonia, managing to move with their armies to Orestida, a southwestern border province of Macedonia.[425]

---

[423] "Historia e Popullit Shqiptar," Volume I, Tirana, 2002, p. 146.

[424] *Titus Livius* is the most important historian of the Roman Augustus time. He was born in Patavium (Padoa) in 59 or 69 BC and died in the year 17 AD. Unlike many of his predecessors he did not participate in political life. All his life he was a rhetorician and literarian. He wrote a history of Rome entitled "Ab urbe codito" (From the establishment of the city). His entire work consisted of 142 books. Livius' work is of great importance as it keeps some data stored on Alexander Molo's and Pyrrhus' campaign in Italy and on Illyrian-Roman wars. For the latter he meets in many respects what has been lacking or lost from Polybius.

[425] "*Historia e Popullit Shqiptar,*" Volume I, Tirana, 2002, p. 147.

The successful Dardanian campaign in Macedonia made Philip V eventually and with all strength turn to Dardania, in order to remove the main obstacle in its efforts to fully concentrate on the wars against the Romans, in which it was already engaged with their side being decisive on the next greatest power of the time, although the chances for Macedonians to restore the former fame was growing smaller while those of the Romans to cross over the other side of the Adriatic increased, as they saw their chances there for expansion and further strengthening. This war began in 208 B.C. and lasted two years.

The long war against the Macedonians, on one hand, and that of the Romans against Macedonians on the other, which would define a new factor of power that transcended the narrow dimensions, made Dardanians, and Illyrians in particular, generally enter into occasional unnatural and even inconsistent alliances with their opponents, in which they had more disadvantages than benefits. Such agreements appeared to be the two that the Dardanians reached with Rome between the years 200 B.C. and 197 B.C. when they tried to gain from the Macedonian wars against the Romans. Therefore, in the year 200 B.C. as the Romans marked considerable success during their campaign in Dasareti, the Dardanian King, Bato, Longar's son, offered the Romans military assistance against the Macedonians, provided they gained something from it, by extending southward.[426]

Evidently, from these wars only the Romans would benefit, while Dardanians remained where they were, without any benefits, but in further enmity with Macedonians, who in the circumstances of suffering losses against the Romans, were able to gather forces to fight them, as indeed happened in 199 B.C. when the Dardanian armies, retreating in Macedonia, were attacked by the forces of Philip V. Though they did not suffer any great loss, it still made them realize they would not benefit from any unnatural alliances such as those with the Romans, who were rather interested in using their overture of conquest in the East, which followed

---

[426] See Livius: *"Ab urbe condita,"* Book XXXI/28. *("As the war ended with this very fortunate expedition, many little kings and princes neighbors of the Macedonians came to the Roman camp; Pleurat, son of Scerdilaidis, and Amynandris, the Athamanian king, and from the Dardanians, Bato, son of Longar. Longar had fought against Demetrius, Philip's father. Their promises to help the consul were responded that he would use the help of the Dardanians and Pleurat once he brought his army into Macedonia; He appointed Amunandrit to boost Aetolians for war.")*

shortly, to divide and use both Illyrians and Dardanians against Macedonians and vice versa so as to weaken the opponents as much as possible and consequently increase their own benefits by their weakening prospects.

Indeed that is what happened. In 197 B.C. after the Battle of Cynocephalus, which ended in the Romans' favor, a truce was settled between Rome and Macedonia. Dardanians, despite fighting alongside the Romans, did not get any gains. Rather, Macedonians benefited from this peace, as they used it for a tough campaign against the Dardanians, upon which Philip V, with multiple forces attacked Dardanians at the Battle of Stobi in Paeonia, defeating them but not completely destroying them.[427]

It is very likely that this campaign interested the Romans, who wished to have two weak opponents instead of one strong one, as could be the case with Dardanians, who from a strategic point of view appeared more dangerous to Rome as they were of the same family with the Illyrians and they could join forces against them anytime.

Aware of the fact that they were dealing with a very resolute and unbending enemy while they were already involved in wars with the Romans, the outcome of which would determine a future victor and the epilogue should have extracted a future winner of imperial dimensions, the Macedonians did everything they could to prevent Dardania from becoming a key factor that would decide that fate. Therefore, both descendants of Pelasgians were involved in actions against each other, something that was to the benefit of the Romans in order to permanently remove them from the social and political scene.

Therefore, evidently, Philip V, in order to finally defeat the Dardanians as an important power, or at least, hold them under constant pressure, decided to do this through the Bastami, a tribe that lived in the Danube provinces, after having settled there on Dardanian lands. This was best described by Titus Livius claiming that "Philip's goal was to erase the tribe of Dardania and settle the Bastami on their lands instead. He (Philip) thought this would be of double benefit for him, as, on one hand, the Dardanian tribe, which had always been a dangerous enemy of Macedonia, disturbing its kings in difficult moments, would be wiped out, and on the other hand, he would send Bastami to Italy in order to devastate it after leaving their women and children in Dardania."[428]

---

[427] *"Historia e Popullit Shqiptar,"* Volume I, Tirana, 2002, p. 148.
[428] Titus Livius: *"Ab urbe condita,"* Book XLI/19.

Indeed, according to ancient sources, the Bastami were deployed to the Dardanian lands, but it was the death of Philip V that ended his plans to disintegrate and weaken the Dardanians in their own lands by settling the Basami there. Perseus, however, after taking the Macedonian throne, attempted to ignite a war between the Bastami and Dardanians, at least to weaken them, aware that if not Dardanians, it would be the Romans who would be dealing with the Bastami, who could even by them be used against the Macedonians. According to Titus Livius,[429] together with the Bastami, Thracian and Scodriscan forces were deployed in Dardanian lands, who after the death of Philip V would be withdrawn, while the Bastami still hoped they would be able to stay on in the promised land where they felt good. Therefore, in the winter of 176 B.C.-175 B.C. Dardanians attacked the Bastami settlements in Dardania and after a war of turns (as a part of the Dardanian army was almost defeated), the Dardanians with the rest of their army managed to force the Bastami to leave Dardania.

The expulsion of the Bastami did not rid Dardanians of the Macedonian threat to which they already were accustomed. In 172 B.C., Perseus undertook a new large campaign against the Dardanians, with an army of 20,000 men, part of which was from the ranks of the famous Macedonian Phalange, led personally by him. Perseus scored a victory in this fight, but eventually did not manage to kneel to the Dardanian Kingdom. On the contrary, the Dardanian Kingdom was able at this time to stand back on its feet mainly thanks to two important actions. The first concerned the strengthening of friendship, even temporarily, with the Illyrians (the marriage of the King Moun's daughter Teuta to Gentius), which was associated with an alliance, also temporary, for joint military actions against Macedonia. The second was another alliance with the Romans, since Gentius had cut his ties with Rome carrying them over to the Macedonians, which eventually turned away from the first and were approached by the latter, and that made the Dardanians, in order to be protected from Macedonian destruction, being more threatened than ever and alone, seeking protection from a new connection with the Romans, which eventually happened.

In fact the second and last Dardanian alliance with the Romans, and that of Gentius' Illyrian Kingdom with Macedonians, after it cut its almost

---

[429] Ibid, Book XLI/19.

vassal connection with Rome, marked the beginning of the end of both the Macedonians and Kingdom of Illyria led by Gentius. It also marked the end of ties between Dardanians and Romans for long wars with them, ending in Rome's victory and the inclusion of the Illyrians and Dardanians under a long Roman occupation, permanently losing their numerous kingdoms and states, being mostly disconnected from each other, but as noted, they also gained an administrative, social and cultural union, which they never had before. The later emergence of Illyricum as the main province on the eastern side of the Roman Empire (one of four in the Empire at the time of Diocletian and beyond), and the acceptance of Christianity from the fourth century onwards, unified for the first time the Illyrian-Dardanian factor in imperial dimensions around a universal concept of global world governance that the Roman Empire represented, whose authors came from their own ranks (Emperors Diocletian, Constantine the Great, and Justinian I).

The reason for the ultimate engagement of Dardanians in a permanent enmity with the Romans, which eventually turned into a long war ending in defeat, was exactly the Roman occupation of Paeonians and Macedonia, leaving Rome's allies without any kind of benefits. The Roman historian Livius describes the cause of this breakdown claiming that "To the Dardanians, who sought Paeonia, sharing a border with them, the Roman commander replied that he gave freedom to all who were under the rule of Perseus. Refusing to grant them Paeonia, as they demanded, he granted them the right to the salt trade instead."[430]

Dardanians felt not only deceived by the Roman "salt concessions" but also underestimated, and after settling accounts with the Macedonians and setting their power over nearly the entire Illyrian Kingdom of Gentius, they turned into masters of most of the Balkans. This made them launch occasional attacks against the Roman forces located in Paeonia and Macedonia. For some time this was done in collaboration with Scordicses, and after they withdrew from military actions against the Romans, Dardanians had no choice but to engage themselves in a war against the Romans alongside their eastern neighbors, the Maedans.[431]

Evidently, the Dardanians together with Maedans conducted a successful defense for decades against the Romans, who were already stationed in Macedonia and other parts of Illyria. In the year 84 B.C., Roman

---

[430] Titus Livius: *"Ab urbe Condita"* (From Rome's Foundation), Book XLV/29, pp. 12-13.
[431] *"Historia e Popullit Shqiptar,"* Volume I, Tirana, 2002, p. 151.

sources agree that between 97 B.C. and 85 B.C., some Roman expeditions against Dardanians, did not succeed. In the year 84 B.C. Dardanians marked an important victory over the Roman forces in Macedonia, from where they managed to penetrate as far as Delphi. However, the Roman consul Gaius Scribonius Curio was the one to regroup some good legions deciding to end the Dardanian Kingdom in order that their further expansion in the Balkans would not be impeded. Roman sources describe Scribonius Curio's campaign in Dardania as extremely bloody, as after the victory over the Dardanian forces, which were fewer in number than the well-prepared Roman forces, he engaged in great terror against the defenseless population. However, despite this, some subsequent events show that although Dardanians were weakened by wars against the Romans and their consequences, they continued to oppose Rome's occupation policies.[432]

Long Wars against Rome

> *Beginnings of the first Illyrian-Roman war, and its consequences. – Queen Teuta tries to establish internal alliances with other Illyrian tribes, especially with Dardanians and Epirotes. – Defeats by the Romans and sending of an Illyrian delegation to Rome for the signing of peace. – Empowerment of Demetrius of Pharos and his links with Macedonia. – Illyrians and Dardanians in an alliance with the Romans against Macedonia and peace with Rome for which nothing was gained. – Coming to the throne of Gentius and the third Roman-Illyrian war. – Gentius' defeat in 168 B.C., the fall of Shkodra and Gentius being sent prisoner to Italy. – In 167, the Roman military commander, Lui Ancinius announced the decision of the Roman Senate, dividing Illyrian lands into three separate administrative units.*

Among the first internal wars between the Illyrians and Dardanians was unequivocally that of the year 229 B.C., caused when a part of Epirus Illyrians, belonging to Teuta, engaged in military operations in the South, left and joined the opposing Dardanians.[433] This "episode" is especially characteristic in highlighting the social and political realities which the

---

[432] Ibid, 152.
[433] See Polybius: "*Histories*," Book II/9.

descendants of Pelasgians experienced: Illyrians, Macedonians, Epirotes, and Dardanians, together with their numerous branches under circumstances of a slave system of the 4th - 2nd centuries, which determined the behavior of the dynasties in accordance with their interests to expand by waging wars against each other regardless of the fact that by doing so they were weakening in relation to their main opponents: Greeks and Romans. This behavior is especially noticeable after the defeat of Pyrrhus that brought an end to the illusion of an expansion of the Epirotan state in Italy and not in their own ethnic space, as happened between the Macedonians and Dardanians.

In fact, when Teuta entered a war with the Dardanians, she was already engaged in another war in Epirus, in her efforts to expand to the South. She summoned Scerdilaidis to return immediately with his forces to the North. However, before he left Epirus he reached a very favorable agreement that put the Epirotes in a dependent position from the Illyrian state,[434] making it clear that the Illyrian Queen was determined to present both a significant naval and land force, by strengthening from the mainland at the expense of Epirotes and others. The latter went through the challenge of an inevitable confrontation with Dardania, given their important position in the central and southern part and, unlike other tribes which Teuta was able to force in accepting her conditions without any threat. With the Dardanians things were different, as they represented an important land power, and although in constant wars with the Macedonians, they would still be able, if necessary, to put aside these enemies, as would happen in this case, and return to a confrontation with the Illyrians. Evidently, Teuta left the Dardanians undisturbed because she knew what it meant to enter into a long battle with the Dardanians, so after a peace without agreement, she returned once again to the coast with the intention of targeting Greek colonies in South Illyria (Dyrrhachion and Apollonia).

Obviously, this move did not remain unnoticed by the Greeks, and also Romans, who received clear messages of Teuta's goals, especially when they already had begun to emerge with their colonies in the southern Italian Adriatic, expecting to do the same in the rest of the Adriatic, in Illyrian lands, where the Greeks had their colonies for a long time and from where they were supervising trade in that important area.

---

[434] Stipcevic, Aleksandar: *"Ilirët,"* Prishtina, 1980, p. 55.

Under such circumstances, with the Romans wishing to expand into the eastern part, and Illyrians still safeguarding their naval force in the Adriatic and Ionian Seas and their fast ships able to oversee the important water ways, one could expect a confrontation between the Illyrians and Romans, as happened with the launching of three Illyrian wars, which began shortly and lasted very long. The issue at hand was if the Illyrians would enter the confrontation alone or with the help of Dardanians and Macedonians, without excluding the possibility of Greeks having some hand, although chances were little for the latter for the sole reason that the principle "the enemy of my enemy is my friend" applied here. This principle, in relation to the Illyrians and Dardanians, left the Greeks to decide any connection, regardless that the latter were more likely smaller, since this principle in relation to Illyria and Dardania always prevailed.

Illyrians were determined to go on their own, going through an internal struggle first with the Epirotes, and others around them (Antinates, Parthians), forcing them into submission, and then with Dardanians, engaging in an open war, but unable to gain them over. However, Dardanians too were trying to maintain a cautious stance in the conflict, as they were facing the Macedonians, who were constantly engaged in unsettled issues, having entered alliances with the Romans to this cause, which explains the fact that the Dardanians were ready to accept the Illyrian Kingdom as a naval force, and as a possible ally against the Macedonians, but not as a continental force, which they claimed to be. It seems, indeed, that the Illyrians held the position that as a naval force, which would inevitably confront them with the Romans and Greeks, they had to have their back protected by Dardanians, and this depended on their testing of power with the Macedonians. In any case, the Illyrians remained a naval power and they could keep their sails open or drown with them.

It has been repeatedly claimed that the wars with Rome were provoked by Teuta, and generally by the Illyrians, who had been controlling the Ionian coast and Adriatic shores for long, from where their pirates set the order. Alleged "extremely arrogant" behavior by Teuta in relation to the Romans has also been mentioned, as she makes a mockery with its messengers (brothers Guy and Luc Coruconis, joined also by a Greek of Isis, Clemporos) when she said that "the state was not able to guarantee for private behavior, that is, of the pirates at sea, because they were right,"[435] and so on, something that looked more like a trigger that the Romans would need to launch an attack against the Illyrians, rather than "a failure of the Illyrian state to control the behavior of the pirates."[436] Even if Teuta would be so insensitive towards Rome, as stated, and as powerless as to not be able to supervise over the sea pirates, she would certainly never send to Rome special emissaries to reflect the real situation and this had to do with her approach of supervising the Greek colonies on the Adriatic and Ionian coast.

In fact, Teuta became convinced that the colonies had not belonged to the Greeks, whose power was declining, but to the Illyrians, to which they naturally were entitled as the colonies were located in their lands and mostly based on agreements with them. The Greeks, on the other hand, realizing that they could not defend colonies any longer without any great tribute, reached a decision that it would be better to leave them under Roman supervision, naturally based on a mutual agreement with them, than let them fall into the Illyrian hands. Of course, Teuta, knowing that games were being played and that therefore she needed a diplomatic approach, invited the Romans to come to an agreement in regard to the colonies, given that in this case, concessions, even sensitive ones, had to be made, but which would prove beneficial to the Illyrians.

It was exactly the question of concessions, which the Romans were indulged by, over which swords would break between Teuta and Rome, an event that continued for years, ending finally at the expense of the Illyrians. What Polybius and other Roman authors claim, with the exception of what Justin says, being somewhat more realistic,[437] is to overwhelmingly retain Rome's policy language, appearing seemingly "peaceful" and without any interest on the eastern Adriatic and Ionian Sea, and hiding its true goals for an incursion in these parts in order to expand its power in accordance with its pretentions it nourished dating back from the fourth century onwards, when it withstood the effects of Gaul and barbaric invasions from the North, coming out, surprisingly much stronger.

Polybius and other ancient authors saw the measures undertaken by Teuta, such as sending warships before Dyrrhachion and Korkyres to prevent certain demonstrations in these lands that the Greeks had planned to provoke the Illyrians. War actions of the Illyrians sufficed for

---

[435] Ibid, II/4; II/8, p. 8.
[436] See Stipcevic, Aleksandar: *"Ilirët,"* Prishtina, 1980, p. 56.
[437] See Justin: *"Epitoma Historiarum Philippicarum Pompei Trogi,"* Book VII-XXXIII.

the Romans to prepare in the spring of 229 B.C. their naval fleet of 200 warships with a strong army of 20,000 men and two thousand horsemen, who, led by Gaius Fulvius Centunam was headed for Dyrrchachion, which marked the beginning of the first Roman-Illyrian War.

That Rome was prepared for such a war and that it only was a pretext, is plainly explained by the behavior of Demetrius Pharos, who without any contradiction handed over Corcyra to the Romans putting even himself at their service. Some other tribes (Antinates, Partines, and others) acted similarly by not only opening the way to the Roman Army, but even "asking" them to be accepted as allies.[438] These curves in the Illyrian contingent, that were at the expense of Teuta, made it known that Rome had long since prepared for combat action against the Illyrians, and had taken all measures to detach from Queen Teuta, one by one, all the factors on whom she could rely. Demetrius Pharos was one of them, as will be seen, with his games, which turned fatal to the Illyrians, but also to himself, since all his actions were to the liking of the Romans.

Against these circumstances, i.e. when the Roman legions without difficulty managed to break the naval and land forces of the Illyrians, while the chieftains of the coastal cities (Dyrrahum, Apollonia and others) were turned over to the Romans and even welcomed seeking their protective umbrella, Teuta could do nothing but retreat to Rizon and there seek peace, which was very costly.[439] With the peace imposed by the Romans she first took leave from his royal throne in favor of Pyni, while her kingdom was partly in control of Rome,[440] which marked the beginning of

---

[438] Stipcevic, Aleksandar: "Ilirët," Prishtina, 1980, p. 57.

[439] For more on the first Illyrian-Roman War see ancient authors: Polybius: "*Historiae;*" Appian: "*Historia Romana*" and "*Rimska Iliria od Apiana Alexandrinskog*" translated by Ante Stipcevic, and other authors, among whom the following: Zippel, Georg: "*Die römische Herrschaft in Illyrien bis auf Augustus,*" Leipzig, 1877; Dominico Mustilli: "*La conquista romana dell sponda oreintale adriatica,*" Napoli,1941; Novak, Grga: "*Prošlost Dalmacije,*" Zagreb, 1944; Walser, G: "*Die Ursachen des ersten römisch-illyrischen Kriges,*" (History), 2-1952-1953, Wiesbaden; Karl-Ernst Petzold: "*Rom und Illyrien. Ein Beitrag zur römischen Aussenpolitik im 3. Jahrhundert,*" History, 20-1971 pp. 199-223.

[440] According to the historian Polybius, in the spring of 228, when Illyrian Kingdom had begun to disintegrate, Teuta sent its representatives to Rome signing peace with the Senate. According to Polybius, Teuta was compelled to pay tribute to the Romans, to relinquish the main part of Illyria while saving only a few areas and bar from sailing in south of Lissus with more than two unarmed ships.

incessant penetrations of the Romans inside Illyrian territories and generally in the East from where it took on the path of a world empire.

However, from all this war which started from a pretext by "unattended Illyrian pirates," Rome managed to achieve some goals, two of which were determinative of the Roman Empire beginning its expansion into the western part of the Ionian and Adriatic, which further paved the way for the Roman conquests in the Balkans. Under goal one, the Greek colonies on the Illyrian coast, Dyrrhachion, Apollonia, Isa, and others maintained political autonomy, but under the protectorate of Rome. And under goal two, under the agreement Illyrian armed ships could not sail further south of Lissos, meaning that the Kingdom lost its oversight of the Adriatic, which was Rome's main purpose.[441]

But the loss of the naval force of Teuta and thereby the Illyrian Kingdom was not the only evil that befell Illyria. Besides the sea, she lost the coast and the mainland together with most of its allies or other Illyrian tribes, many of which she had forced into a position of subordination, who defected to Rome or declared themselves "neutral" from Rome to create the oases depriving the Illyrian Kingdom of any possible connection with its family, a small area north of Lissus. With the creation of the dynasty of Demetrius Pharos (from Durrahum to Shkodra) it suffered a counterweight to the North, detaching it completely from its center to date, its main support. This separation, as noted, was also fatal to other Illyrian tribes in the North (coastal parts), not able to connect among themselves, which, as separate, their opposition to the Romans would be weak or quite useless.

There are several other issues that this war highlighted. A seed of discord was planted among the Illyrians, Epirotes, Macedonians and Dardanians, which had already been present among them, but now was gaining a strong incentive, as they could benefit concretely from it, while it set further opportunities for the Greek-Roman affinity to the detriment of the Illyrians. On this occasion, Rome not only defended the Greek colonies on the Illyrian coast, but, placing them under its own protectorate, it simultaneously strengthened their weakened positions in these parts, especially as their trading ships could sail freely by the Ionian and Adriatic coast, something that they could do only with the permission of the Illyrians and under their supervision, of course, paying a fair tribute. As a token of

---

[441] Stipcevic, Aleksandar: *"Ilirët,"* Prishtina, 1980, p. 58.

gratitude for this assistance and believing that they had found the right allies against the Illyrians, Greeks allowed the Romans to participate in the Isthmic (Olympic) games recognizing them as a civilized people,[442] something of which the barbarians were deprived.

Providing the treatment of a "civilized people" for the Romans and allowing them to compete in the Isthmic (Olympic) Games, in this case, was very important for explaining the internal circumstances between Greeks and Macedonians, because neither they, nor the Illyrians, Epirotes and Dardanians were allowed to participate in the games on the grounds that they were barbarians, that is, foreign. This is contrary to the attempts of some ancient authors to present the Macedonians as Hellenes, or Hellenized, although they remained as a permanent bond, more so when they conquered the Greeks, they were also occupied by them from within, i.e. in terms of ideas, rather than in accordance with any Greek political concept about a global empire, as was said, as it did not even exist.

The alliance of the Greeks with Romans that went to the detriment of the Illyrians, but also Macedonians, despite the vassal acceptance by Demetrius Pharos and forced alliances of numerous small Illyrian tribes with the Romans, would not serve the appeasement of this part, at least for a while, as Rome expected. It would be the aggravations between the Carthaginians and Romans, and later Punic Wars that rose to a certain obstinacy of Pharos, in connecting with the Macedonians to get rid of the Roman bondage, from which, he had expected something else. These scores were not entirely without support knowing that the Greeks were not able to resist a possible alliance between the Illyrians and Macedonians, which could be also joined by Dardanians. The Romans, at the same time, occupied with the Punic concerns, would not be able to enter into a new war with the Illyrian-Macedonians on behalf of the Greeks, a mutual reckoning that started to produce new realities, among worth mentioning is the alliance between Pharos and the Macedonian ruler, Antigon Doson, and his successor Philip V. An encouraged Demetrius Pharos sent several military units into Greece to be put at the service of the Macedonian campaign against the Greeks. After a while, Pharos fully rebeled against Rome when attacking many of Rome's allies in Illyria, and shortly thereaf-

---

[442] Ibid, p. 58.

ter attacking with his fleet the Greek cities, even those on the Aegean Sea.[443]

Expectedly, Demetrius Pharos, although in the role of the main despot of Illyria, which he attained from Rome, on the occasion of this alliance with Macedonians, was not able to represent all the Illyrian "unity," as Scerdilaidis appeared, a former supporter of Teuta, who would not accompany him in his campaign to extract some of the Illyrian tribes from the Roman influence and also, his units occasionally attacked Macedonia, which went against the Illyrian-Macedonian alliance signed with Doson and later Philip V.

The Roman Senate, concerned by these developments that were spoiling its plans, invited Demetrius to Rome to explain his positions. Demetrius did not respond to the invitation of the Roman Senate, so in 219 B.C. a powerful Roman army was sent against him led by two Consuls: L. Emilius Paulus and M. Livius Salinator. Powerless to resist the attacks, he initially fled to Dimallium, an Illyrian city, and from there he moved to his hometown in Pharos, never managing to resist the Romans. He somehow escaped by secret roads, and entered Macedonia, where Philip V received him amicably. Jointly, hoping to restore former power, they sealed an anti-Roman alliance with Carthage and Syracuse, which were at war with Rome,[444] signed by Philip V and Hannibal.[445]

The Macedonian king, excited by Hannibal's victories in Italy, on the advice of his now dethroned ally, Demetrius, attacked Scerdilaidis who had acquired the Illyrian throne formerly belonging to Demetrius, an ally of Rome who conquered also a part of the Illyrian coast. Of course, Rome, after having defeated Carthage, without any hesitation initiated opera-

---

[443] For more see: Frank W. Walbank: *"Philip V,"* Hamed, 1967; John Antwerp Fine: *"Macedon, Illyria and Rome 219-220,"* (Journal of Roman Studies, 26/1936, pp. 24-39; John M. F. May: *"Macedonia and Illyria,"* Rome, 1964, pp. 48-57; Henrry J. Dell: *"The Western Frontier of the Macedonian Monarchy in Ancient Macedonia"* (International Symosium), Thessaloniki, 1970, pp. 115-126.

[444] Stipcevic, Aleksandar: *"Ilirët,"* Prishtina, 1980, p. 60.

[445] In the year 215 Philip and Hannibal made a treaty alliance according to which Carthaginians pledged to help each other in the war against Rome. The treaty totally ignored Illyrian state interests. The clause under which the Romans should not remain "masters of Corcyra, Apollonia, Epidamnos, Pharos, Pathinians, Dimales, and Amathia" practically recognized Macedonia's right over the rule in Illyria.

tions against Philip V. After a series of battles, in 197 B.C. Rome achieved a decisive victory in Cynoscephalae, Thessaly.[446]

Before the Roman victory against the Macedonians, which however did not mean the end of the Macedonian state - because the Romans did not want this, knowing that as the consul said "Greece' freedom was threatened by the power of Macedonian kings, and if that kingdom was destroyed, Thracians, Illyrians, and others would be immigrating into Greece,"[447] – there occurred an internal development that was reflected in the so-called "anti-Macedonian coalition." This coalition further estranged Illyrians, Epirotes, and Dardanians from Macedonia, sending them under the tutelage of Rome, appearing also as allies of Greece, which went against their basic determination, becoming prey to foreign accounts, not depending on them, but rather forced to be subject to them.

However, this anti-Macedonian coalition, which suited Rome, and in no way their potential strengthening against the Greeks, was forced by the Roman successes in war against Carthage when, by submitting Syracuse and Capus (212 B.C.-211 B.C.), the Romans began to taste the first fruits of their superiority over Hannibal. The anti-Macedonian coalition was, in fact, extensive and including all the opponents of Philip V could be called regional. Initially, the alliance was launched with Etoles, which involved several states, such as the Attalus of Pergamos, which was then joined by the Illyrian state represented by Scerdilaidis, Pleuratis' son. Philip V, however, hastened to attack the alliance before they created a joint military force, and managed this by attacking the lands of Orichum and Apollonia, devastating them. He did the same against the Greek lands, where he was not as successful since the Greeks had time to prepare their defenses. However, over two to three years the situation did not change, as Rome was still occupied in final wars with Carthage, so it helped Philip V to hold on. Only in the beginning of the year 205 B.C. a little more concentrated action by the Romans was noticed while moving into Dyrrahum with 10,000 footmen, and a thousand horsemen. Sources from that period, however, do not talk about any tough battle, but rather about a twist, ending in sudden peace with Macedonia, which suited the Romans, who were still occupied with the wars with Hannibal (although he was suffering losses) trying to distribute their forces into other fronts, keeping them internally divided, as was the case with the related alliances.

---

[446] Stipcevic, Aleksandar: *"Ilirët,"* Prishtina, 1980, p. 60.
[447] See: *"Historia e Popullit Shqiptar,"* Volume II, Tirana, 2002, p. 129.

Philip V, in turn, appeared convinced that there was no other way but to strengthen the position in the region as much as possible, where the future clash with Rome was expected. In subsequent years, while Rome was finishing the war with Hannibal, Philip V undertook a series of diplomatic and military actions in the East. He concluded an alliance with Attali III of Syria, extended his conquests in the Aegean stretching to Hellespont, raised the pressure on Greece, and took the land of Aetolians. In the North he attacked Dardanians and in violation of the Treaty made with Phoenicia he achieved small conquests in Illyria and was allowed to detach Parthinians from the Romans.[448]

In 201 B.C., when the Romans finally defeated Hannibal and forced Carthage to embrace peace, an evil hour began for Philip V and Macedonia as a kingdom. Soon, the Romans began the decisive campaign against the Macedonians and the Illyrian lands. In the autumn of the year 200, the Roman legions landed in Apollonia and raised camp near the River Apsos. There it started attacks against Philip's positions in Desaretia. On this occasion, another Illyrian "alliance" against Macedonia was marked, attended by Pleuratis of Illyria, Bato of Dardania and Alexander of Athamania.

This war, which lasted three years, could not end other than with Rome's victory and Macedonian defeat, being unable to resist the coalition of anti-Macedonian and Roman forces. Under these circumstances he sought peace, and was forced to accept more serious conditions, such as those that demanded giving up all of Greece and his Asian possessions, returning the conquered lands in Illyria granted by the peace of Phoenicia to the Romans, and dismantling its fleet to five vessels.

Evidently, Illyrians and Dardanians did not gain anything from this peace. Dardanians even expected to recover their extension in Paeonia, but were left empty-handed.

Here indeed lies the cause for the third Illyrian-Roman War, the consequence of which would be the fall of the Illyrian state of 168 B.C., preceded by the third Roman-Macedonian war and the military hostilities of the year 171 B.C.

In fact, the political situation in the region and in Illyria after 196 B.C. was characterized by a careful concentration of Rome to create opportunities for a general penetration into this space as occurred nearly three

---

[448] Ibid, p. 127.

decades later when it gave the last blow to the Illyrians and others, despite the long resistance in various parts of the Roman conquest. In the meantime all passed in two directions, sealing the final conflict. The first involved Rome's efforts to strengthen its position in Greece, replacing Macedonia. And, the second was to further weaken the Illyrians by means of internal rifts. For this purpose, Rome skillfully exploited the contradictions among the Greek states; initially by supporting the League of Achaea it annihilated the Nabis movement in Sparta, and then ended the Etole League claims for hegemony in Greece, simultaneously breaking the goals of Antiochus of Syria over the land.[449]

In these circumstances, even Philip V took the side of the Romans. He hoped that by doing so he could improve his own position at the expense of the Greeks, but it was impossible having in mind that Rome made clear its ultimate goals, namely to exterminate all the factors East of the Adriatic: the Greeks, Macedonians, Illyrians and Dardanians, one by one, or all together, when conditions were ripe for this, but that it was inevitable, as they, although they knew this already, were trying to escape from drowning by pulling each other down.

As these purposes were easily identifiable, Macedonians and Illyrians began to come closer together somehow standing in Rome's way if not to stop it at least to inflict a heavier price on it. This aroused anti-Roman forces in Illyria and in Macedonia as well. The Illyrian King, Pleuratis, who inherited Scerdilaidis, although in position of vassalage to Rome, began to show signs of cooperation on his own with Macedonia, though moderately, something that troubled Rome, which still showed restraint wishing to consider all the developments before undertaking the final campaign, in order to do this as best as possible and with the least losses.

This concentration gave rise to Gentius coming to power, which followed Pleuratis in 181 B.C. and played the Macedonian card. On this occasion, Rome, looking for a pretext to act when necessary and to see that it looked as a mobilization of the Romans, reacted similarly to the way it had acted in Teuta's time when it launched piracy charges in the open sea and treated the Roman citizens in Corcyra Nigra poorly. Aware of this threat, Gentius tried to improve the economic situation in the country, as the economic strengthening of the country also meant political hardening. Of course in this direction he made a monetary reform, cut

---

[449] Ibid, p. 130.

independent currencies in many cities, bearing his portrait on one side and on the back the symbol of an Illyrian ship, where the town legend was substituted with the name of the king.

In addition, Gentius' efforts for a much greater proximity with the Macedonians are noted, and with the Kingdom of Dardania linked through a marriage, but nothing more was done, as Dardanians had shown that they could be approached by anyone, but Macedonians and Greeks.

However, relations between Gentius and Perseus served as a trigger for the final Roman campaign against Macedonia and Illyria. Rome had begun to prepare the ground for this by means of various "complaints" coming to the Senate from the consuls and militaries. One of them, being more significant, was concerned with the murder of Artetauris, a tiny dynast somewhere in Illyria who maintained Rome's policy. Perseus and Gentius were indicted for this "conspiracy" and their justifications that they had nothing to do with the case were all in vain, though indeed it seemed they had nothing to do with it.

Of course, Rome would like to separate Gentius from Perseus, so that it could first launch its campaign against Macedonia without fear of getting into trouble with the Illyrians, but Gentius refused to do it convinced that together they could force Rome to regard them as regional allies, while they would strengthen also through a new alignment in relation to the risk from beyond the sea, for which they could seek support in the East, towards Asia Minor, where further unexhausted opportunities for political union still existed.

Therefore, in November 172 B.C., the senate ordered the deployment of the first forces in Illyria. A number of them were also sent to Greece. Once they had been positioned in Thessaly, in the spring of 171 B.C., Rome decided to start fighting against Perseus, being more important in strategic and tactical terms.

This war, which lasted over five years, brought even closer Gentius and Perseus of Macedonia. In January of the year 168 B.C. they concluded an alliance against the Romans, which was the last for them, but first of all fatal for Gentius and the Illyrian Kingdom, as the Illyrian king went to war against Rome, even though he knew there was no chance for any long term success, but this being inevitable as he had sealed his own fate with the Macedonians from which there was no going back, even though it seemed increasingly clear that they were not a strong card. This gave reason to Rome to attack the Illyrians in a strong campaign, subdue the southern Illyrian province directly, and destroy the Illyrian Kingdom. The Roman military leader of 30,000 soldiers, Lucius Anicus Gaul, went forth toward the fortified Shkodra, the capital of the Illyrian state, where the King was sheltered.[450]

But the third Illyrian-Roman War lasted a month total. King Gentius surrendered in 168 B.C. Gentius King and his family was sent into exile in Italy, exiled first in Spoletium and then in Gubbium. This marked the end of Illyrian Kingdom and simultaneously a decisive step toward the conquest of Illyrian lands by Rome.[451]

Losing the war against Rome this time was different from those suffered during the time of Teuta or later when the losers, through peace agreements, were subjected to conditions of Rome, which typically was satisfied with heavy tributes, as was the case with Teuta, or vassalage, as happened with Pleuratis and Demetrius of Pharos. Rome had now decided to end the Illyrian Kingdom, the Macedonian Kingdom and other similar creations across the sea, in order to eventually establish its hegemony in the region and other parts of the East. Therefore, after the war, Rome dealt with the administrative division of the land of the defeated states. This measure was preceded by the decision of the Roman Senate to declare Illyrians and Macedonians "free." In Shkodra, in the year 167 B.C., the Roman Army commander Anicius Manlius, in the presence of five special Roman envoys and representatives of pro-Roman Illyrian leadership, announced the decisions of the Roman Senate, whereby Illyrian lands were divided into three separate administrative units.[452]

The first province, with Lissus as its center, included the lands around the city and to the River Mat in the South.

The Second administrative unit was composed of regions inhabited by Labeates, the center of which was Shkodra.

In the third region were parts of Illyrian coastal areas north of Shkodra and River Narona, including the cities Rizon and Olcin (Ulqin).[453]

Noticeably, the Roman conquerors used various measures to attract people who had not taken part in wars against them. Those were released of taxes, while others would give the Roman state half of what they had

---

[450] Stipcevic, Aleksandar: *"Ilirët,"* Prishtina, 1980, p. 60.
[451] Ibid, p. 60.
[452] *"Historia e Popullit Shqiptar,"* Volume I, Tirana, 2002, p. 140.
[453] Ibid, p. 140.

been paying to King Gentius. They also left military garrisons placing representatives from among the Illyrian chieftains over their administrative units.[454]

Interesting to note, the Romans behaved differently with Illyrian territories. Once they divided Gentius' Kingdom into three autonomous administrative units "civitates," they kept the Antinates and Parthines under their protectorate, and those who had not taken part in hostilities (Bylines, Amantians, Desaretes, and others) were left on their own, while the cities of Corcyra, Apollonia, and Durrahum maintained their autonomy, even though they continued to be Roman military bases. So, this was a selective attitude of Rome towards the conquered territories and peoples included within the bosom of the empire, which as noted would not remain without consequences, since tired of the long wars and the damage they brought, there were many of those who succumbed to new imperial circumstances, which opened the way for economic development, among the most powerful one of the time.

Roman Conquests and Uprisings against Them

> *Illyrian occupied areas included within the autonomous "civitates" and respect for their social structures of governance. - Rome aimed to keep Dardanians detached from the rest of the Illyrians in order to more easily penetrate to the North. - The emergence of the Dalmatian League in the North as another powerful rival of Rome and efforts to subjugate it by all means, using their political disunity. – Wars against the Japodes and Pannonii. – Detachment of Ardiaei against Rome and displacement from their lands after their defeat. - Two Dardanian victories in the years 97 and 85 B.C., together with the Meades against the Romans.- The great Octavian and Antonius campaign against Dalmatians and other parts of Illyria and the destruction of their state structures. – The uprising of Breuci and two different pathways of the two Batos.*

The collapse of the Illyrian Kingdom of Gentius and the inclusion of Illyrian territories in the new imperial administration based on the model

---

[454] Ibid, p. 140.

of autonomies (civitates) did not conclude the process of the Roman conquest as envisaged in the scenario for the complete submission of Illyria, Macedonia and Greece under its rule. The removal of the Illyrian Kingdom of Gentius and the Macedonian Kingdom, accomplished a lot of what would be a completion of the Roman triumph over the sea, but not their ultimate victory. Because, as obstacles to be seen were great, they had left the Dardanian Kingdom and the Federation of Dalmatians, which appeared independent and with exceptional power, which as noted, became a big hindrance to Rome.

Obviously, in this invading strategy of Rome, Dardanians were looked upon as a priority for many reasons, with those of a strategic nature certainly as most deserving, because they showed once again the great importance of the Dardanians and Dardania as an old power dating as early as Troy, connecting Central Europe with Asia Minor and beyond. There was also a possibility of it taking over a broad front of anti-Roman resistance, which would be identified on the basis of the common root of the Pelasgic family, of the Illyrian, Epirotan and even Macedonian foundation, although the latter was seen as Hellenized, but appeared in the political sense as opposite from the Greeks in their determination of barbarian peoples.

Aware of these issues, the Romans took all measures to initially keep Dardanians and Dardania separate from the Epirotan and Macedonian parts in the South and East, establishing a Roman circle, as they would do their best to cut any connection with other parts of remaining Illyria outside the conquest in the western part (Dalmatians, Ardians, Pleraei and others). Later, partitioned, they would be subject to new circumstances, meaning to accept the role of a privileged vassal, similar to what had happened to Labeates, Japodes, Doarses and a few others, rather than be submitted to war.

The strategy of keeping Dardanians disconnected for a long time would probably have been useless and even harmful, if they were not denied the opportunity of having allies, or co-actors in their front against Rome. Therefore, it was quite natural for the Romans to keep settling accounts in the North of Illyria with the Illyrian "remnants," as were Dalmatae, and also Ardiaei, Pleraei, Japodes, and other kingdoms, so that the part west of Dardania would be restored to "pure" Roman space.

Indeed, Dalmatians in North Illyria emerged as a major political force in the 2nd century B.C. Their lands were in the inner region of the Dinaric

Alps in the South, where their center was situated in the Delminion castle.⁴⁵⁵ Here they created a powerful federation, stretching toward the Adriatic coast, with lands reaching as far as Tilur River, adjacent to Liburnians. In the South they stretched from River Tilur (Cetina) to the lower flow of Narona (Neretva), on the southern shores of which dwelled the Doarsi.⁴⁵⁶ In the East it reached the areas of Desidiates in Bosnia. Ancient sources claim that Dalmatians appeared as a coastal power, and that besides the port of Solana it also had other cities.⁴⁵⁷

The Federation of the Dalmatians, during the time of Pleuratis, was under the Illyrian state. Upon the arrival of Gentius as the head of the Illyrian state in 181 B.C., they became independent again.

From the separation from Gentius to its final collapse in 168 B.C., that is, once there was space for action, they used Dalmatians to further strengthen that which went against Rome's interests, which aimed to keep both the planned vassals and "independent kings" as innocuous and dependent. But, after the conquest of the Illyrian state, it was the Dalmatians and the federations targeted by them that were in line with their plans for the invasion of northern Illyrian lands from the Adriatic, Dalmatia and up to the Danube (Pannonia) and the Alps.

As with the case of Teuta and later Gentius, Rome began here to look for pretexts for war in the behavior of the Dalmatians towards the residents of Isa, who complained their country and cities of Epetis and Tragyrius were being violated. Furthermore, similar complaints were invoked by the Daorsi, who were denounced for what was reported by Gaius Fanis, who reported to the Senate that Dalmatians not only refused to correct their mistakes against those who constantly complained of suffering from them, but were also refusing to even hear about them, saying that they had nothing to do with Rome.⁴⁵⁸

What was hiding behind the "complaints" of the Roman delegate before the Senate, is best explained by Polybius saying: "by undertaking a campaign against the Dalmatians, on one hand they would encourage and raise the fighting spirit of their people and, on the other, they would give a lesson to the Illyrians forcing them to submit to the Roman rule. For this reason the Romans waged war against the Dalmatians, posing before

---

[455] Ibid, p. 154.
[456] Ibid, p. 154.
[457] Strabo: *"Geographica,"* Book VII/, pp. 3, 4, 7, 8.
[458] Polybius: *"Historiae,"* Book XXXII/, p. 9.

other peoples as if they were doing so because of Dalmatians' bad behavior against their representatives."[459]

Once they had created the "reason," the Romans launched a campaign against the Dalmatians in 156 B.C., but as noted, things did not go well even in the beginning or later. Notably, the Roman consul Mark Gaius Figulius, during that attempt, could not manage to get into Dalmatian areas. Furthermore, during his first confrontation with them, he suffered huge losses forcing him to retreat to where he came from. This did not stop the Romans. They came back, this time with a better prepared consul, Cornelius Scipio Nasica, succeeding, after attacks from many directions, to penetrate Delminium, and devastate but not "pacify" the entire country as desired, as they continued to remain as independent parts, where the Romans failed to enter.

But this did not stop them from moving further. So, after the Dalmatians, whose main cities and larger living space were destroyed, the Romans continuously attacked the northern Illyrian countries, those of Japodes and Pannones.

Along with the northern countries, in the second half of the 2nd century B.C. the Romans dealt with *Ardiaei*, one of the mighty Illyrian peoples stretching in the Middle Adriatic coast to the vicinity of Lake Shkodra. The Ardiaei, having been included after the year 168 as one of the provinces created by the Roman state, changed their mind about Rome and declared independence. As usual, Rome found pretexts to attack the Ardiaei in their "disobedience," thereby sending military legions to their lands, which, as it became known, only after several years of fighting, in 135 B.C. they managed to force them to drop their weapons.[460] In this case, to avoid a new insurrection, Ardiaei were forcefully moved from the seaside to the interior mountainous areas of present-day Herzegovina.[461]

Evidently, Rome still had work to do with Dalmatians, Japodes, Liburnians, and others, who refused submission, although these would be separate tough wars that took a lot of energy, since a good part of the legions were forced to stay engaged in these parts.

Before it returned to them for a second time, especially to the invincible and rebelling Dalmatians, Rome had to remove the Dardanian issue

---

[459] Polybius: "*Historiae,*" Book XXXII/13.
[460] Titus Livius: "*Ab urbe condita,*" Book XLV/43
[461] "*Historia e Popullit Shqiptar,*" Volume I, Tirana, 2002, p. 157.

from its agenda, to deal with the kingdom of Dardania, an important stronghold in the middle of the peninsula, connecting eastern parts with the west, where it oversaw the rivers flowing into the Aegean, Adriatic, and Black Sea, which enabled this country and people, with their geographical position, to forever hold the keys of inter-connectivity of the West with the East.

Contrary to the wars against the Illyrian coastal states and those of Macedonia, where Rome could undertake repeated expeditions by sea, or by their legions stationed in coastal cities, where supplies and refueling were easier and faster, the war against the Dardanians, besides the obvious military force, demanded other preconditions for action. And, one of them was facing the great defensive ability of Dardanians under continental circumstances that did not suit the Romans.

Despite the collapse of the Illyrian Kingdom of Gentius (year 168) and the various campaigns in the North against other Illyrian tribes, Rome would not undertake any significant military action against Dardanians, keeping some legions in the occupied parts of Macedonia and Greece in its vicinity, pressing against them to refrain themselves from taking any action that went against Roman interests. At this time, Dardanians, although not showing any significant interest in any open conflict with the Romans, did not sit back. With their military moves they occasionally disturbed the Roman garrisons in Poenia, undertaking expeditions reaching as far as Astibo (Bregalnica) and Erigon. They made similar actions in terms to the West, in the lands of Autoriates, reaching to the North to Scordican lands, with whom the Dardanians had scores to settle from long before.[462]

Faced with continued "provocations," after having waged numerous campaigns against the Dalmatians, Japodes, Ardiaei and others, as discussed earlier, the Romans, finally, decided to turn to the Dardanians before it became too late. The resistance of the northern Illyrian tribes in Dalmatia and Pannonia drew the attention of Dardanians turning into an important center of anti-Roman movement, which would have unforeseen consequences for them and their plans to subjugate the entire region of Illyricum. The risk was even greater after Dardanians had already begun to connect with their eastern neighbors, Maedi (large Thracian tribe), who also had an important position in the eastern part of the

---

[462] Droysen, J. G: *"Das dardanische Fürstentum,"* Small writings on ancient history, Bd. I, Leipzig 1893, pp. 87-94.

peninsula. So over the years 97 B.C. through 85 B.C. Rome undertook a few military expeditions against Dardania and Maedi, but failed to do much. Dardania and Maedi joined forces together in several battles achieving victories against the Roman legions as they withdrew to Macedonia and occupied parts of Illyria.[463] In the summer of 84 B.C. Dardania even without the help of Maedi attacked the Roman province of Macedonia reaching as far as Delphi.[464]

Dardanian victory greatly troubled Rome for the fact that they, alongside Maedi and other Thracians were already starting to turn into a powerful shield that not only deterred their plans to expand further in the North and East but also made vulnerable those who were under subjection. Therefore, it was expected that they would turn back to a large-scale military campaign. In 76 B.C., Gaius Scribonius Curio was sent to Macedonia in charge of five new legions, which, together with those already there, would launch war against the Dardanians. Ancient authors admit the fear that had overwhelmed the Roman soldiers at the moment they were about to fight when an entire legion near Dyrrahium rebelled in order to avoid this war.[465] However, despite this, Curio Gaius attacked Dardania from three directions and after fighting long and extremely tough battles, with great losses for the Romans managed to enter Dardania. As recorded, although he was unable to penetrate the whole of the country, following along the river streams of Ibër and Morava, he reached the Danube in order to later celebrate his triumph in Rome.[466]

The triumph, however partial, against Dardanians and Dardania, was important to Rome by all means, as this would succumb the Dardanian Kingdom almost entirely and it already had opened up the ways towards the Danube from where it was able to move to the eastern parts, and through gorges of rivers of Vardar, Ibër, and Morava move further northeast from the occupied Greece and Macedonia, straight to Thrace and further to the lands it envied.

Although Dardanians continued to resist, they no longer controlled any major communications to the North, which Rome had on hand from where she had begun setting up new administrative zones in accordance

---

[463] Ibid.
[464] Ibid.
[465] See: Frontini *Stratagema*," cited according to *"Historia e Popullit Shqiptar,"* Volume II, Tirana, 2002, p. 152.
[466] Ibid, p. 152.

with its concept, as it had done in the occupied Illyrian lands, and in Macedonia and Greece.

For the completion of the Danube and Pannonia outlet from the west side, i.e. from the lands of the Adriatic coast to inland, Rome needed to completely subjugate the Dalmatians and other Illyrian tribes, who continued to remain separate or with supervised autonomies, being nevertheless not safe. Both the Dardanians in the central part of the Balkans, and Dalmatians in the coastal part leading towards the Danube and Pannonia, with an extremely broad extension, represented an obstacle for further Roman conquests. Although they received some bloody lessons, as those of 135-130 B.C., however, they continued to be obstacles in these parts. This is best told by Roman sources, indicating that even after a century of bloody confrontation with Dalmatians and repeated punishments, they continued to raise their arms against them even succeeding to inflict significant losses to the Roman army, as the ones in the 50's B.C. when forces led by Caesar's consul Aulus Gabinus near the town of Synodium came and he fled wounded to Solana. The same fate was incurred by Senator Balbus (year 44 B.C.) when he attacked the Dalmatian territories with the four cohorts but suffered complete defeat and fell in the front. In this case, evidently, Dalmatians took Solana and some other parts they had previously lost.[467]

Only after dealing with the concerns resulting from the assassination of Julius Caesar, Rome succeeded in recovering some of the Dalmatian cities that they had recovered in 40 B.C. Octavian and Antony, in the year 39 B.C., sent large military units against the Dalmatians led by poet Asinus Polonius, who, although not able to subdue the whole of Dalmatians, nevertheless, from the plunder he brought from there, built the first public library in Rome.[468]

This too was not the end as it was being trumpeted in the imperial capital. It took four more years and numerous legions of the Roman army led by Octavius, who had become the sole ruler of the Roman state. The army he was leading consisted of 10 legions (1/5 of the entire Roman army) first attacked in the North the lands of Japodes, with their centers evidently falling one after another into his hands: Monetium, Avendo, Arupium, and Terponus crossing over to Metulis, the center of Japodes. Octavius was also wounded there, but the Romans managed to conquer it

---

[467] Stipcevic, Aleksandar: *"Ilirët,"* Prishtina, 1980, p. 65.
[468] Ibid, p. 66.

and broke their resistance.[469] Japodes were powerless to do more in the face of the Roman army.

As he reached Siscis taking the city and turning it into a fine base to attack the Dacians and Pannonians, Octavius, convinced that the campaign would go well, returned to Rome. He left Phuphi Geminis behind, but several weeks later Octavius had to return again to Illyria, after a rebellion against the Romans broke out. The emperor saw it fit this time to continue the campaign against the Dalmatians, who appeared to be the main drivers of the resistance against the Romans, threatening to become a broad front, with the inclusion of other peoples beyond the Danube, who had already accepted submission.[470]

This time, though well started with the submission of Promona, forcing Versinus to surrender and leave the city, the emperor was not given the opportunity for a final battle, as he saw it. Dalmatians, led by warlord Testimotis, decided to wage a partisan war, beyond frontal confrontation, as had happened until then. He began to attack with small groups and surprises. Therefore, it lasted for almost seven years, but the Romans had decided not to return without subjecting the Dalmatians, or at least without taking custody of all the strategic crossings to the Danube and Drina, which provided an oversight of the other parts. With patience and a lot of losses, Octavius invaded the Dalmatian cities of Synodium and Andetrium, and then managed to take the city of Setovis, where the main Dalmatian power had been concentrated. As recorded, Octavius was wounded again, almost being forced to withdraw, but he turned back and laid an insurmountable siege to the Dalmatian city, which faced starvation, disease and other difficulties. This led to the surrender of the Dalmatians. This marked the end of the Dalmatian independence and the end of the independence of Illyrians in general.[471]

---

[469] Stipcevic, Aleksandar: *"Ilirët,"* Prishtina, 1980, p. 66.

[470] For more on Octavian's campaign in Illyria see: Johannes Kromayer: *"Kleine Forschungen zur Geschichte des Zweiten Triumvirats." V. Die Illyrische Feldzüge Octavians 33 und 34-33 v. Chris.* "Hermes," 33-1989; Georg Veith: *"Die Feldzüge des C.Iulius Caersar Octacians in Illyrien in den Jahren 35-33 v.Chr,"* Vienna, 1914; Erih Swoboda: *„Octavian und Illyricum,"* Vienna, 1932; Roland Syma; *"Augustus and the South Slavlands"* (Revue intgernationale des etudes balkaniques, 3/1937-1938, pp. 33-46; Frantz Miltner: *"Augustus' Kampf um die Donauzgrenze,"* 1937; N. Vulic: *"Oktavijanov ilirski rat i izgnanje Skordiska iz Gornje Mizije,"* Belgrade, 1926.

[471] Stipcevic, Aleksandar: *"Ilirët,"* Prishtina, 1980, p. 66.

Octavian's bloody campaign in Illyria eventually overturned all the Illyrian state and tribal remains but not the will of the Illyrians for opposition, as illustrated with numerous uprisings and persistence, among which the most powerful were those of the years 6-9 AD.

These and several similar uprisings that followed later did not aim at restoring the Illyrian state and their kingdoms stretching in various places. First of all, they opposed the policy of Rome, in regard to future wars, which it had already begun in the North against the Germanic Marcomanni, who had created in the lands of present-day Czechia a powerful tribal federation.[472] In this case, Rome had provided a large army of 12 legions, which would be complemented by ancillary units to be recruited mainly from among big northern tribes: Dalmatians, Daesitiates, Pannonians and others. As these recruitments were done by force expectedly they had to be answered likewise. Therefore, the first to react were Daesitiates, who enjoyed some tribal independence. Their leader Bato, who by the rapid successes against the Romans won back the hopes of other tribes that something more could be achieved, at least not to engage in military campaigns in the North of Rome, which were at a great loss. Therefore, he was soon joined by Breuci with their king Pinnes and military leader also named Bato. The two Batos became central figures of this glorious uprising in which a large number of Illyrian tribes, for the first time in their history, were united against the common enemy.[473] The two Batos took different directions, with the Breuces heading towards Sirminium (Sremska Mitrovica), and the Daesitiates towards Solana. The first Bato was defeated, while the second one was wounded and could not get to Solana, but continued toward the South, reaching up to Apollonia in Middle Illyria.[474]

The Illyrian uprising caused great concern in Rome after rumors of a large-scale uprising in which 800,000 rebels were included, with 200,000 warriors and 9,000 horsemen.[475] Evidently, Emperor Augustus facing the

---

[472] *"Historia e Popullit Shqiptar,"* Volume I, Tirana, 2002, p. 158.
[473] Stipcevic, Aleksandar: *"Ilirët,"* Prishtina, 1980, p. 68.
[474] Ibid.
[475] For more on the proportion of these wars see: Otto Hirschfeld: *"Zur geschihte des pannonisch-dalmatischen Krieges"* (Hermses), 25/1890, pp. 351-362; Adolf Bauer: *"Zum dalmatinisch-pannonischen Krieg 6-9 n, Chr.,"* (Archeaelogische-epigraphische Mittetheliungen aus Oesterreich), 17/1894, p. 153-148; Nikola Vulić: *"Dalmatski-panonski ustanak,"* Glas Srpske kraljevske akademije, libr. 121, 1926, pp. 55-72; Reinhold Rau:

risk of this army heading towards the Italic lands, ordered Tiberius to immediately sign peace with Marcomanni and Cuadi against whom he was fighting until then so that he would take his army to Illyricum. Another powerful military leader, Germanicus, was sent to his aid, meaning that all the forces were to be used against the Illyrian insurgents from all sides. The decisive battle took place on the River Bathius (most probably in present-day Bosnia), in which the Breuci Bato suffered heavy defeat. Presumably, the Breuci King Pinnes sought to continue the war against the Romans, but his military leader Bato did not think so. He proposed surrender which was followed by his soldiers. King Pinnes was also handed over to the Romans, and the latter as a token of gratitude recognized Bato as leader of the Breuci.[476]

The submission of one Bato was not approved by the other, the Daesitiates Bato. So, he turned against his former comrade-in-arms, captured him, and sentenced him to death. However, this action did not help him win back the Breuci so he was forced to return to Dalmatia to continue the war against the Romans alone.[477]

Bato achieved some success in Dalmatia, winning back the towns of Splodum, Sertium and others, but soon he faced two powerful commanders of Rome: Germanicus and Tiberius, and suffered serious defeat at Raetinium (the present-day Golubici near Bihac in Bosnia). Bato managed to leave and fortified himself in Andetrium (a place near the present-day Split in Dalmatia), but he left the place again and moved to the town of Arduba, where he was finally defeated.[478] Evidently, after the defeat, the Roman armies acted with exceptional rigor against the Illyrian population. Those who could not manage to hide in the mountainous areas were

---

"Zur Geschichte des pannonisch-dalmatischnischen Kriges der Jahre 6-9," CHr. Klio, 19/1925, pp. 313-364; Erich Köstermann: "Der pannonisch-dalmatische Krieg 6-9 n. Chr," (Hermes), 81/1953, H. 3, pp. 345-378; Tibor Nagy: "Der Aufstand der pannonisch-dalmatinischen Völker und die Frage der Zweitailing Illyricums."

[476] Stipcevic, Aleksandar: "Ilirët," Prishtina, 1980, p. 69.

[477] Ibid, p. 69.

[478] For more on the last Illyrian war against the Romans see: Nikola Vulić: "Oktavianov liriski rat 35-33 i 6-9," Belgrade, 1961, Stefan Josipović: "Oktavijanovo ratovanja u Iliriku," Zagreb, 1965; Walter Schmithenner. "Octavians militärische Unternehmungen in Jahren 35-33 v. Ch.," Wiesbaden, 1958.

massacred terribly. In some parts, in order not to fall into the hands of the Romans, Illyrian women threw themselves into precipices.[479]

Rome had decided to render the Illyrian lands desolate so that no more troubles and uprisings would come from there that would hinder Rome to move on, as was the case with other penetrations in the German lands, even though there, after losing a battle at the Tutinburg Forest, it suffered a setback.

The last resistance of Daesitiates Bato, however powerful, could not turn back the wheel of history nor change anything in Rome's concept of advancements.

Its only achievement, if one may call it so, was that it strengthened the Roman belief that against the Illyrian population the strategy of acquisition and its involvement in imperial structures, the army administration should be used in order for it to become supportive, convincing it through self-governance and maintenance of its own autonomous social structures to be part of the common imperial concept.

---

[479] For more on brutal repression waged by the Roman Army in Illyrian areas (Dalmatia) see Strabo: *"Geographica"* (Geograhphy), Book VII/, pp. 3-6.

CHAPTER 4

Illyrians and Dardanians during the Roman Empire

The Emergence of Illiricum

Rome recognizes forms of civil and military administration of the conquered Illyrians. – Agrarian reforms and the creation of communes as large economies benefiting the locals. – The creation of the province of Illyricum with a very wide territory from the Danube in the North and Mat in the South producing the first administrative and economic unification of the Illyrians. – Formation of other provinces: Dalmatia, Pannonia and Epirus, along with domestic governments, marked the beginning of new connections of Illyrian provinces. – Opening of new roads and the inclusion of the Illyrian and Dardanian territories in the economic and political life of the empire. – The strengthening of urban centers and the return of coins in several cities (Apollonia, Amantia, Naissus) of the Illyrian and Dardanian time. – A rapid urbanization of numerous centers of Dardania. – A broad Illyrian participation in the Roman army and their rapid rise to the top military hierarchy. – Decius, the first emperor of Illyrian origin coming from military layers (240-251). – Other Illyrian-Dardanian emperors were: Claudius II (262-264), Aurelian (270-275), Mark Aurelius Probius (276-282), Diocletian, the most powerful (284-305), and Dardanians: Constantine the Great and Justinian I.

The crushing of the latest Dalmatian uprising in the early new millennium marked the beginning and end of an era in Illyrian and Dardanian history as the leading peoples of a common trunk of Pelasgic root. Included as part of the Roman Empire, they shared the fate of the empire.

Frequent important events for Rome took place on its territory, which played a decisive role in its development and protection,[480] and would be seen later in the circumstances of conquest of many centuries. Opportunities for social and political union were found which did not previously exist with which emerged the appearance of their great power acquired from within the Roman Empire in a natural process. From the second half of the 2nd century A.D., the self-governing, administrative and spiritual (religious) identity of Illyricum was highlighted as their state identity as they became a key factor of the Roman Empire, on which it relied together with all its edifice from the time of the reforms and on, when Illyricum turned into a symbol of the Western spirit based on the spirit of the concept of global universalism.

Before dealing in more length with this uncommon historic development, when the conquered turned into the "conqueror," which occurred in the time of Emperor Diocletian of Illyrian origin, when Rome, after occupying some Illyrian territories in 168 B.C. when King Gentius was defeated, started working to get the occupied parts under its administration. Initially, they associated them with autonomous independent units (civitates), and later split them into separate administrative self-governing parts. Even the lands initially recognized as "neutral," or those that were bypassed and treated as "allies," would impose an administrative organization and other forms of governance similar to the Roman Empire in order for their involvement to help their inclusion in the space it considered under its influence or in the imperial part that would be concluded through military conquests.

Therefore, since the second half of the 2nd century, (i.e. before the time of Roman incursions in Illyrian lands along the Adriatic) certain forms of Roman military and civilian administration were recognized in these parts. However, a complete suppression of the Illyrian and Dardanian resistance throughout their space, as well as Roman penetrations in the North towards the German lands, to the East in the Thracian lands in Asia Minor and Middle East, demanded a new administrative and state rearrangement that would enable the already powerful Empire to have an overall supervision over the social, political and military space stretching over three continents.

---

[480] Stipcevic, Aleksandar: *"Ilirët,"* Prishtina, 1980, p. 68.

Therefore, the Roman slave owner state, faced the great challenge of its internal strengthening, which was not possible without an involvement of the numerous conquered peoples and an economic development that enticed the conquered peoples to become part of a new civilization with imperial pretensions where property, power, and opportunities for prosperity in all areas appeared as a new opportunity for the ruling aristocracy of the country where the representatives of the peoples involved in the Empire, especially those of Illyricum needed to find a place. Notably, the Roman state began the implementation of an Agrarian reform in its early stage in the occupied Illyrian and Dardanian parts, which began with the confiscation of the best arable land, which was declared "*ager publicus.*"[481]

Clearly this reform, aimed at uniting large land holdings held by the state, in fact relied on favoring Roman citizens, mostly Italic settlers and military veterans, who lived on the outskirts of cities or in special habitats.

Despite the intentions of Rome to influence some areas through an agricultural policy, a change in the population structure favoring what was called the Roman citizen through the so-called "*ager publicus*" benefited locals, as well as with the creation of large agricultural economies, called *latifundio*. These were located near major roads and cities, supplying the latter with agricultural products.

Evidently, latifunds (communes) did not affect much the internal parts of the country, which pursuant to the agreements that the central Rome authority had with local tribes and units, recognizing their autonomous status, the land was owned by the tribal or rural communities to be governed in accordance with their interests, while the key say belonged to the lords of the feuds, who were locals.

With changing circumstances, namely as in the occupied areas, new roads connected them to other parts, which meant a break through a certain closure, an acceptance of the new of possession and handling of agricultural property was noted, which incited the local latifundists to be included in the overall system. Therefore, Roman sources show that such large latifunds appeared also in the vicinity of Ulpiana, Skupi, and in many other parts of Dardania, where patricians emerged from among the slave-owning nobility, such as Pomponius Atticus and theTure family in Dardania, and many other similar ones.[482]

---

[481] "*Historia e Popullit Shqiptar,*" Volume I, Tirana, 2002, p. 161.
[482] Ibid, p. 162.

Before dealing with the social, economic and political factors that the new circumstances produced, arising during and after the Roman conquest of the mid-2nd century B.C. to the beginning of the 1st century A.D., namely when the process of submission of the Illyrians and Dardanians and other surrounding peoples' inclusion in the Roman Empire was over, it is appropriate to reflect on their administrative organization within the Roman Empire, which during the next four centuries shared their fate and turned into supporters and ultimately into its main defenders. It came to a point when the Empire turned into their own identification insignia, which must be protected from the challenges that came from the North by the penetration of barbarians who aimed at destroying the overall civilization of antiquity on the foundation of which stood their very own forefathers, the Pelasgians, upon whom the entire Hellenism was built.

Consequently, five centuries before this awareness, it should be remembered that the Illyrian-Dardanian space, being forcefully included in the Roman Empire, passed through an organizational form that began by the last century B.C. creating the Province of Illyricum. It included the provinces of North Illyria. The Province of Illyricum was comprised of a very wide area: in the North it reached as far as the Danube, in the South to the Mat River, and in the East extending to the center of the Balkans.[483]

The conclusion of conquests, following the early 1st century B.C. as well as the need to recognize the ethnic, economic, and other realities in the new lands, somewhat retaining their known characteristics similar to the ones under the circumstances of Illyrian states and kingdoms and Dardania, paved the way for a new administrative division. In this case strikingly Rome established the Province of Moesia, in which Dardania was included with all its space, followed shortly by the emergence of its separate status as a province, in which Dardania enjoyed having a special treatment related to the development and stability of the Roman Empire in this part and the protection from barbarian attacks from the North (Avars and Slavs), where they had a special role. They had the same role during the creation of Byzantium.

The wars between the years 6-9 A.D. were very severe and caused the Illyricum Province, for strategic reasons, to be easily monitored and also caused the creation of separate ethnic realities. Therefore, it was divided into two: in the North the Province of Pannonia was formed with the

---

[483] Ibid, p. 166.

Province of Dardania in the South. Alongside these, the Province of Epirus was established, comprising the Illyrian provinces south of Vjosa, the entire Epirus, with Acamania and Etolia in its South.[484]

These subjugated and appeased provinces were supervised by the Roman Senate, while the provinces of strategic importance, where the situation was uncertain and where there was a need to hold military units, depended directly on the Empire. Later this concept would also affect the pyramid of imperial leadership and administration led by Rome, removing it from its center to the provinces, which emerged as states within the state, as was the case with Dardania and some other Illyrian lands. Soldiers of local origin, backed by that same local power, were rising to imperial posts, a power coming actually from the "periphery" and previously subjugated peoples turning into leading peoples, whose behavior determined its fate. This fact justifies the conversion of the Illyrians from being conquered to becoming "conquerors" from within the Empire. However, initially the imperial provinces of Illyricum were comprised of Pannonia, Dalmatia, Moesia of Epirus, with Macedonia depending on the Senate.[485]

Leading the provinces were special rulers, viceroys, who, based on the importance of a province, differed in ranks. Therefore, notably, in the Province of Dalmatia the viceroy enjoyed the rank of a Council (*legatus, Augustipropraetore*). The Province of Epirus fell in the group of second-hand provinces and was being ruled by viceroys coming from the layers of Roman knights. But leading the Province of Macedonia were senators of the rank of a *properator*.[486] Viceroys were appointed to the provincial administration for a one-year term. They were also in charge of the high court and fiscal policy. In provinces where there were military units they also held leadership over military power. They had their *quaestors*, who carried out duties with finance, and *prosecutors*, who did the work in the army and courts. In time, this administrative, judicial, and military structure, coming mainly from the "center," little by little was supplemented by locals, in order for them to reach the level of being the sole representatives, as the entire administrative, judicial, and military system fell into their hands, on condition that a local leader accepted the status of

---

[484] Ibid, p. 167.
[485] Ibid, p. 167.
[486] Ibid, p. 167.

a Roman citizen in the year 212 A.D. when Emperor Caracalla issued an edict on this.

It is worth noting that the Roman Empire had a well-built tax collection system, ensuring its quick flow into the state coffers. The main tax was the one on land and soul (*tributum soli* and *tributum capital*). At first these taxes were only paid by "*pelegrini*" (foreigners), as the Romans called local residents, but later they extended them to Roman citizens settled in Illyrian and Dardanian Provinces as well. Another source was also customs or border taxes that were due for certain imported goods passing by land, river or sea from one administrative-customs unit to another. Illyricum constituted a separate customs unit (*portorium Illyrici*), which included the provinces of Dalmatia, Pannonia, Moesia, Noricus, and later the province of Dacia.[487]

The Roman Empire did not keep all the taxes to itself. A portion of them went to the provinces as well to be administered in accordance with their needs, primarily for domestic infrastructure. As a result it increased its tax collection focus being in the local interest. Furthermore, a general tax went to Rome, in return for opening new roads, called imperial and linking different provinces of the empire, which largely helped trade and circulation of ideas.

The Imperial administration allowed for an inner self-administration of the municipalities called *civitates*. At the top of *civitates* there was a prefect (*praefectus civitatis*), who came from nearby military bases. Over time, Rome decided to have the prefects come from representatives of local layers, i.e. nobles, who had received Roman citizenship. They were called *praeposites* (heads). *Praeposites* had a tribal council, composed of representatives from various local leaders - *principies*, from whom later came those who made efforts to restore the early Roman empire and to keep slave-ownership that was being dismantled alive.[488]

To conclude the shrinking appearance of what the Roman administration represented in the Illyrian and Dardanian lands and on what basis it acted, it is appropriate to say that the Roman organization in major language-administrative provinces, called conventions (*conventus provinciae*), also a form of internal governance, intended to attract Illyrians and Dardanians to the life of the Roman state, which was proven successful, given that a large part of the Illyrians and Dardanians within a

---

[487] Ibid, p. 167.
[488] Ibid, p. 168.

short time submitted to the system turning it into an important tool to penetrate to the highest administrative political and military hierarchy of the empire reaching as high as the throne of the Emperor. These conventions did not only produce the rulers of the country, but they also selected annually a chairman of the convention and the priest of the cult of the Emperor.

In these circumstances it may be said that in the Illyrian and Dardanian lands the population was largely involved in the life of state administration, military and economy, attaining upon themselves their own destiny, at least those dealing with local concerns.

The latter began with large agricultural economies, latifunds, producing good opportunities for agricultural products, but also benefits, as the agricultural economies supplied the major centers, including the state itself, which had a need for them. This also made possible the development of trade, which in addition to agricultural products, also circulated various goods, which thanks to new roads and the security of caravans, passed freely from one part of the Empire to another.[489]

Among the major and important arteries one should by all means distinguish those leading from coast to inland directions Solana-Sirmium, Narona-Sirmium, Jader-Suiscia and many others from Sen, Epidaurum, Scodra and other cities leading to the Danubian basin towards the East and, or around the coast of Tergeste through Tarsatika to Jader, Narona and south to Dyrrhachion, and further towards Greece. Via Egnatia, one of the most famous Roman roads out of Italy, passed through Illyrian territories, going from Dyrrchachium and Apollonia to Thessaloniki. It was built by the Romans on the ancient route through which since the Neolithic period cultural influences from the East toward the Adriatic and vice versa passed. Another trans-regional road of great importance for the Illyrian and Dardanian lands commenced at the southern Adriatic coast. It passed through Lissus, over the Drin and emerged into Dardania reaching Naissus and connecting to the road coming from the North

---

[489] On roads in the Roman Province of Illyricum, Macedonia, Pannonia, and Moeasia, see in particular: Philipp Ballif: *"Römische Strassen i n Bosnien und der Hercegovina,"* Vienna, 1893; Anton Mollinary: *"Die Römerstrassen in der europiäischen Türkei,"* Zagreb, 1914; Esad Pasalic: *"Anticka naselja i komunikacije u Bosni i Hercegovini,"* Sarajevo, 1960; Anton Premerstein – Simon Rutar: *"Römische Strassen und befestigungen in Kraina,"* Vienna, 1899.

(Danube) from the Singidunis and Viminaicis and ending in Thessaloniki.[490]

These economic developments brought about changes in the civic life in the Illyrian and Dardanian provinces, being mostly self-governed. Therefore, in addition to the main provincial centers, other towns flourished, especially in the coastal regions, but on the mainland linking important passages. Here roads were of great importance, as trading goods and mail passed through them, including all the fruits of Roman civilization, which in turn had an important role in the process of Romanization of a good part of Illyrian and Dardanian lands in the continental parts. Therefore, in these circumstances the local centers were the first to see those changes and it was natural they were experiencing significant development, besides administrative and military importance, they both turned into accumulators of a good part of the population, descending from former strongholds in remote mountainous areas and settlements, which were cut off, to shed its energy by the means of which even better prospects were created.

Strengthening of new urban centers, where the Roman way of life was noticeable, as they were subject to imperial models, and the loss of importance of some fortified settlements in hilly-mountainous parts, had no impact on the loss of importance of many Illyrian other cities, especially the coastal ones, which kept their autonomous governance and their social-cultural traditions, cutting even their own coins until the early 3rd century A.D. Among these were Apollonia, Amantia, Phoenicia, Naissus in Dardania and others.

In these cities, along with settlers, soldiers and Italic colonists began to settle in major Illyrian and Dardanian cities as businessmen, entrepreneurs, or administrators, representing what already appeared as an elite of Roman citizenry; rich Illyrians and Dardanians also appeared, belonging to the slave-owning class or old tribal nobility, who had received Roman citizenship and the right to join the elite of the country.

This originated the beginning of the involvement of the Illyrians and Dardanians in the high hierarchy of governance and administration of the Empire, where many of them were included in the economic, social, political, and cultural life reaching to the highest military and political levels, to be crowned with achieving the imperial throne, which was dealt with later.

---

[490] Stipcevic, Aleksandar: "*Ilirët*," Prishtina, 1980, p. 72.

Of course, this development could not have attained such a large scale and could not have been so profound in terms of social, economic, cultural and political view, if it did not bear the seal of *free citizenry* that would include a good portion of the population which benefited by this status primarily socially and economically.

Although the Roman Empire, after its extensions to the East and West retained and evolved elements of the slave-owning society in parts of Illyricum and Dardania, the population was granted the status of free population, which constituted an important prerequisite to win Roman citizenship, a status that carried in itself civil rights; such would be the little land owners, craftsmen and traders. Evidently, in the Illyrian and Dardanian provinces, along with city-colonies, which provided good opportunities for development and rise to distinct social strata from which they could become involved in wider imperial life, was called *municipes*, as local centers – settlements that would set the nucleus of the free population, where it found its own economic, social and cultural interests.

Municipes had limited self-government, with merchants, craftsmen and others engaged in these economic activities defining their own interests, as they made use of part of the taxes for their own needs. *Municipes* also existed in the interior areas, some of them associated with mining. One such a municipality was that of Ulpiana in Dardania (near Prishtina), established in the early 2nd century A.D.[491]

Besides the municipes, some of which, thanks to economic development, rose to communities and even cities, in Illyria and Dardania was noted the presence of fortified centers-settlements, called *castella* or *opida* (castles or towns), whose residents initially were entitled to Roman citizenship. However, after the Edict of Caracalla in 212 A.D. they enjoyed the entitlement, which had a positive effect on their social and economic status. These castles and towns appeared mostly as centers of internal units of *civitates*, upholding local chiefs and provincial authorities of the empire, which were independent in many respects.[492]

The preservation of fortified settlements in several Illyrian provinces, especially in Dardania, where ethnic identity was preserved, however outside the known tribal profusions characterizing the pre-Roman Illyricum had to do with a certain urban structure, characteristic of

---

[491] "*Historia e Popullit Shqiptar*," Volume II, Tirana, 2002, p. 164.
[492] Ibid, p. 165.

continental countries, where social elements intertwined with those of security, which were important to the Empire. In those parts they faced various attacks by barbarian peoples coming from the East who occasionally incurred the imperial space, jeopardizing greatly its safety and its progress of economic life. Viewed from this perspective, in the new imperial circumstances, Dardania saved a lot of its life, as this suited the Roman Empire as well, which regarded the province that was originally included in that of Upper Moesia, emerging later as a province on its own,[493] since it overlooked the main river flows (Morava, Iber, Drin, and Vardar) and linked imperial roads from East to West and those in Ulpiana or Naissus ramified towards East or Southeast. These connected southern, eastern and western parts of Illyria and Macedonia with Greece and the central and northern parts to the Danube.

Therefore, the urbanization of Dardania in the Roman conquest circumstances was less subject to the enforcement policy called "*Pax Romana*," and more so to maintaining the economic basis and social order aimed at keeping the native element within its long-standing structures, which would be put in use by those of the economic and especially strategic nature of the empire.

This was proven by different archeological evidence in the Dardanian space, although it was believed that a lot has remained undiscovered and unresearched including those in Theranda (former Suhareka,[494] *Municipium DD Soçanica)*, where the topic and ethno-cultural continuity has been noted.[495]

---

[493] For more on the emergence of Dardania into a province, from the beginnings of the 4th century AD see: M. Fukss: "*Moesie,*" PWRE XIV, 1928, col. 2389-2390, cited according to Zef Mirdita "*Studime Dardane,*" Prishtina, 1979, p. 109. According to this author the administrative boundaries of the province of Dardania during the Roman Empire were significantly narrower than the ethnic ones, but nonetheless in the West they included parts of Shar Mountains and beyond Nish, while in the North they went as far as the River Ibar and south Morava up to the Western Morava including the Timok Province up to Dacia, while in the South they lay in the watershed of Upper Vardar up to Vodno and more in the south to Byzolorsid (present-day Veles in Macedonia).

[494] For more see: N. Slavković-Djurić: "*Ilirski tumuli kod Suve Reke,*" in GMKiM. IX/1964, pp. 537-549; E. Cerskov: "*Municipium DD kod Soçanice,*" Prishtina-Belgrade, 1970; Esad Pašalić: "*Period vladavine do kraja III vjeka nase ere,*" in Kulturna istorija Bosnje i Hercegovine, 186-187; M. Suić: "*Problems de Palegenese et d'urbanisation des centrues illyriens,*" in St. Alb.X (2) 1973, pp. 105-116.

[495] Mirdita, Zef: "*Studime dardane,*" Prishtina, 1979, p. 112.

The research indicates that indigenous elements of proto-urban settlements were largely maintained even at times coinciding with foreign elements, especially the urban ones, coming from Rome, subject to the imperial strategic and economic concept, in which, as will be seen, Dardania, as a separate entity, was of great importance, reflected best in its political and administrative status as a separate province, won once the Empire was convinced that part was key to preserving security by its presence in the regional nodes. This is clearly seen in the development of the settlement system of the types of *castella, urues, stationes, villae, canaboe* (Timocum minus e Timocum maius at Knjazevci in present-day Serbia), which were subordinated to economic and strategic aims.[496]

However, the basic features of the urbanization of regions of Dardania, at least in terms of the third and fourth centuries A.D. was seen in the fact that the settlements, as indicated by the details of itineraries, were concentrated along roads and in ore-rich regions (Ulpiana, Municipium DD at Socanica), and, in turn, their own establishment, including the colony of Scupi, was not made based on deduction. The emergence of these three centers in the central part of Dardania with Naissus and Arribantios in the eastern part does not mean that only these four-five cities made up the urban and administrative relief of Dardania. Rather, they are inevitable in all the chronicles and maps, being pre-Roman, that is, coming from the time of classical antiquity (7th-1st centuries B.C.), while maintaining their continuity in terms of importance. But Roman sources indicated that the Dukagjin Plain as well as other parts had towns, castles and other venues of Municipal tribal communities treatment, namely civitates, among which, thanks to the epigraphic materials too had already been proven both in the Sopina-Popovljan-Mushitishtë region, 18 kilometers to the northeast of Prizren,[497] and the second at Lower Tërsnik, in the vicinity of Klina.[498]

Furthermore, another municipal center of *civitate* character in the Kosova Plain was known, somewhere near Kllokot, not far from Vitia, whose thermal springs have been known since antiquity, as other *civitates* centers in other parts of Dardania, such as the territorial tribal ones, one in the region of the present-day Leshak, a second in the valley of Ku-

---

[496] Ibid, p. 113.
[497] E. Čerskov: *"Rimljani na Kosovu i Metohiji,"* Belgrade, 1969, pp. 40-41, cited according to Mirdita, Zef: *"Studime dardane,"* Prishtina, 1979, p. 115.
[498] Ibid, p. 116.

manova, and a third in South Morava with its main center Davidoc,[499] centers of legal-administrative nature *(ordo decurionum duoviri dicundo iure)*, in which the local population lived away from the influence of Romanization, which not only prevented Romanization, but also their extensive involvement in the dynamics of the imperial social and political development, as happened with other provinces. However, the reasons for such a "delay," which went in favor of preserving the ethno-cultural elements of Dardanians, should probably be sought in the very strategy of Rome in preserving the local ethnos (i.e. indigenous Dardanian) in these parts, as this alone kept them tied to their land and environment. Therefore, preserving the province's defensive ability later, in the circumstances of internal cracks and barbarian attacks from the North, proved crucial to the survival of the Empire further, even in the form of Byzantium, which appeared in the 5th century A.D. and maintained for about 10 centuries in the edifice of the Western civilization in these parts.

In this respect, the military element, which in the Roman Empire, as noted, was randomly chosen from the background of the layer enjoying Roman citizenship status, were recruited from the local element, i.e. Dardanians, who would soon rise to the highest military posts of the Empire.

This opens the question of the role of the military factor in the spread of Roman civilization among the Illyrians and Dardanians, but also of the Romanization of this population in its known proportions, which could not be nearly comprehensive on a social, economic and political plain, not excluding the cultural one. The ethnic identity, which for the aforementioned reasons had to be preserved, created the circumstances for the maintenance of some specific features of life, reflecting the spiritual identity of this population among the oldest of the Indo-European civilization.

It should be said that the Roman army, which, thanks to long wars with Illyrians, Dardanians and Macedonians was the first to create opportunities to further imperial conquests and restoration of its overall administrative, social and political infrastructure in the occupied territories, simultaneously appeared in a dual role factor: the one that helped the spread of Roman civilization among the Illyrians and Dardanians, and the one that by including them in this process turned into its main factor. The

---

[499] Ivan Mikulčić: *"Teritoria Skupa,"* Skopje, 1971.

Roman army, whose numerous legions were located near the cities-colonies, and other important settlements throughout the country, as is known, participated in the social and economic life of the country by a factor of safety, which first led to the head of the empire, occurring from the mid-2nd century, when most of the emperors came from the military caste, mostly of rural Illyrian and Dardanian background.

This powerful class was representative of Roman citizenry, and also the first liaison with the local population, the Illyrian and Dardanian one, being the first to open the doors for many young people of this population. Knowing what the military capabilities of Illyrians and Dardanians were, after facing them for more than a century in many bloody battles, Rome felt likely to include their power among its ranks and through this move forward in search of increased imperial space in the South, East and elsewhere. Therefore, the inclusion of many Illyrians and Dardanians among the ranks of the imperial army and the time these soldiers spent in other provinces of the Empire, far from homeland, caused them to soon learn the official language of the army - Latin, and to know many new things without excluding social and cultural relationships that enabled mixed family ties, which were naturally opposed to such circumstances. Tacitus writes that the Illyrians were the majority in the Roman navy, both that based at Mysetum on the Tyrrhenian Sea, and the one seated at Ravenna, on the Adriatic.[500]

What Tacitus said about an Illyrian majority in the Roman navy and their participation in the overall structure of the imperial army, gave them the opportunity to rise to its command hierarchy, and thence to the social and political elite of Roman citizenry becoming among the most prominent and important ones to achieve as high as the position of powerful emperors, becoming famous for their domestic, economic, and political reforms, and for their efforts to protect the empire from barbarian attacks coming from the North.

Therefore, the emperors of Illyrian or Dardanian origin, coming from the army, with the first one recognized being Decius (249-251 A.D.), were not accidental, but rather part of the power that this population had within this powerful institution, which became crucial in the social and political scene of the empire from the times when signs of its crises were seen, which led to its known destruction two centuries later.

---

[500] Tacitis, cited according to Aleksandar Stipcevic: *"Ilirët,"* Prishtina, 1980, p. 73.

However, in these circumstances the appearance of the emperor by the army marked the decline of the authority of state institutions and those of Roman citizenry (Senate and legislation), as a consequence of which an economic crisis followed as part of the unraveling of the slave-owner system, marking also the authority of the provinces, especially those in Illyria and other eastern parts, where the military emerged as the leading authority to secure the Empire from external attacks, and to simultaneously oversee local government in the provinces, becoming increasingly more independent from the authority of the center.

In these conditions, the role and say of the military was key, and seemingly the leadership of the Empire was taken over by "people of the provinces," mostly Illyrian and Dardanian, who could not be other than military men, dominant in terms of the power they attained and because of local support, which became increasingly significant in accordance with the deepening of the internal crisis and the degree of danger from abroad coming from barbarian attacks.

Therefore, the first among Illyrian emperors of Rome was Decius (249-251 A.D.). He was originally from the Pannonia Babala in North Illyricum. Reportedly, troops under his command forced him to accept the Emperor's throne.[501] During his short rule he was mainly preoccupied with the war against the invading Goths.

Claudius II was another senior Illyrian military having been placed to the throne by the military (262-264 A.D.). He distinguished himself in successful wars against the Goths, so for that reason he was nicknamed "Gothicus." Claudius came originally from a little known family in Dardania.[502]

Occasionally, while Caesar was busy in long military campaigns in Persia or Spain and the barbarians threatened the Empire left without a leader, it could happen, in special cases, for a legion to declare its general an emperor. Therefore, in the year 267 A.D. Aurelius was proclaimed emperor by his legions in Illyria. He immediately took possession of Northern Italy, but was killed in battle a year later.[503]

His successor, too, Aurelian, the Illyrian (270-275), from Sirmium, was among the most successful emperors. He stayed on the throne for five

---

[501] Edwin, Jaques: "*Shqiptarët,*" Tirana, 2007, p. 150.
[502] Stipcevic, Aleksandar: "*Ilirët,*" Prishtina, 1979, p.75.
[503] Edwin, Jacques: "*Shqiptarët,*" Tirana, 2007, p. 150.

years, but did so much to strengthen the empire that he was called *"Resittutor Orbis"* (Restorer of the World).

Another Illyrian emperor from the military elite was Mark Aurelius Probius (276-282 A.D.), also of Sirmium origin in Pannonia, in the northern border of Illyricum. Thanks to his military ability Emperor Tacitus appointed him Governor of the East. Upon the Emperor's death, the Sirmium armies forced him to accept the appointment. He was eagerly confirmed by the Senate, people and legions. He was among the most successful emperors, who managed to secure the Empire from barbarian attacks and simultaneously, thanks to public investment, in which he engaged his military apparatus as well, was able to promote economic development. Evidently, this move turned fatal for him, because many of the soldiers who refused to "reduce their authority" by the involvement in public affairs, conjured up an assassination in which he died.[504]

One of the most powerful emperors of Rome, without ambiguity remains Valerius Diocletian, who ruled from 284-305 A.D. Diocletian came from a common Dalmatian family of Dioclea, in the basin of Lake Shkodra. As most of the Illyrians and Dardanians he won fame in the army, serving under Probius. He was proclaimed emperor in 284 A.D. Contrary to numerous military leaders, who saw an enemy from without, Diocletian saw the causes of the crisis in which the Empire was plunged from the inside. This led him to turn to sweeping social, political and economic reforms of the country, through which he restored internal stability and confidence of the Empire. Diocletian showed that he was not absolute but rather committed to ruling for general benefit by appointing a co-ruler, Maximian, also an Illyrian, entrusting him with power over the western part of the Empire.

He continued further to share power with others when in 191 A.D. he appointed two other Illyrians to serve as Caesars: Constantine Chlorus and Galerius. Therefore, Diocletian ruled over the eastern part, Maximian over Italy and Africa, Constantine ruled over Britain, Gallia, and Spain, while Galerius ruled over Illyricum, bordering with the Danube. After a 25-year rule, the most successful of the Empire, Diocletian was seized by the desire to live in peace and tranquility. He abdicated the throne in 305 A.D. moving to the shores of Solana (today's Split on the Adriatic coast of

---

[504] Ibid, p. 151.

Croatia). There he devoted himself to meditation and gardening. He died in 313 A.D.

For a brief period after Diocletian his co-rulers passed through the imperial throne: Maximian, Constantine Chloris and Galerius. Chloris became Augustus after the abdication of Diocletian from the throne, but he died 15 months later in 306 A.D. during the battle of York, Britain. Briefly, the position of Emperor was entrusted to Galerius, but he was unable to remain on the throne for long because of a sordid disease known as *"Morbus pediculosus"* (scabs) from which he died in 311 A.D.[505]

The Illyrian dynasty on the imperial throne did not end with Constantine Chloris and Galerius. It was Chloris' first son, Constantine, nicknamed "the Great" who led the Empire from 306 A.D. to 337 A.D., rightly considered one of the most successful and important emperors of the Empire not only because he made major social and political reforms, and not only because he was able to protect it from barbarian attacks, but because he embraced Christianity, which will be discussed later. Constantine was a Dardanian, as was his entire family. He was born in Naissus (present-day Nis). He fought alongside his father, who was killed at the fatal battle of York. Constantine became Caesar in 306 A.D. and Augustus in 308 A.D. Over the next few years he waged severe struggles to unite the Empire and managed to defeat his opponents who kept it separated. Therefore, in the year 324 A.D. he was the only emperor of Rome. Two years later he moved the seat of Empire from Rome to Byzantium, giving it his own name, Constantinople, and dedicating it in 330 A.D. In the new organization of the Empire, Illyricum was one of the largest provinces. It was divided into two parts: *Western Illyricum (Illyricum Occidentale)*, comprising Illyricum, Pannonia and Noricum, and *Eastern Illyricum (Illyricum Orientale)*, including Dacia, Moesia with Dardania, Macedonia and Thrace. His three incapable sons inherited the throne, Constantine II, Constantius II and Constans. The latter inherited Illyricum, Italy and Africa.[506]

Although the fame of Constantine the Great ended with his death, however, there was another emperor from the family (his nephew Julius), who remained remarkable for two reasons: he was among the youngest emperors to come to the throne (thirty), and he was both a general and philosopher, who, led by ancient Greek and Roman philosophy, renewed

---

[505] Ibid, p. 152.
[506] Ibid, p. 152.

the persecution of Christians, trying to return to the worship of gods and goddesses of his great-grandfathers, the Pelasgians.[507]

Military involvement on the imperial throne by mid-2nd to the 4th century A.D., which usually came from Illyrian and Dardanian areas, and recognized for their devotion to the imperial cause, in fact highlights the crisis of the Roman Empire, which was first of all of social and economic nature and secondly of political nature, reflected in the loss of central authority at the expense of strengthening the military power coming from the province.

Therefore, the social crisis was constrained primarily by the crisis of the slave order, which in new circumstances when the Empire was extended to three continents, began to turn into an obstacle, not being able to convey the proper development and economic dynamics that imposed it. This was seen particularly in jams that appeared in several important branches of economy such as mining, metal processing, agriculture and public works.

The slave system, although showing weaknesses in almost all the pores of society, especially in the ancient way of production, appeared without alternative because the slave-owner class was not ready to accept changes, which brought down its social and political power. This prompted the central government to lose its authority, particularly in the province, where there were numerous slave rebellions, which joined the impoverished settlers and the dispossessed villagers, who were increasingly dissatisfied, and exposed to further deepening of the crisis, which became worse by the barbaric attacks that began to seriously threaten the imperial existence by the 2nd century A.D.

However, in these circumstances, it was the Illyrian and Dardanian provinces, that somehow slowed the headlong fall first by preserving the indigenous manufacturing method they had even before the arrival of the Romans to their lands and later by including high military leaders in protecting the country from the barbaric attacks and in leading the country, including even the emperor's post.

Saving the traditional way of production began with family economies, tribal economies and latifunds, which were embraced by the Roman organization, which proved successful, and went as far as metal extraction, with the Dardanian mines rich in gold, zinc, tin and many other

---

[507] Ibid, p. 153.

metals known since early antiquity, representing the greatest mining basin of the empire.[508]

This was a combination of household economies and slave-owners and the settlers economies, which helped the Illyrian and Dardanian provinces appear increasingly economically and politically stable as opposed to other parts of the empire, especially in the Italic lands and in the Middle East and Africa.[509] Therefore, it was no accident that the emperors of the times of crises (from 2nd to 5th centuries A.D.) primarily were militaries coming from the Illyrian and Dardanian lands, where the economic situation appeared to be better off.

Even the administrative and military reforms and fortification constructions made by Diocletian, which although did not prevent the fall of the Empire, managed to push it for a little while, being that in the Illyrian provinces and in Dardania imperial power was more stable, although it was mostly challenged by the barbarian attacks. This can be explained by the important role that the northern and northeastern Illyrian and Dardanian provinces played against the barbarian attacks at the Danubian frontier. This defensive war, for the Illyrian and Dardanian commanders and soldiers at the stage when the fall of the overall imperial edifice was being threatened, was also a struggle to protect their own country, which was so closely related to their interests.

Romanization and Illyrian-Dardanian Ethnic Identity

> *Why wasn't Romanization in Illyricum as strong as in Thrace and some other parts? – How was "the accommodation" of the Illyrians in the Roman Empire and its "taken from the inside" explained? – Why did some ancient authors see the Roman Empire as a continuation of*

---

[508] According to ancient authors in the cities of Dardania, Naissus, Theranda, and others, numerous metals were not only extracted but the processing of iron and workshops were also extended, producing some 40% of the Roman Army weapons. It is known that the city of Nais of Dardania was one of the cities with the largest imperial workshops for weapons production.

[509] For more on this see: Borivoje Čović: *"Osnovna karakteristika materijalne kulture Ilira na njihovom centralnom području,"* Sarajevo, 1965; Droysen, J.G.H: *"Das dardanische Fürstentum,"* Leipzig, 1893; Egger, Rudolf: *"Balkan pod Rimljanima,"* Belgrade, 1937; Vulic, Nikola: *"Dardanci"* in Glas SKS CLV/1933.

> *Troy? – The role of "pax romana" for admission by the Illyrians of the Roman Empire. – The edict of Emperor Caracalla of the year 212 and the free citizen status for all Illyrians and Dardanians. – Dardania's boom at the time of Emperor Justinian I and its return to a province with special protected status of the Empire. – Construction of new cities in Dardania and building of 100 castles from Naissus (Nis) to Scup (Shkup). – Justiniana Prima rises to the rank of Archdiocese of Illyricum with direct ties to the Holy See.*

What was seen as the interest of Illyrians and Dardanians in protecting the overall edifice of the Roman Empire that was also a struggle to protect their country, frequently is associated with their Romanization as a natural process that included the Illyrians and Dardanians as well, as it included almost all the others who were encompassing the greater part of the empire who were subject to its social political, economic and cultural frame in accordance with their interests.

However, the understanding of this phenomenon on these bases, not always first in line with the nature of the case, often with dilemmas turning occasionally into unfounded and even erroneous interpretations, like those on Romanization of the Illyrians and Dardanians are seen as a blank paper as "a number of tribes scattered and mostly hostile to each other," of having nothing to defend, or holding nothing whatsoever.[510] Interpretations include even assessments of them having been accommodated so well in military and political structures of the Roman Empire that they turned into its defenders as in the case of war against barbarian attacks, as they fought to protect an authority gained based on human power.[511]

These and similar conclusions are not only far from historical truth, such as those dealing with the two-century-old struggles of Romans to subdue Illyrian, Macedonian, Dardanian, and other lands across the

---

[510] For more on this see: Garašanin, Milutin: *"Istorijska i arheoloska razmatranja u ilirskoj drzavi,"* Belgrade, 1974; Geza, Alfördy: *"Die römische Gesellschaft-Struktur und Eigenart,"* 1975.

[511] For more on this see: Hans Urlich Istinsky: *"Sichercheit al politisches Problem der römischen Keisertum,"* Baden-Baden, 1952; I. M. Rostowetz: *"Gesellschaft und Wiertschaft dr Römische Staat;"* A. Morscy: *"Untersuchungen zur Geschichte der römischen Provinz Moesia superior;"* Gavela, Branko: *"O ilirskom substratu na Balkanu,"* Belgrade, 1965.

Adriatic, commencing from the mid-2nd century B.C. and ending in the early 1st century A.D. which, if there had been nothing to fight about would never have happened, but they are also far from the truth on what they call "a voluntary accommodation of the Illyrians" in the new empire as if they had nothing to keep. The Roman Empire even after conquering their lands with so much blood would, in a large measure, accept and also save a lot of their ethnic and cultural organization from tribal self-governance, economic life, and urban structures, which, from a political perspective was sanctioned with an administrative organization in the provinces on a self-governing basis, where Illyricum, together with Dardania enjoyed special treatment, with parts being almost states within the state.

If issues relating to the rise and fall of the Roman Empire from its inception to the end are viewed from the perspective of its constituent factors, it appears that Illyrians and Dardanians may also be taken as its founders, an awareness with a dual function. Ancient sources, especially those from important ancient writers, those of literary ones from Homer,[512] Hesiod,[513] Virgil,[514] and others, as well as historians, geographers, philosophers, and various chroniclers: Herodotus, Thucydides, Isocrates, Scylax, Scymnus, Polybius, Apollodorus, Strabo, Pliny, Lucanus, Ptolemy, and others,[515] offering more information concerning the role of Dardanians and Etruscans in the founding of Rome and then in raising it by Etruscans and other Pelasgic tribes that were there since prehistoric times, that is, since they settled there once detached from the common trunk somewhere in India in the 6th millennium. Literary sources, those from Homer to Virgil target Trojan War and the fate of the Trojans (mostly Dardanians) who followed the land routes (through Epirus), as did Aeneas, and moved from there to southern Italy, where they settled and found Rome.

The literary versions also found in Roman legends, and also various Roman chronicles, where the founding of Rome is constantly linked with the crossing of Aeneas and other Trojans to Italy, tried to compensate for the loss of Troy by building another one in the West, which they did.

---

[512] *"Iliada,"* "Odisea," Tirana, 1979.
[513] *"Theogonia"* (Carmina), fragment 134 (156).
[514] *"Aeneidos,"* (Eneid), Book III, cited according to *"Ilirët dhe Iliria te autorët antikë,"* Prishtina, 1979.
[515] For more see: *"Ilirët and Iliria te autorët antikë,"* Prishtina, 1979.

Something of this consciousness, probably as historical memory or left to the grandchildren of Aeneas' offspring, who although founding Rome, always kept in their minds that they had to one day go back to Troy, to their roots to raise its spirit, as Constantine the Great once said, a Dardanian from Naissus, who transfered the center of the great empire from Rome to Byzantium, closer to Troy, in order to extend there the life of the Eastern Empire for another 1,000 years. The transfer of the center from West to East, i.e. from Rome to Constantinople was not only a matter of a strategic decision, that circumstances of survival dictated to the great emperor from Dardania when the slave-owner society was in its highest crisis, but it was also a testament to return to the root. This had become an obsession to Constantine. After all, wasn't this feeling as strong among all those Illyrian-Dardanian emperors who raised Byzantium to such a high level as to be called "Illyrian Byzantium," [516] on the foundations of which, from the 6th century A.D. onwards stood Dardania and Dardanians with Christianity as a postulate, which was accepted by them and followed by others (Greeks, Romans, even the Slavs who accepted 7 centuries later) turning it into a common denominator of a spiritual civilization that was different from the Western one?

Even without the assumptions of this nature, which draw on literary and mythological sources from antiquity and as such already belong to human memory, even historical ones do not deny the crossing by Aeneas and the defeated Trojans (Dardanians) to southern Italy and their settlement there as a new beginning, as they do not deny also the Pelasgic presence in these parts from the first movements of peoples. Although dispersed, in a factographic light, they enable a reconstruction of the event. Furthermore, this "detail," would not be ignored by historians of centuries later, although many of them still did not follow strictly the historical course of this development, or even when they did, they left this factor aside, only because they wanted to see the Roman empire in continuity with an eastern civilization, like that of ancient Troy, but as a universal imperial western concept that would arise as its antipodal point.

If despite this fact increasingly based on historical data from ancient authors, the historiography of modern times was not able to accept in whole, it has also not been able to deny it, along with Aeneas and the Trojans, who were transferred to the South of Italy, where Dardanian

---

[516] Budimir, Milan: "*O etničkom odonosu dardanaca prema ilirima,*" Belgrade, 1950.

tribes Galabri, Thunans, and Daunes continued their dynasties in Calabria and Sicily and the whole of southern Italy. They were later joined by the population of the Peloponnese and Epirus (an immigration that with different intensities continued until Middle Ages reaching its peak following Skenderbeg's death), also the Pelasgian tribes from the North (Etruscans, Venetians, and others), as part of a pan-European prehistoric stratification, that was also involved in the founding of Rome and all the development derived from the Roman Empire. Numerous historical sources, from ancient and more recent authors, not only do not deny the presence of the important Illyrian tribes in northern and central Italy, but they were given an important place in all the pre-Roman and Roman complexity without excluding their influence in shaping the Latin language seen directly related to the Illyrian language.

This applies especially to Etruscans, whose presence is known in these parts from the 8th century B.C. Even today, Etruscan inscriptions and other traces of their civilization represent a huge puzzle where, only the eagle holds the key to unlocking the truth about the major role that the descendants of Pelasgians played in the Hellenic and Roman civilization.

When to this factor – which is very important to show that for Illyrians, Dardanians, and Macedonians as descendants of the ancient Pelasgians as the first foundation of Indo-European stratification in the old continent and beyond the Roman Empire was neither unknown nor strange, but was also part of their past – we add the fact that even after the Roman conquest, Illyrians and Dardanians, under the auspices of the Roman Empire, joined in with their own internal structures from the tribal ones to those of slave-owner dynasties. These structures were accepted and vindicated within the new imperial and administrative reorganization with self-governing autonomy and other forms of preservation of ethnic identity. It appears quite clear why Romanization served as a convenient tool for Illyrians and Dardanians to be able to manage their fast rise in the political, military and economic hierarchy of the Roman Empire acquiring from within to such an extent as to fight for it to the last moment.

Even beyond this historic observation, which is very important to see some ignored or forgotten truths of the common values among the Illyrians, Dardanians and Rome, it defined their attitude towards the Roman Empire, and even Romans towards them. If we turn to new realities created after long Illyrian-Roman wars ending with the conquest of Illyrian and Dardanian lands in the rest of the Adriatic and in the central part, it was in their interest to gain as much as they could in the newly-created circumstances achieving this only through their inclusion within an advanced social, administrative, economic, political, and cultural system such as the the Roman system.

Sensibly, the Roman concept of "*pax romana*," which provided an opportunity to act and gain from within, especially in the economic, military and cultural aspect, represented not only an appropriate political formula, but the spirit of a concept as well, being also supported by the common roots since antiquity, although this remains a hypothetical, rather philosophical than historical issue. However, if between Virgil's fantasy on Aeneas' yearning for Troy to return to Rome and the dedication of Constantine the Great to transfer the center of his empire to the East, 20 centuries passed before the action that turned history back to the same point, then there is no point in overlooking the fact that the same actors being on the scene (Illyrians and Dardanians), descendants of ancient Pelasgians, where Romans have their own roots too, were entitled to behave in accordance to that historical awareness.

If the arising question such as Romanization of Illyrian-Dardanians is relieved of all historical and literary reminiscence, then even without them one may conclude that since the space of Illyricum, which according to the Roman concept included the Roman province of Dardania as a special province, was one of the largest and most important strategic and economic points, being crisscrossed by the main roads linking the West with the East and Central Europe with its South and North. Simultaneously, by the opening of roads, circulation of people, goods and ideas in various directions, it was natural that the population benefited, particularly from an administrative point of view as it was entitled to keep a part of customs duties and other revenues to use for its own needs.

If one adds to that the military factor, which was discussed earlier and the importance it represented to the involvement of youth in this area, finding a place in its structures in which they seized the opportunity to climb up to the highest military hierarchy, gaining top civic Roman treatment of the most privileged scale, then clearly these conditions implied a high degree of social, economic, political, and cultural integration, the latter standing upon a platform of a recognized system of values to which the Illyrians and Dardanians together with the others began to contribute to come up to the stage of an awareness that by doing so they were defending their country, an empire that in its final stage was called Roman-Illyrian, the same as it would happen a little later with Byzantium when it was called "Illyrian Byzantium."[517]

The Romanization of the Illyrians, Dardanians, Macedonians, Thracians, and others occupied or other populations included within the Roman Empire occurred on a large scale being even a natural phenomenon, since, evidently, it related to the very nature of the Empire as a cosmopolitan concept that relied on known principles of Roman citizenship, with Latin as the official language and culture. Therefore, this component alone would be sufficient, i.e. Romanization as a state framework, where many peoples involved in it would gain the opportunity to exercise their rights as ordinary citizens, which did not mean that they should be different in order to fulfill "a precondition" to seek the status of Roman citizenship in order to be equal in a social and legal sense with the others.

Even the latter, the Roman citizenship, which at least nominally would be able to have an impact on Romanization, by the famous decree of Emperor Caracalla in the year 212 A.D. was entirely removed, by which the policy of "pax romana" practically turned into a further incentive to internal peace, since alongside self-governance tribal and latifundist communities gained the right, in terms of production in agriculture and mining, to turn into an important economic axis. This, in its turn, conditioned further strengthening of the provinces, being at the same time a political factor, as it affected the hierarchy of the imperial powers from the center to the provinces, from the Senate to the army, which could only be strengthened through political and economic self-governance on the ground, where the native factor, in this case Illyrian and Dardanian, gained increasing weight in order to reach a decisive point.

Evidence of the time, particularly that arising from late antiquity, shows that the economy did not only preserve its own native element, but it had strengthened further, as *free peasants (in colae),* and other similar strata, during the reign of Valentinian, Gratian, and Valen were mentioned as very important economic factors, which had helped the country to maintain stability when it was threatened.[518]

---

[517] For more on this see: Budimir, Milan: *"O etnickom odnosu dardanaca prema ilirima,"* Belgrade, 1950; *"Grci i Pelsci,"* Belgrade, 1951.
[518] Mirdita, Zef: *"Studime dardane,"* Prishtina, 1979, p. 128.

These and similar examples suffice in throwing some more light on the essence of Romanization and its specific nature during the time of the Roman Empire as a process that meant inclusion of all of its citizens in a common administrative, social, judicial, and cultural system, but not a necessary and full melting of indigenous entities, as were the Illyrians, Dardanians, and others in its eastern part, for the sole reason that something like that was not in its interest, especially knowing that it would be that very indigenous population in these parts that would best protect the Empire from barbarian threats coming from the North and East, and this they could do best if they felt bound to it in all aspects (social, political and economic).

From this perspective, as noted earlier, Rome, by means of administrative organization and in line with its security and defense (*securitatis populli romani*) allowed for an extensive self-governance of many provinces from higher to local levels through the maintenance of many independent *"castellas"* and *"optidas"* (castles and cities), which mostly served as defense points or as settlements of economic character and distinct warehouses.

Such independent settlements were numerous in Dardania as well, and they were situated in central and strategic points of communication, where there was virtually no opportunity for an intensive Romanization to take place, although a naturalized assimilation should not be excluded, which occurred among the elite layers of the population, which for economic or trade reasons was compelled to accept state and administrative norms, as well as social standards of the Empire, as part of a common system of values that brought benefits. Even what can be called natural Romanization, in Dardania was almost entirely excluded following the military reforms of Diocletian at the end of the 3rd century A.D. since at that time the army not only spoke no Latin, but it did not know the language at all.[519]

In this process, however, one should make a distinction between social and spiritual Romanization, though they go together, with the first helping the second and the second defining its character.

Indeed, it must be admitted that from the 1st century A.D. with the occupation of Illyria and Dardania and other neighboring parts complet-

---

[519] See: Eusebius: *"Vita Constantini,"* IV/19, cited according to Mirdita, Zef: *"Studime dardane,"* Prishtina, 1979, p. 123.

ed, the Roman culture began to spread, albeit intertwined with ethno-culture, especially with those forms that could turn into shared values.

This process was accompanied by a positive development, since the incorporation of local culture extinguished the cultural differences that existed hitherto between the Illyrian provinces and Illyrians and Dardanians themselves as the large Illyrian family, and Dardanians too, from a political standpoint, had no internal permanent connection. Therefore, the main hearths for spreading Roman culture, which should be seen as a cosmopolitan culture, became the settlements *municipe,* those cities that turned into important economic centers and which provided a vibrant cultural life too.[520]

In these new urban environments, alongside new urbanism, the Romans brought in their cultural institutions, from the small and covered theaters (Odeon) to libraries and various museums. Also, in some cities, amphitheaters were built with large arenas where sports and cultural competitions were held.

As some of the coastal cities, either as colonies or as popular trading centers enjoying autonomy (Butrint, Apollonia, Dyrrachium, and others) had public cultural facilities (large auditoriums, theaters, and libraries), they expanded the amphitheater of Apollonia and Dyrrachium, built close to the others, but much larger, and in accordance with new requirements.

In the first three centuries A.D. a significant development occurred in the plastic art, especially sculptures. In the ruins of Apollonia, in Dyrrachium, Butrint, and other coastal cities, sculptures based on Hellenistic and Roman arts were discovered. Similar sculptures were also found in parts of Dardania, in the locality of Ulpiana, the Justiniana Prima, Naissus, Scubi and other areas. Small plastics occupied the main place of bronze figures, produced mostly in series, related to divinity and secular characters.[521]

The mosaic art was also widespread. Mosaics and their development too, just like the beautiful works of architecture and sculpture, were associated with high layers of provinces, both the cities and rural settlements, owners of villas and latifundists.[522] Of this nature are some of the monumental mosaics discovered recently at Vendenis, near Podujeva.

---

[520] *"Historia e Popullit Shqiptar,"* Volume I, Tirana, 2002, p. 177
[521] Ibid, p. 178.
[522] Ibid, p. 178.

Similar mosaics are also found in Theranda and Ulpiana, most of them with motifs from ancient mythology.

But, unlike other parts of the Empire, where a decline of urban centers in the 3rd and 4th centuries A.D. is evident, the urban culture in Dardania had a significant increase as the most notable. This has to do less with the fact that the emperors of this time came mostly from this part and the military caste, which had begun to have the main say on the highest levels, than with political and administrative reforms undertaken to ensure the existence where it was mostly threatened by barbarian attacks, namely in strategic parts as those of Illyricum and Dardania. This component, of course, had its positive turns, as in addition to strengthening the political class from the provinces (mainly military, of local origin) and its influence in the imperial hierarchy, as reflected in the transfer of its pyramid of power from capital to the periphery, also influenced the establishment and development of urban centers from fortresses (*castellas*) to cities (*oppida*), which turned into important political and economic factors.

Notably, in this respect it was Dardania that benefited the most, especially from the second half of the 2nd century to the 5th century B.C. Evidence from the time indicates how in these territories many of the old settlements were restored with many more coming into existence. Obviously it would be the strategic aspect (possibility of protection from barbarian attacks) that played a role in this development, which sometimes is seen to be the main factor. However, in this case one should not forget that Dardania and parts of surrounding Illyricum were populated above the average of other areas, and also, important urban centers were located in these parts, either because most of the metal mines were in Dardania, where they were also processed, or because in this area, river streams also flowed (Vardar towards the Aegean, Ibar and Morava towards the Danube and the Black Sea, and White Drin to the Adriatic). The old routes connecting the West with the East were mentioned in the case of Ptolemy's records identifying the city of Naissus in Dardania, along with several others surrounding major centers of extraction and processing of metals, as well as other important cities in these parts (Scubi, present-day Shkup-Skopje, Ulpiana, Theranda and others). Ancient authors also spoke of these places to which during the Roman era many others were added, such as Justiniana Prima, Justiniana Secunda and many others.

Reportedly, Emperor Justinian I (527-556 A.D.), who came from the Taurus of Dardania, built and rebuilt in these areas 94 castles.[523] Yet in addition to the numerous castles, Emperor Justinian I, built near his city of birth, Bederiana, a magnificent city which he called Justiniana Prima, surrounded by a square-shaped wall with four tetrapyrgos towers.[524]

It is known that the emperor also built a magnificent water supply system providing water for all seasons. Procopius of Caesarea wrote how the emperor had adorned the city with temples, galleries, public squares, palaces, baths and shops.[525] Further on, Procopius reports how he turned it into a great city, very popular and rich, so that it not only rose to the dignity of a metropolis, but was also elected as the center of the Archbishop of the Illyrians, as other cities left that honor to the greatest city in the country.[526]

Besides the construction of Justiniana Prima and its rise to a magnificent city, Procopius of Caesarea provided crucial data for the reconstruction of other centers, such as Ulpiana, after having lost for various reasons their former importance.

---

[523] *"Historia e Popullit Shqiptar,"* Volume I, Tirana, 2002, p. 179.

[524] *Prokopii Caesarensis (Procopius of Cesarea)*, the great Byzantine historian of Justinian's time. He was born in Cesarea of Palestine by the end of the 5th or the beginning of the 6th century AD. After completing studies at the School of Sophists in Gatta, he settled in Constantinople occupying an important place in Byzantine administration. Procopius wrote three books: "De Bellis" (History of Wars), *"De aedificiis" (On Ediffices)* and "Historia arcana" (Secret History). His treaty "On Ediffices" provides notes on constructions made by Justinian throughout the Empire, with the ones on geography and toponomy of Illyria and Dardania as most interesting. Therefore, the long list of castles built or rebuilt by Justinian, as provided by Procopius, includes a number of towns and localities of Illyria and Dardania. Among them he brings the names of eight new castles: Laberion, Castimon, Rabeston, Acrenza, Terios, Drullos, and Victorias. Among the rebuilt castles he mentions: Cesiana, Tezule, Usiana, Mascas, Liste, Celiriana, Zysbaes, Genzana, Petrizen, Euttyhia, Mulato, Belas, Cataros, Catareos, Pentza, Catafeteros, Dabanos, Cubinos, Germatza, Viktoriana, Azeta, Durbulina, Surikon, Cusines, Tutiana, Balesiana, Bella, Caltrelates, Casyella, Maniana, Priskupera, Mitetes, Dardapara, Kesuna, Beriniana, Lasbaros, Castellobretara, Edetzio, Dinion, Kekola, Emastos, Castelona, Kapamolba, Seretos, Ptoheion, Kuino, Berzana, Arsa, Bleza, Labutza, Kuintu, Bermezion, Rotun, Cobenciles, Markeliana, Primoniana, Pamilinos, and Aria (See: "De aedificiis," Book IV/4).

[525] Ibid, Book IV/17-26.

[526] Ibid, Book IV/27.

"There was a town called Ulpiana in Dardania, since ancient times. Its walls (which were falling down) he built anew. And after decorating it with the brilliance and beauty it has today, he named it Justiniana Secunda."[527]

The establishment of another city named Justinopolis, after his brother, was made known on the occasion. It is also worth mentioning four important centers of Dardania, whose walls were rebuilt: *Sardis*, *Naispolis*, *Germana* and *Pantelis* among which three other cities were also established: *Cratiscara*, *Quimedaba*, and *Rumisiana*.[528]

It is to Justinian I's merit that at his time, after having dislocated the Archdiocese of the Dardanian Church from Thessaloniki to Justiniana Prima turning it to the Vicariate of Illyricum directly connected with the Holy See, he started building more churches from the Naissus area up to Astibo. Nearly all the centers of Dardania earned their churches, while in the cities cathedrals were built. These objects were accompanied by gardens, chattels and other spaces in order for them to be rich and open to the public.

The mention of the magnificent Justinian Prima, although associated with Justinian I and his time, which belonged to the Byzantine period, however, highlights the Dardanian ethnic identity expanding under the circumstances of the Roman Empire, carried over to the realities of Byzantium, where Dardania's importance as a province continued appearing from the 4th century as separate. Therefore, as such, Justinian Prima, along with its role for the future (5th-6th century as ecclesiastical center), further explains Dardania's cultural and political development during the previous centuries, from the time of Diocletian and Constantine the Great reforms when Dardania practically turned into a "transition center" from where the power of Rome was transferred to Byzantium, whose importance has been overlooked because the first metaphor of its connection to Troy is implied, highlighting again the Pelasgians and their heritage as a key factor defining relations between East and West, but this time under the aureole of Christianity.

However, Justinian Prima, although reappearing in the 5th century in ancient Scupi, ruined by a devastating earthquake of catastrophic conse-

---

[527] Ibid, Book IV/30.
[528] Ibid, Book IV/33.

quences in 518 A.D,[529] represented the epicenter of power stretching from Naissus and continuing down towards Thessaloniki, interconnecting other important centers: *Ulpiana, Theranda, Hersonissos, Bederiana, Taurisium* and others, a force that speaks of the importance that Dardania had at the crossroads of events related to Byzantine history and what is known as the Middle Ages.

---

[529] According to the chronicle of Comes Marcelini *"Chronicon ad an 518,"* in MGF AA, 100, among others, states that "the earthquake that occurred in Dardania destroyed 24 castelas, among which Scubi, whose inhabitants, while running away from the enemy were saved." Cited according to Mirdita, Zef: *"Studime dardane,"* Prishtina, 1979, p. 138.

CONCLUSION

Antiquity or ancient time has long been identified only with historical time, although it was rather obvious that having the concept of civilization as only shrinking to historical time, namely to what started with the 2nd millennium and beyond, were incomplete without its connection to prehistory, regardless of the secrets that it kept, and regardless of the objective disconnections it may create.

For the sake of history, it was impossible to maintain that concept as such, that is, excluded from prehistory to history in a non-historical way. The opening of this matter and its given legitimacy in almost all scientific areas exposes a deliberate circumvention, through which science had a duty to protect certain social issues, which should even serve political conjunctures!

Such was also the part regarding Hellenism and the Greek role in it, which excluded others, primarily the people that the Greeks had found in Greece, that is, Pelasgians, forefathers of Albanians.

This theory, which originated and was developed in the 19th century in Europe, especially by the Germans and the Nordic countries, in fact, had less to do with turning the attention of the European opinion in favor of the Greek war of liberation "as pioneers of Hellenism" against the Ottoman rule, (although such militants were not absent), than promoting the "leading" role of the northern peoples (Germans and the Balto-Slavs) in the formation of the Indo-European family.

As Germans, Balts, and Slavs were united by the Nordism theory as carriers of Indo-Europeanism, it was imperative to recognize the merit of this civilizing "mission" to the Greeks and Greece as Arians, who through the well-known Doric penetrations from the 10th century B.C. created circumstances for the emergence of Hellenism in Hellada. This recognition meant a victimization of prehistory and its decisive role in antiquity, on one hand, and on the other it sought for the exclusion of any possibility of Hellenism having any connection with the Sumerian culture, which meant also an exclusion of any possibility of the Greeks arriving from the Mediterranean, or even Egypt, as stated in the "Iliad" and as many scientific arguments testify.

This scientific instability, seen from the very beginning, in the 19th century, as something shaky that could not have a long life, as it had many opponents among scientists from the German and Nordic countries, became even more volatile when viewing the Greeks as the only carriers of Hellenism. This idea was rejected by Greek sources, initially from mythology, then by literature (Homer and Hesiod), and later by ancient Greek philosophers, who not only admitted with honesty and appreciation for those who they found and were still there – the Pelasgians, whom they called "divine people" from whom they received and learned a lot, but also excluded the Greek self-identification with Egypt and their culture without which they come up short.

However, the most unacceptable in all this matter was, no doubt, first ignoring the Pelasgians, whom the Greeks had found there - and who, always according to ancient authors, had the highest civilization, and secondly – the stubbornness to accept the fact that the Pelasgians had left a lineage behind: Illyrians, Dardanians, and Macedonians, as part of a tree with many branches sharing the same root.

Even though the biased science, in the face of these facts, tried to manipulate the facts on the grounds that the Pelasgians, who should have been there when the Greeks came, were extinct, whereas Illyrians, Dardanians, and Macedonians, as "barbarian" peoples, meaning outside of Hellenistic culture, did not belong to Hellenism, there was a bulk of testimonies from mythology, history, archeology, anthropology, and linguistics that made it clear that from the Pelasgic-Illyrian continuity came Albanians with their Albanian language, a daughter of the Pelasgian.

The Pelasgians were the ancestors of the Albanians and the Albanian daughter of the Pelasgian was claimed since the mid-19th century by several scientists, among them the German Johann Georg von Hahn, who in his "Albanian Studies" touched the issue of the Pelasgian script and the alphabet they assumed from what they say were Phoenicians, or the other way around, just the same, since Phoenicians too were considered to be Pelasgians, with the Greeks seemingly having appropriated it from the Pelasgians as soon as they showed up in Greece. Even though what Hahn said about the Pelasgians and their language as early as in 1845 to many seemed mere fantasy, gradually but steadily, it would be accepted by many scientists *admitting the role of the Pelasgians as the basis of Hellenism, as they paved the way for the issue of Illyrians being their descendants, confirming the acceptance of an Albanian connection to them.*

However, this change needed tangible scientific facts, which were foremost historical, and also spiritual. The first represented material evidence is kept by archeology and anthropology, and the second by linguistics from Albanian toponyms, as a living testimony being spoken exactly in the core of what Homer testifies on the Pelasgians, "the divine people," and Herodotus speaking of a "barbaric" language they spoke, which was still in use by "barbarians" in Hellada and its vicinity.

Under the pressure of these facts, and others as well, which tied the Greeks to the Mediterranean and Egypt, the Nordic theory was not only deprived of the exclusive viewing of the Greeks as the cradle of Hellenism, and thus the foundation of antiquity, but the theory would also "tame" the stance of ignoring the Pelasgians by not treating them as "indigenous with traces scattered among others, "i.e. part of prehistory and also associated to the historical time, with traces and a continuation among the Illyrians, Thracians, and Albanians, without excluding Basks and many other peoples too, who were seen as "disconnected" or without a root.

Of course this turn toward the Pelasgians and the Albanians would be highly beneficial for the Indo-European doctrine itself, because through the Albanian within its system, it explains a lot of issues, such as those on the "confounding" of kentum-satem division, which had cast trouble for a long time in this family, appearing to some with a row of gutturals, to some others with one, two, and never three, as the Albanian has, with which the presence of centum-satem elements in it prove a common Indo-European factor with a broad East-West dispersion, which in linguistics was called pan-Pelasgianism, while the Pelasgians were called "classics" of Indo-Europeanism."

There are also some other issues that allow the Albanian language to provide answers to the dilemmas considered previously as "unsettled," such as those dealing with Greek mythology, where many of the deities and idols could not be explained otherwise except through Albanian. Also, in the toponymy and onomastics the Albanian appears as the sole decoding key.

Accepting the role of the Pelasgians in antiquity and the Illyrian-Albanian continuity helps in explaining the pre-Hellenic civilization, like that of Troy, Mycenae and Crete, which is of a much earlier date than the Hellenic.

In many segments, science has admitted that Troy, Mycenae, Crete and the Aegean-Mediterranean civilization has been the precursor of Hellenism, but even when proving this, considering it sometimes as prehistoric and other times as pre-Greek and the like, it has tried to avoid the Pelasgian factor and its role in it, whenever they appear as builders, kings, or carriers of an entire ancient civilization.

The failure to address the issue lasted until recently, when the "secret" of Troy was revealed together with the Mycenaean, Cretan and cyclopic remains, inevitably associated with the Pelasgians.

Thus, what the Greek mythology signifies about Pelasgic deities, on what Homer says of them as "divine people" and many deities and idols that are admittedly appropriated from them, would be proven by the material culture at Troy, Mycenae, Crete, and its expansion in the Balkans, Central, West and North of Europe, as well as evidently in the entire Mediterranean, North Africa, in Asia Minor and as far as India.

However, this issue opened the social and political role of the Pelasgians as a kingdom with a wide Eurasian expansion, with Troy playing a special role as a bridge connecting the West with the East. Dardanians appear there as its founders, who, after the Doric and Aegean immigrations and long wars with various Hellenic tribes, were finally forced to flee, with some of the tribes (Galabri, Thunates, and Daos) crossing over to Italy, where they laid the foundations of Rome, as "compensation" for Troy.

Today, historiography has been increasingly treating the hypothetical version of the Trojan War by Homer as historical reality, rather than a creative imagination (though this eternal frame stays on) from where through detached facts a historical truth may be rebuilt as announced in art nearly 30 centuries ago.

Regarding Pelasgian return to historical time and their role for civilization, a role from which we will learn more, the theory has so far affected the Illyrians and Illyrian language, upon which Albanian continuity was supported.

Although the Revivalists accepted the Pelasgic origin, giving it broad support, Albanian science, especially the ideological one, showed no interest whatsoever in linking with the Pelasgians or Pelasgia.

Until yesterday the "alibi" was found in ideology and its dogma, (though it does not free from responsibility certain authorities that compiled the "History of the Albanian People" for this unscientific detachment, which has been in accordance with the interests of hegemonic Serbian, Greek, and

Russian ideologies in the last century, to keep the Albanians, at most, tied to the Illyrians, although nevertheless contested). However, the current position of Tirana Albanian historiography, refusing to liaise with the Pelasgians and Pelasgian language claiming that Illyrian association "is a sure issue," while the Pelasgic one is "fuzzy and unstable," speaks of an unforgivable subversion to the Albanian history, which in a liaison with the Pelasgians, not only did not lose anything, but rather provided strength, as it leads to the foundation of antiquity and hence to a key factor of world civilization.

Claiming that "we are not interested in Dardanian traces in the East" as "they have to do with Troy," that is, Asia, as stressed in the "History of the Albanian People," First Volume, published in Tirana in 2002, by a group of authors, who brag on having made "revisions," while Homer and other ancient authors claim that "Troy is Dardanian," whereas others (Romanians, Bulgarians, and even Serbs) do their best to somehow be associated with it, appropriate it, conjure it up, and everything else, is not only incomprehensible, but also inexcusable.

However, because of known historical circumstances Albanian studies were initiated by foreigners - it is safe to say that, as is the case with the science of Albanology, the foundations of which were laid by German scholars, for which we should be deeply grateful - - it is to be expected that one day the attitude toward the Pelasgians was imposed by them.

PART TWO
MIDDLE AGES

CHAPTER 1

Illyricum and the Emergence of Byzantium

> *Christianity was declared official by Emperor Constantine the Great – a precondition for the emergence of Byzantium. – Byzantium as a new period of history of the Roman Empire. – The Council of Nicaea and the expulsion of the Aryan doctrines. – Church dogma and social consequences. – The first administrative division of the Empire into two parts at the time of Emperor Theodosius brought the division of Illyricum, with northern provinces of Noricum, Pannonia, and Dalmatia belonging to the Western part, and Dardania, and Macedonia belonging to the Eastern Empire. – Despite the administrative division, in ecclesiastical terms, Illyricum and Dardania Illyricum remained under the jurisdiction of the Church of Rome. – The appearance of three Illyrian-Dardanian identities within the imperial one: self-governing, administrative, and ecclesiastical awareness associated with the imperial one.*

There were two curves of historical developments that led to the collapse of the Roman Empire and emergence of Byzantium, or the Christian Roman Empire. The first was the demise of the slave system, a consequence that was inevitably the social and political downfall of the Empire. The second had to do with the start of incursions by barbarians (Huns, Goths, and other tribes) in the eastern parts of the Empire. However, these developments had no significant weight without the factor of Christianity, which appeared in 1st century A.D. and directly affected the emergence of Byzantium during the Medieval Ages.

It should be pointed out that this stage of historical development, which marked the shift from Illyrian and Dardanian lands, as established centuries ago with the emergence of the Roman Empire by the expansion of Illyricum, Dardania, Macedonia, Greece and other areas, as the Goths, Huns, and Slavs from the East crossed Illyrian and Dardanian space, they changed its ethnic, cultural and state realities.

However, the descendants of the Pelasgians, in a tough match with barbarian invaders in the Middle Ages appeared with their Arberarian identity relying on a self-governing, administrative and religious identity from the emergence of Byzantium, connecting their state identity to Illyrians and Dardanians who were most deserving.

Before this change occurred, during the Middle Ages and Byzantium, the Illyrian-Dardanians were seen as *Albanë, Arvaniti, Albani, Arbanasi, Rabani* and otherwise, and their living space as *Alabani, Albaniae, Albanon* respectively, in line with different languages, lasting for more than 1,000 years. It is important to see the very circumstances that preceded them.

The key Roman emperors were of Illyrian-Dardanian origin that composed Illyricum as the main province of the Empire. The main efforts were conducted in order to affect and also accelerate this historical development. Therefore, it was Emperor Diocletian (284-305 AD) of Illyrian origin, who began the most profound and comprehensive reforms that granted Illyricum an important role in the economic and political revitalization of the Empire. The Dardanian Emperor Constantine the Great (306-337 BC) continued reforms in Illyricum and other eastern parts of the empire, which started the project of its division in the East, Byzantium.

Thinking that the crisis could have been overcome through administrative reforms, the central government finally moved to the provincial one where the military class had its largest support; Diocletian divided the imperial power between the two, and then among four co-rulers, all of them of Illyrian-Dardanian origin.

This measure in the late 3rd century practically marked the beginning of the division of the Empire into two parts. The eastern part was formed of two major prefectures: the East and Illyricum. The center of the latter was Sirmium (Sava's Mitrovica). Furthermore, the Illyricum prefecture was divided into 3 dioceses, including several smaller administrative units or provinces. The first included provinces of Southern Dalmatia and northern Illyria, with its center Shkodra (Prevalia), the Province of New

Epirus (Epirus Nova) from Durrahium to Old Epirus (Epirus Vetus) and the lands south of Vjosa with its center Nicopolis (Nikopoja).[530]

Following this measure, which also briefly extended the life of the slave regime but did not save it from ultimate failure, Constantine the Great was aware that the Empire was faced with another even greater social and political crisis because the release from slavery required a certain social dividend, which the free stratum demanded.

He accepted Christianity as a proper tool to support his decision and strengthen his absolute imperial power through the authority of the Church, turning it into his own ally. This historic decision that changed the social and political direction of the Empire was led by the famous order to stop the persecution of Christians in the year 311 A.D., which two years later was accompanied by another order granting support to Christianity and ultimately making Christianity the faith of the Empire. It was also granted a share in power, replacing the *Roman Universe* with the *Christian Universe*, although such an aspiration suffered permanent disappointments in the face of the political reality.

In 325 A.D., Emperor Constantine the Great called the Christian Council of Nicaea or the Council of Nicaea, which was attended by 318 bishops from all over the empire. The subsistence of Christianity in the Illyricum and Dardania was evidenced by the 13 signatures of the bishops present at Nicaea, among who were Bishop Dacus of Scupi (present-day Shkup), the Council "Dacus Dardaniae," and Budius of Stobi in Macedonia and Corcyra (Corfu).[531]

After instituting Christianity, Emperor Constantine the Great announced in 326 A.D. that he was permanently departing from Rome for Constantinople, moving headquarters from Rome to Byzantium four years later. In 330 A.D. he gave his own name, opening a new page in the history of civilization in which Christianity became one of the major determinants of change.

Prior to the consideration of further actions of the followers of Constantine the Great, who was already bearing his own seal, which remained in the framework for 10 centuries of historical development, clarification was needed about Byzantium as a political-religious organization with a Roman state structure, Greek culture, and Christian faith. This synthesis was made possible by the shift of gravity of the Roman Empire in the East,

---

[530] *"Historia e Popullit Shqiptar,"* Volume I, Prishtina, 1967, p. 126.
[531] Edwin, Jacques: *"Shqiptarët,"* Tirana, 2007, p. 163.

and by the 4th century, created the environment, a result of which was the Christianization of the Roman Empire and the establishment of a new capital in Bosphorus.[532]

Indeed, the Byzantine history is primarily a new period of Roman history, and the Byzantine state is a continuation of the old Roman Empire. As known, the term *"Byzantine"* came rather late, and true "Byzantines" did not recognize it. They continued to be called "Romans" (*romei*), while the Byzantine emperors called themselves Roman emperors.[533]

This "continuity" implied also the so-called leap to catch up with the last three centuries B.C. and the three centuries beginning A.D. led by the Roman Empire to the medieval Byzantine, where the forms of ancient Roman life were gradually extinguished yielding to the new phenomena of the country emerging Byzantine civilization, which appeared in circumstances when the state emerged as a *political-religious* organization of the Emperor's *political-religious* cult, while its citizens became his slaves.

Of course all this change wouldn't have been possible without a sublime unification of the ancient civilization between Roman state organization and Greek culture, which merged into a new concept of life melted in Christianity, in which ancient state culture experienced complete denial.

Emperor Diocletian declared war on the Republic of Rome. As known, Diocletian, who came to power at a time of deep political and economic crisis in the empire, was forced to undertake measures of a difficult situation and resort to radical reforms. Drawing conclusions from previous experiences of the Roman state, he systematically shuffled changes restructuring the entire state system.[534]

Diocletian's reform was perfected by Emperor Constantine the Great, which gave birth to a new administrative system, and the starting point of the Byzantine system.[535]

The reconstruction of the provincial administration, undertaken by Diocletian, ended the privileged position of Italy and wiped out the difference between the senatorial and imperial provinces, led by the militaries. Consequently, Italy, enjoying earlier the position of a metropo-

---

[532] Ostrogorski, Georg: *"Historia e Perandorisë Bizantine,"* Tirana, 2002, p. 17.
[533] Ibid, p. 17.
[534] Ibid, p. 21.
[535] Vogz, J: *"Constantin der Grosse und sein Jahrhudert,"* Berlin, 1960.

lis territory was divided into provinces and forced to give up its attributes as every other province of the empire.[536]

The administrative division of the country into provinces, prefectures, dioceses and other units, weakened the central government, but strengthened the power of the emperor and the military on which he relied more and more. Therefore, the emperor through the prefects and governors watched over everything, becoming an absolute ruler. Evidently, a huge bureaucratic apparatus was created out of this centralized hierarchy, which was effective, but expensive for the state. However, it was maintained because it was an important tool in the hands of the Emperor in order to exercise the power of a limitless sovereign.

The most important trait of the Diocletian-Constantine administrative system was a strict separation of the military from civilian authority. Therefore, the civil administration of a province was in the hands of the governor of the province, and the military controlled the Duke (*dux*), who held command over the military in several provinces.

However, Diocletian and Constantine performed substantive military reforms. Initially, the army was mainly a border army. The time of crisis highlighted its inability to deal with problems of internal and external security of the country, specifically protection from barbarian attacks in various parts. Diocletian took measures to strengthen the army on the border, making it mobile and prepared for action. By doing so, he created special units, called *exercitu comitatensis*. These units were later evolved by Constantine, who did not rely on the Praetorian Guard, known for its long-standing claims to produce emperors.[537] Constantine went even further, reforming and training the army by dividing mobile forces (*comitatensis*) from the border forces (*limitanei*).

Besides the Roman state structure factor, which was a prerequisite for creating the Byzantine synthesis, due to the reforms of Diocletian and Constantine the Great remaining on its foundation, there was Christianity, as one among many important factors that influenced the state to turn it into a *political-religious* organization, while the Emperor's regime turned into a *political-religious* cult.

One of the most debated issues of historiography is Constantine's stance towards Christianity. Some think that Constantine was religiously

---

[536] Ostrogorski, Georg: "*Historia e Perandorisë Bizantine,*" Tirana, 2002, p. 21.
[537] For more see: Mommsen, T: "*Das römische Militärwesen seit Diocletians,*" Leipzig, 1899; Ensslin, W: "*Zum Heermeisteramt des spätrömischen Reichs,*" p. 129.

indifferent and that he supported Christianity simply for political purposes. Others believe in his conversion and attribute to him the great turnaround marked in the religious policy of the empire. In fact, there is good reason to speak of his union with Christianity and many more reasons to defend the thesis of his allegiance to the old pagan traditions.[538] Even though this issue continues to be debatable, political goals were decisive for Constantine to accept Christianity as the religion of the Roman Empire, which he made in its known form. This, however, does not mean that he devoted himself entirely to Christianity, breaking his relations with pagan traditions and becoming Christian in the sense that his Byzantine successors gave to the term.[539]

On the contrary, the powerful emperor did not ban paganism. This should be noted in this case as well in order to clarify the true relations between politics and power, which influenced the acceptance of Christianity. Indeed, he took part in some of these rites, especially in the sun rite, a characteristic ritual that he survived in his hometown in Dardania up to our time despite the great impact that Christianity and later Islam had in these parts, trying to attribute his strength to the Creator (God).

Regardless of Constantine's personal behavior towards Christianity and the beliefs he maintained, it remains an undeniable fact that he turned it into a political instrument, replacing the *universal vision* of the Roman Empire with the *Christian vision*. This gave the church influence over politics, with politics using the church for its own aims, which was important to the Emperor, in terms of gaining the title of a divine representative.

The most historically significant example the impact of Christianity had over the Roman Empire at the time of Constantine was the Council of Nicaea in 325 A.D., the first of a whole series of ecumenical councils, setting the dogmatic and canonic basis of the Christian Church.

Notably, the Council included in its agenda the issue of the Alexandrian Presbyterian Aria who did not accept monotheistic *parity of the*

---

[538] In the entire wide bibliography existing in relation to this issue Georg Ostrogorski (History of Byzantine Empire) limits himself to the following authors: Burckhardt, J: "*Die Zeit Constantins des Grosse,*" Second full edition, Stoccard, 1929; Schwartz, E: "*Keiser Constantin und die chistlische Kirche;*" Zeller, J: "*Quelques remarques sul la "vision" de Constain "likuide;*" Lietzman, K: "*Der Glaube Konstatins des Grossen,*" Berlin, 1937; Vogt, J: "*Costantin der Grosse und sein Jahrhundert.*"

[539] Ostrogorski, Georg: "*Historia e Perandorisë Bizantine,*" Tirana, 2002, p. 29.

Father and the Son, thereby denying the *divine nature* of Christ. The *Arian* doctrine was condemned by the Council, recognizing the dogma of *co-substance of the Father with His Son*. This is how it became an article of faith that later, after completing it by resolutions of the Second Ecumenical Council of 381 A.D., became the creed of the Christian Church.[540]

Therefore, the relationship between the state and the church yielded many benefits to both, as many of the state problems became problems of the church as well, intermingling church and political debates which continued to be a permanent factor in the history of the Church, and in the history of the state and politics.

These phenomena sprung up in the time of Constantine the Great, especially *Arianism*, which did not fade away with the decisions of The Council of Nicaea, though it received an answer, while as was seen, its final outcome came at the Second Council.

From the First Council in Nicaea to the Second Council in Constantinople, over half a century of strife and dissension continued involving sons of Constantine the Great. Constans, who ruled over the eastern half and declared himself in favor of Arianism, died in 340. Constantius ruled the western part and was supporting the Nicaea doctrine.

Disagreements between the brothers about the church doctrine continued for a long time, until the older brother died in the war against the usurper Magnetius in 350, who then was defeated by Constans in a bloody battle.[541]

Constans' victory brought a growing political weight to the eastern part of the Empire. The Emperor intended to equate to the power of Constantinople to Rome, which went to the detriment of semi-pagan Rome. On this occasion, he declared Arianism as his state religion in 359. The temporary victory of Arianism in the Roman-Byzantine state had another long-term consequence since the time that marked the Christianization of the Goths, when the Germanic peoples recognized Christianity in its Arian form.

In 343, Ulfilas translated the Bible into Gothic and was ordained bishop by the Arian Eusebius of Nicomedia, who had great influence in the western parts of the empire, particularly in Illyricum and Dardania,[542]

---

[540] Ibid, p. 29.
[541] Ibid, p. 30.
[542] Ibid, p. 31.

where religious differences were carved, continuing to divide Christianity and the Empire as well.

This period of religious conflict in the Empire was culminated with Constans' decision to restore Arianism. Emperor Julian Apostate responded by declaring war against Christianity to restore paganism from 361-363. Julian's actions, being the last representative of Constantine the Great's regime, were of more philosophical nature than political. Finding support on the intellectual and political elite of Rome satisfied certain levels of society, but not the wide layers, which were under the influence of Christianity and promises of an eternal afterlife.

They then resorted to preaching about the hope, which only the Christian Doctrine of equality was able to offer, which was both tempting and exhilarating for the masses. This "elixir" sparked violent social and political movements.

It was clear that freedom of religion was not able to defend free faith, which condemned Julian to failure, an idea people wouldn't support, even if it appeared in such a manipulative format. This failure was sealed with his death from a wound he received in a battle against the Persians. His deed died with him, while his failure showed that the victory of Christianity was unstoppable due to majority support. This evolved into a hostage of promises of equality and afterlife that turned into mostly destructive ideologies.

For the given situation, the final victory of orthodox Christianity created a breath of relief, as it stopped the bloody persecutions that had continued for more than two centuries in the Empire, though it did not bring change to the social and political situation in the country, much less quiet the strife within the church that continued for a good long time with tremendous intensity among Arianism and supporters of the Council of Nicaea, and among the Orthodox *monophysite* and *dyophysite* dogma, and the "*undecided*" as well.[543]

---

[543] "*Dyophysites,*" or supporters of "two natures," held the position about the existence of "two natures" of Christ, divine and human, which is explained by means of the concept of "human God." The founder of this doctrine was Nestorius of Alexandria, who managed to also become Bishop of Constantinople. The "*Monophysites*" deny Christ's human nature, supporting only the divine. In the Fourth Council of the Christian Church in Chalcedon in 451 a dogma was shaped of two natures of Christ, both perfect, inseparable, but distinct. On this occasion both Nestorism and monophysitism were condemned. In relation to them, the Chalcedon formula represented in some way a

This case showed that the great power released after the collapse of the serf system was not able to create better economic or social circumstances. However, many of the economies working on the serfdom basis, rapidly lost production as happened similarly with farming economies, mining and other public works. Craftsmanship too marked stagnation losing its importance in many cities. The only advancing branch, following the fall of the serf system was noted in agriculture, as free peasantry won the opportunity to increase its properties, while the landowners, involved in a latifundist system, benefited from the new forms of exploiting it through the use of the settlers, who appeared as renters, coming from among the dispossessed peasantry. They rented land from large owners (*peculia*) together with the necessary equipment to work and were forced to yield to the owner of the land part of the production as well as to work some days without pay. Settlers were also joined by surfs who gained freedom, slaves captured in war, as well as small declining slave owners.[544]

Generally, the colonies marked a great development in the eastern provinces since the beginning. However, although the condition of the settlers was better than that of the slaves, it brought new forms of exploitation, and a different tax system from that on land, animals and others that the state required, which made things difficult for the social stratum, which appeared as a new hope for the economy, largely justifying the serf system.

Against these circumstances came colonists' discontent, which was reflected by their abandoning this new system of work, which began to create significant difficulties, forcing the central government to take measures against the settlers who refused to respond to their duties. Decrees by Emperor Valentin in 371 in regard to Illyria were noted. Under the new system, settlers who were previously *free citizens*, began to lose their freedom in terms of the binding laws that linked them to the use of land and by numerous taxes, which became more excessive as the empire plunged into wars with barbarians, who had greatly increased their incursions in the north-east and east, plundering the country and causing widespread destruction.

Barbarian destructive expeditions became more common especially after the second half of the 3rd century A.D. when large crowds of nomadic

---

middle position, whereby salvation could come only from the Savior who was at the same time both the perfect God and perfect man.
[544] *"Historia e Popullit Shqiptar,"* Volume I, Prishtina, 1976, p. 124.

barbarians, the Huns first of all, were able to break the borders by crossing the Danube, settling on the territory of the Central Balkans. Imperial armies proved unable to resist these attacks, and it was up to the Illyrian-Dardanian population to try to face the barbarians in order to protect their own lands.

Here lies the reason why the barbarian tribes were not so successful in these parts, as were the Goths and Visigoths in the eastern parts (Thrace), who succeeded at the Battle of Adrianople in 378 in defeating an unprepared imperial army for such opponents. There were also factors who used all of this for their own ends, as later developments showed (the issue of the "vitalization" of the empire with fresh blood and other settling of social and political accounts between the centralist supporters of the empire and provincial "militaries"), paving the way toward the western provinces of Illyricum, well-known incursions that brought the Goths as far as the Adriatic coast.

This made Valentin's successor, Theodorus I, having no other option to evict the Goths from the occupied lands, to enter into agreements with them, giving them land in northern and western parts of the Peninsula, provided that they perform the duty of military service for the Empire under the leadership of their commanders. Under this agreement that was called *foedus*, Ostrogoths were to settle in Pannonia, while the Visigoths in the northern Thracian diocese. Thanks to this agreement, Teodorius was able to avoid for some time new attacks by barbarians and to ensure internal social "peace."[545]

However, agreements with the barbarians brought neither internal peace nor did they increase the security he wanted from outside threats. However, the Empire already divided into two parts according to reforms that Constantine the Great made, was drawn into internal social and economic contradictions resulting in political upheavals in the year 395.

After the death of Theodosius, the Empire was divided in two separate parts: the Roman Empire of the West and that of the East of Constantinople, led by his sons Honorius and Arcadius. This division also touched Illyricum as its northern provinces (Noricus, Pannonia, and Dalmatia) belonging within the Diocese of Illyricum, and, consequently, the political and religious part of the Western Empire. On the other hand, the Illyrian

---

[545] *"Historia e Popullit Shqiptar,"* Volume I, Prishtina, 1967, p. 126.

provinces comprising the Diocese of Macedonia eventually joined the Eastern Empire.[546]

Surprisingly, although these provinces were placed under the political dependence of Constantinople, religiously they remained under the jurisdiction of the Church of Rome, as seen in subsequent discussions of this unfortunate discrepancy between the political and ecclesiastical jurisdictions in the Prefecture of Illyricum, giving the bishops a big opportunity to express their growing rivalry and test forces that became fatal.[547]

Clearly, this separation was inevitable because even after the reforms of Diocletian and Constantine the Great the center of gravity moved from West to East, in which the central provinces, especially those of Illyricum, gained great importance and a function of significance, shifting considerably the ratio of forces in East's favor.

Despite this division, the idea of the unity throughout the Empire was maintained up until the fall of the Western Roman Empire. Even under those circumstances it was no longer spoken of two empires, but rather of the two parts of a single empire, which were governed by two emperors.

Governance of the two emperors and their apparently unified decrees did not bring the East and West closer together. Instead, the West began to weaken even as a consequence of barbarian incursions, as those of Alaricus, who headed towards Italy and after three attempts was able to conquer and plunder Rome in 410.

In the early 5th century a long relative calm period began, proving that the barbarians, with whom peace was reached after their victory at Adrianople, brought benefits to the East, while challenging the West with destruction which would come soon, exactly from the Goths and other barbarians, who were admitted to "protect" the Empire, the same as would happen indeed with the Slavs. After three centuries, when Emperor Heraclius allowed them in to protect the East from other barbarians, they settled them in Thrace and Illyricum, where they turned into inducers of their destruction and suffocators of the western spirit, which affected the final change of Byzantine into an Eastern Empire, supervised by easterners.

However, before the annihilation of the western spirit by Slavs occurred, a university was founded in Constantinople, which helped spread

---

[546] Jacques, Edwin: "*Shqiptarët,*" Tirana, 2007, p. 165.
[547] Ibid, p. 165.

the *Codex Theodosianus*. This new university became an important cultural and educational center of the empire, in which ten Greek and ten Latins taught alongside five Greek and three Latin orators, and one philosopher of two lawyers.[548]

Codex Theodosianus, distributed East and West in the name of emperors Valentian Theodosius II and Valentian III, was of significant importance, as the new code was expected to provide new and more solid basis for the administration of justice as an expression of the legal unity of the empire. It actually opened a period of peace between the two halves of the empire, but failed to prevent its separation process, which was inevitable and increasingly vulnerable.

However, this division attained its most visible expression by the deepening of the linguistic division. The Western recognition of the Greek language gradually disappeared, and in the East, the Latin. Therefore, the "Greekizing" of the East advanced without hindrance, especially at the time of Emperor Theodosius II and Empress Eudocia Augusta.[549]

The increasing linguistic separation, representing a division between two political, social and cultural views, Eastern and Western, led to the creation of a *national-ecclesiastical* culture in the East. This continued into neighboring Armenia, where the *Armenian alphabet* and the *Armenian Bible* appeared.[550]

This was an important step in the formation of *national-religious consciousness* that Byzantium sought and gradually managed to raise to a general degree that Christians were fed to keep connected to Byzantism.

Determination of the Byzantine Church for national religious consciousness found no support from the Roman church. Although the Western Empire, because of barbaric attacks from the Huns, was in dire straights, it continued to show determination for Roman unity among familiar attitudes of the Roman Church around the universal concept of civilization, which it claimed to remain faithful.

It was Pope Leo the Great (640-661) who pointed out that the Roman church remained powerful which did not give up the universal Christian dogma, despite the fact that the Western Empire would eventually come down from the historical scene precisely because it lacked ethnic and

---

[548] Ostrogorski, Georg: *"Historia e Perandorisë Bizantine,"* Tirana, 2002, p. 32.
[549] Ibid, p. 33.
[550] See: Stein: *"Geschichte,"* I, p. 425; A. Mikelian: *"Die armenische Kirsche in iren Bezihungen zur byzantiniscchen,"* 1892.

national identity as happened with the eastern church that gave in, and with the acceptance of regional dioceses, turned it into a powerful tool of survival, governance, and even political rule.

In accordance with Roman unity, which found its basis on the Christian dogma and through extensive administrative, political and social reforms to turn into a common denominator of the empire with the "two wings" (the Easter and Western ones), came the emergence of three Illyrian-Dardanian identities within the imperial one:

a) *self-governing identity*
b) *administrative identity*
c) *church identity*

A) Self-Governing Identity - known since the first Roman conquests beyond the Adriatic, when the Roman army, forced King Gentius to accept vassalage. This prepared grounds for other occupations in the direction of Ardiaei, Dalmatians, and tribes and kingdoms in Epirus and Dardania. Indeed, internal self-governance and autonomy originated on the basis of ethnic identity, and therefore self-governing was also called ethnic identity, with ethnicity being its basis.

This principle was in accordance with the famous Roman policy of *"pax romana,"* by which the involvement of other parts within the Empire, weren't subject to total submission in accordance with the invasion, but as an agreement to a common empire built on the principles of global universalism, which would later be supplemented by those of Christian axis (ecumenism). Therefore, these principles were based on the statutes of self-governing provinces, internal (tribal) autonomies, where besides a slight tribute and military obligations, were managed by the locals to govern and develop, provided that internal development was based on common imperial priorities for the service of everyone.

Forms of self-government and internal autonomies were different and evolved accordingly with respect to the interests of the Roman Empire in these parts. These forms of administrative organization of the Empire continued even after the complete conquest of Illyrian territories from the mid-2nd century B.C. onwards. They represented the most important instrument of incorporation and integration of Illyria in economic, social, and political structures of the Empire from which began the process of Romanization considered as a rather natural development.

At a certain stage, especially with the commencement of the barbarian attacks in the north and northeast, which usually passed through the Illyrian and Dardanian lands, integration produced an awareness that protected the empire from the barbarians.

B) *Administrative Identity* - represents another stage, when the ethnic identity preserved and developed during the internal self-rule, rose to a higher social and political degree, where certain circles expanded into a larger circle and mutual functioning implied a larger space. This form of administrative organization broke the recognized tribal and provincial barriers closed from an economic and social aspect, while their opening created new opportunities that needed adequate forms of governing, despite the fact that they melted in a joint stratification, which remained within their familiar ethnos.

During the time of Diocletian the numerous self-governing units and those enjoying domestic and tribal autonomy in the context of other forms of popular organization were included in joint administrative units. According to Diocletian's reform, the largest province of Illyricum was created as one of the four prefectures of the Empire, divided into 12 dioceses. This was similar to the decision of 292 A.D., when the Empire was divided into four prefectures led by four Caesars, two of them of Illyrian origin: Constantine Chloris and Galerius. The latter was left to govern Illyricum, whose space went from *Dalmatia* to the Danube in the North, including Scodra as its center in *Prevalitana* and South Dalmatia, Dioclea (the present-day Montenegro) in addition to *Dardania* with its center Scupi comprised of the central regions of Dardania (with the present-day Macedonia up to Astibo), while the province of *New Epirus* with its center Dyrrahum included the provinces from the Adriatic to the river Vjosa. *Old Epirus* with Nicopolis as its center included lands south of Vjosa down to the Bay of Preveza.

The union of these provinces in an administrative province benefited both the internal union of self-governing and autonomous units with the status of *civitates, muncipes, casteles* and *autonomous colonies*, as well as for the external one, as they turned into large administrative units, where local government mayors were of the first rank. They were independent to govern and administer dioceses, relating to common interests within the province, where they were equally represented.

Therefore, Illyricum's administrative governance with four large dioceses, created the first administrative identity of a character that was a form of citizenship, as in the new organization local mayors were directly represented in the province, in which the principal authority and the second in rank of the Empire was the Caesar, co-ruling emperor of Rome.

Besides the right of collecting taxes, supervising the imperial roads crossing through this part, representing a knot that tied the West to East (Via Egnatia, the Adriatic road and the one linking Durrahum with Thessaloniki and Constantinople and others in many directions), there was also the aspect of security making these parts even more important, since they, with the preservation of fortifications, directly participated in the strategic concept of the Empire.

Apparently, Illyricum's *administrative identity* gained more weight, especially at the time of Constantine the Great, after accepting Christianity. Because the church was built on this organization, the Illyrian diocese took one of the leading places in the imperial ecclesiastical hierarchy, which meant both political and social power. It was the bishops from Illyricum and Dardania from the First Council of Nicaea in 325 up to the Eight Council of Constantinople in 870 who were committed with religious jurisdiction to remain disconnected from the church of Rome, while administratively belonging to the East, Constantinople, representing a precedent on which all the known East-West delimitations fell leading to the clash of civilizations for six centuries.

C) *Church Identity* – in the Byzantine Empire appeared also as state identity only on the grounds of an agreement with the church empire by which it was "God's representative" on Earth, and that the church appeared as the virtual co-ruler of the imperial throne. Therefore, the emperor and the church, exercised joint power in all areas of life, from which the spiritual aspects led by the church ran aspects of consciousness, which had to totally submit to the Christian dogma and find expression in social, intellectual, and creative life.

With ecclesiastical organization most of the churches of Illyricum (except for Dyrrahum diocese) belonged to the Roman church. Initially their center was at Thessaloniki, and at the time of Justinian I at the vicariate rank, it transferred to Justiniana Prima, remaining there for more than 250 years when it finally fell under Constantinople control.

Even before the center of the church of Illyricum passed over to Dardania attaining the role of a vicariate, in Illyricum and particularly in Dardania, within the popular theological outlines and controversy, reflected in the division within the church (*Arianism* and different doctrines for and against the *Trinity*), this important factor was represented as a catalyst of these currents and often extreme confrontations. It was known that St. Paul made his first apostolic travels in western parts beginning in these lands, and there, having introduced the idea of the Christian gospel, simultaneously established the first ecclesiastical settlements in these areas. In the meantime, St. Jerome appeared in the area with the translation of the Bible into Latin (Vulgate) in 399, which further paved the way for instituting Christianity, as Emperor Constantine the Great later did from rural Dardania.

However, what might be called ecclesiastical identity emerging from the organizational level that Dardania had attained at the time of Emperor Justinian I makes way for the possibility of assessing it as part of national identity within the imperial one. This was reflected not only in spiritual terms, when the vicariate of Justiniana Prima rose to the highest rank of direct connection with Papacy of Rome, but also in the social and political aspect on a broad plain. Therefore, during the time of Justinian, in view of giving the center of Illyricum Diocese a material containment, in addition to building and restoring Justiniana Prima into a superb city, much was done with other centers of Dardania from Naissus, which was rebuilt, to Ulpiana. Destroyed by an earthquake in 518, it was renamed to Justinian Secunda, and many other cities erected over a hundred castles across the country. Although dedicated to security concerns for protecting the country from barbarian attacks, especially those of the Goths, Avars, and a little later the Slavs, these castles strengthened the social and economic life of the country, turning it into a center of powerful linkage between East and West.

Evidence of the time indicates that this spiritual, social and political level conditioned the establishment and strengthening of a new military class and local aristocracy, which felt equally valued with that of the imperial elite.

Therefore, one may say that the church identity of the Dardanian Church in Illyricum tied to the Roman one remained a pluricentennial part of a church tradition that affected the emergence of Byzantine pre-state structures. However, the Dardanian Church came under the jurisdiction of the Eastern Church of Constantinople in the 8th century by order of Emperor Leo III, as did the *themes* created in Durres and Nichopolis, which later preceded those of the feuds, zupanias, and principalities even as vassals of the empire from which the first states emerged.

Christianity in Illyricum and Dardania

Illyrians and Dardanians fall into the group of peoples who embraced Christianity first. – Saint Paul introduced for the first time sacral literature in Illyricum in the year 59 AD.- Dardanians Florus and Laurus from Ulpiana were the first martyrs of Christianity in these areas.- The first Saint of Illyricum, Saint Jerome (347-420)was the first translator of the Bible in Latin.- At the Council of Nicaea of 318 two bishops of Dardania attended, Dacus of Scupi as "Dacus Daradaniane" and Bishop Budius of Stobi, and the Bishop of Corcyra from Illyricum. – The Prefecture of Illyricum, initially divided in two parts, upon insistence of Pope Boniface was placed under the jurisdiction of the Church of Rome. – Establishment of the Diocese of Dardania in Justinian Prima, first tied to Thessaloniki, by a decree of Emperor Justinian, Novellae XI of 14th of April 535 AD, become an Archdiocese of Illyricum directly connected to the Holy See.- Dardania with two more Episcopal centers: Nentana and Diocletiana. – Saint Niketa, or Nikëtë Dardani of Dardania – the author of Byzantium Hymn "Te Deum."

It may be said that in Illyricum and Dardania the key processes were initiated (imperial reforms of Diocletian and Constantine the Great, and the first penetrations of the barbarians from the East towards the West) leading to the birth and later to the creation of Byzantium. The same can be said of the emergence of Christianity, which began its most important challenge in gaining the treatment it won in the 4th century when it became an official creed of the empire, as through these countries passed major roads connecting the East with the West and vice versa, being unavoidable for both the circulation of goods and armies, and also of ideas.

Evidence by various ancient authors and church sources make it plain that Christian missionaries came into view in the space of Illyria and Dardania since the 1st century A.D. The author of the 6th century A.D., Cosmas, included the Illyrians within a group of peoples that embraced Christianity in his own time.[551] During the first centuries AD, in urban centers in these areas Christian communities were first mentioned, and the first edifices of such a cult were erected.[552]

---

[551] *"Historia e Popullit Shqiptar,"* Volume I, Tirana, 2002, p. 200.
[552] Ibid, p. 20.

Church sources claim that St. Paul was the first to introduce sacred literature in Illyricum, such as the Christian Gospel, after appearing in Phillip in Macedonia. He then traveled west across the Egnatia road and preached in Thessaloniki where, in the year 59 AD, he reached the heart of Illyricum for the first time. He said the following about this:

"So that from Jerusalem, and round about unto Illyricum, I have fully preached the gospel of Christ."[553]

This was not the only evidence of St. Paul mentioning Illyricum. Approximately 66 A.D. he wrote to Titus as he remained in Nichopolis during the winter, in the most famous city of Epirus, in a location near Illyricum, which he called "City of Victory," established by Augustus in 31 B.C. after he defeated his opponent Antony.[554]

Church records explain that on this occasion St. Paul founded a Christian community in Durres, the first in these parts, during his sermons in Illyria and Epirus.[555] This might mean that at the time in Durres there were 70 Christian families, with a certain Caesar or Apollo as their bishop.[556]

Sources from the Roman church make it known that of this time was the martyrdom of the Bishop of Durres, St. Astios, who was martyred by Emperor Trajan during his reign (98-117).[557]

The surfacing of Christian emissaries, who were declared saints, such as Paul and others, as well as the presence of their supporters in Illyricum is testified by historian Pliny the Son, who in the years 111-113 A.D. ruled Bitinia and Ponty. Pliny wrote "The epidemic of this fraud," as he called Christianity," had swept not only the cities but villages as well."[558]

The presence of religious cults in *"the world center"* (in media mundi constitutae) as many authors called Illyricum then[559] is also found in Tertullian (200-206) when speaking of the universal spread of Christianity among the Thracians and their neighbors, implying that the Dardanians as well, lived in a common province with them in Moesia Superior.

---

[553] Gjini, Gaspër: *"Skoposko-prizrenska biskupija kroz stolejća,"* Zagreb, 1986, p. 21.
[554] Ibid, p. 21.
[555] See Farlati: *"Illyricum Sacrum,"* I, 254; VIII, 1.
[556] Ibid.
[557] Jacques, Edwin: *"Shqiptarët,"* Tirana, 2002, p. 159.
[558] Ibid, p. 21.
[559] Irenaeus, Lugdunen: *"Contra haereses,"* Book I, cap. 10, PG 7 553/4, cited according to Gjini, Gaspër: *"Skopsko-prizrenska biskupija kroz stoljeca,"* Zagreb, 1986, p. 21.

Dardania, as a center in which Christianity was largely spread by the beginning of the 2nd century A.D. one may learn from the two Dardanian saints Florus and Laurus, who ended up as martyrs in Ulpiana. Although the time of their martyrdom is not exactly known, indirect sources indicate it may be related to the early 2nd century B.C., as church records show the teachers of Florus and Laurus, Poculius and Maximus were exhorted to torture during the time of Emperor Hadrian (117-138); it may be assumed that their students suffered as well.[560]

The influence of Christianity in Illyricum and Dardania was growing and it was not by accident that martyrdom was bursting, which can be inferred by the famous missionaries from these areas having been declared saints. First among them is Gregory of Nish, born in 344, followed by St. Jerome (Hieronymus), born in 347 in Stridom, on the northern border of Dalmatia, and Arius, writer and bishop of the city of Amasea in Asia Minor.

St. Jerome, called Hieronymus (347-420), represented one of the most prominent fathers and theologians of the church among all the saints of Illyricum and Dardania. He is remembered especially for the translation of the Bible, known as *Latin Vulgate*.[561]

The issue of the saints and martyrs in Illyria and Dardania was not outside the deepest sensitivity to Christianity, proven by a number of land names referring to the first martyrs of the East, whose cults were widespread in the 4th-6th centuries, such are the toponyms *Shirgj* (St. Sergius), *Shumbak* (St. Bacchus), *Shëndekla* (St. Tecco), *St. Vlashi* (St. Vlassis), found in Shkodra, Durrës and down to Çamëria, *Shnanou* (St. Andrew) in Gjakova, etc.[562]

Even before the great missionary work of St. Jerome, who translated the Old Testament into Latin and put it in first contact with the Western world with its contents, the existence of Christianity in the Balkans was noted and particularly in Illyricum and Dardania with the presence of the bishops of these areas at the Council of Nicaea, in the year 325, called by Emperor Constantine the Great.

In the ecumenical Council of Nicaea, of the 318 bishops attending from all over the empire, 13 were from the Balkans, two of which were

---

[560] *Acta Sanctorum,* die 18 Augusti, III, Antverpiae 1737, 520-522, cited according to Gjini, Gaspër: "*Skopsko-prizrensaka biskupija kroz stoljeća,*" Zagreb, 1986, p. 23.
[561] Jacques, Edwin: "*Shqiptarët,*" Tirana, 2002, p. 170.
[562] "*Historia e Popullit shqiptar,*" Volume I, Tirana, 2002, p. 200.

from Dardania and one from Illyricum respectively. Those representing Dardania were the Bishop of Scupi (present-day Shkup), Dacus or *"Dacus Dardaniae"* and Bishop Budius of Stobi (present-day Stip in Macedonia) and Bishop of Corcyra (Corfu) representing Illyricum. It seems that Bishop Budius of Stobi was under the supervision of Dacus of Dardania, which speaks of the extension of the church of Dardania up to parts of Macedonia.[563] Harnacus hereby affirms that in 325, in Illyricum, church centers were present in Nikopoja, Buthrotum (Butrint) and Corcyra (Corfu).[564]

At the same time in the country toponomastics of Christian names were introduced, such as *Shëngjin, Shupal* (Shën Pal), *Shmil* (Shën Mëhill), *Shën Koll* or *Shën Nik* (Shën Nicholas), *Shëndill* (St. Iliah) *Shëngjergj* (St. George), *Shtish* (St. Mathias), etc.[565]

Following the recognition of Christianity as the religion of the Empire accepted by Emperor Constantine the Great, Christianity in Illyricum and Dardania took off after being organized on the basis of administrative provinces during the Diocletian era.

Therefore, in the center of each province there was a metropolitan church and the archbishop's headquarters. Under the jurisdiction of the latter were the bishops of subordinate (sufragane) dioceses. In the main centers of Illyricum were the archdioceses of Shkodra (Prevalitana), Scupi (Dardania), Durrës (New Epirus) and Nikopoja (Old Epirus). The Archbishop of Shkodra had 3 bishopric subordinates under its jurisdiction, Scupi had 5, Durres and Nikopoja had 8 and 9 respectively.[566]

Within this organization in the provinces, the Archbishop summoned the provincial synod. Archbishops attended the ecumenical Councils, as the first one of Nicaea, was attended by the Metropolis of Durres. At the Council of Chalcedon in 451, when dogmatic quarrels on the nature of Christ were permanently settled, Luke, Metropolis of Durres, Vendors, Bishop of Dioclea, and Eugenio, Bishop of Apollonia attended.[567]

Church organization in Illyria shared the fate of the difficulties facing the overall organization of the church from its recognition by the Empire in

---

[563] Gjini, Gaspër: *"Skopsko-prizrenska biskupija kroz stoljeća,"* Zagreb, 1986, p. 29.
[564] Jacque, Edwin: *"Shqiptarët,"* Tirana, 2002, p. 163.
[565] *"Historia e Popullit Shqiptar,"* Volume I, Tirana, 2002, p. 201.
[566] Ibid, p. 201.
[567] Ibid, p. 202.

the 4th century by Constantine the Great to the Council of Chalcedon when dogma about the nature of Christ and the thought of the inner peace of the church prevailed. However, as Illyricum was situated in the most strategic part of the empire, representing the hub of all known implications starting from the political, social, cultural, to religious ones, it was natural that all the crises were reflected there in particular.

Therefore, it was not by chance that the first and toughest confrontation between Rome and Constantinople about ecclesiastical hegemony started, emerging from the Second and Third Council, culminating during the so-called *"Accacian Crisis"* (484-519), when bishops of Illyricum confirmed their allegiance to Rome. The provincial clergy of Dardania, Old Epirus, and Prevalitana communicated with the Pope.

Indeed, this crisis was due to a continued political crisis between the two centers: Rome and Constantinople, each fighting for leadership, even though the Council of Chalcedon in 451, according to its Canon 28, equalized bishops of Rome with those of Constantinople, so they were equivalent. Pope Leo refused to accept the canon, which he rejected, acting not upon the political superiority of Rome but rather under the religious primacy of St. Peter. This was something that made the bishops of Illyricum and those of Dardania follow him, having had also the support of a recent decision of the Council, which set the eastern dioceses under the dependence of the Patriarch of Constantinople, but gave it no authority over Illyricum.

In these circumstances, it was again the political movements of imperial leadership that affected the lining of the Church, through which the unity of the Illyric dioceses to preserve the Roman association was broken. It was the bishopric of Durres which began leaning towards Constantinople for the sole reason that the Emperor Anastasios I (491-518) originated from Durres, which affected a reflection toward the Eastern Church.

These religious confrontations of imperial nature, i.e. first those with Arianism and later between the "dyophysites" (the two natures) and "monophysites" (human gods), of course, that a particular scene of action gave the church organization that followed the administrative division of the provinces that had been originally modeled first by Diocletian and later by Constantine the Great, in which Illyricum was divided into two parts: the western part under the direction of *"praefecturas pr.Italie, African et Illyrie"* and eastern part, which had its own mayor *"praefectus pr. Illyrici."*

The Eastern Illyricum, comprised of the dioceses of Dardania and Macedonia, was entrusted by Emperor Graciani to the governance of his co-ruler Theodosius in 379. A bit later, in 423 and 437, the western part of Illyricum joined the Eastern Empire.

However, this division was rejected by Pope Boniface who immediately headed to the western part of the empire to bring the Church of Illyricum back to Rome. Honori wrote a letter to Theodosius presenting the request of the Holy See *"sanetae sedis apostolicae desideria."* Theodosius accepted his request and issued a decree under which the prefect of Illyricum was ordered to preserve the old order *"aniquuom ordiner specialitet faciant custodiri."*[568]

This situation, before all the eastern provinces of Illyricum went independent but were de facto linked to the jurisdiction of the bishop of Rome, continued until the first half of the 9th century. However, this does not mean that there was no attempt to detach them from the Western church affiliation, such as those of the Archbishop of Constantinople Anatolius, who wrote to the bishops of the eastern province of Illyricum asking them to give their consent regarding Canon 28 of the Council of Chalcondil in 451 by which the headquarters of Constantinople was given priority. A letter by Pope Leo indicated that the bishops of Illyricum would reject the demand of Patriarch Anatolius.[569]

Delimitations within these congregations, which influenced the social and political life, should be seen in the role of the Diocese of Dardania, as one among the initiators of church organization in what Emperor Diocletian included in the part of Illyricum as an independent province of particular importance.

Indeed the term Illyricum, of an administrative nature to become official at the time of Diocletian, was accepted by Constantine the Great to remain during the Byzantine period, also political in nature. The first time, the wide Illyrian space, implying for a long time an ethno-geographic term, i.e. a space of Illyrian tribes, which at some time some of them were independent kingdoms, but without any internal political connections, gained the attributes of an independent set of a certain imperial identity.

---

[568] On contested issues of the correspondence between Bonificius and Honorius see for more: *"Acta et diplomata res Albaniae mediae actatis illustration, colleg."* Thalloczy L.-Jericek C.-Sufllay E, Vol. I, Vindibonae MCMXIII, 2, no. 9-10.
[569] Gjini, Gaspër: *"Skopsko-prizrenska biskupija kroz stoljeca,"* Zagreb, 1986, p. 35.

Therefore, it was natural that in accordance with this concept, the church organization of Dardania would be at the level of a diocese. This is testified by the Council of Nicaea in the year 325, summoned by Emperor Constantine the Great, when among the 315 delegates to the Council were Hosius of Cordoba, Nicholas of Smyrna, Anastasius, and also the Bishop of Dardania, Dacus, signed as *"Dacus Dardaniae."*[570]

Although there is no official data about the exact time of the establishment of the Diocese of Dardania, the Council of Nicaea, announced that with the participation of Bishop Dacus, signed as *"Dacus Dardaniae,"* Dardania had its own Diocese under the jurisdiction of which also fell Budis of Stobi of Macedonia. At the Second Council held in Sardica, on the border of the two parts of the Empire in 342, the Diocese of Dardania was represented by Bishop Gasdens from Naissus (present-day Nis), who also attended on behalf of the bishops of Illyricum.

He became familiar with the proposal of Canon 5 about the powers of the Holy See over the appointment of bishops, being supported by the Metropolis of Dardania, who signed the council document as *"Paregorius a Dardania de Scupis* (Progory of Scupis from Dardania)."[571]

Episcopate of Dardania was mentioned by Bishop Eustace of Sebe as an important religious center during his stay in this province, forced to move to those regions by a decision of The Council of Constantinople in 360. Bishop Eustace was a famous proponent of Arianism, and his stay "as punishment" in Dardania had to do with the support that this movement enjoyed in these parts, and a number of Dardanian bishops were held responsible because of this at the Council of Chalcedon in 451 charged with supporting the "schism" as the famous stance against Arianism was reached.

Both the bishops and Diocese of Dardania continued to be involved in many of the hottest issues of the church that the "two churches" were dealing with when trying to influence the imperial political life. One of these was that of the *"three heads"* (Tria Capitula), which included the Council of Constantinople. All the bishops of Dardania attended it: Focca from Stobi, representing Archbishop of Justina Prima, Benenatis, Sabian from Zapora, Project from Naissus (present-day Nish) and Paul, Bishop

---

[570] Ibid.
[571] Farlatus D: *"Iliricum Sacrum,"* VIII, 4, cited according to Gjini, Gaspër: *"Skopsko-prirenska biskpupija kroz stoljeca,"* Zagreb, 1986.

of Justinian Secunda (former Ulpiana) who, with the exception of Benenatis and Focca, signed Pope Virgil's "*Constitutum.*"

However, the Diocese of Dardania was connected with the Church of Thessaloniki from the beginning. This big and important city of the Empire gained even more weight after the administrative reforms of Diocletian and Constantine the Great once it was appointed as the seat of the Prefect of Illyricum.

Therefore, the bishops of Thessaloniki earned the title of Pope's vicars for that part, which represented a huge and sensitive responsibility for them knowing that there is where the border between eastern and western parts of the empire was drawn, being also the border between the Church of Rome and that of Constantinople. The Vicariate, as a way of delegating the primary power in the space of one or several provinces has been known in church organization since the 5th century. The first vicariate was that of the Church of Thessaloniki, while vicariates also appeared at the Church of Arles, that of Justiniana Prima, and two in Spain.

However, the importance that the Church of Dardania gained has to do with its position in support of the Church of Rome, a stance which in this part of Illyricum had always represented the necessary balance between East and West, between the two parts of the Empire, which had gone different ways due to known differences in the church, and actions undertaken by Emperor Justinian I granting this province the weight of one of the key provinces of the Empire in the internal connection of Illyricum as part of the West.[572]

Although this became a heavy and detrimental burden during the time of Justinian I (527-565) from an ecclesiastical, social, and political point of view, it was an important center of Byzantium.

Therefore, one may say that at the time of Justinian I, who came from Dardania, began a successful era in the life of the Church of Dardania among the most successful ones in its history. The Emperor, under the reorganization of the Illyrian churches founded an independent church province, granting it a special role in this part of the empire. At that time, in ecclesiastical terms, the Eastern Illyricum represented an entirety. By the Emperor's decision it was divided into two parts, which were independent and had separate centers.

---

[572] The true name of Emperor *Justinian* is *Flavius Petrus Sabbatius Justinianus*, or *Anicus Julianus Justinianus*. (See: Diehle, Ch: "*Justinien et la civilisitarion bizantine au VI-e siecle,*" Paris, 1901.)

The center of the southern part still remained in Thessaloniki, while in the newly formed province the new center of Illyricum became Justiniana Prima. So the emperor had a clear purpose, to raise his own homeland to a new administrative center by transferring the center of the prefecture from Thessaloniki.[573]

In response to this, on April 14, 535 AD, Emperor Justinian announced his Novelae XI through which he established a vicariate for that part of the empire. The new Exarchate included the following regions: Mediterranean Dacia, Dacia Ripensis, Moesia Prima, Dardania, Prevalitana, Macedonia Secunda, and part of Pannonia Secunda in Baciensi civitate, which broken down by present-day geographical aspects, implies that Justiniana Prima introduced under its supervision provinces that included today's Serbia, Eastern Srem, Western Bulgaria, Northern Macedonia, Dardania and Montenegro. Ten years later, with *Novella CXXXI*, the Emperor issued a decree by which he legally sanctioned the judicial position of Justiniana Prima.[574]

According to the Emperor's decree, the new ecclesiastical province had the character of an independent ecclesiastical province, extending up to its maximum extension. Bishop of Justiniana Prima did not only carry the title of the Metropolis (the same title was also carried by the bishop of the ruined Scupi), representing the highest rank in the ecclesiastical organization of the new province, but also the title of an Archbishop, or of the highest rank in the province, to whose authority several provinces were subject. The new Archbishop was entitled to *"summus honore, summa dignitas, summum sacerdotium, summum fastigium"* (greatest honor, greatest dignity, greatest title, and greatest rank).[575]

These high titles were not only titles of honor, but they also carried a certain power of law, under which the archbishop of Justiniana Prima directed the bishops of his province, and at the same time he was the direct representative of the Bishop of Rome in these parts. By that time, neither he nor his bishops depended on the Diocese of Thessaloniki.

Furthermore, the archbishop of Justiniana Prima, as the first of the diocese, summoned and chaired over the regional councils. He made the final decisions on all deliberations and disagreements arising among the bishops. The new archbishop was elected by all the metropolises and

---

[573] Gjini, Gaspër: *"Skopsko-prizrencaka buiskupija kroz stoljeća,"* Zagreb, 1968, p. 41.
[574] Ibid, p. 42.
[575] Ibid, p. 42.

bishops in the Common Council without the consent of the bishop of Thessaloniki.[576]

It should be noted that the written language and all decrees of Justiniana Prima were written in Latin. Many of the archaeological materials of the time, including the Justinian's monograms in the discovered basilicas were written in Latin, which explains that the language of liturgy and church administration was conducted in that language rather than in Greek. Even the names of titulars of Justiniana Prima (Catellianus, Benenatus, Johannes, and others) attest to the Latin language sphere in these parts, connected in every aspect with the West.

Although the exact ubication (location) of Justiniana Prima is still not known, research carried out in the vicinity of Skopje (Shkup), and elsewhere, especially in the direction of Prishtina, makes it known that this, among the most important cities of Dardania and eastern part of Illyricum, lies near Skopje, in the North at the mouth of Lepenc in the village of Zllakuqan.

There were a considerable number of exhibits of the time, among which a basilica from early Christian times was found. As this ubication of Justiniana Prima is linked to that of ancient Scupi, ruined in a devastating earthquake in 518, it is quite reasonable that Emperor Justinian decided to build the city in its vicinity, carrying it a bit further to the north, skirting the Lepenc River, which continued to be at the important junction of Naissus-Scupi-Thessaloniki roads, connecting the Aegean and Singidunum in the North, while to the West the Adriatic through Ulpiana and Lissus (present-day Lezha).

The destruction of ancient Scupi and reconstruction of Justiniana Prima, which at the time of Justinian turned into the center of the Diocese of Illyricum and an important center of the Empire, did not interrupt the continuity of the Diocese of Scupi or ecclesiastical life in Dardania, with a tradition of almost two centuries.[577] Furthermore, besides Scupi, ancient authors revealed other Christian dioceses in Dardania. Hierokleus, along with Scupi marked also Ulpiana as a church center.[578]

---

[576] Ibid, p. 42.

[577] The first data on the first Dardanian Diocese of Scupi are provided by Ptolemy (See: Ptolomeaeus III 9/4.Bekkerus I), confirmed also by Procopus (See: Procopus, Caesar, *De Aedificiis* IV I) and Hierocles (See: Hierocles, Synecdemus: *Provincia Dardaniae sub presime, urues 3: Scupom metropolis,* Merion "Ulpiana," rec. Bekkerus I Bonnae 1844).

[578] Gjini, Gaspër: *"Skopsko-prizrenska biskupija kroz stoljeća,"* Zagreb, 1986, p. 51.

The ancient city of Ulpiana was situated north of ancient Scupi in the central part of ancient Dardania. Archaeological research has shown that the city was located ten kilometers south of Prishtina, near the present-day Gracanica.

Ulpiana is mentioned in 343 as an important city by St. Anastasius. The big city *"urgus splendidissima"* was visited in 380 by Emperor Theodosius I, on his way from Sirmium to Thessaloniki.[579]

According to Jordan's transcripts in 472, Ulpiana was occupied by the son of the King of the Goths, Tiudimer Teodoricus, who after conquering Naissus with 3,000 warriors headed towards this city, which had suffered damages at that time as did most of the lands through which the army of Teodoricus passed.

Like other parts of Dardania, Ulpiana, and especially Scupi, suffered by the great earthquake of the year 518. Emperor Justinian built Ulpiana naming it Justiniana Secunda. In church terms Ulpiana must have been an important center as this place produced the first Dardanian martyrs, Florus and Laurus. Ulpiana was also known as the birthplace of the Monophysite bishop Gergentius, who served as bishop at Safara of the Black Sea. According to ecclesiastical records Ulpiana was known as episcopacy in the 4th century. At the Council of Sardica in 342 its representatives attended, signing the acts of assembly as *"Machedonius a Dardania de Ulpiana."*[580]

The Synod's letter sent to Emperor Leo in 458 by the bishop of Dardania Ursilis and that of Dalmatia, Maximus, reveals another two Episcopalian centers in Dardania: Nentiana and Diocletia,[581] where many Christian missionaries worked, among whom is St. Niketas or Nikete Dardani, who together with his friend Paulianis from Nolea was listed among the church fathers.

For Niketas one mostly learns from his friend Paulianis, who was twice in Rome accompanied by St. Niketas in 398 and 402. St. Niketas left behind many theological works and reviews, some of which have been preserved in their entirety and some in part. Above-mentioned sources indicate that St. Niketas or Nikete Dardani was born around 340 in

---

[579] Ibid, p. 51.
[580] For more on St. Niketas as author of Byzantine hymn see: Ramadan Sokoli: "16 shekuj," Eurorilindja, Tirana, 1996, pp. 29-49.
[581] These dioceses are identified by Farlattus as Naissus and Duclea (See: Farlattus, D-Coletus: *"Iliricum Sacrum,"* VIII, 5, Venetiis, 1751-1819).

Remesiana of Dardania. At that time, this thriving center with bishopric headquarters was formally included within the province of Mediterranean Dacia. There is no approximate notification about his family, childhood and youth.

Information about him appeared from his adulthood as it happened with other prominent people who were recognized only at that age, especially at their late parable. For the first time Niketas is mentioned in 366 in a letter by Germain of Serminium, which included a list of bishops of that region, explaining that Nikëtë Dardani was bishop of Remesiana at the age of 26.[582]

Besides his activities as a bishop, Nikëtë Dardani was focused on research and creative work. Although artists' creative activity was not easy in such circumstances, Nikëtë Dardani brought up with literary and musical affinities, compiled songs and hymns and taught the believers to sing together.

What makes St. Niketas or Nikëtë Dardani famous is the well-known hymn *"Te Deum laudamus"* and treatise *"De psalmodiae bono."* His work *"Te Deum Laudamos"* is one of the most famous and prevalent hymns worldwide. This hymn of praise, widespread in Western Europe as early as 523, has come through early manuscripts in four variants with minor changes: a) Milanese, b) Moese-Arabic (Spanish), c) Irish, and d) Gaelic. Besides these known variants there is an alteration in *"Graduale vaticamo"* with melodies carried in a key higher. [583]

Besides the hymn *"Te Deum,"* Nikëtë Dardani also composed other songs as one may learn from indirect sources. He appears as the author, although in some countries it is attributed to St. Ambrose, but reinforced that St. Niketas of Dardania is the sole author of the hymn,[584] which shows the importance of the church of Dardania at the time of the great clashes of the church for political and spiritual dominance between East and West, and also of the commitment of its bishops and the consecrated to contribute directly to its spiritual identity with their artistic creations, as was that of St. Niketas in music, and of many others in creativity, especially in plastic arts from icons, reliefs and monumental mosaics, which adorned sacred and public objects throughout the empire.

---

[582] Sokloi, Ramadan: "16 shekuj," Tirana, 1996, p. 12.
[583] Sokoli, Ramadan: "16 shekuj," Tirana, 1996, p. 46.
[584] Gjini, Gaspër: *"Skopsko-prizrenska biskupija kroz stoljeća,"* Zagreb 1986, p. 58.

However, it should be known that the great contribution in the field of jurisdiction of Emperor Justinian I are his famous codices, which sanctioned the Roman law, serving even today as an irreplaceable judicial model.

As the spiritual identity in the Byzantine Empire was part of national identity, and thus also of political identity, it is appropriate to mention the carriers that have helped this superstructure and institutions established by the diocese, bishopric, vicariates to the capital of Illyricum prefecture, as the one declared by Emperor Justinian in 535, through his Novelae XI, pointing out the social and political realities that produced this situation, which might be seen in the context of imperial delimitations of the time to be dealt with later.

Of course these reports cannot be explained nor properly reflected in accordance with the importance they had outside the official church relations, since only there can they be confirmed as such. Even the Emperor's decisions, despite his religious independence, were to be corroborated by the Archbishop of Constantinople (if they were related to the eastern province) and the Pope, i.e. the Holy See of Rome (if they had to do with its jurisdiction).

In this regard there is an interest in the documents dealing with ordinances and papers addressing the Church of Dardania and bishops by the Pope and the Holy See, followed by emperors as well as the letters that the bishops of Dardania addressed to the Holy See and the Emperor. Not only did they help develop and understand the relationship between the church of Dardania and the Holy See, but also the relations of the emperors with the church and its titulars, being at the highest level, which confirms the assessment that the strengthening and establishment of the church of Dardania on such a level by Justinian I was part of the concept that Dardania, and the entire Illyricum were to turn into central factors of the Byzantine Empire, with which both of its wings would be held.

Viewed from this perspective, some of the preserved letters of Papacy sent to the bishops of Illyricum and Dardania indicate the high position of this church and the role it played in many of the delimitations, ranging from *Arianism* (carried from the First Council of Nicaea of 325 to the Third Council of Chalcedon in 451), followed with the fierce disputes about dyophysitism and monophysitism to the issue of *"the three heads."*

It is noted that the bishops of Dardania and Illyricum always appear in the center of these squirms, influencing the decisions of the

Council, or by opening issues concerning the top leaders of churches and the emperors. Of this nature are the letters of Pope Celestine I, sent in 424 to nine bishops, in all probability leaders of ecclesiastical provinces, including the Church of Dardania, being ordered to submit to Rufius, Bishop of Thessaloniki, who was Vicar General.[585] Previously, a similar call to the bishops of Dardania was issued by Pope Innocent I through the circular *"Magna me gratulatio,"* demanding a final stand against the heretics and heresy arising from the actions of Bishop of Naissus, Bonosius.

That the issues of heretics would still continue, and that they disturbed the Holy See, can be seen from a letter that Pope Gelasius I addressed to the bishops of Dardania in 493. It bears the title *"Ubi Primum"* and demands loyalty to the Holy See and its teachings. The same message was repeated by the Pope a year later entitled *"Audientes orthodoxam"* to all the bishops of Dardania *"universis episcopis per Dardaniam sive per Illyricum constitutis."*

Here too a demand is made to stay away from "the errors of Eutyches" and not rely on the Bishop of Thessaloniki, who did not respond to the Pope's request to judge Accacius.[586]

Pope Gelasius I addressed two letters to the Church of Dardania, in which he constantly reminded it of its obligations to the Holy See and its attitudes in relation to the matters concerning East and West in the circumstances of the worries regarding the barbaric attacks in the East and efforts to ease them through various alliances with them, as would be the ones with the Goths, Visigoths, or Huns, passing as domestic affairs of the Empire, especially when they were used as reasons for settling accounts among internal rivalries.

Of the same nature was also the letter of Pope Symmachus in 512 addressing all the bishops, deacons, archimandrites, and church leaders throughout Illyricum, Dardania and in both Dacias.

Following the emergence of Justiniana Prima to the rank of a vicariate and ecclesiastical center of the province of Illyricum, the Holy See addressed the leaders of this center on several occasions bearing the main authority after the Vatican. Thus, Pope Gregory the Great addressed the vicar of Justiniana Prima in 592 with the letter *"Post longas,"* and in 594 he sent them the letter *"Manifestum bonitatis."* The same Pope addressed the

---

[585] Ibid, p. 61.
[586] Ibid, p. 62.

vicar of Dardania in the year 599, demanding they not submit to the Church of Constantinople, but rather respect earlier decisions passed by Emperor Justinian I, which were still valid. The last letter of Pope Gregory to the vicar of Justiniana Prima was sent in 602. It demanded that measures be taken to restore order in the Metropolis of Shkodra after the brawls that occurred between the Metropolitan Constance and Bishop Nemison, which speaks of the powers that Justinian Prima had in the entire Illyricum.

Of some significance are letters that emperors sent to the Diocese of Dardania as they surfaced the high level it enjoyed for a long time in the spiritual and administrative hierarchy of the Empire. Therefore, the first letter of this nature was that of Emperor Augustus Leo I, which brought the imperial attitude about two issues: the first concerned the top acts of Bishop Timotheus Elurius, who took leadership over the Diocese of Alexandria after the death of Bishop Proterius, displayed his non-compliance with this act and required adequate sanctions. And, the second had to do with the Council of Chalcedon, with the Emperor asking all the bishops for their opinions about the issues raised therein.[587]

Emperor Justinian I also sent two letters in the form of decrees to the Diocese of Dardania, when it was raised to the highest position as ecclesiastical center of Illyricum. It concerned Novelae XI of the year 535 and Novelae CXXXI of 545, which granted it the status of Archdiocese and Vicariate defined as *"secundum ae quae definita funt a sanctissimo Pope Virgilio,"* as sanctioned by Pope Virgil.

Finally the superb relations of the Church of Dardania with Papacy and the Empire were also filled with the letters that its bishops sent to them. They certainly went beyond ecclesiastical matters, opening matters of political and social nature, characteristic of known and unknown relations between East and West.

These letters and the relations between Dardania and the Holy See, and the emperors, continued for two centuries. Diocese and the rest of Illyricum, except that of Durres and some others, remained on the side of the Western Church, that is, Rome, implying a Western determination in the circumstances of eastern administration. This situation was not quite natural, being under the eastern administration of Constantinople and ecclesiastically belonging to the Western Church of Rome. This ended by

---

[587] Ibid, p. 64.

an arbitrary decision of Emperor Leo III, who detracted Eastern Illyricum and many other provinces from the Church of Rome to submit them to the jurisdiction of the Patriarch of Constantinople in 733.

Rome's attempt to preserve its jurisdiction under Bulgarian occupation that penetrated into some old Illyrian provinces brought no fruit. Therefore, in the Eighth Council of Constantinople (869-870), despite objections by the Pope's legates, it was decided that all parts of Illyricum under Bulgarian occupation were to remain under the Patriarchy of Constantinople. This would be the last time that the term "Illyricum" would be mentioned.[588]

With this decision stripping Dardania of its diocese and vicariate that it had since Justinian, ended also what might be called a self-governing identity with Illyrian-Dardanian statehood elements. The continuity of six centuries (from 284-870), beginning with the reforms of Emperor Diocletian of Illyrian origin, promoting Illyricum as a separate part of the empire in the East, and continuing with Emperor Constantine the Great of Dardanian origin concluded with those of the Dardanian Justinian turning Justiniana Prima into the second ecclesiastical center, after that of the Holy See.

Under the structure of imperial hierarchy, the Church was co-member of the administrative and political power with the bearing of a two-headed power. The Dardanian state experienced its origin at the time of Justinian and continued for 250 years before being conquered by Eastern Byzantine and Bulgarian occupiers.

Dardania and Byzantium

The restoration of the Church of Dardania to an Illyricum Vicariate by Emperor Justinian I aimed at preserving the spirit of world universalism of the Empire.- Illyricum and Dardania – the main parts of which the Empire was to be defended from the Slavic and other eastern peoples barbarian conquests. – Granting Dardania a special treatment from a military point of view as an imperial knot and its importance. – Accession to the throne of Emperor Heraclius (606-630) and the begin-

---

[588] See: Manna, S: *"L' Ilirico e i suoi problemi"* (Oriente Cristiano, a. XVIII, no. 4, Palermo, 1978 – 64), cited according to Gjini, Gaspër: *"Skoposko-prizrenska biskupija kroz stoljeća,"* Zagreb 1986, p. 66.

ning of the end of the western identity of Dardania and Illyricum with the settlement of the Slavs in Illyricum parts.- The devastating role of Slavs against the Dardanian and Illyrian ethnicity in the central part of the Empire with the building of their first tribal structures, tolerated by Constantinople.- The emergence of themes as forms of military-feudal organization, directly supervised by the center to the detriment of local self-governance set from the time of Diocletian and on. – Rapid "Greekization" of the eastern part and its detachment from the rest of the western part to the detriment of Illyricum.

Through Constantine the Great and Emperor Diocletian's reforms, the concept of Illyria as ethno-geography emerged, which in the memory of the Romans was taken by the Greeks sometime from 4th century B.C. through 4th century A.D. when an Illyrian emperor (Diocletian) with radical reforms changed the character of the Roman Empire turning Illyricum into the main eastern province. It was another Dardanian emperor, Justinian I, who restored the center of Illyricum – Dardania, an ecclesiastical center of Illyricum as a vicariate directly connected with the Holy See.

This granted one of the most powerful and important church, political, and state identities, which remained for the next 300 years until Byzantine destroyed it, starting the known flounders of the eastern empire in the long wars with itself and with those from the outside who also led to its end.

Emperor Justinian I, who succeeded in turning Illyricum and Dardania into a spiritual center of the eastern part of the Empire, was led by a vision to restore the ancient Roman Empire to its power and glory of universal dimensions. To become so, it also needed the power of ecumenical Christianity, which was likely to be promoted in a highly strategic area, exactly where since antiquity it represented a knot of world connections where Troy had its strong foundation as an image of world civilization. It also provided a platform where Dardanians, if not as its founders (as supported by ancient sources and legends) emerged among the key stakeholders participating in its development and protection, from where they remained the only ones to turn it into a new continuation in time and space, to be followed towards Epirus and from thence to the south of Italy, where branches of Dardanians (Galabres, Thunates), together with the Etruscans (Tyrrhenians), established Rome.

In the new circumstances, the last Roman emperor on the Byzantium throne, also a Christian sovereign aware of the divine origin of his imperial authority, did his best to restore the former glory of the Roman Empire. Justinian, although for a short time, returned the space that was and remains the universal empire, which was now considered possible with the help of Christianity.

How was he able to make this historical twist, when the old Roman Empire revealed all its power experiencing the last moments of its greatness in the political, cultural and spiritual sense? This twist subsequently turned toward a different direction, opening the way for the Middle Ages, through which despotism, divisions, intrigues and power struggles have been known as Byzantinism, when an imperial concept of universal size turned into a bad government policy.

To better understand all this, one should consider the social and political circumstances created in that transitional time of more than two centuries as the noted crises, such as that of the slave-owner system, contributed to imperial crises. Since the 1st century A.D., Christian monotheism was presented to the polytheists with the formula of spiritual life and equality, a promise that attracted the broad strata and all those who felt used in the slave-owner system hoping that the injustices of this world could be redressed through the eternal life of the afterworld.

When added to the difficulties arising in the North and East Empire from barbarian attacks, initially the Goths, Huns and later the Slavs, it seems quite clear why the Roman Empire confronted the challenge of failure, which could be avoided or rather postponed only by changing the basic concepts on which it was initiated and established, so as to fit the circumstances of the time such as doing away with the slave system and finding common language with pervasive Christianity that relied on the triumph of monotheism over polytheism.

Of course this historic leap was also encouraged by the administrative, political, social and military reforms and contributions made by emperors of Illyrian and Dardanian origin: Diocletian and Constantine the Great, when they accepted Christianity as the state religion of the Empire but they were not able to avoid the approaching precipice because of a past hostage that did not allow radical disassociation (parting from the slave-ownership order to a feudal order), just as Christianity did not allow for a spiritual concept to be attached to the universal concept of the

Empire in its very harsh internal war for its dogma (that of Arianism, Dyophysites, Monophysites and others).

At the time of such a great squirm, Justinian was the one who tried to restore its former fame to the old Empire, by restoring it through Christianity as a powerful tool. Even as a Christian, Justinian remained Roman and the idea of the autonomy of the religious sphere was quite foreign to him, as he considered the popes and patricians as his own servants. He directed the affairs of state as those of the church, by intervening personally in any problem that had to do with church organization, giving him the right to decide on questions of dogmatic liturgy, chair councils, and the writing of theological tracts and church hymns.[589]

Suffice it here to mention his *Novellas* (XI and CXXXI) by means of which he first announced Justiniana Prima (his birthplace) archbishopric of Illyricum and then raised it to the level of a vicariate, directly connected with the Holy See. Of this nature are also his famous stances on Arianism, monophysm, and other theological issues, which mostly burdened the ecclesiastical life when they were not given a final answer to where they stemmed from before turning into political issues. Therefore, one may say that in the context of the historic relations between church and state, the epoch of Justinian represents a moment of the greatest impact of the imperial power in the ecclesiastical life.

No emperor before or after him had such unrestricted power over the church, as there was no emperor like him who attempted to subject the church life to the concept of a universal empire.[590] Although he failed here, Emperor Justinian showed that the universal concept was feasible if the church would define the boundaries of behavior, even though she appealed to the "Creator's" word and his boundless power.

Besides the superior attitude toward the Church and its internal problems carried over to the imperial social and political life, Justinian initially faced the barbarian invasions and the difficulties that their incursions from the East had caused while his predecessors (Valentian and others), unable to stop them, not only made space for them but also started to use them for certain political purposes. The same was happening with the Goths, who after the battle of Adrianople, were allowed to settle in Thrace and a part of them also in Pannonia and Western Illyricum from where they continued their attacks against Italy.

---

[589] Ostrogorski, Georg: *"Historia e Perandorisë Bizantine,"* Tirana, 2002, p. 47.
[590] Ibid, p. 47.

Indeed, when Justinian came to power, the situation in the eastern part of the empire, especially in its northern and eastern borders was almost beyond any control. On one hand, the barbarians who penetrated deep into the rubble and began to settle there, behaved without respect for any law. On the other, Persians constantly tried to acquire the extreme border provinces, especially those who had begun to lose faith in the empire. A worse situation prevailed in the West, especially in Illyricum, where the Germans had begun to settle and got through to Italy and Spain without any difficulty, placing their power outside imperial control. So, a part of the Roman Empire had already begun to accept the authority of the barbarians, while the Germans were turning into an important military factor not only as regular troops, but also in the commanding hierarchy.

Despite these major troubles, which threatened to demolish the empire in both of its parts, especially the western Roman one, the Roman Emperor continued to be considered the head of *Orbis romanes* (Roman world) and of the Christian *ecumen* (sphere). By this doctrine even areas that were once part of the Roman Empire were considered as its eternal and irrevocable possessions, regardless of the fact that they were governed by German kings, they later accepted the sovereignty of the Roman Emperor and what they exercised was only the power delegated by him.[591] Therefore, recovering Roman legacy was a natural right of the Roman emperor. It was his sacred mission to liberate the Roman territory from the yoke of foreign barbarians and Arian heretics, returning the old borders of the Empire, as inherent and Christian. Justinian I (527-565) put his policy in the service of this mission.[592]

It is rightly said that Justinian of Tauresios of Dardania began to act in accordance with this mission in order to run a lot of the imperial policies even during the reign of his uncle, Justin I (518-527). The intellectual with military ambitions rose quickly in the power hierarchy from which he was marked with his ambition to reach its peak, which he achieved by being appointed Emperor after the death of Anastasios I. Upon becoming Emperor, Justinian was put in charge of military campaigns, but didn't put himself in charge of specific state affairs, as was the action for the legal codification, or the announcement of administrative measures. Simultaenously, he began the most important campaigns of the

---

[591] Ibid, p. 42.
[592] Ibid, p. 42.

empire to settle accounts with barbarians in the East and North and worked on legal codification, as well as the major administrative reforms whereby the state created a lot of opportunities to act in accordance with its projects standing above everyone and everything.

In this regard Emperor Justinian chose the best collaborators, such as Balisarius and Narsetius, those who led the large-invasive campaigns; it was Tribanion who ran all the work on legal codification together with the prefect of pretoratis Johan of Cappadocia, the one who got the most important administrative measures. Despite the hard work that his foremost associates did, Justinian stood as the inspirer of all the great enterprises of his era, including those associated with the modernization of cities, fortification of vital parts of the Empire, as Illyricum and Dardania, where he built magnificent castles (46 from Naissus to Shkup) and many churches, especially in Illyricum and Dardania. Therefore, the total restoration policies pursued by Justinian were the greatest expression of this aspiration, although it didn't matter that they did not last long, and that their failure had severe consequences for the Empire.[593]

In his struggle to restore the power of the empire and to make it even bigger, Justinian led his powerful commanders into Africa and western Europe in settling accounts with the Vandals, a people who had put under surveillance the African North, and since 468, when it defeated the imperial army, appeared independent. Belisarius landed in Africa in 533 with thirteen thousand soldiers near Decimes and Tracaricus, having beaten the Vandal army badly. He took their king Genseric prisoner, after totally surrendering.[594]

In this case Belisarius waged heavy fighting with some other Mauritanian tribes, which for many years rivaled the Byzantine rule.

Simultaenously, when the Byzantine army scored successive victories in Sicily, Belisarius engaged in fighting against the Ostrogoths which he conquered, then Naples, and headed towards Rome, where after a pretty long siege, he captured the Osthrogoth king, Vitige, and took him to Constantinople (540). On this occasion, a large part of Illyricum was for half a century occupied by the Goths. They were allowed back in 376 to cross the Danube and it was they who represented a barrier to the Huns' penetration. However, as was seen, the Gothic "dam" did not hold. Under the leadership of Attila, "God's whip," after crossing the Danube in the

---

[593] Kulakovskij: *"Istorija,"* II, 93.
[594] Schmid, L: *"Geschichte de Wandalen,"* p. 125.

years 441-442, they devastated a good part of Illyricum. During the course of their attacks they destroyed seventy cities and forced the Eastern Empire to pay heavy tributes, besides vacating the Danube Valley. In 447 Attila devastated Illyricum and Dardania again, penetrating as far as Greece.[595]

Unlike the Huns, Goths came to invade the country and settle in it. They were introduced into the army, and by declaring Theodoric as their king, they won the right to become part of the Empire. Of course, they were used to this "new treatment" for internal purposes in the rivalries between East and West. Therefore, Emperor Zeno led Theodoric to stand against Italy. With an army of 200,000, Theodoric extended in 489 his possessions in Illyricum and other provinces in North and East, as well as in Italy and Gallia. The Roman army was able to temporarily stop the expanding Goths, but not inflict them a final blow. When it seemed that they had decided to obey the imperial orders, led by Totilas, they rebelled and began to reap consecutive successes against the Romans. Narses, another powerful military of Justinian, was sent to Italy to subdue them but this time the punishment was too severe, from which they never recovered. So, the Ostrogoth Kingdom fell in 552 and the Goths disappeared from history entirely as a nation.[596]

After 20 years the old power was restored in this part. On this occasion the latifundist aristocracy regained estates which they had been deprived of by the Ostrogoths. However, Spain was also expected to loosen itself of the Germanics. There were the Visigoths, who gradually lost control of many parts of the Iberian Peninsula after which with the victory against the Ostrogoths in Italy; the Mediterranean once again became the lake of the Empire.[597]

The period of successes in Africa and against the Vandals, Goths, Visigoths and others in the West was not repeated in the East. Therefore, the main concern began to come from Persia, which was increasingly infiltrating the extreme parts of the Empire. Although Justinian had signed peace in about 532 with the Persian king Khusrav I Anoshakravan (531-579), which he paid for, having had to pay tributes to the Persian Empire, in 540 Khursava broke the agreement attacking Syria, entering Antioch, where his troops caused havoc. The Persians did the same in the North

---

[595] Jacques, Edvin: *"Shqiptarët,"* Tirana, 2002, p. 171.
[596] Ibid, p. 171.
[597] Ostrogorsi, Georg: *"Historia e Perandorisë Bizantine,"* Tirana, p. 43.

upon entering Armenia and Hiberia and invading the province of Lazica in the Black Sea.[598] Further progress of the Persians was stopped somewhat through a new peace lasting for half a century and with additional attributes, which caused Persia to increasingly expand its power in the East.

The peace achieved with the Persians, though it cost Justinian, did not stop the penetration towards China in a sideway path bypassing Persian territory through the Byzantine bases of Cersona and Bosphorus towards the Crimean Peninsula and Lazica in the Caucasus. China was important for Byzantium being a huge market, from which there was a lot of give and take. The interest here focused on Chinese silk. The so-called "war for securing the silk" brought about for the first time an alliance between Byzantine and the Turks, who, at that time extended to the north of the Caucasus and, like the Byzantines, were enemies with the Persians on silk trade issues.

Justinian's vision for a global scale Byzantine Empire, alongside those towards Central Asia and China, passing through the Black Sea and Caucasus, also led him in the direction of India, where he made great efforts to go as far as possible. Its new trade routes providing raw materials, such as Chinese silk and other products in the East, brought the Empire great developmental opportunities with an increasing presence of its products in the world markets. Therefore, it increased its revenues needed for such targets.

Besides the great successes achieved by restoring the space the Empire had lost and adding others, the greatest and most lasting act of the Justinian era certainly remains the codification of the Roman law. Even here, his right hand was his close collaborator Tribanus, quickly concluding and completing the work of Justinian. Therefore, the whole work, called the *Codex Justinianus* was published in 529 with a complete publication four years later. Besides the *Codex* and *Digest* (summary with endless sentences by Roman jurists), *Institutiones* was also published, provided as a guide for the study of law, including parts from two of the major works. Therefore, the entire *Corpus iuris civilis* is complemented with the *Novellae* collection, with laws emerging following the publication *Codex*, *Digest* and *Institutiones*, which were published in Latin, with the great bulk of the *Novella* in Greek.

---

[598] Ibid, p. 43.

Codification of Roman law served as the legal basis for the unified centralized Byzantine state featured by the emphasis of imperial absolutism. However, the code of Justinian also declared freedom and equality for all the people, regardless of how much and how such a principle was applied.

As noted above, the Empire of Justinian was unable to resist the test of time. It shined for a time and continued to be as such only for as long as he was on the top of it, being able to reconcile a glorious past, which could not be repeated, and a future, which could not be consistent while lacking emperors of vision such as Justinian.

So after the death of Justinian, the Empire began to suffer blows and shocks from where its recovery had begun - Italy and Africa. In Italy the Longobardies attacked in 568, occupying a part of the country. In Spain again Visigoths took to the stage, conquering Cordoba in 572 followed with the larger parts of the country. In Africa, besides Mauritanian tribes, Arabs emerged with their powerful and unstoppable attacks to its North, warning their approaching involvement in developments that gave special coloration to the world civilization. Therefore, the center of gravity of Byzantine policy shifted again towards the East, where it remained for long in the vortex of many abortive squirms until its well-known end.[599]

The decline of imperial power, which had been restored by Justinian, was not only a waste of something that could return in certain circumstances. Rather, this loss represented a milestone in the transformation of the old state structure of the latter Roman period to a new system, that of the medieval Byzantine Empire, which practically, in the historic scene appears as what is known as the Middle Ages.

The emergence of what was called the Middle Ages is also associated with post-Justinian settlers and their efforts to renew the Western Empire through eastern vivacity and political governance associated with the military one. This paved the way for the militarization of the imperial government, which led to a new crisis of governance concerns and major unrest that produced tyranny such as that of the Emperor Phocas on October 5, 605 when it was abrupted by Heraclius, who, after the bloody events was crowned emperor by the patriarch of Constantinople, bringing an end to the Roman Empire once and for all and concluding what has been called the late Roman or early Byzantine period.[600]

---

[599] Ibid, p. 49.
[600] Schevill, Ferdinand: "*Ballkani – historia and qytetërimi,*" Tirana, 2002, p. 56.

It was precisely his right arm, Maurice, who after two emperors succeeding Justinian, Justin II and Tiberius Constantine (578-582), came to the imperial throne holding it for the next 20 years (582-602), succeeding to strengthen the Empire from within, after so many disorders, and simultaneously waiving the continuing threats of the Persians, with whom he was engaged in long wars, which he was able to successfully complete thanks to the commitment of all the internal resources of the empire, and sign a long-term peace treaty with the Persians, by which a large part of Persian Armenia passed over to the Byzantine Empire.

Maurice's victories in the East against the Persians and the stabilization of the Empire from within were not at the expense of the western part of the Empire. Instead, he made great efforts and ceaseless commitment to keep its possessions from the time of Justinian, particularly those in Africa and Ravenna, where the Longobards appeared with their known claims. Unlike Justinian, who saw the extension of the imperial powers as a civilized affair and something he was attempting everywhere, Maurice turned to strict military organization in the western provinces. Therefore, he set up *exarchates* of Ravenna and Cartagena,[601] a form of military dynasties able to defend themselves.

These vicariates were subject to the exarches thus inaugurating the period of Byzantine administration militarism, and forewarning the future system of *themes*, which extended a new and direct supervision over the various parts of the empire from the center and their governance in accordance with its interests.

The militarization of the Empire, though it seemed to have brought stability, was not able to repay the claims to stay on the known course set by Emperor Justinian as a world power. Slavic invasions on one hand and domestic boils against absolute governance on the other opened domestic fronts, reflected in a tough battle between the "blues" and the "greens" (political currents between the demos and depos), which led to the weakening of government authority.

If one adds to this the grievances facing the army (lack of payments, demoralization by long campaigns in the North against the Goths and Slavs, who were increasingly insistent on penetrating into the eastern part), the situation became ripe for a military response that came from the

---

[601] Exarchate of Ravenna is mentioned for the first time in 584, and that of Cartagena was first seen in 591. For more see: Diehl, *Exarchate*, 6; Hartman: "Byzantinische Vervaltung," 9 and on; Gelzer: *"Themenveerfassung,"* 6 and on.

Danube, where a semi-barbarous petty officer called Phocas, leading the rebel soldiers, marched on to Constantinople. This prompted a major uprising in the Byzantine capital, which therefore led to the dethroning of Maurice and the declaration of Phocas as Emperor.

The arrival of the semi-barbarous officer on the imperial throne, as an expression of the first military coup, opened the bloody chapter of the Byzantine government, followed by uncontrollable terror, internal plots and intrigues of the most severe kind. All of this started with terror against Emperor Maurice, who once dethroned was cruelly slaughtered and dragged to see his own sons massacred. These executions were followed by mass murder with terror striking mainly distinguished families, which turned to resistance by means of different plots, as a consequence of which new massacres followed, taking place under the direction of certain "lodges."[602]

In this bloody squirm, while losing domestic support, from aristocracy in particular, which stood against the involvement of the military apparatus in the state terror turning it into a factor of decisive force, reportedly Emperor Phocas sought and gained the support of Rome, which was equally harmful and even fatal for both parts, especially for the Holy See, which eventually lost its influence on the East not only on the spiritual plane, but also on the administrative and cultural one. After the fall of the tyrant Phocas, the Church of Constantinople became the full-fledged owner of the East and removed Latin from official use and liturgy, starting the period of "Greekizing" of the Orthodox Church throughout the eastern empire.

Indeed, the wily Emperor made his return to Rome by sending an edict to Pope Boniface III in 607, in which he pledged recognition to the primacy of the Apostolic Church of St. Peter over all the churches, by which he broke an earlier edict of a century ago when the patriarchs of Constantinople bore the title of "ecumenical patriarchs."[603]

Rome's support, and the power it granted, in addition to the glories platted for the tyrant of Byzantium in the West, did not bring anything but further loss of confidence in Constantinople, which began to be expressed in various forms of civil war, becoming inevitable when his

---

[602] Ostrogorski, Georg: "*Historia e Perandorisë Bizantine,*" Tirana, 2002, p. 51.
[603] For more see: Gelzer, H: "*Der Streit ber den Titel des ökumenischen Patriarchen;*" Gaspar, E: "*Geschichte des Papsttums,*" 1933, cit. 364, 452; Haller, J: "*Das Papsttum.*"

orthodox-church policy relapsed into bloody persecutions of Monophysites and Judaists.

In these circumstances of internal weakness, the outside danger reappeared. It came from the Persians, who felt it was the right moment to recover what they had lost to Emperor Maurice. King of Persia, Khosrau II, the one who Maurice brought to power, who remained bound to the forced peace treaty, attacked Byzantium in 605 conquering the Castle of Dara. He didn't stop there, continuing further into Asia Minor whereby he invaded Caesarea and approached Chalcedon.

As the Empire was on the edge of collapse salvation came from the side-line. Heraclius, the Exarc of Cartagena rebelled against the terrorist regime of Phocas. He was joined by Egypt, and Heraclius sent his son, also named Heraclius, to Constantinople at the head of a powerful fleet, where he was received with enthusiasm and on October 3, 605 Phocas' terrorist regime was overthrown and the tyrant was publicly burned at a hippodrome. Two days later, Heraclius was crowned Emperor by the Patriarch of Constantinople.

This was the real moment of the beginning of Byzantine history, the history of the Medieval Greek Empire and the "Greekizing" of Byzantium.[604]

Factors that led to this historic shift are customarily sought from outside (attacks by the Goths, Huns, Slavs and others in North and East), although their role cannot be denied in some cases, while the crucial internal ones on this occasion have been undervalued or mitigated, which would radically change the concept of Justinian's idea about a universal empire, a world empire with Christianity subject to the Emperor with its spiritual center being the Holy See, the West.

Unequivocally, the external factors, the Gothic, Avarian, Hunic, and Slavic attacks, weakened the defensive power of the Empire, as was with other crises that would produce administrative and economic reforms, but used by the Eastern Church and the new military caste, which brought to power the tyrant Phocas for its own purposes, bringing to an end once and for all the influence of the Church of Rome in the East. This occurred after the arrival of Heraclius on the imperial throne in 605, and also with the help of the *church-military factor* to open the way to the "Greekizing" of Byzantium. This was well the beginning of an alliance between the

---

[604] Ostrogorski, Georg; *"Historia e perandorisë Bizantine,"* Tirana, 2002, p. 52.

church and the army, which in future events played an important role, as this link militarized the Church and the frequent acts of military coups had the blessing of the Church spirit.

Indeed the arrival of Heraclius and the significant support of his military fleet in Constantinople was part of an agreement between the Church of Constantinople and the Exarchate of Cartagena. Heraclius was to eliminate tyrant Phocas from the throne and invalidate the Edict of 607 that recognized the primacy of the Holy See throughout the Empire. It happened.

This was best seen with the crowning of Emperor Heraclius under the blessing of the Bishop of Constantinople, who was the first to turn the leader of the Orthodox Church into an Emperor's deputy.

With increasing threats from Avars, Huns and Slavs in Danube, Heraclius, vigorously supported by the Church of Constantinople was to undermine the administrative system of internal governance of the Empire. This was followed by emperors coming from Illyricum: Constantine the Great, Justin and Justinian, who placed the Byzantine foundations by virtue of the concept of the Roman Empire, empowering Christianity in partnership granting the Emperor spiritual blessings. This was also used by Constantine the Great and separately Justinian I to get the support of the masses who believed in the promise of Christianity on social equality. So, Heraclius made the first schism from the concept of Byzantine emperors who came from the West exploiting Christianity for political needs, starting with the profound changes in the structure of the army and provincial administration of the medieval Byzantine rule, which at the time of Emperor Maurice was divided into exarchates. Therefore, based on exarchates, like that of Carthage and Ravenna, he set the *theme* system,[605] upon which the territory of Asia Minor, prior to being stamped by the Persians, was divided into administrative counties of a clear military character.

Military strategists had great power, after more provinces were placed under their supervision. This system, which included the local armies,

---

[605] The word *"theme"* indicates a military body later used to mark new military districts. In fact they did not represent administrative units alone, but also territories colonized by the military. Soldiers were given an inheritable fund of land, which in later-date sources was called "military property." From the time of Heraclius themes of Opsicans, Armenians, and Anatolians were born. The navel theme of Carabisians, on the southern coastal wing of Asia Minor, is also of that date.

called *"stratioti"* affected the change of the shape of local government, which with the emergence of *themes* and military strategists at their helm lost that of the prefectures that existed from the time of Diocletian onwards.

There were strategists alongside their clergy, who had gained all the power of local government, which was proven successful. This success was reflected with Heraclius gaining strength to begin a military campaign against the Persians, which was provided after reaching peace with the Avars (619), being forced to pay them a heavy tribute. This meant keeping them at bay for as long as he would be dealing with Persians.

After four years, Heraclius started war with the Persians. After initial battles, he won the war, entering Ardashir's residence, the first of the Sasanians, and one of the most important religious centers of the Persians. On this occasion, Khusravi was forced to abandon the city, which fell into the hands of the Byzantines. The Temple of Fire of Zarathustra, the most important temple of the city, was destroyed in retaliation for the plundering of Jerusalem.[606]

The successful campaigns of Heraclius in Persia were followed by a sudden counter-attack in 626, when their leader Shahbaraz penetrated Asia Minor, taking over Chalcedon and appearing in Bosphorus.

Simultaneously, Constantinople came close to numerous hordes of Avars, joined by Slavs, Bulgarians and Gepids. In July they surrounded the city and came near the main gates. The battle was decided at sea, when the strong Byzantine fleet broke off the Slav skiffs, unaccustomed to such a confrontation, and unable to undertake an organized fight. This led the Avarian ground forces to withdraw in panic, which led to the Persian forces abandoning Chalcedon in the direction of Syria. His brother, Shahin, was badly defeated by the Emperor's brother, Theodor.[607]

The Avar-Slav-Persian failure before the walls of Constantinople gave wings to Heraclius, who felt the time was right for a military demonstration against Persia, launching a hard blow by invading Khursavi's capital, Destagerd, in 628. The dethroning of Khursavi a little later and his son, Shiro Kavadh, boarding the throne to be overseen by Heraclius, returned all the territories to the Empire: Armenia, Roman Mesopotamia, Syria, Palestine, and Egypt.

---

[606] Ostrogorski, Georg: *"Historia e Perandorisë Bizantine,"* Tirana, 2002, p. 69.
[607] Ibid, p. 70.

This compelled Heraclius to go to Jerusalem in 680 and restore the Holy Cross, kidnapped years before by the Persians. This solemn ceremony sanctioned the completion of the first victory of the great religious struggle of the Christian era.[608]

Although Heraclius's significant military victories in the East did not last long before they were ambushed by Arab attacks, the Heraclius era in the history of Byzantium still represents a turning point not only in political and cultural life. With Heraclius the Roman stage closed and the Byzantine one opened in the true sense of the word. Complete "Greekizing" and a powerful clericalization of the entire public life gave the country an entire new face.[609]

Additionally, Emperor Heraclius was attributed with another "merit,"which changed the appearance of the internal imperial life. The word was to allow the settlement of Slavs in the Balkans, these barbarian tribes from the Carpathians, which were threatening western civilization for quite some time with their westward incursions, and whose "acceptance" was made on the account of them being "mitigated" for the benefit of the Empire. However, detrimental to its main ethnic and social factors, Illyrians and Dardanians, had great merit in the establishment and rise of Byzantium turning it into a great power in the East. Illyrian and Dardanian emperors: Diocletian, Constantine the Great, Justin and Justinian I, in the context of imperial reforms did not accidentally raise Illyricum to the level of a key province between western and eastern parts, becoming the scene of important developments in the following centuries in which the vitality of the Roman Empire as a world power would be tested.

By allowing the barbarian Slavic tribes to settle in the areas mainly inhabited by Dardanians (from the Danube in the direction of Morava and Ibar rivers) and toward Sava and Dalmatia, where Illyrians dwelt, Heraclius began the process of deregulation of an already existing Illyrian-Dardanian administrative, social and spiritual ethnicity, among the most stable in that part bearing the balance of an imperial edifice.

For more thn 100 years they withstood the attacks of barbarians from the North, by turning into an anti-Slavic fortification, such as envisaged by Emperor Justinian, who had done so much administratively and militarily for Dardania in particular and Illyricum generally to gain additional protective powers by means of fortifications, which were once

---

[608] Ibid, p. 71.
[609] Ibid, p. 71.

part of a separate imperial identity, where the western spirit and Christianity met.

And as noted, the beginning of the Slavic settlement in these parts (a process that continued intensively over the next two centuries) as well as their involvement in the army (not as mercenaries as it happened occasionally when they were committed to specific needs and had conducted numerous services) - by granting the right to create their own communities, which were of an extremely primitive mentality compared with what Dardania and Illyricum were (just enough to mention here the magnificent cities that Justinian built in Dardania such as Justiniana Prima, Justiniana Secunda and many others, the first having become a vicariate and center of the Church of Illyricum directly linked with the Holy See) - started the period of forced Slavization of the Empire in the western Balkans, as well as the exclusion of the ancient culture that was based on values of world universalism, exactly what the Roman Empire and the people who built it had cultivated. It was done initially with the return of the Greek language as an official language and, later, with its introduction into the liturgy and local administration, which brought about a total "Greekizing" and powerful clericalization of the public life.

Indeed, in the eastern part the Latin language as the language of administration as well as of the army had long since begun to break down. "Bilingualism" as the first measure of preparation to one day have Greek win over in the East, came from the Church of Constantinople on the grounds that people were seeking mass in a language they understood, namely Greek. Heraclius ended this state and the Greek language became the official language of the Byzantine Empire.[610] The language of the people and the church became the state language. In order to further strengthen "Greekization" and turn it into the foundation of the state of Byzantium, Heraclius renounced his imperial Latin title and was named *Basileus*, according to a popular Greek name.

Basileus became the official title of the Byzantine emperor and was considered a true imperial title, phasing out Caesars, Roman Emperors, and paving the way for the final separation of the churches in the Latin rite, with the Vatican as its center, and that of the Orthodox rite with its center Constantinople, a division that since the eleventh century onwards, passing through the middle of Illyricum and what would later appear as

---

[610] Zilliacus, H: *"Zum Kampf der Weltschprache im oströmischen Reich,"* Helsingfors, 1935, p. 36.

the Arberarian and later Albanian ethnic space, represented the boundary of separation of civilizations and fierce and unstoppable wars that were waged on the basis of this division.

Illyrians and Dardanians within the Framework of Early Byzantine Mentality

Illyricum and Dardania and Illyrian provinces were generally targeted by the first missionaries of Christianity. – Efforts to resist the campaign of monotheism by maintaining the divine conscience as part of antiquity inherited from Pelasgians.- Despite accepting Christianity as the official religion of the Empire, Constantine the Great did not give up his ancient Pelasgic creed. – The Code of Theodosius "De paganis sacrificiis et templis" did not stop the old tradition of sacrifice.- A great number of supporters of Arianism in Dardania, including those from bishopric ranks – an expression of free thinking .- Emperor Julian and his decree on allowing worshipping of deities.- Ultimate victory of Christianity did not end the church dogma as reflected in the fierce battle between supporters and prohibitors of icons, with the first enjoying larger support in Illyricum and Dardania.- Numerous Dardanian and Illyrian artists from the 4th to the 9th century, such as Niketë Dardani (author of Byzantine Hymn), St. Jerome, translator of the Bible, and others reaching the peak of Byzantine art.

Opening the road for Slavic barbarian tribes to settle in the Balkans and turning the Greek language into official use directly hit the Illyrian-Dardanian administrative, social and cultural identity, which had begun to gain legitimacy from the time of Emperor Diocletian, Constantine the Great and Justinian, and favored the "Greekizing" of Byzantine Empire turning it ultimately towards the East, eventually harming the spirit of world universalism that characterized the Roman Empire in past centuries when it had reached its peak of power and glory.

Emperor Heraclius, who came to power with the help of the army of the Exarchate of Cartagena and the Church of Constantinople, accepted the help of the latter rather as an alliance that the Crown needed in order to gain the trust of the population there, while making use of the social and political dividends among the largest ones, to turn it into permanent capital and with it becme a co-member of the imperial crown, and power for centuries until Byzantium ceased to exist and Constantinople fell into the hands of the Ottomans. When it fell under the Ottomans, the Orthodox Church quickly adapted to circumstances, keeping something from her position during the Byzantine period, which may be said that although her ruling was not like before, it, however, was in the service of the new power.

Connecting with Constantinople and its cross, Heraclius finally broke away from both the Roman Church and the West in general, a disconnection that resulted not only in separation but also alienation, a move that hit Illyricum worst of all because administratively, as a province it belonged to the East, and in ecclesiastical terms to the West, that is, to the Church of Rome. It remained so until the 9th century when, as is known, after an arbitrary decision of Leo III, belonged to the jurisdiction of Constantinople, a decision that was justified at the Seventh Council of Constantinople of 869-870, where pats of Illyricum occupied by the Bulgarians would pass over to the Church of Constantinople, by which, for the last time, the name Illyricum was mentioned, a fact resulting in a deliberate disregard for Illyrian-Dardanians for four centuries, in so that their trails "suddenly" reappeared in the 12th century, as *Arbër, Albanë, Rabanë*, an issue that was discussed upon reviewing the historical passage from Illyrian to Arberian and from the *Illyrian* to *the Albanian* language.

Prior to this development, it should be said that Illyricum played an increasingly active role in what would appear as medieval mentality, which emerged in the historical scene from the acceptance of Christianity as an official religion and onwards, initiated by Emperor Constantine, a Dardanian, in 319, to continuing in all its stages until it turned into a social and political dogma of which is actually known.

Since, as is known, the emergence of Christian missionaries, and with that traces of Christianity in the Illyricum and Dardania date back from the 1st century AD,[611] it is expected that in this space first clashes of monotheism and polytheism occurred between Christianity and paganism in a considerably fierce form as the pagan Roman Empire set its key eastern challenge at this knot, connected with land and water routes, connecting the West with the East for a long time.

---

[611] For more see: Gjini, Gaspër: "*Skopsko-prizrenska biskupija kroz stoljeća,*" Zagreb, 1986.

This new challenge, emerging in the East and spreading on all sides implied an inevitable confrontation with it among the most important crossroads from where penetration to the West depended on the support it could get in these parts. Furthermore, aware of this, it is no accident that the Roman Empire took tougher measures against the missionaries in these parts, among who were the first martyrs of Dardania, who according to Farlati were four: Florus, Laurus, Proculius, and Maximus, spreading from this part to the West and Northeast going as far as Italy.[612] *Acta Sanetorum* also cites their homeland, Dardania, and the name of the city where they were tortured, Ulpiana. It becomes known that they were stone carvers and could even be twins. Although the exact date of their martyrdom is not known, it still refers to the time of Emperor Hadrian (117-138), known for his toughness against any Christian teaching that appeared in these parts.[613]

Besides the first day martyrs, generally the Province of Illyricum also experienced numerous missionary movements before and after the acceptance of Christianity as an official religion by Constantine the Great. However, *a priori* setting of the medieval mentality in Illyria and Dardania within Christianity as a doctrine that has to do with the victory of monotheism over polytheism, overcame the clichés of efforts to have Christian missionaries accepted with open arms. It may result from several sources or even Byzantine church annals of the time, as neither the consciousness of polytheism managed to beat it once and for all even when pagan Christianity was accepted as the official religion of the empire, nor has the Christian dogma been able to cut the link with the pagan belief and heretical conscience and heresy (Arian schism and other beliefs) that continued for a long time to be faced and even confronted at these parts, with some of them, such as Arianism, occupying the main space.

Regarding the former, the pagan and occult beliefs, it suffices to mention the fact that even Emperor Constantine the Great, who officiated Christianity, had personally not given up his pagan consciousness nor did he do so after accepting Christianity. Apparently, he sought communion on his deathbed (even though this has not been found anywhere outside church sources, which can also be taken as speculatory for the needs of the church), his request being to have his sarcophagus and burial be done

---

[612] Farlattus D: *"Iliricum Sacrum,"* Volume, VIII/2, Venetiis, 1751-1819,
[613] *Acta Sanetorum*, die 18 augusti, III, Anverpiae 1737, pp. 520-522, cited according to Gjini, Gaspër: *"Skopsko-prizrenska biskupija kroz stoljeća,"* p. 56.

according to a pagan rite and adorned with grape vines, which was an important Dardanian cult since the time of Pelasgians (and so it happened). This explains best the dilemmas, squirms and all those that accompanied this piece before and during what was taken as medieval mentality.

That this was a long and fierce struggle between extremely unacceptable differing mentalities, with sometimes unpredictable turns, is best reflected by the decree of Emperor Julian, of the year 361, which announced the renewal of polytheism, restoring ruined temples and exempting priests from various duties, even tempting the "returnees" with awards. Emperor Julian was convinced that Christianity as it was explained by the clergy and accepted by the part of senior officials, was nothing but a struggle for power from bottom-up of the slave class, which required new social and political treatment at the expense of the aristocracy, which played the leading role of the main instigator using the trust to these purposes, which simultaneously consented with despotic inclinations of the Emperor.

However, Julian failed after two years precisely because freedom of religion was not able to defend free faith from the Christian dogma, which by now had already passed as nourishment for the masses with the promise of equality and afterlife, seeming much more acceptable than the entitlement to free belief from which they did not see any benefit. And, soon after Julian's death in 363, Emperor Theodosius declared Christianity by decree as the only official religion. Moreover, a year later it was decided not only to deny any assistance to pagan worship, but also to confiscate the assets of temples and temple worshippers persecuted. An order issued in 392 banned any proponent in private places being viewed as an offense threatened with fines and strict punitive measures.[614] Of this nature is the famous Code of Theodosius *"De paganis sacrificiis et templis"* (On Pagan Sacrifices and Temples) stating the following:

"We command the temples anywhere to close ... no one should make sacrifices. If anyone makes such violations, let him fall by the sword revenge. We command that the property of those killed and punished be confiscated and the governors of the provinces be punished if they fail to act accordingly for the obliteration of these crimes."[615]

---

[614] Sokoli, Ramadan: "16 shekuj," Tirana, 1996, p. 20.
[615] Ibid, p. 20.

This social development, namely the presence of extremes, may serve in understanding Illyricum and Dardania within it as a space in which they found an almost permanent place and nourishment. Therefore, it is no wonder why the extent of their social, political and spiritual spheres would make their administrative and later church boundaries emerging from the 11th century and on, turn into a space of harsh clashes between the Christian eastern and western rites, while four centuries later, with Islam emerging, it turned into a space of clashes of civilizations as well.

Indeed, the Illyrian and Dardanian mentality during the Middle Ages, in circumstances where the Christian dogma made ceaseless efforts to absolutize any spiritual, social and political truth, should rather be seen in its determination to maintain the space of a "different" thinking or heresy, even within what was seen as the church doctrine pursuant to the teachings of the scripture.

In Dardania, along with the first appearance of the Old Testament translated into Latin, or in what was called "vulgate" by the Illyrian St. Jerome or St. Eusebius also called Saint Jeri, the differences between *monophysites* and *dyophysites* in these parts find an extremely suitable plot, coming from the remote parts of the empire (Armenia and Egypt), two known currents within the church, with one side protecting the stance of the nature of *man-God* spirit and the other seeing it as represented by the son of God, Jesus as his spirit. Although this contention came to a close at the Council of Nicaea when a consensus was reached about the nature of Trinity, i.e. Father, Son and the Holy Ghost, the doctrine was ultimately legitimized in the Third Council of Chalcedon, in 451.

However, it was heretical thinking that was circulating quite freely in Dardania and Illyricum as a powerful faction within the church, based in Alexandria, supported by the Armenian Church and a good part of the bishops of Dardania, turning Arianism into a major threat to the church dogma, as this instruction does not accept the divine nature of Jesus nor the claim of him being an "illegitimate" son of God brought to life by Mary.

The Arians, being influential at the beginning and even a majority, excluded this teaching and were evidently very powerful and influential, particularly in the part of Dardania and Illyricum, where "different thinking" was maintained. What impact Arianism had in these parts is best explained by the acceptance of Christianity of the Arian variant by the Goths, which, from Dardania, spread rapidly in the northern parts of the Empire, with the impact continuing even after the end of their kingdom in Italy and Dalmatia.

That the so-called schism among the Dardanian bishops was not only "an accidental case of the Arian position in Dardania,"[616] being reprimanded by the Second Council held near Constantinople at the request of Constantine the Great, who demanded order in the Church instead of bickering about the spirit of God among men, is best illustrated by the case of the Bishop of Naissus, Bonosus, who openly opposed the virginity of Mary, the same as heretics Jovinian and Helvidius had done. According to Bonosus, Mary, after Jesus, had other children with Joseph.

This heresy disturbed the church, which at the Council of Chalcedon would demand that the bishops of Dardania and Illyricum distance themselves from the heretical bishops led by Bonosus.

Obviously, an investigation of the Council, by a majority vote, announced Bonosus a heretic ousting him from church activities. But knowing that the bishop is not only proud to accept the punishment and would not repent, but would continue on his own for a long time in Dardania and other parts wherever he went; clearly Arianism was still supported in these parts.[617]

Despite these delimitations, which were severe, regardless of the "reconciliation" achieved in Council after Council, and regardless of formal conservation of jurisdictional alignment between the Church of Rome and that of Constantinople, the internal struggles of one or the other church for greater impact continued through different methods often mean-spirited, in which usually political strengthening or weakening of one or the other side would be used for church favors.

However, the situation that Justinian had set up with his first and second novella of 535 and 545 respectively, when Justiniana Prima was declared the capital of Illyricum Diocese and its vicariate was linked directly with the Holy See, the Dardanian Church rose to the highest state level. Despite popular disturbances and destruction of political and social changes that occurred after Heraclius came to power, when the "Greekizing" of life in the East and the secession process began leading to separation from Rome, Dardania, at least formally, continued to preserve something of the old situation, although with less opportunities for action

---

[616] Gjini, Gaspër: "*Skopsko-prizrenska biskupija kroz stoljeća,*" Zagreb, 1986, p. 33.
[617] Ibid, p. 33.

that it once had. This certainly had something to do with maintaining further ties with the Holy See, by continuing to respect its jurisdiction until the Emperor Leo III arbitrarily removed it, in 733, as legitimized by the Seventh Council of Constantinople in 870.

When speaking of Emperor Leo III and what followed later at the Eighth Council when Dardania and Illyricum lost once and for all the position they enjoyed since the time of Diocletian, Constantine the Great, and Justinian, i.e. in an attempt to reverse everything of the administrative, social, and church identity they enjoyed in their connection with the western church and civilization, a war against the icons should be pointed out turning into an internal conflict of the Church, among the biggest and most debated one, in which Dardania and Illyricum in general were mostly involved, as they administratively were included in the eastern part of the Empire, while in the ecclesiastical aspect they were included within the Western church, the Holy See. At the core of that long and tough conflict, with great social and political consequences for the entire empire, stood the different interpretation of the role that the sacred images (icons) had in the Christian faith.

The unbending war for and against icons turned into a very harsh ecclesiastical conflict, which brought to the open, among others, the big cultural, social and political differences between the Western Church and the Eastern Church. The Western Church demanded that arts and creativity in general not be suffocated by the church dogma, having instead freedom of the artists in the church as well to be more creative, consistent with the pagan culture still preserved in a large part of Illyricum, and among others in the West. The Eastern Church, Constantinople, demanded harsh dogma in art and creativity with artists abides by the twelve apostolic orders around the image (icon) with nothing else appearing. This was in line with the influence exerted on the Byzantine Christianity, by Islam and Jewish faiths, which prohibit paintings of the saints and motifs dealing with them.

During the time of Justinian, who upgraded the church of Dardania, then its center Justiniana Prima, to a vicariate and archdiocese of Illyricum directly affiliated to the Holy See, in the local churches of this area art of icons would blossom art and everywhere they were adorned with these motifs. The Church images (icons), turned into some kind of creative freedom, almost similar to that which appearred at the time of the Renaissance, when art and creativity, after centuries of slavery, was released from Christianity submitting itself to the free momentum.

Even during the time of Justinian, *iconolatry* (admiring of icons), greatly supported in Illyricum and other western parts under the church jurisdiction of the Holy See, there was an attempt by *iconoclasts* (haters of icons) to increase their influence bringing an end to what could be perceived as a creative free space in Christian art. In the East, iconoclasts not only strengthened, but they turned into a Pavlican sect standing against every form of religious cult and did so by brutal interventions destroying works and afflicting severe punishment to artists.

Thus, the struggle between supporters of icons and their haters continued even after Justinian's passing to be turned into a bitter dispute between the church of Constantinople, which, after the coming to power of Emperor Heraclius, gained full legitimacy in the East, and the Holy See continued for more than a hundred years, until Leo III showed up with his famous decree on protection of iconoclasts. Using the pretext of iconoclasts and their numerous supporters of the Dardanian Church taking the side of the holy teachings and proper views of the church, Leo III justifying his views that the heresy appearing in the Western side had to come to an end, arbitrarily separated the Church of Dardania in 732 from the Holy See placing it under direct dependency of Constantinople's Patriarchate. According to this measure, the Christian clergy gained "better opportunities" to be supervised and not go astray.

This action, however, was not able to stop the worshipping of the icons, nor could it convert the Dardanian Church into a wishful follower of the Church of Constantinople, as was supposed to have happened after these unilateral measures. Rather, Illyricum, with the exception of the Diocese of Durres, continued to maintain its links with the Holy See, which was tolerated by the son of Leo III, Constantine V, who after coming to power following his father's death in 746, had to deal more with Arab attacks, whom he clashed with that same year in Syria causing a defeat to the Omaiads, who after a long struggle were replaced by the Abbasid dynasty (750) which moved its state center from Damascus to Baghdad.

The Emperor's mother, Irena, who was from Athens, where the worshipping of icons continued, sought to find a language of reconciliation with the worshippers of icons, but her son refused. He became even more severe demanding to justify his iconoclast position through a Church council, that of February 754, which took place in the imperial palace of Hiera on the Asian coast of Bosphorus. In August of that year, the forum of the Synod of Constantinople announced its decisions, banning in most severe terms religious images, ordering the destruction of all statues of worship and condemning the Orthodox party supporters, among whom Patriarch Jesus with paintings of profane subjects, where ornamental trimmings of animal and plant motifs, among them portraits of the Emperor hunting, filled the church walls and doors.

Although the secular art was almost completely neglected in Dardania and Illyricum, as well as in the largest parts of the jurisdiction of the Holy See, while the relation between the mother, Irene, and her son Constantine V was to the point of a conspiracy that brought to power the next youngest son, Constantine VI, who was also killed by his mother on 15th of August 797, the the worship of icons returned. However, he did not return the Church of Dardania and Illyricum under full supervision of the Church of Constantinople, even when it was clear that after Pope Stephen II's agreement with the king of Longobards, Pipi, in January 754, the state had laid the foundations of the Roman church with the Kingdom of the Franks, in order to permanently turn its back to the Byzantine emperor, even though knowingly, such a connection, after a century, brought life to the Western Empire.

Despite this large discrepancy, from 3rd to the 9th century, which from a social and political aspect should be assessed as the time of the appearance of Illyrian-Dardanian citizenship within Byzantium – as both from an administrative, social, political and spiritual (faith) aspect, this empire was erected and built also thanks to the Illyrian-Dardanians, who, along with others (Greeks, Armenians, Dacians) became its main supporters – they should also be seen as part of a cultural development that would fulfill this identity even within the church dogma and all that the medieval mindset allowed and enabled, where numerous Illyrian and Dardanian artists achieved the peaks of Byzantine art, from music, architecture, and theological thinking. The emergence of Niketë Dardani and his musical works that would provide the seal to all medieval art, the major role of St. Jerome, who translated the Old Testament to disseminate its views to the west and help admission of Christianity on a large scale, the appearance of numerous architects and artists in all fields, depict a material and cultural development of Illyrian-Dardanians.

Archeological excavations brought to light streets paved with large stones, remnants of temples and shrines, baths, houses, water supplies, inscriptions, and a lot of other finds from pottery, ceramics and construction, architectural models, mosaics and coins, providing proof of appropriate conditions for cultural and artistic flowering of the country accordingly. Archaeologists assure us that all the findings of the 5th and 6th centuries in Prevalitana, Dardania, Northern Albania and Old and New Epirus in the South reveal a uniform material culture.

Therefore, close to Naissus (today's Nis) traces of a splendid palace were found built during the 3rd or 4th centuries by Emperor Gallery, Diocletian's son-in-law. Residues of magnificent palaces are also found near Prishtina (those of Ulpiana and Justiniana Secunda), in Theranda near Prizren, at Justiniana Prima with those of old Scupi near Skopje, several blocks of buildings at Vendinis near Podujeva and many other parts of Kosova and Macedonia.[618]

At that time, in the early 4th century, began the tradition of genuine basilicas, associated with precursor makers, who used the pagan tradition of high pillar art on the ruins of previous art; a new Paleo-Christian art appeared by absorbing elements of antiquity, to express through them the content of a new civilized worldview also.

---

[618] For more see: Shukriu, Edi *"Ancient Kosova,"* Prishtina 2004, *"Dardania paraurbane,"* Pejë, 1966; *"Fortifikata e Veletinit,"* Arheološko društvo Jugoslavie, Lubjana; *"Gradina e Gushicës and mu nicipium Labuza,"* Vjetar XXVII –XVIII, Prishtina; Kovaljević, G: *"Kasnoantička palata u Nerodimlji"* in *"Starine Kosova IX,"* Prishtina, 1989.

CHAPTER 2

Slavic Invasions and Deepening of Divisions between East and West

With the beginning of the Slavic invasions, from the beginning of the 7th century onwards and their settlement in Illyricum, with the permission of Emperor Heraclius, began the demolition of ethnic and cultural identity of the Western Roman Empire. - Slavs caused changes in the social, political and cultural relations in the Empire at the expense of the Western and in favor of the Eastern civilization. - Acceptance of Christianity by the Slavs in the 9th and 10th century and creation of their tribal structures in Bosnia and Dalmatia to the detriment of Illyricum and Byzantium. - The first Christian missionaries from Thessaloniki, Cyril and Methodius and the introduction of the Slavic languages as church liturgies strengthen the influence of the eastern Slavs, although they flirted with the Holy See for more privileges.

It has been said that Christianity and Slavic incursions (invasions) altered the direction of the Middle Ages and the course of European history in general. The first is justifiable on a spiritual, social and political plain, not only in the emergence of Byzantium as a continuation of the Western Empire, whose spirit was gradually turning into an Eastern Empire, but also as factors that gained proportions dealing with the mainstream of our civilization. As for the Slavs and their invasions, it may be said also that they produced major changes with social and political consequences but they were not those who changed the direction of history, nor provided any particular direction, but they turned into actors to be used for important social and political changes supported by Byzantium until recently, issues that depending on certain observations and interests are assessed in different ways.

Despite this, one may say that Slavic incursions (invasions) and the Slavic settlement in the Balkans, regardless of their true occurrence, were accompanied by many uncertainties and even speculation. Regardless of external and internal factors that conditioned and favored this, their emergence deeply impacted three main peoples of the Balkans at the time:

Illyrians, Greeks, and Latins,[619] and this impact and its consequences, was reflected in various ways in each and every people.

These obvious changes, seen in line with the consequences but not conditioned by factors outside of historical continuity from ancient times onward, often created an unclear picture of the developments, this becoming more evident whenever the same factors are evaluated differently. Such was the case with the Illyrians and their descendants (from the late Middle Ages Arberians and later Albanians), who in relation to the Greeks and Latins, unilaterally seceded from the imperial Byzantine complexity, to be seen in its margins or even standing "unnoticed," as a consequence of which an impression was conjured up to see them appearing "by chance" five or six centuries later, feeding up the biased and unscientific approach to the issue, which was given special attention.

If one is to accept the view that Slavic incursions (invasions) in the Balkans profoundly affected the position of the Illyrians, Greeks, and Latins, this first applied to the Illyrians, with negative and grave consequences for them, who were faced initially and thereafter with them, leaving the space occupied and their civilization destroyed in most barbaric ways. While the appearance of Slavs in the Empire, as a social factor, accelerated the process of separation of Latins from Greeks, with the first joined the Western holy empire rising after the time of Charlemagne onwards. The latter, the Greeks, with the situation started by Emperor Heraclius, that of "Greekizing" the Eastern Empire, turned the Slavic presence into an almost permanent favor, where the officiating Greek language also became the language of liturgy while the inclusion and accommodation of Slavs in the Eastern Empire was under the direct influence of Greek supremacy and its empowerment.

This was best reflected upon the acceptance of Christianity by the Slavs, who although initially their best links were with the Western Church (speaking of the tribes centered in Bosnia, Zahlumia and Dioclea, where the true social and political nucleus was before being carried over to Rascia by Nemanja and his dynasty), in accordance with various

---

[619] For more on the issue see: Schewill, Ferdinand: *"Ballkani – historia and qytetërimi,"* Tirana, 2002, pp. 72-75; Ostrogorski, Georg: *"Historia e Perandorisë Bizantine,"* Tirana, 2002, pp. 108-149; Jireček, Konstandin: *"Historia e serbëve,"* Part One, Tirana, 2010, pp. 87-108; Malcolm, Noel: *"Kosova një histori e shkurtër,"* Prishtina, 2001, pp. 23-42; *"Historia e Popullit Shqiptar,"* Tirana, 2002, pp. 203-209; Shufflay, Milan: *"Histori e shqiptarëve të veriut,"* Prishtina, 2009, pp. 21-35.

alliances they were subject to from the twelfth century onwards, they passed under the umbrella of the Orthodox Church, turning into its militants in the war against the Church of Rome, as occurred during Dusan's time in the 14th century, preserving that same spirit up to the present day. The other part, however, the one in the West, remained under the supervision of the Holy See, with the acceptance of Catholicism and turned into Croats or Slovenians.

This Slavic division, defined by the acceptance of Christianity and related to the middle of the 9th century and early 10th century, is of particular importance, since it actually represents the first social and political structuring at the family and tribal level within Byzantium. This structuring did not occur at the sixth century or earlier, as stated, when they penetrated from the North across the Danube, or when they joined the Huns and Goths, as in the case of their attacks on Constantinople at the time of the Huns, Avars and Persians during the time of Heraclius, or those of the Goths during Theodoric, which were supposedly linked with the beginnings of the "medieval Serbian state," which is also known as Rascian or Slavic-Rascian, appearing from the mid-13th century as the Dynasty of the Nemanjas in Rascia, a vassal of the Byzantine or Bulgarian Kingdom, of Boris and, later, of Simeon.

The "medieval state," as a large part of Serbian historians and historiography shows, is a construct of the 19th century, especially after the emergence of "Nacertanja" of Garasanin, which was dealt with later. Therefore, the titles such as "Zupanja," "sevastokrat," "despot" and "princes," which occur throughout the Orthodox Church documents, although devised for the church and placed inside "authentic chronicles" led to biased history in accordance with hegemonic Slavic-Orthodox claims,[620] and were part of the domestic hierarchy of Byzantium, divided according to the degree of self-governance, autonomies or even vassalage.

---

[620] Forging of church documents and their invention in accordance to the church needs, especially those of the Orthodox Church has been admitted by many authors, receiving them with reservation and even assessing them in a critical way. Among them is the renowned historian Konstandin Jireček, author of "History of the Serbs," in two volumes, published for the first time in German in Gotha, in 1918, expressing distrust over numerous Orthodox Church sources, including those written in Latin, such as Mario Orbini's history about the "Slav Kingdom" of the year 1601. For more see *"History of the Serbs,"* Tirana 2010, p. 245. The lack of authentic documents of Slav Orthodox churches, particularly those of Decan, Peja, and Prizren, which are inevitable reference

This matter was given greater attention because it directly affects historical relations between the descendants of the Illyrians, Arbërians (later Albanians) and Slavs in general from the Middle Ages. It must be said that since the first friction with the barbarian tribes from the North (originally with Goths, then the Huns, Avars and more recently Slavs), Illyrian-Dardanians had a dual role: as loyal defenders of the imperial space and the pervasiveness of destructive tribes, as with this they were also defending their own country, being the first to fall prey, and also, in this long and tough war they often were left alone to protect also the Christian civilization, which they had been among the first to accept.

In this dual role, Illyrian-Dardanians had their own interests. From the time of Emperor Diocletian of Illyrian origin, after his popular reforms when the Province of Illyricum was established as the eastern part of Illyricum of the Roman Empire, they saw it as their own Empire to be protected at all costs, as in so doing so they were protecting the high social, political and cultural status they had achieved from the declaration of the codices of Emperor Caracalla on free citizenry. In addition, with the well-known ecclesiastical reforms of Justinian, when the center of the Church of Illyricum passed from Thessaloniki to Justinian Prima, i.e. Dardania, and it was linked directly with the Holy See, the Western Church turned into a part of their spiritual identity, simultaneously satisfying the imperial or state identity.

That this was not a formal issue nor of political geography, although in this respect too Illyrian-Dardanians as genuine Byzantines exhibited their Western spiritual identity, was best reflected in the so-called crisis of icons, which for more than 100 years turned into a religious and political war between East and West, which consequently led to further developments of the final separation of the church, which took place in 1054. This division passed on the trunk of their ethnicity hitting them mostly, as that line turned into a line of political divisions and clashing of civilizations with serious consequences for the Albanians.

---

when it comes to "the Serbian medieval state" in Kosova, and conjuring of some of them "in accordance with the original" (though it is not known which are the original ones when they do not exist) is also admitted by Jastrebov in his work *"The History of the Serbian Church,"* published in 1879.

As is well known and discussed earlier, the Dardanian Church was within the administrative space of the Province of Illyricum, with some small exceptions. One exception was the time when the Diocese of Durres, being that Emperor Anastasius came from this city, was pretending more towards the Patriarchy of Constantinople. The church continually protected the views of the Holy See, meaning it ranked itself along the supporters of icons, not only because this was consistent with the spirit of tolerance, which stretched into the western part of the Empire, but also because freedom of creativity had its roots in pagan traditions as a consciousness of free belief rooted from the early stage of antiquity which it never abandoned even in the new circumstances.

Regarding the former, that is, defending the Empire as part of their own country and complete identification with the empire, the Illyrian-Dardanians were the first to face up to the challenge as early as 376 when the Goths were allowed to cross the Danube to get away from the Huns, settling on a strip of land between the East Rhodopes and Timok in the West, which actually featured some dividing line between Dardanians and Thracians known as Thrace, a line that Herodotus and other ancient authors also mention.[621]

Although historical sources do not say much about the temporary positioning of Goths at this corner of the Empire and the consequences this caused to that part, they were evidently able, however, as expected, to turn into a dam against the Huns or to stabilize the situation, rather into precursors of the new realities which the western part of the Empire faced, always at the expense of Illyricum, from where in the historic scene they played a special role in dealing with the future of Western civilization in that part dominated by German peoples (Franks, Longobards, and others).

Since the time of Charlemagne onwards these peoples took over the direction of what became the Holy Western Empire, with the Holy See as their ally, where papacies tried to make policy, but not similar to the patriarchs of Constantinople, turning the state government into a direct church and spiritual interest. Led by Attila, the Huns broke the Gothic cordon and in 441-442 devastated a good part of Illyricum. During their attacks they destroyed 70 cities and forced the Eastern Empire to pay a heavy tribute.[622]

---

[621] *"Historiae,"* Book V/15.
[622] Jacques, Edwin: *"Shqiptarët,"* Tirana, 2002, p. 171.

After the Huns campaign, which ended in 447 when Attila once again devastated the Balkans, the Goths turned into composing factors of the Empire, from the moment they decided to remain in it and be subject to imperial loyalty. Participation in the military and the willingness to engage in defensive fighting against the attacks of barbarian tribes coming from the North rewarded them with fertile land, which originally stretched along the course of the Danube at the Black Sea to be expanded shortly to Pannonia, where the Illyrians were expanded.

They were allowed a Kingdom of Ostrogoths, led by Theodoric, who had spent his youth at the court of Constantinople under the protection of the Emperor and was regarded as a supporter of the "middle line," that is, of an East-West balance. From his proclamation, as the King of Ostrogoths, in 489 Theodoric expanded his "kingdom" in the West at the expense of Illyricum. He was able to penetrate northern Italy and Gallia, and from there, having been the ones who were accepted by Empire in order to protect it, became its new threat.

But was this unexpected threat something that could have been foreseen? Or, was it part of an ongoing development, which appeared as though Illyricum even as a new province proclaimed by the Illyrian Diocletian and reformed by the Dardanian Constantine the Great would not be able to turn into a protective shield against the intrusions of barbarians, as it had been thought, despite the huge expenses that were made throughout the system of fortification that covered northern Illyricum (Danube) and Dardania?

Indeed, the emperors of reform, Diocletian, Constantine the Great, and Justinian, felt the risk of barbarians in the North, they differentiated them according to who could be less dangerous, and who even useful, in circumstances when the Empire was in need not only of soldiers but also of labor to work the lands, especially in its extreme parts. The need for workforce became even greater in the empire after the reforms began to form a clearer economic unity, interconnecting three continents through the Mediterranean. In these circumstances the barbarians posed a major threat, but also an opportunity to give new blood to the Empire.

Emperor Valens was among the first to allow the Goths to settle in parts of Thrace and Illyricum as they saw them different from the Huns, who came from the steppes of Mongolia and in their attacks only caused havoc and destruction. Why the Goths were seen differently certainly had to do with the tendencies of Oriental Germans towards Christianity.

Descending from the Black Sea coast, the Goths had fallen into contact with the old cult of the Greeks of Sarmatia of Crimea, where they learned the art of ornamental silversmithing, which later spread throughout Europe under the name "barbarian."[623]

As Christian-minded barbarians, Ostrogoths, followed by the Huns, were bound to Pannonia, i.e. Illyricum, while the Visigoths to Thrace beneath the Danube. It was in 276 when they left their country forever and settled in the eastern parts of the Empire. With their entry, a foreign body had pierced the Empire, which coming from the East gradually shifted toward the West, only after having measured their strength exactly where they were expected to defend the Empire in Thrace and near the walls of Constantinople, when during a rebellion they managed to kill Emperor Valens in May 378. After this victory, the buoyant Goths, still with their status of barbarians (according to both the law of Valens and that of Velenian in 370 and 375, marriages between Romans and barbarians were banned under the weight of the death penalty), attacked Illyrian lands from the East towards the South. After having plundered many cities of Dardania and Thessaly, they reached as far down as Athens and the Peloponnese and from there they also assailed Epirus. Probably if it were not for the intervention of Emperor Arcadius, who reached an agreement with them allowing them stay in the Empire under a special "federal" status, they would have continued with further destruction and mischief.

Arcadius' agreement with the Goths, which prescribed they be placed in the province of Illyricum (in the West towards Italy) was directly detrimental to Illyricum, as their leader Alaricus was given the title *"Magister militum per Illyricum"* by the Emperor. This made the Goths feel not only as new owners of a good part of Illyricum granted to them in return for becoming its defenders, but also self-mandated them to further expand what they now saw as a Gothic Kingdom, perhaps with the pretention to one day turn the Roman Empire into a Gothic Empire.

With such acts, Alaricus, who had already plundered Rome and was headed back North again, targeted Illyricum again in the North, as he aimed at connecting the space of "Romania" with that of "Gothia." This same route was followed by Alaricus' descendant, Athaulf, who took lead of the Goths in 410 after his father's death. Ravages of Goths and conjunc-

---

[623] Pirenne, Henri: *"Muhamedi dhe Karli i Madh,"* Tirana, p. 19.

tures of the emperors to settle various scores with them continued, especially as they were being threatened by the Huns, as the case with Attila's assaults and his notorious plundering from 447 to 451, launched from Thrace and up to the Thermopylae, from where they turned against Gallia and from there crossed the Rhine, destroying everything they found as far as Laurel River.

Obviously it was Aetius supported by Germans, Franks, Burgondans, and Visigoths that beat Attila, who two years later met death in the war of Troy, France. With this victory the Goths became owners of the western part of the Empire, while their allies, the German tribes, were complicit in the power-sharing chopped into many pieces, at a time when the West had but a mosaic of barbarian kings: Ostrogoths in Italy, Vandals in Africa, Suebi in Gallia, the Visigoths in Spain and to the South of the River Laurel, and Burgonda, the Rhine valley.

Obviously, it would be the Dardanian Emperor Justinian I, who militarily resolved the matter of the Gothic threat for good in 552 when his commander Narses, after profoundly defeating them, ended the Kingdom of the Ostrogoths after which they entirely disappeared from history as a nation.

The end of the Goths, as it happened, brought back brief domestic tranquility to Illyricum, but not the sure future that Emperor Justinian had wished as he was supposed to play the role of the bridge linking the West with and East. It was precisely the threat of Slavic tribes from the North, and their subsequent penetration across the Danube, that began to disturb not only the concept of Illyricum as the main province in the eastern part of the Empire, but also in maintaining internal social and political balance of the Empire, which in this part was also being challenged from the East.

After the death of Justinian and the crises that the Empire endured under the governance of Justin, Mauritius, and Heraclius, the pressure of the Slavic tribes affected the latter by using them as a "soothing" factor. Therefore, by allowing them to settle in Illyricum, the Eastern Empire won the opportunity to remove the Persian risk in the East, a move that harmed the Illyrian-Dardanians and weakened the positions of the western portion of the Empire in relation to Constantinople, paving the way for the known alliances between the Eastern Church and Heraclius, diminishing or entirely removing all Western influence.

This was best reflected by the introduction of the Greek language as the official language in the East and language of liturgies, by which Illyricum, under the administrative jurisdiction of the East and ecclesiastical jurisdiction of the Holy See, was brought to a very serious situation over which domestic and foreign fractures occurred, leading to well-known developments. On one side, the western portion of the Empire collapsed and, on the other, the churches separated with most of Illyricum belonging to the ecclesiastical jurisdiction of Constantinople, by which socially, culturally and politically it was subject to the East.

But, who were the Slavic tribes and where were the tribes coming from, those who became important factors with whom the Illyrian-Dardanians, and their later descendants, Albanians, had frictions, and sometimes fragile co-existence in the same areas, many of which the Slavs eventually succeeded in adopting, while the natives with their roots in antiquity were forced to assimilate or shrink across the gorges of the mountains and mountainous parts?

This then raises the question about the general behavior of the Slavs in Byzantium (from their introduction into service of various emperors, as it was in the beginning, to the creation of their social and political structures a little later, to the creation of their states, as in the last phase of the Eastern Empire) to continue subsequently to direct Arberian-Slavic relationships from the late Middle Ages and on, to the emergence of the Ottomans in the Balkans and the occupation of this space by them, where these peoples also behaved specifically to this factor, an issue that was dealt with later.

Initially it should be said that the Slavs appeared as blurred in history somewhat by the 6th century A.D. due to their mixing with the Avars and other nomadic peoples of Central Asia, who occasionally attacked and devastated the western parts returning again to their steppes. Some of the more visible historical evidence makes it known that the homeland of the Slavs was the barren land of River Pipet, north of the present-day Ukrainian city of Kiev,[624] although there is much more evidence that their first nest could not have been the plains, but a mountainous country, or the steppes, which produced nomadic mentalities.

Shortly afterwards, they were seen in groups spreading towards the Carpathian Mountains, from where they began to approach the Roman

---

[624] Schevill, Ferdinand: *"Ballkani – historia and qytetërimi,"* Tirana 2010, p. 73.

Empire, solely because in Thrace and Illyria the living conditions were better and, like many nomadic and barbarous tribes of the East heading towards this part, the Slavs did as well. In their early lands they were engaged in hunting and later also with cattle-breeding, but without any trend for agriculture, which apparently they acquired after settling in Illyricum and Thrace, by which the search for arable land also determined their subsequent movements to river valleys and fertile parts, mostly owned by the Illyrians.

Their internal organization was tribal, and without any strong cohesion, so that in the face of Avars, Mongols and other nomadic peoples from the East, they were not able to wage any resistance but rather joined them in their campaigns, benefited from their prey, while following the withdrawal or their defeats, as those of the Avars and Mongols. Avars were defeated by Byzantium in the 5th and 6th centuries, returning to their tribal organization in independent groups approaching the imperial territories, crossing the Danube in the North, dealing first with the Thracians and later with Dardanians and Illyrians, without excluding marginal encounters with the Greeks. Some authors say they penetrated as far as Thessaloniki and the Aegean, suffering losses, and reappearing there again after two centuries. Here, the word is about certain eastern tribes, which at times were at the service of the Empire for certain purposes, as mercenaries, but were withdrawn to the parts beyond the Danube.

One may speak only from the 7th-11th century about a permanent settlement of the Slavs in the Balkans after first being settled by Emperor Heraclius in some parts of Thrace and Illyria. A permanent presence of the Slavic tribes in the Balkans became known by their settlements as *"slavinen"* (Σκλαβιναι) in Greek and *"Sclavenia, Sclavonia"* and rarely as *"Sclavinica"* in Latin from where then begins their differentiation from what Nikephiris Bryennios called "the people of the Slavs" (Σλαβινων εσνος). In 1072, Michael Rhetor of Thessaloniki calls the Serbs *"slavinen,"* while Niketas Akominatos (ca. 1204) "the people of the Slavs" saw *"Dalmatians,"*[625] continuing with this uncertainty even later, when zupanias and principalities emerged in the beginning of national Romanticism, on the part of historians, whose aim was to conjure up by all means Serb and Croat states from the Middle Ages, seen as "princedoms" and Serb or Croat "kingdoms."

---

[625] Ibid, p. 142.

This was also the case with Dioclea (Dukla or Zeta), Zahlumia, Rascia, and others, although their affiliation, even according to some Serb objective sources continues to remain unclear,[626] although this ambiguity has been noticed by many foreign authors of scientific authority, including historians who had been engaged by Belgrade to write the history of medieval Serbia in accordance with Serbian hegemonic interests.[627]

However, these "uncertainties" were raised to the level of issues that continue to be present to this day causing troubles, not because the Slavs often "lose" their tracks among eastern nomadic peoples (Avars) and northern Goths, in whose actions they were often present, or because it is not known when they were received in the Balkans. Related to the actions of Emperor Heraclius in 626 they were granted land in order for them to become a shield against other barbarian intrusions from the North, the true role of the constituent peoples of the Byzantine Empire is being circumvented, linked to the penetration of the Barbarians which began to affect the Byzantine Empire state view only in the 9th century.

Bulgarians collapsed and only nearly three centuries later did the first Slavic social and political structures appear (zupanias, despotates and principalities), which were dependent or in the service of Byzantium from the fall of Bulgaria to the weakening (12th century) and complete collapse of Byzantium (15th century).

In this development, conditioned by the well-known Christian Crusades (seven of them) toward the East (12th -14th century) when states within states were created within Byzantium, such as the Latin Empire, Despotate of Epirus, Anjou Kingdom and Arberian Kingdom, the Arberian identity could not be excluded because they, along with zupans, princes of Rascia and Greek despots, were the Arberians, who played an important role in the delimitations between the churches and their efforts to restore the imperial power in the new circumstances.

What is even more important at this turn of four centuries (5th-9th) from the crisis and concerns that the empire faced as a result of attacks by barbarian tribes (Goths, Avars and Slavs) to the appearance of their first

---

[626] On this see: Relja Novakovic: *"Gde se nalazila Srbija od VII-XII veka;"* Stanojevic, M: "Byzant und die Serben," Belgrade, 1893; Manojlovic, S: "Das Adriatische Künstengebiet im 9 Jahr," Belgrade, 1902; Svejović, Dragan: *"Balkanski istoćnjaci Milana Budimira,"* Belgrade, 2001; Grujič, Radoslav: "Legenda iz vremena cara Samuila o poreklu naroda," (Glasnik skopskog naučnog društva), 13/1943.

[627] See Jiriček, Konstandin: *"Historia e serbëve,"* Tirana, 2010.

social and political structures, although those among the most primitive ones, such as tribes and other forms within the empire, is the process of rounding a certain Byzantine identity of its founders: Latin, Illyrian-Dardanians, and Greeks as a social, political and spiritual identity. Illyrian-Dardanians benefited the most, since it was in harmony with their ethnic-social identity dedicated to the new imperial edifice, and the emergence of barbarians and their subsequent settlement in the parts of the Empire.

The issue opens the question of the behavior of the Slavs during the time they were settled in parts of the empire, first in the Thrace and Illyria, to their introduction and involvement in the social, cultural and spiritual life, a time that began in the 12th century continuing in the 7th and 9th centuries to be somehow rounded up in the 11th century with the emergence of zupanias, principalities, and later their states, sometimes interim ones, always within the Byzantine space.

Some historians saw them outside of Byzantium, marked in various wars with the central government of Constantinople, which were mostly in the nature of their involvement in permanent conflicts between the eastern and western churches for control over the imperial space rather than any national state autonomy, as they are customarily described in the views of the 19th century, which would affect the future Balkan state political map.

Indeed, the first traces of Slavic tribes' participation in the social and economic life of the country are found in the context of the existing ones, such as the *themes* of Durres and Dioclea, found also in Bosnian "krainas" and in Zakhumina. In the first two Slavs are mentioned as separate tribes.[628] In Dioclea, in the year 996, a certain "nobleman," Vladimir, is mentioned as a Slav, after it had been occupied in the same year by Samuel. In Dioclea, during and after the Bulgarian conquests several zupans were noticed, such as Vladislav (1074), who had several relations with Durres, then Stefan Vojislav, Mihal, Vojislav's son, who had a correspondence with Pope Gregory VII (1077) to continue so with Vlakan, second son of Nemanja, who appeared as the prince of Dioclea.[629]

These data are unclear, being but church documents many of which are forged or fabricated in accordance with the political needs of the time, as certain documents of Diocletian "kings" do not exist, as they never

---

[628] For more See: Jeriček, Konstantin: "*Historia e serbëve,*" Tirana 2010, pp. 215-220.
[629] Ibid, p. 245.

existed, except for earls, nobles, zupans, and others, associated with this important part, where more than anywhere else eastern and western interests crisscrossed, as economic and spiritual relations were also interconnected.[630]

While the documents of this nature were written in Slavic they were only kept from the year 1180. They too appear flawed, confusing the titles attributed to simple zupans, as were those recognized locally either as leaders of a tribe as "princes" and "kings" or even according to Church affiliation and pertaining to their scribes.

The confusion found support in the chronicle of Dioclea, a priest called Dukljanin (Pope Dukljanin in Slavic), a Slavic priest from Ragusa who brought a semi-literary tale about the appearance of Slavs in these parts, rather than a document of merit, which, however, was commonly used by many historians, regardless of the fact that literary narratives do not always represent complete historical evidence.[631]

Of these stories, such as that of Dioclea and Popov (the first written document in Slavic from the year 1180),[632] the highest titles of Slavs found in Dioclea, Zahlumnia, and later Rascia, are those of zupans, who appeared as leaders of communities or tribes, which only from the 12th century and onwards were recognized as dynasties, while their dynasty leaders, dependent on Byzantium, or as vassals of Venice and others in the West were dealt with later.

---

[630] Ibid, p. 246.

[631] *"Letopis Popa Dukljanina"* – Belgrade, 1971. This refers to a rather literary than historical work more by a priest from Dioclea, called Pop Dukljanin, published first in Latin under the title *"Presbyteri Diocleatis Regunum Slavorum."* In 1601, Mavro Orbini published it for the first time in Italian "Il regoni de gli Slavi." This work served numerous historians as historical material, treating this rather literary tale as a "document," which in most part does not address the factual data of the time or history. This literary construct, together with that of Mavro Orbini "Il regoni de gli Slavi," which is also a literary fantasy liaisoned with some facts devised for the purpose of the church, turned into the main "source" of the largest part of Serbian historiography nourishing also some foreign authors, unable to examine these documents otherwise but accept them as served by Serb historians of the last century. Orbini and Pop Dukljanin, although being anathemized in time as inventions, continue to remain particular historical references because of the failure of objective scientists to duly denounce them, finding it difficult to bring down the stereotypes they have created during the last two centuries.

[632] Jiriček, Konstandin: *"Historia e serbëve,"* Tirana 2010, p. 247.

This passage, dealing with less than a clear view of Slavic society within the new relations from the time they were accepted by Emperor Heraclius and their settlement in the central parts of the Balkans as citizens of the Empire, opened the process of factorization of the Slavic element in the part of Illyria (the space around the Danube to the Alps in the north and central part of Dalmatia to the Adriatic coast in the West), where they were concentrated until the early ninth century, organized in tribes and led by pagan customs.

Other external factors were crucial that created conditions for radical changes in the Empire so that its parts (West and East) took opposite directions, resulting in their full separation, while its founding peoples (Illyrian-Dardanians, Latins and Greeks) took on different sides. Latins went West, Greeks went East, and Illyrians remained in neutral grounds swept in the vortex line in an environment in which each side saw its own beginning and the end of the other, while there was no political or spiritual clarity and constant clashes and wars with dire consequences.

As stated, the external factors, Arabs from the southeast and the Mediterranean and Bulgarians from northeast accelerated the inevitable division of the Empire, while the remaining Byzantium circumstances created eventually turned the Greeks into spiritual factors, turning the Slavs into the main political factor, while the population of Illyricum, which from the late Middle Ages was recognized as Arber (from *Alban* to *Arban, Arvanë, Rabanë, Arvanites*) was subject to further partition, assimilation and reduction starting from the central part of the Peninsula (Dardania), maintaining its ethnicity in the South, in Macedonia, Thessaly and the Peloponnese to the Aegean islands.

The western part extending from the Ionian and Adriatic seas, north near Ragusa, including Shkodra with Dioclea (Zeta), the last capital of the Illyrian kings and the first space to be included in the Roman Empire, turned into an arena of fierce social and political encounters between the Slavic lords and invaders, primarily those appearing as Hasians (from Rascia), in which local zupans and despots crossed swords in their efforts to break away from an exhausted Byzantium, or find protection by it against others, an issue that was addressed shortly thereafter.

It should be emphasized that with this development by external factors (the Arab – affecting the western part of Illyricum as far as Italy to become fully and permanently detached from the entirety, and the Bulgarian – spurring the Slavs to further invade their space in the East from

Thrace and in the West by subjugating Dalmatia and the entire portion of northern Adriatic), Illyrian-Dardanians - territorially, but also spiritually – were excluded from the Western Empire.

Within Byzantium, they began to be marginalized on an account-settling dime on which Balkan princes respectively broke alliances against Byzantium, and broke Byzantine agreements with various contenders to maintain internal relations, and sometimes setup alliances and internal links with external ones, such as those starting from the Christian Crusades onward through to the final collapse of Byzantium.

However, in this historical development, the oldest people of this area and most deserving of Byzantium had no more supporters nor potential allies, but only opponents and oppressors. This severe squalor was of a social, political and cultural nature, resulting precisely from the obliteration of the concept of the Byzantine Empire in the new circumstances, that broke almost all the natural rules of an inevitable end being among the most typical on the passageway from the Middle Ages to modernity.

Despite this, one may say that the emergence of Islam and the Arab factor (as external), on one side, and the Bulgarian factor (as internal), on the other, were the main drivers of this historical development, outside of which can be explained neither the fate of Illyricum nor Slavic penetrations and Slavization of a substantial portion of the eastern wing of the Empire, conditioning the West-East allocation, as they conditioned what is called Byzantinism of the West (according to the concept of Justinian) and the "Greekizing" of the East (the model of Heraclius).

It was exactly Heraclius, who after the victory over the Persians in the East was left with the impression that perhaps he permanently got rid of the Persian threat, that almost suddenly faced Islam, before which the Empire was withdrawn, losing possessions in Africa, and being threatened on its holdings in Italy, as the Arabs had settled in Sicily, while it was not able to defend from within because the Visigoths inside were destroyed. This situation drew the attention of both Heraclius and the entire Empire suggesting that Islam and with it the Arabs had already affected the transformation of global equilibrium that had been imposed by them.

But was this confrontation of Heraclius with the Arabs quite unexpected as the opponent was unknown, or was it an intentional omission? This, however, is best explained by the appearance of Islam as a new factor, turning shortly into a world factor, which, just like Christianity, was used for imperial purposes, but this time in an opposite direction from Christianity.

Truly, the Empire had never paid attention to the Arabian Peninsula nor had it ever noticed what was going on with Islam, which was turning into a great power setting in motion social issues, as Christianity had done six centuries before with its emergence, becoming an existential challenge for the Roman Empire. In these circumstances, its entire attention had turned to Syria sufficing itself to protecting that country from the nomadic tribes of the desert people, by building a wall, as in Bretagne, as it had built one against Pictes invasions.[633] But, this *limes*, which were built in Syria, had nothing comparable to them, built on the Rhine or Danube.[634]

The Persian Empire acted similar to the Byzantine Empire, as no one felt the need for protection from some wandering Bedouins of the Peninsula, whose state of civilization was tribal, whose religious beliefs had barely overcome fetishism, and who spent time fighting each other and looting caravans, wandering from South to North. Busy with their conflicts, neither the Roman nor the Persian Empire felt the importance of propaganda, with which Muhammad, through a confusing tribal war, gave his people a religion, which he had designed, and together with that religion a ruler, who according to some assessments of the time, Islam was not seen otherwise but as some schism of a previous nature.[635]

However, no more than two years after the death of Prophet Muhammad, in 614, did Byzantium feel the first fist of the Arabs on both sides, losing the provinces it had just restored from Persia. Heraclius celebrated the return of the Holy Cross to Constantinople with such a triumph, seeing it as a world "triumph" saw that the great stress had exhausted the empire in all directions. Therefore, in the year 635, the Arabs, marching under the banner of Allah, conquered Damascus in 636 at the Battle of Yaramak with Syria falling entirely into their hands.[636]

Only after that happened did Byzantium realize the Arab danger. Heraclius attempted to remove any disagreement he had with the Western Empire to the favor of Franks, Longobards, and other German kingdoms, which had begun to turn into full lords of the Western Empire, turning Illyricum further into a hostage of the Slavs.

---

[633] Pirenne, Henri: *"Muhamedi dhe Karli i Madh,"* Tirana 2006, p. 124.
[634] Ibid, p. 124.
[635] Ibid, p. 124.
[636] Ostrogorski, Georg: *"Historia e Perandorisë Bizantine,"* Tirana 2002, p. 73.

Strengthened by lightning successes, the Arabs, who had already strengthened the navy, focused on destroying Constantinople in order to become the lords of the global empire. Evidently, they had acquired the same ideas from Christianity and were following suit. In the year 674, the decisive battle for the Byzantine capital began, and the Arab fleet entered the waters of the Bosphorus and appeared before the walls of Constantinople.

After four years, the battle, ending in a deep defeat for the Arabs was of great importance, as Islam failed to defeat Christianity at its castle; it did not remove the Arab threat to Byzantium and the Western Empire and with it the rapid penetration of Islam in different directions.

Realizing what was possible at that time and what was not, the Arabs instead remained attached to the walls of Constantinople taking them one by one. In 688 it was Jerusalem's turn to open its gates, while in Asia they had conquered Persia and Mesopotamia with Egypt waiting for its turn.

This spread continued without a break, flooding over Byzantine possessions in North Africa from where the Arabs headed towards the Mediterranean to master it almost entirely, especially after being deployed in Spain and southern Italy.

The disembarking of Arabs in Spain and the Mediterranean brought about that big breakaway between the Eastern and Western Empire, as the one in the European part, in the West, brought other factors to the stage, such as Charles the Great, while in the East, the continued weakening of Byzantium, too, after the Slavs, who were already accepted in Illyricum acting there to the detriment of the indigenous population makers of the Empire, introduced eastern barbarian peoples into the game. First came the Bulgarians, a Turkish people, which greatly flooded the area causing Byzantium its first great historic loss, being forced to accept an "empire" within its own space and even pay a tribute in gold, with the highest price. From that time onward, however, it became subject to internal vibrations, giving into exhaustion, eventually causing its collapse.[637]

Viewed from a social, political and spiritual standpoint, the emergence of the Arab factor with Islam as its shield spread tremendously, gaining ground and winning over other peoples within the Western part. With the Arab domination in the Mediterranean it was physically disconnected from the East, stirring up the spirit of a general social emancipa-

---

[637] Ibid, p. 82.

tion (as the Arabs had given importance to highlighting the knowledge of ancient teachings that Christianity had anathemized for centuries), while in the East it had been so far excluded from the impact of Mediterranean basin.

Byzantium was a Greek empire that leaned on Illyricum as a center linking the East and West of the Empire, although that too was losing importance in line with the strengthening of the Slavic factor in it.

Against these circumstances, the western identity in the western part of the West was greatly stimulated in competition with the Arab mentality and Islam, while Byzantium was forced to defend itself with the spread of Christianity among the barbarian peoples. Slavs and Russians had already surrounded Arab and Turkish invasions with Islam, and confronted the West, which made Catholicism a bulwark against Islam. A new civilization identity was seen as the only salvation for survival, considering Slavs and Russians could be used for some link with the West.

They shared the same Christian flag for a long time with various emblems, the eastern eagle with its yellow background, once the furious penetrations of the Ottomans commenced in its main part, not hesitating to enter into open or sealed alliances against the Catholic eagle; with a red background, opening new avenues to the Ottoman penetrations in the West, although they had to cross through the East. These were movements with very absurd actions, as on one side the West benefited from the Arab penetrations by cutting off from the eastern Byzantinism to build its civilization identity in the West in order to protect itself from the Arabs. On the other hand, Byzantium made efforts to protect itself from internal demolition but also from the risk of renewed domination from the West, linking alliance with the Russians, but also with the Ottomans, without excluding the Islamic factor accompanying it, viewing it as an ally in the war against Catholicism!

The first Byzantine attempts to turn towards Russia, ending in the Christianization of Russians and their incorporation under the Patriarchate of Constantinople, were made in a manner beyond the rules of friendship, under the circumstances of a Byzantine threat coming suddenly from the North, when the Emperor returned from a recently launched campaign against the Arabs in 860 and was forced to turn back after he received news that the Russians had appeared before the walls of Constantinople. They had already devastated the area when the emperor was able to break their siege and adjourn. This defeat brought the two empires with different ambitions closer (the new with occupation purposes and the old in order to survive), as the Patriarch of Byzantium had understood that the conversion to Christianity and the involvement of the Russian people in the Byzantine sphere of influence was the best means of removing the danger that threatened the empire from that side.

Two years later the Russians accepted their inclusion into Christianity. The spread of Christianity among the Slavic peoples passed through an internal competition between the Patriarch of Constantinople and the Holy See for the full benefit of it, as they were already spreading out from Illyricum to Moravia and Czechia at an interim stage of passing from paganism to monotheism.

The Greek Church was included in this missionary work accepting an invitation by the Prince of Moravia, Rastislaos, who asked Constantinople for Christian missionaries to help him spread Christianity in these parts. The reasons why the Prince of Moravia asked for Byzantine missionaries were political ones, as he sought a counterweight to the danger of a Franco-Bulgarian siege. The fact that the political leadership of the Byzantine Church entrusted this important mission to two brothers from Thessaloniki, Constantine (Cyril) and Methodius and that it preached the new religion in the Slavic lands in the Slavic language, is indicative of its vision, to spread Christianity in the large Slavic world outside the Empire in a rather tempting way for the barbarian peoples, who were not able to shift from one spiritual mood to another in Latin, but rather in their native language.[638]

The Eastern Church was much more practical in this direction, compared with that of Rome using Latin as its main code of liturgy and script. In line with this attitude, being more political than religious, but by all means emancipating, Constantine (Cyril) created a Slavic alphabet, a so-called Glagolic alphabet inserting thereafter the translation of the Holy Scripture into Slavic (in the Slavic-Macedonian dialect).

The mission of Cyril and Methodius and their activities in favor of the spread of Christianity among the Slavs touched Illyricum. As the Bulgarians were mixed with the Slavs acquiring their language and assimilating into Slavs, part of southern Illyricum was attacked by the Bulgarians, who devastated everything. On this occasion, Boris of Bulgar-

---

[638] Ibid, p. 161.

ia, after returning to Orthodoxy, founded the Bulgarian Archbishopric in Ohrid in 870, where brothers Cyril and Methodius were seen working.[639]

Despite the missionary work of Cyril and Methodius, as they left behind traces of culture related to the South Slavs and the West, the history of the conversion of religion from Slavs was accompanied with many uncertainties. Some may be known, especially those dealing with the big race of the Greek and Latin Church, being close to the Slavs, who tried to win over new believers under their influence. Therefore, many Slavic princes and leaders accepted the new religion, not by divine promise, nor because they were spiritually changed by them, but rather by appropriate political allegiances that could be created by accepting the new religion.

However, the spread of Christianity among the Slavs was incited by the Bulgarian element, succeeding briefly to turn the barbaric people coming from the North, after accepting the Slavic language and Christianity, even formally at first, into a very important factor with which the fate of Byzantium was linked. Their arrival and settling in the Balkans also led further to an inclusion of Illyricum and the furrowed part of Arbërians in a social and political development characterized by a fierce struggle for power among the Bulgarians, seeking to expand and dominate in the Balkans and Byzantium trying to maintain and also further transform the administrative and social identity within the political realities of a Slavic-Orthodox world, which by now was entirely overseen by the Church of Constantinople, which was increasingly turning towards the East and against the West.

As seen in this development it was exactly the Byzantine administrative structures, *themes*, as an organizational form, which had originated from the time of Emperor Heraclius onward, (through which, the power of the former rulers of the time of Justinian was replaced by the military-administrative governance, which supervised the center and had to be strictly supervised), that forewarned the restoration of the local government and its use for generating autonomous state structures up to independent ones, exhibited through zupanias and principalities, which eventually led to the weakening, dissipation and fall of Byzantium.

---

[639] Jacques, Edwin: "*Shqiptarët,*" Tirana, p. 179.

Illyricum and Bulgarians

Bulgarians emerged as a Euro-Asian race phenomenon, mingling with the Slavs in the ninth century and acquiring their language. – The first Bulgarian conquest in 679 was recorded in the territories between the Danube and the Balkan mountains. – Heavy defeat of Constantine IV by Bulgarians beyond the Danube led to the invasion of Varna. – The first Bulgarian state under the leadership of King Boris (853-879). – Simeon (897-923) strengthened the Bulgarian Kingdom turning it independent from Byzantium, which included many parts of Illyricum and Dardania. – The emergence of Bogumil at the time of the Bulgarian Kingdom and the expansion of its influence in the West. – At the Seventh Council of Constantinople the occupied territories of Illyricum passed under the jurisdiction of the Patriarchy of Constantinople ending the mentioning of Illyricum. – The last Bulgarian King, Ivan Vladislav (1015-1018), lost his life in Durres in an attack on the city.

Besides the recognized penetrations (invasions) of Slavic barbarian tribes from the North, pouring down from the Carpathians and mostly accompanied by Avars, Huns and others across the Danube, in order that at the time of Emperor Heraclius a part of them remained permanently in Thrace and Illyricum as a "bulwark against the Avars," however, about the end of the 7th century, another barbarian people crossed the Danube assailing the Balkans with plundering purposes. These people were called Bulgarian and were tied to the terrible Huns and Avars.

Evidently, the first group of Bulgarians that crossed the Danube in 679, managed to occupy the territory between the Danube and the Balkan Mountains. Initially, the Byzantine Empire did nothing to prevent this, as it was involved in war with the Arabs. But shortly after that being able to sign a peace treaty with the Arabs, Emperor Constantine IV understood the new threat coming from the North and began to deal with the Bulgarians before they crossed the Danube.

Indeed, the Bulgarian or Onogur-Bulgarian Kingdom, with which the Byzantine Empire had established friendly relations at the time of Heraclius, was put in motion toward the West out of pressure coming from the Hazars, a people that was becoming increasingly dominant in the central part between the Carpathians and the Ukraine. Therefore, a large group of Bulgarians, under the leadership of Asparukh, moved towards the West appearing at the seventies at the mouth of the Danube. Emperor Constantine IV came out to meet the Bulgarians beyond the Danube, but his army was confined to marshland, becoming prey to Bulgarian attacks and was defeated. Therefore, the failed expedition of Constantine IV, unprepared for a fight with an opponent who still struggled with the logic of quick plundering and unpredictable movements, did nothing but open the way to the Bulgarians in making the last step, as they crossed the Danube and conquered Varna.[640]

In these circumstances, the Bulgarian state was founded, based on the southern region of the Danube (called Moesia in Roman times). It began to expand towards the South and West as much as space allowed. But the greatest power of Bulgarians increased after they began mixing with the Slavic population appropriating their language, and starting from the mid-9th century they were called a Slavic people. The truth is that a thorough mixing of the Bulgarian and Slavic population is a mixture between an Indo-European people (Slavs) and another non-Indo-European people, or between a white race and the yellow Tatar-Mongol race. Therefore, the Bulgarian state of Asian origin became a Slavic state, thus becoming the first Slavic state in the Balkans.[641]

The Bulgarian state in the Balkans was not only a mixture of different Euro-Asian races. From the early acceptance of Christianity, it sought to strengthen and even provide a crosslink between Rome and Constantinople, exactly what Illyricum had between the eastern and western parts since the time of Diocletian and that of Justinian, when the equilibrium of the Empire was being preserved or tested. Boris, who was recognized as king by Byzantium, after Bulgaria accepted Christianity and became a Christian state, built a partially independent church from the Constantinople Patriarchate, as this was a new phenomenon that Byzantium needed.

Besides the Eastern Church, Boris established parallel connections with the Church of Rome. To prevent any connection with Rome, the Church of Constantinople allowed them their own church, organized with archbishops and bishops. Despite this, Boris frequently attempted to introduce the Western church into the game in order to win a special status in the West as well to a dual benefit. When this did not succeed, he turned entirely to the Greek influence and he sent his son Simeon to

---

[640] Ostrogorski, Georg: "*Historia e Perandorisë Bizantine,*" Tirana 2002, p. 83.
[641] Schevill, Ferdinand: "*Ballkani – historia dhe qytetërimi,*" Tirana, 2002, p. 91.

Constantinople to get Greek education, after which he replaced his father as he was drawn into a monastery and died soon thereafter. Obviously, Simeon (897-923) succeeded in strengthening the Bulgarian Kingdom in the Balkans and turning it independent from Byzantium.

As such, the Bulgarian Kingdom reached the Illyricum area, extending its conquests in Dardania and Macedonia, which is known were being administered from the East but were under the jurisdiction of the Holy See. Although this condition had already ended with the Eighth Council of Constantinople of 870, when the occupied areas of Illyricum were transferred to the jurisdiction of the Patriarchy of Constantinople, the Bulgarians, however, showed willingness to preserve the western identity of the Dardanian Church, if this would turn to their benefit in their relations with the Holy See, which wanted to maintain them as separate.

This would not happen and King Boris eventually turned east; the behavior of Bulgarians on the issue was in accordance with that policy, so that the center of the state and the church along with it shifted to Illyricum, in Ohrid, where the center of the Holy Church during the last three centuries had been. So, what Justiniana Prima was once for the Holy See, the Ohrid Diocese was for the Bulgarians.

Before that happened, King Boris (852-879) had to extend his power in these parts, which he did by including in his conquests the belt between the Devoll and Vjosa rivers. So, the castles of Devoll and Puleropolis (Berat) became the bases of the Bulgarian rule in these parts.[642]

In Simeon's time Bulgaria reached its widest scope in Illyricum and Dardania. With the exception of Durres and Shkodra, Simeon occupied the entire territories of southern Illyricum. He took possession of Vlora in the South and a good part of the Theme of Nicopolis.

With ambitions to extend the power to as far as Byzantine bordered with the Western Empire, beyond the Western Illyricum, Simeon originally brought other Slavic tribes under his crown, who had begun to form a principality in Zahlumia, connecting them to Croats, but failed to go further in that direction, as in 924 he lost a war with Tomislav of Croatia.

As noted earlier, the Bulgarian conquests in Illyricum (in Dardania and a good part of Macedonia), influenced the extent of a Slavic-Byzantine culture, which was utterly prejudiced against the Catholic West, to which its church belonged from the time of Constantine the Great, and

---

[642] For more see: Jiriček, Konstadin: "*Historia e serbëve*," Tirana, 2010, p. 256; "*Historia e Popullit Shqiptar*," Tirana, 2002, p. 218.

especially from the time of Justinian, who bound the Bishopric of Illyricum in Justinian Prima, as a vicariate, with the Holy See, and as such it functioned for more than three centuries. Its main promoters, brothers Cyril and Methodius and missionary Clement of Ohrid, who in the area of Ohrid, Korce, Devoll, Berat, and beyond towards Macedonia and Dardania, worked for years to establish Slavic schools and churches. This activity was made possible as Bulgaria turned Ohrid into the center of an independent Bulgarian patriarchate.[643]

When speaking of spiritual issue and issues that were set in motion by the emergence of Bulgarian rule in Illyricum and other parts of Dardania all the way to the South, it should be said that the full involvement of the Church Dioceses of Illyricum, which until then was under the jurisdiction of the Holy See, now under the jurisdiction of the Church of Constantinople, brought about the emergence of the sect Bogomils, a fierce enemy of the Church, by the decision of Eighth Council of 830.[644]

The doctrine of its founder, Pop Bogomil, was justified by the Messalian doctrine and especially of Pavlicans, who, after being massively moved to Thrace by the government of Byzantium, lived in close contact with the Slavic population of Bulgaria and Macedonia. Further spreading of the Bulgarian Empire in the Balkans, especially towards the West, provided Bogumilism with an opportunity to spread to these parts. Therefore, in the space of today's Bosnia, they created a powerful center from where teachings dispersed towards the West and South. The Bogumil Center was maintained until the arrival of the Ottomans in these parts where many believers of this sect, refusing to fall under the pressure of

---

[643] Ibid, p. 218.

[644] *Bogumilism* represented a dualistic doctrine, according to which the world was run by two principles: *Good* (God) and *Evil* (Satan) and the struggle between these two opposing powers determines all the events of the world and every human life. The entire visible world is the work of Satan, tempted by Evil. Like their predecessors of the Orient, Bogumils propagated a religious life purely spiritual and a strictly ascetic lifestyle. They firmly rejected any foreign cult, every church rite and all church body. The Bogumil rebellion against the official was at the same time a rebellion against the existing secular order itself, which had found its strongest spiritual support in the Church. The Bogumil Movement was an expression of protest against the government, the powerful and the rich. Bogumilism grew deep roots in Bulgaria, especially in Macedonia. It had great influence far away from the borders of the Bulgarian Empire appearing in different names in Byzantium, Bosnia, Italy, and in the southern part of the Kingdom of France as well.

Christian dogma, from which they departed long ago, accepted Islam, and joined the Shiites, as a belief that offered them the opportunity to preserve the spiritual philosophy of duality that could be plugged through eastern mysticism and Western philosophy, which maintained the concepts of war and of good and evil.

Despite the Bogomil sect and their impact, following its submission to the Byzantine Empire, when King Samuel (976-1014) came to the Bulgarian throne, under his rule, the center of the Bulgarian state moved from the East, Preslavia, to Prespa and Ohrid, where its Diocese was. It was the first time that the territories of Illyricum, under the Byzantine *themes*: Durres and Nicopolis, became involved in the long Bulgarian-Byzantine conflict with serious consequences for the country, as they turned into polygons of wars resulting in widespread destruction, and above all social and political uncertainty.

Aware of the importance of this founding factor of Byzantium, which still maintained its role as a hub between East and West, Samuel not only made no attempt to overthrow the military-administrative structure occupied by him, but it was maintained and even strengthened. Evidently, in Dioclea he transferred power to Prince John Vladimir, offering him his daughter's hand, Kozara. In Durres, after the year 997, Samuel had not affected the privileges and power of the nobles of the city, represented by the powerful family of Krisilis, John Krisilis, *proteuon* of the city. In the region of Vlora and Berat, Samuel entrusted the command to the progeny of a local noble family, Elinger Freng. He acted similarly in Devoll, Kolonja, Vagenetis, Scupi, Naissus, Ulpiana, and elsewhere.

"Allies" that Bulgarians found at the *Theme* of Durres, Nicopolis, and in other parts all the way from Dardania to Dioclea, even despite the titles and properties maintained or acquired by them, would not prevent them from being viewed as permanent, as their rule did not show signs of helping a social and political development consistent with the early emergence of feudalism.

Rather, the noble prodigies and families, which had been part of a dividing but also conciliatory space between East and West, yielding economic benefits (free trade with both sides) but also an exchange of ideas and other values, in circumstances when they realized they were unable to overcome the suffocation, soon joined the Byzantine movement to restore its power in these parts. The restoration of power had begun with the appearance of Basilius II (976-1025), who was nicknamed "killer of

Bulgarians" due to the severity and sadism he used against Bulgarian soldiers in his wars with them, when he took the eyes out of several thousand soldiers who were captured in Macedonia, sending them to King Samuel in Perlep, who, horrified by the sight, died. This marked the beginning of the dissolution of the Bulgarian Empire in Thrace, Illyricum, and Dardania.

And, as in an inevitable prediction of the fate of Illyricum - for better, as happened to King Boris on his rise, or for worse, as happened to the last king, Ivan Vladislav (1015-1018), this happened to the Bulgarian Kingdom as it was trying to restore the Bulgarian hegemony in its parts. The last Bulgarian king was killed in Durres in February 1018, during an attack on the city. The Emperor of Byzantium, Basilius II headed from Durres to Ohrid, the first Bulgarian spiritual capital from where he quenched one by one all the hearths of Bulgarian resistance at the top of Tomorri, Vlora, and Thessaly.[645]

Although ruining the Bulgarian Kingdom in Illyricum and Dardania, where it had reached its peak and experienced its inevitable downfall by failing to become a factor of balance between East and West, intending instead to become a rival of the West aimed at eradicating Byzantium, or rather at least turning its position into a vassal, Basilius II, while newly restoring Byzantine power in these parts, used caution in preserving the mechanisms of local administration it had from the time of Heraclius and Leo III in this part of Illyricum, such as *themes*, even increasing them in harmony with the power they represented in the strategic parts for Byzantium from where the Empire aimed at restoring the power lost by the Bulgarians.

Therefore, besides the existing *themes*, that of Durres and Nicopolis, Basilius II established that of Scupi, which, as a strategist, he entrusted to the Illyrian patrician David Arianiti, who was one of the most prominent commanders of the Emperor against the Bulgarians. This theme, which included the central parts identical in importance to those in the provinces of Dardania, established by Emperor Justinian, rose to the rank of *catepanate* and later that of the *duchy* at which time the one in Durres was also raised, retaining the status of the most strategical base of the Byzantine Empire on the Adriatic coast.

---

[645] *"Historia e Popullit Shqiptar,"* Volume I, Tirana 2002, p. 219.

Besides the Illyrian themes, Basilius II began organizing other western parts of the Empire to gain them over in the service of restoring the Byzantine influence in these parts and preventing various influences, especially those caused by the appearance of the Arabs and Turks, acting in the East, but emerging also in the Mediterranean and even the Adriatic. In accordance with these goals, Basilius II formed on Bulgarian lands, in the Danube downstream, the theme of *Paristirion* or *Paradunavon* with Silistria as its capital, on the banks of the Danube. This theme later rose to a *catepanate* and further to a *duchy*. Even the limited territory from the Danube and Sava was organized based on a theme with Sirmium as its center. Zadar on the Adriatic coast to the North and Ragusa in the South formed the Theme of Dalmatia.[646]

The territories of Dioclea, Zahlumia, Rascia, and Bosnia were not organized in themes, but along with Croatia, remained under local princes forming unreal provinces, zupanias (family and tribal-based local governments bound together by one or more of them), and vassals to the Byzantine Empire.

Evidently, two of these themes, Dalmatia in the North and Scupi in the central part of Dardania, were of particular interest, as they were outside the known form of themes, with an experience of over a hundred years represented in these parts. Instruments of the central government at the local level, directly related to each other, the announced the emergence of local dynasty formations. This went as far as vassal principalities, which, in the new circumstances, following the arrival of Slavs and their settlement in these parts, highlighted new internal realities of both the indigenous population and invaders. Out of these positions their fight for or against Byzantium, waged with rigor, and resulted in disintegration processes, which continued for two centuries.

From Themes to the First Arberian Principalities

Return of the Byzantine power in the Bulgarian occupied areas followed by the creation of the two other themes in Illyricum and Dardania. Besides those of Durres and Nicopolis, Theme of Dalmatia on the Adriatic and Theme of Scupi in Dardania were established. – Basilius

---

[646] Ostrogorski, Georg: "Historia e Perandorisë Bizantine," Tirana 2002, p. 206.

II allowed for local despots of the Slavs as their forms of autonomous organization, such as that of Rascia, Dioclea, Bosnia, and Zakhumia. – After the arrival of Emperor Constantine IX Monohomos (1042-1055) the role of farmer-soldier (stratiote) began to weaken and that of feudal aristocracy strengthened. – Military strategists of Themes of Durres and Nicopolis against Constantinople. – Alex Comnenus and the revival of Byzantium. – The first appearance of name Arvanites by Byzantine chronicler, Mikhail Atalias in 1072 and the country Arvanon by Anna Comnenus, daughter of Emperor Alex Comnenus. – At this time Kruja was called Arbanum *by Latins and the Bishop of Kruja "episcopus Arbanennsis."*

The return of Byzantium in its space after the long Bulgarian rule, which, although gone, left behind some new social and cultural realities that affected further developments, among which one should mention the seal of the Eastern Church sited throughout the country after its transfer to the jurisdiction of the Patriarch of Constantinople, and the forced alteration of the ethnic structure in some parts of Illyricum by Slavic settlements, where they turned into feudal lords after having acquired large possessions.

However, with the new organization of themes in Illyricum and Dardania (the Danube and Skopje) and allowing zupanias or local despots, as were those of Dioclea, Zakhumia, Bosnia, and Rascia, opened the issue of a rivalry between the local autonomous rule, based on despots, carriers of which were Slavic settlers, mostly Illyricized or mixed with them, and the local government related to the central government (Illyrians, Latins, and Greeks), a rivalry resulting in the weakening and eventual fall of the Empire.

Actually, accepting a dual form of the country's administrative organization with centralized themes and despots (local self-government), soon brought them into conflicts, as the situation here was not one of the "mixing" of competences among *themes* representing the local government connected to the central and local autonomies, but rather of social changes of the ruling class whose power was measured not in administrative terms, but in property. Strategists managing the *themes*, although senior officers of merit in maintaining the stability of the country, began to lose power and prestige against local feudal lords and despots who operated independently within their feud, by which they became rich fast emerging as a true factor of power.

The reason for this major change was the social relations within the Byzantine Empire, connected with the development of feudal relations, which produced different consequences, affecting the whole society, especially the middle and lower class, which was being dispossessed, with their properties being transferred to the hands of the great feudal lords. One may say that after the death of Emperor Basilius II and the end of the Macedonian dynasty, with Constantine IX Monohomos (1042-1055) the era of small property characterized by the *farmer-soldier* (stratiot) ended.

This form of property, based on the concept of *themes*, where the leading factors were local soldiers, during the last two centuries, was in fact a mainstay of Byzantine power in the parts of Illyricum and Eastern provinces, where forms of administrative autonomies of the provinces initiated by Emperor Diocletian and continued by Constantine the Great achieving their highest level with Justinian's reforms, were replaced by a central military surveillance, while during the Bulgarian occupation, when violent changes took place among the population (settling of the Slavs in some parts as well as their economic enforcement to the disadvantage of the natives through properties acquired by invading wars), it began to lose its importance.

Aware of this new reality, Emperor Basilius, despite restoring former *themes,* that of Durres and Nicopolis and adding two more: that of Skopje and Dalmatia, raising them a bit later to the level of *catepanates* and *ducates*, accepted local despots, such as those of Dioclea, Zakhumia, Bosnia, and Rascia, with a mixed population dominated by Slavs who had been awarded land from the time of Heraclius becoming richer during the Bulgarian invasion. This opened a rivalry among local autonomies, which although raised to the level of *dukates*, deepened the gap of differences between local feudal lords and the military and the noble class, backed by the Byzantine Empire and with Byzantine resolve.

This removed the center of power from the existing factors to the others, who were subject to neither command nor centralized management, but to economic power, sucking it to the detriment of the impoverished social strata.

This pyramid-shaped development was reflected in the highest imperial echelons and structures, shaking the current military government from that of the feudal and increasingly bureaucratic aristocracy of

Constantinople, which needed finance acquired from the rich feudal lords. While this change was immediately reflected in the layers of farmers, soldiers (stratiotes), who were not only being impoverished, but were also losing their social significance, something that came to be understood as a factor able to discriminate the local and imperial defense, the military layer and its favoring of the feudal factor by Bulgarian-Slavic despots strengthened in all aspects to the detriment of the first.

This was sufficient for the first discontent and insurgent movements appearing at the *themes* of Durres and Nicopolis, well incited by the rebelling Gregory Maniac, Commander of Sicily, who in 1043, after having rebelled against the central government, with the help of troops, many of them from Arbëria, was declared Emperor. With this aureole he disembarked at Durres and with an Arberian-Byzantine army, achieving significant successes in Macedonia, headed towards Thessaloniki and certainly would have taken it if he had not been accidentally killed on his way there.[647]

Maniac's uprising worsened the relations between the *theme* of Durres and the central government, as it had already become a fertile ground for such events. This is best reflected in a note by the Byzantine historian of the 11th century, Mikhail Ataliatis, saying that at that time Arberians, once allies of the Byzantine Empire (*symmachio*), became "suddenly" its opponents (*polemioi*).[648]

What historian Ataliatis says about the "allies" of the Byzantine Empire that "suddenly" lost faith, turning into "opponents" (*polemioi*), seems more of a description than an expression of a deeper condition, which followed future relations of the domestic imperial crisis. For, the issue of the *themes* and the expropriation of their power of over one hundred years and the establishment of the feudal aristocracy, which was a source of income, but at the same time a determining factor of the ratio of forces, was not at all an issue of ally-opponent relations, differing in accordance with particular circumstances. It represented a difference, on one hand between those who felt the Byzantine Empire as part of their state consciousness, such as Arberians (descendants of the Pelasgian-Illyrians) and Greeks, who had built and developed it to that extent, and, on the other, the invading Slavs, Bulgarians and others from the East, who had begun to

---

[647] *"Historia e Popullit Shqiptar,"* Volume I, Tirana 2002, p. 220.
[648] Mihal Atalati, cited according to *"Historia e Popullit Shqiptar,"* Tirana 2002, p. 221.

conquer the Empire from within demolishing it with pretensions to turn it into an empire of their own.

Initially the Bulgarians and then Zupans of Rascia in the 12th-15th centuries (by Nemanja, Uros II, and Stefan Dusan) fought with all means against Byzantium's central power using its own crown, without hesitation implicating others in the same fight, especially the Western Empire, including the Ottomans themselves, with whom, as noted, reached numerous secret and later open pacts of vassalage against Byzantium, and generally against the West.

This fact, mainly deliberately overlooked, unearths the founders and invaders of a large edifice such as the Byzantine Empire, as well as highlights its true defenders and demolishers. Slavs and other barbarians, coming from the North and East, factored quickly because of their great potential of human force, never having accepted the proper imperial rule, as it meant emancipation and submission to state rules and laws, as it required social culture and creativity.

They remained outside these concepts remaining loyal to their barbaric tendencies, as best illustrated by their late acceptance of Christianity (ninth and tenth century), and even when they accepted it, this was rather a matter of its use for power, that is, as it was the religion of the Empire, with Christianity being an inevitable co-ruler, rather than for the domestic needs of spiritual emancipation. Christianity remained a power tool, shown by the inclinations of Slavs and Bulgarians to settle scores with it, making efforts to move from one church to another (East to West and vice versa).

This game was particularly emphasized by the mid-10th century, namely in those Illyricum despots where they already were turning into a factor, such as Dioclea, Zakhumia, Bosnia, and Rascia, recognized by Byzantium after the ejection of the Bulgarian Kingdom by Emperor Basilius II, taking on one or another cross, by mostly linking alliances in favor of strengthening them and weakening the central government of Byzantium.

This situation culminated by the mid-11th century in order to become an open arena where now more than ever the interests of East and West collided, which is not by accident that in 1054, the boundary of the separation of the church was drawn on this "race," as a consequence of which was not only the alignment of the rulers in compliance with this limitation and movement, but also a fierce struggle for survival between the Byzantine and Western Empires.

Even the most bitter and bloody appearance of the Ottomans became more ferocious by the emerging Ottomans, who were not only involved in it but also benefited from it, by opening the way to incursions that affected Byzantium from the early 10th century to turn into its conquerors by the early 14th century continuing towards Central Europe.

In the forerun of these developments, with Byzantium being protected by changing from bottom-up, Arberian lands were included, as the foundation of Byzantium, but also as a very important space where the power of one or the other cross could be determined.

One of the first efforts paving the way to the power struggle by local militaries was that of the strategist Nicephorus Bryennius of 1077, rising up against Constantinople. This strategist was known for his imperial patriotism in numerous wars against Slav despots in the North, including wars against Norman ships in the Adriatic.

Nicephorus proclaimed himself Emperor, the same as Gregory Maniac did as he headed towards Constantinople to dethrone Emperor Mikhael VII Dukas. On the way he was joined by other nobles and an expropriated layer of *theme* stratiotes, seeking revenge. At the gates of Adrianople he met his end by the imperial army under the command of Alex Comnenus, who four years later, on April 4, 1081, was declared Emperor of Byzantium.

The accession of the famous imperial general on the Byzantine throne was made after a challenge he had once again with the Duke of Durres, Nicephorus Basilicas, who had replaced Nicephorus Bryennius. As a representative of western military aristocracy in his efforts to take the throne of Constantinople, Basilicas had a military eastern rival, Nicephorus Botonia, who succeeded in gaining the imperial throne, by the support provided by Suleiman, grandson of Sultan Alp Arslan.[649]

The support that Nicephorus Botonia the Elder got from the Turks and the subsequent one of Melisen, indeed, eased their path to the conquest of Asia Minor. It paved the way to rapid penetration of Islam towards the West. The Church of Constantinople used its influence for a short time to expand at the expense of the Roman Church, something that emanates historical doubt, not without support, in regard to the fact that

---

[649] Osrtrogorski, Georg: *"Historia e Perandorisë Bizantine,"* Tirana 2002, p. 243.

charges Orthodoxy in its war against Catholicism with abhorrence of open and concealed alliances with the Ottomans was a strategy that surfaced especially through the vassalage of Orthodox princes with the Ottomans after their penetration in the Balkans, a matter that was addressed later.

Conversely, around the year 1080 Suleiman administered the entire territory of Asia Minor, from Cilicia in Hellespont, establishing in this ancient Byzantine territory the Sultanate of *Ar Rumi*, i.e. "Roman Sultanate."[650]

This is worth mentioning as Byzantium sought to compensate for the losses in the East, being irreversible and even fatal, by reforming beyond Bosphorus, in the Illyricum space, whereby with the creation of two new *themes* (that of Dalmatia and Scupi) and, in particular with permitting independent despots: Dioclea, Bosnia, Zakhumia, and Rascia, the situation changed considerably from both the crisis of *themes* and intrusion of coastline states (Venice and Genoa) for as many allies as possible among the new settlements on the Adriatic coast and Mediterranean.

One should not forget here the implication of the Holy See as well in drawing Slav despots, who were seeking to profit with their games with the churches, although these two issues shared a common dissatisfaction with the central power, but not with its aims. The military aristocracy did not wish to ruin Byzantium but rather to attain its imperial throne in order to lead it in maintaining its entirety for as much as possible, while the Slav despots and princes aimed at possibly transferring it into some kind of *Slavia* or through as many independent principalities as possible have it under their armpit, not hesitating to even connect with the West to obtain it.

This multi-turn development, bearing an internal drama, was challenging Illyricum for worse, as following the division of the churches (1054) this line crossed through its body where supporters and beneficiaries of Byzantium submitted to a thorough war between Byzantium and the West, which was waged under circumstances of the beginning of the era of military feudalism, characterized by an expansion of conditioned military property (*pronies*), in which another "outside" and powerful factor was involved. The Normans had an impact on sobering up an

---

[650] For more see: Laurent, J: *"Byzance et les origines du Sultanat Roum,"* 1930; Wittek, P: *"Deux chapitres de l'historie des Turcs de Roum,"* 1936; Cohen, C: *"La premiere penetration turque en Asie Naeneasre."*

exhausted West reflected by moving towards the East and facing Byzantium; with many difficulties, the new invaders from the West, who, together with those from the East (Turks), set conditions for its internal and external demise.

In this new development with many actors notably and inscrutably, acting on stage and behind the scenes, the central character remains Byzantium and its edifice condemned to collapse as its time was running out, while in the arena of this match was Southern Illyricum, by now as medieval Arbëria, or even as Byzantine Arbëria as it was often called, where everything began and was tested as the West saw in it its crucial start eastward, while the East saw its protection block against the West. This split (into two administrative parts), which occurred in the 4th century during the time of Emperor Theodosius, and the latest division of the churches, was by now turning into a social, cultural, and political division among the largest of the time, becoming eventually a boundary for the divisions of world civilizations.

However, in this squirm, it was Emperor Alex Comnenus (1081-1118), known as the most successful Byzantine general of all time, who as a military man that strengthened the military aristocracy, succeeded in preventing, at least for some time, and not entirely removing, the dual pressure which he had begun to face - from the East with the Turks and from the West with the Normans. From both internal and external movements, now an already defunct Empire managed to afford the humiliation after a century in its very heart, in Constantinople, as it was occupied by Western crusaders and destroyed to the ground, which would come two centuries later by the Ottomans.

But, why can it be said that Alex Comnenus and his dynasty were decisive, that Byzantium once again, even temporarily, was back into the whirlpool of these developments with a certain military and diplomatic sense, continuing to remain in the game for some time, but doing so not in terms of its own power, but of the extraction of profits by foreign cards, that is, of its opponents admitted into the game?

As a noted military, Alex Comnenus was tested as a skilled diplomat in several respects. However, his actions focused primarily in using the assistance of the Western countries, especially Venice and Genoa, in facing the Norman danger, as this people, full of energy coming from the North, was by now becoming a very important factor in the Mediterranean threatening to place under its control Constantinople, after Rome, which was facing multifaceted troubles.

In addition, another Comnenus' action, relating to the first, was the one dealing with his attempt to exploit the euphoria of the crusade movement, which had broken out in the countries of Europe to liberate the tomb of Christ in Jerusalem, in the struggle to prevent the Turks in the East, who had snatched many of Empire's parts in Asia Minor and it was a matter of when they would approach Constantinople.

Both for the first issue, that of the Norman threat and its confrontation with it, and the second issue, namely the Crusades (eight of them), with which Byzantium would be dealing for the next two hundred years with them becoming the cause of its downfall, the starting point was in the lands of Arberia, where the Arberians were included in what would turn into a war between Byzantium and the West.

When speaking of the lands of Arberia and Arberians in general becoming a factor at this stage of Middle Ages it is important to see the issue of passing from *Illyrian, Illyria, Illyricum* to *Alban, Albaniae, Albani*, as they were called at that time and externally their country as *Arbër, Arbëri* or *Arben, Arbni* internally so that from the 18th century onwards they called themselves *shqiptar* and their country *Shqipëri*.

With this phenomenon being not only linguistic, but also of a social and cultural nature that requires an historical explanation, it should be said that the name *Alban* is known since antiquity and for the first time is mentioned by the Alexandrian geographer, Ptolemy (Ptolemaion) in the second century AD. The famous geographer, describing the country of Macedonia and its boundary, in Paragraph 20, presents "the land of Albans, *Albanoi*, with the city *Albanopolis*.[651]

After nine centuries from the time of Ptolemy, Michael Ataliates, a Byzantine chronicler, mentions Albanians in 1072 under the name of *Arvanites*; in 1079, the Byzantine princess Anna Comnenus, daughter of Emperor Alex Comnenus, upon her father's wars with the Normans speaks of the country that she calls *Arvanon*, while George Acropolitia calls it later *Alvanono*. At the same time the Latins called Kruja *Arbanum* and the Bishop of Kruja *Episcopus Arbanensis*.[652]

Noticeably, a little later, the Anjou called their possessions *"Regnum Albaniae."* Along with this name, from without and within, there is also

---

[651] Ptolemy: *"Gjeografia,"* Book III, 20.
[652] Çabej, Eqrem: *"Studime gjuhësore"* III, Prishtina 1977, p. 85.

Epirus, Epirote going as far back as antiquity, when it comes to Epirus and Epirotes, a large Illyrian tribe, associated with Molossians, which later, at the time of Pyrrhus onwards, as a kingdom played a political role, turning eventually into an ethnic, social and cultural identity.

Thus, in the Middle Ages, many of Arberian princes carried the title *Epirotan* (the case of Castrioti and Skenderbeg family), but the toponym Epirus and Epirotan also maintained a wide cultural and social identity, which up to the 15th and 16th centuries was competitive to the Arberian one, when speaking of *Epirotan* as a language, as found in some church documents and reports, such as those dealing with Bogdani and his work.[653]

Regardless of these linguistic and ethnic parallelisms as their internal and external use, with the dominating *Alban - Albanien /Arbër-Arbëri/* in all their variants in different languages, from where then in the 18th-19th centuries it developed into *shqiptar-Shqipëri*, still, from a linguistic point of view it may be said that from the Latin *Albaneuses* came the Italian *Albanese*, Greek *Arvanitis* as a continuation of the Byzantine name of the Albanians, taken from the Greek by the Turks, turning it through metathesis into *Arnaut*. The Serbs turned it into *Arbanasi, Rabans*, and Aromanians into *Arbinisi*.[654]

All these names show that the name *Shqiptar, Shqipëri* (Albanian, Albania) in the Middle Ages had not yet emerged as the national name of the people of the country. This truth is tested by the situation of Albanians in Italy, who moved there by the end of the Middle Ages, and were called *Arbëresh*, and Albania *Arberia*, as it can also be witnessed by the Albanians of Greece who use the name *Arberesh*. Also the inhabitants of the colony Borgo Eriggio in Dalmatia (Zadar), who moved out in 1734 from Kraja of Shkodra, call their country *Arbënesh*.

This situation, that of maintaining the name *Arbër - Arbëri* in the South and *Arbën - Arbëni* in the North, is also proven by the old literature written by old Geg authors. The old name is often met in these authors:

- at Buzuku we find - *"gjithe populine e chersteen andeh Arba-niit,"*[655]

---

[653] For more see: Marquet, Odette: *"Pjetër Bogdani – letra dhe dokumente,"* Shkodër, 1997; Rugova, Ibrahim dr: *"Pjetër Bogdani ,"* Prishtina, 1983.

[654] Ibid, p. 85.

[655] *"Meshari i Gjon Buzukut,"* 1, Prishtina, 1987, (Ad Laudes VIII/68), p. 105.

- at Budi - *"..ke ndarbene setiu lecht," " perëndimete githe kersotenimit arbenit," ."..Ndarbene meua derguom,""Priftenet e Scerbe-torevt kiscesse tinezot chi te gindene ndegiulm te arbanesce;"* [656]

- at Bogdani we find - *"dheu i Arbenit, nde dhe te Arbinit,"* then *"ghiuhesse Arbenesce, scium fjalë t'Arbensecia, arbenescit, t'Arbenes-cete,* and *Arbenorete."*[657]

All this evidence is proof that the name of the Albanian people in the Middle Ages was *Arbëresh, Abënesh,* and the name of the country *Arbër, Arbën.* This name, for unknown reasons, was withdrawn in more recent times and replaced by *Shqiptar, Shqipëri, Shqipni.*[658]

However, the latter is first only seen designating the *Albanian language*. It is neither found as the name for a people nor for a country.

Thus, Buzuku has *"Embas andaih thuo prift Paster noter qi vien me thasune sqip."*[659]

Budi says: *"schip te na thoete mbechete arresye."*[660]

Bogdani says too: *"gramatike Latin e Scqip."*

Professor Çabej thinks that the name *shqip* was used to determine the Albanian as a language. The language seems to have overlaid naming both the people and place,[661] a development, which necessarily implies a complexity of issues of the social, cultural and political nature dealing with the totality of the Albanians and Albania as an entity that has been preoccupying many scholars and researchers who share the opinion that an explanation of this, however approximate, holds the key to overcoming many issues dealing with the explanation of the transition time from antiquity to the Middle Ages, as a development, where social changes reflected in the spiritual plane highlighted certain ethnic and cultural identities, which later passed as a hallmark of national identities.

---

[656] *"Dottrina Christiana,"* 1618, pp. 233, 226.
[657] Bogdani, Pjetër: *"Cuneus prophata."*
[658] Ibid, p. 87.
[659] *Meshari i Gjon Buzukut,* Prishtina 1987, XXV.
[660] *"Rituale Romanum,"* p. 74.
[661] Çabej, Eqrem: *"Studime gjuhësore"* III, Prishtina 1977, p. 87.

Arbenians between Byzantium and the West

The emergence of the Normans and drawing of the West from lethargy. – The inclusion of the Arberian lands in the Christian Crusades. - The Return of Jerusalem by the Westerners and the beginnings of the weakening of Byzantium. - The emergence of the Despotate of Epirus 1204-1214 and the "Kingdom of Arbëria" 1272-1286 - as foundations of the Albanian national identity in the Middle Ages. - The inclusion of a part of the nobles and feudal lords of Arberians on the side of the "Kingdom of Arbëria" and the remaining side of the few and the inclusion of some others on the side of Byzantium against it. - Successes and failures of Charles I Anjou in Arberia and his departure due to backstage games played by the Byzantines against him in Italy. – Manfred's return and the second recovery of the "Kingdom of Arbëria" as an expression of the will of a majority of the Arberian nobles and feudal lords who see it as being in their own interest in their struggle for survival between Byzantium and the invading aims of Rascia. – The joint war of Byzantium and Rascia in destroying the Arberian principalities. – The evidence of the Archbishop of Tivar, Gulhelm Adae, in the year 1332, regarding Arberians and their language written in Latin script.

The unsuitable situation of some of the Arberian lands and generally their living space in the circumstances of the separation of church since the mid-eleventh century, began to change, after the fall of the first Bulgarian empire, and then upon the appearance of Normans and their strong penetration from the northwest and southwest, occupying some of the exhausted European kingdoms in the North, such as the English, those of Spain, and finally the Mediterranean coastal kingdoms from Genoa to Sicily.

With the emergence of the Normans and their great willingness for changes, the European kingdoms and coastal cities of the North received a new energy, which revived many of their former ambitions to move towards extending their power towards the East. In order to put into action the will to new conquests in cooperation with the Papacy and the spirit of Catholicism, which compared with the Orthodox, being for a long time in retreat, rediscovered the Holy See, namely Palestine, and the tomb of Jesus Christ, which had to be returned once again from the Seljuk Turks into the hands of Christians.

Therefore, the Normans along with the Vatican and the republics of the Adriatic and the Mediterranean, "discovered" crusades as a means for returning the sacred places in the East and this attained the proportions of waves of mobilization of all social strata from the countries of the North of Europe, especially those who thirsted for turning adventure into a profit tool by being included in a popper campaign towards the Eastern countries, lasting for more than 150 years in seven major crusades, in which most of the "success" consisted of destruction everywhere and in failure to turn the Holy See and its Christian temples in Jerusalem under constant control.

Historical records and various chronicles of the time show that the period of the Crusades marked the time of outburst among the wildest, leaving behind trails of unredeemed blood, in which the values of Christian civilization would greatly suffer, including two of the occupations of Constantinople itself and the ruthless destruction of Byzantine temples, as occurred during the Fourth Crusade.

Regarding the Norman danger, threatening from all sides, the Crusaders and their role, at least during the First Crusade (1097-1099), there were many indications that Alex Comnenus not only would have desired it as such, but also urged it in various forms. He used the slogan of a "holy war" to liberate the tomb of Jesus in Jerusalem, which was used to mobilize broad layers of Christians across the old continent where Catholicism had its main say, not only leaving behind the differences between the churches, which were considerable but also harmful. It created circumstances for all the great energy to be poured into the East, against the Turks, so that with their settlement in Asia Minor, they would turn into a protective dike.

It seems that this was motivating not only for the large layer of ambitious adventurers, eager to benefit from something, but it was also motivating for feudal lords, expecting to get rich from the eastern parts of Asia Minor, with large properties and climatic conditions for agriculture. This issue seems to have been a very thoughtful account for many of the Catholic clergy, assessing that the euphoria of the crusaders in the East should be primarily used for the relocation of a large part of Catholics in those parts in order to increase the influence of the Western church, being entirely excluded until then.

Before the actions of the crusaders were understood with all the developments relating to them and their behavior, it must be said that

Byzantium would initially face the Norman challenge, which was neither new nor unknown, as they had already become lords of the Mediterranean, and the Holy See with the coastal cities under the pressure of their conquests.

The Normans, as a vital force coming down from the North inverting or occupying old European kingdoms one after another, emerged in the Mediterranean headed by the famous Robert Guiscard, who long ago, after he had managed to unite all the possessions of Norman princes of southern Italy, founded a powerful kingdom and immediately looked to the other side of the Adriatic. At last, Guiscard, after having expressed openly his claims to the crown of the Byzantine Empire looked at conquering Durres as his immediate goal, which would open the gates to Constantinople.

In this case one should say that even for the Arberian lands and circumstances where initially *themes* (independent administrative-military units under Byzantium, as that of Durres in the 8th century and Nicopolis in the 9th century) were and later nobilities and feuds divided into both parts of an already divided and alienated Christian world, the Norman penetration and the beginning of the Crusades had a special importance, waking up hope.

On one hand, the Normans would set in motion a great energy, which primarily would be used to push the boundary of the separation of the church further eastward, so that the space of the West and therefore Catholicism would go as far as Constantinople. On the other hand, it would create awareness that Arberians too could be part of these changes seeing their own interest in accordance with the developments, attaining an unstoppable direction. The Norman King Roger never hid his intentions by saying that his aim was to restore Old Rome,[662] that was actually a rather settling of accounts with the eastern empire than fighting for the return of the Holy Sepulcher and Palestine, as found in the oath of the Crusades, although the First Crusade achieved that, but with the price of blood and further divide among Christians, as the so-called "Latin Kingdom of Jerusalem" was mostly be fought by Constantinople, even with the help of the Ottomans and Arabs!

Noticeably, in these circumstances, the penetration of the Normans in Arber areas initially started with the occupation of Durres and later of

---

[662] Ostrogorsi, Georg: *"Historia e Perandorisë Bizantine,"* Tirana 2010, p. 140

the greatest part of the coast and then in the North and the interior. When the Princedom of Dioclea accepted the Norman vassalage, he determined to join the Crusades provided they ensured the eastward expansion of Catholicism,[663] representing a positive development at the sight.

As the new situation promised the abolition of the separation boundary, or at least pushing it deeper towards the East, it opened up a good opportunity for union with the eastern part, which in the circumstances arose from the separation of churches, linking them more naturally economically and politically with that part of the world than the eastern association, which had begun to shrivel, below the original imperial dimensions. What is worse, it was turning into a shooting range where the Bulgarians, Greeks, Slavs and others were trying to realize their own interests over those of Arbërians or even to the detriment of the latter.

On the initiative of Pope Gregory VII, the Norman leader Guiscard and Dioclea, Mikhael agreed on a military alliance against the Byzantines, with several other countries of the Western Balkans joining in, such as the Republic of Ragusa and the Kingdom of Croatia, which were under the influence of the Catholic Church.[664]

Venice was left outside this alliance, which although against the restoration of Byzantium, also, saw the danger to its vital interests in the strengthening of the Normans and their claims to becoming lords of the East, particularly when their strength could benefit Genoa and other Mediterranean cities, threatening its position as a supervisor of navigation and trade in the Mediterranean, from where its goods moved in and out of Asia and Africa.

Furthermore, when the Normans began their deployment to the rest of the Adriatic, the Venetian fleet answered the call of Alex Comnenus to join the war against them, opening the way to several alliances that Byzantium signed with them, at a dear cost to Constantinople and with grave consequences, as behind them there were always hidden tricks that the famous navel republic of the Adriatic played, using every situation without hesitation to break and impose conditions in accordance with its own interests.

---

[663] *"Historia e popullit shqiptar,"* Volume I, Prishtina, 1969, p. 140.
[664] *"Historia e popullit shqiptar,"* Volume I, published "Enti i Teksteve and i Mjeteve Mësimore i Krahines Socialiste Autonome të Kosovës," Prishtina, 1969, p. 165

However, in May 1081 the Norman armies led by Guiscard's son, Boemund, descended on the bay of Vlora, conquering the city and taking Jerik and Kanina to reach Butrint where he joined Guiscard's armies, who had occupied Corfu. Byzantine Emperor Alexis Comnenus tried to cut their path to unity as once united the Normans would come close to Durres and surround it.

Historical sources also indicate that Alex Comnenus, finding himself at an edge played the "Catholic card." He asked the Venetians for assistance, promising them settlements on the Albanian coast, but this would not help to protect Durres from the Norman Conquest. After some tactical victories, Comnenus, the next October, suffered losses by the Normans and fled to Ohrid with George Paleologos. On this occasion, Guiscard addressed the Arbëresh population with a message to join him, as "the missing freedom awaited them."[665]

On this occasion, the Norman commander gave a promise to the inhabitants of Arberian lands that his intention was to take back the Orthodox principalities under the Vatican's direction, announcing big turns, through which the Christian world was to be relieved of internal divisions which had reached the degree of hostility from which Arabs and Ottomans in the East already benefited, cutting the arms of the eastern empire little by little.

With Durres falling into his hands in October of that year, Guiscard opened his way to Constantinople. The Norman armies penetrated deep into imperial territory, crossing Epirus, Macedonia, and Thessaly, finally surrounding Larissa. But in spring 1082, Robert Guiscard was forced to return to Italy, where a riot broke out promoted by supporters of the Byzantine emperor, Alex Comnenus passing his command to his son, Boemund.[666]

Guiscard's departure to Italy created a liberating situation for Byzantium, as it provided it with an opportunity, on one hand, to prevent the penetration of the Norman forces in Epirus, Macedonia, and the Adriatic, and on the other, it created conditions for reaching an agreement with Venice against the Normans, managing to recover Durres from the Normans.

Despite the alliance with Venice, the fortunes of war probably would not smile at Alex Comnenus as they did, if Guiscard would not have fallen

---

[665] Ibid, p. 165.
[666] Ostgrogorsi, Georg: *"Historia e Perandorisë Bizantine,"* Tirana 2002, p. 255.

victim to an epidemic, after he crushed the revolt in Italy incited by Byzantium and Venice, upon returning to Vlora in 1085, from where he resumed his successful operations against the Byzantine armies. Guiscard's death had a double impact: on the Byzantine front, and also in the resumption of unrest in Italy, which briefly relieved Byzantium of the Norman risk, that was reappearing, but now with the help of the Crusaders.

Meanwhile, the alliance reached with Venice, would cost Byzantium dearly, for Venice demanded a high price for the assistance provided for the return of Durres to Byzantium. By a treaty of May of 1082 the Dodge of Venice attained for himself and for his descendants the title of a *protosebasto*, with a good annual fee, and the Patriarch of Grados was honored with the title of *hypertimos*, while the Church of Venice with an annual contribution of twenty golden books.

Venice got the greatest benefits from this agreement in the area of trade, as from now Venetians would be allowed to trade freely in all the areas of the Byzantine Empire, including Constantinople itself, without paying any customs duty. Therefore, they were privileged against local dealers. In this way, Venice laid the foundations of its colonial power in the East, simultaneously opening a deep rift in the Byzantine state trading system. The fact that Venice continued to recognize the sovereign rights of the Byzantine emperor did not change anything. The Italian maritime republic was a determining factor in the history of Byzantium.[667]

At the time when Alex Comnenus brought his temporary security from Venice against the Normans at a high price, it was facing the Pechens, an eastern Turkmen people, most militant and largely Bogumil, who for years threatened Byzantium and at last found the support of the Bogumils in the eastern part of the Balkan Peninsula at a time when the Empire was facing the Norman risk on the Adriatic and "guard" began to crack.

After fierce battles with them, where the Romans proved helpless, the Pechens came near the walls of Constantinople. The risk increased even more as they were joined by the troops of Emir of Smyrna, Chaha, one of the heir emirs of Suleiman, who had allied with Pechens to conquer the Byzantine castle, who died in 1085.[668]

---

[667] Jireček, K: "Die Bedeutung von Ragusa in der HandelsGeschihte des Mittelalters," 1899, p. 9.
[668] Ostrogorski, Georg: "Historia e Perandirisë Bizantine," Tirana 2002, p. 257.

The cunning Comnenus faced the risk again by playing the card of "the enemy of the enemy," as he had done in Durres when at war with the Normans calling Venetians for help. Now, he called on the Cumans against the Pechens, another nomadic people, Turkish by language but not by ethnic origin. They arrived fast in the Byzantine territory, being promised accommodations and good properties by the emperor, provided that they gave up plundering, and in April 1091, at the foot of Levunion Mountain, they waged the final battle against the Pechens, which they not only won, but massacred the Pechens to the last one. This rather shocking massacre was also described by the Emperor's daughter, Anna Comnenus, saying: "An entire people, which amounted to tens of thousands, was wiped out in a single day."[669]

In this way, killing two birds with one stone, the Byzantine Emperor succeeded in settling accounts with Chaha of Smyrna against whom he sent his son-in-law, Amir Nicaea, as well as Abul Qazim, while spurring the latter against several other emirs who entered the war against the Sultan of ar-Rumi, which was dissolved by internal struggles between emirs ruled by Byzantium, creating good opportunities for Comnenus to reoccupy Asia Minor.

The way to regaining possessions in Asia Minor, was blocked to Alex Comnenus exactly from the West, where he had thought that by the agreement with Venice he had managed to remove the Norman threat once and for all, once they left Durres and moved to the other side of the Adriatic, landing on their way to Constantinople, and remaining stuck for four years between Epirus, Macedonia and Thrace.

It was the Crusaders, at the call of Pope Urban II at the Council of Clermons who liberated the Holy Sepulcher, which since 1077 was occupied by the Seljuk Turks, who had conquered Jerusalem. The Papacy was strengthened at that time and saw the idea of the crusade to extend its power as far deep as possible in the East. The Pope's call found great resonance among the feudal lords eager for land and adventure and among the masses of the West, devastated by economic hardship and incorporated by religious fervor. This call also found support in the East, as the Holy See was once a Byzantine province, which had to be liberated, as this was a state obligation and not an obligation of Christianity in general. The advantage of state coercion against the Christian one had to

---

[669] Gyboni, M: "*Le nom de Βλαχη dans l'Alexiade d'Anne Comnene,*" 1951, p. 44, cited according to Ostrogorski, Georg: "*Historia e Perandorisë Bizantine,*" Tirana 2002, p. 257.

do with the schism between the two churches, which allowed no cooperation with the West.

There are many sources, ecclesiastic or diplomatic of the time showing that Alex Comnenus would have been the one, who through his emissaries, and also directly, asked Pope Urban II to have Crusaders head as soon as possible to "their holy mission,"[670] because in that way he would be able to mobilize his war against the East, where the crusaders and their bigotry would be used for these purposes, as did happen. This score, however, brought trouble to him and the Empire, with what appeared as a Latin Empire in the East, turning into a further fuse to Byzantium and Christianity in general.

Furthermore, that was shown by the "vanguard" of Crusaders, who came from the Amien eremite. Notably, he was followed by a promiscuous crowd of fanatics who were on their way through Hungary and the Balkan regions and went after the spoils. With the momentum they reached Constantinople on the August 1, where they continued to plunder, but the emperor who had accounts with them, ordered to have them forwarded from the Bosphorus to Asia Minor, where they were badly crushed by the Turks and only a small number of them managed to return to Constantinople.

The debacle of the vanguards of the crusaders, however, did not end plans for their organized initiation, as everyone was interested in them regardless of what every side expected. So in early 1096 in the capital of Byzantium the cream of western cavalry came ashore, the one that was expecting the most from the enterprise. Among them was the Duke of Lorraine - Gottfried of Bouillon, Count Raymond of Toulouse, Hugo de Vermandua, brother of the King of France, Robert of Flanders. There was

---

[670] For more see: Holzman, W: *"Studien zur Orientpolitik des Reformpapsttums und zur Enstehungen des ersten Kreuzzuges"* (Hist.Vierteljahrscht, 22 (1942), 167, and *"Die Unionsverhandlugen zwischen Keiser Alexios I und Papst Urban II. Im Jahr 1089,"* 1928, p. 38. The assessment that Emperor Alex Comnenus had asked Pope Urban II for help is confirmed by Byzantine sources as well, particularly those provided by Synopsis Sathas (Teodor Skutariotis), accepted by the notable historian P. Lemerle *"Byzance es la Croisade, Relazione del X Congresso internacionale di scienze storiche,"* Rome, 1955, III, 600. According to the latter, the essence of the problem is not in learning the truth if Alex I did or did not ask the West for help, as he surely repeated such a request many times, but rather what were his intentions for such a demand for help: did he ask for troops to help his empire or did he intend to organize a Western Crusade?

also the Norman Prince Boemund, the son of Robert Guiscard, who ten years earlier led the first Norman campaign in Epirus, Macedonia and Thessaly, succeeding to even temporarily take Durres, which was forced to give up after being attacked by the Venetians.[671]

Under such not so natural circumstances for Byzantium, with Constantinople having forgotten for quite some time the presence of western notables and counts, Alex Comnenus used his apparent cunningness once again, being in need of the crusaders, fearing, on one hand, their power in the future, by drafting an agreement by the means of which he would be able to cook the meat without getting burned.

So, from all of this came an agreement under which Byzantium recognized their entitlement to property, provided they returned them to the Empire after which, by a decree, their property and management rights would be recognized, in accordance with imperial law. Through this compromise the Emperor was taking over the supply of food and military equipment for the crusaders. The Emperor also pledged that he would personally grab a cross, putting himself at the forefront of the crusaders with his entire army. On these terms an agreement was signed with particular princes, also Boemund, Guiscard's nephew, who would soon break it, but not signed by Raymond of Toulouse.[672]

Under this pretense, the First Crusade began in the spring of 1097. Guiscard's son, Boemund, after having passed once again with his armies through the lands of Arber while the people had not yet recovered from the damages suffered from the Normans, appeared again with the attitude that *"the lands of Arber had the honor to know the crusaders who had gathered from all the European countries, starting forth from there towards Jerusalem to restore the holy tomb and Christian holy lands that were under the occupation by the Seljuk Turks."*[673]

Along with numerous Norman crusaders that landed again in Vlora and Himara following the path along the rivers Vjosa and Devoll, crusaders came also from two other directions. Crusaders of the Provence (South France), led by Count Raymond of Toulouse, through Dalmatia, came to the lands of Arber by the way of Shkodra. The French crusaders of Flanders and Normandy, passing through Italy, were thrown to Durres by the

---

[671] Ostrogorski, Georg: *"Historia e Perandorisë Bizantine,"* Tirana 2002, p. 258.
[672] Ibid, p. 258.
[673] *"Historia e Popullit Shqiptar,"* Volume I, Prishtina, 1969, p. 167.

sea. Both these groups went across the country following the royal road Egnatia, over Shkumbin valley.[674]

The first important success of the crusade was the occupation of Nicaea, in June 1097. On this occasion, the crusaders held their word, handing over to Emperor Alex Comnenus the city they took with blood, where an imperial garrison was hastily positioned. The crusaders, with some small exception, such as that of Baldwin, brother of Gottfried of Boulogne and Tancred, nephew to Boemund, making a detour at Cilicia to take over for himself cities in Turkey, from where Baldwin continued his march in rural northern Mesopotamia, founded an autonomous princedom based in Edessa.[675]

In fact, there emerged, on one side, disagreements between the crusaders and Alex I, and, on the other, among the crusaders as to how they should act in the new circumstances as they, with the newly occupied territories went beyond their agreement with Alex I. The cause was the invasion of Antioch, capital of Syria, where the crusaders entered on June 3, 1098. In this appraisal over Antioch, the Norman Boemund proved to be the most able one, who was also fulfilling Guiscard's wish he left behind in Vlora, in 1081, when he swore he would establish a Norman Rome.

After three months the army of the crusaders crossed the Bosphorus moving into Asia Minor where a part of them was drawn in numerous invasions of lands where they stayed forever, while the rest approached Jerusalem keeping the siege for more than two years. At that time Jerusalem was under the rule of the caliph of Egypt, Fatim, who made great efforts to resist the crusaders. On July 14, 1099 Jerusalem fell into their hands. Notably, on that occasion they committed terrible massacres against the Arab population, which was almost entirely exterminated.

The massacre opened a permanent blood gap between the Franks and Turks and Arabs on the other side. Hereby the Crusaders declared the *"Latin Kingdom of Jerusalem"* under the leadership of the Duke of Lorraine, Godfrey de Bouillon, who took the title *"Defender of the Holy Sepulcher"* in order to rule over Palestine as the deputy of the Pope. Once Bouillon died a year later, he was replaced by his brother, Baldwin, who opened the centennial way of the "Latin Kingdom of Jerusalem," which included Palestine and other parts of the East. Besides the creation of the

---

[674] Ibid, p. 167.
[675] Ostrogorski, Georg: *"Historia e Perandorisë Bizantine,"* Tirana, 2002, p. 229.

"*Latin Kingdom of Jerusalem*," another success of the First Crusade, at least in maintaining the Western influence in this part of the world, was the Principality of Antioch, whose ruler was the Norman Duke, Boemund, who in the new circumstances, never gave up his ambition for the conquest of Constantinople and the collapse of Byzantium in accordance with what King Roger had once demanded.[676]

Under these circumstances, Emperor Alex Comnenus could tolerate the "Latin Kingdom of Jerusalem" in Palestine under the leadership of Duke Bouillon, but not Boemund's settling in Antioch, as the Norman principality in Syria represented a direct threat to its interests in its most important part. The Norman Principality in Syria was regarded with an evil eye by the Turks, who already had an agreement with Alex. So, the Norman Prince was found simultaneously targeted by two strong opponents: Byzantines and Turks.

After a nearly two-year war he was captured by Amir Malik Gazi of the Danishmmendia dynasty, but was released on disbursement by the crusaders and returned to Antioch. But after a heavy loss in 1104 that the Latins suffered from the Turks near Harran, he left Tarkend in Antioch and returned to the West to prepare a broad campaign against the Byzantines. It was noted that the Normans, led by Count Boemund, with an army of 250 thousand, and with the blessing of Pope Gregory, in the spring of 1107, began his war against the Byzantines by conquering Albania.

Boemund went down to Vlora from Apullia, with the Byzantine fleet unable to stop the incursion. Then the Normans turned to Durres, surrounding and capturing it thanks to the Arberian population which joined him. Similarly, during the assault and capture of Kruja and Dibra, the Byzantine army led by Commander Cantacusenus suffered big defeats, something that was repeated upon the capture of Kanina and fortresses along the river valley of Erzen.

The Normans weren't so lucky to bring down the Byzantine fortress from the Arberian lands and to promote the Roman Empire there. It was the military power of Byzantium, which at war with the Normans had lost most of its military strongholds in the lands of Arber. What prevented the Normans from realizing their historical aims was the disease of cholera, which struck the Norman winter camps, decimating and debilitating them

---

[676] Ibid, p. 230.

all, insofar as Count Boemund, as the Prince of Antioch, had no other choice, but to accept declaring himself vassal of the Emperor of Byzantium, without any fight. He returned to Italy with the soldiers that escaped cholera and as soon as he arrived there he again declared that he got back to Albania to destroy Byzantine from there. It did not happen, as he died in the summer of 1111, which extinguished forever the Norman ambition to achieve that goal.

Although the Crusades eventually continued from the Second Crusade and on circumventing the lands of Arber, they weren't able to inspire hope for the restoration of what was known dominance of the Western Empire with Rome as the leader in all the areas of Christian countries, which, as noted, had more trouble among themselves than with the Ottoman threat that was soon turning into a calamity for the eastern portion.

The Normans, originally representing as their driving force, becoming possibly successful in restoring former glitter to exhausted Christian kingdoms and principalities, were deemed to fail, by the reluctance, even fear of the West! Multiple sources make it known that even the Vatican, the main inspirer of the Crusades and supporter of Norman conquests towards the East, at the moment realized that the Normans were able to make an historic turnaround, started its known intrigues in order to sabotage their success.

As usual, they started from its main supporters: Venice and Genoa, which were included in various games, with the Normans suffering troubles and defeats without even being aware that they were coming from their main consecrators, the Papacy.[677] Surely this backdrop of the Vatican had to do also with its score that despite popular opposition and disagreement with Constantinople, it had to be saved from final destruction.

This strategy became even clearer by the stance of Pope Bonieca III, when in complete despair and with reprimand, during the Fourth Crusade, addressed the Marquis of Montferrat about what had happened in the capital of Byzantium after the Crusaders went in:

"You have despoiled the sacred purpose for which you went forth, fighting against Christians instead of the Saracens, occupying Constantino-

---

[677] See Ostrogrski, Geogie: *"Istoria Vizantije,"* Belgrade, 1969. The author provides numerous testimonies on secret agreements between the Vatican and Constantinople in preventing the Normans from reaching their military gains of retaking Jerusalem.

ple instead of Jerusalem, preferring the material wealth of this world instead of divine happiness in the hereafter."[678]

A part of the Papacy strategists thought that Byzantium should be supported in resisting the Ottoman invasions and the increased risks posed to Christianity from the East and West with no interest to destroy the natural dam of defense against them. After the weakening of the Normans, it was the Venetians who would do their best to attain Byzantine power from within, in order for it to become a puppet of the commercial republic of the Adriatic, known for her role in this regard.

The strategy to weaken Byzantine power, even through its direct destruction began as early as the Second Crusade, when after the fall of Jerusalem in the hands of the Saracens, in October 1187, led by Prince Salahuddin, the call by Pope Clement III for a general crusade, which involved the German Emperor, Friedrich Barbarossa, was inspired by the Venetians to take the way to Palestine through Constantinople, and there, before settling accounts with the Saracens, to restore order, even though the Papacy would be against this scheme.

The tragic death of Barbarossa, on his way to Asia, and with Heinrich IV taking leadership over the Fourth Crusade, spared for a while the Byzantine capital from Catholic punishment, but not for long, as after the failure of the Second and Third Crusades, it was Pope Innocent III who provided that the Fourth Crusade pass through the sea and that the crusaders land in Egypt, and from there turn to Palestine, considering this to be an easier way. The Pope, who after the dissolution of the Western Empire remained the only authority in this part, mediating between Latin remains and German power of Heinrich who claimed the throne of Byzantium, put the eastern policy at the foreground, which according to him Byzantium should not be brought down by the force of arms, but had to submit to the Seat of St. Peter through a merger of the church taking part in the Crusades along with Western Christianity.

The reasons why the Pope was already playing the card of preserving Byzantium were also purely ecclesiastical, as he had already been successful in the former part of Illyricum in winning over Slavic principalities and the Bulgarian Kingdom, which after the weakening of Byzantium, had begun to turn their eyes towards the Holy See and seek its spiritual attention, which meant nothing other than a return to the West.

---

[678] Zavalani, Tajar: *"Historia e Shqipnis,"* 1998, p. 106.

Therefore, the house of Nemanjas, which had passed from Zakhumia to Rascia and there the son-in-law of the Emperor of Byzantium, Stefan, bearing the title of a *sebastocrate*, removed his father Nemanja, who became a monk locked at the monastery at Mount Athos, and instead of linking with Byzantium, turned his back on his father-in-law to connect with Rome. Why Stefan did not succeed in this in his first attempt his brother Vukan is to blame, who had stayed behind in Dioclea (Zeta). Brothers Stefan and Vukan, one the master of Rascia and the other of Dioclea (Zeta), engaged in a power struggle with each other with each one trying to gain alliances with Hungary and the Papacy as allies.

In this bloody struggle Vukan was assisted by Hungary and having recognized the power of the Pope and Hungarian sovereignty, in 1202, he rose to power; however this would not suffice forever, as his brother Stefan restored his power with the help of the Bulgarians. However, this does not imply that he had renounced Rome and its tutelage in which Slavs were involved. Instead, it was the Bulgarians who had accepted the Roman Church, as "guarantor" of the game between the brothers, where the Holy See added the Slavic-Rascian part to the Balkan pie with the Bulgarians.

Therefore, Rome, on the eve of the fall of Constantinople had laid not only Slavs but Bulgarians as well under its spiritual hegemony extending its sphere of influence in most of Illyricum. This was a situation almost similar to that which six centuries earlier Emperor Justinian had set in Prima Justina of Dardania, which was within the large province of Illyricum, placing it under the jurisdiction of the Holy See, where it remained until the Eighth Council of Constantinople of the year 870, when the Bulgarian-occupied territories of Illyricum passed under full supervision of the Eastern Church bringing an end to the administrative and spiritual subjectivity of Illyricum within the Empire.

However, it should be pointed out that the situation that the Holy See had created in favor of the West, where the Slavs and Hungarians were already included under her crown, went to the detriment of Arberian lands, as during that time a good part of Dardania and Macedonia were seized by Zupan Nemanja, meaning that for the first time Rascia spread its conquests in these parts. This action was preceded by the strengthening of Bulgaria, expanding on Byzantine territory, with which Zupan Nemanja reached an alliance with Peter of Bulgaria to share together the Balkan parts of Byzantium.[679]

Therefore, he captured Nis and destroyed the Timot Valley, causing great devastation. Multiple sources make it known that Nemanja totally destroyed the ancient city, which was the leading city of Dardania in Justinian's time. In order to secure these conquests, Nemanja, unaware that the next Crusade to Jerusalem would be started by the Germans, who together with Hungarians appeared as its main supporters, rushed to send his own representatives on Christmas of the year 1188 to the imperial court at Nuremberg, where king Friedrich was delivered letters, according to which, "Rascians" were waiting with great joy the passing of the army of the Crusaders through their country and there was nothing that would please them more than to personally greet the Emperor."[680]

In the spring of 1189 the great crusader army led by Friderich of Hungary crossed the Danube and Morava valley reaching Nis. On July 27, before the great Emperor appeared, Nemanja and his brother Strazimir, brought many gifts and thanked the German Emperor for the many benefits that the penetration brought (invasion of Nis and the surrounding parts, where they showed up for the first time), and asked to become vassals of Germany, suggesting they were ready to show support with all means against the Greeks.

Emperor Friedrich, whose mind had been drawn to Jerusalem, did not prevent his allies (Rascians and Bulgarians) from using his penetrations eastwards to exploit them for their purposes, such as those benefits they gleaned in the South. Indeed, it happened. A good portion of Nemanja army continued with the crusaders led by Friderich towards Adrianople, but at the same time, Nemanja led a good number of his troops to the Valley of Morava and Ibar to conquer Skopje and Prizren, as well as the provinces of Upper and Lower Polog. So, in January 1190 Nemanja's Army destroyed the Byzantine of Serdice all the way to Prizren, conquering also Scupi and provinces of Polog. On this occasion he set under vassalage the Arberian Prince, Progon, whom he married to his daughter, Komita.[681]

This was the first appearance of Rascia in Arberian lands, which until then had been part of Byzantium and were governed by noblemen,

---

[679] Jiriček, Konstatindin: *"Historia e serbëve,"* Tirana, 2010, p. 305.
[680] Ibid, p. 306.
[681] Ibid, p. 328.

despots and local princes. This fact is of great importance because it lifts the mist created by some makeshift church documents re-written in the 19th century, which were dealt with later, according to which the social and political Slavic presence in these parts, dates back to the 5th century A.D.

Although after the agreement of German Emperor Friedrich with Byzantium at Adrianople on February 14, 1190 for the crusaders to move through Hellespont towards Asia, by which the Rascians and Bulgarians could no longer count on the German help to continue with their conquests in the parts of Byzantium, many of which were already occupied, the Zupan of Rascia, Nemanja, succeeded even after the defeat he suffered by the Byzantine Emperor, Isaac, at the Battle of Morava, to sign a favorable peace treaty with Byzantium, which legitimized their invasions in the Dardanian areas, where their civilization stretched from ancient time enjoying special exfoliation from the time of Justinian I when Dardania turned into an administrative and spiritual center, among the most known in Illyricum.

Therefore, the Rascians held on to an important part of the area of "Arberian Byzantium" from Nis, Leskovac and Sitnica and Llab Rivers with Lipjan. At the White Drin Basin they kept the conquered provinces belonging to the Episcopate of Prizren, Peja, and Decan, as well as the provinces in the north to Shkodra. Nemanja was empowered on the coast too with the new conquests in the part of Dioclea, including Tivar and Kotor.[682]

The reasons why Byzantium sought to strengthen Zupan Nemanja with new commitments from the central part of the Adriatic (mostly parts belonging to Arberian lands) should be required in Rascian determination, by acknowledging vassalage of Constantinople, to emerge as the main supporter between the Bulgarians and the West. However, the Byzantine edifice was guarded, which was by now faltering from both within and outside. For this reason a marriage was agreed with Nemanja. His son Stefan married the niece of Emperor Eudoch, his brother Alex's daughter.

Besides the acquisition of the major central and western part, the Zupan of Rascia showed skill in consolidating the part between Dioclea and Zahlumia, where the true nucleus Slav social and political organiza-

---

[682] Ibid, p. 310.

tion of the 9th century and on was located, where it moved to the East as far as Rascia. This had to happen through an outlet to the Adriatic, providing the "center" with two wings. As Nemanja had joined the Crusade of Friedrich I stating support for his campaign to Jerusalem, even accepting German vassalage – although he soon changed his words upon engaging in secret agreements with the Normans - Pope Clement III (November 25, 1189) asked the Catholic archbishops of Ragusa and Tivar to be on friendly terms with Nemanja. The Pope, indeed, had asked the newly appointed archbishop, Bernard of Ragusa, to do honors to the sons of Nemanja *(dilectis filiis, nobilibus viris megaju-pano, Straschimiro et Mirosclabo),*[683] which they, as their father had done, responded by loyalty to the Western Church.

In all this development to restore to the Holy See its lost spiritual space in the former parts of Illyricum, where other factors (Slavs and Bulgarians) now entered the game, they were trying to remain submissive to Catholicism, though at the same time they were doing the same towards the East and Byzantine areas in order to preserve the broken balance of the Church on both sides especially after its division in 1054.

There was also another factor in all this discussion standing for the opposite, for a complete destruction of Byzantium and creation of a new Rome. The old Dodge of Venice, Henry Dandal, who was in charge of crusade preparations, had become convinced that Byzantine should be ruined to the ground. Although for the circumstances this seemed somewhat excessive, as Venice was long an ally of Byzantium and in terms of the agreement with Emperor Alex Comnenus of 1081, it managed to conquer all the markets of the Empire thanks to the privileges it enjoyed. However, after the death of Alexis I, and the coming to power of his successor, Manuel, Venice felt its interests were at stake in Byzantium.

It was its rivals, Genoa and Pisa, which had already been strengthened and in a new agreement with Manuel, that would be able to remove Venice from the game. So, it was time to use all the Norman mood and rage for this purpose.

On these premises and on the account of Louis VII, Venice took over the running of the crusade. Crusaders gathered in Venice and as the fleet of the city was the only one able to make the transfer of thousands of Christian volunteers to Egypt with its fleet, it needed a preliminary

---

[683] See: Theiner: Mon. Slav. 1, 6, (no date, response to Pope's letter of 2nd of January 1199), cited according to Jiriček, K: *"Historia e serbëve,"* Tirana, 2010, p. 311.

agreement with the Dodge Henrik Dandal, who asked the crusaders to leave the costs of the trip to Venice through a military intervention to take Zara (Zadar), which was held by Hungarians.

In November 1202 Zara was captured. The crusaders waited for the following spring at Zara. They were joined by the son of Isaac II, the young Alex, who had managed to escape from prison with his blinded father, where he had been placed by Alex Angel. In May of 1203 in Corfu an agreement on the diversion of the expedition was signed.[684]

Of course, the deviation of the expedition that took place in Corfu was part of Venice's games, managing to convince the leaders of the Crusade in disembarking in Constantinople and settling accounts there with Byzantine "conspirators," led by Emperor Alex III, who collaborated with Arabs and other enemies of the Catholics.

The crusaders found no difficulty in entering the Golden Horn, once they broke the chain that blocked access to the bay. From there the crusaders began the demolition of city walls from the ground. Efforts to defend the capital of Byzantium proved futile. On July 17, 1203, Constantinople fell to the crusaders. Emperor Alexis III fled with the treasure, while the crusaders restored blind Isaac II to the imperial throne, while his son, Alex IV was appointed co-emperor.

However, it was soon realized that the blind emperor was not able to hold to the throne, as the crusaders were dissatisfied with him being unable to pay the compensation which was agreed upon in Zara soon after they restored him to the throne, and the Byzantines, who could not tolerate an emperor supervised by the Latins and worked to take the Empire hostage.

This was cause for a rebellion that broke out in Constantinople in the beginning of January 1204, as a consequence of which the Emperor was dethroned losing both his crown and his life. Alex V took the throne. Duke Murzuflis, son-in-law of Alex III, husband of Eudoclea, and former wife of Despot Stefan, once again campaigned in Byzantium for the anti-Latin trend, giving reason to the crusaders to shed their anger over the Byzantine capital.

Therefore, the capital of Byzantium replaced Jerusalem in the summer of 1204, turning into a Papacy ploy of the crusaders, in which works of art were lost, and other values looted, while the leadership was entrust-

---

[684] Ostrogorsi, Georg: *"Historia e Perandorisë Bizantine,"* Tirana, 2002, p. 288.

ed to Alex IV, a blind old man, released from prison and on an unstable throne, which he soon lost, as the Crusaders were wrenching the Byzantine Empire, which they baptized as the "Latin Empire of Constantinople" with Emperor Count Baldwin of Flanders.[685]

This intervention layed preconditions for the destruction of Byzantium, which before it happened in general, opened the way to some crumbling developments everywhere, with emerging ambitions of many different principalities to inherit it or benefit from its fall, triggering multiple internal wars. This suited the Arabs and Turks, who after one and a half centuries turned the 10-century-old Byzantium rule over to the showcase of history.

The time of more than a century remained increasingly scarce to the internal and external defenders, users, and destroyers of Byzantium, to end the edifice that passed through different unbundling conflicts, wars and most volatile alliances, with the lands of Arber and Arberians forcefully included in all the important developments. These represented the foundations of the Arberian state in the Middle Ages as a natural extension of the edifice of the Byzantine Empire in the establishment of which they had participated since the beginning, being its founders together with the Latins and Greeks.

Of this nature was the *Despotate of Epirus,* 1204-1253, and the *Kingdom of Arberia,* 1272-1286. The first was founded by Mikhael Angel the Second and the latter by King Charles the First Anjou. The first was an effort that the legacy of Byzantium be used to create a state structure competitive with others. The second was within state structures that the Westerners had begun to create out of their royal crowns in order to create conditions so that Byzantium would be restored into a western empire.

The latter, namely the Arbërian Kingdom, although there were some stiff "repetitions" and returns for almost a century, remaining in some stages but external "crowns," was politically promoting the existence of "Regnum Albaniae," in a meaningful report of the bitter fighting of the West against the East, with Arberians appearing as a kingdom.

---

[685] Zavalani, Tajar: *"Histori e Shqipnis,"* 1998.

Despot of Epirus and the Arberian Kingdom

The establishment of the Despotate of Epirus was associated with the Fourth Crusade and its consequences for Byzantium. – The Latins occupied Constantinople and proclaimed the "Latin Empire of Constantinople." – Emperor Alex V escaped moving to Nicaea in Asia Minor, declared it as the capital of the newly formed "Empire in Exile," which mainly included the European provinces of Byzantium not occupied by Latins, part of which were also some feuds from Drin to the Bay of Corinth, known as Epirus. – Mikhael Angel I was proclaimed Despot of Epirus, by opposing the Emperor of Nicaea. – Michael of Thessaloniki went to Durres, and there, with the assistance of Arberian and Vlach soldiers fortified the city managing to keep the Despotate of Epirus strong for ten years. – Emperor Paleologus war against the Despotate of Epirus and its destruction by means of Turkish, Tatar, Slav and Greek mercenaries. - Charles I of Anjou and the announcement of the "Kingdom of Arbëria" "Regnum Albaniae," on September 21, 1272. – Splits among Arberian nobles and feudal lords on the basis of loyalty to the "Kingdom of Arbëria" and Byzantium. – The failure of Charles of Anjou after sixteen years and the conquering of parts of "Kingdom of Arbëria" by Uros II of Rascia. – The return of the "Kingdom of Arber" and the union of a good part of nobles and feudal lords under the crown of Philip of Tarentum. – Rascian and Byzantine attacks against the "Kingdom of Arbëria" and the call for a European campaign by Pope Gregory in defense of the "Kingdom of Arbëria." – Western volunteers in Arberia and their defeat from Rascians and Byzantines. – The collapse of the "Kingdom of Arbëria" and occupation of its largest parts by Stefan Dusan.

It has been rightly said that rarely in history has something gone as planned as in the case of the division of the Byzantine Empire after what happened during the Fourth Crusade. In fact, it was all part of settling an account between the crusaders and the Great Dodge of Venice, Henry Dandal, who had played a crucial role in recent events, being an inspirer of the treaty of division and becoming also a figurehead in its implementation.[686]

---

[686] Ostrogorski, Georg: *"Historia e Perandorisë Bizantine,"* Tirana, 2002, p. 302.

The first step of implementing the division of the Byzantine Empire was naturally to start with choosing an emperor in Constantinople, an act that would be under the influence of the Venetians, who were determined for Count Baldwin of Flanders, who on May 16 at St. Sophia Church was crowned Emperor of the Latin Empire of Constantinople. He was consecrated by the first Latin Patriarch of Constantinople and the Venetian Tomazo Morazini. On this occasion, as the Emperor of the Latin Empire, Baldwin took over a quarter of the entire territory of the Empire, and of the remaining three quarters, half belonged to the Venetians, and the rest was to be divided into imperial feuds to be distributed to knights.

However, the biggest benefits from this division, as expected, went to Venice. Although it relinquished territories of Epirus, Acarnania, Etolia and Peloponnese, it acquired the ports of Corona, and Modones in the Peloponnese and a little later that of Durres and Ragusa on the Adriatic. The Adriatic Republic took the Ionian island, Crete, the largest part of the archipelago of islands, among others Euboea, Andro, and Naxos, the most important gates of Hellespont and Marmara Sea: Gallipoli, Rodos, Heraclea, and Adrianople on the mainland. Venice also took two thirds of the city of Constantinople, becoming the master of a quarter of the Byzantine Empire. Therefore, the Byzantine Empire was torn apart into a number of large and small principalities with a complex system of diversified feuds.

The establishment of the Epirus Despotate is associated with the Fourth Crusade and its consequences for Byzantium. After the Latins occupied Constantinople proclaiming the "Latin Empire of Constantinople," Emperor Alexis V escaped. He took the treasure with him and settled in Nicaea in Asia Minor, which he declared the capital city. As Alex V lost authority, an army man, Theodor Lascaris, son-in-law of the Comnenus appeared, forming the *"Empire in Exile,"* which included mainly European provinces of Byzantium, not occupied by Latins, or enjoying some independence through the composition of certain feuds. This setup included some feuds from Drin to the Bay of Corinth, known as Epirus. Mikhael Angel I, who was in Thessaloniki, was announced Despot of Epirus, by opposing the Emperor of Nicaea. Mikhael went from Thessaloniki to Durres and with the assistance of Arberian and Vlach soldiers, fortified the city and managed to keep the Despotate of Epirus strong for ten years.

Before he died, his heir was appointed, Theodor Angel, his half-brother, who did his best to transform the Despotate of Epirus into a Byzantine Orthodox stronghold in the war against Westerners, who with the "Latin Empire in Constantinople," was in Constantinople and the part of the Latin Empire in Thessaloniki. After taking the throne from his brother, Theodor attached his own name to three imperial dynasties: Angels, Dukes, and Comnenus,[687] calling himself Theodore Angel Duke Comnenus, and this evoked the Byzantine rivalry between the two centers, fighting to regain the throne of Byzantium in Constantinople.

Under the leadership of Theodore Angel the Despotate of Epirus attained contours of a state, gaining increasing importance. The noble warrior had already seized lands from Durres to the Bay of Corinth with its center in Arta. Therefore, the Epirotan state, as a Byzantine principality in the center of the Balkans, just as the Empire of Nicaea in Asia Minor, represented an important center of Byzantine cultural continuity and a unifying political core.[688]

On these principles, as an independent principality, it opposed the Latin kingdom of Thessaloniki, Venetians on the Adriatic, and the Slavs in the North and northeast. In 1216, Theodor achieved a major success cutting one of the Latin arms that held Byzantium hostage as was the Latin Empire of Thessaloniki. Before achieving this, Theodor captured in Durres the Latin Emperor of Thessaloniki, Peter de Courtenay, who had previously stayed in Rome where he put on the crown of the Latin Empire by Pope Honorius III himself.

Peter de Courtenay, married to Yolanda, Baldwin and Henry's sister, in order to witness the crowning triumph in Rome had to go through Durres and then continue his journey to Constantinople. After this great success, Theodor Angel Duke Comnenus undertook an extensive campaign against the Latins. Of course, his first destination was the neighboring kingdom of Thessalonica, as the knights that established it had gone back to their own countries. The Epirotan Prince held the Latin Kingdom of Thessalonica under siege for some time, and in late 1224 he went in. This was the same time as the end of one of the crusader states created on the Byzantine land. The Principality of Epirus was now stretching from the Adriatic to the Aegean Sea and included Thessaly and a good part of Macedonia.

---

[687] *Mikhael* and *Theodor* were the sons, the first being illegitimate and the latter legitimate, of Sebastocrat Johan Angl. He took his name Dukas from his mother, and that of Comnenus from his grandmother Theodora, Alex I's daughter.
[688] Ibid, p. 309.

These successes made Theodor Angel Duke Comnenus see himself as emperor. He was called *basileus* and autocrator of Romeys, holding himself as the heir to the throne of Byzantium as well as the leader of the Battle for Constantinople, fighting openly against the Empire of Nicaea.[689]

The success of Theodor Angel Duke Comnenus against the Latins, with the participation of the Arberian military and feudal lords from the territories of Epirus, greatly intimidated the West, which did its best to save the *"Latin Empire of Constantinople"* from Theodore Angel and his Epirotan power. However, what Rome was unable to do to prevent Theodor Angel Duke Comnenus from ending up in Constantinople as Emperor of Byzantium, was done by his "rival," the Czar of Bulgaria, Asen II, who played a game with Theodor, cutting in his way with a large army, at Edirne. There, Theodor Angel Duke Comnenus suffered defeat by the Bulgarians, being captured and blinded.

With this loss from the Bulgarians, the Byzantine Empire of Thessaloniki was destroyed, while the Despotate of Epirus went back to its former boundaries continuing as a separate kingdom for several more years.[690] However, the Bulgarian Jan Asen II soon returned to the old dream of the former czar Boris, and after invading Macedonia, he also brought under submission Arberian lands up to Durres.[691]

During this campaign the Bulgarians were gaining strength again in the Balkans, either by linking them to despots of Rascia, or by keeping good connections with the descendants of the German King Heinrich, with Latins and Normans as common rivals. On these alliances, and committed to eliminating at all costs the rivalry of Nicaea for the throne of Byzantium, the Bulgarians sought to be relieved of the Roman Church crown. However, as they did not wish to do that by falling into the hands of the Eastern Church, meaning that of Constantinople, whose "authorizations" were already in Nicaea, Asen II presented the idea of establishing an Orthodox Patriarchate at Trnovo, which was recognized by both Nicaea and eastern patriarchs.

The church leaders of Nicaea accepted this heartbroken, fearing rejection would push Bulgaria into the bosom of Rome, with major political

---

[689] For more see: Langon, J: *"La reprise de Salonique par les Grecs en 1224, Actes du VI Congres Intern. d'Etudes Byz.,"* I (1950), cited according to Osgtrogorsi, G: "Historia e Perandorisë Bizantine," Tirana, 2002, p. 309.

[690] Ibid, p. 109.

[691] Vasilev, A: *"History of the Byzantine Empire,"* p. 525.

consequences, which the Empire wished the least waiting a return. Therefore, with the establishment of the Bulgarian Patriarchy, Bulgaria won its independent church, as would the Church of Rascia, using almost the same stratagem as Bulgaria. However, these churches had to recognize the primacy of the Patriarch of Nicaea, mention the name of the Byzantine Patriarch in their religious services, and pay tribute to him.

A treaty of tolerance among the three Byzantine churches was signed in the spring of 1235 at Gallipoli, where a new post for the Bulgaria Church was issued. This "reconciliation" was solemnly celebrated with the marriage of the son of Emperor Theodor II Laskar with the daughter of the Czar of Bulgaria.

Despite this marriage, the Bulgarian Kingdom of Jan Asen II didn't last long. It crumbled in 1241, after the death of Jan Asen II, while trying to reach an alliance with the Latins and Cumans against Nicaea. This gave reason to Jan Vatace to take back Byzantine lands of Thrace and Macedonia and conquer Thessaloniki in 1246.

The Despotate of Epirus, with lower intensity, continued to be included in internal delimitations of Byzantine emperors for power. This was clear after the accession to the throne of Byzantium by Michael Paleologos, in 1259, declaring himself emperor, something that was challenged by the Despot of Epirus, Manuel II, who used the mess in the Empire of Nicaea, to turn the Despotate of Epirus independent from Paleolog's influence.

Therefore, he called on the King of Sicily, Manfred, the illegitimate son of the German Emperor Frederick II for help, as well as the Prince of Morea, Gulhelm de Villehardou. At the same time Michael Paleologos assembled a mercenary army made up of Turks, Tartars, Slavs and Greeks, and marched against Manuel II. The battle took place near Pelagonia near Castoria. Manuel and all his allies suffered a humiliating defeat. This was the end of the Despotate of Epirus, becoming a province of the Byzantine Empire.[692]

A little later the *Latin Empire of Constantinople* was destroyed. On August 13, 1261, exactly 130 years later, Mikhael Paleologos entered the historic capital of his kingdom with great ceremony and was solemnly crowned in St. Sophia Cathedral.[693]

The fall of the *Latin Empire of Constantinople*, as was thought, would not stop the final downfall of Byzantium. Rather, the disintegration

---

[692] Ibid, p. 527.
[693] Zavalani, Tajar: "*Histori e Shqipnisë*," Tirana, p. 110.

processes continued further, but in the final stage did not move toward the restoration of the Byzantine center by Latins. The former vassal princes of the Byzantine Empire, a Slav, Bulgarian and Greek, played a decisive role in the collapse of the Empire, and, in this process, were used in different ways by the Catholic countries of the West, led by the Vatican.

Evidently, the Arberian lands and factor in general, scattered through various principalities, gained special and perhaps insurmountable weight, because since the Despotate of Epirus, aware of their role, acted towards becoming a factor and this caused the Catholic countries of the West led by the Vatican, to focus on them and their power, so that it be used as much as possible for their interests.

Indeed, finding themselves at developing events among the worst for their turns involving the Byzantine Empire between the 11th and 14th centuries, especially from the time of the beginning of the Crusades and the appearance of the Normans as the driving force in the West, from the First Crusade (1097 and to the Fourth 1104), the Arberians were found on the defense lines of Byzantium and its edifice, as they rightly felt they were its legitimate founders.

Although the circumstances in their area differed significantly from the time of Emperor Heraclius, when their very important status was called into question as an important liaison factor between the West and East (as the eastern province of the empire - from the reforms of Emperor Diocletian, and under the jurisdiction of the Holy Church of Rome so - by the Novella of Emperor Justinian I), a status they would lose in the 9th century after the appearance of the Bulgarian Kingdom and their fall under long occupation, however, the Byzantine roof, no matter how much it would protect them from "foul weather," remained their only support.

The same was repeated during the developments following the First Crusade and on, when they lined up in defense of Byzantium. They did the same even when the Slavs, who had narrowed their ethnic space in the North and East, turned into their main opponents and destroyers of their ethnic and spiritual identity. Even after the Fourth Crusade when Constantinople fell into the hands of the Crusaders and his Empire became fragmented into four parts (two in the West: Latin Empire of Constantinople and the Latin Kingdom of Thessaloniki, and two in Byzantium: the Empire of Nicaea and Despotate of Epirus), Arberians turned to defend Byzantium.

They did that with strong commitment for nearly half a century. Angels and Comnenus acted to keep the tree and spirit of Byzantium alive in the western part, i.e. Epirus, Macedonia and Thessaly up to the Bosphorus, mostly threatened by Westerners. Of course, Theodore Angel Duke Comnenus was able to take the Latin-held Constantinople from Thessaloniki, facing collapse if it were not for the rivalry of Jan Vatace of Nicaea, in the detached part of Asia Minor. He then demanded the crown of Byzantine for himself, and also, if it were not for the Bulgarian Ivan II Asen, who in alliance with the Despotate of Rascia and Latins, in 1230, he would have been stopped in Thrace, after having occupied Adrianople and being near the Bosporus.

From that time on, the Despotate of Epirus, though turning into a vassal of the Emperor of Nicaea, grasped the new realities, speaking of the end of Byzantium and the idea of a great empire. It was condemned to fall forever, so the new factors had to line up and act accordingly.

And, the "new" factors of power, along with the Turks who had begun to come in from all sides, especially from the East, creating through both open and concealed alliances with favorable conditions for themselves, were by now the western countries, which entered the game leaning mostly on the local factor (Bulgarian, Slav, Greek and Arberian despots and princes). Aware that Byzantium could not be turned to Rome, as had been attempted with the Latin Empire of Constantinople, the Holy See and its allies focused on the local factors, opponents of Byzantium, and all those who had ambition for power, in creating western states or kingdoms in this space, which would defend their interests in this part, first of all by turning them into a protective block against the Ottomans.

The emergence of the "Kingdom of Arbëria" was a result of this project, founded in 1272 by Charles the First of the Anjou Kingdom, after having gained the crown of the Kingdom of Sicily in a battle with the King of Sicily, Manfred Hohenstaufen, as Pope Innocent IV asked the brother of the king of France for this, who by dethroning the Hohenstaufens aimed at creating opportunities for the Anjou to fight against the Byzantine Empire reeling in its land with its component factors. Arbëria represented one of the most suitable countries for this purpose, from where they could move further eastwards.

Prior to the establishment of the *"Arbërian Kingdom,"* which represented a significant twist, not only for Arberians, but also for the further developments taking place in Europe on the eve of the pervasiveness of the Ottomans, which changed the direction of history, one should consider several developments leading to the emergence of the Arberian factor to the level of an important subject, an ally of the West in its struggle to profit and assimilate as much as possible by the weakening of Byzantium.

Because, the throe of Byzantium for the West did not only mean the end of an opponent, but was the beginning of a concern about who would be able to inherit it, especially when it was known that the leading contenders - Rascians, were more unpredictable, as they had already been tempted for possible alliances with the Ottomans, who were also related to the undeclared position of the Patriarchate of Constantinople to maintain the orthodoxy space from "Catholic re-conquest" even with the help of the Ottomans!

In these circumstances, the Holy See, although cautiously, again openly announced the aims of the West to penetrate Arberia, in order from there to take over the falling edifice of Byzantium, before it became prey to Slavs or Bulgarians, who were strengthening at its expense and by day were taking its place by giving the issue an unpredictable direction full of risks for the West. This development for the West was equally disturbing as was the loss of power and defense of Constantinople in the East at war with the Seljuk Turks.

Therefore, it was Pope Innocent IV, who was positioned openly on the side of Charles the First Anjou, a promising European force to be incited, first against the king of Germany, Manfred Hohenstaufen,[694] and then against the Byzantines, wars that he won, first in 1266 at the Battle of Benevento against the Germans and then against Mikhael II of Byzantium. Pope Innocent IV did so in a different language from what the Holy See had been using before, constantly attempting to separate the issues of church unity from the political ones, which in fact had caused Western

---

[694] The circumstances establishing the rule of Manfred Hohenstaufen in Epirus are not quite clear. It is only known that at that time an uprising against Byzantium had broken out, which Georg Akropolites calls "an uprising of the Albanian people" (το των Αλβανιτων ετνος), in which the Byzantine administration was in complete disarray and the Byzantine governor, Constantine Habaran, fell victim to a conspiracy conjured up by Despot Mikhael II Angel of Epirus. Apparently, this was considered the most suitable moment for Manfred to start implementing his ambitious plan in the East. In a private act prepared some time before February 1258 in Durres, Manfred Hohenstaufen was the lord of Durrës, Vlora, Berat, and "Highlands of Spiranica." (See: Xhufi, Pëllumb *"Nga palelogët te Muzakajt,"* Tirana, 2009, pp. 106-111)

concerns, as the ability or inability to resist the East to the existential challenges, such as that of the Ottoman penetration would determine its future and that of all Christianity.

The Anjou, of course, in agreement with the Pope, in their efforts to conquer the uncertain Byzantine edifice, aimed mainly at taking over the Arberian lands and placing them under surveillance as a balance against the Slavs, Greeks and Bulgarians, erecting a kingdom of their own, which appearred as a permanent ally of the West and Western Christianity in general. Arbëria was being seen as an important point towards the restoration of the Roman Empire in the East. Furthermore, even though with the Zupans of Rascia and Bulgarians, Charles of Anjou, on the eve of landing on the other side of the Adriatic, had some conversations to frame his plans, in which he was successful in reaching some secret alliances with Rascians in addition, such as those on Dioclea and Ragusa.

However, he wouldn't change his attitude about the role and place of Arberians in this development, which included many local factors associated with Byzantium, or having an interest in its weakening or collapse. By focusing on Arberia as an impassable gateway, which always opened the doors for Constantinople, Charles of Anjou sought to find a "trump" in his rights of succession to the holdings of Manfred in Arberia, by turning Manfred's associates in Arberia into vassals. Therefore, Charles I of Anjou appointed Gazo Cinardi, as viceroy in Arberia, a relative of the slain vicegerent of Manfred, Philip. Evidently, before he was deployed on the Arberian coast, by means of two Catholic priests: John from Durres and Nicholas from Arberia, he had established a good relationship with some of the aristocrats of Arberia. As supporters of King Charles and his great ally, Pope Gregory X, they made several trips between Naples and Durres, relaying the king's orders to the chiefs of Arberia.[695]

With the promise of unifying and strengthening them towards independence under the Catholic cross, Charles the First of Anjou did not find it difficult to win over the Arberian nobles and feudal lords, upon his arrival in Durres in 1272, and from there, with a well-prepared army for another war against Mikhael the Second succeeded, without much difficulty, to return the properties and possessions taken by Byzantium to the Arberian nobles. As during further incursions on the mainland, the well-known Arberian families were rewarded with high posts, but also with

---

[695] *"Historia e Popullit Shqiptar,"* Part One, Tirana, 2002, p. 240.

large properties, Charles of Anjou had established all the necessary conditions for the formation of the *"Kingdom of Arbëria"* (*Regnum Albanaie*) in order to proclaim himself *"King of Arberia"* (*Rex Albanaie*).

In these favorable circumstances, suitable to its emergence in Arberia, however, one should by all means mention those preceding the time when he took measures to have Arberians recognize him as a sovereign for life "without violence and pressure," implying an agreement under which Charles of Anjou recognized all the privileges to Arberian nobles and gentry granted to them earlier by the Byzantine empire, respecting all the "their good customs and traditions."[696] The preservation of property and guarantees provided to local feudal lords and despots were a precondition for accepting vassalage, which satisfied them, but also the new owners, regardless of what kind of crowns emerged.

On these principles Charles I Anjou acted, announced "Regnum Albanaie" and himself "Rex Albanaie" in Naples, on February 21, 1272.[697]

The establishment of the *"Kingdom of Arbëria,"* in 1272, surviving internal and external challenges for fourteen years, is an important factor not only for Arberians, who were most devoted in the past to defend the edifice of Byzantium at all costs, as they felt it as their own, but for other factors from within and without as well, as the lands of Arberians turned again into a vital force determining relations between East and West.

Therefore, in the new circumstances when Byzantium could not hold, while the West had made it known that Arberians and Arbëria were those that could turn into a significant western power in the Byzantine space, on which they could rely by creating a wide defense dam against Ottoman intrusions, a constant fight with two open fronts began. On one side what appeared as a remnant of Byzantium, was nothing more than a Bulgarian-Greek mixture. Meanwhile, principalities, primarily the Slavic ones, tended to play double games, but mostly at the expense of Arbërians and their social and political structures from those of nobility to their principalities.

In this battle, an already unraveled Byzantium required by all means to restore the lost power of the West doing this in the Arberian lands, as they had a strategic importance, because, evidently, through them crossed

---

[696] Among the circumstances dealing with missionaries of Charles I Anjou sent by him to Arberian nobles and feudal lords are mentioned by all means. (See: *Acta Albaniae*. I, p. 802).

[697] "*Historia e Popullit Shqiptar*," Part One, Prishtina, 1969, pp. 188/189

waterways and land roads connecting the East with the West, the surveillance of which, along with political power meant economic power as well.

Rascia, aided by Greeks, saw a double danger in the further strengthening of the "Kingdom of Arbëria." Arberians became a factor in the Balkans and this could not be done without cost, for the Slavs increasingly opened claims for appearing as successors of the crumbling Byzantine Empire. On the other hand, it was unacceptable to the Rascians for Arberians and their kingdom to become a supporter of Catholicism, assessing that with its help the West would gain an opportunity to penetrate further in the direction of Constantinople, and one day to conquer it all.

Therefore, the "construct" of the Holy See called the "Kingdom of Arbëria" had to be prevented at all costs before turning into a key factor that could eventually ultimately decide the internal struggle for the cross in favor of Catholicism, and with this, the line of Emperor Theodosius from the 4th century for moving further towards the East, to where the West was interested, but now turning it into a line of confrontation with the Ottomans.

Viewed from the perspective of spheres of interest and wider East-West relations as defined in long efforts for power between the Catholic and Orthodox churches, the emergence of the "Kingdom of Arbëria" and of Charles I d'Anjou, as "King of Arbëria" rightly opens the question of the importance of the Arberian factor since the Middle Ages and its big role for determining the boundary of spheres of interest to one side or the other.

Although the Albanian historiography, out of the known ideological concepts of the past had overlooked this fact, and the Serbian, Greek and Russian historiography had tried to minimize it, seeing it only as a *"failed attempt, or as an insert most frequently of the Papacy nature and the Anjouine Dynasty to weaken Byzantium through the use and manipulation of the population to those ends.*[698] However, what happened during the 14 years of the *"Kingdom of Arbëria,"* represents more than an open war between East and West for domination, where the majority population of Arbëria was included in the West, which through the assistance of the Papacy and the Italian-French alliance to eventually become part of it, a part of Arberian nobles and gentry stuck with Byzantine commitments,

---

[698] Ostrogrorski, Georg *"Historia e Perandorisë Bizantine,"* Tirana, 2010, p. 281.

such as Pal Gropa and Gjin Muzaka, masters of the Dibra zone fighting on the side of Byzantium, standing for the first time on opposite sides and at war with each other since the emergence of Byzantium.

Even in these circumstances, at least regarding the behavior of Pal Gropa, who although remaining outside the sovereignty of Charles of Anjou and the "Kingdom of Arbëria," was still on the side of his vassals. All the authority he possessed in the territory of Dibra and Ohrid (Manastir) was recognized, even when there was news of him being about to be found on the Byzantine side.[699]

Various sources indicate that mobilization for and against the "Kingdom of Arbëria"were, on one side for the Orthodox cross and the East, and on the other for the Catholic cross and the West. In this decisive war for the relocation of Theodosius' line from the 4th century and the final separation of the churches and their open hostility in 1054, the Arberian factor not only had the role of a simple object, as in the time of the *Despotate of Epirus,* which had to decide on the power relations among the Byzantines, but rather the role of a subject that could decide upon the new relation of forces between the two wings of the former empire, struggling for domination.

In these circumstances, a part of Arberian nobles, feudal lords, and gentry, having lost their confidence of Byzantium and its power, understood that there was only the Arberian royal crown on the head of Charles I d'Anjou, brought in from Naples. This could have motivated them to protect it and it was the social position of the builders of the kingdom, in which they now stood united in almost all their lands realizing for the first time that they were fighting for an internal power, which, although supervised from outside, was turning into a state of their own and acting as one. Indeed, the Arberian population gained a sense of self-sufficiency even when Mikhael VIII Paleologos succeeded through promises sent by various emissaries in 1275 in sparking a few rebellions by some local feudalists tied to the Gtreeks in various forms, declaring themselves as Arberians to encourage others with the pretext that the nobles coming from Italy and France had allegedly usurped many of the local properties behaving as invaders against the native population.[700]

The Arberian feudal lords, nobles, counts, and gentry, despite some fluctuations, as were those Blinishti and Sguraj, to a large extent still

---

[699] Xhufi, Pëllumb: "*Nga Paleologët te Muzakajt,*" Tirana, 2009, p. 124.
[700] "*Historia e popullit shqiptar,*" Part One, Prishtina, 1969, p. 189.

supported Charles I of Anjou in the war against Byzantium. They kept doing this even when Paleologos, thanks to help arriving from the Greek and Rascian volunteers, fanatics of the Orthodox cross, caught up to the walls of Durazzo (Durres).

Before the "Byzantine connection," in which, besides Greeks and Rascians, also a number of Arberian noblemen were involved, fighting for the first time "on different sides" to conquer Durres, a decisive battle would take place for Berat where Byzantines and their allies were concentrated, whose primary aim was the destruction of the "Kingdom of Arbëria." King Charles of Anjou was obliged to undertake a campaign in these breakaway parts that had joined Byzantium, although this would put the Arberian noblemen and counts in an internal struggle, instead of representing the main core of the "Kingdom of Arberia."

However, in order to fight less with each other and more with Byzantium, Charles of Anjou reached an alliance with what appeared as the remnant of the Despotate of Epirus, led by Despot Nicephorus, who appeared to have an impact on this part, especially on some Arberian feudal lords. He was proclaimed vassal to Anjouin king and handed the latter the castle of Butrint, Sopot, and Porto Palermo, showing that Nicephorus, who hitherto stood between Byzantium and Charles I Anjou, who was a leading exponent of the West in the war against the Empire of Constantinople, decided in favor of the West, accepting the "Kingdom of Arberia," despite the fact that it was not recognized and was even fought by some Arberian noblemen who were on the side of Paleologus, who no longer cared about the plight of Byzantium. This was done by dividing Arberians who had already turned into a factor between East and West. To prevent their wastefulness, that went to the detriment of the "Kingdom of Arberia" and thus to the detriment of the West and in favor of Byzantium which was no Byzantium any longer, but rather a creature held by Slavs, Bulgarians and Greeks, while playing with the West on its back, Charles of Anjou made another attempt to unite Arberians around him. In this context, he released a number of noble Arberian rebels from Italian prisons, among whom were Gjin Muzaka, along with Demetrius Zgura, Kasnec and Guliem Blinishti, etc.[701]

Evidently, the release from internment of these nobles wasn't able to save Charles I of Anjou from the ruin that was on the verge of happening.

---

[701] *"Historia e Popullit Shqiptar,"* Volume I, Tirana 2002, p 244.

The fate of Anjou was sealed in Berat with the war ending in the defeat of the Anjou forces and that part of Arberian nobility and gentry fighting on their side. The Anjouin Commander, Hugo de Sully was captured, while the rest of his forces were able to find refuge in the castle of Vlora.

Therefore, the Byzantines and some Arberian noblemen with them had managed to halt the expansion of the "Kingdom of Arbëria" to the South creating circumstances for Mikhael VIII Paleologos to appear as a winner. Why it did not immediately happen had to do with the fact that the Seljuk Turks had crossed the borders of the Empire and had invaded Pelagonia.[702]

Despite the return of attention from the East, Paleologos did not renounce his commitment to ruin the "Arberian Kingdom" as soon as plausible, which for him and others was seen as a springboard of the West towards Constantinople. The Papacy, which was following with concern the developments on the eastern Adriatic coast, where by now a great battle between East and West was taking place, could not allow the West to experience a significant loss from Byzantium, which could represent some kind of revenge against the Fourth Crusade when Catholics conquered Constantinople and ruined many of its cultural values. Therefore, it engaged Catholic volunteers from the Italian, French, Maltese, and even Spanish lands in defense of the "Kingdom of Arbëria" deciding, on one side, on the direction the continuation of the campaign would take in moving towards the East, and on the other, the East possibly defended as a result of a premature end, coming naturally. Furthermore, the "Arbërian Kingdom" could either be turned into a symbol of Western triumph or into the tomb of Byzantium.

And, as this was the case, it was expected that the spiritual inspiration of the project, the Papacy, with a very dramatic coloration, would address the West for help. Through it, the Catholic countries of the West, heard for the first time of the "Kingdom of Arbëria" and the role it had for the interests of the western cross, interests that were by now of a much wider nature, being motivated also by the interest to be protected against the Ottomans and the penetration of Islam in the old continent, which had begun to horrify the Europeans.

Indeed, the dramatic call for help for the "Kingdom of Arbëria," viewed by western interests, was more than a relief to a country that was

---

[702] D. Geanakoplos: *"Emperor Michael Paleologus,"* p. 343, as quoted by Xhufi, Pëllumb *"Nga Paleologët te Muzakajt,"* Tirana, 2009, p. 132.

threatened, as was said, by the "Byzantine fury" of Paleologus. This referred to a new policy based on the Papacy doctrine of "Roman universalism," as announced by Pope Nicholas III, and made possible after the death of Pope Gregory X (1276). Evidently, Pope Gregory X was one of the followers who had kept walking, forasmuch as the tense East-West circumstances allowed the Roman-Byzantine union.

As noted, it could not hold on any longer, as this went against the interests of the West, being seriously challenged with its ally, "Arbërian Kingdom," which was being attacked from all sides, while Charles of Anjou was unable to act outside the concept of the Holy See, which required some kind of "coordination" with the Byzantines, who were viewed as a dam against the Ottomans. The accession to the Papacy throne of the Frenchman Pope Martin IV, the Roman Curia was determined that the position of sovereign Arberians, i.e. the "Kingdom of Arbëria" be aligned to "the recovery of the Roman Empire usurped by Paleologus," which raised this project to the scale of missionaries, almost similar to that of the Crusades.[703]

Naturally, a good part of the Arberian feudal lords and gentry considered the generous help coming from the West, primarily, as support for their kingdom, despite the fact that it was in the service of the Anjou and for the maintenance of their presence in this part of the world in fierce rivalry with Byzantium and its interests. It was seen that the feudal lords and nobility of Arbëria, and the growing layers of local notables sincerely fought in defense of their kingdom, even after repeated attacks by the Byzantines, aided by the Bulgarians, Greeks and Rascians. It was forced to admit defeat which would come by the end of the year 1281, not because of relation of forces in that war, where they were able to continue to resist, but due to the partial withdrawal of the forces of Charles of Anjou from the defending Durres due to his return to Italy to quell a large uprising that had broken out in Sicily.

It was realized soon that it too was part of a Byzantium plot, which, seeing that the Arberian lands, despite some internal rifts, were invincible and that occurred thanks to the determination of most of Arbërians to defend their kingdom, introduced into the game the King of Aragon by attacking Sicily and thus sealing the ill fate of the *Arbërian Kingdom* as a project of the West, built on the Arberian factor and its growing role.

---

[703] Norden: *"Papstum und Byzanz,"* p. 489.

After this stratagem, which weakened the military strength of Charles the First, the Anjou weren't able to protect the "Arbërian Kingdom." The efforts of the Arberian feudal lords to do so were futile, despite the fact that most of them engaged sincerely in this regard. The new Byzantine Emperor Andronicus II Paleologos, aided greatly by the allies he found among some Arberian nobles and gentry that were not included in the "Kingdom of Arbëria," or who left it depending on the movement of frontlines, continued the attacks to conquer other cities of the "Arbërian Kingdom" by getting back on and exercising terror against the "traitors of orthodoxy." Indeed, more than Catholicism defended their own interests, feeling that they could opt for the first time for a state of their own, even as a vassal, as in those circumstances, this was an almost inevitable way. After Vlora, Kruja and Durres eventually fell in 1286, the Anjou left the Arberian lands and the latter fell once again under the rule of a meticulously fragile Byzantium.

The departure of the Anjou from the Arberian lands after fourteen years of rule and building of the throne of "Arberian Kingdom" left deep scars among the Arberians, because on one side the old conviction about Byzantium as their foundation and roof and their only supporter was broken, and, on the other side stood the western factor, which provided something that in the East was either lost or could inevitably become lost. So, from that time onwards, the Byzantium, as it appeared - connected to the canister of the Slavs, Greeks, Bulgarians, and unable to resist the Turkish invasion – would be unacceptable for many of the Arberian feudal lords and nobles. Therefore, the Byzantines were challenged everywhere without being able to restore the former administrative or church order, and much less have the trust of spiritual counsel. Instead, the Arberian feudal lords and nobles began to rebel in defense of the "Kingdom of Arbëria," because during its time many of them were able to increase and strengthen their social and political positions, while the relationship with the West opened their direct trade route and circulation of goods on both sides of the Adriatic, where others were acting as mediators and main beneficiaries.

The efforts to restore the *"Kingdom of Arbëria,"* though badly and loosely aligned, outside any joint force led by a local center, weren't wasted. There were moments when the Arberian feudal lords and nobles were declared followers of the *"Kingdom of Arbëria,"* regardless of the fact that they were lacking a central crown, which the Anjou kept shining for many years.

However, it was another opponent, who took over the reins of the oppressive central government of Byzantium. This refers to the Slav-Orthodox and the state of Rascia, who used the departure of the Anjou, with whom they had some "contained" agreements in the North, to conquer a large part of the "Kingdom of Arbëria." There were penetrations from the East and Northeast conquering Durres, which they kept for some time. As the Despot of Rascia, Stefan Uros II Milutin (1282-1321), had already occupied Skopje and Prizren, seeking to break even at the rest, all the way to Ohrid in the South, in order to focus on that important triangle, as the Bulgarians had once done. Ohrid was protected by the Arberian nobleman, Progon Skurra, who held a high Byzantine title of the *great heteriarc*. He married Eudocia, the niece of the Byzantine Emperor Andronicus II Paleologos.[704]

Based on an agreement with Byzantine concluded in 1299, the Rascians were drawn above the Shkumbin River while Byzantium held Southern Arberia. It was a deal reached between Rascia and Byzantium, strengthened by the marriage of Milutin with Simona, five-year-old daughter of Andronicus II. The Treaty of friendship between Rascians and Byzantium led to the rising influence of Byzantium on the Slavs, who began to be articulated by successive extensions of their territories snatched from the Arberian lands.[705]

The "Kingdom of Arbëria," founded by the Anjou royal gate and led by Charles I, who was proclaimed "King of Arbëria," after its subjugation by Byzantium and the Kingdom of Rascia, and its division into two parts, continued to remain a political and state concern of the feudal lords, nobles and gentry of Arberia. This was shown by the wars they waged against Byzantine and Slavic invaders during the next eight years. However, they were never able to strengthen their state and administrative presence. This led to the Anjou, and the Pope never giving up their efforts to restore the *"Kingdom of Arbëria,"* as a factor of power and ally of Catholic Christianity on the other side of the Adriatic, which opened the door towards Constantinople.

---

[704] That the Arberian noble *Progon Skurra* carried the title of a Grand Heteriarc is testified by an epigraph in Saint Clements's Church of 1295.

[705] Ostrogorski, Georg: *"Historia e Perandorisë Bizantine,"* Tirana 2002, p. 348.

Therefore, the *"Arbërian Kingdom"* was turned into a lighthouse for the West, where they hung their hopes of being protected from the Ottomans, something they saw during the period of George Castrioti Skenderbeg.

The Arbërian crown was by now sought by the Arbërian feudal lords and nobles, who were ordered against the Byzantines because it hindered the implementation of the "Kingdom of Arbëria," while with the Slavic invasion everything would be lost. They did not expect for the "royal crown" to come from the outside, as had happened sixteen years earlier when it came along with Charles the First d'Anjou, after being proclaimed in Naples on August 21, 1272, but rather sought it as an internal force, which would unite them, in order to replace the situation of conquest and vassalage with that of a royal conscience.

Thanks to this war and this commitment lasting for nearly 30 years, it weakened the Byzantine and Slavic invasion in the Arberian countries – Philip of Tarento, grandson of Charles I of Anjou landed taking back Durres by defeating the Byzantines. Therefore, in 1304, in Durres the "Arberian Kingdom" came back to life once again, recovering now from the inside and in full cooperation with the Arberian factor, aware of the role and importance of the throne understanding ultimately who sought to defend it and who wanted to destroy it to the ground.

The return of the *"Kingdom of Arbëria"* under the leadership of Philip of Taranto, nicknamed *"the Despot of Romania and King of Arbëria"* in relation to the natives represented an even higher degree of independence of the Arberian feudal lords, nobles and gentry, who had fought for it to be consistent with their interests for as much internal power as possible.

Indeed, this was also requested and was the main condition for the Anjou intervention in the Arberian areas. As a part of Arberian gentry included in territories occupied by Rascia, and those who were under Byzantium and under despots of Epirus, were ready for a rebellion, in the spring of 1304, when their representatives arrived in the Neapolitan Court with a proposal for a new Arberian-Anjouin connection. On September 5, 1304, Philip of Taranto addressed Arberian gentry of Durres and Arberia promising he would acknowledge all their rights and privileges recognized by his grandfather, Charles I of Anjou.[706] On this occasion, Shpata, Bua, Zenebishti, Arianiti, Sgura, Blinishti were among the Arberian leaders

---

[706] *Acta Albaniae,* I, no. 637, cited according to P. Xhufi *"Nga Paleologët te Muzakajt,"* Tirana 2009, p. 139.

joining the Anjou, being quite widespread, with the absence of Muzakaj, who was still trying to keep the equilibrium between the two sides.[707]

As soon as he restored the royal throne of Arberia, Philip of Taranto,[708] the feudal lords, nobles, and gentry solemnly gathered in Durres to share with them the possessions and power they had lost and promote them with various high posts they had not previously held, or to restore some to the posts they had lost during the time of Charles I of Anjou, who in his efforts to fight against Byzantium had not always been able to understand why some Arberian nobles and gentry were at his side but still had fought on behalf of the Greeks and Serbs in the past.

Philip not only restored the possessions but also named the famous Arbërian lord, Guliem Blinishti, Marshal of Arberia, whom Charles I of Anjou, after some disagreement held his uncle in internment camps. There were many similar cases and as a result the confidence towards the representative of Charles I was restored.

Philip's strengthening to power in Arberia went against the similar goals of Despot Uros II Milutin, who kept in his grip some of the Arberian lands up to Ishmi and held, like Philip of Taranto the title of the *"King and Suzerain of Arbëria."* Although the Anjou had a deal "for a joint struggle against Byzantium" since the time of Charles I of Anjou, which was kept to some extent, the Rascians were neither interested in the strengthening of Philip of Taranto nor in the restoration of the imperial crown of "Kingdom of Arbëria." This they would show as early as during the Durres campaign of Philip of Taranto in 1308, when they put themselves at the disposal of the Byzantines, helping them to keep the city in the hands of Byzantium. Even after Durres was taken by Taranto's forces the Rascians continued to assist the city's fall into the hands of the Byzantines or in their own hands. From 1312-1315, they entered it several times, so that in the spring of 1318, after a new offensive in the South of Mat, they invaded Kruja and Durres.[709]

With the Despot of Rascia gathering much strength with Greek and Bulgarian troops, Philip of Taranto managed to recoup a European coalition of Catholic powers against Rascians that included Hungarians

---

[707] Ibid.
[708] In a letter dated April 28, 1311, Philip of Taranto, brother of Robert, is called "Dominus Regni et Despotus Romanie." (See *Acta Albaniae* and G. Monti *"Recerche sul domino angioino in Albania,"* Studio Albanesi, V-VI, 1935-6, p. 182)
[709] *Acata Albaniae,* I, no. 526, 626

and Croats. The Pope also urged the French bishops who had filled the churches of Arbëria to help the Anjou. In separate letters, the Pope invited Arberian nobles placed under the Slavic rule to turn their arms against their invaders and do their utmost against the Rascian Kingdom, "the enemy of the faith," as the Pope called the Rascians.

Indeed, in the spring of 1319 a number of Arberian nobles and gentry of notable families: Blinishti, Ionima, Arianiti, Matrënga, Muzaka, and others, through the Bishop of Kruja, Andreas, appealed to Pope John XXII that "they were ready to rise up and throw away the yoke of the Kingdom of Rascia." On this occasion they said they would abandon the Orthodox rite and accept Catholicism, being well separated church-wise from the invading Rascians.[710]

Philip of Taranto personally addressed Pope John XXII for help suggesting he should assist them against the schismatic Byzantines, and especially against King Uros. The call by Arberian nobles, gentry, and Philip of Taranto caused the Catholic Church represented by the Pope of Rome to become an instigator and inspirer of the coalition against Rascia. For this purpose he sent for the Bishop of Kruja, Andrea, to organize the uprising. In addition, with a special letter for help and the importance of anti-Serbian insurgency, the Pope addressed Manuel Muzaka – Count of Kelcyra (*Comiti Clissanie*), Andre Muzaka - Marshal of the Kingdom of Arbëria (*regni Albanie marescalco*) and Teodor Muzaka – *protosebast*.[711]

July 1319 marked the first major war of the European allies against Rascians in defense of the "Kingdom of Arbëria." Later they withstood the armies of the coalition and even temporarily occupied Durres. Although the Rascians were forced to leave Durres, never leaving it in peace, they continued their conquests in almost all parts. The crumbling Byzantine Empire made efforts to oversee several cities, Berat among them, after having become a despotate and keeping ties with a number of Arberian nobles giving them despot titles, thus recognizing them as local governors. Such a high title was granted to Andrea I Muzaka, a powerful lord of territories between Ohrid, Kolonja, and Berat. Other nobles were honored with the high title of *Sebastocrator*.

Byzantium's silent withdrawal and Rascian commitment to occupy Arberian countries and from there to create their own state, which would close the ports of the West to the East, with westerners already concen-

---

[710] *"Historia e Popullit Shqiptar,"* Volume I, Tirana 2002, p. 272.
[711] Acta Albaniae, I, pp. 649, 650.

trating in order to turn the "Arbërian Kingdom" into a vanguard of the West, caused an activation of the Catholic clergy as well, in organizing a new European crusade for the defense of Arberia from Slavic occupation. The Archbishop of Tivar, Guiliem Adea, by order of Pope John XXII, presented the King of France with a report in 1332, which was later wrongly attributed to a monk named Brocard. According to him, the main role was played by the Arberian feudal lords, who extracted 15,000 horsemen and soldiers.

In this letter, one finds the famous phrase that made him famous in history referring to the fact that *"even though Albanians have a completely different language and different from the Latin, they use the Latin script in all their books."*

Among other things, the letter points out the following:

Observe, my Lord King, the ones mentioned above (Rascians and their kings) emperor and king, and their home, I describe as confirmed throughout the Orient, and for the most part I know from sure experience. Now he who sees the care of your attention, and learns if one is to trust the promises, oaths, and loyalty of others who have been born as a perverse generation and children of misfaith of a low nation, and of a monstrous family trunk, who feel bad about God, who do not obey the church, who kill parents, who do not spare children and kill brothers, etc…Conquering the Kingdom of Rascia would be so easy… How would it suffice to have a desire for such an action? That Kingdom possesses little, almost no fortified place at all, but it entirely consists of village homes and huts, without defensive trenches and with no walls inside. Buildings and premises, of both the King and other notables, are of straw and wood. There one cannot see palaces or houses of stone or clay anywhere but in Latin coastal cities... Arberians, being the largest nation, may master in war areas more than 15 thousand horsemen for any war activity. They are brave and skilled fighters, according to their customs and habits. And, since the latter, both Latins, and Arberians, are oppressed under the unbearable and heavy yoke of slavery of that heinous and inhuman Slavic rule: people squeezed, clergy removed from positions and humiliated, the bishops and abbots often imprisoned, nobles stripped of heritage and kept in captivity, churches, both Episcopal and others, looted and underprivileged, monasteries ruined and destroyed, all or each of them wanting to plunge their hands in the blood of the above-mentioned Slavs, once they saw a French prince among them, whom they would make commander in their fight against the aforesaid Slavic criminals and enemies of the truth and of our faith. With the foregoing Arberians and Latins, 1000 French riders and 5000 or 6000 infantrymen, would, without a doubt, easily conquer this entire kingdom.[712]

The call for the crusade was left short of a proper response as the French had trouble with the Germans, while the Kingdom of Sicily was also involved in different conflicts with the Spanish, continuing to weaken its full commitment to gather strength for further intervention beyond the Adriatic in order to prevent the Arberian space from falling prey to the Byzantine and Slavic invasions. King Robert of Anjou, right after his accession to the throne, in 1333, appointed his son Captain of Durres and supported the hopes of the Arberian feudal lords in the war against Rascians.

He already conquered Macedonia and part of Thessaly, and didn't want to risk turning the Balkans, into the main force of the "Arbërian Kingdom," as Dusan did.

In the efforts to defend the "Kingdom of Arbëria" against Dusan, two of the feudal lords of Arbëria were of great importance: Tanush Topia, whose possessions lay between Durres and Tirana, and Andrea Muzaka, whose properties were located between the rivers Shkumbin and Seman.[713]

The other son of King Robert, Louis, was deployed in Durres in 1336 with a considerable army, reaching an agreement with Andrea Muzaka, whose title *"Despot of Arberia"* he recognized. Efforts to move closer to Arberian feudal lords by being associated with different properties and titles continued, as it was already clear that the *"Kingdom of Arbëria"* could succeed in the war against Slavic invasions only if it was supported by internal factors, and they saw this as being in their interests.

Simultaenously, Tanush Topia was included, whose title of the *Count of Arberia* was recognized and he was granted properties between the rivers of Shkumbin and Mat. Topia received an annual income of 1000 grosches (monetary denomination used at the time) from the Durres saltworks.

Despite the full involvement of Arberian feudal lords in key positions of the "Kingdom of Arbëria," understandably as vassals of the Anjou king – which could not be otherwise in those circumstances - these measures did not impede Stefan Dusan on his way to invade Arbëria. In 1343 he

---

[712] *"Ekskluzive,"* No. 28, August 2002.
[713] Ibid, p. 192.

took Kruja. Two years later he conquered Berat and in 1347 invaded Vlora and Kanina. But, in order to become "emperor," as he had announced, and thereby gain the right to inherit Byzantium, Dusan had to have the consent of the other side, i.e. the West, with whom he was constantly in ties and alliances, as his predecessors from the time of Nemanja and Dioclea in the 10th century and 11th century when Rascians settled there.

This Western "wing" was Venice, which also had its own accounts to settle with Dusan, as the latter could serve to weaken Constantinople by adding its influence in the central and western parts of the Balkans. Dusan and his family had been citizens of Venice for years, whom they constantly addressed for help and with whom they tied connections. These links were set in 1340 when he received a commitment that Venice would send soldiers (up to 500 horsemen) upon his command. On this occasion, Venice granted him and his family the right to Venetian citizenship.

Therefore, as a Venetian citizen, in January 1346, Dusan sent from Ragusa a delegation to Venice to inform about the next crowning of the King (*coronation sua in imperiao Constantinopolitano*), asking for an alliance for the conquest of the Empire. Naturally, for Venice, any such alliance was unacceptable. Evidently, Venice was opting for a different strategy, engaging them in a war and yielding the benefits for itself. In this situation the Venetians were satisfied with Dusan's conquests and his expansion eastward, so they responded to him with heartfelt congratulations. After the congratulations, Dusan decided to be crowned Emperor on Easter Sunday on April 16, 1346 in an assembly in Scupi by the Orthodox Patriarch Joanikij and Bulgarian Patriarch Simeon of Trnovo. Queen Helena was crowned empress, the son Uros king, by which the megazupan of Rascia had managed to gain over the key regional factors to reach what he had dreamed.[714]

Besides the parts that once belonged to Justinian's Dardania, who served as an example to Dusan to choose to perform his crowning at the ruins of Justiniana Prima (near Skupi), the self-proclaimed emperor continued his conquests towards the South, so that he would add Epirus and other areas to the South of Greece, in order for him to complete his dream of becoming a great emperor. On his way Dusan received assistance from the plague of the 1348, which spread in Europe by the King-

---

[714] Ostrogroski, Georg: "*Historia e Perandorisë Bizantine,*" Tirana, 2010, p. 428.

dom of the Tartars. Even though the plague had devastated many parts of central and eastern Balkans, this did not stop Dusan to continue his invasion campaign. Moreover, it helped him, as he encountered very little resistance. Angelos fell victim to it.[715]

In these circumstances, Dusan, facing more ailing people than opponents, came in and conquered Epirus Ioannina, Arta and other cities to the borders of the Franks – the Anjou, at that time, rulers of Butrint and Lepantos, Brienes, the former dukes of Athens.

Notably, the Arberians, who were alienated with the Greeks at the time of Andronicus III, joined Dusan. They managed to preserve their lands and property long threatened by the Byzantines.[716]

Since he saw no danger from a divided Byzantium diluted by internal struggles for power between Paleologus (supported by him) and Catacusenes, backed by Genoa and Hungary and, to avoid any risk of the "Franks" or the Anjou, who appeared on the side of Arberian nobles and gentry (fresh in their memory the "Arbërian Kingdom" of the time of Charlemagne and Philip of Taranto, as a western creation, was increasingly becoming a fixation as compensation for the dissolving Byzantine), Dusan again turned to his good links with Venice, offering them some of the occupied lands in this part as well as full support if they decided to invade Constantinople. Needing Dusan in its expected and soon-to-ignite war against Hungary and Genoa, Venice congratulated him granting him additional properties in Venice. Furthermore, in order that this support seemed more solemn, Venice sent a large Venetian and Ragusian delegation to Rascia headed by Count Nikola Giorgi of Bodanica.

Links with Venice and his efforts to gain as much as possible from them didn't help Dusan gain peace with the alliance between Hungary and Genoa. Evidently, the Hungarians, who claimed Bosnia, Croatia and the Adriatic coast, increasingly gained strength through time. As the Turkish threat was becoming increasingly greater, and Catacusen associated increasingly with them to restore his lost power and win the race with Paleologos, Dusan was encouraged by the Holy See to go to war with the Turks even at the price of occupying the Byzantine throne in Constantinople. He also had the support of the Germans with this work. It was the conflict taking place between Ludwig of Hungary and Dusan that prevented him not only from getting the flag of a western crusade against the

---

[715] Dil, Sharl: "*Istorija vizantijskog cartstva,*" 1919, p. 97.
[716] See: Catacusenos IV, Chap. 20.

Turks, as Rome had hoped, but also in restoring his power. His "tower" was facing a rapid collapse, more due to external factors (internal weakening of Byzantium and plans of Venice and the Holy See to demolish it once and for all as in that last gasp was unable to turn into a bastion against the Turkish invasions approaching Europe) than internal strength.

In the summer of 1354, Ludwig entered Belgrade, at a time when an exhausted Dusan wore a heavy crown on his head and turned south for the Rudnik Monastery. During that winter and spring, Dusan could not be relieved of the Hungarian anxiety, although the Venetians would intervene to bring peace between them, afraid of further Hungarian strengthening. The intervention could not bring an end to the true decline of the "emperor" of Rascia, as he, in December of that year, on the 20th day of the last month of the year 1355 died somewhere near Nerodima and was buried in Prizren, at the Archangel Monastery that he had built himself.[717]

Even though he ended up where he expected with "spiritual" power, while his dream to become Emperor of Byzantium turned into a nightmare for his temporary edifice, rapidly disheveled despite these reverses, Dusan's Rascia was the one that in a long struggle against Arbërians, targeted some strategic goals of some importance for it, which had implications for further developments and circumstances in which the Balkans and Eastern Europe in general passed during the next five centuries. Here, relations between Arberians and Slavs remained at the spotlight determining the delimitations of East-West direction, which rose to the highest level of spheres of interest.

These goals consisted of the following:

- *Firstly* - to bring down any state core of Arberians linking them to Byzantium. They targeted nobles and gentry as well as their commitments that could turn them into a factor within the empire becoming its supporters. In this case the Despotate of Epirus and the role it played from the Second Crusade and on was being considered;

- *Secondly* - to bring down any core that would allow the recurrence of the Kingdom of Arbëria, similar to that of the Anjou or otherwise, that would be the fruit of joint efforts of the Catholic West and emerging Arberian feudal lords, nobles and gentry to provide support from across the Adriatic exactly where the boundary of separation was, and

---

[717] See: Orbin, p. 268, writes that Stefan Dusan died of fever in Nerodimje.

- *Thirdly* - that thanks to this war and victory against the Arberians, Dusan's state would rise to the level of an Empire, replacing Byzantium and becoming a balance power in relation to the West.

Unlike Byzantium, which in many cases treated the Arberian feudal lords, nobles and gentry with respect, trying to keep them in service using their strength in forms of internal local governance with limited powers (themes, bounties, and principalities) and keeping them connected, Dusan did the opposite, even when during celebrations and promotions of his crown, in his proclamation dispatches he constantly added the attribute "King of Arberians," proving that he considered the strength of the Arberian factor, which he wanted to supervise and use for his own purposes, but without allowing it to become strong.

Even when solemnly pledging to respect the local feudal lords, wherever his army passed across Arberian lands he carried his rulers along to be named as full-fledged administrators. On this occasion he raged all the local autonomous structures, while forcing Arberian nobles, gentry and feudal lords to completely submit to his strict supervision.

Through his "zakonik" ("codexes") he introduced harsh rules and laws, theretofore quenching any past forms of "elders councils," "assemblies," and tribal alliances, which regulated domestic life, and managed ownership and trade relations for centuries. This was accepted by Rome and Byzantium as well, which based much of the local governance on these traditions. In line with these prohibitions, the nobles and gentry that had any ties with Constantinople or the Adriatic countries (Ragusa, Venice, Genoa, and others) were denied any direct connection with them. Even marriages and family connections of this kind were banned. It was just he and his officials who permitted and defined relationships with others.

The depreciation of the local factor by the invaders was followed with measures undertaken by him to strengthen the Orthodox Church, which was granted large properties and entire Arberian villages.[718] The opposite happened with the Catholic Church as it was stripped of properties, with

---

[718] For more on Arberian properties granted to the Orthodox churches (that of Deçan, Prizren, and Hilandar on the Holy Mountain in Greece, see: Miloš, Milojević: *"Dečanske hristovulje,"* Belgrade, 1880; Novaković, St: *"Zakonski spomenici srpskih država srednjeg veka,"* Belgrade, 1912; Solovjev, Aleksandar: *"Odabrani spomenici srpskog prava srednjeg veka,"* Belgrade, 1912; Ivanović, R: *"Dečansko vlastelinstvo,"* Belgrade, 1954.

Catholics required to convert to Orthodox. This was especially true for those who in any form wanted to keep their properties and positions.

Another measure undertaken by Dusan against the Arberians was that of destroying the structure of their ethnicity, especially of what appeared as homogeneous living in fertile valleys, forcing them to emigrate to parts of Thessaly and Greece replacing them with Slavs instead brought from the northern parts of the country, although completed later because death prevented Dusan from carrying out his project. He failed in implementing the second, bringing Slavs from the North to Arberian lands, but he moved in various forms a great number of Arberian families to Thessaly and Greece, who settled in those parts and stayed there forever.

What was obvious during the reign of Dusan in the Arberian lands, is that he made great efforts to turn the most vital part, ancient Dardania and Macedonia, into an institutional and spiritual "core," as Bulgarians once did, especially during the rule of King Simeon. Therefore, the main center of the Rascian Kingdom became Prizren and Scupi, where he moved both his administration and church institutions. Over old Illyrian castles and churches, as well as other fortresses of local feudal lords, reflecting the historical and spiritual identity of Arbërians, he placed Slavic edifices, Slavic and Orthodox churches.

Therefore, this, Dusan's not very long rule, reveals the efforts of spiritual Slavization of the Arberian ethnic space that was done through brutal and repressive measures (both administrative and ecclesiastical) unseen before. In this regard, the Orthodox Church played a great role as the main promoter of complete identification of religious consciousness with ethnicity, upon which the identity of religious association was to determine the ethnic identity, meaning that whoever was an Orthodox should be a Slav, and whoever was a Slav had to be Orthodox.

Even before Dusan came to power and before Rascia expanded its invasions of Arberian territories, an open war was waged by the Orthodox Church and Rascian invaders against Catholic believers of Arberian lands that cannot be explained other than a prudent strategy serving a dual purpose: on one side to prevent Arberians from maintaining their affiliation with the Western Church, and by this their western affinities, and, on the other side, to help the Easter Church maintain its supervision in this important part of the world, where Byzantism was entirely identified with the Slavic domination.

Interestingly, the church sources explain that before Rascia began its campaign against the Arberians of the Catholic faith and the Catholic Church in general, the Rascian Zupania headed by Nemanjas belonged to the Catholic rite. Stefan of Nemanjic kept a correspondence with the Pope Innocent III calling him *"spiritual father."*[719] In 1217, Stefan Nemanja received a crown by Pope Innocent III, delivered to him by a special legate, a "Bishop of Alban."[720] In a letter of reply that Stefan sent to the Pope, he said "that he feels like a son of the Roman Church," swearing allegiance to the Pope by *"wishing to remain loyal to the teachings of this holy mother."*[721]

Good relations between the Vatican and Rascia ceased in 1307, at the moment when Milutin (Stefan Uros II) addressed Pope Clement V demanding as a return for his acceptance of Oneness, as his brother had done, to intercede with Karl Valois, contender for Emperor of the Western Empire, to gain some Byzantine lands and cities in Macedonia,[722] which although promised by the representative of Rome, he would renounce the agreement with the explanation of *"fear from the powerful Orthodox clergy."*[723]

It seems that the "fear from the powerful Orthodox clergy" had to do with some other Rascian ties with Greek princes, who provided Rascia an expansion into Thessaly in favor of an alliance with the Greeks and strengthening the axis between them to the detriment of Bulgarians, which actually were never sincere, as Rascians changed their allies accordingly, something to be realized soon by the Greeks, who were never spared during Dusan's conquests.

He also proved impervious toward the Greek language and church, while being condescending even to Byzantium in general, who's throne he tried to take, demanding to do so in an alliance with Venice and other

---

[719] Theimer, A: *"Monumenta Slavorum"* I, 6 nr. 11. Cited according to Gjini Gasper *"Skopsko Prizrenska biskupija kroz stoljeća,"* p. 88.

[720] Plasari, Aurel: *"Skënderbeu,"* Tirana, 2010, p. 84.

[721] Ibid, p. 88.

[722] See Purković M: *"Avinjonske pape i srpske zemlje,"* Pozarevac, 1934; Novaković St. *"Nemanjićke prestonice Ras-Pauni-Nerodimlje,"* published in SANU 88 (1911) no. 14, cited according to Gasper Gjini *"Skopsko Prizrenska biskupija kroz stoljeća,"* p. 89; Radinić dr Jovan: *"Vizantija i rimokatolička crkva u prvoj polovini XV veka,"* Belgrade 1905.

[723] Ibid, p. 90.

Western powers, without excluding the Holy See, whose believers he savagely persecuted in the occupied lands. However, Uros II started the fierce campaign against Catholics, first by ousting liturgy in Latin and later by banning the opening of Catholic monasteries in Trepca, Novo Brdo and several other places, as provided by a late agreement with the Vatican.

Arberians found themselves targeted by these measures and opposed them. This was proven by a delegation of their leaders from among the nobles, who in the spring of 1319 sent representatives to Pope John XXII in Avignon to inform him about the wild Slav terror against the Catholics and their church. They also sought permission from the Pope that in case the Rascians would not end their terror, they would organize themselves in an uprising, which would be assisted by volunteers from Catholic countries.[724]

The state of terror, persecution of Catholic followers, mostly Albanians, would not change even after the arrival of Pope Clement IV to the Holy See, who seemingly would respond to the Serb terror with harsh measures. In 1346, Dusan wrote a letter of protest, but he, always according to Serbian diplomacy, trying to cast a stone by hiding his hand, responded that *"what was being rumored were but slanders of irresponsible missionaries, and that he had plans to open further monasteries for Catholic believers, whom he respected."*[725]

Dusan told this to the Pope while at the same time he publicly proclaimed his famous *"Zakonik,"* according to which Catholics weren't persecuted, but were declared *"false believers"* and Catholicism a heresy.[726]

---

[724] See Gasper Gjini: *"Skopsko Prizrenska biskupija kroz stoljeća,"* p. 90. Among others, it provides details of Albanian representatives, many of them from Prizren, and led by the notable nobleman Mentulus Musatius. Evidently, the Pope received them well promising thorough support and advising them not to undertake any rebellion before all negotiations with the Rascians had been exhausted.

[725] Ibid, p. 92.

[726] See Solojev A. V: *"Zakonik cara Stefana Dušana* 1349 i 1354 godine," SAN Belgrade, 1980, pp. 10-11.

The Agony of Byzantium and Arberian Principalities

The beginnings of Arberian principalities should be seen in the former themes of Byzantium, Durres, and Nicopolis in the 9th century and of Scupi and Dalmatia in the 11th century and in their efforts to protect themselves from the Slavic and Greek despotates acting against Byzantium as well.- David Arianiti was the first policymaker of Scupi.- Progon (1190-1198) Archhondrite of an Arberian independent ruling dynasty.- Gjin, son of Progon (1198-1206) leading the Principality of Arber.- Demetrius, son of Progon (1206-1216) and his links with Nemanjas.- The emergence of the Despotate of Arta (Epirus) in 1213.- The rise of the Balsha families in the North from zupans to princes.- Topia and their role in alliances with westerners as well as their possession of territories between the rivers Mat and Shkumbin.- Andrea Muzaka and the Principality of Muzaka (1335-1372).- Internal conflicts of Arberian princes and the consequences for the country. - The role of Dukagjini and Castrioti families in creating a state founding awareness.

The sudden death of Stefan Dusan on December 20, 1355, opened the last page of Byzantium's agony, though it continued for a century, until the last stronghold, Constantinople, fell into the hands of the Ottomans, causing a great mess in the Balkans and beyond, with a few "bases" left such as Morea and some half-independent Arberian and Greek despots in Epirus and Thessaly, who quickly declared independence. This mess grew even larger, as neither Paleologus nor the Catacusenes, "co-governing" Byzantium mostly by quarreling with each other at the expense of the remaining part, was able to supervise the troublesome space, which Stefan Dusan had left behind.

Even before the crisis, Byzantium was such a wreck as the only problem remaining was who would get the last pieces of the Empire: the Turks or another Christian power.

As the Turks already had managed to invade all the major cities of Asia Minor and with their "excursions" in the Mediterranean and the Adriatic had ambushed their prey from all sides, waiting for its fall, so in the face of this concern, as early as August 1354, the Venetian Ambassador in Constantinople informed the Dodge Andrea Donaldo that the Byzantines, threatened by the Turks and the Genoese were ready to submit to any power: Venice, Rascian sovereignty and even to the King of Hungary.[727]

Unable to impose any kind of central authority in most of what appeared as a remnant of the Empire, in circumstances when the Ottomans were at the gates and getting ready for their decisive attacks, the local "authorities" began to appear, at first with powerful nobles and despots with their principalities, whose empowerment necessarily required mutual links or wars.

Arberian lands faced the same sitiuation after the death of Stefan Dusan, whose 30-year conquest altered the approach of nobles, feudal lords, and zupans. They were using them in accordance with their interests, and not those of the Byzantine edifice. Contenders for this thrown were ruined by the Ottoman Empire, which was gnawing at it from all sides. This then opened a mutual war from all sides, looking for salvage by the acquisition of separated parts, which led to a disupute with no permanent solution.

This trend became even more pronounced because the Rascian "empire," aimind at creating a ruling hierarchy in different occupied parts to be held by its family members (brothers, sons, sons-in-law), had appointed "kings," despots, and numerous zupans, who had run various parts and were inclined to use it in the new circumstances for their own needs. They always had boasted claims of having been part of a "crown" that was still standing, although the realities spoke of the contrary. Therefore, after the sudden death of Dusan the power struggle started from the top, from Stefan's son, Uros, and Stefan's half-brother, Simeon, to be carried in all directions. This power struggle could not be terminated by Dusan's widow, "Empress" Helena, who withdrew by converting herself into a nun in a monastery because she was unable to withstand the collapse of what was seen as her husband's empire.

However, the successor to the throne was passed to Uros, although he was only 19. He was married to Ana (1360), daughter of the prince of Vlachia, whose sister was the wife of the successor of the Bulgarian throne, King Strazimir, suggesting he had been advised to turn to alliances with the Bulgarians in order to turn into a hereditary factor of Byzantium regardless of the large dimensions this implied.[728]

---

[727] Contasmeno, G: *"Byzintanische Geisterwelt,"* Baden-Baden, 1958; *"Zeitgeschihte in der Rhetorik des sterbenden Byzanz,"* 1969, p. 152.

[728] Jiriček, Konstandin: *"Historia e serbëve,"* Tirana, 2010, p. 456.

Stefan's half brother, Despot Simeon, Governor of Epirus, advised by Byzantium, still counting on making a comeback through a connection among Slavs, Greeks and Arbërians, hastened to declare himself *"Emperor of the Greeks, Rascians and of all Arbëria"* and, in accordance with this claim, called himself Simeon Uros Paleologos, appearing formally as a pretender of the highest throne that had to be backed by three leading nations of Byzantium. Previously, he appeared in Castoria with an army of 5,000 soldiers, many of them Arberians, previously involved in Dusan's army as mercenaries or those coming from the obligation that nobles and zupans had granting their loyalty for the benefit of properties and high posts. However, at this precise time, Simeon Uros Paleologos, having been self-proclaimed "Emperor of all Arbëria" faced Arberian opposition, which cost him the loss of his army in Epirus, after which he was forced to leave for Thessaly, while other Byzantine-Rascian officials were forced to take refuge in Ioannina.[729]

Desiring to exploit this situation, namely the removal of Rascian forces beaten by Arberians, Despot Nicephorus II Angel, who had descended in Thessaly and Epirus with a corvette from Arnos, counted on replacing the invading Slavs in these parts by returning there some of the noble Greeks from Morea. He was also counting on evicting the Arberian population from these areas through a military campaign. Furthermore, he sought to do this with Simeon Uros Paleologos, who had suffered a defeat by Arberians. But, Nicephorus II Angel, along with his Greek Stratioses and Turkish mercenaries in Achelos (Astropotamo) suffered a heavy loss from Arberian nobles, where he died (1358).[730]

Though supposedly after this loss of Nicephorus II Angel, Simeon restored the Rascian rule in the South from Castoria for some more time; in Epirus, his influence was limited by the victors over Nicephorus. Arberians, being the true rulers in Anhelos and Arta, were in the process of seeking "partnership" with other factors in these parts.[731]

Similarly, in the North, Dioclea (Zeta), one of Dusan's generals Djuras Ilic, was not seen anymore, whereas in 1360 the Balsha brothers appeared: Strazimir, George, and Balsha, who as princes, together with others in the North and South, filled the parts of the mosaic of Arberian state formations in the 14th and early 15th centuries, who nonetheless

---

[729] *"Historia e Popullit Shqiptar,"* Tirana, 2002, p. 281.
[730] For more see: *Kantakuzenos IV*, Chap. 43 – Janina Chronicle, August 31, 1358.
[731] Jiriček, Konstandin: *"Historia e serbëve,"* Tirana, 2010, p. 459.

remain separated, even when opportunities emerged for a political union between them on the basis of a broader relationship, something that helped maintain their reputation of power without politics.

Before this important development occurred, that is, the multiplying factors in Byzantium's "no man's land," where Arberians also were used, nobles, gentry, and local zupans, creating state formations without being politically connected. They were part of the self-governing structures that emerged from the 4th century onwards, i.e. since the time when in the Province of Illyricum, Byzantium was established with its known provinces, in the 9th century with the *themes* (that of Durres and Nicopolis), and in the 10th century, at the time of Basilius II was completed with those of Nis and Dioclea, in order that they get back to the foundation of what in the 12th century appeared as Despotate of Epirus" (in 1204) and in the 13th century as "Arbërian Kingdom" led by the Kingdom of Anjou (1272).

The circumstances and developments that conditioned these Arberian state governance structures divided the political and social scene of Byzantium for more than 100 years. Within the focus of the Despotate of Epirus, *"Byzantine Arberia"* can also be seen as a self-governing social formation, the same as the divided Empire of Nicaea acted on the other side after calling for the protection and restoration of Byzantium. Meanwhile the second part of the 13th century brought the emergence of the *"Kingdom of Arbëria"* created by Westerners, but not outside the interests and claims of Arberian nobility, gentry, and feudal lords.

The emergence of the *"Kingdom of Arbëria,"* although seeming like a parallel construct to *"Byzantine Arbëria,"* dealt with the Empire of Nicaea and its emergence, as the Despotate of Epirus led by Angels, turning into a rival of the Eastern Empire of Nicaea for the throne of Constantinople. This reflects the growing of Arberians into a factor in the fierce fight between East and West, rather than dividing them into these fronts, although this was an emphatic reality. The return of Byzantium in the areas of the Adriatic bordering with the West, after the triumph of Nicaea against the Latin Empire of Constantinople, and the appearance of the Normans, Anjou, and Venetians in those parts, eventually caused Arberians to lose faith in Byzantium as their own creature, to be protected at all costs, where for centuries they had poured all their efforts and dedication into it and its edifice.

The *"Arbërian Kingdom,"* although initially did not include many of Arberian nobles and gentry, even with some others fighting against it on the side of Byzantium, with the appearance of the Slavic, Bulgarian and Greek factor in the games between East and West and claims to benefit as much as possible from them to the detriment of Arberians, as such and under the suspicion of "coming from the outside," soon turned into an existential commitment for them. It occurred during the second return of the Anjou through Philip of Taranto, as the "Kingdom Arbëria," as such, turning into a challenge of war between East and West, between Constantinople and the Holy See, when it eventually fell in the hands of the East due to a Slavic-Greek-Byzantine alliance.

From that point on, there was also the appearance of the so-called *"Rascian Arbëria,"* a construct devised by the Slavs and their plans to turn the Byzantium into a Rascian Empire, as Dusan did. On one hand, they wanted to ultimately bury the *"Byzantine Arberia,"* with no theoretical chance for survival, and on the other hand, eventually prevent the occurrence of a western, Catholic, *"Kingdom of Arbëria"* that the Anjou had started in order to turn it into a project of Papacy, and other western factors, upon which rested the penetration of the West to the East, a project that reappeared at the time of Skenderbeg, and even later, to continue to the present time.

The *"Rascian Arberia"* construct was not only a particular political plan set to appear due to certain circumstances, such as those that would appear after the *"Kingdom of Arbëria"* in 1272 when Charles I Anjou announced this kingdom as part of a project of the westerners to move to the East, fighting at any cost and by all means to eliminate any competition in relation to Byzantium. It was also seen in accordance with a social and ethnic consciousness of the Rascians whose origin was not always seen related to the Slavs, coming somewhere from the 6th century from the Carpathians, but perhaps with an old stratification, such as the Tribals, a Dardanian tribe in Moesia, in the part between them and Thracians, which could have changed their language due to pressure from the Slavs, but not their ethnic identity. This dilemma must have been supported by Nemanja's gate emblem, as a late center of Rascians, demanding a confrontation of multiple constructions and counterfeits made by the Serbian Orthodox Church and certain Serbian political and intellectual centers during the 19th century for hegemonic purposes, including the creation of certain clichés through deliberately forged documents that provided the origin of the Nemanjas. However, some Serbian and foreign authors[732] are skeptical of the "evidence." It remains unclear whether or not they are Slavic, while their relationship with Dardanian Tribaldines remains open, having acquired the Slavic language and preserved some of their features of nobility, which also led to a "compromise" that Nemanja and his family be seen as of "pre-Slavic origin" and Rascia be assessed as a Dardanian "fortress" connecting Byzantium with the new realities created after the settling of Slavs in these parts. Here, they began to accommodate themselves into the social and political structures of Byzantium.[733] Therefore, in this process, a mixture between the Tribals and the Slavs could have possibly highlighted Nemanjas' pre-Slavic formation, from which later appeared this noble family to be related to the emergence and establishment of the Dynasty of Rascia and its empowerment, as occurred during Dusan's time.

Despite these dilemmas, remaining at a level of speculation still to be proven, while the question of when and how this can happen against such stereotypes that are not able to accept any hypothesis that denies them, almost all the serious authors dealing with the history of the Slavs and their rise are of the opinion that Rascia was not the starting point of their state. Rascia is *Arsa*, Justinian's famous castle, which had a major strategic importance in protecting Illyricum and Dardania from the Slavic invasions precisely at that place.[734] It was the modern name of ancient Dardania and the Upper Moesia.

However, it would become a target of the Slavs only after they weathered their tribal formations known in parts of Bosnia, Dalmatia and the

---

[732] Mauro Orbini: *"Il Regno degli Slavi,"* Pesato, 1601; Johann Christian von Engel: *"Serbien und Bosnien,"* Halle, 1911; Jiriček, Konstandin *"Historia e serbëve,"* Tirana, 2010; Sharl Dil: *"Istoria vizantijskog carstva,"* 1919; Josef von Hamer: *"Istoria osmanskog carstva,"* Zagreb, 1967;

[733] See: Solojev, A: *"Zastava Dušana nad Skopljem godine 1339,"* Skopje, 1936; S. Ristić: "Serafim, Dečanski spomenici," Belgrade, 1864.

[734] For more See: Svejović, Dragan: *"Balkanski istoćnjaci Milana Budimira,"* Belgrade, 2001. The book states the following: *"Recent linguistic and archaeological research has proven that Dardanians, the eponym Dardan passed from the Balkans to Troada and through his son Illyus linked with the Trojan royal connection, probably by mid-fifth millennium BC, populated the central Balkan area, remaining there during the Roman period as well until the arrival of the Slavs, whose center was Rascia, deriving from the Dardanian name ARSA."* p. 91.

Coast, formations constantly challenged from Venice, the Holy See and other Western factors and stimulated in various ways to weaken Byzantine in its central part, so that together with the Bulgarians, would touch upon the most sensitive point of Illyricum, in Dardania.

The truth of this may be best found in the history of the rise of the Nemanjas Dynasty, when the first signs of its rising are seen from Zahlumia and Dioclea in the early 10th century, with its progenies distinguishing themselves in the war against rival families in these parts, followed with attention by Ragusa and Venice in order to support the "strongest" becoming even stronger, as long as that strengthening served their interest. Once strengthened in that fashion, the Nemanjas passed over to Rascia in the early 11th century where the most dedicated conjurers of this family's "history," Mauro Orbin and Pop Dukljanin,[735] were not able to indicate against whom the Nemanjas won when they moved to Rascia, who their enemies were and, most importantly, who their many "followers" were, as they say, on whom they relied and began turning into power factors in these spaces inasmuch as to jeopardize Byzantium.

In the absence of such an explanation, that the main "biographers" deliberately kept the Nemanjas silent, representing also the "Achilles heel," it is also an undeniable reality that such popular fiction cannot hide for certain hegemonic purposes, on which a large part of the "historical truth" is based, such as that which appeared in the 19th century. This refers to a famous historical development - that explains the emergence and rise of zupans and multiple Slav zupanias, among which the most emblematic was that of the Nemanjas - which refers to the Edict of the Emperor of Byzantium, Basilius II. After destroying the Bulgarian Kingdom of Simeon (894-927), which had included almost all the regions of Dardania and Epirus, they performed administrative and military reforms in parts being for some time under Bulgarian occupation, which favored the emergence of independent Slav tribal formations and their further implication in the well-known social and political processes of Byzantium.

Among these reforms, the strengthening and expansion of *themes*, as social and military formations, from originally two in the Illyricum space (Durres and Nicopolis) to four, in addition to the *Theme* of Scupi and that of the Adriatic with Dalmatia, further beyond Dioclea. However, with these reforms, the space outside the *themes*, in which less than half of the

---

[735] *"Il regono degli Slavi,"* Pesero, 1601; Sišić, Filip: *"Letopis Popa Dukljanina,"* Zagreb, 1928.

former Province of Illyricum formed by Diocletian was included, the so-called social "independent" formations were allowed for Bosnia, Zahlumia and Rascia, where Slavic tribes expanded, accepted in Illyricum by Emperor Heraclius in the 7th century.

Historically, the first social and later political formation showed the Slavic tribes located in the Balkans from the time of Heraclius as organized Zahlumia. This was a province located in the northern coast of Ragusa up to the lower valley of Narenta (present-day Neretva in Dalmatia), called Hum, *Humska zemlja* (Huma's land), which in Latin was called *Chelmo - land*. So, it is the same center, which from the 9th century, after the Slavs accepted Christianity, began an internal social differentiation among the Slavs, which remains for science with many unknowns. According to Constantine Porpyrogennetos, inside the country away from the sea and the Danube laid the first true Slavic country,[736] a description that so far seems to be closer to the truth. Even Emperor Constantine, being also among the most important historians of his time, whose works have become an inevitable historical reference, presents the Rascians as eastern neighbors of the coastal tribes Diocleates and Travunires, meaning they were namely across the water strip between the Adriatic and the Danube. Here for the first time, Rascia (Ρασον, Ραση) near the river Rascia was mentioned, but only as an eastern border, while according to this important historian, the nucleus of the Slavs, possessing rich sources, was the land of Bosnia, called in Latin *Bosonmo, Bossina* (Βοσωνα) in the Middle Ages, a province that took its name from the River *Basanius* of the Roman period.[737]

The Slavs with their tribal structures from family to zupan ones, between the 9th and 12th centuries, were mostly located in the eastern part of the River Drina, but not excluding their appearance here and there during their noted "excursions" to *Pagania* as Cecaumenos called the part of Drina going from the Danube to the North and Morava in the South called Moravia, or Viminacium in Latin, which bordered on the Bulgarians (ο Μοραβον ητοι Βρανιτςαβαν). The author of the imperial history, Constantine Porphyrogennetos, announced the tribal-prince structure of the Slavs, saying that the *"prince" (dux)* was the first of a fraternity, who was also the first of a tribe, often providing cause for rivalries and animosities among brothers and cousins.

---

[736] Jiriček, Konstandin:"*Historia e serbëve*," Tirana, 2010, p. 148.
[737] Ibid, p. 151.

Therefore, Emperor Constantine, in his *Book of Byzantine Ceremonies* enlists a certain Vlastimir, grandson of Radoslav (ca. 850). This does not show numerous Slav "princes" in Dioclea between the 9th and 11th centuries, as seen by some later ecclesiastical sources, such as the "notes" of Pope Dukljanin, which are rather creative figments than part of reality, related more to the history of medieval Slavic written literature rather than historical realities.[738] Rather, the *Byzantine Book of Ceremonies*, shows a zupan as leader of Travunieres, Krainas, Belajs' son, to whom, as the story goes, Prince Vlastimir marries his daughter naming him prince (αρχων), stating that thereafter Travunien's princes, Krainas, and his predecessors Hvalimir and Cucimir remained subject to him.[739]

Indeed, the Slavs, from the 9th century to the 13th century, appeared in multitudes, zupans constituting a major factor of governance from tribes to zupanias and principalities. Since Slavic tribes knew no nobility, as the Arberians, Latins and Greeks did, the system was replaced by the patriarchal-tribal hierarchy. On the basis of this, in the 12th century, after having come from Dioclea, the Great Zupan is displayed in Rascia as becoming more powerful than the "king." As seen, the title of zupans was distributed to Arberians and others as well during the known invasions of 1191 when Nemanja, after having opened the way to the German King Friedrich and Crusaders from Hungary to Constantinople, invading and destroying the Dardanian Nis with all its castles, captured Scupi and Prizren reaching as far as Ohrid, which, in these parts, with interruptions, marked the beginning of Rascian conquests of nearly two centuries.

Therefore, the time from the 9th century, as mentioned by the Byzantine Emperor Constantine Porphyrogennetos, when in his *Book of Byzantine Ceremonies* a certain Vlastimir as the first Slavic "prince" is marked down and up to Stefan Nemanja, Zupan of Rascia, in the 12th century, represents the time of establishment and strengthening of the authority of these communities at the local level to independent behavior referred to numerous and diverse titles *(sevast, prince, despot, king* or even *emperor)*, many of which wer conjured up by present and later churchmen for certain purposes mostly religious but also political. The Church was also co-governing, something that has troubled historians in presenting the true social and political situation of the time, while making it more

---

[738] For more on this see Dučić-Ruvarac: "*Prilozi k objašnjenje izvora srpske istorije,*" in "Glasnik," Belgrade, Vol. XLVII, XLIX.
[739] Ibid, p. 153.

suitable for the conjurers in creating constructs according to the political needs, such as those emerging from the 19th century onwards.

Regardless of the intricacies that these titles created and their highly controversial descriptions in terms of their genuine social and political power under the circumstances, it remains an undeniable fact that the local prince and royal "crowns" scattered across different provinces, neither prevented the extension nor the acceptance of central authority, as the local "kings" paid tributes to the center for which the military troops were most important to the Empire. Therefore, during the Comnenus time, the Great Zupan of Rascia was forced to send 2,000 troops during the Emperor's campaign in the West, 30 in Asia, and later 500, since, at this time, the Bulgarian invasions commenced, and the Rascian zupans were subject to this obligation, doing it in the form of "mutual alliances."

However, developments within the South Slavs in general from their first appearance in the 6th century settling in northern and central parts of Illyricum in the 7th century by Emperor Heraclius, as well as those between the Slavs and Rascians in particular, open a chapter of ties and also of ongoing confrontation between these peoples. On one hand, it focused on the maintenance and utilization of Byzantium as a common edifice while it was possible, especially between the 11th and 13th centuries. On the other hand, it was used for taking possession of its throne, as did the Rascians between the 13th and 14th centuries, when with the invasions of Uros II and those of Stefan Dusan conditions were created for its destruction.

During the first phase, when Byzantium was used to maintain it as a common edifice, and this has to do with the time from the Fourth Crusade and on, when after the collapse of Constantinople by the Latins, the Empire of Nicaea in the East came into existence, having the Despotate of Epirus as its rival in the struggle for the return of the imperial throne, Arberian countries were constantly targeted by invasions of the Dynasty of Rascia, as occurred during the first Nemanja incursions in Scupi and Prizren in February 1190.[740]

This time Nemanja of Rascia played the German, Byzantine and even Greek and Bulgarian cards, using them all to expand and strengthen their occupations in the Arberian lands, mostly in Dardania, since they provid-

---

[740] For more See: Zimemert, K: "*Der deutsh-byzantinisch Konflikt von juri 1189 bis Februar 1190,*" 1903, pp. 42-77; compare also Nichetas Akominatos speech, pub. Miller in *Recueil des historiens dea croisades, Historiens grecs* 2, pp. 737-741.

ed them with a very powerful position in relations between East and West on which they counted on acquiring the throne of the Byzantine Empire. Dusan pretended, either to become a leading partner of the West or to act in alliances with Venice and alternately with Hungary.

In the second phase, after the collapse of the Despotate of Epirus by Nicaea and the return of Constantinople, when Charles of Anjou showed up in the Arberian lands with the "Kingdom of Arberia" under his crown, the Rascians tried not only to fight against any idea of an Arberian kingdom associated with Westerners, but also to suffocate it by any means including shrewdness, as was that of the *"Rascian Arberia,"* a governing Arberian structure, which could emerge and be maintained within the royal tutelage of Rascia, defining its limits from all points of view. This card was promoted widely, first publicly by Uros II in 1308, when after extending his conquests to the coast and central parts of Scupi and Epirus, he declared himself "The King of the Arberians" (*"Urossio Slavi, Dioclie ac Albanie regi"*).[741]

In line with this idea there were also the known intrigues by Nemanja and Uros in trying to gain over the Arberian nobles and gentry, mainly those from Dardania, through their alliances with Venice, Bulgarians, but also the Greeks, making efforts to prevent them by all means from creating a common political stance among themselves. It can be said that in certain circumstances, as those arising from the emergence of the Anjouine *"Kingdom of Arberia,"* both the Rascians and Byzantium succeeded in winning over some of the Arberian nobles, or in keeping them out of connections with Latins and the Holy See, something that was of importance.

From this point of view Stefan Dusan was most direct. Previously, during the military campaign against Byzantium he included a significant number of Arberians within the military forces (estimated to be over 5,000, even as elite troops), while as he entered their lands he recognized the Arberian nobles and gentry and their past properties and privileges, while those who supported him with the troops or in other forms he awarded with zupan's titles. During the invasion of Kruja, Ohrid, Castoria, and Arberian cities and centers, in the cards issued he declared himself "King of Arberians," although in some of these rewritten "novel-

---

[741] See: *Acta Albaniae*, I, no.594, cited according to P. Xhufi *"Nga Paleologu te Muzakajt,"* Tirana 2009, p. 150.

la," of course, this was omitted with certain sources remaining, preserved in Latin and Greek bringing proof of this.

But as noted, the efforts to involve Arberians mostly forcefully in the Slavic "crown," as would occur during the time of Uros II and Stefan Nemanja when the latter occupied most of Arberia between 1340-1355, and in the circumstances when he also under the signature of the "King of Arbërians" attempted to start the most violent Slavization of Arberia (through expropriations and imposition of Orthodoxy at the expense of Catholicism and destruction of ethnic structure through forced deportations of some of the rural population to dry Greek areas, turning them into simple laborers), all this sensitized most of the nobles, gentry and those bearing titles of zupans that "the common kingdom" with the Slavs was nothing but a hoax, coming to subject them completely in order to have them dissolved under the Slavic "crown."

Consequently, following Dusan's sudden death (1355), the nobles, gentry and zupans from among the Arberians soon exploited the situation to be released from the trap of the Rascian "Imperial Crown" in a "quiet" way, by continuing with their local independence they had before Dusan, or by declaring the secession from the "portion" beginning to separate from his family (son and half brother), with Balsha being the most keen in the North, Topiaj, Muzakaj, Aranitis and others, who acted vigorously not only to restore the properties and the positions they had, but also to enhance and strengthen them in any respect.

Even though some of the Arberian princes and nobles succeeded in creating independent principalities joined in a political and social development, as was the confrontation with the Ottoman conquest, among the most vulnerable to their fate and to a civilization to which they belonged for centuries and shared together with others as they poured their being into its existence, they did not succeed in connecting politically among themselves, as the Slavs and Bulgarians had done long ago.

During that crucial century there were Arberian princes and noblemen with respective Byzantine titles issued by Slavic princes, but they remained only family principalities without an Arberian crown, such as that of the *Arbërian Kingdom* that the Anjou brought in, when for the first time they were confronted with an alternative other than Byzantine, from which most of them reflected. But this passage was interrupted or failed altogether, failing rather by those that started it (the West headed by Papacy) than by their assumptions to join, as happened in the beginning, even though they were present and noticeable, so that one day the Westerners began to design their own Eastern agenda to insure the success of their project.

Before considering this very meaningful development that can be assessed as a war of everyone against everyone for as many possessions as possible, with a mosaic of feuds or principalities of Arberian lands without any internal political connection and state framework, attention should be turned slightly back at the Byzantine state consciousness and its logic, from where the Arberian behavior actually originates, consistent with maintaining its common edifice and that of the others - primarily the Bulgarians and Serbs - as its users in acquiring it, benefiting from it, or bringing it down as soon as they had a chance and circumstances were ripe.

In this case, there is a distinction between Arberians and their social and political structures, and Slavs, Bulgarians and others, whereas the first were in accordance with the needs of Byzantium for internal strengthening, as was the case with *themes*, emerging from the ninth century onwards, and for the latter, they were in compliance with ambitions to break away from it in accordance with alliances and the difficulties that would arise to Constantinople.

This brings us back to a social and political reality, which within the specific relations that Byzantium had since the time of Basilius II with Arberians with the establishment of the *themes* of Durres and Nicopolis, (and later those of Scupi and Dalmatia) created a "partnership" with them, being more or less equivalent to the Roman federation (*foedus*), implying a military alliance with the Empire and an extensive self-governance of local structures.

The Roman model, on which indeed Byzantium was built, through the establishment of *themes* rises to a higher operational scale, whereby implying strengthening of certain social formations (tribes, nobles, gentry, counts and others) within the imperial structure by turning them into powerful factors. In these circumstances, from the 9th century onwards, within these imperial models of local government there was an emergence of famous families, such as Arianiti, Muzakaj, Skuraj, Matrëngaj and others.

The role of these families increased even more by the beginning of the Crusades onwards and particularly after the intrusion of the Normans in the East, so that Byzantium being forced to keep more connected to them began to attract them with enviable privileges and high posts in the army and administration. The title *Sebast* was among the most common with which noble families of Arberia were honored.

Therefore, one of these families rising in accordance with the Byzantine *Izopolitia* was that of the Arianiti. David Arianiti, a strategist of the Theme of Thessaloniki, was subsequently appointed strategist of the Theme of Scupi (1001-1018). This was done by the Emperor for his merits as a military man in the fight against Bulgarians. Certainly the military worthiness of David Arianiti, to have his family raised to the rank of a local military authority, connected with the center, was important for the subsequent prosperity of the Arianiti, playing an important role.

There were some other circumstances that brought this family and others in the spotlight not only of Byzantium, but also its rivals and opponents from within and without, as they already appeared as unsurpassed in the delimitations between East and West.

The growth of this trend, i.e. empowerment of the Arberian factor within these Byzantine structures, appeared during the Comnenus Dynasty, especially from the time of Manuel I (1147-1181), as he would promote many of the Arberian nobles and gentry with senior titles, among them that of princes. Therefore, in 1166, during the inauguration ceremony of the St. Trifon Church in Kotor, attended by the Byzantine Commander for Dalmatia, Dioclea, and Arberia, Isaac, along with other senior holders of clergy, a certain *Prior Arbanensis* (Prince of Arberia), Andrea, was mentioned who recognized Byzantium's sovereignty.[742]

Sources of the time indicate that Pope Innocent III, in 1208, called a noble Arberian, named Demetrius, by the title of the "Prince of Arbëria" (*Princeps Albaniae*).[743] This may refer to the son of Progon, the founder of a princedom family, emerging in 1190, which as such was recognized by the Papacy, whose influence had been increased from the time of Emperor Manuel, after he had allowed the opening of churches in Epirus and other parts of Arberia, previously closed during the time of the separation (1054) and onwards. Although there are no clear sources indicating as to what family Progon belonged, who according to Byzantine terminology

---

[742] "*Historia e Popullit Shqiptar*," Volume I, Tirana, 2002, p. 228.
[743] "*Acta et Diplomata res Albaniae Mediae aetatis illustrantia*," by L, de Thalloezy, C. Jericek et E. Sufflay, Vol I, Vienna, 1913, Vol II 1916.

carried the title of the *Grand Archon (megas archon)*,[744] it can be assumed that the rulers of Arberia in the early twelve and thirteen centuries belonged to the family of Skurra from the highlands of Tirana, where the name Skurrë occurs constantly in the records of the most important of Arberian times. The family tomb of the *Sebast* Mikhael Skurra at St. Mary's Church of Berat in 1201 also speaks about the high social position of this family, or another tomb of this family, that of the noble Anton Skurra, in St. Andrew's Church in Lezha.[745]

However, originating from the Skurra family of Kruja, or even from Dukagjin, Progon remained a prince until 1198, when after his death, his sons inherited his power, first Gjin (1198-1206), then Dhimitri (Demetrius - 1206-1216). It is known that Demetrius, approx. 1208-1210, also kept the title of *Judge of Arbanum* in Kruja, which speaks of his great power.

But there is another element that makes this prince even more important, justly turning his principality into a node of various high level interests of the time. This refers to him as being son-in-law of Zupan Stefan Nemanja, married to his daughter Comina, who was also the niece of the Byzantine Emperor, Alexis II Angel;[746] he proved to be "untrustworthy" for the Venetians,[747] who, after the peace with the Romans, sought the provision of a maritime route to Constantinople placing all the rulers of the coast under its rule, among whom is also mentioned the *Arbanesis pinceps, iudex Albanorum.*

Indeed, as mentioned, the relation of Progon's son, Dhimitri (Demetrios) reveals the circumstances where Zupan Stefan Nemanja after the Fourth Crusade had entered into an alliance with Venice, among many he made at the time even with Byzantine adversaries taking advantage, as he benefited from an agreement he made with the German King Friederich when he took over Nis, Scupi, and Prizren penetrating as far as Ohrid, when the Albanian prince, as it is said, compared with vassal Greeks of Epirus, was "untrustworthy," meaning that power should be taken away

---

[744] A. V. Soloviev: "*Eine Urkunde des Panhispesbastos Demetrios. Megas Archon von Albanien,*" in "Byzantinische Zeitschrift" 34/1934, p. 304.

[745] "*Historia e Popullit Shqiptar,*" Volume I, 2002, p. 228.

[746] For more see: Jiriček, Konstandin: "*Historia e serbëve,*" Part One, 2010, p. 328 (Αρχων του Αρβανου), Arbanesis pinceps, udex Albanorum: Dem. Chomationo no. 1, 3; Inocenti III te Theiner, I, 45. Compare Drinov in Viz. Vremenik I (1894) 321, 326. By the same author, see also papers in archives. Slaw. Phil. 21 (1899), no. 87.

[747] Ibid, p. 328.

from him little by little. To "remove the threat" from his son-in-law, Nemanja began conquering his lands from Prizren, taking the region of Pulti (highland on both sides of the River Drin), which were part of the *"Principality of Arberia."* At the same time, Despot George of Dioclea, Nemanja's vassal, in July 1208, concluded an agreement with Venice to give his support in "giving a lesson to the Prince of Arbanum, Demetrius."[748]

Faced with this pressure, that is, by his father-in-law and his vassals in Dioclea and Venice, which had begun to exercise their power on the Adriatic coastal cities, Demetrius turned to the Roman Catholic Church to seek protection. Pope Innocent III did promise protection. On this occasion, he switched to the Catholic rite, though still retaining his Byzantine titles of *Panhypersebast* and *Megas Archon* (Grand Archon).

Although Venice, with the help of the Despot of Dioclea, did not succeed in "persuading" the Prince of Arber, events that followed in the wake, during and after the conquering of Constantinople (1225-1254), whereby the Despotate of Epirus turned into an important actor of war between the two Byzantine "wings" for restoring their imperial center from the Latins, erased the traces of the Progon nobility, depicting trails of some others, such as the Gilliam of Arberia, who tried to keep the Byzantine balance in favor of the Despotate, which saved the possessions and privileges of the nobles, gentry, and those of the clergy and citizens.

However, since the time of the "Despotate of Epirus," when the Byzantium's core had to be preserved from menacing dissolution to the time of the *"Kingdom of Arbëria"* initiated by the Anjou, a large number of Arberian families (nobles, gentry, sevasts, archons, and princes) were found in an altogether new situation, having realized that the real Byzantium not only did not exist (except for the fortress of Constantinople), but holding on to its remnants posed a genuine risk, as this turned them into prey directed from all sides.

Therefore, under such circumstances, nothing else remained other than in the absence of an internal alternative (unsecure alliances with Slavs or Greeks under the defamed Byzantine signature) to fight for support from outside, i.e. from the West, but even this advance required prior internal testimony that could be reflected in the form of an inde-

---

[748] Ljubić: *"Archiv slaw. Phil."* 21/1899.

pendent nobility or principality, which would be considerable in its representing power.

The process of self-testing through independent social and political structures, as were the principalities, under the vassalage of Byzantium, started by Progon and continued by Gilliam and some others noticed or unnoticed, appeared with difficulty for the Arberian nobles, gentry, and princes. On one side were the Nemanjas with Bulgarians, who were very determined to use all means to hinder the process in this respect (as they knew what their empowerment meant), it actually happened (they were occupied) once they were conquered by Uros II and Dusan, and on the other side stood the "fictitious Byzantines" (Paleologus and Cantacusenes), who continued to claim that any kind of strengthening be measured by their war for imperial loyalty, regardless if Byzantium remained but a shadow.

In these circumstances there were only the Westerners (Anjou, The Holy See, Venice, Hungary, and Genoa), who offered conditional protection, and they too aimed at turning the lands of Arberia into a passing point for conquering Constantinople.

Indeed since the emergence of the Anjou in Durres in the spring of 1272, when Charles of Anjou would come down with the crown of the Kingdom of Arbëria, the nobles, gentry and princes of Arberia, were caught up in over half a century of development, pouring down their inner strength in two opposite directions: for Byzantium, which was in agony and, for their first kingdom, as was that of Arberia, which although coming from abroad, represented their first royal crown, and with Western backing, closely linked to their interests in the new circumstances.

The mutual struggle on one or the other side, or even standing aside, as occurred in some cases with some of the nobles and gentry, no matter the consequences, sensitized them in creating an internal social and political link. However, they learned the hard way by lining up on two lines with some being listed on the Byzantine side and some on the Anjou side. On this occasion they first recognized the importance of the royal crown, even coming from abroad and serving certain foreign interests, as they also recognized the futility of delay after Byzantium, which provided nothing other than loss and collapse of the common destiny.

The biggest lesson in this incurrence would be the one regarding a final understanding that it was Rascia with Nemanjas and Dusan as its latest exponent, that were fighting against whatever their state and spiritual identity was, even when appearing with the rouge construct of *"Rascian Arberia"* during the time of Uros II and Dusan who claimed during their crowning upon conquests of Arberian lands, as happened in Castoria, in 1348, when the crowning card read: *"Dušan car samodržac Srblem, Grčkoa, Blgaromi i Arbanasom."*[749]

Therefore, it is not by chance that the Arberian nobility and zupans, announced during Dusan's time, were so dedicated, that after his death, they acted for a rapid collapse of Dusan's state, which was filed on conquests that he had made over Arberian countries.

As Dusan's state was built on bases of hegemony and not of true power it rather gained from Byzantium's weakness, whose space was turned into an easy prey for everyone, it was natural that it began to collapse from inside by the heirs themselves, who fought for their own share. But this process was accelerated by composing factors, being forced, as were first of all the Arberian nobles, gentry, and zupans and their properties included in Dusan's state through conquests, who, despite having their ownership recognized and zupan titles granted, rose up to drive away their invader.

Thus, among these families, there was Shpataj and Zenebishi in the South, Topiaj in the middle parts, Muzakaj in the Castoria area, and especially Balsha in the North. Along with these families at this time were some other families, like that of Dukagjini and Castrioti, who played an important role within the social and political spectrum of Arberia on the eve of Ottoman conquests, so that they can rightly be regarded as Arberian state formations in the 14th and 15th centuries, by which Arberians too, as well as other Balkan peoples (Slavs, Greeks, Bulgarians, and Romanians) became part of the puzzle with many pieces, thus making things easier for the Ottoman invaders, as their social and political being, before entering five centuries of captivity, passed through a process of vassalages that included almost everyone.

The collapse of Dusan's state had set in motion everyone including the last descendents of Byzantium, who tried to exploit the new situation to somehow get back to where they were. Such was the Despot of Epirus, Nicephorus II Angel, who in order to strengthen himself had to face Arberian nobility. In Acarmania, his army enforced with Ottoman mercenaries, was badly beaten and the Byzantine despot was killed. After

---

[749] Bogdanović, Dimitrije: „*Knjiga o Kosovu,*" Belgrade, 1986, p. 112.

this battle, the southern provinces of Epirus, Acarmania, and Etolia were incorporated within two new despotates. The first one based in Arta, was led by the nobleman Pjetër Losha, and the second, based on Angelokastron (Acamania), was led by Despot Gjin Bue Shpata.[750]

Arberian despots faced the remains of Rascian rule in Epirus, as Prelubevic aimed at restoring these parts under his occupation, which he led from Ioannina. Gjin Bua Shpata, after marrying Prelubovic's sister, concluded some kind of peace with the Despot of Ioannina, but he was never at peace by the intrigues of the latter. They became even greater after Shpata's death. He was replaced by his son, Pal Shpata, who wasn't able to withstand the various pressures with those of the Anjou and the Greeks. Therefore, he made peace with Venice, from which he retained some possessions, but lost the control over the main parts, as was the stronghold of Lepantos on the coast and the capital, Angelokastron.

Another noble family from the South was that of the Zenebish, who possessed lands from Gjirokastra, Delvina and further on in Vagenetis (Chameria). The Zenebish rose during the time they lived next to Gjin Bua Shpata of Arta, with which they had family ties, as Gjon Zenebish was son-in-law of the powerful despot of Arta. Like Shpataj, Zenebishi's main opponent was the Despotate of Ioannina, led by the Italian Ezau Buondelmonti Achajuoli (1386-1411), with whom he had several battles, one of which, in Dhive (Mesopotamia) the Italian was captured by Zenebish and later released against a hefty reward of 10 thousand gold pieces.[751] Being in possession of the coastal area with Parga, Zenebish fell into conflict with Venice, which did not stop acting to remove his control over those parts, which for the maritime republic were of great interest to keep the free navigation on these parts from where its goods went through to the East and vice versa.

In 1386, Venice occupied Corfu, while grabbing also some of the main economic and military centers of the coast, Butrint Ksamil and Sajadha.[752] Although the Sajadha saltworks were returned, Zenebish was not able to protect it and other coastal parts. Venice was very assiduous, but there were also other circumstances, such as the Ottoman penetration and intrigues of Rascian despots together with those of the Greeks in Epirus, which forced him in 1414 to reach an alliance with Venice,

---

[750] *"Historia e Popullit Shqiptar,"* Volume I, Tirana 2002, p. 281.
[751] Ibid, p. 285.
[752] Ibid, p. 285.

guaranteeing him and his family refuge in Corfu in case of an Ottoman risk, which eventually happened, where Gjon spent the last days of his life.

Compared with Shpataj and Zenebish, who ended up seeking refuge from the Ottomans in the Bay of Venice, there were two large Arberian families, Topia and Balsha, which although included in different alliances from both the East and West, turned into main protagonists of the developments preceding the Ottoman conquest.

These two families turned the fight for liberation from Dusan's occupation into a struggle for an enlargement of their possessions on all sides, reaching a critical point by entering into an internal struggle with one another that ended in their common loss. In the War of Savra in 1385, although the outcome was the loss of Balsha and his fall in the battle, coming from an intervention by the Ottomans, who briefly withdrew and the "fruits" of that victory were "enjoyed" by Topia who returned to Durres. This defeat directly opened the curtain for the five-century invasion of the Arberian lands by the Ottomans.

Topia came on the scene sometime in the early 13th century, being among the first to pull away from Byzantium joining the Anjou of Naples instead. In return for recognition by the Papacy they promised they would convert from the Orthodox into the Latin rite. Therefore, the door of Topia, run by Tanush, was among the first to accept the crown of the Kingdom of Arberia that the Anjou brought. Tanush's son, Andrea, even though married to the daughter of King Robert, was killed by his men, as they disliked him. However, the Topia experienced their greatest power during the reign of Charles, who came to power in 1359, when Arberian countries had begun to reject Dusan's occupation. Although an ally of Naples, Charles had set out to recapture Durres, as by having possession of the city he increased his power, becoming a much more important factor.

To prevent this, Venice even ordered his fleet to sink Topia's fleet before it gained enough strength. When Topia broke a powerful attack by George Balsha towards Durres in 1366, the Venetian Senate pronounced him an honorary citizen of Venice. This did not stop him from taking Durres, in which he entered two years later. Topia was extended to the South, by annexing the possessions of sebastocrat Vlash Matrënga, stretching between the Shkumbin and Seman deltas.

This expansion caused the Muzakaj, ranging from Castoria to Berat, to bind an alliance with Balsha, entering into a direct conflict with Topia, which triggered what appeared as an internal promotion of Arberian princes to the detriment of each other and their weakness against foreigners, sharing together the suffering of their defeat.

Topia was now surrounded by foreign and domestic enemies. The Anjou briefly succeeded in 1372 to regain the Anjouine sovereignty in Durres, one hundred years after Charles I of Anjou had declared an "Arberian Kingdom." It did not last long, as the campaign of George of Navara, with the blessing of Pope Gregory XI, failed to do other than hand over the fate of Durres to Topia, which he bought from Anjou two years later, thus becoming one of the most powerful Arberian factors.

The dominance of Karl Topia would not last long either, as it would be the Balsha, his sworn enemies, who owned Vlora and were connected with Muzakaj in the South, wanting at all costs to be the first. In 1384, Balsha II, with a surprise attack captured Durres. He added to his title also that of *"Duke of Durazzo."* Balsha did not have it for long as it was the Ottomans, led by Hayredin Pasha, who was already in More with his army, who on September 18, 1385, in the field of Savra in Muzeqea, crossed swords with Balsha II and his allies scoring a victory, while Balsha was killed in the battle. Durres was left in Topia's hand on which the eyes of everyone were directed with ambitions to expand their power from West to East, while the Ottomans withdrew, according to some sources called by Topia to help restore his center.[753]

Of course, his return to the center was the grand prize of ransom that the Ottomans asked the Count of Durres to pay, which he thought he could circumvent by being able to get an alliance with Venice or any other western power. In this regard he made some efforts in Venice, but was left out of the game, because, as the Venetians knew very well that Topia's possessions in Durres and in general in his principality were targeted by the Ottomans, and knowing that, whatever settlement with the Topia affected Ottoman interests, they moved cautiously.

After the death of Charles, his son, George failed to do more than make an agreement with Venice, stipulating that after his death the whole city came under the dominion of Venice, a matter that remained in suspense, as in 1415 the Ottomans conquered Kruja, the old capital of Arberians and Topia. Ballaban Bey appeared as "Subash of Kruja and Arberia."

---

[753] Gelcich, Guiseppe: *"Zeta and dinastia e Balshave,"* Tirana, 2009, p. 147.

Princedom families of Muzakaj and Arianiti experienced a similar rise. Muzakaj were known as a noble family from the time of Comnenus, when Ana Comnenus mentioned the name of a nobleman from the Muzaka family, who in around the year 1090 was among the trusted commanders of Emperor Alex I Comnenus.[754] One of the princes of this family, John I Muzaka, was known for failing to support the "Arbërian Kingdom" of the Anjou.[755] But Andrea II Muzaka was seen heading a movement against Byzantium of 1335-1341, whereas in Durres he signed an agreement with the Anjou of Naples. After the failure of this anti-Byzantine movement, many of the nobles of Muzakaj family were dispossessed and forced to seek refuge in the Peloponnesus in Greece. During Dusan's conquests the Muzakaj were inspirational in a resistance against him and the Byzantine governor of the area of Berat and Vlora, Despot Ivan Comnenus Asen. After the dissolution of Dusan's state, the Muzakaj expanded the boundaries of their possessions towards Korca and Devoll.

In this confrontation he had to deal also with the ruler Vukasin, then the master of Dardania and the entire Western Macedonia, when in 1370 he defeated his army at Castoria. This caused the Emperor of Byzantium, Johan V Palelologus to confirm his title of a despot. A year later, Andrea Muzaka II took Castoria back from Vukasin's son, Mark Kralevic.

His sons John, Theodor, and Stoja encountered the invading Slavs later on. But, in the famous Battle of Dardania Plain of 1389, Theodor, leading Arberian fighters, was killed along with his former permanent opponents. The last of the Muzakaj, Theodor III, accepted Ottoman vassalage in 1417 until 1478, when Shkodra fell under Ottoman rule, keeping hold of a small fraction of their former possessions. On this occasion, Gjon Muzaka, the famous author of the genealogy of Muzakaj family (1510), left the country and settled in the Kingdom of Naples.[756]

The Arianiti family was related to the famous strategist of the Theme of Thessaloniki and later Scupi, Patrician David Arianiti (1001-1018), appointed by the Emperor of Byzantium for his military merits in the war against the Bulgarians. His son, Constantine, was mentioned in the years 1049-1050 as a noted military officer at the service of Byzantium. In 1274, the *Sebast* Alex Arianiti is mentioned. The importance of the Arianiti

---

[754] See: Anna Comnena: *"Alexios,"* pub.Schopen, Vol. I, Bonn, 1938, pp. 451,452.
[755] For more on the genealogy of Muzakaj family see: Pëllumb Xhufi: *"Nga Paleologët te Muzakajt,"* Tirana, 2009, pp. 415-459.
[756] Ibid, p. 380.

family and its power was increased later in relation to the Castrioti family when George Arianiti's younger brother, Vladan, married the daughter of John Castrioti, Angelina. His family remained connected with the Castrioti family even during the time of Skenderbeg, and these ties continued to remain strong even during the Ottoman era, when one of George's nephews, according to a recent document of the 15th century, acted as a high Ottoman official in the region of Vlora, to be recorded as part of *"Arianiti's Arberia,"* a name used in addition to *"Skenderbeg's Arberia."*[757]

One of the most powerful families of Arberia that utilized Dusan's death, for its own rapid rise, turning into an important factor, is that of the Balsha. For Balsha it is known that they came from a noble door in the North, appearing at the whirlwind of events by the mid-14th century remaining as an important factor for more than a century. Brothers Balsha: Strazimir, Gjergj I and Balsha II were among the first to benefit from the new situation, running Dioclea (Genta or Zenta) and from there towards the South and East. On the way they captured Ulqin, Tivar, and then turned to Shkodra and the port of Shirgj. In 1367, they took Budva overseeing commercial movements across the Adriatic. Then the Balsha, through Drin Valley, headed toward Dukagjin reaching Dardania, which was kept occupied by Uros.

Penetrations into the South (through Dukagjin, Zaharia, and Topia possessions) confronted Balsha with the main Arberian noble families, which made equal efforts to take back their possessions conquered by Dusan and Byzantines in Epirus and Thessaly. Durres, Vlora, and Berat were also some of the strongholds that the Balsha targeted to take hold of through alliances, as happened with Muzakaj, or by means of war, as would happen with Topia of Durres. However, the struggle for Durres with Topia was most severe for its consequences in the Arberian lands, as it transpired that at those most crucial circumstances, the pretentions and ambitions of princes had a priority over the common fate of the country, with which internal divisions became an easier prey to foreign occupations.

Obviously, Balsha's determination to increase his possessions on all sides through a strong hand aroused the curiosity of neighbors, first of all Venice. The Adriatic fox was interested to see a force that would free the dissipating space of Dusan's state from a condition of turbulence with

---

[757] *"Historia e Popullit Shqiptar,"* Volume I, Tirana, 2002, p. 298.

numerous unpredictable zupans and princes, but not a very powerful prince who would dictate terms, as happened soon with Balsha. After accepting Catholicism and a direct connection with the Vatican, granted by Pope Urban V, Balsha would turn into a decisive factor for the West across the Adriatic. It was not only the military power what made Balsha already strong in these parts. It was also the Vatican Church that turned him into a two-fold competitor: on one side against the Slavic countries and on the other side against the Orthodox Church, making it a target of the Ottomans, as would happen in the Battle of Savra in 1385, who watched closely in their preparation for an entrée in these areas to see everyone weakened, but not wanting to see anyone rising above anyone else in that internal struggle. Of course, Venice shared the same attitude of having obedient allies and vassals, who could be controlled with defined roles and tasks in accordance with its interests, but rather unable to dictate conditions, which it would not accept.

After the loss of Savra, the grandson of Balsha II, George II Strazimir (1385-1403), faced with the realities tried to preserve the former holdings as much as possible, not through war, but rather by alliances, first with the Venetians, notwithstanding efforts to connect with the Hungarians, even though opponents of Venice. George's relationship with Venice, after which he gave up much of his lands in favor of the Republic of the Adriatic, accepted within the Venetian nobility and the Grand Council of the Republic, provided him with a defense - especially after he got rid of his Crnojevic rivals (one of whom, Djurasin, he killed in April 1396 during a punitive campaign) - but did not give him permanent protection for his steadfast opponents from Dukagjin, Jonimes, Zaharia, and Prince Vuk Lazarevic, had all become vassals of Sultan Bayazid, increasingly threatening him from all sides.

Against these circumstances, the son of George II, Balsha III (1403-1424), once looked up to Hungary, signaling also towards the Ottomans, indicating he could be useful to them if they did not obstruct him to restore Shkodra and Drishti from Venice, which happened in 1405. This was a dangerous adventure in which the young Balsha ventured himself, lasting for about 15 years, with mutual attacks and counter attacks, and some peaceful agreement that would not be respected by Venice, so that all ended in an expected defeat of Balsha III in April 1421, marking the descent from the historical scene of this powerful family, not as vassals, as would happen with most others, but as losers as predetermined by a force which was among the most refined able to turn diplomacy and political guile into force.

However, in this squirm with the new circumstances, which required tremendous vigilance by those behaving similarly, i.e. in closed circuit operations, where the slightest mistake was punished severely, it was two Arberian families, those of Dukagjini and Castrioti, who played a special role in the developments that preceded the Ottoman conquests, since they turned into the carriers of what might be seen as part of a particular Arberian social and spiritual identity, stemming from an historical consciousness, which refers to the antiquity on which it was based.

Therefore, the Dukagjinis highlighted awareness of the law as part of internal social and institutional rule that was supposed to protect the Arberian society from foreign laws, such as those of the Ottomans, related to a completely different civilization from their own, while Castrioti highlighted the factor of a common state and behavior in accordance with it, which although appearing on circumstances of vassalage, it was necessary so that the Arberians, like others (Slavs, Bulgarians, Greeks, Romanians), were subject to this logic in a turn of almost one century. This logic set their consciousness on statehood even as vassals, no matter how valid it could be in the existing circumstances, such as those that preceded a multi-century Ottoman subjugation, as one day it could return only if it were historically marked as part of an indelible memory.

In this historic mission, these families, which, along with others, were included in popular developments such as those that would occur from the time of the collapse of Dusan's conquering state to direct confrontation with the Ottoman invaders, had a rather appropriate opportunity to behave in accordance with this awareness, as graphically they appeared at a link between the coastal and mid-section part and that of Dardania and Macedonia, territories held under Rascian occupation by the late thirteenth century onwards when the Nemanja, after German Crusaders under the leadership of Friederich opened their way, appeared for the first time in these parts.

As Dardania and Macedonia, especially the part of Epirus, have always represented a core of social and spiritual Illyrian-Dardanian identity on which for centuries the Byzantine Empire based itself, it was natural for these parts to turn into targets of beneficiaries and leading destroyers of Byzantium - Bulgarians and Slavs from the 10th century on. When their social and political formations emerged, as was initially the Bulgarian

Kingdom and then Rascian zupans, beginning with Nemanja and ending with "Mega-zupan" Dusan, who, after breaking through the western part (Bosnia and Zahlumia), where their establishment nucleus was, acted mostly at the expense of Byzantium to the detriment of its constituent peoples, primarily the Arberians. The invasive behavior of the Slavs against Arberians and their land became apparent since the time of Boris of Bulgaria in the second half of the 9th century and later of Simeon when they occupied a portion of Dardania and southern Illyricum. But the Rascian behavior against the Arberians was manifested by a greater severity after the Fourth Crusade, along with the campaigns of the Westerners to either conquer or ruin Byzantium.

Therefore, it was quite natural that Arberian countries be attacked from both North and East by both Bulgarians and later Rascians, because it was from there that the foundations of Byzantium, erected by them during the time of Emperor Constantine the Great and Justinian, would be conquered and ruined, while they, admitted in it as barbarians by Emperor Heraclius in the 7th century, for more than two centuries, did their best to dishevel the ethnic and social structure of Illyricum, where they were located and from where they incessantly acted.

This behavior, which started with the Bulgarian conquests of the 9th, 10th and partly the 13th centuries, continuing with the Nemanja of Rascia and tolerated by the "Greekized" Byzantium, seeing enemies among the Bulgarians and Slavs but also potential rescuers, severely damaged the social and spiritual structures devoted to the Empire. Indeed, Byzantium, in accordance with this account, which turned into its boomerang, allowed the collapse of the traditional *izopolitias* relations, a model of partnership of autonomous government (*foeedus*), inherited from the Roman times. Therefore, it was not by chance that the Bulgarian Kingdom at the time of Simeon would bear its own administrative center and church in the occupied parts of Dardania and Macedonia (Ohrid), and it was not by chance that the Nemanjas as soon as they broke the Rascian siege intended to occupy it, and also to destroy the entire Dardanian civilization there from Naissus, as Stefan Nemanja did in 1191, when he flattened all the castles up to Scupi.[758] From the 13th century onwards it carried its administrative and spiritual center (Prizren and Scupi), where the "mega-zupan" Stefan Dusan started one of his most severe campaigns

---

[758] See K. Jiriček: "*Historia e Serbëve,*" Part One, Tirana, 2010, p. 306-309.

against what had already appeared Medieval Arberia, whose center was deliberately set in that of the ancient Dardania in order to keep most of the former Illyricum space surrounded.

Since, knowingly, the former Dusan's zupan, Balsha, succeeded only for a while from the northern areas (Ulqin, Tivar, Budua and Shkodra) to get rid of Dusan's occupations extending the northern principality towards Durres and Vlora in the South, reaching through the Valley of Drin as far as Prizren, his penetration to Dardania led him through the family holdings of Dukagjin, which allowed the passage of his troops across the only road leading there, but staying out of submission.

However, after the fall of Balsha at the Battle of Savra, marking the first shrinking of his holdings, the Dukagjinis emerged as landowners of Lezha keeping possessions on both sides of the valley of Drin up to Prizren. Also, Dukagjinis supervised the Dukagjin Plain from Prizren to Peja. Through their son-in-law, Koja Zaharia, who controlled the part of Deja, they also connected directly with the west of Dardania, linking it with Shkodra and Durres.

Although after the Ottomans temporarily flooded the northern and middle parts, invading Kruja, Ulqin, Shkodra and Deja in 1393, holding them for some time, the Dukagjinis handed over Lezha to the Venetians, thus temporarily yielding their supervision over the Lezha-Prizren road. However, the Dukagjinis, in addition to interconnecting Arberian territories (Prizren and Peja) with the northern coast (Shkodra and Lezha), which had been kept for a long time under the Rascian occupation of Dusan and Nemanja, rising to a level of a key principality, left behind their *Kanun* (Code), a piece of legislation that held most of Arberia together in a spiritual, social, and political sense. The Code of Lek Dukagjini, or as it is called, the Canon of the Mountains, was almost the only legal document that authentically regulated the inner life of Arberians in the circumstances of the Ottoman occupation as well.

The Code of Lek Dukagjini, as a legal and moral institution, an internal constitution linking most Arberians, was not something accidental, the case, much less being in any way part of Dusan's "Zakonik" often called "a product of mega-zupan's mentality" of law and order that he had left to Arberians, but it was a continuation of the famous Justinian Code of the 6th century, succeeding to codify the laws and rules which governed the Illyrian-Dardanian society since ancient time. This Code continued to be used by Arberians since the first Bulgarian invasions, with the breakdown of the imperial legal system, which was a product of their social awareness about the law codified by their Emperor, Justinian I, to be continued during Slavic invasions as well from the 13th century onwards.

Therefore, viewed from this perspective, Dusan and the Nemanjas in general, since their emergence as invaders in Dardania by the late 12th century when they came into contact with Arberians, did not bring "law and order" as alleged, as they never had any but rather received it from the Arberians, as they previously had their own Canon, which had arranged their inner life even before Justinian that was quite natural for him to support his famous imperial code.

Even certain legal forms of "Zakonik," besides those of ecclesiastical nature, viewed from the perspective of the issues addressed in them (property, family, blood feud, etc.),[759] if plainly seen, seem to be taken out of the Arberian Canon. These forms they acquired little by little, as long as their publication by Dusan represented nothing but an adoption of a few articles of the Arberian Canon, to which was then added some more code, of a repressive and discriminatory nature against others (especially against the *Arbanasi*, as they were called, and Vlachs).

After all, if Dusan's "Zakonik" were a "genuine" social and spiritual code of the Slavs, as pretended, and Dukagjini's Code its imitation, then why did it not stay in use among the Slavs during the Ottoman occupation, as occured with the Arberians, when it, within the system of *bulukbasches* was accepted by the Ottomans as a basis that self adjusted over half of its population for centuries?

Hence, one may say that the Canon among Arberians, in its Lab variants, of Skenderbeg, and its form as codified by Justinian I of the sixth century, was part of an internal legal institution of their forefathers, Pelasgians, the forms of which, such as the Council of Elders, warfare behavior, the regulation of property and many other issues we find described in Homer's "Iliad," to which von Hahn relates the institution of law among the oldest of antiquity. The German researcher brings many more examples of the spreading of moral and legal norms not only among the descendants of Pelasgians, but also to other nations: Germans and the Balto-Slavs.[760]

A case issue states that the *"Council of Elders,"* as it acted in most of Arberian lands, when making decisions such as those dealing with crimi-

---

[759] Jeriček, Konstandin: *"Historia e serbëve,"* Part Two, Tirana, 2010, p. 59.
[760] For more see: J. G von Hahn: *"Studimet shqiptare,"* Tirana pp. 235-249.

nal cases, property, or family, and the way of sanctioning of these issues and their application have many affinities with that of Old Rome, where the Senate proposes and adopts such laws by its representatives, who, in this case, come from the tribes, as organizational forms known from antiquity.[761]

Viewed from this perspective the next princedom family, that of the Castriotis, presented an extremely important reference between the social awareness of Arberians for their internal adjustments through legal institutions, such as the Code of Lek Dukagjini and awareness for a common state and affiliation with Western civilization. As the rise of the (John) Castrioti family was associated with the weakening of two large families, Topia and Balsha(j), its social and political position was of importance as it interconnected two main goals of Arberian nobility in those circumstances. On one hand, they sought a fast liberation from the impact of the Rascian state, which even after Dusan's death was on its downfall, although his successors were still making efforts to prevent a social and political alignment of Arberian principalities and, on the other hand, they were fighting for establishing conditions for an alliance with the Western countries in facing the Ottoman conquests, which had already affected Arberian countries from many directions.

Regarding the former, liberation from Rascia, the Castriotis continued the path followed by Balshaj and other nobles. Numerous sources indicate that Castriotis extended in the direction of Dardania (up to Prizren and Scupi), but cannot say exactly what was the nature of their possessions in these parts, as Brankovic, appearing as holder of a part of this area (parts between Prizren and Scupi) had entered vassalage relations with the Ottoman, by which he could own certain parts, as allowed under free possessions. However, rather than for power over those parts, which without any historical evidence were seen as "part of Castrioti's state" attributing to him even a family genealogy from this part (Has),[762] one may speak about economic presence in this part, through trade and other operations he had with certain Ragusian and Venetian merchants, quite viable in the time of their intensification, being that even the Ottomans, now appearing in many parts of the Arberian lands, were interested in free trade with western countries and for an economic development that enabled them good benefits in this region.

---

[761] Ibid, p. 277.
[762] See *Historia e Popullit Shqiptar,*" Volume I, Tirana 2002, pp. 316-318.

However striking in these circumstances, John Castrioti managed to transcend the narrow limits and behave in accordance with the appearance of an important nobleman, who was careful to respect the churches, which reflected the social and even political reputation, necessary to feed and maintain spiritual being with authentic Christian identity, even when, in the threatening circumstances of the conquest, this could bring other mechanisms to a halt. Therefore, along with his links with Venice and the Roman Catholic Church, he was also attentive to the Orthodox Church by granting it two of his villages from the Gostivar region to its center Hilandar on the Holy Mountain, in 1426. He also purchased there St. John's Knoll (also known by the name of Arberesh Knoll - *arbanaški pirg*), where one of his sons, Reposh, remained as a monk for his life until he died on July 25, 1431.[763]

Regarding the second issue, namely on creating conditions for closer affinities with western countries to face the Ottoman conquests, Castrioti's behavior was consistent with the logic of vassalage, which was already accepted by all other Balkan princes after losing the Battle of Dardania in June of 1389. John Castrioti accepted vassalage to the Sultan in 1409, where he was forced to hand over one of his sons as hostage, which seems to have been Reposh and he sent his youngest boy, George, six years later, as *içoglan* (Saray juniors) to Sultan's court, where children of nobles, gentry and zupans accepting Ottoman vassalage were educated.[764]

Noticeably, John Castrioti's possessions achieved a major expansion precisely after having accepted vassalage from the Sultan. Even after the fall of Kruja into the hands of the Ottomans, Castrioti was attentive so that his relations with the Ottomans would not cause a decline of his

---

[763] Ibid, p. 316.
[764] Ottoman institution of *iç-oglan-lari*, in *Edrene*, where John Castrioti's son, George (Skenderbeg), differs from the order of *janissaries (acemi oglan)*. It was established in Bayazed's time aimed at distinguishing the dervish from the mobilized janissaries from *raja*, peasants, representing the core of the famous military order in the Ottoman Empire, with which great military achievements are connected. They served at Sultan's Saray and were called "Saray Acemi oglanlari," or "Celeb," meaning – Saray juniors. Wishing to create a greater difference from the junior janissaries (acemi oglan), they were also called "Sadi," meaning in Persian: happy, fortunate. The most handsome and smart boys were chosen for iç-ogllans. (For more see: Zeki, Pakalin: "Osmanli Deyimler ve Terimleri Sözlügü," Istanbul, 1951, pp. 28-29; "Resimli Osmanli Tahiri Ansiklopedis," Istanbul, 1985, p. 151, cited by Rizaj, Skënder: "Kosova gjatë shekujve XV, XVI dhe XVII," Prishtina, 1982, p. 26.)

power. At this time he reached some agreements with Venice and Ragusa, maintaining open communication links with this part of the world, which through northern routes allowed for free movement of goods from Shkodra to Prizren and Scupi. He tried to keep this balance to the end, even though it was very difficult, especially at times when he could not decide any longer on the fate of alliances with the big powers (the Ottomans and Venice), who were settling accounts between themselves at his own expense.

In these circumstances, one may say that John Castrioti managed to create an Arberian state structure, even as a vassal to the sultan, equal to the ones that the Orthodox Slavs, Bulgarians, Greeks and others had, in order to host further developments relating to the Ottoman conquests, which were on the verge, where Arberians did not enter "under foreign armpits," as Slavs and Greeks claimed, but wearing "their own skin."

Evidently, this historic authentication, i.e. organizing the state in the circumstances of bondage, was embodied by Skenderbeg as an inspiration, so that one day he restored the royal crown his country had since the time of the Pelasgic Kingdom.

Ethnic Relations between Arberians and Slav Invaders during the Middle Ages

The Slavic invasions in Dardania and North Arberia from the 13th to the 14th century almost entirely destroyed the material infrastructure of Arberians built during the Byzantium, but not the spiritual one. – The Christobulate of Decan Monastery of the year 1330 and that of St. Archangels in Prizren, 1341, although devised and rewritten in accordance with hegemonic concepts of Serbian historiography of the 19th century, in all probability, based on Ottoman civil registers covering the 15th and 16th centuries, provide evidence for the preservation of the ethnic structure of Arberians as a majority people.

Nothing more than the Slavic invasions affected the Arberian ethnic relations from the Middle Ages onwards bringing them to a situation where they on many occasions and in various forms were influenced socially and culturally. This was rather natural, as it was about different people and about a different social and spiritual situation, with the first bearing their roots in antiquity and appearing among its founders that had affected the entire Hellenic civilization, with kings and kingdoms as far back as the time of Pelasgians and Illyrians, who had helped build the Roman Empire even after they were conquered by it - as they had built Byzantium and were among the first to have accepted Christianity - while the Slavs were barbarian peoples. Other barbarian tribes from the 5th century threatening Roman civilization were accepted by Emperor Heraclius in the northern parts as servants in the 7th century, to prevent further penetrations by Avars and barbarian peoples from the North.

Indeed, the acceptance of the Slavs by Emperor Heraclius in the 7th century would not only serve to "protect the Empire from barbaric attacks," but accelerated the process of intrusion and destabilization of Byzantium from within by them, which also led to its complete destruction centuries later.

However, it can be said that this ongoing process of collapse of the Empire from within started in Illyricum and among the Illyrian- Dardanians, who were the first to be faced with the barbaric behavior of the Slavic tribes located in their parts. As known, Emperor Heraclius, initially allowed the Slavic tribes to settle in the northern part of Thrace and Illyricum along the Sava River as they were used for different services in the Empire, mostly as mercenaries and servants to which relates also the etymology of their name *serbros* (in Latin) and $αεμπρος$ – half peasant, half renter $αεμπρα$, in Latin (*sebra*), a word that even in the old Russian (*sjaber*) has the same meaning, i.e. one who performs services of hirelings or servants.[765]

Simultaneously, as mercenaries performing various services, they were subject to some specific social rules, allowing them certain primitive tribal organization, as they had them in the Carpathians, from where they came. This, however, led to adverse consequences for the Illyrian population, living according to imperial rules and organized in accordance with an internal self-governance. Additionally, the Illyrians, who had accepted Christianity by the 4th century, although retaining many of the positive traditions of paganism, had great spiritual inconsistencies with the Slavs, who led a barbaric life and behaved in a barbaric way with others.

Therefore, this affected the population resulting in frictions with them, to either leave, or for those who for various reasons could not do so,

---

[765] For more see: Jiriček, Konstandin: "*Historia e Serbëve*," Part One, Tirana, p. 162.

adapt and even Slavicize, which, according to many sources, this happened in Dalmatia and Bosnia from the late medieval period with a situation where a good part of the former Illyrians were seen by both churches (western and eastern) as assimilated into Slavs.

The Slavic tribal social life outside the imperial rules was legitimized during the time of Emperor Basilius II through his famous decrees on establishing *themes*, that of Durres and Nichopolis, joined by other two, those of Dalmatia and Scupi, as forms of military-feudal organization directly supervised by the center, while the Slavic tribes were allowed to continue with their independent zupanias and despotates, as were those of Dioclea (Zeta), Zahlumia, Bosnia and Rascia, from where they started their known penetrations in the western and southern parts of Illyricum and Dardania conditioned by the biological expansion of barbarian peoples as compared with the indigenous population. From this point of view, the latter was increasingly shrinking, due to both the retreat under barbarian pressures for protection in urban centers or close to them, and two plague epidemics that affected Illyricum in the 6th and 8th centuries. According to the Byzantine and Roman sources, the reduction of population and economic and defensive decline of the Empire was one of the reasons why they demanded that the barbarian tribes, whose services were hitherto utilized in various ways, be accepted as equal citizens of the Empire.

Thus, from the 10th century onwards the first penetrations of Slavic tribes in the parts of Shkodra and coastal cities (Ulqin, Tivar, Budua) occured, while in the 11th century onwards, after the conquest of Rascia by Nemanjas, the Rascian despots constantly made efforts to extend their conquests toward the center of Dardania. They achieved this in 1191, when Nemanja utilized the Fourth Crusade and the penetration of the German king Friedrich to the East to conquer Naissus and then to penetrate to Scupi, Ulpiana and Prizren, from where they never left.

Besides the Rascian efforts to keep the western parts hostage (Bosnia, Zahlumia and Zeta), from where they had come, areas which in different forms were subject to different influences of Catholic countries (Venice, Ragusa, and Hungary) and pursuant to this also accepted Catholicism, the Nemanjas of Rascia and their followers from Uros to Dusan, turned to the East in the 13th century, after cutting the last ties with the Holy See and declaring their own independent church. However, they shortly gave it up and returned to the Byzantine mentality. This, however, did not turn them into followers of Byzantium in its proper concept as promoted by Justinian and its Illyrian-Dardanian ancestors. Rather, as it happened with the Bulgarians, who as soon as they were strengthened declared their own state at the expense of Byzantium (initially as vassal - during the time of Boris, and later as an independent kingdom - at the time of Samuel); the Nemanjas too used every possibility and game to harm Byzantium, as to one day go as far as to declare themselves its sole heirs, as Dusan did (1331-1355).

However, by the late 12th century when the despot Stefan Nemanja made his way into Dardania and from Naissus (Nish) to Scupi (Shkupi-Skopje) destroying the entire ancient civilization raised by the mighty Emperor Justinian I, coming from Dardania, one of the most deserving for turning once again to its concept of a universal empire, direct relations took place between ethnic Arberians and Slavic invaders, remaining, more or less the same until the Ottoman conquests.

Although Slavic sources, primarily those devised by the Orthodox Church and one-sided Serbian historiography of the 19th century tried to reflect these relations in a vary distorted light, where according to them, Dardania by the second half of the 19th century and on was called *Kosovo (Kosova)*.[766] This was seen as "the center of the medieval Serbian state," but also "as the Serbian spiritual center" with "numerous Orthodox monasteries" where "the Serbian Orthodox Church was born," and others,

---

[766] In Middle Ages the name *Kosova* was not known in naming any wide province, as it appears in the 19th century. In *"Letopis Popa Dukljanina"* a little settlement in Bosnia named Kosova is recorded. Even the Battle of Dardania of 1389 of the Alliance of the Balkan Christians against the Ottomans, in Serb sources is explained as *Kosovo Polje (Plain of Ravens)*, which has been literally translated by the Germans (Amsenfeld). In Turkish it is called *Küs-ova (Great Plain: "ova" - "plain" and "küs" - "great," "large")*. In Arabic it is called *"Kusure,"* while some western sources of the time called it as the battle that took place in Albanicum or Illyricum. In the administrative organization of the Ottoman Empire after 1455, Kosova is not mentioned as sanjack, or as nahije. Most of the territory of Dardania was included in the territorial and administrative unit called *"Vilayet Vilk,"* according to holder Vuk Brankovic, who accepted Ottoman vassalage turning into their right hand in future campaigns to the West. The Vilayet of Vilk became a Sanjak that in the time of Sultan Mehmed II was known as Sanjak of Vuçitërn. Kosova as a vilayet appears in 1876 within the new organization of the Empire following the Tanzimat reforms. (For more see: Tërnava, Muhamet: *"Popullsia e Kosovës gjatë shekujve XIV-XVI,"* Prishtina, 1995; Rizaj, Skënder: *"Kosova gjatë shekujve XV, XVI and XVII,"* Prishtina, 1982.)

namely as an "ethnic Serb stronghold" with "a few Arberians, some Vlachs and Greeks,"[767] still, Dardania and the largest part of Illyricum, called since Middle Ages and on as *Albania, Albaniae, Arvanien, Arbania*, and its inhabitants called *Albanians, Albanoi, Arvanites, Albani* and by the Slavs *Arbanasi* and *Rabans* kept its Arberian ethnic character with a Slavic minority.[768]

As such, even with its Arberian character, *Dardania* went even further in the coming13th through 19th centuries, even when appearing by the name of *Kosovo* (*Kosova*), as a political amputation incited by the Slavs and unusable and unknown in that form by its ethnic residents since antiquity, crumpled in a single vilayet, as that born out of the imperial reforms of 1876 intended to detach it from its ethnic wholeness, and above all from its sense and dimension of antiquity connecting it with Troy.

However, what often comes out as unilateral "evidence" to prove the alleged ethnic Slav association of Dardania and northern part of Arberia, narrowed in the contour of *Kosova-o,* has to do with the affiliation of the Christian Orthodox rite, which connects with the largest population of this part since the time of the acceptance of Christianity in the 4th century onwards, where the Dardanian Church appeared among the first in Illyricum. At the time of Justinian, it became an independent vicariate

---

[767] For more on unscientific views see the following Serb authors: Jovanović, D. K: "*O Arbanasima,*" Belgrade, 1880; Veselinović, M. V: "*Srbi u Makedoniji i u Južnoj Srbiji,*" Belgrade, 1888; "*Geografsko-etnografski pregled Makedonije i Stare Srbije,*" Belgrade, 1898; "*Pregled kroz Kosovo,*" Belgrade, 1895; Gopčević, Spiridon: "*Stara Srbija i Makedonija,*" I-II, Belgrade, 1890; Orlović, Pavle: "*Pitanje o Staroj Srbiji,*" Belgrade, 1901; Cvijić, Jovan: "*Osonove za geografiju i geologiju Makedonije i Stare Srbije,*" Belgrade, 1906; Filipović, Milenko: "*Etničke prilike u Južnoj Srbiji,*" Skopje, 1937; Jovičević, Andrija: "*Malesija, Naselja i poreklo stanovništva,*" Belgrade, 1923: Hadživasiljević, Jovan: "*Muslimani naše krvi u Južnoj Srbiji,*" Belgrade, 1924; Stanković, Todor: "*Putne beleške po Staroj Srbiji,*" Belgrade, 1910; Nušić, Branislav: "*Kosovo-Opis zemlje i naroda,*" Novi Sad, 1902; Urošević, Atanasije: "*Novobrdska Kriva Reka,*" Belgrade, 1950.

[768] For more on the Arberian character of Dardania as part of Arberia, see the following authors: Hahn, Johan - Georg von: "*Studime Shqiptare,*" Tirana, 2007; L. Thalloczy – K. Jeriček: "*Zwei Urkunden aus Nordalbanien,*" in "*Illyrisch-Albanische Forschungen,*" band. I, München und Leipzig, 1916; M. Šufflay: "*Die Grenzen Albaniens in Mitelalter,*" in "*Illyrisch-Albanische Forschungen,*" I, 1913; M. Šuflllay: "*Acta des Albanesischen Volkstammes,*" in "*Ungarische Rundschau,*" I, 1916-17; M. Šufflay: "*Srbi i Arbanasi,*" Belgrade, 1925.

associated with the Holy See, something that rightly promotes Illyrian-Dardanians to be among the first Christians in the western part of the Roman Empire.

Indeed, at this point both understandings and misunderstandings occur, turning them into "arguments" and "counter-arguments," as it is the Slavic Orthodox Church appearing with its own records and "title-deeds" pretending they represent a real situation of believers and their properties from the time of their establishment, which in this case relates to the thirteenth century onwards, when the first Orthodox churches were built by the invading Nemanjas, first Stefan, Uros II, Stefan Decanski and Stefan Dusan (1335-1355).

However, if the churches were really built by Nemanjas invaders, although this is not evidenced by independent sources of the time (both Latin and Byzantine), it has been omitted that in these parts churches existed from the 4th century and on, and that the Dardanian Church, as noted, appeared as independent bishopric from this time onwards and remained for more than three centuries (5th-8th). Meanwhile the Slavs accepted Christianity in the 9th and 10th century, and with Christian adolescence they appeared in these areas in the late 12th and early 13th centuries after Stefan Nemanja of Rascia occupied a large part of Dardania from Naissus to Scupi, Ulpiana and Theranda, finding there Christian Arberians with their churches and monasteries among the largest of the Empire, built by Emperor Justinian I (over 80 of them in the triangle Justiniana Prime – Naissus - Scupi alone); they also faced real Christianity and their temples for several centuries.

Although one cannot exclude the possibility of the invaders having built a church, though this seems unlikely, given the fact that in their first incursions from Naissus to Scupi, despite the destruction of a good part of Dardanian civilization, they inherited the Christian temples they found.[769] However, even if they were repaired, they could not possibly be seen as separate from the existing ecclesiastical culture and building traditions.

The monastic cristobula and various charts dealing with their "histories," keeping an absolute silence over the Dardanian church factor and emphasizing the Slavic-Orthodox one, outside century-old continuity,

---

[769] For more on the Nemanjas penetrations and occupation of Dardania see: Osgtrogorski, Georg: *"Historia e Perandorisë Bizantine,"* Tirana, 2002; Jeriček, Konstandin: *"Historia e Serbëve,"* Part One, Tirana, 2010; Guiseppe, Gelcich: *"Zeta and dinastia e Balshave,"* Tirana, 2007.

confirms this biased and unscientific approach, in which an inherited church culture with numerous temples were entirely kept silent, as was the native population, the Arberian one. In accordance with this view, this history had to be omitted, or even when seen, shown as entirely reduced, as actually happened in the "documents" of the Slav-Orthodox Church.

As during the Byzantine Empire there was no census, except records of property (*pronia*), while the Ottoman ones appeared immediately after the conquest, with the start of its administration, then remained the "Cristobula"[770] of Orthodox monasteries as the only "source" of this nature, and as such did not transmit the entirety of church affiliation, as during that time too, despite the prosecution of Catholics carried out by Uros II and especially Dusan, Catholic churches and Catholic followers existed in Dardania.[771] For if there were no Catholics, who certainly had been in a significant number causing reason for concern for the Orthodox, then why would Dusan even start his campaign against the Catholic "schism?"

But, although much such church "evidence" of Orthodox monasteries, as mentioned earlier, is charged with justified suspicion of being fabricated later for hegemonic purposes, as is the case with the actions of the Serbian Orthodox Church, which, consistently in the 19th century onwards, announced "discovering" many of them, appearing inasmuch as four or five versions,[772] while some of them as "testimonies of the time" were biased (being written by the clergy, they hid or distorted information for the interests of the church, as noted, ignoring believers who did not belong to their church and others on similar grounds).

---

[770] *Cristobulae* are written testimonies on events of legal character, with permanent form and insignia that change according to the place, time, and legal events. Namely, the cristobulae are some kind of diplomas, testimonies, cards, gift certificates, and others in use in the Middle Ages. As such they were issued by both Byzantine and local rulers and despots. This type of solemn testimonies was passed from Byzantium to Balkan despots. (For more See Dr. Stjepan Antoljak: *"Pomone istorijske nauke,"* Kraljevo, 1971, pp. 52, 59.)

[771] For more on the distribution of Catholic churches in Dardania and believers in Middle Ages see: Gjini, Gaspër: *"Skopsko-prizrenska biskupija kroz stoljeća,"* Zagreb, 1986.

[772] For more on the appearance of cristobulae of Serb Orthodox Monasteries in three or four versions see: Krasniqi, Mark: *"Dulje - Nasjelje u Prizrenskom Podgoru,"* Glas Etnografskog Insitutua, II-III,(1953-1954), Belgrade, p. 365.

However, even as such, certain realities related to the fact that most of them were written and described upon Ottoman civil registers covering the 15th century onwards, not having been able to distinguish the definite and indefinite forms of the names, with the definitive being a prominent feature of the Arberian language and similar "trivialities," and even as such they highlighted data providing certain historical evidence proving Arberian autochthony even with Slavic names and designed Slavic toponomastics.

The Cristobula of Decan Monastery is one of the documents of this nature, which provides valuable historical data, without taking into account the intention and limited objectivity of the scribe for the circumstances, and regardless of the fact that its original was missing, and that one is dealing here with a rewritten form, allegedly "fully adhering faithfully to the genuine document,"[773] although this "faithfulness" cannot be scientifically ascertained.

However, the Decan Cristobula bears the signature of Stefan Decanski, saying as its author, that he had prevailed against the Bulgarians,[774] which all relates to historical data, such as the one proving the occupation of a good part of Dardania by the Nemanjas, which had begun in the summer of 1191, as the Rascian army invaded Nish, Scupi, and Prizren up to the Sharr Mountains. Therefore, it comes in the context of the historical documents building up an historical frame of the church life of Orthodox rite in medieval Dardania, focusing the Monastery of the Decan

---

[773] Jastrebov J.G: *"Podaci o istoriji srpske crkve,"* Belgrade, 1879, who admits that most of the documents dealing with the history of Serbian Orthodox churches, are not authentic, though many have been lost, and even those found elsewhere in northern monasteries, are incomplete. Jastrebov acknowledges that both the book and documents of *"Dečanski Prvenac"* of the year 185, compiled by Monarch Joseph of Decan Monastery is not complete. Similarly, he considers the publication of "Dečanski spomenici," published in Belgrade in 1851, which, according to Jastrebov, lacks many of the original documents, while "the complete" and rewritten ones are not meritorious, because they are not accompanied with the Ottoman civil registers, orders, and others, which, according to him, fill the "grave situation of the Serbian Church in the Ottoman Empire and the injustices it witnessed by the devastating Arnauts"! (For more see pp. 36-78).

[774] Although the Decan Cristobula bears no date, it has been assessed that the mentioned battle has to do with that of Velbuzhd (present-day Kystendil) taking place between the Rascians and Bulgarians in 1330, won by the Rascians led by S. Decanski.

Orthodox Church and its property in this part of Dukagjin in a space of about 2500 square kilometers.[775]

It provides anthropogeographic data, especially those dealing with the settlements, ethnic makeup of its population and professions, with toponomastics being of particular interest,[776] even in the one given in the inevitable Slavic-Orthodox version, which, at least from this viewpoint is verifiable with Ottoman civil registers immediately after the establishment of their rule in these parts, which carry the actual situation found, although even Ottoman recorders lacked knowledge of the local language, knowing only that they were dealing with Christians.

Thus, according to this Cristobulae one learns that the feud of Decan Monastery included several villages (*katunde - selo*) and hamlets *katundthe* (*zaseoci*), being part of the following *zupas* (provinces in a narrow term): *Zatrnava*, Altin (present-day Gjakova), Reka (the area between Decan and Gjakova), *Parkova* and *Podrima* (area of Drin). *Zupa of Zatrnava* included the villages in the present day vicinities of Decan: *Decan, Brezhan, Carrabreg, Pridvoc* (preserved neither as a settlement nor a toponym), *Beleg* (with 11 houses and 30 men), *Locan* (with 60 houses and 200 men) and *Upper* and *Lower Lluka* (with 20 houses and 73 men).[777]

The western part of the Medieval Zupa known as *Hvosno* or *Hvostno* also belonged to the Decan Feud, an area between Bistrica of Peja and Decan. In that part the following villages were recorded: *Strellc* (with 70 houses and 130 men), *Lublolik* (with 74 houses and 230 men), *Bohorik* (today's Bohoriq with 24 houses and 78 men), *Lubusha* (with 9 houses and 24 men), *Istinik* (present-day Isniq with 37 houses and 127 men), *Bivolar* (with 7 houses) and *Papracan* (today's Prapaçan with 52 houses and 174 men).[778]

Based on the anthroponomical data of this document most of the names appear to be Slavs. But, it is precisely this issue that reveals some of the truth about the Slavic names, which, as given, reveal the presence of a population of Arberian origin, which even the Orthodox church records were not able to withhold as well as those fabricated later in accordance

---

[775] Ivanović, R: "*Dečansko vlastelinstvo*," Istorijski časopis, Belgrade, 1954, knj. IV. 173-225, cited according to Tërnava, Muhamet: "*Popullsia e Kosovës gjatë shekujve XIV-XVI*," Prishtina, 1995, p. 27.
[776] Novaković, St: "*Selo*," Glas 24, Belgrade, pp. 189,213.
[777] Milojević, M: "*Dečanske hristovulje*," Belgrade, 1880, p. 184.
[778] Ibid, p. 185.

with the Ottoman civil registers, as is the case with many of them, mentioned by Jastrebov in his book *"Podaci o Istoriji Srpske Crkve"* (Facts about the history of the Serbian Church) of 1879, where he examines the very documents of Decan Monastery and several churches in Prizren and its environs. Therefore, in the village of *Strellc* the anthroponym *Beroje* is found, in *Lubolik, Shishman, Beran,* and *Bohoriq* one finds the Arberian anthroponym *Preno, Milesh* in *Lëshuna,* in Isniq, *Bukur* and *Tolaj* and in *Prapacan* one finds the name *Milesha*.[779]

When speaking of Albanian anthroponomy, such as those, it must be said that they are also found within the Slavic families, which shows that the church registration had not been able to entirely conceal the ethnic reflection of the Arberian indigenous population, as intended by identifying it with religion, which for the Orthodox Church was identical with the Slavic autochthony. Therefore, in the village of *Bohorik* there is a note confirming this situation: "*A u njih Boloje a sin mu Priboje, a brat mu Mirsha i Prenko(At Baloja son Priboje, and brothers Mirsha and Prenko).*"

Similarly, the presence of Arberian names among the Slavic ones is also found in a family from the village of Isniq: "*Preljub a sin Bogoje i Branko i Miloslav a ded im Bukur...Tolaj a sin mu Priboje i Radoslav*"(Preljub and his son Blagoje and Branko and Miloslav and his grandfather *Bukur.....Tolaj* and his sons Priboje and Radoslav.)[780]

If, however, transiently one considers the first case of a family where brothers appear one with a Slavic and the other with an Arberian name from a Slavic father (Boloje), then one may not claim it to be a "mixed" Slavic family, as there was no reason for this when the church was Orthodox, the writing was Slavic, zupan (governing area) was Rascian, as Stefan Decanski was from the family of Nemanjas, who came from Rascia.

Therefore, it seems that one is dealing with an Arberian family, Slavicized by obligation or interest or being registered as such because of their Orthodox affiliation (all the same), trying to "hide the root," as actually happened during the Ottoman period, when many families, for economic or other interests would accept Islam in the eyes of the government, while maintaining their Christian names or surnames at home. The phenomenon of "Laramans" (crypto-Catholics), not in terms of maintaining a double belief (Christian-Muslim), but in an ethnic *Arberian-Slavic* sense is the best explanation. Even the second case, the one of *Bukur* family from

---

[779] Tërnava, Muhamet: *"Popullsia e Kosovës gjatë shekujve XIV-XVI,"* Prishtina, 1995, p. 28.
[780] Ibid, p. 29.

Isniq confirms this in a rather "natural" form, namely when grandfather *Bukur* of *Tolaj* family had his son *Prelub* and sons *Blagoje* and *Branko*.

This phenomenon was made possible as the Church only took care of the rite affiliation, in this case the Orthodox one, with the Catholic one being its "rival," and not for others.

The occurrence of "mixed" name families within Orthodoxy is not limited only to the immediate environs of the Decan Monastery. Rather, it extended to other Zupas, everywhere its possessions were reaching as far as Prizren, Tropoja, and other parts in the direction of Prishtina.

In Zupa of Reka, north of the present-day Gjakova, which had three villages and a hamlet: *Hrasovica* (with 34 houses and 103 men), *Prekiluk* (with 18 houses and 48 men), *Prilep* (with 21 houses and 52 men), besides the names mentioned one notes the names *shok*, *Trashan*, *Tolijak* and *Milesh*. In the village of *Babaj* the anthroponym "*Shin*" is found.

In *Gramacel* a family had the following men members: *Gjin, Radislav* and *Bogoslav*. Here, the first bears an Arberian name *(Gjin)*, and the others Slavic names.

Even the Zupa of *Altin*, stretching between the Zupa of Reka and Valbona River had ten villages, with the following being the largest: *Tropoja, Lluzhan, Babjan, Shoshan, Goraj, Shipçart, Bunjaj,* and *Balubi*, most of them with mixed Slavic-Arberian names, although the Decan Cristobula marks them as *"Serbian villages."* Even based on anthroponomy, the village of *Greva* (with 11 houses and 34 men) comes out to be overwhelmingly of Arberian origin, with an "interference" of Slavic or Christian names in the Slavic form. It notes the following:

> Bogiša a brat mu Magoje a sin mu Andreja, Martin a sin mu Andreja i Šuško, pavi Duraš a sim mu Zaharija Bogša a Ivan a sin mu Nikola a brat mu Đuđ Tanuš Đurđ a sin mu Mihal d Minko a sin mu Andreja Koprc a sin mu Grdan i Dolin i Duraš Dimitri Gon Ivan Đuđ a ded im Marko Vojgo i Gon i Dobrave a si mu Nikola Đurđ i Nikola i Gin a dem im Zagarije.[781]

Similar cases are found in the villages of Podrima, included in the feud of Decan Monastery. The village *Serosh* indicates a mixture of names, in which almost every house, along with Slavic or Slavicized church names Arberian names are also found. Here are some typical examples:

"Runka a brat mu Rad sin mu Hodan a brat mu <u>Prenko</u>."

---

[781] Milojević, M: *"Dečanske hristovulje,"* Belgrade, 1880, pp. 34-35.

Or:

"Pribislav a brat mu Bušat a sin mu Dragoš."

The Decan Cristobula, even in the way it is "(dis)cribbed" or fabricated (all the same), shows an interesting distinction between the village anthroponomy for the village: *Selo* (for Slavic composition, though, evidently they were mixed by names) and *katun* (Arberian composition). In the case of granting villages to the Decan Monastery, Stefan Decanski writes the following:

"I jeliko mi bist v z mono priložiti semu sel u katun vlaških i arbanaškiH."[782]

So the saying is about *"Vlachian and Arberian villages"* (ten of them with only one qualifying as having Arberian population), in which case, the presenter (despot Stefan Decanski) comes out with an ethnic segregation, if it could be said, who, even outside a thorough analysis, brings to light the Arberian ethnic factor, which even "defined" in that fashion, lying amidst Vlach and Slav villages, as shown also by the phenomenon of the "laramans," accepting Slavic church and Slavic names, which is explained in no other way but by social and political factors that were unavoidable in the circumstances when Rascia aimed at extending its rule as deep as possible into occupied Arberian areas so as to change their ethnic and spiritual character, in which in addition to its administration and the official language, the Church appeared as a very powerful ally, obliged with the task of performing that job.

Therefore, as "Vlach villages" were: *Radishevc*, stretching near *Rizniq* (with 17 houses and 62 men), *Upper* and *Lower Ratish, Sashiqan* (with 29 houses and 181 men), Vardishtan (with 11 houses and 48 men), *Lepqinovc* (with 18 houses and 71 men), *Gjurashevc*, near the present-day Gjakova, (with 53 houses and 110 men), *Tudoriqevc*, near Rogova (with 29 houses and 104 men) and *Gojilovc*, near *Lloqan* not far from Decan, (with 35 houses and 90 men). The only *"katun Arbanasa"* (Arberian village) according to the Cristobulae descriptions should be sought on the right side of the river Drin, near *Zerzeva*, present-day Xërxa.[783]

In the Vlach *katuns* (villages) along with Slav and minor Vlach names, Arberian names are found in majority. Arberian characteristic anthroponomies are found there such as: *Gjin, Lesh, Tol, Milesh, Gon,*

---

[782] Ibid, p. 3.
[783] Tërnava, Muhamet: *"Popullsia e Kosovës gjatë shekujve XIV-XVI,"* Prishtina, 1995, p. 36.

and others of that nature. As in "Slavic katuns (selo)," whenever a father appears with an Arberian name, even among the "Vlach" ones there is almost the same pattern. The father bears an Arberian name (*Lesh, Gjin, Tol, Milesh, etc.*), and the children have Slavic names:

"*Radoslav a brat mu Radomir i Hrane a otas im Leš*" (Radoslav and his brother Radomir and Hrane from father Llesh).[784]

But the only *"arbanas katun"* (Arberian village) mentioned in the Decan Cristobulae, even if designed to shrink to a minimum the Arberian population in parts of the ancient Dardania, occupied by the Nemanja more than a century before, even if it presents a realistic picture of an ethnic situation seen with the eye of the Orthodox churchmen to whom all the followers of their church are seen as Slavic-Orthodox and in no other way, it still refutes the position that anthroponomy, as presented here, can be taken as the main and absolute criterion for determining the ethnic structure of these villages. Instead, it refutes its very construct, as that same reflection repeats itself, more or less, in all the villages, providing the phenomena with a seal of an insurmountable fact speaking in favor of the dominance of the Arberian factor in the registers of the Orthodox Church, written in Church Slavonic and sealed by Slav despots. In this case the "exceptions" (the occurrence of Arberian anthroponomy phenomena in the Slavic one) not only return to a natural rule, but they explain how an "exception" cannot turn into a rule. Therefore, it is interesting that it is reflected as in the Cristobulae:

Leš Tuz i s detiju Braislav Čurko s bratijom i s detiju.
- Svinoglav i s detiju Gon Bušat i Gon i Petreč.
- I Gin Gratan Georgie i Budan.
- Petr Suma i s bratiom Mataguž s bratom Lazor i Prijezda Kreč s detiju Gonom.
- Domin'ko s detiju, Reč s detiju.
- Leš i Lazor Progon Mira.
- Dminko s detiju.
- Reč s detiju.
- Leš i Lazor Progon Mira.
- Petr Kuč s bratiom Pavls s detiju.
- Reč s detiju Nikola, Pavl s bratiom.

---

[784] Ivanović, R: "*Istorijsko geografski značaj Dečanske hristovulje iz 1330 godine.*" Belgrade, 1951, Book II, p. 185.

- Mihal i Dmitri.
- Golub i Gon s bratiom.
- Đurđ i Šok i Lešmir.
- Marko Suma i Mizko i Pelegrin...S Gonc.
- Lazo...(pi) Serak Dejak s detiju Bogoslav.[785]

Along with the Decan Cristobulae, most probably of the year 1330, that is, what the Serbian historiography admitted to have been "written on the basis of the original," which however was missing, and even as such provides ample evidence of the Arberian association of the majority population in this part of Dardania, which by the early 13th century was under an occupation by the Nemanjas, who had penetrated from Rascia, was also that of Megazupan Stefan Dusan (1331-1355) given to the *St. Michael and Gabriel* Monastery near Prizren. Although this Cristobulae too is burdened with a reasonable doubt being rewritten in the 19th century, like numerous other Slav-Orthodox church "poveljas" and documents of this nature, in order to nurture the "Serbian medieval history" with "its truth," it is of interest because of the anthroponymic and toponymic data, even with the Slav-Orthodox full version, because of its dealing with Prizren and wider area of this ancient Dardanian city, called Theranda, which, in Byzantium appeared with a new name.

The feud of this monastery, according to the Cristobulae, had its earthly possessions in Dardania, Dukagjin, the outskirts of Shkup, Tetova, Ovçepole, Veles, Strumica, Vranje, Toplica, Plava, Pulti, like in the district of *Shkodra* and the coast. The city of Prizren itself, at the time of the construction of the monastery, featured a part of Upper Pulti and Dukagjin.[786]

Interestingly, the Cristobula does not mark the names of farmer residents, but only those of cattle-breeding residents, the so-called Vlachs, who lived in villages, where, according to previous typologies, besides Slavic and Vlach names, a large number of them are typical Arberian names. Equally varied appears the structure of the anthroponomy of inhabitants in other settlements, classified as "katuns" (villages) in the Cristobulae, where for the first time, a resident head of family of the katun of *Kostercan* carries a Slavic name with a typical Arberian last name but with a Slavic suffix:

---

[785] Ibid, pp. 120-121
[786] Ibid, p. 345.

"*Bogdan Tanušević s sinovi*"(Bogdan Tanushevic with his sons.)

In the *katun* of *Blace* the following record is found:

"*Gonc Arbanas s sinovi*"(Gonc Arbanas with his sons.)[787]

The Arberian presence in these parts is also evidenced in being discriminated against by the famous Dusan's "Zakonik," whereby they were forbidden access to "public property" and banned from use of "common" pastures.[788]

Thus, a Dusan's decree of May 2, 1355, granting privileges and properties to the Hilandar Monastery in the vicinity of Rahovec, banned the use of land to others, emphasizing resolutely Vlachs and "Arbanansin":

"*da ne pase tei zabelje nikoj vlastelin, ni mal, ni velik, ni Vlah, ni Arbanansin.*"[789]

But, in an authentic diploma of Dusan of the year 1355, providing wealth and privileges assigned to the monastery of St. Nicholas in Dobrusha, the following anthroponomies are recorded:

"*Negomir, Gin, Beli, Vasil od Zuričani, Nemat i Prkač i Bratisljak.*"[790]

The name *Gin* comes out here, identical with the anthroponym *Gjin*, which is typical for Arberians.

Arberians appear as well in the cards that the nun Evgenija with her sons, Stefan and Vuk granting the village of *Livoc* to St. Basilius of the Holy Mountain, in which, when describing the village a person of the name of *Lesh* is mentioned, with two of his brothers bearing Slavic names, coming from Gracanica.[791]

In addition to the Cristobulae of Orthodox monasteries, representing certain ethnic realities, by which one may get a picture about the autochthony of Arberians in these parts even in circumstances when most of Orthodox churches treated them as Slavs, while Rascian occupiers from Stefan Nemanja to Stefan Dusan had made constant efforts to force them

---

[787] Tërnava, Muhamet: "*Popullsia e Kosovës gjatë shekujve XIV-XVI,*" Prishtina, 1995, p. 39.

[788] For more on Dusan's discriminatory measures against Arberians see Article 82 of "Zakonik" (O Vlasima i Arbanansima).

[789] Novaković, St: "*Zakonski spomenici srpskih država srednjeg veka,*" Belgrade, 1912, p. 430.

[790] Solojev, A: "*Dva priloga sa proučavanju Dušanove države,*" Glasnik-Skopskog naučnog društva, Notebook 1-2, Skopje.

[791] Tërnava, Muhamet: "*Popullsia e Kosovës gjatë shekujve XIV-XVI,*" Prishtina, 1995, p. 41.

out of their own lands in various ways, as it happened in the final years of Dusan's rule when a good part of them had been deported to Thessaly and other parts of Greece, there are other sources indicating the presence of Arberians in their ethnic lands, having inhabited them since antiquity.

There are Ragusian documents too, showing the trade and also economic ties, such as the Trepca mining, Novobrdo and others, whose presence was maintained later as well.

Thus, a book by a Ragusian merchant, Mihail Lukarevic of the thirties of the 15th century, contains such anthroponomic data, which indicate the presence of Arberian ethnos in Novobrdo in several villages of its surroundings and in several other villages of other suburbs of these parts. Among such anthroponomic data are also the following:

- Andrea Gan foxer de Pod (gradie),
- Gin e Mechxa de Ostatuozi,
- Gonaz Arbanaxo de Hroipsinzi,
- Gon Mali foxer e Peia de Miralia,
- Andria Gon focer de Podgradie pego per Macho Stranieuich foxer,
- Andria Gonouich focer Trupostiza,
- Gurag de Gon Arbaneco chruzmar e foxer e Andria suo frar mortor sono in Chratoua de gruan temo dreno dere per resto,
- Andria Nicholich Arbanexo de Matia foxer...
- Andria e Tanus conpari ostri de Liuada...
- Todor surela de Balich die dar piego per lui Vlaia de Gon,
- Llex conpare de Gurcouzi.
- Tanus Bogdanouvich de Gurchouzi piego per liu Lex conpare diedare...[792]

These and similar data stored in the archives of the countries with which the Arberians were in good ties in the Middle Ages are of great value for the understanding not only of anthroponomy but of patrimony as well of the residents of these areas and settlements in the first half of the 15th century, depicting also the changes emerging under the influence of church factors in the circumstances of Slavic invasions when their patronymics began to emerge with Slavic suffixes.[793]

For a most faithful reflection of ethnic relations between Arberians and Slavic invaders during the Middle Ages, and especially at the turn of

---

[792] Dinić, M: *"Iz Dubrovačkog Arhiva,"* Book I, Belgrade, 1957, pp. 37-90.
[793] Tërnava, Muhamet: *"Popullsia e Kosovës gjatë shekujve XIV-XVI,"* Prishtina, 1995, p. 42.

the time of Byzantium to the Ottoman conquests, most deserving are Ottoman defters (registers), commencing from the very start of the Ottoman Empire. These defters link the ethnic situation from the latest time of Slavic invasions with the first decades of the Ottoman conquests, with the establishment of the new administration together with an overall economic, social, and political system that remained for the next five centuries.

The first defter of this kind is that of the *Vellk Vilayet* of Brankovic territory of the year 1455, which marks the end of Slavic rule and the beginning of the Ottoman one. This and other similar defters appearing in the 15th-17th centuries were dealt with extensively in the second half of the book within the coverage of ethnic relations and the process of Islamization of Arberians. However, within the range of coverage of ethnic relations between Arberians and Slav occupiers in the late Middle Ages, the light was cast on toponyms matters whenever maintaining their native character since antiquity, or whenever appearing in a foreign vocabulary altered or rewritten but safeguarding the nature of the Arberian (Albanian) language.

As the toponyms belonging to the Pelasgian-Illyrian-Arberian autochthony, such as: *Naissus – Nish, Skardous mons – Shar, Scupi – Shkupi, Scodra – Shkodra, Lissus – Lesh, Drivastum – Drisht, Drinus – Drin, Barbanna – Buena, Buna, Mathis – Mat* and others have been discussed earlier within Pelasgic antiquity and its connection with the Illyrian, toponyms that despite the changes best explain this language relationship. Nevertheless, the Slavic invasions in Dardania and other parts of Arberian territories (first the Bulgarian in the 9th-11th centuries, and Rascian in the 13th-15th centuries), brought about onomastic, anthroponomistic, and toponomastic changes.

Thus, in a diploma issued by Despot Stefan Uros I to St. Peter and Paul Monastery in Lim (the hydronym *Lim* is etymologically explained by Albanian),[794] among others, several place names in Dardania are mentioned, among them is a recorded toponym in Slavic locative "*Arbanasju Potokju.*"[795]

---

[794] See: Çabej, Eqrem: "Gjurmime të reja në fushë të shqipes," in Studime Filologjike, 3, Tirana, 1974, p. 7.
[795] Tërnava, Muhamet: "*Popullsia e Kosovës gjatë shekujve XIV-XVI*," Prishtina, 1995, p. 169.

This name appears in determining the land boundaries of the village of Krusevac, near the Devic Monastery in the present-day Drenica. The diploma reads:

."..Ot Kruševca u Djal k Djeviču, ot kuda...k Arbanašju Potokju..."[796]

Even the Cristobula of Despot Milutin granted to the Banjska Monastery between the years 1314-1316, among some 500 toponyms, presents the toponym of "Jaćimovo Katunište." Since the attribute "katunishte" is based on the Albanian word katund (village) it refers to a village with Arberian population, like many others associated with the Orthodox Church, as they belonged to Orthodoxy, being under the spiritual jurisdiction of this Church, which registered as Slavs all those that belonged to the Orthodox faith. This is best explained with the case of the name Arbanas, repeated in some villages appearing as Slavic. One of them was the village of "Arbanaš," with seven houses in the Lab area, found in the defter of Vilk Vilayet of 1455. Although the defter does not mention any resident belonging to Arberian affiliation, there is no doubt that it refers to Orthodox Arberians, who even after the end of Slavic and the start of the Ottoman invasion, were registered according to their church association, that is, the Slav-Orthodox one.

These are not isolated cases, as it can be seen from Milutin's Cristobula given to the Banjska Monastery and that of the village "Arbanaš," but a general phenomenon already known since the separation of the Church in 1054, when most of Arberian territories, after the Slavic invasions of Stefan Nemanja in 1191, when he conquered parts of Nis, Scupi and as far as Prizren, appropriated by the jurisdiction of the Rascian Orthodox Church, this is confirmed by the example of a charter (povelje) issued by Stefan Decanski in 1327, when the toponym "Tanušev Laz" is found.

The basis of the toponym "Tanušev Laz" is the anthroponym Tanush, typical for medieval Arberians. The microtoponym "Tanušev Laz" speaks clearly that someone by the name of Tanush lived nearby, whose name attained a toponomystic function.[797]

---

[796] Ivanović, R: "Srednjovekovni baštinski posjedi – Humska eparhijska vlasništva," Belgrade, 1960, p. 93.
[797] Tërnava, Muhamet: "Popullsia e Kosovës gjatë shekujve XIV-XVI," Prishtina, 1995, p. 171.

In Decan Cristobula of 1330, among numerous toponyms of the feud of Decan Monastery the toponym *"Ujnemir"* is also found, determinative of the village of Çabiq.[798]

"Ujnemiri" of 1330 is none other than the present-day *Ujmir* in Klina. Serbophones call it *"Dobra Voda,"* being a very recent translation from the Albanian.[799]

An analogy with *"Ujnemir"* of 1330, from Çabiq, which some Serb historians and linguists try to connect to a Slavic origin,[800] comes also from the toponym *"Onamir"* in the defter of the *Vilk Vilayet* of 1455, in this sense backing up the Albanian association and rejecting that of the Slav origin.

This village too is situated in the Lab area and is explained by the *"good earth," "good place,"* as was the case with *"Ujin e mirë,"* (Good Water), *"Ujmir"* near the present-day Klina, recorded in its genuine form as *"Ujnemir,"*[801] which later, by the 19th century, with the launching of the notorious hegemonic campaign of Serbian science by devising cristobulae, charts, and all sorts of documents by means of which it needed to devise "the old medieval Serbia," based in Dardania, which it calls *Kosovo,* by which in 1876 it was named the Vilayet of Kosovo, bringing this toponym translated as *"Dobra Voda,"* precisely by realizing that the medieval toponym *Ujnemir* registered by the Orthodox Church had Albanian roots.

Therefore, based on certain data provided by the medieval Slav-Orthodox Church, though acknowledging that most of them have been rewritten, as is the case with Decan Cristobula, the first document of such kind devised with the rest, one can say that the ethnic relations between Arberians and Slavs in the Middle Ages, in the Dardanian area, where the most severe friction between them took place, between the 13th and 15th

---

[798] Novaković, R: *"Zakonski spomenici srpskih država srednjeg veka,"* Belgrade, 1912, p. 25.

[799] Çabej, Eqrem: *"Rreth disa çështjeve të historisë së gjuhës shqipe,"* in Buletini i Universitetit Shtetëror të Tiranas, seria e shkencave shoqërore, No. 3. Tirana, 1963, p. 83.

[800] For more on this see: R. Novakovic: *"Zakonski spomenici srpskih država srednjeg veka,"* Belgrade, 1912; M. Milojević: *"Dečanske hristovulje,"* Belgrade; Sindi, Dušan: *"Ko je autor osnivačke povelje Hrama sv. Nikole u Hvosnu,"* Belgrade, 1972; G.A. Krivanić: *"Vlastelinstvo Sv. Stefana u Banjskoj,"* Belgrade, 1965.

[801] Kaleshi, Hasan: *"Die Albaner in Kosovo im 15 Jahrhundert,"* published in "Akten des Internationalen Albanologischen Kolloqiums" - zum Gedächtnis an Norbert Jokl, Innsbruck, 1971, p. 518.

centuries, emerged as relations between the indigenous population - Arberians, with historical and ethnic continuity from antiquity and as state-forming in Byzantium, and conquerors – and the Slavs, who appeared in Illyricum as barbarians from the 7th century. Even having accepted Christianity in the 9th century, the Slavs would not cease their invading behavior and actions against the Arberians and Arbëria, stopping only with the emergence of the Ottoman Empire when they were rebuffed for the possibility of "confusing" church affiliation with ethnicity.

Social and Political Relations between Arberians and Slav Invaders

> *Why are the social and political relations between Arberians and Slavic invaders in North Illyricum – Dioclea and Dardania different from those in Dalmatia? – Why do both the Nemanjas and Dusan constantly mention Arberians as part of the occupied space and what was hiding behind the construct of "Rascian Arberia?" – Why did the Ottoman Empire, seeking a supportive factor in the center of the Balkans, focus on the feudal lords of Dardania, who turned into its main allies? – Were the Brankovici, Markovici and others "Slavicized Balkanians" or "Slavicized Dardanians?" – The Rascian invasion of Dardania from the 13th to the 15th centuries was not able to alter the ethnic picture of this part, which even by Orthodox church documents, even fabricated, relying on the Ottoman civil registers of the 12th-15th centuries, was largely populated by Arberians.*

Ethnic relations between Arberians and Slavic invaders in the 13th-15th centuries, namely those representing the circumstances from the Stefan Nemanja Dynasty in 1191 until the death of "Mega-zupan" Stefan Dusan in 1355, reflect the situation of an invasion that was not classic, as it was done in circumstances where over the social and political situation stood the Byzantine imperial crown and a war of rivalry and limited war for larger possessions taking place among the feudal lords, despots, zupans, and self-proclaimed princes within a certain area.

However, the reflection of these relations, of being complete and highlighting their true nature, requires special treatment, because they differ significantly in Illyricum (in the area of Dioclea) from that of Dardania, because of various social, ecclesiastical, and ethnic backgrounds conditioned by various factors.

Therefore, in Dioclea, the first encounters and also frictions between the Illyrians and the Slavs date back from the first half of the 8th century, just as the Slavs would be allowed by Emperor Heraclius to settle in a part of Thrace and north of Illyricum in order to prevent the incursions by barbarian tribes from the North. From the second half of the 7th century, when they were accepted in these parts, up to half of the 8th century, when in an area between Bosnia and Zahlumia their first organizational forms of tribal nature were mentioned, no significant change, ethnic or social, occurred. Even the appearance of the Bulgarian Kingdom in Boris's time, which was noted in passing during a penetration of some of its units in the vicinity of Dioclea and Shkodra did not create an impact of the kind that was reflected later in the Dardanian area. Changes occurred by the 9th century when Dioclea was seen at the intersection of interests of several Slav zupans and Ragusian counts, whose claims for much larger possession extended as far as Shkodra, and in the west towards Narenta and Zahlumia, when the first Slav zupans emerged entering various services in the coastal cities, including Venice.

Of course here was the factor of the Western Church, controlling the situation, being the one that defined in most part the ratio of forces among claimants for larger holdings. It was keen to create Slavic constructions such as *"Slavic Kingdom,"*[802] which were used as a convenient tool in the game, not only to acquire Byzantium's "natural eastern allies" in order to be used against it, as would happen on several occasions, but at the same time to be utilized, as needed, in designing the relationship among the Venetians, Ragusians, Hungarians, and other allies, which happened more than once.

However, Arberians too could not be left aside in this game with their highly strategic space keeping the sea lanes open, and the land leading eastward through Dardania, a part that was turned into an epicenter of all developments deciding on events that ultimately determined Byzantium's fate and future relations between Christianity and the Ottomans, as would happen in the battle of Dardan Plain of 1389.

---

[802] Orbin, Mario: *"Il regno degli sllavi,"* 1601.

As in the Dioclea area and generally in the southern part of Illyricum the relations between the Slavs and Arberians would be mostly relations outlining the interests between the Western Church and its contenders who took over a defending banner in its favor, when there were severe frictions for large area invasions of particular importance, in Dardania and generally in the central part. The battle was about who would become the claimant to the throne of Byzantium, whether to acquire it or give it a final blow. In both cases it was the Slavs (Bulgarians mixed with them and eventually Slavicized and Rascians), who in the last two centuries, that is, from the time of the Fourth Crusade (1204), turned into key stakeholders benefiting from the weakening of Byzantium, while their rise hurt Arberians and others.

In this case it must be said that the strengthening of Nemanjas as Slav zupans, appearing in their struggle for power in Dioclea a century before, after being distinguished in the triangle among Bosnia, Zahlumia, and Narona occurred precisely in Rascia (Arsa), the former castle of old Dardania, which for more than 200 years had been one of the most fortified centers of Dardania in one of the main points from where the most successful Emperor of Dardanian descent, Justinian, had originally planned a defense from Slavic incursions in these parts.

There are many indications that Nemanja's drive from Dioclea in 1047, and his takeover of the castle, may have been in accordance with a plan by the Venetians and the Holy See to take over Byzantium's main fortification post so that, as was done during the First Crusade when the Normans reigned over Durres and other parts of the Illyricum coast evicting Byzantine power for a while and prepared for Sicily (with Hohenstaufen and later with Anjou). The same was done with the occupation of Dardania, but this time by a Slavic Zupan, who as a Catholic, turned into a contender for the throne of Constantinople increasingly supported by the Holy See and its known interests.

Although the forged Serbian historiography of the 19th century saw the advent of Nemanjas in Rascia and the rise of their power from there towards the South as "Serbianization under the banner of Orthodox Christianity," bypassing the fact that this Zupan and his heirs up to Uros II, whoever was crowned was associated with the Western Church receiving blessing from the Papacy. It does not mention the fact that Stefan Nemanja concluded an alliance with the Hungarians and a little later with the German king, Ludevic of Bavaria, to join his campaign toward Constantinople in 1191. There he accepted it after crossing the Danube with 20,000 soldiers when he invaded Naissus with a part of his army fending off towards Scupi (today's Shkup-Skopje) taking it from the Byzantines and continuing with Ulpiana and Theranda, which were led by Arberian nobility,[803] although the Nemanjas suffered defeat by a Byzantine counter-offensive near Stobi that summer. However, after a peace treaty between them and Byzantium, as the Byzantines needed a Slav supporter in this part to withstand western attacks, the Rascians kept most of their conquests in Dardania, marking the beginning of nearly two centuries of occupation, which was not a classic kind of occupation, but put them (Rascians) as the main owners of these parts even with Arberian feudal lords and nobles appearing as local governors.

This position was strengthened for the benefit of Nemanjas even after Byzantium beat the Catholic Empire of Constantinople returning to its castle after half a century of residing in Nicaea. The Rascians were getting additional concessions to the detriment of the Greek and Bulgarian despots after demands by Stefan Uros to the Patriarch of Constantinople to restore their church back to the family it left, after having "unilaterally" declared autocephaly, which was given up in favor of the "Imperial Crown."

These and similar "high gamble" actions caused the Nemanjas through 13th-15th centuries to maintain their holdings in most of Dardania. Furthermore, in these parts, they remained even after Dusan's death (1355) when what he had built as Rascian Kingdom began to collapse rapidly. Most of Arberian lands were included in his kingdom with a good part of the nobles and feudal lords maintaining their properties, while others, who fed his army with soldiers, were appointed zupans. Various data indicate that Dusan included senior Arberian advisers in his court, which he moved from one place to another.

However, even in these circumstances, the social and political relations between Arberians and Nemanja conquerors in Dardania, before, during, and after Dusan's death, followed a line aimed at linking a classic occupation with the project of a *"Rascian Arberia,"* a construct that would stand between the model of *"Byzantine Arberia"* and *"Kingdom of Ar-*

---

[803] For more see: Ostrogorski, Georg: *"Historia e Perandorisë Bizantine,"* Tirana, 2002; Jiriček, Konstandin: *"Historia e serbëve,"* Part One, Tirana, 2010; *"Historia e Popullit Shqiptar,"* Book One, Tirana, 2002; Gelcich, Guiseppe: *"Zeta dhe Dinastia e Balshave,"* Josef von Hamer: *"Istoria osmanskog carstva,"* I, Zagreb, 1965.

beria" by the Westerners, as was the case with the one declared by Charles of Anjou in 1272-1288. This was repeated in another variant by his nephew Robert from 1314 and similar projects of the "Kingdom of Arberia" to be repeated by that dynasty constantly until the arrival of the Ottomans, sometimes successfully and sometimes unsuccessfully.

However, if the construct of "Rascian Arberia" is viewed from a slightly more analytical prism, never explicitly revealed, but always present in the Rascian actions during their occupying campaigns towards Arberian lands, appearing somehow from the marriage of Progon's son, Demetrios, with Stefan Nemanja's daughter, Comita and repeated through other marriages, ranging from those of the Balshaj family with zupans of Zeta and Nemanjas, Castriotis and Arianitis with Nemanjas (Skenderbeg's half sister Angjelina would marry Rascian King, the blind Stefan, for which she was subsequently declared a saint by the Serbian Orthodox Church), and many similar marriages on both sides, one can understand the confusion that took place in the 13th and 15th centuries.

It is not surprising why Rascians from Uros II to mega-zupan Stefan Dusan emphasized the Arberian factor in their crowns and various charts, scattered throughout the Western chancelleries and Papacy,[804] although some of them have been damaged, deliberately destroyed or omitted from reference during subsequent rewriting, so that Rascia and its power appears as a "clean" issue of the power of "Medieval Serbia," not associated with any other factor, the least of all Arberian, for whom many Serbian historians, supporters of nationalistic and hegemonic concepts of the 19th century onwards, should never have existed in such contexts.

Despite this attitude, the continuous alignment of *"Rascian Arbëria,"* to the extent it may be seen in the original documents and those that could escape known interventions and inventions, rather than the political issue of the Rascians to use this card to certain purposes – as the Anjou and the westerners acted out of interest to help the Arberarian factor, as an important force in these parts, converged with their own in order to penetrate the eastern part of Byzantium - highlights the possibility of their identification with this factor in those circumstances where Dardania represented an important knot of ancient identity, on which it Byzantine identity was built, associated with Troy. The efforts by Nemanjas to reach

---

[804] For more see: Farlati, Daniel: *"Illyrici sacri tomus septimus,"* Venetiis, 1817; Evans, Johen Artur: *"Antiquarian researches in Illyricum,"* Ports I-IV, London, 1883-1885.

the imperial throne, especially those by Dusan and their actions in this regard, may have developed upon that goal.

If it were to take away a bit of the Serbian amalgam from Rascia and Nemanja, as being unilaterally adopted by the Slavic community and conjured up by the Serbian hegemonic historiography of the 19th century onwards, if there is room for the possibility that Rascia is a continuation of Dardania and the Tribaldine Rascians a possible Slavicized Illyrian-Dardanian exfoliation - which is most likely so - it is quite possible that the emphasis on "Rascian Arbëria" is a reflection of "Dardanian Rascia" in its orthodox version, which cannot be ruled out.

Although this remains a speculative observation, however, such unprecedented consistency by the Serbian Orthodox Church and the Serbian Academy of Arts and Sciences during the last century onwards, to destroy or conceal original documents of the medieval church (despite the flaws they carry as such against the nature of the issue) and to present others, reprinted and fabricated – being admitted also by many Serbian historians, without excluding the evidence of the Russian Jastrebov in his book *"Podaci o Istoriji Srpske Crkve" ("Evidence on the history of the Serbian Church"*), published in Belgrade in 1879 - does not exclude the possibility of Rascia and Nemanjas not being Slavs, but Tribals or a Slavicized Illyrian-Dardanian exfoliation.

This dilemma, however, was fed by the Serbs, even when they made efforts to fabricate the medieval Serbian myth of Kosova, on what supposedly had to represent the Serbian historical epic, which had its own formulas in Vienna, in the workshop of Vuk Stefanovic Karadzic and his numerous aides from the French school of Cvijic and Garasanin, author of "Nacertanje" from 1844 out of the fear that one day they may be faced with evidence of a possible emergence of a *"Dardanian Rascia"* as a historical reality.

Therefore, if one reads the folk epos *"Royal Dinner" (Kneževa večera)*,[805] taking place at the Knjaz Lazar's "royal court" in Krusevac one night before the decisive battle of the Dardana Plain, even as a 19th century construct, it is clearly seen that Lazar is surrounded by sons-in-law (Vuk Brankovic and Milesh Kopili - Kopiliqi, Obilic in Serbian), looked upon with distrust for being "foreign," meaning they were not Slavs, but as

---

[805] Karađič, V. S: *"Srpske narodne pjesme,"* II, Vienna, 1846.

coming from Dardania could also be "Serbianized Balkanians,"[806] (from the ranks of Tribals, Arberians, and others), "joined" by Orthodox faith, making them "equal in the eyes of God." [807]

The possibility that the construct "Serbianized Balkanians" could best cover all the dilemmas, as presented in this case, simultaneously opens the possibility of showing through it the alleged superiority of the Serbs in contrast to others, as big as to be able to assimilate them, although it is quite clear that this can have no scientific or historical backing, being that at that time there was no Serbian people or Serbian nation (it appeared by the mid-19th century) but a Slavic association existed there, as a common ethnos with many unknowns. In the 12th-14th centuries this appeared with regional differences (Dioclea, Bosnia, Zahlumia, Rascia, etc.), and religious differences within Christianity (of Catholic or Orthodox rite) from where the dynasties were named, that of Rascia among them, which shortly left its matrix in order for it to expand over the ancient Dardanian space.

Despite these evident developments, however, the social and political relations between the Arbërians and Slavic invaders remained open, where Serbian historiography, in line with its most nationalistic and hegemonic resolves tried to see among these ethnicities only "Serbs" as a majority and a few "Arbanas and Vlachs," acting similarly with the social and political ones. Furthermore, beyond the social and economic logic, although numerous impartial documents of the time and Byzantine ones (Michael Atalati, notes of Constantine the Philosopher, Anna Comnenus, and many others) disclose, it became known that many nobles and princes of Arbëria were recognized by Byzantium. For example, Progon, married the daughter of Stefan Nemanja, or Dushan kept some Arbërian zupans and nobles in his court, granting them new possessions, which if such things did not take place, why would they be recorded in the "poveljas" and marriage "charts?"

Therefore, the evidence, although scattered, indicate that the social and political relationship between the Arbërians and Slavic invaders was identical to the ethnic one, meaning that the Arbërians had their own

---

[806] Kosić, D: "*Miloš Kopilić, Kobilić, Obilić*," Revue International des Etudes Balcaniques," Tom. I, Belgrade, 1934-1935.

[807] For more see: Arapi, Fatos: "*Këngë të moçme shqiptare,*" Tirana, 1986, p. 200; Popovic, Milorad: "*Vidovdan i časni krst,*" Belgrade, 1976, p. 18-23; Šobajić, Peter: "*Malesia,*" II, 1923, p. 221.

feudal and aristocratic structures, as well as their feudal lords, counts, and princedom families that were accepted by conquerors too in order for them to continue functioning as such in accordance with the logic of internal vassalage.

Of course there were zupans from among the invaders too, but they could not eradicate the local hierarchy similar to what others had in the Byzantine space, a structure that continued to stand under the new circumstances up to the emergence of the Ottomans. A few of them kept their positions even after the Ottomans came through and established vassalage relations with them, with a few profiting and turning into allies of the Sultans during their invasion campaigns in Europe.

At the issue of Ottoman vassalage of certain nobles of Dardania, as the Brankovic family or some others from the year 1389 until 1455, when Dardania was conquered by the Ottomans, beginning the five-century-long era of the Ottoman Empire in these parts, rightly opens the issue of ethnicity of these nobles. Serbian folk epos, though designed by the mid-19th century, charged them with suspicion of "disloyalty" for the loss of the Battle of Kosova, because of "being others." It was their social and political behavior after the defeat, when they, like the rest of the local nobility under the occupation of Nemanjas, were ranked on the Ottoman side remaining alongside them for more than half a century, until 1455, when the Ottoman Empire would end vassalage in these parts to eventually establish its own administrative and political power at all levels. Even after its fall from the scene, like the rest, the Ottomans included most of Dardania under the so-called *"Vulk Vilayet" (Vuk's Province)* in the new administration of occupied territories. [808]

If this was a behavior of common vassalage, neither the Brankovics nor Lazarevics (sons of the despot killed in the Battle of 1389, Stefan and Vuk, who linked with Bayazid through his marriage to their sister Jelena), would surely never be mentioned any longer, as the Balkans were full of such behavior even without the defeat. One could even say that the logic of vassalage represented not only survival in the current circumstances of the accession but the power of the fittest. During the Byzantine and Ottoman Empire, a form of different social and political profiling existed, as many of the Balkan nobles, gentry and despots benefited by it, not only by extending their possessions, but also by reversing a social state with

---

[808] Rizaj, Skënder: *"Kosova gjatë shekujve XV, XVI and XVII,"* Prishtina, 1982.

another that did not exclude the possibility that by transferring to the Ottomans one could mark the removal of a despotic state invasion by replacing it with a new perspective, as the one that the Ottomans had to offer.

The Brankovic case (initially Vuk and later Djurad), and their links with the Ottomans exceeded the proportions of vassalage of the time and circumstances, giving reason for justified suspicion of a replacement of a social and political situation with another. Numerous historical sources, including Ottoman, which compared with the western ones are somewhat sparing in this regard, indicate that Brankovic's relations with the Ottomans were relations of a high-level trust. This particular family had special connections that cultivated with three sultans, Bayazed, Mehmed I, and Murad II. Despite the "troubles" that Vuk faced with Bayazed which could have been fatal for him, Djurad and his family were generally actors involved in all important events of the Ottoman Empire. In these circumstances, it was facing two crucial challenges: that of their intrusions to the West, and protection from the East, having to fight the Mongols and others at the same time.

The Brankovics were direct participants in both these challenges. They were all involved in supporting military operations of Ottoman forces against Hungarians, Romanians, and others in the West. In addition, they were present in the eastern challenges of the Empire, including the most dramatic and crucial ones as the power struggle among the Sultan's sons after Bayazed's death. Djurad Brankovic was seen on the side of the winner Mehmed I, while in the wars for imperial power, Lazarevics were noted too, changing sides, alternately supporting Mousa and Mehmed I, remaining, however, on the winner's side with great benefits.

In this outline, it was Djurad Brankovic who benefited through his connections and friendship with the Ottomans reaching as far as Murad II, upon which his sister Mara's marriage with the Sultan, not only "strengthened his position, but it turned him and his family into one of the most reliable families of the Empire at that time. Therefore, his sister had the last say on spiritual matters, those of the Church, while Djurad acted as a senior regent in the western part, who also decided upon the war plans there, certainly on the side of the Ottomans against the Christians.

The last Brankovic (Djurad) also remained known for sabotaging the Second Battle of Dardans of 1448, which pretended to represent a new

Christian Alliance against the Ottomans, held at the time when Hungarians, supported by the Poles, the Holy See and others represented a new hope that the Ottomans could be stopped, after which the Christians would proceed with a counter response. He not only failed to duly attend, but also impeded Hunyadi and other forces to duly deploy, which caused their defeat. Although it was anticipated that George Castrioti – Skenderbeg would also participate in the battle, he arrived too late (two days later) and returned sometime after passing Skopje, having learned the news of the defeat of the Christian forces, which had largely occurred as a result of the attitude of Brankovic as an Ottoman ally.

His (Djurad's) behavior as a reliable ally and his selection by the Ottomans for such a role was natural, although the Ottoman attitude seemed to be in favor of finding a Christian power for this region, which would become supportive, and the Rascians could hereby meet this requirement,[809] it is still open to suspicion that the Ottomans may, however, have been leaning more toward local native despots than defeated princedom families, such as Lazar's, who had been beaten, and whose center was not in Dardana, but rather in Krusevac, in the vicinity of Rascia.

The Ottomans relied on indigenous despots from Dardania, which, in strategic terms, oversaw major roads between East and West, and even in the new circumstances continued to remain a crucial factor (Brankovics, Mark Kraljevic and others, coming from the ranks of local feudal lords and nobles), who appeared independently even when in these parts the zupans of Rascia spread their power from Stefan Nemanja in 1191 through to Stefan Dusan, in the years 1340-1355.

These local despots were held under suspicion of treachery, as happened with Brankovic and Milesh Kopili before the Battle of Dardana, despite the fact that the Serbian historiography of the 19th century tried to place them within the frame of Serbian nationalism. Not only were they not part of the "medieval Serbian state in Kosova (as such did not even exist after the demise of the state of Dusan until the battle of Dardana)." They were typical representatives of the native nobility of Dardanian origin, who, after the fall of the Rascian power of the Nemanjas, looked at any opportunity for independence. The Ottomans represented a good opportunity for them for their fast and certain rise instead of becoming pawns in the Westerners' game aiming to turn them into "defensive

---

[809] Salabi, Muhamed Ali: *"Perandoria Osmane,"* Prishtina, 2009, p. 76.

trenches" against the Ottomans, which inevitably placed them in the position of being sacrificed.

The assessment that at the brink of the Battle of Dardana of 1389 "Serbianized Balkan nobles" appeared, with Milesh Kopili and Vuk Brankovici mentioned,[810] with their quandary over "what side should they take" comes to light here with the only correction that at the time there was no way for "Serbianized" nobles to exist, but rather Slavicized ones, as the Serbian nation did not exist at all at that time. In Rascia, from the 11th century and on there was a dynasty, mainly a vassal towards Byzantium, which after a century began to extend its possessions towards Dardania. These possessions were, in fact, supported upon the feudalist reasoning, being led by local feudal lords, who even when attaining power from "without" always preserved it from within.

The question of "Slavization" too, if it were to be accepted as an alternative to "Serbianization" was conjured up in the 19th century to feed Serbian nationalism and hegemonic views shown in the same time by means of which Serbian conquests were kept in the southern parts was the Orthodox Church that was creating the platform of what appeared as "Slavization" in circumstances where the bulk of Illyricum and the entire Dardania, after the separation of the Church in the 11th century belonged to the jurisdiction of the Eastern Church of Constantinople. Despite the games that the Nemanjas played by passing from one church to another (initially starting as Catholics, when Uros II was crowned with the blessing of Papacy, and ending up as Orthodox fanatics), a good part of the Dardanian nobility and its feudal lords remained loyal to the Eastern Church, being in line with the trust towards the central Byzantine state and realities that the Eastern Church in these parts were plenipotentiary during the last two centuries, although the presence of the Catholic Church was not excluded, even as a minority.

Nemanjas' final breakup with the Holy See and the beginning of Dusan's fierce campaign of prosecuting Catholics and the forced conversion of Catholics to Orthodox in Dardania, was another factor identifying slavization with Orthodoxy, which would be accepted as a natural state that continued unvaried until circumstances changed by the Ottoman invasion. This radically demolished social and political stereotypes, with matters of autochthony and "national identity" appearing more signifi-

---

[810] See: Kostić, Dragoljub: *Miloš Kopilić, Kobilić, Obilić,* Belgrade, 1934/35.

cant than others, as through them opportunities could rise to get rid of the rule of a conquering despot, which mainly Rascian zupans were, by means of an imperial power, from which they could benefit, as indeed happened.

The Brankovics, Kraljevic Marko, and others, whether belonging to *"the Serbianized Balkanians,"* as indicated in the twentieth century in a formula that concealed the truth regarding the *"Slavicized Dardanians,"* or dealing with the Christian Arberians of the Orthodox rite, which is much closer to the truth, did not see any great reason for not joining the war against the Ottomans, after losing the Battle of Maritsa in 1371. This justification was not unjustly seen by the "muses" and manufacturers of Serbian folklore of the 19th century as "traitors," while justifying the "loss" of the battle by the "treason" of in-laws, who, based on feudal rules of the time, were definitely "others," non-Serbs in this case, who as such could only be Arberians, allegedly willing to join in with anyone (this time with the Ottomans) against the Slavs.

There is an additional argument, perhaps the most important one, that justifies the behavior of Brankovics and others, which has to do with the fact that it puts into question the initial formula of the *"Serbianized Balkanians"* the only alternative of which may be that of *"Slavicized Dardanians"* to turn to the real formulation of *"Christian Arberians of Orthodox Rite"* being in compliance with this awareness, as was natural for others as well, although later they were amputated of their "national and ethnic awareness."

This refers to ethnic relations in Dardania during the Nemanjas occupation (from Stefan Nemanja in 1191 through to Stefan Dusan in 1335), which as noted in the previous chapter, were relations entirely between the Dardanian indigenous people with roots in antiquity, and transitory invading Slavs, who appeared in this part for the first time as unstable conquerors and vassals of Byzantium, an invasion ending with Dusan's death, after which emerged the numerous Arberian nobles and gentry with despotates and principalities. This lasted as long as Ottomans appeared with the vassals they gained from the Battle of Maritsa of 1371, after that of Savra of 1385, the Battle of Dardana in 1389, and ending in 1455 when Dardania fell under Ottoman rule.

Although documents of the Serbian Orthodox Church were mostly fabricated and rewritten in the 19th century, together with the drawings of Serbian historical epics based on a myth, which fed Serbian nationalism and hegemony, they still revealed the Arberian factor as dominating in their lands. It is quite natural that this population had their own feudal lords and nobles, regardless that they were Christian, who may have accepted the extension of Nemanjas in their possessions, but in no way renounced them, as ownership was an issue of Byzantine general order, respected under all circumstances, with any power built on them, whether temporary, vassal, or permanent.

Therefore, it was quite natural for the Ottomans, seeking supportive indigenous factors at the center of the Balkans, to have opted for nobles and feudal lords indigenous in the central part, with Brankovic and others being as such, who turned into intended vassals and main allies of the Ottoman Empire. After all, isn't this admitted by the Serb historical epos itself, as fabricated as it is in the 19th century, as Brankovic (Vuk) was not interested in a war with the Ottomans, but in maintaining an adequate vassalage, for which he was charged with "treason?" There were others in Dardania and Arberia like Brankovic, who were not interested in a war with the Ottomans, where the loss was inevitable, while even if it produced something, it went to the interest of those who even in the existing circumstances were sharing scores with the Ottomans.

It was precisely the Christian formula with the Orthodox rite and even a pathetic cry of nationalism, which finally highlighted the social and political relations of Arberians with the invading Slavs, in which it was only natural for Brankovics, Kopilics, Kraljevic Marko and the likes, to have been part of the local nobility and aristocracy, which in the circumstances of big turns, as those of the Ottoman invasions, behaved in accordance with their interests.

History may not accept this fact, but it can no longer deny it with the previous anti-historic constructions.

CONCLUSION

The difference between Antiquity and Middle Ages often appears unclear when based on certain years rather than on events and developments, which marked this important historic leap.

However, sometimes certain years, even as dates, are significant, as they define the beginning of an era and the conclusion of another. Viewed from this prism, the definition between Antiquity and the Middle Ages could be related to the year 312 AD, when an Illyrian Emperor from Dardania, Constantine the Great, accepted Christianity, although personally he would remain faithful to divine worship, while twenty-five years later, on his deathbed he was baptized, which created conditions for the emergence of what in the historic scene appeared as Byzantium, prolonging the life of the Empire for ten more centuries.

The emergence of Christianity as the official religion of the Empire, constituting one of the three components characterizing Byzantium (Roman rule and Greek culture), could not be legitimized for quite some time as the nephew of Constantine the Great, Emperor Julian, known as Flavius Claudius Julianus (361-363), turned back to worshipping gods and goddesses of his Pelasgian ancestors. It took a long time until Emperor Theodosius, who in addition to dividing the Empire into two administrative parts, made Christianity official. On this occasion, he also issued a special Imperial decree by which he forbade idols practically starting the era of unification of the imperial throne with that of the church, with the Emperor appearing with the Creator's "blessing" as well.

Despite these breakthroughs associated with this definition, for the Illyrian-Dardanians, the late antiquity and early Byzantium, i.e. 4th-7th centuries, represents the time of their administrative, governing, and spiritual identity that can be taken as identification with state identity.

This is related to the actions of two other Illyrian-Dardanian emperors: Diocletian (284-305) and Justinian I (527-565), who were remembered for their great reforms, with the first dividing the Empire into four major administrative provinces (one of which was Illyricum belonging to the eastern part), and the latter with the creation of Diocese of Dardania in Illyricum, transferring it from Thessaloniki to Justiniana Prima and upgrading it the level of an independent vicarage directly connected with the Holy See. The situation linking Illyricum administratively with the eastern part of the Empire (Constantinople) and spiritually with the West (the Holy See) lasted for three centuries, until 852, when following the Bulgarian conquest of Illyricum, its Church with archdiocese in Dardania (Justiniana Prima) was transferred to the jurisdiction of the Patriarchy of Constantinople. Concurrently, it was the last time in the Eastern Church records that Illyricum and Dardania were mentioned.

Diocletian's administrative reforms, according to which Illyricum, as the largest province of the Empire occupied a key place between the eastern and western parts, and those of Justinian I, spiritually linking the Dardanian Church with the West, were of great importance, as they turned Byzantium into an administrative, spiritual, and state identity, of medieval Arberians, while turning Illyricum and Dardania into a center of social and political developments, actually sealing Byzantium's ultimate fate.

This situation, although it was broken from the 9th century onwards, first by two Bulgarian invasions (by Boris and Simeon) and later by the invasions of the Nemanjan Dynasty of Rascia - when for the first time, in 1191, several cities of Dardania (Nis, Scupi, and Prizren) were conquered, while Mega-zupan Stefan Dusan, between 1336-1355, occupied the largest parts of Arberian lands, previously governed by Byzantium or Arberian gentry and nobles - represented the foundations of administrative, self-governing, and Christian church identity.

The history of the Arberian state is closely linked with the establishment of Byzantium from the 4th century onwards, to the foundations of which they deposited awareness as part of a known isopolitic state, which began to be reflected from the time of Roman conquest onwards, when Illyricum and Dardania acquired the status of the interior provinces with tribal self-government (foedus) or municipal treatment. Illyricum's status as one of four federal provinces of the Empire, granted by Emperor Diocletian, the acceptance of Christianity as the official religion by Constantine the Great, The Dardanian, and the direct connection of the Church of Dardania with the Holy See, Illyricum, and Dardania, clearly point to being an integral part of the state edifice of the Empire. These should be attributed to the history of the Arberian medieval state, bearing on its own emblem at least Justinian's Novella of 525 for declaring Justiniana Prima as vicariate of Illyricum, standing until 852, when it was destroyed by the invading Bulgarians replacing the western Illyrian-Dardanian awareness, on which the Roman civilization and the concept of universal empire was based, with eastern Balkan awareness.

But, even after the departure of Bulgarian invaders, the state administrative identity deposited on the foundations of Byzantium, for whose defense Arberians struggled throughout the Slav invasions, beginning by the end of the 12th century to the mid-14th century, ending with the emergence of the Ottomans and their occupations, was reflected through the creation of Themes (military-feudal forms of local government associated with the Empire), originally that of Durres and Nichopolis, and later in Scupi and Moesia, governed by Arberian chieftains of Arianiti and Skuraj.

Committed to preserving Byzantium's power even when attacked from all sides by the Slavs, Bulgarians, and Greeks, making different alliances at its expense and doing their best to undermine the central government, the Arberians demonstrated dedication also during the collapse of Constantinople, by the Crusaders in 1204 and declaration of the Latin Kingdom, when Byzantium was divided into two: one part in Asia, Nicaea, and the other in Epirus with the announcement of the Despotate of Epirus, which gathered mainly the main nobles and feudal lords of Arberian lands not included in the Rascian and Venetian conquests in the Adriatic. Allegations that Arberians gave up the Byzantine consciousness from the 10th century onwards or having fought its foundations, as did the Bulgarians, Slavs, and sometimes Greeks are unfounded.

Arberians showed their commitment to the Byzantium rule as part of their national identity in the most critical moments for Byzantium, as were those it faced from the Fourth Crusade when Constantinople was conquered by the Latins and its values collapsed terribly. This is best shown by the establishment of the Despotate of Epirus and the great efforts of all Arberian nobles and gentry to strengthen and raise it to a situation as it was at a time when Byzantium expected Constantinople to give back its crown forcefully taken away by Latins.

This assessment does not preclude the occasional actions of some Arberian lords, nobles, and zupans, who joined in numerous games played by despots of Rascia, Bulgarian, or even Greek despots in their ongoing struggles, open at times and under the rug at other times, to take or ruin Byzan-

tium, as reflected with the alliance between Rascians and Bulgarians during the time of Stefan Dusan.

But only after the failure of the Despotate of Epirus by internal rivalry with the Empire of Nicaea to reassign the Byzantine throne to Constantinople, which turned into an open war, when the Arberian nobles and gentry realized there was nothing left of Byzantium in its fierce struggle for survival against Slavic and Bulgarian threats, they started turning their eyes toward the West, although that was followed by some with doubts and fears, which, in those circumstances, were reasonable.

Involved in the devastating earthquake that struck Byzantium, seeking to protect their space from the invasions coming from those with whom they had lived under a common roof, they became a factor, and it was in them that the Western countries, primarily the Anjou of Naples and Papacy, saw the power that would help the West cross over to the East in order to occupy the disintegrating throne of Byzantium or demolish it altogether.

It was the Anjou, more specifically Charles I, who after having established links with many of the Arberian nobles and gentry disembarked in Durres, in 1272, with the crown of the "King of Arberia." Even though a number of Arberian nobles were neutralized (especially those of Epirus being under the influence of Paleologus and later Cantacusens), some others were indecisive (Muzakaj). They realized that the crown of the "Kingdom of Arberia," even on the head of a foreign king, as Charles I, was more useful and safer than that of a failing Byzantium held by helpless Paleologus, or the subjugating alternative that the invaders of Nemanja's and Dusan's dynasties offered a little later.

Though the squirmishing life of the "Kingdom of Arbëria" was short, the first (16 years) and the second, under Manfred, (8 years), however in the last stage, its protection turned into a fight to protect the Arberian state against a dogged opponent, the Dynasty of Nemanja and that of Dusan, on one hand, and on the other side the Byzantine Paleologus, determined to extinguish everything that was Arberian out of the fear they might be supportive of the West in its route towards the East.

In this war, Paleologus did not hesitate to take advantage of their links with the Ottomans to destroy Arberian despotates and principalities, suspecting them of connections with the West. One is aware of some of the "excursions" of the Ottomans towards Epirus, undertaken with the incitement of Byzantium, to punish Arberian despots, in addition to the known intervention by Ottomans at the Battle of Savra in 1835, in which Balshaj *and his allies suffered a heavy blow after having restored a large part of their possessions they had previously lost to Dusan's conquests.*

However, in the final stages of the Middle Ages, when the period of the Ottoman conquests began, and the Christian Western civilization was faced with a new social and spiritual challenge lasting for five centuries, Arberians and Arberia went through the same pathways and processes which others faced as well. The filter of vassalage and afterwards long-lasting bondage quenched their state identity, but not their language and historical memory, as a people coming from antiquity, which would nourish their national consciousness.

LITERATURE

Adamidi, D: *"Les Pelasges et leurs Descendants les Albanias,"* 1903.
Attaleiates, Michal: *"Historia,"* Bonnae, 1837.
Alföldy, Geza: *"Bevölkerund und Gesellschaft der römischen Provinz Dalmatien,"* Budapest, 1965.
Alföldy, Geza: *"Die Personennamen in der römischen Provinz Dalamtien,"* Heilderberg, 1969.
Andrea, Zhaneta: *"Gërmime arkeologjike në tumën ilire të Kuçit të Zi (Korçë),"* Tirana, 1969.
"Anonymi Descriptio Europae Oreintalis," O. Gorka, Cracoviae, 1916.
Anamali, Skënder: *"Ilirët dhe qytetet e Ilirisë së jugut në mbishkrimet e Greqisë,"* in "Iliria" 1982, I.
Anamali, Skënder: *"Epoka e Justinianit në Shqipëri,"* në "Iliria," 1997, 1-2.
Akademia e Shkecave e Shqipërisë, Instituti i Historisë: "Historia e Popullit Shqiptar," I, Tirana, 2002.
Aref, Mathieu: *"Shqipëria – odiseja e pabesueshme e një populli parahelen,"* Tirana, 2007.
Aref, Mathieu: *"Mikenët=Pellazgët,"* Tirana, 2008.
Arapi, Fatos: *"Këngë të moçme shqiptare,"* studime. Tirana, 1986.
Barišić, Franjo: *"Dosadašnji pokušaji ubikacije grada Justiniana Prima,"* Zagreb, 1963.
Babinger, Franc: *"Das ende der Arianiten,"* München, 1960.
Benac, Aloiz: *"Prediliri, Protoilir i Prailiri – neki novi aspekti,"* in "Balcanika" VIII-1977.
Benac, Aloiz: *"O identifikaciji ilirskog etnosa,"* in Godišnjak CBI XI-1973.
Benac, Aloiz: *"O učešću Ilira u Englesjkoj seobi,"* AR JAZU IV-V, 1967.
Beck, H.G: *"Kirsche und theologische Literatur in Byantinischen Reich,"* München, 1925.
Bernal, Martin: *"Athina e zezë,"* Tirana, 2009.
Budimir, Milan: *"Iliri i prailiri,"* Beograd, 1952.
Budimir, Milan: *"Grci i Pelasti,"* Beograd, 1950.

Budimir, Milan: *"O etničkom odnosu Dardanaca prema Ilirima,"* JIČ III-1973.
Budimir, Milan: *"Pelasto – Slavica,"* Beograd, 1951.
Budimir, Milan: *"Iliriski problem i leksićka grupa Teuta,"* Beograd,1953.
Budimir, Milan: *"Mesto arbanskog u krugu indoevropskih jezika,"* in "Gjurmime albanologjike," 2/1965.
Budimir, Milan: *"O Ilijadi i njenom pesniku,"* Beograd, 1940.
Buzuku, Gjon: *"Meshari,"* 1, 2, Prishtina, 1987.
Bozić, Ivan: *"O Dukađinima,"* in "Zbornik Filozofskog Fakulteta," VIII, Beograd, 1964.
Bozhari, Koço: *"Dokumente bizantine për historinë e Shqipërisë,"* Tirana, 1978.
Bourcarts, J. L: *"L' Albanie et les Albanais,"* Paris, 1821.
Benac, Aloiz: *"Mbi proceset etnogjenetike dhe përcaktimin e kufijve tokësor të fiseve ilire,"* in "Studime Historike," 1972, 4.
Buda, Aleks: *"Ilirët e jugut si problem i historiografisë,"* in "Kuvendi i Studimeve Ilire," (15-20 shtator 1972), I, Tirana, 1974.
Buda, Aleks – ZAMPUTI, Injac - FRASHËRI, Kristo - PETRO, Petraq: *"Burime të zgjedhura për historinë e Shqipërisë,"* II shek. VIII-XV," Tirana, 1962.
Cantacuzenus, Joannes: *"Historiae,"* I-III, Bonn, 1828-1832.
Choniates, Nicetas: *"Historia,"* Bonn, 1835.
Ceka, Hasan: *"Problemet e numizmatikës ilire,"* Tirana, 1976.
Ceka, Hasan – ANAMALI, Skënder: *"Mbishkrimet latine të pabotuara të Shqipërisë,"* in "Buletini i Universitetit Shtetëror të Tiranas," seria e shkencave shoqërore, 1961, 1.
Ceka, Neritan: *"Ilirët,"* Tirana, 2000.
Ceka, Neritan – KORKUTI Muzafer: *"Arkeologjia,"* Tirana, 1993.
Cerović, I: *"Nalazi iz praistorijskih tumula u Donjoj Bitinji kod Uroševaca,"* Beograd, 1991.
Comnena, Anna: *"Alexias,"* I-III Bonn, 1928.
Choniates, Nicetas: *"Historiae,"* Bonn, 1835.
Çabej, Eqrem: *"Studime gjuhësore"* I-VIII, Prishtina, 1976.
Ćović, Borivoje: *"Osnovne karakteristike materialne kulture ilira na njihovom centralnom području,"* in "Simpozijum o teritorialnom i hronološkom razgraničenju Ilira u preistorijsko doba" (15-16 May 1964), Sarajevo, 1964.

Čerškov, Emil: *"Antička bista zene iz Klokota,"* Glasnik Muzeja Kosova i Metohije III-1958.

Dašić, Ljubomir: *"Praistorijsko naselje na Širokom,"* in Glasnik Muzeja Kosova i Metohije II-1957.

Demiraj, Shaban: *"Gramatikë historike e gjuhës shqipe,"* Prishtina, 1988.

Demiraj, Shaban: *"Rreth disa bashkëpërkimeve midis mesapishtes dhe shqipes,"* in "Studime filologjike," Tirana, 2000, 3-4.

Drançolli, Jahja: *"Raguzanët në Kosovë (prej fundit të shek.XIII deri në vitin 1455),"* Prishtina, 1968.

Drini, Faik: *"Ilirët dhe Epirotët (Paralele dhe veçanti),"* in "Iliria," 1982, 2.

Drysen, J. G. H: *"Das Dardanische Fürstentum,"* in "Kleine Schriften zur alten Geschichte," Bd.I, Leipzig, 1883.

Dil, Sharl: *"Istorija vizantijskog carstva,"* 1919.

Dobruna – Salihu E: *"Plastika dekorative dhe figurative e stelave mbivarrore të perudhës romake në Kosovë,"* in "Gjurmime albanologjike," 14/1985, Prishtina.

Dušanić, Slavko: *"Novi Antinojeve natpis i metalla municipii Dardanorum,"* in Živa Antika, XX/1, Shkup, 1971.

Egger, Rudolf: *"Balkan pod Rimljanima,"* in "Knjiga o Balkanu" II, Beograd, 1973.

Evans, Johan Artur: *"Antiquarian researches in Illyricum,"* Parts. I-IV, Westminster – London, 1883-1885.

Farlati, Daniel: *"Illyrici Sacri tomus septimus,"* Venetiis, 1817.

Fallermayer: *"Geschichte des Kaisertums Trapenzunt,"* München, 1827.

Fashëri, Mehdi: *"Historia e lashtë e Shqipërisë dhe e Shqiptarëve,"* Tirana, 2000.

Falkenhausen, Vera von: *"Untersuchungen über die byzantinischen Herrschaft in Süditalien vom IX bis XI Jahrhundert,"* Wiesbaden, 1967.

Fermendjin, Eusebius: *"Monumenta spectantia historiam Slavorum meridionalum, Acta Bosnae,"* Zagrabiae, 1892.

Ferri, Naser: *"Monumentet ushtarake të periudhës romake në Mëzi të Epërme,"* Pejë, 2001.

Flus M: *"Illyrioi,"* Supplement V, Stutgard, 1931.

Franke P.R: *"Alt Epirus und das Königtum der Molosser,"* Kallmunz, 1955.

„Fjalor i mitologjisë" (compiled by Todi Dhamo), Prishtina, 1988.

FINE, J. V. A: *"Macedon, Illyria and Rom,"* in „Journal of Roman Studies," XXVI/1936

Gatti, Ettore: "*Gli Iliri,*" 1-2, Chiaravalle, 1981.
Galović, R: "*Predionica, neolitsko naselje kod Prištine,*" Prishtina, 1959.
Garašanin, M: "*Rugovo 'Fushe', Djakovica - praistorijska nekropola sa humkama,*" Beograd, 1966.
Garašain, M: "*Istorijska i arheološka razmatranja o ilirskoj državi,*" Glas CCLX-1974.
Garašanin, M: "*O poreklu i hronologiji balkanskog neolita,*" in Starinar, r.s.VII-VIII/1956.
Garašanin, Draga: *"Iliri"* in *"Iliri i Dačani,"* in Narodni Muzej Beograd, 1971.
Gaspër, Gjini: "*Skopsko-prizrenska biskupija kroz stoljeća,*" Zagreb, 1986.
Gavela, Branko: "*O ilirskom substratu na Balkanu,*" in Godišnjak CBI III/1, 1965.
Georgiev, Vladimir I: "*Ilirët dhe fqinjët e tyre,*" in "Studime filologjike," 1927,4.
Georgiev, Vladimir I: "*Illyrien et leurs vosins,*" in "Studime albanologjike" V/1971.
Gelich, Giuseppe: "*Monumenta spectantia historiam Slavorum Meridionalium Monumenta Ragusana,*" I-V, Zagrabiae, 1879-1897.
Gelich, Guiseppe: "*Zeta dhe dinastia e Balshave,*" Tirana, 2009.
Gerlach: "*Geschichte des lateinischen Kaiserreiches,*" Hamburg, 1905.
Graham, Walter J: "*The palaces of Crete,*" 1962.
Glišić, J: "*Iskopavanje na lokalitetu Gladnice kod Gračanice,*" Beograd, 1959.
Glišič, J – Jovanović, B: "*Fafos II – Kosovska Mitrovica, naselje vinčanske grupe,*" Beograd, 1961.
Gibbon, E: "*History of the Decline and Fall of the Roman Empire,*" London,1896.
Hahn, Johan Georg von: "*Studime shqiptare,*" Tirana, 2009.
Hammond, Nicol G.L: "*Varrimi në tumat në Shqipëri dhe probemet e etnogjenezës,*" in "Studime historike," 1972, 4.
Hamp, Eric P: "*Albanian and Messapic,*" in "Studies presented to Joshua Whatmogh on his sixtieth birthday," S.Gavenhage, 1957.
Hunger, Herbert: "*Das Regiester des Patriarchats von Konstantinopel,*" I, Wien, 1981.
Hopf, Ch: "*Geschichte Grichenlands vom Beginn des Muittelaters bis auf unser Zeit,*" 1876.
"*Historia e Popullit Shqiptar,*" I, II (group of authors), Prishtina, 1969.

"*Illyrisch albansiche Forschungen,*" vol. I-II, München and Leipzig, 1916.
"*Ilirët dhe Iliria tek autorët antikë,*" Prishtina, 1979.
"*Ilirët dhe gjeneza e shqiptarëve,*" Tirana, 1969.
"*Ilirët*" (S. Islami, S. Anamali, M. Korkuti and F. Prendi), Tirana, 1985.
Holleaux, M: "*The Romans in Illyria*" in CAH vol. VII/1953.
Hertzerberger: "*Geschichte der Byzantiner und des Osmanischen Reiches bis gegen Ende des XVI Jahrhundertes,*" Berlin, 1883.
Heyd, W: "*Geschichte des Levantehandels in Mittelalter,*" Stuttgard, 1879.
Jacques, Edwin: "*Shqiptarët – historia e popullit të lashtë nga lashtësia deri në ditët tona,*" Tirana.
Jokl, Norbert: "*Illyrier, Reallexion der Vorgeschichte,*" 6, Berlin, 1926.
Jubani, Bep: "*Tiparët e përbashkëta në ritin e varrimit tek ilirët e trevës së Shqipërisë,*" in "Ilirët dhe gjeneza e shqiptarëve," Tirana, 1969.
Jireček, Konstandin: "*Historia e serbëve,*" I, II, Tirana, 2010.
Jireček, Konstadin: "*Albanien ind der Vergangenheit,*" in "Illyrisch-Albanische
Forschungen," band I, München und Leipzig 1916.
Jireček, Kontandin: "*Skutari und sein Gebit im Mitteilatter,*" in Illyr.Alba. Forshungen I band, 1916.
Jorga, N: "*Breve Historie de l'Albanie et du Peuple Albanais,*" Bucarest, 1919.
Katičić, Radoslav: „*Die illyrische Personennamen in ihrem südostlichen Verbretingsgebit,*" in „Živa Antika," Shkup, 12, 1962, flet.1.
Katičić, Radoslav: "*Antroponime ilire dhe problemi i etnogjenezës së shqiptarëve,*" in "Studime filologjike," 1972, 4.
Katičić, Radoslva: "*Liburner, Pannonier und Illyrier,*" in "Studien zur Sprachwiessenschaft und Kulturkunde," Insbruck, 1968.
Knolles, Richard: "*The General History of the Turks,*" London, 1620-1621.
Kola, Aristidh P: "*Arvanitasit dhe prejardhja e grekëve,*" Tirana, 2002.
Koka, Aristotel: "*Kultura ilire parahistorike në Shqipëri,*" Tirana, 1985.
Kovaljević, G: "*Kasnoatička palata u Nerodimji,*" Prishtina, 1958.
Kovaljević, G: "*Antičku novci u Janjevu za Zbirku Zemaljskog muzeja u Sarajevu,*" Prishtina, 1984.
Korkuti, Muzafer: "*Paleoliti në Shqipëri,*" në "Iliria," 1995, 1-2.
Korkuti, Muzafer: "*Parailirët, Ilirët, Arbrit,*" Tirana, 2007.
Konda, Spiro N: "*Shqiptarët dhe problemi pellazg,*" Tirana, 1964
Krahe, Hans: "*Die Balkanillyrischen geographishen Namen,*" Heidelberg, 1925.

Krahe, Hans: "*Die Sprache der Illyrer,*" I, Die Quellen, Wisbaden, 1955.

Krahe, Hans: "*Von Illyrischen zum Alteuropäischen ,*" in IF 69/1964-65, Berlin.

Krahe, Hans: "*Sprache und Vorzeit. Europäische Vorgeschihte nach dem Zeugnis der Sprache,*" Heilderberg, 1954.

Kretschmer, E: "*Einleitung in die Geschihte der griechischen Sprache,*" Götingen, 1896.

Kretschmer; E: "*Die Leleger und die ostmediterrane Ubervölkerung,*" in Glotta XXXII/1953.

Krahe, Hans: "*Das Venetische. Seine Stellung im Kresi der verwandten Sprache,*" 1950.

Leveques, Paul: "*Pyrrhos,*" Paris, 1957.

Lubić, Sime: "*Listine o odonošajih izmedju Južnog Slovenstva i Mletačke Republike,*" I-X, Zagreb, 1876-1891.

Neumann: "*Der vierte Kreuzzug,*" Berlin, 1898.

Norwich, John Julius: "*Bizanti – shkëlqimi dhe rënia e një perandorie 330-1453,*" Tirana, 2005.

Novaković, Relja: "*Gde se nalazi Srbija od VII – XII veka,*" Beograd.

Novak; Grga: "*La nazionalita dei Dardani,*" in Arhiv za Arbanasku Starinu, Jezik i Etnologjiju, knjiga IV/1, Prishtina, 1969

Nikol, Donald M: "*The Despotate of Epiros,*" I-II, Oxford, 1957, 1984.

Marić, Zdravko: "*Doarsi,*" Godišnjak CBI X-8, Sarajevo, 1973.

Mayer, Anton: "*Die Sprache der alten Illyrier,*" I-II, Wien, 1957-1959.

Malcolm, Noel: "*Kosova,*" Prishtina, 2001.

Malltezi, Luan: "*Përpjekjet dhe synimet e Venedikut për pushtimin e Durrësit në 20 vjetët e parë të shek XV,*" in "Studime Historike," 4/1980.

Makušev, Vikentij Vasilijev: "*Istoričeskije razyskonija o slovjanah v Albanii v srednjie veka,*" Varšava, 1871.

Miklosich, Franz – Müller, Johannes: "*Acta et Diplomata Graeca medii aevi sacra et profana,*" 1, Wien 1860.

Mikulčić, Ivan: "*Teritori Skupa,*" in ŽA. XX-2, 1971.

Miočević – Rendić, Duje: "*Iliri u natpisima grčkih kolonija u Dalmaciji,*" in VAHD LIII/1951.

Miočevoć – Rendić, Duje: "*Ilirski vladari u svijjetlu epigrafskih numismatičkih izvora,*" in HZ, XIX (1966-1967), Zagreb, 1968.

Mirdita, Zef: "*Studime Dardane,*" Prishtina, 1979.

Mirdita, Zef: *"Antroponomia e Dardanisë në kohën romake,"* Prishtina, 1981.

Mirdita, Zef: *"Eine Inschfrit aus Ulpiana,"* in "Zeitschrift für Papyrologi und Epigraphik," bnd. 29, 1978, Bonn.

Moscy, A: *"Gesellschaft und Romanisation der romischen Provinz Moesia Superior,"* Budapest, 1970.

Mosso, A: *"The Palaces of Crete and Theri Buildes,"* London, 1957.

Orbin, Mauro: *"Il regno degli Slavi,"* Pesaro, 1601.

Ostrogorski, Georg: *"Historia e Perandorisë Bizantine,"* Tirana, 2002.

Oštir, Karl: *"Beiträge zur alarodischen Sprachwissenschaft,"* I Wien-Leipzig, 1921.

Papazoglu, Fanula: *"Dardanska onomastika,"* in "Beogradski Univerzitet," Zbornik Filozofskog Fakulteta, Book 8, Beograd, 1964.

Papazoglu, Fanula: *"Politićka orgsnizacija Ilira u vreme njihove samotalnosti,"* Sarajevo, 1976.

Papazoglu, Fanula: *"Poreklo i razvoj ilirike države,"* in Godišnjak CBI V-3, 1967.

Papadopulos, A: *"Versuch einer Genealogie der Paliologen 1295-1435,"* Amsterdam, 1962.

Patsch, Karl: *"Dardani,"* in PWRE IV/1901

Patsch, Karl: *"Das Sandschak Berat in Albanien,"* Wien, 1904,

Patsch, Karl: *"Ilirët,"* Tirana, 1923.

Patsch, Karl: *"Realencyclopädia der Classischen Altertumswissenschaft,"* Stuttgart.

Parović-Pešikan, M: *"Neka zapazanja o urbanom razvoju Ulpiane – ispitavanje ulica,"* Ohrid, 1989.

Parino, Guiseppe: *"Acta Albaniae Vaticana, res Albaniae saeculorum XIV atque crucuatan spectantia,"* I, Citta del Vaticano, 1971.

Pedersen, Holger: *"Die Gutturale in Albanischen,"* in Zeitschrift für vergleichende Sprachforschung, 36/1900.

Petzold, Karl-Ernst: *"Rom und Illyrien. Ein Beitrag zum römischen Aussenpolitik im 3. Jahrhundest,"* "Historia," Wiesbaden, 20/1971, H. 2-3.

Përzhita, Luan: *"Mbretëria Dardane,"* Tirana, 2009

Peter, Schreiner: *"Die byzantinischen Kleinchroniken,"* I, Wien, 1975.

Pisani, Vittore: *"Ilirët në Itali,"* në "Studime filologjike," 1972,4.

Pilika, Dhinitri: *"Pellazgët – origjina e jonë e mohuar,"* Tirana, 2005.

Pirenne, Henri: *"Muamedi dhe Karli i Madh,"* Tirana, 2006.

Pirraku, Muhamet: "*Kultura kombëtare shqiptare deri në Lidhjen e Prizrenit,*" Prishtina, 1989.

Praschniker, Camillo: "*Muzakhia und Malakastra, Archeologische Untersuchungen in Mittelalbanien,*" in "Jahresheften des Österreichischen archaologischen Institues," Wien, 21-22/1921-1924.

Prendi, Frano: "*Neoliti dhe eneoliti në Shqipëri,*" in "Iliria," 1976, VI.

Prendi, Frano: "*Epoka e bronzit dhe e hekurit në kërkimet shqiptare,*" in "Iliria," 1998, 1-2.

Prendi, Frano – Budina, Dhimosten: "*Kultura ilire e luginës së Drinosit*" in "Studime historike," 1971, II.

Prifti, Leonard: "*Shqiptarët, grekët dhe serbët,*" Tirana, 2010.

Ptolemaeus, Claudio: "*Geografia*" ed. O. Cuntz, Berlin, 1923.

Popović, Relja: "*Neka pitanja iz Justinianove kodifikacie,*" Beograd, 1928.

Popa, Theofan: "*Të dhëna mbi princët mesjetarë shqiptarë në mbishkrimet e kishave tona,*" in "Bulletini i Universitetit Shtetëror të Tiranas," seria e shkencave shoqërore, 1957/2.

Radojević, Nikola: "*Srpska istorija Mavra Orbija,*" Beograd, 1950.

Radonić, J: "*Dubrovačka akta i povelje,*" SANU, Beograd, 1839.

Rendić-Miočević, Duje: "*Iliri i antički svijet,*" Split, 1989.

Redenić-Miočević, Duje: "*Municipium riditarum në Dalamaci, trashëgimi i tij epigrafik dhe onomastik ilir,*" in "Kuvendi I i Studimeve Ilire," II, Tirana, 1974.

Rizaj, Skender: "*Kosova gjatë shekujve XV, XVI dhe XVII,*" Prishtina, 1982.

Tafel, G – Thonas, G: "*Urkunden zur älteren Handels-und Staatsgeschichten der Repubik Venedig,*" I-III, Wien, 1856-1857.

Tërnava, Muhamet: "*Popullsia e Kosovës gjatë shekujve XIV-XVI,*" Prishtina, 1995.

Todorović, J: "Hisar, Suva Reka," Beograd, 1962.

Todorović, Jovan – Cermanovič, A: "*Bajnica, naselje vinčanske kuture,*" Beograd, 1961.

Tomaschek, W: "*Wo lag Scupi, die Metropolis von Dardanien?,*" Wien, 1882.

Tomovski, Tomo: "*Auf den Spuren der illyrischen Sidlungen Uscana,*" in Živa Antika. XII-2, Shkup, 1963

Thumb, Adalber: "*Altgriechishve Elemente des Albanischen,*" in "Indogermanischen Forschungen," 1910, Band I.

Thalloczy, Ludevicus – Jirecek, Konstantinus – Sufflay, Emilianus: *"Acta et Diplomata res Albaniae mediae aetatis illustrantia,"* I-II, Vindebonae, 1913, 1918.
Sergejevski, D: *"Iz problematike ilirske umjetnosti,"* Sarajevo, 1965.
Srejović, D: *"Karagac and the Problem of the Ethnogenesis of the Dardanians,"* Beograd, 1973.
Stephanus, Byzantius: *"Ethnicorum quae supersunt. Exrecensione Augusti Meinecki,"* I, Berlin 1849.
Simone, Carlo: *"Ilirët e Jugut. Përpjekje për një kufizim,"* in "Iliria," 1986, 1.
Sisić, F: *"Letopis Popa Dukljanina,"* Zagreb, 1928.
Spahiu, Hëna: *"Qyteti iliro-arbëror i Beratit,"* Tirana, 1990.
Stadtmüller; Georg: *"Forschungen zur Albanischen Frühgeschihten,"* Wiesbaden, 1966.
Stipçeviq, Aleksandër: *"Ilirët,"* Prishtina 1968.
Stipçeviq, Aleksandër: *"Simbolet e kultit tek Ilirët,"* Prishtina, 1983.
Suić, Mate: *"Zapadne granice Ilira u svjetlu historijskih izvora,"* in Simpozijum II, 1975.
Soloviev, Aleksander: *"Eine Urkunde des Panhypersebastos Demetrios, Megas Archon von Albanien,"* in "Bytantinische Zeitschrift," XXXIV, 1934.
Sokoli, Ramadan: *"16 shekuj,"* Tirana, 1996.
Svejević, Dragan: *"Balkanski istočnjaci Milana Budimira,"* Beograd, 2001.
Sulić, M: *"Ilirski Deus Patrius,"* Beograd, 1961.
Shafarik, Johannes: *"Acta Archivi Veneti, spectantio ad historiam Serborum et reliquorum Slavorum Meridionalium,"* I-II, Belgradi, 1860.
Schütt, Carl: *"Untersuchungen zur Geschihte der alten Illyrier,"* Breslau, 1910.
Šufflay, Milan: *"Serbët dhe shqiptarët,"* Prishtina, 1968.
Šufflay, Milan: *"Histori e shqiptarëve të veriut,"* Prishtina, 2009.
Šufflay, Milan: *"Die Kirchenzuustände im vrotürkischen Albanien,"* in *"Illyrische-albanische Forschungen,"* I, München, 1916.
Šufflay, Milan: *"Städte und Burger Albaniens hauptsächlich während des Mittelalters,"* Wien, 1924.
Shukriu (Hoti), Edi: *"Dardania prourbane,"* Pejë, 1996.
Shukriu, Edi: *"Ancient Kosova,"* Prishtina, 2004.
Shkutri, Spiro: *"Der Mythos vom Wandervolk der Albaner, Landwirtschaft in der albanischen Gebiten (13-17 Jahrhundert),"* Wien, 1997.

Shuteriqi, Dhimitër: "Arianitët, emri dhe gjenealogjia," in "Studime historike," 1965/4.
Schevill, Ferdinand: "*Ballkani, historia dhe qytetërimi,*" Tirana, 2002.
Schramm, Gottfried: "Anfänge des albanischen Christentums," Freiburg im Breisgrau, 1994. XHUFI, Pëllumb: "Nga Paleologët te Muzakajt," 2009.
Xhufi, Pëllumb: "*Krishterimi roman në Shqipëri, shek. VI-XVI,*" in "Krishterimi ndër shqiptarë," Simpozium ndërkombëtar, Tirana, 16-19 November 1999, Shkodër, 2000.
Xhufir, Pëllumb: "*Shteti i Arbrit,*" in "Studia albanica," 1990/2.
Vulić, Nikola: "*Justiniana Prima,*" 1929.
Vulić, Nikola: "*Dardanci,*" in Glas SKA CLV/1953.
Zavalani, Tajar: "*Histori e Shqipnis,*" London, 1966.
Vulpe, Radu: "*Gli Iliri dell'Italia imperiale romane,*" in Ephem. Docorum, III/1925.
Walser, G: "*Die Ursachen des ersten römisch-illyrischen Krieges,*" in Historia II/1953.
Xylander, Ritter von J: "*Die Schprache der Albanesen oder Schkipetaren,*" Frankfurt, 1835.
Zamputi, Ignjac: "*Autonomitë e qyteteve shqiptare të Principatës së Balshave dhe pasojat negative të pushimit venedikas - Fundi i shek. XIV, fillimi i shek. XV,*" in "Studime Historike," 3/1980.
Zaninović, Marin: "*Iliri i vinova loza,*" Sarajevo, 1976.
Zaninović, Marin: "*Ilirsko pleme Dalmati,*" in Godišnjak CBI IV-V-2-3, 1966-1967.
Zippel, Georg: "*Die römische Herrschaft in Illyrien bis auf Augustus,*" Leipzig, 1877.

Jusuf Buxhovi

KOSOVA
Volume 1

Printed by
"PROGRAF"
Prishtina, Kosova

Buxhovi, Jusuf
    Kosova: (Dardania in Ancient
    and Medieval Times)
Jalifat Publishing, 2013
Houston, Texas
www.jalifatpublishing.com

Volume 1

All rights reserved

ISBN 978-0-9767140-5-7
ISBN 978-0-9767140-8-8